Bridges Not Walls

A Book about Interpersonal Communication

SEVENTH EDITION

Edited by
John Stewart
University of Washington

McGraw-Hill College

Boston   Burr Ridge, IL   Dubuque, IA   Madison, WI   New York   San Francisco   St. Louis
Bangkok   Bogotá   Caracas   Lisbon   London   Madrid
Mexico City   Milan   New Delhi   Sequi   Singapore   Sydney   Taipei   Toronto

McGraw-Hill College

*A Division of The **McGraw·Hill** Companies*

Bridges, Not Walls:
A Book about Interpersonal Communication

This book is printed on acid-free paper.

2 3 4 5 6 7 8 9 0 DOC/DOC 9 3 2 1 0 9

ISBN 0-07-290435-6

Editorial Director: *Phillip A. Butcher*
Sponsoring editor: *Marjorie Byers*
Editorial assistant: *Jennifer Kaldawi*
Marketing manager: *Carl Leonard*
Project manager: *Alisa Watson*
Production supervisor: *Heather Burbridge*
Freelance design coordinator: *JoAnne Schopler*
Compositor: *Carlisle Communications, Ltd.*
Typeface: *10/12 Palatino*
Printer: *R. R. Donnelley & Sons Company*

Library of Congress Cataloging-in-Publication Data

Bridges, not walls : a book about interpersonal communication /
    [edited by] John Stewart. — 7th ed.
        p.   cm.
    Includes bibliographical references and index.
    ISBN 0-07-290435-6 (alk. paper)
    1.   Interpersonal communication.   I. Stewart, John Robert, 1941-

    BF637.C45B74 1999
    158.2—dc21   98-18700

http://www.mhhe.com

About the Author

JOHN STEWART has been teaching interpersonal communication at the University of Washington since 1969. He attended Centralia Community College and Pacific Lutheran University, then got his M.A. at Northwestern University and completed his Ph.D. at the University of Southern California in 1970. John coordinates the basic interpersonal communication course at the University of Washington, teaches upper-division and graduate courses, is Graduate Program Coordinator, and provides communication consulting services to technical professionals. He is married to Kris Chrey, a Seattle attorney. He has two children and two grandchildren and they have a son, Lincoln, who was six years old in 1998.

Books and People

Imagine yourself in a situation where you are alone, wholly alone on earth, and you are offered one of the two, books or [people]. I often hear [speakers] prizing their solitude, but that is only because there are still [people] somewhere on earth, even though in the far distance. I knew nothing of books when I came forth from the womb of my mother, and I shall die without books, with another human hand in my own. I do, indeed, close my door at times and surrender myself to a book, but only because I can open the door again and see a human being looking at me.

—Martin Buber

Contents

Part II
OPENNESS AS INHALING

Part III
OPENNESS AS EXHALING

Part IV
RELATIONSHIPS

Part V
BRIDGING DIFFERENCES

Part VI
APPROACHES TO INTERPERSONAL COMMUNICATION

Preface

This edition of *Bridges Not Walls* maintains the approach and basic format of the previous six editions. It also offers an updated account of verbal and nonverbal communicating, a new chapter on hurtful and negative communicating, a state-of-the-art discussion of gender similarities and differences, a new approach to interpersonal communication by psychologist Ruthellen Josselson, and 23 readings that either replace or supplement materials used before. The book is still designed primarily for college students enrolled in interpersonal communication classes. But the materials discuss topics also included in humanities, social work, counseling, and sociology courses. Chapters treat the standard topics covered in most interpersonal communication classes, and a majority of the readings are authored by communication scholars and teachers. There are also materials from authors in a range of disciplines, including organizational development, education, clinical and social psychology, and philosophy.

Since the first edition of *Bridges* in 1973, the approach to communication that has guided this selection of readings has been a relational one, focusing on the quality of contact that people create *together*. In other words, as the first two chapters explain, *communication* is understood basically as the term humans use for their collaborative processes of meaning-making. To say that humans are "social animals" is to say that we make sense of things *with others*, and "communication" is the general label for these processes. The term *collaborative* obviously does not mean that humans always agree as we make meanings together, but only that we "co-labor" in response to one another. All this implies that communication is not simply an activity that one person performs or does "to" another, but is a process that happens *between* people.

Interpersonal communication is a subset of this process, a type or kind of contact that happens when the people involved talk and listen in ways that maximize the presence of the personal. This approach emphasizes the prominence of culture in all communicating and highlights the ways communication affects social and personal identities. In other words, although it is certainly true that communication is often expressive and instrumental, this approach emphasizes that it is also person-building, which is to say that *who humans are* gets worked out in our ver-bal/nonverbal contact. Virtually all the authors represented here acknowledge these features of communication, and many comment directly on them.

This is a book for people who want practical suggestions and skills that will help them communicate more effectively with their friends, partners, spouses, family, and co-workers. Unlike much of the self-help literature, however, *Bridges* resists the tendency to gloss over conceptual issues and to reduce interpersonal effectiveness to techniques or formulas. The authors represented here recognize that there is much more to effective communication than simply being "open and honest." Included are thought-provoking discussions of the nature of in-terpersonal contact, connections between verbal and nonverbal cues, person perception and social intelligence, listening, deception and betrayal, identity management, interpersonal ethics, types of love, transformational conflict man-agement, and diversity. In addition, four philosophies of communication are de-veloped at the end of the book in Chapters 15 through 18. *Bridges* also includes systematic treatments of dialogue, self-awareness, self-expression, communica-tion spirals, friendship, family relationships, and defensiveness, but no reading claims to offer the definitive "six steps" or "12 easy techniques" for guaranteed success. The authors emphasize that the unique situation, the constancy of change, and especially, the element of human choice all make it impossible to design and execute a purely technical approach to *human* relationships.

This point is rooted in the book's definition of its subject matter, which I've already sketched. *Bridges Not Walls* does not define interpersonal communica-tion as something that happens only in face-to-face settings, during discussions of weighty topics, or in long-term intimate relationships. Instead, the term *in-terpersonal* designates a quality of contact that emerges between people when-ever they are able to highlight in their speaking and listening, aspects of what makes them human. The editor's introductions in Chapters 1 and 2 explain this definition, and subsequent readings extend and develop it. Throughout the book the point is made that different qualities of contact are possible or appro-priate in different situations. "More" interpersonal communicating is not *always* "better." There's much more to it than that, as the readings, in Chapters 8, 13, and 14, especially, demonstrate. At the same time, materials in the first two chapters and the four approaches at the end clarify how most people's personal, educational, and work lives could profit from increased interpersonal contact.

Readings in Chapters 1, 2, 4, 5, 9, 10, 12, 15, 17, and 18 also emphasize the point made earlier that communication is more than just a way to get things done, because it affects who we are. I introduce this idea at the beginning of the book; James Lynch, Harold Barrett, John Welwood, Carole Logan and I, and Ken Cissna and Evelyn Sieburg develop and extend the early discussions, and the person-building dimension of communication is discussed in detail by Martin Buber in Chapter 18.

These theoretical and conceptual commitments are complemented by my commitment to make the book as readable as possible. This is the main reason why there are few research articles from scholarly journals. As in all earlier edi-tions, I have tried to select materials that speak directly to the student reader. I continue to favor authors who "write with their ears," or *talk* with their readers. Selections from past editions by Gerald Corey and Marianne Schneider-Corey, Virginia Satir, Carl Rogers, Hugh and Gayle Prather, and C. Roland Christensen continue to be in this edition partly because the authors do this so well. I have also found this accessibility in some new authors, especially William Isaacs, Julia Wood, and Matthew McKay, Martha Davis, and Patrick Fanning.

New Features

As I noted, one significant addition is the new Chapter 8, "Hurtful and Negative Communicating." For more than a decade, some scholars have been calling attention to the therapeutic bias and emphasis on intimacy that has characterized much of the writing about interpersonal communication. Real relationships are not always therapeutic or supportive, these scholars have argued, and textbooks should equip student readers to understand and cope with deception, hurtful messages, aggression, and harassment. Chapter 8 acknowledges this important insight and provides excerpts from three discussions of what is sometimes called "the dark side" of interpersonal communication. The first is taken from Anita Vangelisti's classic "Messages That Hurt," a discussion of hurtful communicating which cites almost three dozen studies of this topic. The second is a treatment by therapist John Welwood of how to turn relational "lead" into "gold," by distinguishing between what he calls "discernment and condemnation," using "emotional judo," and being willing and able to be each other's teacher. The chapter closes with another communication research–based discussion of deception, betrayal, and aggression from the 1998 edition of Carole Logan's and my book *Together: Communicating Interpersonally.*

A second new feature is the combined treatment of verbal and nonverbal communicating in Chapter 3. Especially over the last decade, communication scholars in a variety of disciplines have been arguing against the historical pattern of separating the two. One main reason is that people experience verbal and nonverbal cues together, so that discussions emphasizing their differences can distort as much as they clarify. The first reading in Chapter 3 outlines both some distinctions and some important connections. Then, primarily because there are still only a few combined discussions in the literature accessible to students, subsequent readings in this chapter focus either on words—Virginia Satir's "Paying Attention to Words" and Amy Tan's "The Language of Discretion"—or on what Ted Grove calls "Nonverbal Elements of Interaction." Taken as a whole, this chapter should enable instructors to emphasize both the benefits of separate treatments and the necessity of considering verbal and nonverbal elements together.

Chapter 16, psychologist Ruthellen Josselson's approach to interpersonal communication, is also new to this edition. The chapter is made up of excerpts from the beginning and the end of Josselson's 1996 book, *The Space Between Us.* In the introduction she outlines eight developmental stages that are the ways each human overcomes the space between people. The first stage is *holding,* being cradled in strong arms. Subsequent stages include *attachment, passionate experience, eye-to-eye validation, mutuality,* and *tending and care.* Healthy and complete development moves through all eight stages, and aspects of the need for each kind of contact continue as parts of our experience. The second part of Chapter 16 is taken from the final chapter of Josselson's book, "Notes on Love," where she uses these eight dimensions to explain what is for most people the most important and sometimes the most baffling interpersonal phenomenon of all—loving. As I note in the introduction to Chapter 16, there is gentle wisdom on these pages.

A fourth important change in this edition emerges in the discussions of gender and communication, especially in Chapter 12. Earlier treatments of gender in *Bridges* followed the research that emphasized differences. In the past few years, some feminist authors have been arguing against the essentializing tendencies of much of this research and the distorting oversimplifications that have been popularized, for example, in John Gray's "Mars and Venus" publications. In 1997, three communication scholars summarized some of the arguments against essentializing and oversimplification in *Sex and Gender Differences in Personal Relationships,* and Chapter 12 begins with excerpts from this book. The two other readings in this chapter address the practical questions that much gender communication research tries to respond to—"How can I develop a close relationship with somebody who seems so different from me?" But they do so without relying on questionable overgeneralizations about "male" and "female" communication patterns.

This feature of *Bridges* may well be controversial. I realize that many communication scholars and teachers, including some feminists, still believe strongly in the importance of gender-based differences and the value of a gendered standpoint in the negotiation of interpersonal relationships. As a male, teacher, husband, and scholar, I am not yet ready to deny the extent to which parts of Deborah Tannen's and even John Gray's writings resonate with my own experience. But I am impressed by the empirical insignificance of differences due only to gender that Canary, Emmers-Sommer, and Faulkner explain in the first reading in Chapter 12. More importantly, I believe in the efficacy of dialogue, as it is explained in Chapters 2, 6, 12, 13, 15, 17, and 18. And while gender undoubtedly figures in the emergence of meaning (*dia-logos*) between people, I do not believe that the flesh-and-blood selves who negotiate actual relationships can best be thought of as "essentially" male or female. My sense is that, in a couple of decades, the research and writing that emphasized gender differences will be seen as one stage in the development of a more nuanced, context-sensitive, and dialogic understanding of human contact.

There are also two new readings in the self-awareness chapter (Chapter 4), "Maintaining the Self in Communication," by rhetorician Harold Barrett, and "In Search of the Genuine, Powerful Male and Female," by therapist John Welwood. Chapter 5, "Awareness of Others," is anchored by the most recent edition of Sarah Trenholm and Arthur Jensen's discussion of person perception, and fleshed out by Julia Wood's comments about stereotyping, an explanation of social intelligence from Daniel Goleman's *Emotional Intelligence,* and a discussion of collective thought by physicist David Bohm.

Chapter 6 includes a new treatment of creative listening, and communication scholar and teacher Steve Duck explains "Expressing Meaning to Others" in Chapter 7. Chapter 9, "Negotiating Relationships," includes Bill Wilmot's recent discussion of spirals, paradoxes, and conundrums, and the familiar and useful article on confirmation and disconfirmation by Cissna and Sieburg. Julia Wood's 1998 discussion of families updates Chapter 11, and two similarly recent readings strengthen the treatment of conflict in Chapter 13. Chapter 14, "Bridging Cultures," is anchored with Letty Cottin Pogrebin's discussion of "Crossing Boundaries of Color, Culture, Sexual Preference, Disability, and Age." Included also are two new readings. The first is a practical description of how to build relationships with diverse others, by social psychologist David Johnson. And the second is Donal Carbaugh's detailed examination of how Soviet and American cultures were mediated in a televised "spacebridge" featuring Phil Donohue.

Plan of the Book

This edition maintains the basic structure of the last one, starting with "basic ingredients," treating the "inhaling" dimensions of communication separately from the "exhaling" dimensions—even as the breathing metaphor underscores their inseparability—discussing relationships and bridging differences, and then concluding with four overall "approaches." This structure makes the materials easy to adapt to each instructor's approach. Although it makes sense to me to assign readings in the order they are presented, both the sections and the individual chapters are self-contained enough to be read in whatever sequence works best.

My introduction tries to show that *Bridges Not Walls* is a little different from the standard, faceless, "objective" text. I want readers to consider the potential for, and the limits of, interpersonal-quality communicating between writer and reader. I also want them to remember that a book or essay is always somebody's point of view. I'd like readers to respond to what's here not as "true because it's printed in black and white," but as the thoughtful speech of a person addressing them. In the introduction I introduce myself, give a rationale for the way the book is put together, and argue for the link between quality of communication and quality of life. I also preview the book.

Chapter 2 of the "Basic Ingredients" section introduces the book's approach to communication, and three readings develop this approach. Then Chapter 3 focuses on verbal and nonverbal communicating.

The introduction to Part Two, "Openness as Inhaling," explains the two metaphors that are used to help organize this section of the book: "openness" and "inhaling/exhaling." As I explain, the first term is fruitfully ambiguous, because it can mean both "open to receive" and "willing to disclose," and the allusion to breathing underscores the organic interconnectedness of the receiving and sending aspects of communication. Chapter 4, "Self Awareness," begins with a discussion of personal meaning and values by Gerald Corey and Marianne

Schneider-Corey, followed by two selections that develop this focus. Chapter 5 shifts focus to person perception via Trenholm and Jensen's outline of "interpretive competence," Julia Wood's comments on stereotyping, Daniel Goleman's description of the rudiments of social intelligence, and David Bohm's discussion of collective thought. Chapter 6 concludes Part Two with four selections on listening. One new reading in this chapter by John Sanford highlights the creative parts of listening, and in the other new reading, Carole Logan and I describe and illustrate the move from empathic to dialogic listening.

Part Three, "Openness as Exhaling," consists of two chapters. Chapter 7, "Expressing Yourself," treats disclosure as a part of the interpersonal process, and Chapter 8, as I have already noted, overviews some of the hurtful and negative parts of communicative expressions.

Part Four is a four-chapter section focused on relationships. Chapter 9 outlines the general processes by which relationships are negotiated in three readings. The first is called "Co-constructing Selves"; the second is Bill Wilmot's discussion of communication spirals, paradoxes, and conundrums; and the third is Cissna and Sieburg's account of confirmation and disconfirmation. The next chapter offers two explorations of friendship, and it is followed by a two-reading chapter focused on families. The final chapter of this section examines intimate partnering.

Part Five, "Bridging Differences," begins with a chapter on conflict and concludes with a chapter on intercultural communication. Chapter 13 is introduced by a fairly comprehensive, recent overview of interpersonal conflict by Folger, Poole, and Stutman. This is followed by Jack Gibb's classic "Defensive Communication," and profound pieces of advice from Hugh and Gayle Prather. Then the chapter's focus broadens as Jeffrey Kottler argues against the blaming that characterizes most conflict, and, finally, Barnett Pearce and Stephen Littlejohn outline a transformational approach to conflict management in an essay called "New Forms of Eloquence."

Chapter 14 starts with David Johnson's suggestions about how to build relationships with diverse others. This is followed by Pogrebin's "The Same and Different" article and Carbaugh's discussion of Soviet and American contact on Phil Donohue's television show.

The book ends with four approaches to interpersonal communication, statements by noted writers that summarize their views of being-in-relation. Chapter 15 presents a teacher's approach; Chapter 16, a psychologist's approach; Chapter 17, a counselor's approach; and Chapter 18, a philosopher's approach. C. Roland Christensen is the teacher, Ruthellen Josselson is the psychologist, Carl Rogers is the counselor, and Martin Buber is the philosopher. Each time *Bridges* is reviewed, I hear some complaints that the final reading by Buber is "too confusing," "too hard to read," and "too heavy." Happily, I also hear and see what happens when students in my classes—and in classes taught by teaching assistants—actually begin to connect with Buber and his ideas. When teacher and student readers are patient and diligent, they often begin to appreciate through Buber the depth and importance of interpersonal communication. Frequently, this motivates them to apply these ideas, even in the face of hardships and challenges. All this continues to make teaching Buber rewarding for me and many of the people I work with. I agree that it is not easy to make Buber accessible to the basic course student, but the introduction to his essay goes a considerable distance in this direction. I believe in the value of high expectations, and I continue to be surprised and delighted by the majority of my students' understanding of his ideas.

Other Features

Two sets of questions follow each reading. The first, "Review Questions," are designed to prompt the reader's recall of key ideas. If the student can respond to the review questions, there is some clear indication that he or she understands what's in the reading. Then "Probes" ask the reader to take some additional steps by extending, criticizing, or applying the author's ideas. Some probes also explore links between readings in various chapters.

Many of the readings include extensive reference lists or bibliographies. There are lengthy lists of additional sources, for example, accompanying the readings that discuss the book's approach, verbal and nonverbal dimensions of talk, nonverbal elements of interaction, maintaining the self, person perception, listening, hurtful messages, deception, co-constructing selves, gender stereotyping, transformative conflict management, and intercultural communication. A detailed index also locates and provides cross-references to authors and key ideas.

As before, I want to remind readers that this book *about* interpersonal communication cannot substitute for direct contact between persons in the concrete, everyday world. This is why I've once again begun the book with Buber's comment "Books and People" and ended with Hugh Prather's reflections on the world of ideas and the world of "messy mortals."

Acknowledgments

This book would not be possible without the cooperation of the authors and publishers of material reprinted here. Thanks to all of them for their permissions.

I am also grateful to reviewers of earlier editions. The following people offered insightful comments that guided the revision process of this edition: Richard Brynteson, Concordia College; Jamey A. Piland, Gallaudet University; David B. Valley, Southern Illinois University at Edwardsville; and Mark Woolsey, Fresno City College.

Many people I am fortunate enough to contact regularly have also contributed in direct and indirect ways to what's here. I appreciate current and former interpersonal communication teachers in the program at the University of Washington, including Milt Thomas, Carole Logan, Kathy Hendrix, Karen Zediker, Jeff Kerssen-Griep, Lisa Coutu, Roberta Gray, Laura Manning, Tasha Souza, and Amanda Graham. Among these, Karen Zediker especially continues to improve my teaching and challenge my thinking, and she and her family are important parts of my family's life.

I also appreciate contacts with the colleagues who support and challenge my ideas, including Gerry Philipsen, Barbara Warnick, Raka Shome, Mac Parks, Bruce Hyde, and John Shotter, and important friends Walt and Tom Fisher, Fr. Ralph Carskadden, Chris Galloway, and Dale Reiger, who do the same. But I notice as time goes on how both the greatest tests and the most solid confirmations of what's in this book emerge in my most important living relationships with Kris, Lincoln, Marcia, Lisa, Mark, Jamie, Josh, Mom, Bob, Barbara, Michael, Helene, and other family members.

Two things that have not changed through all seven editions of *Bridges Not Walls* are my awareness of the difficulty and the necessity of interpersonal communicating and my excitement about the challenge of working toward achieving it. I hope some of this excitement will rub off on you.

John Stewart

PART ONE

The Basic Ingredients

CHAPTER 1

Introduction to the Editor and to This Book

Writing about interpersonal communication, especially in a book that's used mainly as a text, is difficult, because it's almost impossible to practice what you preach. Like many other text authors and editors, I could think of you as just "reader" or "student" and of myself as just "editor" or "teacher" and proceed to tell you what I want you to know. But if I did, we'd have something a lot closer to *impersonal* rather than *interpersonal* communication.

Why? Because, if I write simply as "teacher," and address you simply as "student," or "reader," and if you respond the same way, we will be relating to each other only in terms of our social roles, not in terms of who we are *as persons.* If I use the vocabulary introduced in the next chapter, that kind of contact would connect us as interchangeable parts.

But there's more to it than that. Both you and I are *non*interchangeable, multidimensional persons with distinctive personalities, ideas, convictions, wants, and needs. For my part, my name is John Stewart, I've been teaching college for almost 30 years, and I like just about everything about my job. For the past 5 years I've been in the exciting, demanding, and very rewarding position of being a 50-plus-year-old parent. This is my second time around as a dad. My daughters, who were born just after I finished high school, are in their midthirties, the grandkids are 11 and 9, and our son Lincoln is 5. So Lincoln is an uncle to a niece and nephew older than he, and is also the youngest member of a large extended family of aunts, uncles, and cousins.

I'm a native of the northwest corner of the United States and have been fortunate enough to spend most of my life near where I was born and raised. I love the smell of salt water and the fizz it makes behind a quiet boat; the brisk, wet freshness of our winters; the exhilaration of biking and downhill skiing; the babble of a crowded family gathering; and the rainbow of faces in our church congregation. I dislike phony smiles, grandiose flattery or apologies, pretentious academicians, rules that are vaguely stated but rigidly enforced, oysters, and machinery that runs roughly. I also get impatient with people who have trouble saying what they mean. I was raised in a small town in Washington State and now live in Seattle, near Lake Washington. I like the challenges of helping people in my classes learn new and old ideas, and of translating philosophy into applied insights about communication. I feel very fortunate to have the job, family, and health that I have.

The longer I study and teach interpersonal communication, the more I'm struck by how much the person I am today has been molded by the relationships I've experienced. Some of the most important people in my life are no longer alive: for example, my dad; my father-in-law; my first real "boss," Marc Burdick; college teachers Peter Ristuben and "Prof" Karl; and Allen Clark, the friend who introduced me to Martin Buber's writings. Some others I've almost completely lost contact with, like high school and college teachers, co-workers in the pea cannery, and graduate school classmates. But many other relationships continue to teach and mold me, including those I have with Lincoln and my wife Kris, my mom and stepdad, Kris's mother, my sister Barbara, and close friends Dale Reiger, Karen Zediker, Tim Milander, Father Ralph Carskadden, Chris Galloway, Bill Burgua, and John Paul Olafson. I've also been affected by relationships with many authors who have made themselves available in their writing, especially Martin Buber, Hans-Georg Gadamer, Mikhail Bakhtin, John Shotter, Martin Heidegger, and Carl Rogers. Contacts with all these persons have helped shape me. At the same time, I sense the presence of a continuous "me" that's never static but that's firmly anchored in values, understandings, weaknesses, and strengths that make me who I am.

If I stuck to being just "writer" or "teacher," I could also skip the fact that I am almost as grateful and excited about doing this seventh edition of *Bridges Not Walls* as I was about the first edition, and that I continue to be a little amazed that this book speaks to so many different people. Each mention of the book by a student who has read it or a teacher who has used it is a delight, and I especially like hearing from the communication graduate students and teachers who tell me that this was their introduction to the field. It's a gift to be able to share some ideas and feelings about interpersonal communication in this way, and I'm pleased that readers continue to allow me to talk relatively personally rather than just in the safe, sterile, and distant style of some "educational materials."

The impersonal approach I mentioned would also get in the way of the contact between you and me, because *you* are not simply "reader" or "student." Where were you born and raised, and how has that affected you? Are you reading this book because you want to or because somebody required it? If you're reading it as part of a college course, how do you expect the course to turn out? Challenging? Boring? Threatening? Useful? Inhibiting? Exciting? How do you generally feel about required texts? About going to school? What groups have you been in or are you a part of? A sports team? Neighborhood gang? A band? Campfire or Scouts? Natural Helpers? A church group? A sorority or fraternity? Alateen? What important choices have you made recently? To end a relationship? Move? Change majors? Quit work? Make a new commitment?

I'm not saying that you have to pry into the intimate details of somebody's life before you can communicate with him or her, but I am saying that interpersonal communication happens between *persons,* not between roles, masks, or stereotypes. Interpersonal communication can happen between you and me only to the degree that each of us makes available some of what makes us a person *and* at the same time is aware of some of what makes the other a person, too.

One way to conceptualize what I'm saying is to think about what could be called your Contact Quotient, or CQ. Your CQ is a measure of how you connect with another person. It's the quotient that expresses the ratio between the quality of contact you experience and the quality of contact that's possible. In other words,

$$\frac{\text{Richness or quality of contact achieved}}{\text{Richness or quality of contact possible}}$$

A husband and wife who have been married for 40 years have a huge CQ denominator (the figure below the line)—let's say 10,000. When one is giving the other the silent treatment, their numerator (the figure above the line) is painfully small—maybe 15. So their CQ in this instance would be 15/10,000—pretty low.

But when they spend an afternoon and evening together in conversation, mutually enjoyed activities, and lovemaking, their numerator is very high—perhaps 9,500—and their CQ approaches 10,000/10,000. You and I, on the other hand, have a pretty small denominator. This means that the absolute quality of contact we can achieve by way of this book is relatively low. But we can still work toward a CQ of unity—maybe 100/100—and this is one of my goals in this introduction and the other materials I've written for this book.

It's going to be difficult, though, to maximize the CQ between you and me. I can continue to tell you some of who I am, but I don't know whether what I write is what you need in order to know me as me. In addition, I know almost nothing about what makes you a person—nothing about your choices, feelings, hopes, fears, insights, blind spots—your individuality. This is why *writing* about interpersonal communication can sometimes be frustrating. Interpersonal communication can be discussed in print, but not much of it can happen here.

More can happen, though, than usually does with a textbook. Our relationship can be at least a little closer to interpersonal than it often is. I will work toward this end by continuing to share some of what I'm thinking and feeling in my introductions to the readings, in the Review Questions and Probes at the end of each selection, and in the five essays I've authored or coauthored. I hope you'll be willing to make yourself available by becoming involved enough in this book to recognize clearly which ideas and skills are worthwhile for you and which are not. I also hope you'll be willing and able to make yourself available to other persons reading this book, so they can benefit from your insights and you can benefit from theirs.

WHY APPROACH INTERPERSONAL COMMUNICATION THIS WAY?

Before we begin breaking human communication down into some manageable parts, I want to talk about a couple of beliefs that guide my selection and organization of the materials in this book. I believe that when you know something about this book's rationale, it'll be easier for you to understand what's being said about each topic, and you'll be in a better position to accept what works for you, while leaving aside the rest.

Quality of Communication and Quality of Life

One of my basic assumptions is that *there's a direct link between the quality of your communication and the quality of your life.* I can best explain this idea with a little bit more of my history.

After high school, I attended a community college for two years and then transferred to a four-year college to finish my degree. I took a basic speech communication course at both schools, and noticed that in each, something was missing. The teachers emphasized how to inform others and persuade them to do what you want. They showed our classes how to research and outline ideas, how to move and gesture effectively, and how to use vocal variety to keep our listeners' attention. Students were required to write papers and give speeches to demonstrate that they'd mastered these skills. But the courses seemed to overlook something important. Neither the textbooks nor the instructors said anything about the connection between the quality of your communication and the quality of your life.

Other texts and teachers did. In my literature and anthropology classes I read that "no human is an island," and that "the human is a social animal." Psychology books reported studies of infants who suffered profoundly when they were deprived of touch, talk, or other kinds of contact. A philosophy text made the same point in these words: "communication means life or death to persons. . . . Both the individual and society derive their basic meaning from the relations that exist between [persons]. It is through dialogue that [humans] accomplish the miracle of personhood and community."[1]

The speech communication texts and teachers promised that they could help students learn to make ideas clear, be entertaining, and persuade others to agree with them. But they seemed to miss the communication impact of the point being made in literature, anthropology, psychology, and philosophy. If humans really are social beings, then *communication is where humanness happens.* In other words, although communication is definitely a way to express ideas, get things done, and entertain, convince, and persuade others, it's also more than that. It's the process that defines who we are. As a result, *if we experience mainly distant, objective, impersonal communicating, we're liable to grow up pretty one-sided, but if we experience our share of close, supportive, interpersonal communicating, we're likely to develop more of our human potential.* This is how the quality of your communication affects the quality of your life.

One reason I started teaching interpersonal communication is that I figured out the truth of this idea, and this same point has motivated me to edit this book. I've also been impressed with some recent research that supports this reason for studying interpersonal communication.

Medical doctors have done some of the most impressive studies. James J. Lynch was codirector of the Psychophysiological Clinic and Laboratories at the University of Maryland School of Medicine when he introduced one of his books with these words:

> As we shall see, study after study reveals that human dialogue not only affects our hearts significantly but can even alter the biochemistry of individual tissues at the farthest extremities of the body. Since blood flows through every human tissue, the entire body is influenced by dialogue.[2]

In other words, Lynch is saying that the quality of your communication affects the *physiological* quality of your life. One of his important discoveries is that blood pressure changes much more rapidly and frequently than people used to believe, and that some of the most significant blood pressure changes occur when people speak and are spoken to. Computerized instruments permit Lynch and other researchers to monitor blood pressure constantly and to map the effects of a person's entering the room, engaging in nonverbal contact, reading aloud, and conversing. Speech appears to directly affect blood pressure; in one study the mean arterial pressure of healthy nurses went from 92 when they were quiet to 100 when they "talked calmly."[3] Listening has the opposite effect. Rather than just returning to baseline when a person stops speaking, blood pressure actually drops below baseline when one concentrates on the other person.[4] And this happens only when we talk with people; "conversation" with pets does not produce the same result.[5]

In an earlier book, Lynch discusses some of the more global effects of essentially the same phenomenon. There he reports the results of hundreds of medical studies that correlate loneliness and poor health. For example, people with few interpersonal relationships tend to die before their counterparts who enjoy a network of family and friends.[6] In fact, a study of identical twins found that smoking habits, obesity, and cholesterol levels of the twins who had heart attacks were not significantly different from the twins with healthier hearts. But there were some other important differences, one of which was what the doctors called "poor childhood and adult interpersonal relationships."[7]

What conclusions can be drawn from evidence like this? Lynch puts it this way:

> Human companionship does affect our heart, and . . . there is reflected in our hearts a biological basis for our need for loving human relationships, which we fail to fulfill at our peril. . . . The ultimate decision is simple: we must either learn to live together or increase our chances of prematurely dying alone.[8]

In other words, if you view quality of life physiologically, it becomes apparent that there's more to it than ample food, warm clothing, shelter, education, and modern conveniences. The quality of your existence is linked directly to the quality of your communication.

If you go beyond physiological quality of life, the same point can be made even more strongly. In fact, nonmedical people have been talking about the link between the quality of your communication and the quality of your life for many years. For example, the philosopher Martin Buber wrote:

> The unique thing about the human world is that something is continually happening between one person and another, something that never happens in the animal or plant world. . . . *Humans are made human by that happening.* . . . That special event begins by one human turning to another, seeing him or her as this particular other being, and offering to communicate with the other in a mutual way, building from the individual world each person experiences to a world they share together.[9]

Jesuit psychologist John Powell put the same idea in simpler terms: "What I am, at any given moment in the process of my becoming a person, will be determined by my relationships with those who love me or refuse to love me, with those I love or refuse to love."[10]

"Okay," you might be saying, "I don't disagree with the lofty ideals expressed by all these people, and I can see how quality of life and quality of communication are related, but let's be a little practical. It's not always *possible* to treat everybody as a personal friend, and more importantly, it's not always *wise*.

So you can't realistically expect your communication always to be friendly and supportive. Impersonal communication happens all the time, and often it's exactly the right kind of communication to have."

I agree. And this is an important point. Many factors make interpersonal communication difficult or even impossible. Role definitions, status relationships, cultural differences, physical surroundings, and even the amount of time available can all be obstacles to interpersonal contact. Lack of awareness and lack of skills can also affect your CQ. One person may want to connect interpersonally with someone else, but may simply not know how to do it.

In other situations it may be possible but, as you point out, it may not be wise. The power relationships or amount of hostility may make it too risky. Everyday communication also includes a great deal of deception. One study concluded that 62 percent of statements made in conversations could be classified as deceptive, and in two other large surveys, more than one-third of the respondents admitted to lying to close friends about important topics.[11] I know a man who used to teach interpersonal communication as part of a Living Skills program in a prison work-release facility. Eric also worked there as a guard. His power as a guard—he had the authority to send people back to the county jail—drastically affected what he could accomplish as an interpersonal communication teacher. Some people in his classes responded openly to his efforts to connect with them. Others were so hardened by their years in various prisons that they could think only about maintaining their own power in the convict hierarchy and getting out as soon as possible—legally or otherwise. It simply didn't make good sense for Eric to try to communicate with all the persons in his class in consistently interpersonal ways. The bottom line is that all our contacts certainly cannot be interpersonal, but in most cases, more of them could be. And if they were, the quality of our lives would be enhanced.

Human Being Results from Human Contact

The second, closely related basic assumption behind the materials in this book is that *there is a basic movement in the human world, and it is toward relation, not division.* This might sound a little vague, but I think it'll get clearer if you bear with me for a couple of paragraphs. First, I believe that human life is a process and that the general kind of process we humans are engaged in is growing into fully developed persons. So far, no big deal, right?

Second, humans are relational, not solitary, beings. We fundamentally or existentially need contact with other persons. If you could combine a human egg and sperm in a completely impersonal environment, what you'd end up with would not be a person. This is different from cloning. I'm thinking about an artificial womb, machine-assisted birth, mechanical feeding and changing, and so on. Why wouldn't the being created this way be a person? Because in order to become a person, the human needs to experience relationships with other persons. This point can't be proved experimentally, of course, because it would be unethical to treat any human organism that way. But there is some empirical evidence to support the claim I'm thinking of studies of "feral," or "wild," children—children discovered after they'd been raised for a time by wolves or other animals. One book tells about the Wild Boy of Aveyron, a "remarkable creature" who came out of the woods near a small village in southern France on January 9, 1800, and was captured while digging for vegetables in a village garden. According to the people who knew him, the creature

> was human in bodily form and walked erect. Everything else about him suggested an animal. He was naked except for the tatters of a shirt and showed no modesty, no awareness of himself as a human person related in any way to the people who had captured him. He could not speak and made only weird, meaningless cries. Though very short, he appeared to be a boy of about eleven or twelve.[12]

The creature was taken to a distinguished physician named Dr. Pinel, one of the founders of psychiatry. The doctor was unable to help, partly because "the boy had no human sense of being in the world. He had not sense of himself as a person related to other persons."[13] The "savage of Aveyron" made progress toward becoming human only after he was taken on as a project by another medical doctor named Jean-Marc Gaspard Itard. Itard's first move was to give the boy a foster family and to put him in the care of a mature, loving mother, Mme. Guerin. In this household the boy was able to learn to "use his own chamberpot," dress himself, come when he was called, and even associate some letters of the alphabet with some pictures.

Itard's first report about his year of efforts to socialize the wild boy emphasizes the importance of human contact in becoming a person. Itard describes in detail events that demonstrate the significance of "the feeling of friendship" between him and the boy and especially between the boy and Mme. Guerin: "Perhaps I shall be understood if people remember the major influence on a child of those endless cooings and caresses, those kindly nothings which come naturally from a mother's heart and which bring forth the first smiles and joys in a human life."[14] Without this contact, the young human organism was a creature, a savage. With contact, he began to develop into a person.

Accounts like this one help make the point that *human being results from human contact.* Our genes give us the potential to develop into humans, but without contact, this potential cannot be realized. People definitely are affected by solitude, meditation, and quiet reflection, but mostly because those individualized activities happen in the context of ongoing relationships. As many writers have pointed out, we are molded by our contacts with nature, our contacts with other humans, and our contacts with whatever supreme being, higher power, or god we believe in. This book focuses on the second kind—our contacts with people. This is *why* there is a direct connection between the quality of your communication and the quality of your life. This is also why I encourage you to think about your communicating in terms of its Contact Quotient. You certainly cannot have the same quality of contact with everybody you meet, in every situation. But you can recognize the quality of contact that's possible between you and the other person(s) and work toward a CQ of 1/1.

Again, I'm not saying that if everybody just holds hands, smiles, and stares at the sunset, all conflict will disappear and the world will be a happy place. I'm not that naïve. But the kind of communicating discussed in this book is not just a trendy, pop-psychology, Western, white, middle-class exercise in narcissism or New Age good-feeling. It's grounded in some basic beliefs about who human beings are and what communication means in human life—regardless of ethnicity, gender, class, or age. In the first reading of Chapter 2, I say more about this point. When you read those pages, you might want to refer to the two assumptions I just described.

PREVIEW OF THE BOOK

So far I've tried to say that for me, interpersonal communication differs from impersonal communication in that it consists of *contact between (inter) persons.* This means that for interpersonal communication to happen, each participant has to be willing and able to make available some of what makes him or her a person and to be aware of some of what makes the other a person. This willingness and ability will happen only when the people involved (1) are familiar with the basic ingredients of the human communication process, (2) are willing and able to accurately perceive and listen to themselves and others, (3) are willing and able to make themselves and their ideas available to others, (4) recognize how the basic communication processes work in various relationships, (5) have some resources to deal with differences, and (6) can put the whole complex of attitudes and skills together in a human synthesis that works for them.

This is why I've organized *Bridges Not Walls* into six sections, or parts; the readings in each part are designed to do what I've just outlined. So the next two chapters, which complete Part One, explore the rest of the basic ingredients—your overall view of the communication process (Chapter 2), and the verbal and nonverbal parts of the process (Chapter 3). Parts II and III are organized around two metaphors, "openness" and "inhaling-exhaling." I explain the reasons for both metaphors in the introduction to Chapter 4. Basically, I use the term *inhaling* to highlight the perception and listening parts of the communication process and *exhaling* to focus attention on the messages that are expressed; the allusion to breathing emphasizes the impossibility, in actual practice, of separating these two processes.

Part Two is made up of three chapters treating various parts of inhaling. Chapter 4 consists of three selections about self-awareness. Then Chapter 5 expands from self-perception to perception of others, and Chapter 6 provides four discussions of listening. The two chapters of Part Three are made up of articles talking about self-expression and self-disclosure (Chapter 7) and hurtful and negative communicating (Chapter 8). Together, Parts One, Two, and Three lay out the general communication process and specific information about each of its main subparts.

The last three sections of this book focus solidly on application. The four chapters of Part Four discuss applications to relationships. First there are readings about how relationships are negotiated (Chapter 9). Then I've included two discussions of friendships in Chapter 10, two articles about family communication in Chapter 11, and three treatments of communication between intimate partners in Chapter 12. Following are the two chapters that make up Part Five, where 12 authors grapple with some of the most difficult situations where communication knowledge and skills are applied. Chapter 13 focuses on conflict, and Chapter 14 discusses communicating across cultures. These readings can help equip you to cope with the challenges of defensiveness, hostility, anger, ethnocentrism, racism, and related tensions.

The final part of the book consists of four overall approaches to interpersonal communicating described by a teacher, a psychologist, a counselor, and a philosopher. These readings illustrate how the individual insights, attitudes, and skills talked about in all the other chapters can be condensed and synthesized. They also suggest some additional ways to take this content out of the classroom and into your life.

Before each reading there are some introductory comments that pinpoint what I think are the key ideas that appear there. At the end of each reading I've also included two kinds of questions. Review Questions prompt your recall of key ideas. Probes are questions intended to provoke your thinking and discussion, especially about how the ideas in the reading relate (1) to your own life experience and (2) to ideas in other readings.

One final note: A few of the essays that I have reprinted here were written before people learned about the destructive potential of the historical male bias in the English language. As a result, when these authors mean "humanity," "humans," or "humankind," they write *man* or *mankind*. And when they are using a pronoun to refer to a person in the abstract, it's always *he* rather than *she* or *he and she*. In some cases I've tried to delete offensive uses or to substitute terms in brackets. In other cases, that kind of editing would make the essay very awkward and difficult to read. This is especially a problem in the readings by Jack Gibb (Chapter 13) and Martin Buber (Chapter 18). I hope in those cases that you'll be able to read beyond the sexist language for the important ideas.

I also hope that you can have some fun with at least parts of what's ahead. Sometimes the topics are serious, and occasionally the concepts are complex. But this book is about familiar activities that all of us engage in just about all the time. By the time you're finished with it, you should be an even more effective communicator than you already are. That kind of learning can be exciting!

NOTES

1. Reuel Howe, *The Miracle of Dialogue* (New York: Seabury, 1963), cited in *The Human Dialogue*, ed. F. W. Matson and A. Montagu (New York: Free Press, 1968), pp. 148–149.
2. James J. Lynch, *The Language of the Heart: The Body's Response to Human Dialogue* (New York: Basic Books, 1985), p. 3.
3. Lynch, pp. 123–124.
4. Lynch, pp. 160ff.
5. Lynch, pp. 150–155.

6. James J. Lynch, *The Broken Heart: The Medical Consequences of Loneliness* (New York: Basic Books, 1977), pp. 42–51.
7. E. A. Liljefors and R. H. Rahe, "Psychosocial Characteristics of Subjects with Myocardial Infarction in Stockholm," in *Life Stress Illness,* ed. E. K. Gunderson and R. H. Rahe (Springfield, IL: Charles C. Thomas, 1974), pp. 90–104.
8. Lynch, *The Broken Heart,* 14.
9. Paraphrased from Martin Buber, *Between Man and Man* (New York: Macmillan, 1965), p. 203. Italics added.
10. John Powell, *Why Am I Afraid to Tell You Who I Am?* (Chicago: Argus Communications, 1969), p. 43.
11. H. Dan O'Hair and Michael J. Cody, "Deception," in *The Dark Side of Interpersonal Communication,* ed. Wm. R. Cupach and B. H. Spitzberg (Hillsdale, NJ: Lawrence Erlbaum, 1994), pp. 183–184.
12. Roger Shattuck, *The Forbidden Experiment: The Story of the Wild Boy of Aveyron* (New York: Farrar Straus Giroux, 1980), p. 5.
13. Shattuck, p. 37.
14. Shattuck, p. 119.

CHAPTER 2

Introduction to Interpersonal Communication

O ne of the best courses I took during my first year of college was Introduction to Philosophy. Part of the appeal was the teacher. He knew his stuff, and he loved to teach it. But as I discovered a few years later, I also enjoyed the course because I liked the kind of thinking that was going on in the materials we read and the discussions we had. It seemed as though I usually thought that way myself. As I continued through college, I supplemented my communication courses with other work in philosophy. The topics I talk about in this essay reflect that dual interest.

One definition of philosophy is "the systematic critique of presuppositions." This means that philosophers are interested in first principles, basic understandings, underlying assumptions. If you've read much philosophy, you may have the impression that it can be stuffy or even nitpicky to the point of irrelevance. But it can also be exciting and important, because the philosopher says something like, "Hold it! Before you go off to spin a complicated web of explanations about human communication, or an economic system, or the history of culture, or the operation of a political system, try to get clear about some *basic* things. When you're talking about human communication, for example, what are you assuming about what actually gets passed between people as they communicate?" The philosopher might say, "If each human perceives the world in his or her own way, then I can communicate only with *my perception of you*; I can *never* really get in touch with you. All I can do, when it comes right down to it, is communicate with myself!"

Basic issues like these intrigue me, mainly because they have so many practical applications. People's everyday choices about both big and small beliefs and actions grow out of their assumptions—about what's right, what's important, what's honorable, what will provide the best income, or whatever. So it's important to think about those assumptions and change them when they aren't working well. I know that many potentially exciting conversations have been squelched by someone's dogmatic insistence that all participants "define their terms." But I also know that a great deal of fuzziness can be cleared up, and many unhealthy choices can be revised when a conversation starts with some shared understandings about the assumptions behind and definitions of what's being discussed.

In the following essay I describe my definition of the topic of this book—interpersonal communication. I begin with a five-part description of communication in general that includes a practical implication of each of the five parts. Then I discuss interpersonal communication as a subset of the more general term.

As you'll notice, the views of communication and interpersonal communication that I develop here extend the point I make in Chapter 1 about quality of communication and quality of life. One of the most important things I want to emphasize throughout this book is that communication functions in part to negotiate identities, or selves. In other words, who I am emerges in my listening and talking. This is why the reading begins with an extended explanation of how human worlds or realities are collaboratively constructed (built, modified, torn down, re-built) in communication. And the definition of interpersonal communication grows out of this point. In brief, interpersonal communication, as I put it, happens when the people involved maximize the presence of the personal in their listening and talking.

The reading is a little long, and I apologize for that. But I'm using it to frame just about everything that follows in this book.

COMMUNICATING AND INTERPERSONAL COMMUNICATING

John Stewart

Communication is an intriguing topic to study because, on the one hand, you and I have been doing it since at least the day we were born, so we have some claim to being "experts," and on the other hand, many of the difficulties that people experience are communication difficulties, which suggests that we all have a lot to learn. If your communication life is trouble-free, this book and the course it is probably a part of might not be for you. But if your experience is anything like mine, you might be interested in some help. After 30 years of communication study and teaching, I still experience plenty of misunderstandings, but I've found that some basic insights about what communication is and how it works can smooth many of the rough spots. That's why this introduction describes the general subject matter of communication and this book's specific focus, interpersonal communication. I don't want to make too much out of "defining our terms," but as I think you'll discover, there are some common ways of thinking about these topics that can actually make things harder rather than easier. And there are some important features of communication and interpersonal communication that significantly affect how they work.

COMMUNICATING[1]

In the most general sense, the terms *communication* and *communicating* label *the processes humans use to construct meaning together.* So when somebody says, "She's a good communicator" or "We communicate well," it basically means that contacts with those persons go smoothly and that there aren't many confusions or misunderstandings, which is to say that the meanings the people build together generally work okay. By the same token, people talk about "poor communication" when they experience confusing, ambiguous, frustrating, or incomplete meanings. Interestingly, this construction-of-meanings-together continues even when people are in conflict. When two parties are in the midst of a violent disagreement, they are still co-constructing their meanings of anger, re-sentiment, hostility, fairness, and respect. This can become clear if one party refuses to argue—the opponent has to figure out what this unexpected move *means*. So whether you're talking about written or spoken communication, verbal or nonverbal, face-to-face or e-mail, conflict or cooperation, the process basically involves humans making meaning together.

Meaning is what makes the human world different from the spaces inhabited by other living beings—worms, dogs and cats, and even, so far as we now know, chimpanzees, whales, and dolphins. Since humans live in worlds of meaning—rather than worlds made up of only objects or things—the processes of constructing and modifying these worlds goes on literally *all* the time. This is why communication is such a major part of human living.

To clarify this idea that humans live in worlds of meaning, consider the part of your world that's your "home." If someone asked you to describe your home, you probably wouldn't just talk about how many square feet it has, how tall it is, the distance from your home to some prominent landmark, or the color of the bedroom walls (objective features). Instead, you'd talk about what it *means* to live in a place this small or this big, what you think and feel about the wall color, and what it *means* to live where your home is located. Similarly, the transportation part of your world is significant not simply because you travel by bike or on a bus, in your own old or new sedan or convertible, on foot or on a motorcycle, but because of what it *means* in your family, group of friends, and culture to get around this way. And the meanings of all these parts of our worlds get built up (constructed) and changed in communication—the written and oral, verbal and nonverbal contact people have with each other.

When each of us was born, this process of meaning-making was going on all around us, and we entered it kind of like a chunk of potato is plopped into a pot of simmering soup. The soup was there before we were born, it will be simmering all the time we're alive, and these communication processes will continue after we die. As individuals and groups, we certainly affect our worlds a whole lot more than a chunk of potato affects a pot of soup. In fact, as I said in the Introduction, the *responses* or *choices* people make go a long way toward determining the quality of their lives. But each of us is also a participant in an ongoing process that we do not completely control, a process as old and as large as the history of humanity. All the time, everywhere, in all the contacts that make us social animals, humans are constructing meaning together, and "communication" is the name of this ongoing process.

Interpersonal communication is a subset of this general process, a particular kind or type of communication. I'll describe what it is later in this chapter. But first I want to explain five important features of all kinds of communication, the first of which I've already introduced, and an important implication or practical application of each of the five:

1. Humans live in worlds of meaning, and communication is the process of collaboratively constructing these meanings.
   Implication 1: No one person can completely control a communication event, and no single person or action causes—or can be blamed for—a communication outcome.

2. Culture figures prominently in this process. Ethnicity, gender, age, social class, sexual orientation, and other cultural features always affect communication and are affected by it.
   Implication 2: Your cultures, mine, and the cultures of each author in this book affect what is said about communication in this book and how you respond to it.
3. Some of the most important meanings people collaboratively construct are identities; all communication involves negotiating identities, or selves.
   Implication 3: Identity issues are always in play.
4. The most influential communication events are conversations.
   Implication 4: The most ordinary communication events are the most significant.
5. The most useful single communication skill is "nexting."
   Implication 5: Whenever you face a communication challenge or problem, the most helpful question you can ask yourself is, "What can I help to happen next, and how?"

1. Humans Live in Worlds of Meaning, and Communication is the Process of Collaboratively Constructing these Meanings.

When I introduced this idea, you might have thought it was kind of strange. Most people don't give much thought to their definition of *communication*, and if pressed, a person who's new to this subject matter might just say that communication basically means "getting your ideas across," or "sending and receiving messages." In fact, there's a widespread belief in many cultures that communication

- begins when a sender gets an idea he or she wants to communicate,
- works by having the sender translate the idea into words or some other kind of message,
- also requires the receiver to perceive the message and retranslate it into an idea,
- can be evaluated in terms of the match, fit, or, fidelity between message-sent and message-received, and
- can be analyzed by figuring out who *caused* its successes or failures (who's responsible, who gets the credit, who's at fault, or to blame).

According to this definition, the general process of communication can be diagrammed this way:

$$\text{Idea}_1 \rightarrow \text{Message Sent} \rightarrow \text{Message Received} \rightarrow \text{Idea}_2$$

When idea_2 is the same as idea_1, then communication is successful. When the two ideas don't match, there's a misunderstanding that's somebody's "fault."

This might sound like a fairly reasonable, even accurate, understanding of communication. **But all these common beliefs about communication are misleading, and if you act on them, you're likely to have problems.**

Let's consider each briefly.

Communication Consists Mainly of "Getting Your Ideas Across"   This belief focuses attention on the topic or content of the communicating—the ideas
people talk about. And it's reasonable to believe that idea transmission or information sharing is the most important function of communication. But to test
this belief, look for a minute at an excerpt from an actual conversation:

1. JOHN: So what do you THINK about the bicycles on campus?
2. JUDY: I think they're terrible.
3. JOHN: Sure is about a MILLION of 'em.
4. JUDY: Eh, heh.
5. JOHN: (Overlapping Judy) Duzit SEEM to you . . . there's a lot more people
    this year?
6. JUDY: The re-yeah, for sure.
7. JOHN: (Overlapping) Go-GOD, there seems to be a mILLion people.
8. JUDY: Yeah. (brief pause) YEah, there's way too many. I can't at TIMES the bi-
    cycles get so
9. bad I just get off mine and . . . hhh . . . give up.
10. JOHN: (Overlapping) Oh, really . . .
11. JOHN: I dunno, when I DODGE one then I have to DODGE another one, 'n
    it's an endless
12. cycle.
13. JUDY: Yeah (brief pause), oh they're TERrible.
14. JOHN: 'S so many people.
15. JUDY: Um hmm.[2]

The content of this conversation—bicycles on campus—is only a small part of
what's going on here. John and Judy are college students who have just met, and
they are using the topic of bicycles in part to figure out who they are to and for
each other. In fact, the most important parts of this conversation are probably
not John's and Judy's ideas about bicycles, but the commonality that their similar opinions creates, combined with the subtle power relationship that's constructed when John defines the topic and overlaps Judy's talk, and Judy is willing to go along with this slightly one-up/one-down relationship. In other
words, especially if you remember that John and Judy don't know each other
well, you'd probably agree that the most important features of this conversation
are what communication researchers call the *"identity messages"* or *"relationship
messages."* These are the verbal and nonverbal indicators of how John defines
himself, how he views Judy, and what he thinks Judy thinks of him, along with
Judy's verbal and nonverbal ways of defining herself, what she thinks of John,
and what she thinks John thinks of her. These messages about the identities, or
selves, of the persons involved and their relationships with each other are at
least as important as the idea content, and often more so. So the first part of this
common definition of communication is misleading because human communication always involves more than simply getting ideas across.

*Communication Works by Having the Sender Translate the Idea into Words
or Some Other Kind of Message*   This belief assumes that speech happens

when a speaker changes a mental idea into spoken words. But this conversation didn't just "start" when John got a nonverbal idea about bicycles in his head. He's encountering Judy in a particular context—in this case they're both volunteer subjects in a communication experiment. Their social, political, and religious cultures help define how similar-age men and women strangers relate to one another, and they're probably each looking for ways to make the encounter as comfortable as possible. So the topic of bicycles emerges out of a context much broader than John's mind. In addition, before John spoke, there was probably no clearly identifiable, singular piece of mental content (an idea) located somewhere in his brain. The phenomena called "ideas" are complex and always changing; they're made up not simply of synapse patterns or cognitions but of words, intonation, stress, pauses, and facial expression; and they change as they are being uttered. This means that there is no unitary, identifiable thing inside a person's head (an idea) that gets translated or encoded into spoken words.

Communication Requires the Receiver to Perceive the Message and Retranslate it into an Idea   This belief suggests that listeners are doing the same things that speakers are, only in reverse. But again, human communication is not this simple. First, notice that neither John nor Judy is simply "sender" or "receiver" at any point in this exchange; in fact, they're both sending and receiving at every moment. *As she speaks,* Judy is noticing John's response (she is receiving) and is modifying what she says and how she says it. John is doing the same thing. *As he listens,* he's "saying" things to Judy with his face and body. And this goes on all the time. Human communicators are always sending and receiving simultaneously. As a result, each communicator has the opportunity to change how things are going at any time in the process. When this excerpt of the conversation ends, John and Judy are at a point of potential change, and the next utterance may move them closer together or farther apart. John could pick up on Judy's disclosure that she is a cyclist, for example, or Judy could introduce a new topic that's more important to her than this one. The point is, much more is going on here than back-and-forth translation and retranslation of individual ideas.

Communication Can be Evaluated in Terms of the Match, Fit, or Fidelity between Message-Sent and Message-Received   This belief suggests that you could isolate and define John's and Judy's mental contents (ideas) so you could figure out how well they match or fit. But since ideas are so fluid and dynamic, and since communication happens as much in talk as in people's heads, the fidelity model doesn't fit living conversation very well. In order actually to apply this notion of matching or fitting, you'd have to slow down and distort the exchange to the point where it wouldn't be anything like what actually happened. Communication success has more to do with the people's ability to continue relating smoothly with each other than with matching mental contents.

Communication Problems Can Be Analyzed by Identifying Fault and Blame   To say that a problem is somebody's "fault" is to say that she or he *caused* it, like a temperature below 0°C causes water to freeze, or pushing down on one end of a lever causes the other end to rise. In other words, this belief assumes that human communication is governed by laws of cause and effect. But is it? If Judy noticed the one-up/one-down power relationship with John, she might believe that it's John's fault, because he asserted power by taking on the roles of topic definer and overlapping speaker.[3] John, on the other hand, might think that any power imbalance between them is due to Judy's initial silence, or her willingness to go along with his topic choice. Who's right? Who's fault is it really? Who's really to blame?

One problem with questions like these is that they require somebody to identify where the exchange *started*, so they can determine what's "cause" and what's "effect." But as I've already noted, some of what's going on in a conversation is as old as the participants themselves, or older. And this is literally always true. Every single thing the participants say and do may be understood as a *response* to what preceded it in their lives. No living human is the original Adam or Eve, the first one to disturb the cosmic silence of the universe. An enormous amount of communication precedes everything all of us communicate.[4] Even the first "hi" in a relationship can be understood as a response to a smile, the situation, or a lesson your parents taught you about being polite. In John and Judy's conversation, some of what's said can be traced back to the gender definitions that each of them developed when they were growing up. And these influences could be traced back to John's and Judy's parents' definitions of themselves, which came in part from *their* parents, and so on. This is the kind of complex mess a search for original causes can suck you into. And for the sake of argument, let's assume that John and Judy finally agree on just where the exchange started and whose fault some part of it was. What then? Will the resulting guilt feelings or an apology from the accused party fix the problem? Not usually. Even when people agree on fault and blame, that agreement doesn't usually improve things much. The reason is that human communication is much too complex to be profitably analyzed into simple cause-effect, fault-blame sequences.

In short, two things can be learned from this brief example:

- Some of the most common understandings or definitions of human communication are plausible but misleading.
- Since the way you think about or define something determines what you experience, and what you experience determines the responses you make, it's important to have a workable definition of human communication so you can respond in ways that help you communicate effectively.

The main reason that this common definition of communication is misleading is that it's oversimplified.

Communication Is the Continuous, Complex, Collaborative Process of Verbal and Nonverbal Meaning-Making through Which We Construct the Worlds of Meaning We Inhabit   It's *continuous* because humans are always making meaning—figuring out, making sense of, or interpreting what's happening. It's *complex* because it involves not just words and ideas but also intonation, facial expression, eye contact, touch, and several other nonverbal elements, and it always includes identity and relationship messages, culture and gender cues, more or less hidden agendas, unspoken expectations, and literally dozens of other features that usually become apparent only when they create problems. It's *collaborative,* because we do it with other people. This definitely isn't to say that we always *agree,* but only that we don't communicate alone.[5] Even prize-fighters collaborate, because they show up at the same time and abide by the rules. "Co-labor-ating" just means working together, and collaboration can be as anonymous as obeying traffic laws and speaking the local language, or as intimate as attending to your partner's lovemaking preferences.

Worlds of Meaning   "Worlds of meaning" is simply a label for *the more or less coherent spheres of sense, significance, or interpretation that each human inhabits.* You might think of your world of meaning as your "reality" or your overall view of the way things are. I call it a "world of meaning" partly to indicate that there's a wholeness to it. The geographic world (that is, the earth) is roughly shaped like a sphere, and the sphere is the ancient symbol for wholeness. Even though every human's world of meaning changes and has incomplete parts, people experience their world or reality as relatively whole.

It's useful to think of this world as made up of at least five main elements, or dimensions: space, time, laws of physics, culture, and relationships. Most adults' worlds also include the dimension of work. There are undoubtedly more than these six—for example, religion—but these are the most common important dimensions. The main point about these six dimensions of our worlds is that, as I've indicated, they're all inherited, constructed, modified, and molded in communication.

Space   How big is your living space or your bedroom? How big would you *like* it to be? As I mentioned above, this is part of the spatial dimension of your world, and there are many other spatial elements. For example, how crowded or roomy is the campus, neighborhood, or community where you're currently living? Do you think that everybody in this campus, neighborhood, or community believes it's as crowded or roomy as you do? Probably not, which is one of the ways your world of meaning differs from other people's. How do you think the worlds of people who were born and raised in New York City, Tokyo, Los Angeles, Mexico City, and Chicago are different from the worlds of natives of Wyoming, Montana, Utah, Western Australia, Saskatchewan, or the Dakotas? What are some communication events where the spatial parts of your world are particularly relevant? Looking for a place to live? Interviewing for a job? Negotiating with a roommate? Each of us inhabits a world that's partly spatial, and its meaning is built in communication.

Time   When you're put on hold on the telephone, how long are you willing to wait? How fast do you walk and talk, and does everybody walk and talk at the same speed you do? What time is "really early" in the morning for you, and what time is "really late" at night? What are some relevant meanings of time? For example, if your boss at work asks to meet with you at 9 AM, how late can you arrive before you have to apologize—9:03? 9:10? 9:20? What age people do you think of as "a lot younger" than you? A lot older? How did you develop these time-related aspects of your world? What communicating affects them most? When are the time dimensions of your world most relevant? When you plan a weekend with a friend? Register for classes? Make a commitment at work?

Laws of Physics   Even if you've never studied physics and couldn't name a law of physics if you had do, parts of your world are also governed by your understandings about these regularities or laws. For example, you know that if you lean far enough back in your chair, you'll fall over—because of the law of gravity. The same law makes it harder to pedal uphill than down. You also know that fire melts ice and can burn fingers. Especially if you're a long distance from the equator, it'll be hotter when the sun's directly overhead and colder when it's not. If you don't clean your teeth, plaque will form and eventually decay will probably set in.

Many of these physical regularities are common to just about everybody's world, but others aren't. Aircraft pilots have to apply physical principles of lift and drag that are irrelevant to most people, and the worlds of people who sail boats include not only lift and drag but also a different set of understandings about relative wind, waterline length, and displacement. Auto and cycle racers think about tires in terms of friction and wear, and people who cook learn the temperatures at which butter burns, bread dough rises, and sugar carmelizes. Welders know about combining metals with heat; the worlds of carpenters, baseball players, and furniture movers include important information about levers and leverage; and electricians and auto mechanics understand some of the physics of electricity.

Once again, communication defines, transmits, and changes these parts of our world. Often one's understanding of these regularities stays in the background, but it becomes an important part of your communicating when, for example, you decide with your partner or parents what driving "too fast" is (what conditions create an unacceptable risk of losing control of the vehicle?), when you plan and put on a barbecue (how much fuel is needed to cook this quantity of food?), and when you move heavy furniture (how can leverage help?).

Culture   The 1986 film *The Gods Must Be Crazy* illustrates how laws of physics and culture interrelate in the world of a tribe of bush people. In the film, members of the tribe discover a Coke bottle that has fallen from the sky, and they conclude that it came from the gods. They try to figure out how to return it to its rightful place, and this effort reveals their unusual—to people in Western cultures—view of the law of gravity.

Films and other information about other cultures combined with international travel and intercultural relationships can all help clarify how culture is a part of each person's world. In the next section I'll highlight the importance of culture in communication, but for now I just want to emphasize that culture means more than a group's customs, cooking, and clothing. Think of culture as "the sum total of ways of living built up by a group of human beings and transmitted from one generation to another."[6] This means that ethnicity is an important part of culture—as in African-American, Latino, Asian-American, Anglo or Caucasian, or Arab—but today many groups of mixed ethnicity are also considered cultures or subcultures because they also share distinctive ways of living. Some people say that cultures can be identified in terms of race, class, gender, age, sexual orientation, or religion. Others say that some of these markers—for example, religion—are too general or are not clearly cultural. Contemporary communication theory underscores, though, that cultural identity is not limited to just one feature—like ethnicity—but is made up of "interlocking and overlapping modes of identity" and "the intersection of various subject positions."[7] As a result, most would agree today that not only may various ethnic groups constitute cultures, but so may the Amish people in the midwestern United States, gay men, lesbian women, members of "Generation X," people over 65, stockbrokers, and the blue-collar families inhabiting an area of south Chicago one communication scholar called "Teamsterville."[8] Importantly, this understanding of culture may make it possible for two members of the same *family* to belong to different *cultures.* A heterosexual brother and his lesbian sister may belong to different cultures, for example, or, if you consider gender a cultural marker, so may a heterosexual brother and his heterosexual sister.

The three key features of culture are group identity, the shared ways of living that produce and reflect this identity, and the transmission of this identity from one generation to the next. Every human group with these features could be thought of as a culture, whether the group is relatively small—Australian aborigines living in the state of Nebraska—or large—women or men. The most trustworthy way to determine whether a group makes up a culture is to ask several potential members. Usually, if people identify themselves culturally, it works best to treat them that way.

Most people studying this general topic also agree that culture becomes manifest or concrete mainly in a group's ways of communicating. So cultures are marked primarily by special ways of verbally and nonverbally communicating, including terms for important things and people, appropriate and taboo topics, valued and criticized speaking styles, and so on. Silence, for example, is important in Apache culture. Many Apache ridicule "the whiteman" because they talk so often, so loudly, and so much.[9]

What are the important cultural dimensions of your world? Your ethnicity? Age? Gender? Physical ability? Social class? Where your family lives or where they came from? Sexual orientation? Religion? How many different cultures do you consider yourself a member of? I consider myself to be Western, Anglo, middle-class, middle-aged, heterosexual, male, a parent, and a teacher–scholar. All these features are parts of my world, and each has emerged and taken on its meaning for me as I've communicated over my life span. Sometimes these aspects of my world stay in the background, but at other times they are central parts of my communicating.

Relationships   It's easy to understand how important relationships are to human worlds. Each of us has been molded most of all by our relationships in our family of origin—the people we lived with in our early years. Our senses of ourselves as women and men emerge in our relationships with our parents, as do our definitions of what it means to be a husband, mother, wife, and father.

Family relationships are where we learn how to act—how to express (or hide) anger, deal with money, be polite, tell the truth and lie, work and relax.

Relationships with grandparents, cousins, and aunts and uncles are also important, as are links with playmates, best friends, teachers, and members of organizations we are a part of—sports teams, school clubs, neighborhood gangs. Again, you might think for a minute about the relationships that help define your world. What's the difference in importance and intimacy of your relationship with your mom and the relationship with your dad? How are you affected by relationships with sisters or brothers? What nonfamily relationships have affected you most? If you're married or intimately partnered with someone, how does this relationship reflect the way you get along with your mom or dad?

Work   Many adults also work, at least part of the time, and the worlds of these people can be strongly influenced by the tasks that occupy their day-to-day money-making efforts. Many people think of their work as a major part of who they *are* rather than simply something they *do*. So they introduce themselves with "I'm a stay-at-home mom," "I work in construction," "I'm a nanny," or "I'm at Microsoft." Family members' worlds are also affected by the work of primary breadwinners. My father owned his own business until illness forced him to sell it and take a job as a janitor, and that change dramatically altered the work part of his world. At that same time, mine, my mom's, and my sister's worlds also changed.

Work affects our worlds in other ways, too. For example, the people who hire and supervise us in our first part-time and full-time jobs can significantly affect our definitions of ourselves as competent, trustworthy, creative, and intelligent—or their opposites. Mentoring relationships at work can be almost as influential as family relationships. In addition, work helps determine whom we spend time with. Some police officers complain that their work forces them into constant contact with people who are at their worst, and nurses spend most of their time with people who are sick and needy.

I've gone into detail about these six dimensions of our worlds to emphasize the significance of the point that *communication is the way humans build our reality*. Human worlds are made up not simply of objects but of peoples' *responses* to objects, or their *meanings*.[10] And these meanings are negotiated in communication. Try not to think of communication as simply a way to share ideas, because it's much more than that: It's the process humans use to define reality itself.

Rashad Versey, a friend of mine from a rough urban neighborhood, applied this idea when, as a peer counselor at high school, he talked to friends in trouble about the power of what he called their "mind-set." Rashad used the term *mind-set* roughly the same way I use *world of meaning*. Rashad became a peer counselor partly because, when he was arrested for armed robbery, he was shocked into seeing the difference between a mind-set that gave him a world of aggression and hostility, and a mind-set that gave him a world marked by hope and ambition. He also recognized how he'd built his mind-set in his communication with hostile and aggressive friends. After Rashad's arrest and jail time, the objective features of his neighborhood and situation didn't change much. He still lived in a rough part of the community and continued to suffer from the racism of U.S. culture (Rashad's African-American). But the way he *interpreted* these objective features—their *meaning*—did change. While he was out on bail, on trial, and even while he was in jail, he spent time with people with hope and ambition, and this helped modify his world. Now, in his job as manager of a video store, Rashad is trying to be one of these people with hope and ambition, so he can help affect the mind-set of others.

At this point you might be saying, "Okay, I'm happy for Rashad, but how can I apply all this abstract theorizing? What is the practical payoff of defining communication as the process people use to construct their worlds of meaning?" I'll be responding to this question for each of the five features I discuss. One practical implication of feature 1 is this:

Implication #1: No one person can completely control a communication event, and no single person or action causes—or can be blamed for—a communication outcome.

Many people come to communication classes or workshops wanting to learn how to "do it right." They want to know how to *solve* the communication problems they experience—to get their parents off their backs; eliminate misunderstandings with roommates, co-workers, or dating partners; deal with a critical and complaining boss; end a painful relationship; become a masterful salesperson. Some of these people want to learn the surefire techniques that will give them control over their communication lives. These people are disappointed, and some are even angry, when they learn that it isn't that simple. They are even more uncomfortable when they learn that it's an illusion to believe that surefire techniques of human communication even exist! As philosopher William Barrett put it over 30 years ago in his book *The Illusion of Technique,* "Technical thinking cannot deal with our human problems."[11]

I don't mean that technical thinking is hopeless or that there's nothing to be gained from scientific and social scientific experiments. But one direct implication of the recognition that communication is a *collaborative* process is that no one person can completely control any communication event, and that no technique or set of communication moves can definitely determine its outcome.

Regardless of how clearly I write or speak, you may still interpret me in a variety of different ways. Regardless of how carefully I plan a meeting, one or more people are likely to have agendas very different from mine. Even a successful dictator whose orders are consistently followed can't control how people understand or feel about his or her demands. And as I mentioned, even though I've been working on my communication for years, I still experience difficulties that I cannot completely predict or control in relationships with family members, friends, co-workers, and acquaintances.

I believe that your development as a communicator will be enhanced if you try to manage your expectations about control and perfection. The more you understand how communication works and the more communication skills you develop, the more effective and competent you will be. It is possible to learn how to give and get criticism gracefully, to manage conflict effectively, and to develop relationships smoothly. But not 100 percent of the time.

Cause-effect, fault-blame thinking is one of the oversimplifications people often fall into. I won't repeat what I said in the discussion of John and Judy's communication, but I do want to reemphasize it in this context. Problems obviously happen in communication, and the choices of the people involved help create, maintain, worsen, and solve these problems. But when you understand that communication is *continuous, complex,* and *collaborative,* you cannot coherently blame one person or one set of actions for whatever you might see as problematic. For one thing, fault and blame ignore the continuousness of communication. In order to say someone is at fault, you need to assume that whatever happened *began with the guilty person's action.* But all the people involved have been engaged in communication literally since they were born and have developed and reinforced each other's ways of speaking, listening, and interpreting since at least the time they met. So the person whom you say is at fault because he didn't call you back to confirm the meeting may be remembering your complaints about "getting all those annoying calls" and your insistence that it's only necessary to call if meeting plans change.

Fault and blame also ignore the fact that communication is collaborative. When directions are unclear, for example, it's due to both the direction-giver and the direction-receiver. Did the receiver ask about what confused her? Did the giver check the receiver's understanding? It may have seemed perfectly legitimate to one person to assume that everybody understood that the meeting was at 8 PM and not 8 AM, for example, or that the family would gather for the holiday dinner just like they had in the past. But others might have radically different assumptions that lead to significantly different interpretations.

Does this mean that when there are problems, nobody's responsible? Does this idea eliminate any possibility of accountability? No, not at all. Individual responses still make a difference, and some are definitely more ethical, appropriate, or humane than others. But I'm trying to replace the oversimplified and distorted notions of fault and blame with a broader focus on both or all "sides" of the communication process. I do not mean to replace, "It's his fault" with "It's her fault," "It's both of their faults," or "It's nobody's fault." Instead, I encourage you to give up the notion of fault altogether, at least when you're thinking or talking about human communication.

Another way to put this point is to say that this view of communication redefines what responsibility means. Traditionally, being responsible means that you *caused* something to happen, that it was your fault. But from the perspective I'm developing here, responsibility means *ability to respond,* not fault, blame, or credit. It means "*response-able.*" You are response-able when you have the willingness and the ability to contribute in some way to how things are unfolding, rather than ignoring what's going on or dropping out of the event. "Irresponsible" people are not responsive; they act without taking into account what else is going on or how their actions may influence others. Responsible (response-able) actions consider the larger wholes that they help make up. This idea is related to the basic skill of "nexting" that's discussed in feature 5 below.

2. Culture figures prominently in the communication process. Ethnicity, gender, age, social class, sexual orientation, and other cultural features always affect communication and are affected by it.

I've already explained what's meant by culture. Especially today, with the increasing globalization of sports, music, media, business, education, and religion; with the explosion of international communication via the Internet and the World Wide Web; and with the growing recognition in education and business that diversity in organizations is a strength rather than a threat, culture is on almost everybody's minds. This is partly why I say that culture figures prominently in communication.

But there is a more basic reason: As I've already noted, culture becomes concrete in communication. The shared "ways of living" in the dictionary definition of culture can be observed in a group's ways of relating to each other—that is, in their communicating. What it *means* to belong to a culture is to communicate in certain ways—as I said, to use certain expressions that members of other cultures don't use, to prefer certain kinds of meetings, to honor certain styles of speaking, to maintain certain distances, touch in certain ways, and so on. This means that your culture is present in your communicating and other people's cultures are present in their communicating, too.

Implication #2: Your cultures—and mine—affect what I say about communication in this book and how you respond to it.

Importantly for each author in this book—and for you as reader—*our* cultures are present in our communicating, too. I've already said that I consider myself to be culturally Western, Anglo, middle-class, middle-aged, heterosexual, gendered, a parent, and a teacher–scholar. This means that my communication content and style in this book will embody these cultural features (and probably others I am not aware of). You'll get cultural information about some of the other authors in this book, and none about other authors. If you do *not* identify yourself culturally with an author, you may legitimately ask, "How are this person's ideas relevant to me? If culture and communication are so intertwined, what can I—an African-American, perhaps, or Latino, 20-year old, gay or lesbian, engineering or chemistry student—learn from writings by this person?"

Enough, I hope, to keep you reading. This book offers some knowledge and skills about communication that are supported by evidence from a variety of cultures, and its authors speak from positions in cultures with fairly large memberships and fairly wide ranges of influence. If you are not a member of one or more of the cultures an author belongs to, this material can still be useful to you in at least two ways: (a) You can test generalizations against your experience in your own cultures to determine which apply and which don't, and (b) when an author's ideas don't apply in one or more of your cultures, you can use them to enhance your ability to communicate with people in the cultures the author inhabits.

For example, my first two claims about human communication are that humans live in worlds of meaning that are constructed in communicating, and that culture figures prominently in all communication. I believe that there is ample evidence to demonstrate that these two points are true about all people in all cultures, *not* just Western, Anglo, middle-class, middle-aged, heterosexual, gendered, parent, and teacher-scholar cultures. Do you? I encourage you to test these generalizations against your own experience and to discuss the results with your instructor and classmates. On the other hand, as just one example, this book's readings about nonverbal communication may contain some generalizations about space or eye contact that don't ring true for one or more of your cultures. If so, you can combine your understanding of your own culture with what the author says about hers or his, and use this knowledge about space or eye contact in the author's culture to enhance your ability to communicate outside your own culture, with people in the culture the author inhabits.

And notice that you can do this without being co-opted. If you feel culturally different from some of the writers in this book, you don't have to give up your distinctiveness to profit from what's here. You can operate like a global businessperson. People who have to serve customers or work with producers outside their own cultures routinely learn how to adapt to these other cultures, but from their own position of strength—as a representative of their business. These people want to do business in another culture, so their adaptation is based on that foundation; it doesn't mean that their values or morals are co-opted. Regardless of the culture you enter or the adaptations you may choose to make, you can do so from a comparable position of strength.

3. Some of the most important meanings people collaboratively create are identities; all communicating involves negotiating identities, or selves.

Communication theorist and teacher John Shotter emphasizes this point when he says that our "ways of being, our 'selves', are produced in our . . . ways of interrelating ourselves to each other—these are the terms in which we are socially accountable in our society—and these 'traditional' or 'basic' (dominant) ways of talking are productive of our 'traditional' or 'basic' psychological and social [identities]."[12] In other words, who we are—our identities—is built in our communicating. People come to each encounter with an identifiable "self," built through past interactions, and *as we talk,* we adapt ourselves to fit the topic we're discussing and the people we're talking with, and we are changed by what happens to us as we communicate.

The way communication and identity are closely related became especially apparent in a conversation I had with a friend who was going through a painful divorce. "Mary Kay is not the person she used to be," Dale said. "Sometimes I hardly know her. I wish we could communicate and enjoy each other like we did when we were first married."

The times Dale was remembering were before Mary Kay was a mother, before she completed medical school, before she suffered through her residency in an urban hospital 2,000 miles from home, before she joined a prestigious medical clinic, and before she became a full-fledged practicing physician. They were also before Dale was a dad, before he started his import-export business, before he became active in his state professional association, and before he began attending church regularly. Dale was forgetting that Mary Kay could not possibly still be "the person she used to be." Neither could he. Both of them had experienced many relationships that changed them decisively. Mary Kay had been treated like a medical student—required to cram scientific information into her head and spout it on command—and like a first-year resident—forced to go without sleep, stand up to authoritarian doctors, and cope with hospital administrators. Now nurses obey her, many patients highly respect her for her skills, and prestigious doctors treat her like an equal. And she's treated as a mom by her son. Dale has also experienced many different relationships, and he's changed too. He's treated as a boss by his employees and as "a respected American businessman" by his Japanese customers. Because of the contacts both have experienced, each is a different person. And the process continues as both Mary Kay and Dale continue to be changed by their communication.

Obviously these identity changes are limited. Most people don't change their gender, ethnicity, or family of origin. But some changes are inevitable over time, and others can happen in the short term. For example, a woman can communicate in ways that say she is more feminine—or more masculine—than her conversation partner, and as a person with greater or less authority or power than her conversation partner has. The other person's responses will contribute to the identity as it's negotiated verbally and nonverbally.

Consider the difference, for example, between "Shut the door, stupid!" and "Please close the door." The command projects the identity of a superior speaking to a subordinate. On the other hand, the request identifies the speaker as an equal to the person being addressed. The person who's told to "Shut the door, stupid!" may silently comply, in which case he or she is reinforcing part of the identities of superior and subordinate. Or the person may respond, "Shut it yourself!" which is a negotiation move that says, in effect, "You're not my superior; we're equals."

Implication #3: Identity issues are always in play.

The point is that *identity-negotiation, or the collaborative construction of selves, is going on whenever people communicate.* It definitely is not the *only* thing that's happening, but it's one of the very important processes, and it often gets overlooked. When it does, troubles usually result. By contrast, people who are aware of identity-negotiation processes can communicate more effectively and successfully in many different situations. So whenever you communicate—on the telephone, via e-mail, face-to-face, in meetings, even in front of the television—part of what is happening is identity-negotiation.

Communication content is important too, and sometimes problems can be solved only when the parties involved have more or better information. Policies may be out of date, data may be incomplete, and people may have misread or misheard key instructions. In these cases, the people involved may need to complete, refine, or recalibrate the information they're working with.

But as I noted, effective communicators understand and manage what they're verbally and nonverbally "saying" about *who they are* to the people they're communicating with. Identities are communicated in many different ways. Topic choice and vocabulary are important. Grooming and dress also contribute to this process, as people offer definitions of themselves using nose rings and other body piercing, tatoos, starched white shirts or blouses, and conservative business suits. Tone of voice is similarly identity-defining. Some people foster misunderstanding by unknowingly sounding like they're skeptical, hostile, or bored, and other tones of voice can help their listeners feel genuinely appreciated and supported. Facial expressions also help define a person as attentive, careful, positive, or their opposites.

Especially when you're troubleshooting—or just trying to live through—a disagreement or conflict, it usually works best to start by understanding the identities that are in play. Who might be getting defined as inattentive, insensitive, or incompetent? What communication moves make one person appear more important, trustworthy, moral, or thorough than the other? Does everybody involved feel able to influence the ways they're viewed by the others? Or are identities being treated as unchangable? By the time you've worked through this book, you should have a wealth of ideas and practical skills for constructively managing how you define yourself and how others define you.

4. The most influential communication events are conversations.

If you had to identify one event that humans all over the world engage in characteristically—because they're humans—routinely, naturally, and almost constantly, what would it be? We all breathe, but so do other animals. We eat and drink, but not constantly, and again, other animals do too. The one activity that marks us as human and that occupies a large part of our personal and occupational lives is conversation, verbal and nonverbal exchange in real time, either face-to-face or mediated by some electronic medium (e.g., the telephone).

For a long time, people who studied communication and language tended to overlook this point. Language scholars focused on rules of grammar and syntax, dictionary definitions, and other features of writing, and speech research and teaching paid primary attention to public speaking and deliberation in law courts and legislatures. But in the last third of the twentieth century, an increasing number of scholars and teachers have shown how written and formal kinds of communicating are derived from the most basic human activity, informal conversation. Recently, for example, two well-known psychologists from Stanford University began a report of their National Science Foundation-supported research with these words:

> Conversation is the fundamental site of language use. For many people, even for whole societies, it is the only site, and it is the primary one for children acquiring language. From this perspective other arenas of language use—novels, newspapers, lectures, street signs, rituals—are derivative or secondary.[13]

Another respected scholar puts it more simply. "Conversation," he writes, "is sociological bedrock,"[14] the absolute foundation or base for everything humans do as social beings. This explains the sense of the title of one of communication theorist John Shotter's recent books, *Conversational Realities: Constructing Life Through Language.*[15] Shotter's book explains in detail how human realities get constructed in communication—our point 1 above—and emphasizes that the most characteristic form of this communication is *conversation.*

Implication #4: The most ordinary communication events are the most significant.

The reason I highlight this idea as one of the five main points about human communication is that it justifies paying close attention to something common and ordinary. The fact that humans engage in conversation so constantly, and so often almost without thinking, is part of what makes the process so important. As organizational theorist and trainer Peter Senge puts it, effective conversation is "the single greatest learning tool in your organization—more important than computers or sophisticated research."[16] Whether in a living group, a family-run shop, a small work team, or a multinational corporation, the real organizational structure and rules—as contrasted with what's on the organizational chart—get defined in the subtleties of verbal and nonverbal conversation. Superior and subordinate status get negotiated in face-to-face contacts. Key decisions are heavily influenced by brief informal contacts in the bathrooms and halls as much as they are by formal presentations in meetings. And when the organization needs to change and there are feelings about rights or two worthwhile principles in conflict, the only realistic options are some form of authoritarianism or some form of problem-solving conversation. Similarly, conversation is the primary way families have of making decisions and negotiating differences. And children become effective participants in play groups, classrooms, sports teams, and their own families by learning how to converse well.

This means that one very important way to improve your communication competence is to pay close attention to the most common and everyday kind of communicating—conversation. When you do, you'll discover that you already have a great deal of experience with many of the concepts and skills this book discusses. This means that you have a solid foundation to build on. Even if you don't believe you're very good at conversation, you've done it often and well enough, and it's going on around you so much, that you can build on the experiences you have. One way is with point 5.

5. The most useful single communication skill is "nexting."

Nexting is a strange term, I admit. But it's the best one I've come up with for this skill. If, as you read this section, you come up with a better one, please let me know.

By "nexting" I mean doing something helpful next, responding fruitfully to what's just happened, taking an additional positive step in the communication process. If you've grasped how I've described communication so far, this is the most important single skill you can build on this understanding. Here's why:

Since you realize that communication is complex, continuous, and collaborative, you'll always recognize that, no matter what's happened before and no matter how bad things currently look, you always have the option to take a positive *next* step. No matter how many times the same insult has been repeated, the next response can be creative rather than retaliatory. No matter how long the parties have not been speaking to each other, the next time they meet, one of them could speak. No matter how ingrained and toxic the pattern is that two groups are caught in, the next move one side makes could be positive. No matter how much you feel "thrown" by what the other person just said and did, if you give yourself a little time to regroup, you can make a next move that could help get the relationship back on track. No matter how little power the system gives you, your next communication choice can maximize the power you have. Even when it is very difficult not to strike back, your next comment could conceivably be helpful rather than abusive. Conversely, no matter how well things are going, the next communication move can introduce a problem. No matter how smooth the water, people's next responses can help make it rough.

When you understand that communication is continuous and collaborative, you'll recognize the potential value of what you do next. Why? Because since no one person determines all the outcomes of a communication event, you can help determine some outcomes, even if you feel almost powerless. Since no one person is 100 percent to blame or at fault, and all parties share response-ability, your next contribution can affect what's happening. Since all communication is collaborative—remember, even prizefighters are co-labor-ating—your next communication move can make a change in the situation.

Implication #5: Whenever you face a communication challenge or problem, the most helpful question you can ask yourself is, "What can I help to happen next, and how?"

You can apply the skill of nexting by remembering that no human system is ever completely determined or cast in stone. Regardless of how well or badly things are going between you and someone else, remember that what you do next will help maintain or destroy this quality. It almost goes without saying that in some cases you may not *want* to try to improve a bad situation or to maintain a good one. You may have tried to make positive contributions and have been continually rebuffed, and you may be out of patience, resources, or caring. You may in this particular case decide not to make a positive, supportive, or conciliatory move. You may also decide to let silence remain, to keep your distance, or to let the hostility fester. But if you understand the world-constructing nature of human communication, you can understand these options for what they are—*responses,* choices, decisions about what you are going to do *next.* They have their benefits and their consequences, just as other responses would.

To put it simply, people who understand communication to be the kind of process I've outlined so far are not generally thrown off balance by communication difficulties. They understand that the most important thing to consider is what they are going to do *next.*

INTERPERSONAL COMMUNICATING

As I said at the start of this chapter, interpersonal communication is a subset of communication in general. This means that collaboration, culture, identities, conversation, and nexting are all parts of interpersonal communicating, too. The kind of communication I'm calling "interpersonal" doesn't happen all the time, but it can take place in families, between friends, during an argument, in business situations, and in the classroom. It can also happen on the telephone, on-line, among jurors, at a party, across a bargaining table, and even during public speeches or presentations. The main characteristic of interpersonal communication is that the people involved are contacting each other *as persons*. This might sound pretty simple, but again, there's a little more to it than you might think.

For one thing, as you and I move through our daily family, work, social, and school lives, we tend to relate with others in three different ways. Sometimes we treat others and are treated by them *socially*, as role-fillers (bank teller, receptionist, employer, bus driver, etc.). Sometimes we treat others and are treated by them mainly *culturally,* as people who are similar to or different from us (male, female, young, white, black, Latino, etc.). And sometimes we connect with others *personally,* as a unique individual (not just role-filler or cultural representative).[17] I don't mean that there are sharp divisions; sometimes we move back and forth among cultural, social, and interpersonal contact. But these three terms can anchor a sliding scale or continuum that models the qualities or kinds of communication that people experience.

QUALITIES OF COMMUNICATION

Social————————————Cultural————————————Interpersonal

Communication at the bank, in the convenience store, and at the fast-food restaurant usually fits somewhere on the left-hand side of this scale. In these situations, people connect in accordance with their *social roles.* Even though human beings are obviously involved, they all function pretty much like interchangeable parts of the situation, something like the interchangeable parts of an automobile or laptop computer. The people don't know or care much about each other beyond the social role each is playing.

Often, of course, this is the best kind of communication to have. For one thing, it's efficient. Nobody wants to wait in line while the Burger King cashier has a personal chat with each customer. It's also often the most appropriate kind of communicating. Ordinarily, people don't approach bank tellers or clerks at the motor vehicle bureau expecting or wanting to have a deep conversation.

In other situations, the contact we experience could be called *cultural.* This happens when people connect with each other around the cultural identities they have in common. When you enter a party, for example, you might feel most comfortable talking first with people of the same gender, age, or ethnicity as yourself. Even though you recognize that this is a mild form of stereotyping, you might feel the same way at a pickup basketball game or aerobics class. When you notice that you're in the minority because of some cultural feature, it's often easiest to connect first with people who appear to be most like you. Cultural contacts like these are less generic than social ones, because they revolve around some specific shared similarities. But they're still different from communicating with some *particular* or *special* member of a cultural group.

As with *social* contacts, *cultural* communication is sometimes exactly what works best. As we noted, talking with someone who's culturally similar can help ease the discomfort of an unfamiliar situation. It can also be a relatively easy route to a new friendship. And you can learn important things from culturally similar acquaintances.

But some of almost every day's communication experiences also fit near the right-hand end of the scale. During a committee meeting or team activity you may contact another person as a unique individual, and you may get treated that way by him or her. The same kind of communicating can happen in your conversations with a dating partner, a parent, your brother or sister, or your roommate, co-workers, or close friends. In this kind of communicating, each of you has moved through and beyond social role identities, and your contact is also based on more than cultural similarity. You may be culturally different from each other, for example, but still meet interpersonally. If you do, then even when you disagree with each other, you know that the quality of your contact is not the same as when you disagree with the bank teller or the only other African American in the room.

No one's communication life can be packaged into neat boxes; that's why the model is a sliding scale. At one moment you may be contacting someone socially and at the next moment your communication may turn cultural or interpersonal. But the best way to understand the topic of this book is to recognize the differences among these three general ways of relating to others.

And the best way to understand the sliding scale is to focus first on the ends. If you think about what makes human *persons*, you can begin to see clearly what it means to communicate interpersonally. (I've already said enough about culture to give you a sense of what cultural communicating is.)

Features of the Personal

Many philosophers, anthropologists, and communication scholars have defined what it means to be a person and how persons differ from other kinds of animals. One widely recognized description was created by a philosopher of communication named Martin Buber. (Buber was born in 1878, lived in Austria, Germany, and Israel, visited the United States a couple of times, and died in 1965.) He suggested that there are five qualities, or characteristics, that distinguish persons across many—though perhaps not all—cultures: uniqueness, measurability, responsiveness, reflectiveness, and addressability.[18] These five define what I mean by "the personal," and I will use the five and their opposites to distinguish *social* from *cultural* and *interpersonal* communicating.

Unique   Uniqueness means noninterchangeability. We, as persons, can be treated as if we were interchangeable parts, but each of us can also be thought of as unique in a couple of ways, genetically and experientially. The main reason that genetic cloning experiments are controversial is that they threaten this quality. Unless they are cloned or are identical twins, the probability that two persons would have the same genetic materials is 1 in 10 to the ten-thousandth power. That's less than one chance in a billion trillion!

But cloning wouldn't really threaten uniqueness, because even when persons have the same biological raw material, each experiences the world differently. For example, recall identical twins you've known. Both twins might see the same film in the same theater on the same night at the same time, sitting next to each other. Both might leave the theater at the same time and say exactly the same words about it: "I liked that film." At a superficial level, someone might suggest that the experiences of the two are, in this situation, interchangeable. But additional talk will show that they aren't. Did both twins like the film for the same reasons? Did they recall the same experiences as they interpreted the film? Will the film have the same effect on both of them? Will both remember the same things about it? If you asked the twins these questions, you'd get different answers, and you'd discover what you probably knew before you began the process: Each human is unique.

When people are communicating with each other *socially,* they're overlooking most of this uniqueness and focusing on the similarities among all those who play a given social role. All of us naturally and constantly fill many different roles—student, daughter or son, sibling, employee, and so on. And role relationships are an inescapable part of communicating. But the sliding scale emphasizes that people can move through social communication to cultural and interpersonal contacts.

The next step, to *cultural* communication, happens when the people involved notice some of each other's particular features, but haven't yet paid attention to what makes them uniquely themselves. As I said, often it's much easier to talk with someone who shares your own cultural background, but most people still don't choose a spouse, best friend, or business partner only on the basis of cultural similarities.

So the first feature that distinguishes *persons* is experiential and, in most cases, genetic uniqueness. Some cultures downplay this feature, but most Western cultures emphasize it. The more present this feature is in your communicating, the farther your communication is toward the right-hand side of the social–cultural–interpersonal continuum.

Unmeasurable   Objects are measurable; they fit within boundaries. An event is of a certain duration; it lasts a measurable amount of time. Even extremely complex objects, such as sophisticated supercomputers, 70-story buildings, and space vehicles, can be completely described in space-and-time terms. This is what blueprints do. They record all the measurements necessary to recreate the object—length, height, width, mass, specific gravity, amperage, voltage, velocity, circumference, hardness, ductility, malleability, conductivity, and so on.

Although it's difficult to measure some things directly—the temperature of a kiss, the velocity of a photon, the duration of an explosion—no object or event has any parts that are unmeasurable, in theory at least.

It's different with persons. Even if your physician accurately identifies your height, weight, temperature, blood pressure, serum cholesterol level, hemoglobin count, and all your other data right down to the electric potential in your seventh cranial nerve, the doctor still will not have exhaustively accounted for the person you are, because there are parts of you that can't be measured. Many scientists, social scientists, philosophers, and theologians have made this point. Some cognitive scientists, for example, include in their model of the person components they call "schematas," or "cognitive patterns" that don't have any space-and-time (measurable) existence, but that can be inferred from observations of behavior. Others call the unmeasurable elements of a person the "human spirit," "psyche," or "soul." But whatever you call it, it's there.

Emotions or feelings are the clearest observable evidence of this unmeasurable part. Although instruments can measure things related to feelings—brain waves, sweaty palms, heart rate, paper-and-pencil responses—what the measurements record is a long way from the feelings themselves. "Pulse 110, respiration 72, Likert rating 5.39, palmar conductivity 0.036 ohms" may be accurate, but it doesn't quite capture what's going on in me when you encounter somebody you can't stand or greet somebody you love.

One other thing: These emotions or feelings are *always* a part of what we are experiencing. Psychologists and educators agree that it's unrealistic to try to separate the intellectual or objective aspect of a person or a subject matter from the affective or emotional parts. This is because humans are always thinking *and* feeling. As one writer puts it, "It should be apparent that there is no intellectual learning without some sort of feeling and there are no feelings without the mind's somehow being involved."[19]

Even though feelings are always present, some communication acknowledges them and some communication doesn't. The cashier who's dedicated to her social role will greet people with a smile and wish them a "nice day" even if she feels lousy. Servers in a restaurant are taught not to bring their feelings to work. Two persons who are in a minority may share similar feelings of isolation or exclusion, but they may or may not talk about them. On the other hand, when people are communicating interpersonally, some of their feelings are in play. This does not mean that you have to wear your heart on your sleeve to communicate interpersonally. It just means that when people are making interpersonal contact, some feelings are appropriately acknowledged and shared.

Responsive   I've already discussed this idea in the section about worlds of meaning. Humans are thoroughly and uniquely responsive beings. Objects can only react; they cannot respond. They cannot choose what to do next. Automatic pilots, photoelectric switches, personal and industrial robots, thermostats, and computers can sometimes seem to operate on their own or turn themselves off and on, but they too are dependent on actions initiated outside them. The computers and robots have to be programmed, the thermostat reacts to temperature, which reacts to the sun's rays, which are affected by the earth's rotation, and so on. Similarly, a ball can go only where it's kicked, and if you were good enough at physics calculations, you could figure out how far and where it would go, on the basis of weight, velocity, aerodynamics, the shape of your shoe, atmospheric conditions, and so on.

But what if you were to kick a person? It's an entirely different kind of activity, and you cannot accurately predict what will happen. The reason you can't is that when persons are involved, the outcome depends on *response*, not simply *reaction*. If you tap my knee, you may cause a reflex jerk, but the feelings that occur are not completely predictable, and the behavior or actions that accompany my reflex may be anything from giggles to a slap in the face.

The range of responses is limited, of course. We can't instantly change sex, become three years younger, or memorize the contents of the Library of Congress. But we can decide whether to use a conventional word or an obscene one, we can choose how to prioritize our time commitments, and, as will be discussed in later chapters, choice is even a part of the feelings we experience.

In fact, the more you realize your freedom and power to respond rather than simply react, the more of a person you can be. Sometimes it's easy to get out of touch with this freedom and power. You feel like saying, "I *had* to shout back; he was making me look silly!" or "I just *couldn't* say anything!" These statements make it sound like you don't have any choice, like what you do is completely *caused* by what another person does. But as the discussion of fault and blame noted, even when circumstances are exerting pressure, persons still have some freedom and power to choose how to respond. It may mean resisting a culturally rooted preference or breaking some well-established habit patterns, and it may take lots of practice, but it's possible to become aware of your responses and, when you want to, to change them. The reason it's important to learn this skill is that when you believe you're just reacting, you've lost touch with part of what it means to be a person. Persons are responsive, and the more you remember and act on this feature, the more interpersonal your communicating can become.

Reflective   A fourth distinguishing characteristic is that persons are reflective. Being reflective means not only that we are aware of what's around us, but also that we can be aware of our awareness. As one author puts it, "No matter how much of your self you are able to objectify and examine, the quintessential, living part of yourself will always elude you, i.e., the part of you that is conducting the examination,"[20] the reflective part. Wrenches, rocks, and rowboats aren't aware at all. Dogs, cats, armadillos, and giraffes are all aware of their environments, but we don't have any evidence that they are aware of their awareness. So far as we know, only humans compose and save histories of their lives, elaborately bury their dead, explore their extrasensory powers, question the meaning of life, and speculate about the past and future. And only humans are aware that we do all these things.

Reflection is not a process that affects only philosophers and people who know that they don't have long to live. Healthy "ordinary" people reflect, too. I wonder from time to time whether I'm spending my work time wisely and whether I'm making the right parenting decisions. Sometimes you probably wonder what you'll be doing five years from now. Before you make an important decision, you ask questions of yourself and others about priorities and probable consequences. On clear days you may notice the beauty of the landscape around you and reflect on how fortunate you are to live where you do. Like all persons, you ask questions and reflect.

When people ignore the fact that persons are reflective, their communication usually shows it. For example, you may stick with superficial topics—the weather, recent news items, gossip. On the other hand, when you're aware of your own and others' reflectiveness, you can respond to more of what's going on as you communicate. Questions can be a clear indicator that a person is reflecting. Often people who express their opinions with absolute certainty have forgotten to reflect, to ask what they might be unsure of and what they might not have thought about. But the reflective person will often explicitly express appropriate reservations and qualifications—"I think this is the right thing to do, but I'm not absolutely sure." Or "I know I don't want to lie to him, but I'm not sure how or when to tell him."

Addressable   Beings who are addressable can recognize when they are addressed, that is, when they are called or spoken to in language, and can also respond in language. Addressability is what makes the difference between talking *to* and talking *with*. Neither baseball bats nor dogs and cats are addressable, because you can talk to them, but not with them. You can call them, curse them, scold them, and praise them, but you cannot carry on a mutual conversation, even with an "almost human" pet.

One student described what addressability meant to her by recounting her experience as a child with her imaginary playmate, Sharla. Mary said that Sharla went everywhere with her and was always dressed appropriately. Sharla was also (in Mary's mind) always sympathetic to what Mary was doing and feeling. Mary would talk *to* Sharla constantly, telling her how she felt, complaining about her parents and older sister, and sometimes making elaborate plans. Occasionally Mary would talk *about* Sharla to her friends or her mother. But of course Sharla never responded out loud. She never talked back. Mary could talk *to* and *about* Sharla, but not *with* her. Sharla was not addressable; she wasn't a person.

Communication theorist John Shotter talks about this feature of human communication under the heading of "addressivity," which he defines as "the quality of being directed toward someone."[21] "Addressed" speech is directed or "aimed" speech, and one characteristic of persons is that they can recognize address and respond in kind. So, for example, as you sit in an audience of several hundred, the speaker can single you out for immediate contact: "Holly Tartar? Are you here? Your question is about job programs, and I want to try to answer it now." Or even more commonly and more directly, you may sit across from a friend and know from the touch of the friend's eyes, his hand, and his voice that he means *you*; he's *present* with you, you are being addressed.

Definition of Interpersonal Communication

Remember that communicators are always both talking and listening, sending and receiving, giving off cues and taking them in—this book calls it "exhaling" and "inhaling." These five features—unique, unmeasurable, responsive, reflective, and addressable—can be used to describe how communicators engage in these exhaling and inhaling processes. That is, these five can describe what people are giving out (exhaling) and what they are taking in (inhaling). And **the term interpersonal labels the kind of communication that happens when the people involved talk and listen in ways that maximize the presence of the personal.** When communicators give and receive or talk and listen in ways that emphasize their uniqueness, unmeasureability, responsiveness, reflectiveness, and addressability, then the communication between them is interpersonal. When they listen and talk in ways that highlight the opposites of these five features— interchangeability, measurable aspects, reactivity, unreflectiveness, and imperviousness, their communicating fits on the social end of the sliding scale. When they talk and listen in ways that highlight features that make them culturally but not personally identifiable, their communicating can be placed near the center of the continuum.

So two persons who stick to their (interchangeable) role definitions—"I'm the teacher and you're the student"—ignore feelings, and behave as if they're controlled by outside forces (reacting rather than responding) will be communicating more socially than interpersonally. One way to describe their communication would be to place it near the left end of the sliding scale. A student and teacher who both identify themselves culturally as male and African-American, and who recognize each other's characteristically male and African-American feelings and responses, but who are still teacher and student to each other, and who know little of each other's uniqueness, can be described as communicating more culturally than socially or interpersonally. Their communication could be placed near the center of the continuum.

On the other hand, a different student and teacher might both acknowledge each other's unique features, affirm relevant feelings, actively respond rather than react, and show they're aware of their own perspectives by questioning, or being tentative about some of their ideas. When they both speak and listen in ways that reflect these qualities, their communicating would fit nearer the right-hand, interpersonal, end of the continuum.

Interpersonal communication is easiest when there are only two of you and you already know and trust each other. But it can also occur early in a relationship—even at first meeting—and, as I've already mentioned, it can occur over the telephone, during an argument, on the job, in group meetings, and even in public speaking or presentation situations. The important thing is not how many people there are or where they're located, but the peoples' willingness and ability to choose personal over social or cultural communication attitudes and behaviors.

Importantly, the terms *social, cultural,* and *interpersonal* are *descriptive,* not *prescriptive.* Interpersonal communication can be appropriate, effective, or "good" in some situations, and "bad" in others, and the same goes for social and cultural contact. Sometimes social communication is exactly what's called for, what works best, and what's most ethical. The point of this simple model is to give you some control over where your communication is on the social–cultural–interpersonal scale.

So the basic definition of interpersonal communication is pretty simple. It's the counterpart of social and cultural communication. But as you'll see, I base this book's entire approach on this simple definition. As I've already explained in Chapter 1, each major division of the book, each chapter, and each reading extend a part of the approach to communication, and to interpersonal communication, that I've outlined here. So although this book contains writings by 47 different people, we all view interpersonal communication in similar ways. As a result, by the time you're finished with the book, you ought to have developed not only a deeper understanding of interpersonal communication but also a more powerful and effective sense of how to help make it happen when you want to.

REVIEW QUESTIONS

1. According to this reading, what is the main distinction between the world inhabited by a dog, cat, chimpanzee, or dolphin and the world inhabited by a human?
2. Why is it misleading to think about human communication in terms of senders and receivers?
3. Complete the sentence: Communication is the c_____, c_____, c_____ process of verbal and _____ meaning-making through which we construct _____ _____ _____ _____ we inhabit.
4. Which of the following were included in the discussion of worlds of meaning?
   a. religion   **b.** work   **c.** history   **d.** relationships   **e.** space

   What additional dimensions were discussed?
5. According to this reading, what's the difference between responsibility and response-ability?
6. List three qualities in addition to ethnicity that make up a person's culture.
7. True or False: Identity-negotiation is the only process that's occurring when humans communicate. Explain.
8. Define *nexting* and give an example of it from your own communication experience.
9. What rationale is offered here for the sequence social–cultural–interpersonal rather than cultural–social interpersonal?
10. What is the clearest example of the unmeasurable part of persons?
11. What's the difference between a reaction and a response?

12. The presence of questions in one's communicating is a clear example of which of the following: uniqueness, unmeasurability, responsiveness, reflectiveness, or addressability?

13. Complete the following: This reading defines *interpersonal communication* as the kind of _____ that happens when the people involved _____ and _____ in ways that _____ the presence of the _____.

PROBES

1. At the start of this reading's discussion of worlds of meaning, I outline five common but misleading ideas about communication: that it happens between sender and receiver, that it starts when an idea is translated into a message, that it continues when a message is retranslated into another idea, that it can be evaluated in terms of fidelity, and that it can be understood in terms of cause and effect. Which of these five are part(s) of your understanding of communication? Which are you least willing to give up or change?

2. How often does your communication focus on issues of fault and blame? How productive are these discussions? What alternative do you hear me proposing here?

3. Paraphrase the point I make when I say that collaboration doesn't necessarily mean agreement.

4. What is the most important feature of your own world of meaning *in addition to* space, time, laws of physics, culture, relationships, and work? When—in what communicating—does this additional feature surface most prominently?

5. Implication 1 says, "No one person can completely control a communication event, and no single person or action causes—or can be blamed for—a communication outcome." How do you respond to this claim?

6. How would you describe the greatest cultural distance between you and the author of this reading? Where are you and this author culturally closest?

7. Describe the identity that you understand me (the author of this reading and the editor of this book) to be trying to develop so far in this book.

8. Without reading ahead to Chapter 3, which do you believe are more important in the identity-negotiation process, verbal or nonverbal cues?

9. Which of the five features of the personal—uniqueness, unmeasurability, responsiveness, reflectiveness, or addressability—do you believe is most important in interpersonal communicating?

NOTES

1. "Communic*ation*" or "communica*ting*?" I started with the "-ion" form because it's a little more familiar. But many "-ion" words, like *education, expression, persuasion,* and *sensation,* call to mind the finished product rather

than the ongoing process. Education, for example, is something I get at school and expression is something that comes from my voice or body. "Educat*ing*," on the other hand, calls to mind events, occurrences, and processes, just like such terms as *singing, laughing, arguing,* and *making love.* It's helpful to remember that the topics of this reading are processes. This is why the reading title and main headings use the "-ing" forms.

2. Adapted from an example in Douglas W. Maynard, "Perspective-Display Sequences in Conversation," *Western Journal of Speech Communication,* 53 (1989), 107.

3. Interruptions, or overlapping speech, can manifest a variety of power relationships between conversation partners. Sometimes overlaps can be supportive, and at other times they are denigrating. See, for example, Deborah Tannen, *Talking from 9 to 5* (New York: Wm. Morrow, 1994), pp. 232–234.

4. Russian communication theorist Mikhail Bakhtin put it this way: "Any concrete utterance is a link in the chain of speech communication of a particular sphere. . . . Each utterance is filled with echoes and reverberation of other utterances to which it is related by the communality of the sphere of speech communication. . . . The speaker is not Adam, and therefore the subject of his speech itself inevitably becomes the arena where his opinions meet those of his partners." *Speech Genres and Other Essays,* trans. Vern W. McGee, ed. Caryl Emerson and Michael Holquist (Austin: Univ. of Texas Press, 1986), pp. 91, 94.

5. Some people call talking to yourself or thinking out loud "intrapersonal communication," or communication "within" one person. I prefer to reserve the term *communication* for what happens between two or more people. The main reason is that *common* or *commune* is the root of *communication,* and you can't make something common that's not divided or separated. While any one person obviously has various "parts" or "sides," I think it's most useful to understand the human as a whole, a unity captured by such terms as *I, me,* or *the person.* Talking to yourself and thinking out loud are important processes, but they are fundamentally different from connecting with an *other,* someone who is not-you. In addition, I want to emphasize that humans are first and foremost "social animals," relational beings. Humans become who we are in our contacts with others, not mainly as a result of thinking and talking to ourselves.

6. *The Random House College Dictionary,* rev., unabridged ed. (New York: Random House, 1984), p. 325.

7. Dreama G. Moon, "Concepts of 'Culture': Implications for Intercultural Communication Research," *Communication Quarterly,* 44 (1996), 76.

8. Gerry Philipsen, "Speaking 'Like a Man' in Teamsterville: Culture Patterns of Role Enactment in an Urban Neighborhood," *Quarterly Journal of Speech,* 61 (1975), 13–22.

9. Keith Basso, *Portraits of "the Whiteman": Linguistic Play and Cultural Symbols Among the Western Apache* (Cambridge: Cambridge Univ. Press, 1992).

10. Notice that when I emphasize how fundamental meanings are, I am not claiming that there are no such things as objects. Meanings emerge as people

contact aspects of their worlds. Some of these "aspects" are concrete, material, solid. But humans constantly interpret these objects; we don't perceive them directly. And the results of interpretations are meanings.

11. William Barrett, *The Illusion of Technique: A Search for Meaning in a Technological Civilization* (Garden City, NY: Anchor Doubleday), p. xx.

12. John Shotter, "Epilogue," *Conversational Realities: Constructing Life Through Language* (London: Sage, 1993), p. 180.

13. Herbert H. Clark and Deanna Wilkes-Gibbs, "Referring as a Collaborative Process," *Cognition*, 22 (1986), 1.

14. Emanuel A. Schegloff, "Discourse as an Interactional Achievement III: The Omnirelevance of Action," *Research on Language and Social Interaction*, 28 (1995), 186–187.

15. London: Sage, 1993.

16. Peter M. Senge, Art Kleiner, Charlotte Roberts, Richard B. Ross, and Bryan J. Smith, *The Fifth Discipline Fieldbook: Strategies and Tools for Building a Learning Organization* (New York: Doubleday, 1994), p. 14.

17. In the mid-1970s, a widely cited textbook by Gerald Miller and Mark Steinberg proposed a similar continuum that ran from cultural through social to interpersonal communication. In those days, it made sense to think of the most general features of a person as "cultural" ones. Now, at the end of the twentieth century, cultural features are recognized as more specific than are general "social" features. This is why this continuum is different from theirs. See Gerald Miller and Mark Steinberg, *Between People: A New Analysis of Interpersonal Communication* (Chicago: Science Research Associates, 1975).

18. Buber was an international citizen whose major book has been translated into over 20 languages. So he believed that his definition of the person applied across cultures. Many people agree, but others argue that his view of the person is in some ways more Western than Eastern. Some people in cultures that emphasize group identity (Japan, for example) believe that Buber's emphasis on the individual was misleading. But most people in Western cultures think that his description fits their experience pretty well. What do you think? See Martin Buber, *I and Thou*, trans. Walter Kaufmann (New York: Scribner's, 1970).

19. For a discussion of this point, see George Isaac Brown, *Human Teaching for Human Learning: An Introduction to Confluent Education* (New York: Viking Press, 1971).

20. Fredrick Buechner, *Wishful Thinking: A Theological ABC* (New York: Harper Collins, 1973), p. 64.

21. John Shotter, *Cultural Politics of Everyday Life: Social Constructionism, Rhetoric and Knowing of the Third Kind* (Toronto: Univ. of Toronto Press, 1993), p. 176.

*T*he following pages come from one of the books I quoted in the introductory essay. As I mentioned there, James Lynch has been at the University of Maryland School of Medicine. Since the early 1980s, he's written extensively about the impact of dialogue on our physical health. His books contain a great deal of detailed evidence about how the quality of the communication we experience affects the quality of our lives.

This is the introduction to his book, *The Language of the Heart*. He argues here that "human dialogue not only affects our hearts significantly but can even alter the biochemistry of individual tissues at the further extremities of the body." To some people, that probably sounds like Eastern mysticism or New Age pseudoscience. But Lynch's documentation is impressive; in his book, he cites literally hundreds of medical studies that support his claims. He also points out that it is difficult for some people to accept the link between dialogue and physical health, because we've been taught for years that the human body is essentially a complex machine. We know that talk, human conversation, or dialogue is not reducible without remainder to the programmable, cause-and-effect elements of mechanics. And yet this nonmechanical phenomenon significantly affects our allegedly mechanical bodies. How can that be?

Without trying to provide an easy answer to this question, Lynch briefly describes what he believes are the historical ideas and attitudes that have led us to our current picture of the human body. And he tells how the discoveries he and his colleagues are making are beginning to provide the foundation for a new type of clinic that integrates medicine and speech communication.

I include this essay in order to encourage you to think about how the communication *you* experience is more than just a way to accomplish tasks, negotiate deals, and get your needs met. There's an important link between how you talk and *who you are*. No complete study of communication in any of its forms—public speaking, argumentation, organizational communication, media, or interpersonal relationships—should overlook this link.

THE LANGUAGE OF THE HEART

James J. Lynch

It is obvious that we human beings are distinguished from all other living creatures by the fact that we speak. Whether man or woman or child, we can share our desires, thoughts, plans, and—above all—feelings with each other through

From *The Language of the Heart: The Human Body in Dialogue* by James J. Lynch. Reprinted by permission of Basic Books, Inc., Publishers.

dialogue. Coupled to this is another simple yet sublime truth: that while we speak with words, we speak also with our flesh and blood. As we shall see, study after study reveals that human dialogue not only affects our hearts significantly but can even alter the biochemistry of individual tissues at the further extremities of the body. Since blood flows through every human tissue, the entire body is influenced by human dialogue. Thus, it is true that when we speak we do so with every fiber of our being.

This "language of the heart" is integral to the health and emotional life of every one of us. Yet this vital truth has been largely obscured by a scientific-philosophical perspective we all share and that leads us to think about the human body solely in terms of its mechanical functions. In an age dominated by dramatic images of heart transplants, artificial heart machines, and even the implantation of a baboon's heart into a human baby, it is all too easy to look on the human body solely as a machine incapable of either listening or speaking to others. Nonetheless, the essence of the human being is the body's involvement in dialogue—a process in which no machine can ever engage. For the human heart speaks a language that not only is vital to our well-being but makes possible human feelings and binds human beings together. . . .

To appreciate why we tend to think about the body as a machine, we need only recall an outstanding event of late 1982 and early 1983. For the first time ever, at the University of Utah's Medical Center in Salt Lake City, the life of a human being was sustained by an artificial heart machine. The public's response to this endeavor was electric, perhaps equaled only by the excitement over the first heart transplant operation performed by Christiaan Barnard in Capetown, South Africa, in 1969. And, as in that earlier operation, hourly news bulletins told the world of Dr. Clark's progress, as relentlessly and efficiently pulsating with the timed sighs of its own air compressors, a machine outside of his body kept the life-sustaining fluid—blood—flowing through it. For 112 days, the machine kept beating, pumping blood through his body, until the failure of other organs, his circulatory system collapsed, and he died. Thirteen hundred mourners, including a personal representative of the President of the United States, attended his funeral in the town of Federal Way in the state of Washington.

Clearly, not only Dr. Clark but the medical profession had attempted, and accomplished, a heroic and extraordinary feat. Moreover, this feat, heralded all over the world, was the culmination of a belief on which medical scientists have acted for over three centuries: that is, that the human body is made up of a group of essentially mechanical organs that, when not running properly, can be tinkered with, like any mechanism, in the hope of setting it right again.

At about the same time, my colleagues and I at the Psychophysiological Clinic at the University of Maryland Medical School, were seeing, also for the first time, quite a different aspect of the human cardiovascular system that would lead us to develop an entirely new type of clinic, one based on an understanding of the connection between human communication and the cardiovascular system. For computer technology allowed us to see that as soon as one begins to speak, one's blood pressure increases significantly, one's heart beats faster and harder, and microscopic blood vessels in distant parts of the body change as well. Conversely, when one listens to others speak or truly attends to the external environment in a relaxed manner, then blood pressure usually falls and heart rate slows, frequently below its normal resting levels.

Initially, this discovery seemed more a curiosity than a conceptual breakthrough, especially when contrasted with the human and technical drama in Utah. Yet the data were so clear and so predictably consistent that we could not ignore them. They showed us that centuries of religious, philosophical, literary, and poetic wisdom that had suggested links between words and the human heart contained the core of an astonishingly fertile truth, and one central to medicine. Once aware of this truth, we tested for it in a variety of cases and research studies. We examined thousands of individuals, from newborn babies crying in their cribs; to preschool children reciting their ABCs; to grade-school children reading aloud from textbooks; to nursing and medical students describing their daily work routine; to hypertensive patients in our clinic, and those waiting anxiously for cardiac by-pass surgery; to schizophrenics in psychiatric wards; to elderly patients in nursing homes describing their loneliness, and in patients close to death. In each and every one, the link between language and the heart was clear and undeniable.

Yet, as I shall discuss, there was a powerful force that made it initially difficult for us to appreciate fully that we were indeed creating a new type of clinic. That force had to do, as I have said, with an unexamined philosophical perspective we brought to our own research. It included a vision of the human body shared by virtually everyone in our society, and first formulated by the French philosopher René Descartes in the seventeenth century. Living in an era that witnessed the beginnings of modern science, Descartes harnessed the discoveries of scientists like Galileo, Copernicus, Kepler, Harvey, and Pascal and cast their findings into a new and comprehensive philosophical system. As Descartes himself stated, he intended to create a totally new medicine, one based on the idea that the human body is a machine. He accomplished his goal so brilliantly that his influence, though pervasive, is scarcely understood today. Rather, like the air we breathe, his perspective is simply taken for granted.

Descartes promulaged and defended the idea that the human body functions like all other bodies in nature, according to mechanical principles. He separated mental functioning from bodily mechanics, arguing that the capacity to think has to be the result of the existence of the human soul. While ostensibly innocent, it was an extraordinary vision, one that permeates the way we in the Western world came to understand the nature of human beings, the human body, human health, and the links between our individual bodies and our social existence. After Descartes, issues of health and illness were relegated strictly to medical science; while spiritual and social concerns came to be seen as having little in common with physical health.* Physicians would come to be trained much as were the highly skilled technicians who maintained the French water gardens where statues were cleverly designed to move by means of water pressure, and that helped to inspire Descartes's concept. Three centuries after him, it would make "perfect sense" to think about a heart transplant in a human being much as a mechanic thinks about replacing a faulty water pump in an automobile: heart disease had become a mechanical problem in a faulty hydraulic system. Indeed, as the doctor treating the baby girl with the transplanted baboon heart said, "The heart . . . 'is a muscular pump and is not the seat of the soul.'"[1]

The stage, thus, was set with Descartes. From then on, thinker after thinker, scientist after scientist—including, as we shall see, those seminal masters of modern times, Marx, Darwin, Freud, and Pavlov—thought about the human body in mechanical terms. Whether in social evolution or in social revolution, the body was uncritically accepted to be an isolated, self-contained group of organs functioning strictly according to mechanical principles. In the process, the emotional life of human beings came to be seen as a reflection of mechanical functions inside a well-regulated machine. Unique aspects of human emotional life and the unique nature of human speech were obscured by a scientific perspective that accepted the human body as mechanically similar to other animal bodies, and human emotional life as comparable to the emotional life of animals.

Our thinking about these issues has developed over two decades of research. When we originally began our journey, we sought to understand how human relationships and human loneliness affect cardiovascular health. In 1977, I summarized our findings in *The Broken Heart.*[2] That book was based on the fact that human loneliness is among the most important causes of premature death in modern America. In our studies, for virtually every cause of death—whether suicide, cancer, cirrhosis of the liver, automobile accident, or heart disease—the incidence of premature death was far higher among people who lived alone than among those who were married. While in certain cases—such as suicide, cirrhosis of the liver, or lung cancer—we could easily detect the factors that caused premature death, in others the mechanisms were far less clearcut, especially for heart disease, the leading cause of death in the United States. It was far from obvious why the single, the widowed, and the divorced were two to four times more likely than married people to die prematurely from hypertension, stroke, and coronary heart disease.

While human loneliness appeared to be the single most important and compelling emotional factor in these premature deaths, we were at a loss to explain how this feeling state influenced the heart. Though the statistics were unambiguous, we did not understand how a human experience such as loss or bereavement could lead to premature death from hypertension, stroke, or heart at-

---

*Descartes's influence was every bit as pronounced in religious circles as in medicine. Thus, today no theological school—be it Catholic, Protestant, or Rabbinical—deems it necessary to teach its students elementary anatomy and physiology. The body is considered utterly irrelevant to religious questions, even though the Bible was rooted in such concerns (for example, Talmudic dietary regulations, or Christian and Judaic notions about blood and the heart). Hospital chaplains are today

tack any more than we understood how loneliness caused elevations in blood pressure. While pondering this question, we were equally troubled about how to counteract this problem effectively, since many of the patients who appeared in the coronary-care unit recapitulated the very statistics we had uncovered linking loneliness to increased risk of heart disease.

These questions led us to explore loneliness in hypertensive patients. Since hypertension was, and still is, the single most important medical problem in modern America (it has been estimated that anywhere between forty million to sixty million Americans are hypertensive), we assumed that loneliness played an important role in the problem in at least a significant percentage of these cases.

Yet our efforts to examine the interlocking problem of human loneliness and hypertension quickly confronted us with a whole series of paradoxes. While it seemed intuitively obvious that human dialogue ought to be the best antidote to human loneliness, a large and well-documented literature had amply warned that certain types of social interaction can cause marked increases in the blood pressure of hypertensive patients. Even more to the point, the type of psychotherapeutic dialogue that seemed best suited to delve into issues surrounding the loneliness of hypertensive patients had already been shown to be precisely the type of encounter that would cause their blood pressure to rise to dangerous levels. This problem was compounded further when we discovered a striking relationship between speaking and blood pressure. While the blood pressure of almost everyone we tested rose during speech, that of hypertensive patients increased far more than that of any other group. Sometimes a hypertensive person's blood pressure would surge 50 percent above the resting baseline level as soon as he or she began to speak. Thus, we were forced to recognize that our psychotherapeutic "cure" could make hypertension worse. We began to wonder whether hypertensive patients were trapped inside their own bodies, damned if they withdrew from their fellow human beings and damned if they tried to relate to them.

Through our efforts to reconcile this dilemma, we uncovered a new dimension of the cardiovascular system which allowed us to develop an entirely new way to approach the treatment of vascular disorders, such as hypertension and migraine headaches. And we came finally to recognize that the human cardiovascular system does far more than change in response to internal and external demands: it also communicates. Since our hearts can speak a language that no one hears or sees and therefore cannot understand, we can get sick at heart. . . .

In machines created by humans, it is perfectly clear who and what controls the internal mechanisms and why a particular machine, such as the pump that replaced Barney Clark's heart, was created. That pump was designed to fill a particular purpose, and it was absolutely regulated by its creators. Yet who is in charge of, and what controls, the machinery of the human heart is another matter. Control is exercised from both inside and outside. This idea, though simple

trained so as to feel no need to understand even the most rudimentary aspects of physical disease; instead, they see their job as caring for the soul. Likewise, psychologists can go through college and graduate school without any training in anatomy and physiology. And even the most elementary introductory courses in psychology or philosophy are not required to gain entrance to medical schools, though such schools do require advanced training in calculus, physics, and chemistry.

when it first occurred to us, gradually led us to understand that internal bodily mechanisms, such as blood pressure, long thought to be primarily regulated by the internal machinery of the human body, are also powerfully influenced by the force of human dialogue. Once this force was recognized, we came to understand that dialogue gives the body its very humanity.

Since human dialogue, and its relationship to our hearts and feelings, is the central issue of this book, let me define it as I did in *The Broken Heart:*

> In its most general meaning, dialogue consists of reciprocal communication between two or more living creatures. It involves the sharing of thoughts, physical sensations, ideas, ideals, hopes, and feelings. In sum, dialogue involves the reciprocal sharing of any and all life experiences. . . .
>
> Other characteristics of the process of dialogue are that it is reciprocal, spontaneous, often nonverbal, *and* alive.[3]

At the core of this book is the idea that we human beings are biologically interrelated—and that any attempt to maintain or restore health must be based on that reality. Scientific attempts to understand the human body apart from the most basic of all human traits—the fact that we speak—[are] all too likely to produce a medicine that brilliantly treats isolated parts of the human body, while it seriously neglects the individual as a whole and as part of nature. We can understand and cope with illness only when we are able to view ourselves as part of a complex world beyond the confines of our own individual skin. The response of our hearts, blood vessels, and muscles when we communicate with spouse, children, friends, colleagues, and the larger community has as much to do with our cardiovascular health as do factors such as exercise or diet.

So vital to human health is the language of our hearts that—if ignored, unheard, or misunderstood—it can produce terrible physical suffering, even premature death. For the language of our hearts cries out to be heard. It demands to be understood. And it must be not be denied. Our hearts speak with an eloquence that poets have always, and truly, sensed. It is for us to learn to listen and to understand.

REVIEW QUESTIONS

1. Lynch claims that a "vital truth" has been "largely obscured" by our mechanistic scientific-philosophical perspective. What is this "vital truth"?
2. What is the primary distinctive feature of the approach to cardiovascular health that Dr. Lynch and his colleagues are taking in their clinic at the University of Maryland?
3. Lynch claims that a seventeenth-century philosopher named _____ is primarily responsible for our current mechanical view of the human body.
4. Our mechanical view of the human body begins from the belief that there is a fundamental separation between what and what?
5. What has Dr. Lynch's research shown about the relationships between loneliness, heart disease, and dialogue?

6. Lynch believes that if our efforts to understand the human body don't pay attention to speech, what will occur? What problem will the neglect of speech create?

PROBES

1. Based on your own experience with the medical profession, how do you think most medical doctors might be responding to Lynch's belief that doctors can learn from "centuries of religious, philosophical, literary, and poetic wisdom"?
2. Is Lynch arguing that Descartes single-handedly established our modern view of the human body? What's his point here?
3. Lynch implies that Descartes's scientific-philosophical perspective especially affected the way we view speech. What does he say about this topic?
4. What does Lynch mean when he says that control of the human heart "is exercised from both inside and outside"?
5. What's the relationship between Lynch's definition of *dialogue* and my definition of *interpersonal communication?*

NOTES

1. *The New York Times,* October 31, 1984, p. A18.
2. James J. Lynch, *The Broken Heart: The Medical Consequences of Loneliness* (New York: Basic Books, 1977).
3. Lynch, pp. 217, 218.

*D*avid Bohm was, until his death in 1992, a world-renowned British physicist. He became interested in communication because of his commitment to improve life on this planet, and his ideas about communication emerged from his studies of the natural world. His basic insight was about the pervasiveness of interconnection—that humans and nature are interconnected, cultures are interconnected, and even the things we call "thoughts" are generated and sustained collectively (some of Bohm's ideas about collective thought are in Chapter 5).

In this short overview Bohm applies this insight about interconnection to our basic understanding of the processes we call "communication" or "communicating." He starts by noting how aggression and violence happen when people forget how interconnected we actually are. This often happens, he says, because we get stuck in a "crude and insensitive" way of thinking and talking about communication. We tend to believe, implicitly or explicitly, that communication "makes common" ideas or information that are already known to at least one of the people communicating. But if we examine communicating carefully, we can see that what is often actually happening is that the people are negotiating a variety of *differences* in order to generate something new that they then hold "in common." So the first view treats differences as problems to be eliminated, and the second view treats differences as contributions to the collaborative mix. To put it another way, we could say that the distorted view treats communication as a process whereby one person injects her ideas into another person's head, so they both supposedly end up with the same idea, and the better view understands communication as a process whereby two or more people co-construct a meaning that neither had before they communicated.

Importantly, this doesn't mean that communicators always agree. Opposing political candidates and spouses in a divorce build meanings together just as lovers do.

Bohm argues that even relationships with inanimate objects and with nature are collaborative or mutual in the sense he's developing. For example, in science there is a back-and-forth movement between observation and testing that generates new ideas which are eventually extended into practical applications.

In art, science, and human relationships, the key to this kind of collaborative creativity is effective *listening*. As Bohm sees it, the general human tendency is to believe that we are already listening to the other person in the proper way, even though we may be what Bohm calls "blocked" about certain questions. This condition generates defensiveness—the tendency to protect one's own meanings rather than opening them to collaborative revision. But if we can learn to notice how we are blocking collaborative meaning-making in this way, "then we may be able to create something new between us, something of very great significance for bringing to an end the at present insoluble problems of the individual and of society."

ON COMMUNICATION

David Bohm

During the past few decades, modern technology, with radio, television, air travel, and satellites, has woven a network of communications which puts each part of the world into almost instant contact with all the other parts. Yet, in spite of this world-wide system of linkages, there is, at this very moment, a general feeling that communication is breaking down everywhere, on an unparalleled scale. People living in different nations, with different economic and political systems, are hardly able to talk to each other without fighting. And within any single nation, different social classes and economic and political groups are caught in a similar pattern of inability to understand each other. Indeed, even within each limited group, people are talking of a "generation gap," which is

From *On Dialogue* by David Bohm, 1996. Reprinted by permission of Routledge.

such that older and younger members do not communicate, except perhaps in a superficial way. Moreover, in schools and universities, students tend to feel that their teachers are overwhelming them with a flood of information which they suspect is irrelevant to actual life. And what appears on the radio and television, as well as in the newspapers and magazines, is generally at best a collection of trivial and almost unrelated fragments, while at worst, it can often be a really harmful source of confusion and misinformation.

Because of widespread dissatisfaction with the state of affairs described above, there has been a growing feeling of concern to solve what is now commonly called "the problem of communication." But if one observes efforts to solve this problem, he [or she] will notice that different groups who are trying to do this are not actually able to listen to each other. As a result, the very attempt to improve communication leads frequently to yet more confusion, and the consequent sense of frustration inclines people ever further toward aggression and violence, rather than toward mutual understanding and trust.

If one considers the fact that communication is breaking down and that in the present context efforts to prevent this from happening generally tend to accelerate the breakdown, [one] may perhaps pause in his [or her] thinking, to give opportunity to ask whether the difficulty does not originate in some more subtle way that has escaped our mode of formulating what is going wrong. Is it not possible that our crude and insensitive manner of thinking about communication and talking about it is a major factor behind our inability to see what would be an intelligent action that would end the present difficulties?

It may be useful to begin to discuss this question by considering the meaning of the word "communicaton." This is based on the Latin *commun* and the suffix "ie" which is similar to "fie," in that it means "to make or to do." So one meaning of "to communicate" is "to make something common," i.e., to convey information or knowledge from one person to another in as accurate a way as possible. This meaning is appropriate in a wide range of contexts. Thus, one person may communicate to another a set of directions as to how to carry out a certain operation. Clearly, a great deal of our industry and technology depends on this kind of communication.

Nevertheless, this meaning does not cover all that is signified by communication. For example, consider a dialogue. In such a dialogue, when one person says something, the other person does not in general respond with exactly the same meaning as that seen by the first person. Rather, the meanings are only *similar* and not identical. Thus, when the second person replies, the first person sees a *difference* between what she meant to say and what the other person understood. On considering this difference, she may then be able to see something new, which is relevant both to her own views and to those of the other person. And so it can go back and forth, with the continual emergence of a new content that is common to both participants. Thus, in a dialogue, each person does not attempt to *make common* certain ideas or items of information that are already known. Rather, it may be said that the two people are making something *in common*, i.e., creating something new together.

But of course such communication can lead to the creation of something new only if people are able freely to listen to each other, without prejudice, and without trying to influence each other. Each has to be interested primarily in truth and coherence, so that he is ready to drop his old ideas and intentions, and be ready to go on to something different, when this is called for. If, however, two people merely want to convey certain ideas or points of view to each other, as if these were items of information, then they must inevitably fail to meet. For each will hear the other through the screen of his own thoughts, which he tends to maintain and defend, regardless of whether or not they are true or coherent. The result will of course be just the sort of confusion that leads to the insoluble "problem of communication" which has been pointed out and discussed earlier.

Evidently, communication in the sense described above is necessary in all aspects of life. Thus, if people are to cooperate (i.e., literally to "work together") they have to be able to create something in common, something that takes shape in their mutual discussions and actions, rather than something that is conveyed from one person who acts as an authority to the others, who act as passive instruments of this authority.

Even in relationships with inanimate objects and with nature in general, something very like communication is involved. Consider, for example, the work of an artist. Can it properly be said that the artist is *expressing himself*, i.e., literally "pushing outward" something that is already formed inside of him? Such a description is not in fact generally accurate or adequate. Rather, what usually happens is that the first thing the artist does is only *similar* in certain ways to what he may have in mind. As in a conversation between two people, he sees the similarity and the difference, and from this perception something further emerges in his next action. Thus, something new is continually created that is common to the artist and the material on which he is working.

The scientist is engaged in a similar "dialogue" with nature (as well as with her fellow human beings). Thus, when a scientist has an idea, this is tested by observation. When it is found (as generally happens) that what is observed is only similar to what she had in mind and not identical, then from a consideration of the similarities and the differences she gets a new idea which is in turn tested. And so it goes, with the continual emergence of something new that is common to the thought of scientists and what is observed in nature. This extends onward into practical activities, which lead to the creation of new structures that are common to humans and to the overall environment in which we live.

It is clear that if we are to live in harmony with ourselves and with nature, we need to be able to communicate freely in a creative movement in which no one permanently holds to or otherwise defends his [or her] own ideas. Why then is it so difficult actually to bring about such communication?

This is a very complex and subtle question. But it may perhaps be said that when one comes to do something (and not merely to talk about it or think about it), one tends to believe that one *already is* listening to the other person in a proper way. It seems then that the main trouble is that the other person is the one who is prejudiced and not listening. After all, it is easy for each one of us to see that other people are "blocked" about certain questions, so that without being aware of it, they are avoiding the confrontation of contradictions in certain ideas that may be extremely dear to them.

The very nature of such a "block" is, however, that it is a kind of insensitivity or "anesthesia" about one's own contradictions. Evidently then, what is crucial is to be aware of the nature of one's own "blocks." If one is alert and attentive, one can see for example that whenever certain questions arise, there are fleeting sensations of fear, which push the person away from consideration of these questions, and of pleasure, which attract his thoughts and cause them to be occupied with other questions. So one is able to keep away from whatever it is that he thinks may disturb him. And as a result, he can be subtly defending his own ideas, when he supposes that he is really listening to what other people have to say.

When we come together to talk, or otherwise to act in common, can each one of us be aware of the subtle fear and pleasure sensations that "block" our ability to listen freely? Without this awareness, the injunction to listen to the whole of what is said will have little meaning. But if each one of us can give full attention to what is actually "blocking" communication while also attending properly to the content of what is communicated, then we may be able to create something new between us, something of very great significance for bringing to an end the at present insoluble problems of the individual and of society.

REVIEW QUESTIONS

1. Bohm starts by saying that modern technology has woven a vast network of communication, but that this has also created a basic problem. What is the problem?
2. According to Bohm, what is the major benefit of becoming aware of a *difference* between your idea and somebody else's?
3. Bohm briefly extends his treatment of communication to include not only contacts between persons but also what other type of contacts?
4. What does Bohm mean by "a kind of insensitivity or 'anesthesia' about one's own contradictions"?

PROBES

1. Paraphrase the distinction Bohm makes between treating communication as an "attempt to *make common*" and as "making something *in common*." How might this difference affect the way you communicate with a friend or co-worker?
2. When you're talking with a close friend about a topic that's important to you, is the main point of your talk to *eliminate* differences or to *integrate* them into your mutual understanding?
3. Compare Bohm's understanding of collaboration with the understanding developed in the first reading in this chapter.
4. Talk with an artist you know (painter, sculptor, poet, etc.) about the idea Bohm introduces in the eighth paragraph of this essay. Is it most accurate to see art as an "expression" of the artist or as a negotiated, collaborative, creative engagement?
5. How often do you believe—without thinking about it—that you are "already listening to the other person in a proper way"? How might your communicating become "unblocked" if you were to reconsider this assumption about your own listening?

W illiam Isaacs is a prominent member of a group of people studying dialogue at the Sloan School of Management in Massachusetts. Since the early 1990s, Isaacs and his colleagues have been helping
people in a wide variety of business organizations cope with innovation
and change.

Under the leadership of an organizational consultant named Peter
Senge, this group has developed ways for businesses to become what
are called "learning organizations." Isaacs, Senge, and their colleagues
have discovered that today's global economy and rapidly expanding
technology make the processes of change so continuous and unpredictable that the only way an organization can survive and prosper is to
continually adapt. It is no longer enough for businesses to do a good job
of short-range and long-range planning; today, organizations need to be
learning, almost on a daily basis, how to serve their customers or clients
better and to become increasingly smarter about how to produce their
products and services. So, for example, the Boeing Aircraft Company
now claims that it never makes any two airplanes in exactly the same
way, because it learns from each experience how to do it better.

How does all this relate to interpersonal communication? Well,
these organizational consultants have discovered that a primary element of every successful learning organization is dialogue—collaborative, ongoing, back-and-forth communication anchored in effective *listening*. To put it simply, Isaacs, Senge, and their colleagues have
determined that the main way to become a learning organization is for
the members to learn how to engage in dialogue.

In the next several pages, Isaacs describes this kind of dialogue. He
begins by defining dialogue as "a sustained collective inquiry into
everyday experience and what we take for granted" (this is related to,
but different from, the discussion of dialogue by Martin Buber in Chapter 18). One key idea in this discussion is that the prefix *dia* in the word
dialogue does not mean "two people." *Dia* means "through," and *logue*
is the English version of the Greek term *logos* that can be translated
"meaning." So *dialogue* in this sense means "meaning-through," or the
process of helping meaning flow *through* the people involved in co-constructing it.

Isaacs distinguishes dialogue from *discussion*, which comes from a
Latin word meaning "to smash to pieces." He notes that the point of discussion is often to break ideas down, but the point of dialogue is to
build meanings together.

Isaacs also emphasizes that there is no sure-fire set of techniques or
rules for dialogue. The process involves *people thinking together*, so it requires commitment, focus, attention, and the willingness to risk your ideas
as you explain and describe what you believe. Importantly, this kind of
dialogue is not just "warm and fuzzy." The power of collaborative inquiry
is greatest when people disagree about important things, as they do in
many of the organizations that Isaacs and Senge have worked with.

The second part of this reading describes four phases of dialogue that commonly occur as groups try to communicate this way. The first phase is "instability *of* the container" when the people involved recognize how much they disagree, and that if they are going to cope with their disagreement, each person is going to have to relax the grip on his or her ideas in order to consider other possibilities. Phase two is "instability *in* the container." Here differences really begin to surface to the point where members, as Isaacs puts it, "begin to feel as if they were in a giant washing machine" with ideas and opinions jostling over and under each other in a barely restrained chaos. There's a great deal of "heat" and instability in this phase, but it's exactly what's needed in order for all the differences to get airtime. The trick in phase two is not to panic or withdraw, but to hang in there, usually with the help of a facilitator.

Phase three is called "inquiry in the container." If people survive phase two, they begin to recognize insights they have never had before, understandings that came about only because they lived through the turmoil of mutual confrontation and careful listening. There is often a "crisis of collective pain," and it requires discipline and collective trust to move through this phase.

The final phase is "creativity in the container." Here thinking becomes genuinely collaborative. People's ideas bounce off and build onto each other. There are also periods of silence where mutual understanding may seem too full to be expressed easily. In this phase, as Isaacs puts it, ideally, "the group does not 'have' meaning in its conversation. The group *is* its meaning."

To help clarify what all this means in actual practice, Isaacs ends with a brief discussion of some basic components of, and some general guidelines for, a dialogue session. This kind of group dialogue needs to begin with an invitation so people experience their participation as genuinely voluntary. Participants need to listen "generatively" (compare this idea with the discussion of dialogic listening in Chapter 6). They also need to be open to observing themselves and each other and willing to suspend assumptions, at least for the time of the dialogue.

At the end of the reading Bryan Smith interjects three short paragraphs about viewing disagreement as an opportunity rather than a threat or curse. Then Isaacs and Smith close with six very concrete guidelines. The last one captures the spirit of this kind of communication well. It is: "Speak to the center, not to each other." This is important, because the point of this kind of dialogue is not mainly two-person direct contact but collaborative group reflection and thinking. And "speaking to the center of the group" can help facilitate this kind of communication.

I've seen these ideas about dialogue significantly improve communication in the parts of the Boeing company where they've been applied. Isaacs, Senge, and Bohm have some ideas that are different from the ones I outline in the first reading of this chapter, but we are all working toward a similar end. The kind of communicating that's described here can substantially enhance how well an organization functions—whether the organization is a work team, a committee, a student organization, a board of directors, or a family.

DIALOGUE

William Isaacs

DIALOGUE AND SKILLFUL DISCUSSION

The word dialogue comes from two Greek roots, *dia* (meaning "through" or "with each other") and *logos* (meaning "the word"). It has been suggested that this word carries a sense of "meaning flowing through."

Dialogue can initially be defined as *a sustained collective inquiry into everyday experience and what we take for granted.* The goal of dialogue is to open new ground by establishing a "container" or "field" for inquiry: a setting where people can become more aware of the context around their experience, and of the processes of thought and feeling that created that experience.

As we practice dialogue, we pay attention to the spaces between the words, not only the words; the timing of action, not only the result; the timbre and tone of a voice, not only what is said. We listen for the meaning of the field of inquiry, not only its discrete elements. In short, dialogue creates conditions in which people experience the primacy of the whole.

Dialogue is an old term. There is some evidence to suggest that human beings have gathered in small groups to talk together for millennia. It does not feel like ordinary "civilized" conversation, but it does feel very natural to people once they start. That may explain why it seems to flourish in modern settings, despite a range of institutionalized barriers. The word "discussion" stems from the Latin *discutere,* which meant "to smash to pieces." Discussion is a conversational form that promotes fragmentation. However, skillful discussion differs from unproductive discussion because the participants are not merely engaged in "advocacy wars" of one-upmanship. They develop a repertoire of techniques (encompassing collaborative reflection and inquiry skills) for seeing how the components of their situation fit together, and they develop a more penetrating understanding of the forces at play among the team members themselves.

In skillful discussion, you make a choice; in a dialogue, you discover the nature of choice. Dialogue is like jazz; skillful discussion is like chamber music . . .

A team of people sit in a circle on a stage, talking with intensity. In this form of intimate theater, they are both the performers and the audience. They are arguing, because they do not agree, but there's a quality of engagement about their argument. They listen intently to each other's language, rhythms, and sounds. The silences between statements seem as striking as the words. Every time someone says something, a texture changes subtly; something new has been seen. Everyone knows that everyone in the group has seen it, and that it represents more than just one person's model of the truth. As the people in the circle continue to talk, the sense of meaning they share grows larger and sharper. They begin to gain unprecedented insight into their fundamental views. No one can muster this form of thinking alone, and even in a group it takes a willful desire to build a context for thinking together. It takes a practice like dialogue.

Dialogue is not merely a set of techniques for improving organizations, enhancing communications, building consensus, or solving problems. It is based on the principle that conception and implementation are intimately linked, with a core of common meaning. During the dialogue process, people learn how to think together—not just in the sense of analyzing a shared problem of creating new pieces of shared knowledge, but in the sense of occupying a collective sensibility, in which the thoughts, emotions, and resulting actions belong not to one individual, but to all of them together.

As theorist David Bohm has pointed out, when the roots of thoughts are observed, thought itself seems to change for the better. People can begin to move into coordinated patterns of action, without the artificial, tedious process of decision making. They can start to act in an aligned way. They do not need to work out an action plan for what everyone should do, any more than a flock of birds taking flight from a tree, in perfectly natural order, requires planning. Each member of the team simply knows what he or she is "supposed" to do (or, rather, what's best to do), because they all fit into a larger whole.

At the Dialogue Project at MIT, we have begun to learn how to nurture this process in diverse settings—including an entire health care community in the Midwest riddled with competitive antagonisms, a group of South African professionals and leaders, a steel manufacturer (GS Technologies) with a history of severe labor/management problems, and a group of urban leaders in a major U.S. city. We have sought to translate 100 years of dialogue theory into practice, and to extend that theory, for the first time, so that reliable action can be built upon it. This has turned out to have exceedingly practical applications. As Margaret Mead put it, "Small groups of thoughtful, concerned citizens can change the world. Indeed, it is the only thing that ever has." . . .

Levels and Stages of Dialogue:
The Development of Cool Inquiry

David Bohm has compared dialogue to superconductivity. Electrons cooled to very low temperatures act more like a coherent whole than as separate parts. They flow around obstacles without colliding with one another, creating no resistance and very high energy. At higher temperatures, however, they began to act like separate parts, scattering into a random movement and losing momentum.

Particularly around tough issues, people act more like separate, high-temperature electrons. They collide and move at cross-purposes. Dialogue seeks to produce a "cooler"shared environment, by refocusing the group's shared attention. These environments, which we have called "containers" or fields of inquiry, emerge as a group moves through a dialogue process. A container can be understood as the sum of the collective assumptions, shared intentions, and beliefs of a group. As they move through the dialogue progression, participants perceive that the "climate" or "atmosphere" of the room is changing, and gradually see that their collective understanding is changing it.

The following chart displays the evolution of dialogue:

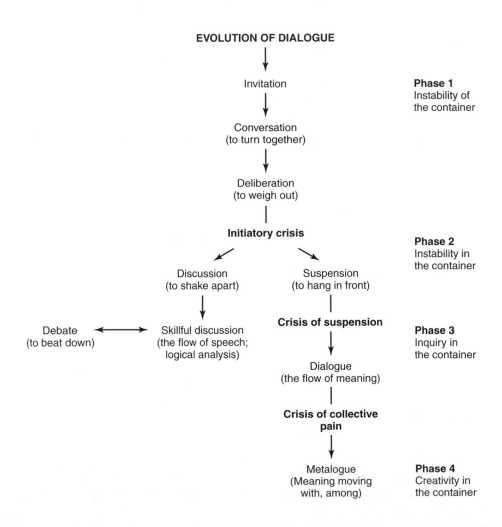

Passing from one phase to the next seems to entail meeting different types of individual and collective crises. Once one moves through a phase, one can return to it. In a sense, all the phases are always present, though one may seem more dominant at any moment.

Phase 1: Instability of the Container   When any group of individuals comes together, the individuals bring with them a wide range of tacit, unexpressed differences in perspectives. At this moment, dialogue confronts its first crisis: the need for the members to look at the group as an entity including themselves as observers and observed, instead of merely "trying to understand each other" or reach a "decision that everyone can live with." In this initiatory crisis people confront and navigate a critical paradox: that you can intend to have dialogue, but you cannot force it to happen.

Gradually people recognize that they have a choice: they can *suspend* their views, loosening the grip of their certainty about all views, including their own. They can observe the ways they have habitually made, and acted upon, assumptions. They can question the total process of thought and feeling that produced the conflict—and everything else—in the room: "Lets see where this divergence, this chaos, this instability came from." That will move them toward dialogue.

Or the group can move to converge, avoiding the challenge of gaining insight into the barriers that are appearing, choosing instead to dissect or defend previously held positions. This convergence can take two very different forms. To the extent that people begin to defend themselves, avoiding evidence that would weaken their view, they are moving toward unproductive discussion. To the extent that they begin to surface the data that leads them to conflict, and the reasoning they use to support their positions, they are moving to skillful discussion.

Phase 2: Instability in the Container   Having chosen to live with chaos, groups begin to oscillate between suspending views and "discussing" them. At this stage people may find themselves feeling frustrated, principally because the underlying fragmentation and incoherence in everyone's thought begin to appear. Normally this would be kept below the surface, but now it comes forward, despite the best efforts of the participants to keep themselves "cool" or "together." The members begin to feel as if they were in a giant washing machine. No point of view seems to hold all the truth any longer; no conclusion seems definitive. They can't tell where the group is heading; they feel disoriented, and perhaps marginalized or constrained by others.

This leads to a "crisis of suspension." Extreme views are stated and defended. All of this "heat" and instability feels distressing, but it is exactly what should be occurring. The fragmentation that has been hidden is appearing.

In our health care dialogue sessions, at this stage, people began to talk about the long-suppressed "myths" different groups felt about each other (physicians versus administrators, for example), and the anger which they felt about each other. Though expressing conflict of this sort was traditionally anathema to "caring" people, the instability in the container compelled them to explore it directly. However, instead of talking about it in terms of interpersonal issues, they could talk about their different collective images of one another. ("You think nurses are less intelligent than doctors, don't you?")

To manage the crisis of collective suspension that arises at this stage, everyone must be adequately awake to what is happening. People do not need to panic and withdraw, to fight, or to categorize one viewpoint as "right" and another viewpoint as "wrong." All they need to do is listen and inquire: "What is the meaning of this?" They do not merely listen to others, but to themselves: "Where am I listening from? What is the disturbance going on in me [not others]? What can I learn if I slow things down and inquire within myself?"

At this crisis, skilled facilitation is most critical. The facilitator does not seek to "correct" or impose order on what is happening, but to model (in his or her own behavior) some ways to suspend assumptions. The facilitator might point out the presence of polarization, the opportunity to learn what they represent, and the limiting categories of thought that are rapidly gaining momentum in the group.

Phase 3: Inquiry in the Container   If a critical mass of people stay with the process beyond this point, the conversation begins to flow in a new way. In this "cool" environment people begin to inquire together as a whole. People become sensitive to the ways in which the conversation is affecting all the participants in the group. New insights often emerge. When we facilitated a dialogue in South Africa, we found people began to reflect on apartheid in ways that surprised them. They could stand beside the tension of the topic without being identified with it.

This phase can be playful and penetrating. Yet it also leads to another crisis. People gradually begin to sense their separateness. Such awareness brings pain. It hurts to exercise new cognitive and emotional muscles, and it especially hurts to feel how you have created your own fragmentation and isolation, throughout your life.

This "crisis of collective pain" is deep and challenging. It requires considerable discipline and collective trust. As areas of lack of wholeness come to the group's attention, its members begin to change, freeing up rigidity and old habits of attention and communication.

Moving through this crisis is by no means a given nor necessary for "success" in dialogue. Groups may need a considerable period of time to develop the capacity for moving to the final level.

Phase 4: Creativity in the Container   If this crisis can be navigated, the distinction between memory and thinking becomes apparent. Thinking takes on an entirely different rhythm and pace. The net of words may not be fine enough to capture the subtle and delicate understandings that begin to emerge; the people may fall silent. Yet the silence is not an empty void, but one replete with richness.

"When the soul lies down in that grass," wrote Rumi, a thirteenth-century Persian poet, "the world is too full to talk about." In dialogue's fourth phase, the world is too full to use language to analyze it. Yet words can also emerge here: Speech that clothes meaning, instead of words merely pointing toward it. I call this kind of experience "metalogue" or "meaning flowing with." The group does not "have" meaning in its conversation. The group *is* its meaning. This kind of exchange allows participants to generate breakthrough levels of intelligence and creativity, and to know the aesthetic beauty of shared speech. . . .

Basic Components of a Dialogue Session

Invitation   The invitation process begins building the container. People must be given the choice to participate. They must understand that their resistances and fears are safely answered. Dialogue can't be shoved down their throats, because that will invoke the memory of previous times when something was forced on them, whether at your organization or elsewhere. You'll get a primitive "fight," "flight," or "freeze" response. Your goal with dialogue is to evoke a higher-level response. Freeing up traditional structures of imposition and hierarchy in a group is essential to allow new energy for collective inquiry.

Generative Listening   To listen fully means to pay close attention to what is being said beneath the words. You listen not only to the "music," but to the very essence of the person speaking. You listen not only for what someone knows, but for who he or she is. Ears operate at the speed of sound, which is far slower than the speed of the light the eyes take in. Generative listening is the art of developing deeper silence in yourself, so you can slow your mind's hearing to your ears' natural speed, and hear beneath the words to their meaning.

Observing the Observer   When we observe the thoughts that govern how we see the world, we begin to change and transform ourselves—and this is as true for a team as it is for an individual. Many of the dialogue techniques—like silence—are based around developing an environment that is quiet enough so that people can observe their thoughts, and the team's thoughts. Once that happens, things can change without conscious manipulation.

Suspending Assumptions   Dialogue encourages people to "suspend" their assumptions—to refrain from imposing their views on others and to avoid suppressing or holding back what they think. The word suspension means "to hang in front." Hanging your assumptions in front of you so that you and others can reflect on them is a delicate and powerful art. This does not mean laying your assumptions aside, even temporarily, to see what your attitudes would be if you felt differently. It means exploring your assumptions from new angles: bringing them forward, making them explicit, giving them considerable weight, and trying to understand where they came from. You literally suspend them in front of the group so that the entire team can understand them collectively. . . .

We have found that to understand the term "suspension" we must see it as several activities, not just one. First comes *surfacing assumptions:* one must be aware of one's assumptions before one can raise them. Typically others are more aware of your assumptions than you are, and less aware of your intentions; as the team inquires into the relationship between assumptions and intentions, the suspension process is begun. Second comes *display* of assumptions: unfolding your assumptions so that you and others can see them. This act of displaying assumptions is itself a kind of suspension. The third component is *inquiry;* to suspend with the intention of inviting others to see new dimensions in what you are thinking and saying.

Disagreement as an Opportunity

Bryan Smith

A dialogue group is always on the lookout for those moments when an almost imperceptible disagreement rises to the surface. Inevitably there will be a temptation to think: "Let's just get on with it. The difference is just semantic." But chances are, if the difference is not easily resolved, it is not just semantic. The facilitator must say, in effect, "Our purpose is not to 'get on with it,' but to use potentially subtle disagreements to show us where to dig deeper."

The moment of disagreement is cause for celebration: "This little discrepancy is intriguing. It's a real opportunity. Let's not lose it. Let's slow down a little bit, play back the tape, and see what's really going on below the tip of the iceberg . . ." In fact, if there is no disagreement, that can be a sign that the group is moving too quickly.

Often an affection develops between members of the group with the most opposing views, as if the affection itself is fueled by diversity: "Isn't that amazing," someone might say, "that you have such a different idea? Why do you feel that way? How did you come to it?"

General Guidelines for Dialogue Sessions

William Isaacs, Bryan Smith

There are no rules for a dialogue session: instead, we offer guidelines that may be helpful, based on experiences that people have recorded.

Allow at least two hours, or more if possible, for every session.

"Checking in" is one of the most powerful ways to kick off a dialogue session. At the beginning and end of every session, give every participant an opportunity to simply speak for a minute about what he or she is thinking, is feeling, or has noticed. Stress the value of speaking from personal experience. When everyone knows that they will have some air time, people tend to relax.

Avoid agendas and elaborate preparations; these inhibit the free flow of conversation.

While meeting over a meal may break the ice, we recommend that you avoid the temptation; restaurant service and eating can be distracting.

Agree, as a group, to hold three meetings before you decide whether to continue or disband. Anything less may not be a fair experiment; it can take time to grow into the dialogue form of conversation.

Speak to the center, not to each other. While challenging to execute, this guideline underlines the creation of a pool of common meaning, not interpersonal dynamics.

REVIEW QUESTIONS

1. What is the main difference Isaacs wants to emphasize between discussion and dialogue?
2. In what ways is dialogue like superconductivity?
3. Look back at the diagram of the evolution of dialogue and explain the main difference between "Discussion" and "Suspension."
4. Explain the difference between "instability *of* the container" and "instability *in* the container."
5. How does silence contribute to dialogue, according to Isaacs?
6. "The moment of disagreement," Bryan Smith writes, "is cause for celebration." Explain what Smith means by this.
7. What does "speak to the center" mean?

PROBES

1. Isaacs says that the word *discussion* comes from the Latin word meaning "to smash to pieces." Bohm notes in the previous reading that the word *dialogue* comes from the Greek words that mean "meaning-through," which suggests a process of collaboratively generating understandings. Give an example from your own experience where each has happened—one where a group smashed a topic to pieces and another where a group actually pooled ideas collaboratively.
2. Why can't dialogue be achieved just by applying a set of techniques?
3. What do you think Isaacs means when he says, "when the roots of thoughts are observed, thought itself seems to change for the better"? How might a group observe "the roots" of its thoughts? What changes might this produce?
4. Isaacs and his colleagues believe that, with the help of a facilitator, disagreements and even hostility need to be surfaced, expressed in the group, rather than covered over. What is their rationale for this belief? Do you agree that it is important to have this happen?
5. Flip forward to the reading "Empathic and Dialogic Listening" at the end of Chapter 6. Make a note there to compare the idea of "dialogic listening"with what Isaacs calls "generative listening."
6. What is the *opposite* of viewing disagreement as an opportunity? What is the main benefit of viewing disagreement as an opportunity?

CHAPTER 3

Verbal and Nonverbal Communicating

This next reading starts with its own introduction and is longer than most, so I'll make this short. These pages come from the 1998 edition of an interpersonal communication text that I coauthor with Carole Logan, a friend who teaches communication at the University of San Diego. As you can tell from the title, the reading reverses the popular tendency to discuss verbal and nonverbal communicating in separate chapters. We explain why at the start.

This selection is broad enough in coverage to give you a fairly comprehensive introduction to both language and most nonverbal cues. We resist the "verbal/nonverbal" dichotomy by locating the main communication building blocks on a continuum or sliding scale that runs from primarily verbal (written words) to mixed (vocal pacing, pause, loudness, pitch, and silence), to primarily nonverbal (gestures, eye gaze, facial expression, touch, and space). Our goal is to encourage you to view these aspects of your communicating as holistically as you can and to notice the ways the various kinds of cues affect each other.

We briefly review the three main ways language has been discussed—as a system of symbols, an activity, and what we call a "soup." Then we discuss some features of mixed and primarily nonverbal cues. If you follow this introductory overview with the three other readings in this chapter, I think you'll have a pretty decent understanding of this final part of communication's basic ingredients.

VERBAL AND NONVERBAL DIMENSIONS OF TALK

John Stewart and Carole Logan

Interpersonal communication texts typically devote one chapter to verbal codes and a separate one to nonverbal communication. This practice began in the late 1960s when communication researchers and teachers first discovered the importance of the nonverbal parts of communicating—eye contact, body movement, facial expression, tone of voice, touch, silence, and so on. For about 30 years, most textbooks treated each subject as significant and distinct.

But now research is focusing more and more closely on conversations as people actually experience them, and it has become obvious that you can't really separate the verbal and nonverbal parts. In the words of two researchers, "It is impossible to study either verbal or nonverbal communication as isolated structures. Rather, these systems should be regarded as a unified communication construct."[1] And as teacher and theorist Wendy Leeds-Hurwitz puts it, "In

From *Together: Communicating Interpersonally,* 5th ed. by John Stewart and Carole Logan, 1997. Reprinted by permission of The McGraw-Hill Companies.

discussing communication as consisting of verbal and nonverbal modes . . . we leave ourselves open to the impression that the two are somehow distinct and should be studied separately. This is not at all the case, and there is now a current body of literature devoted to rejoining the two."[2]

Interestingly, almost this same point was made at the beginning of the 20th century by Ferdinand de Saussure, one of the founders of linguistics. Saussure said that language is like a sheet of paper, where sound makes up one side of the page and the concepts or thoughts make up the other. You can't pick up one side of the paper without picking up the other, and you can't cut one side without cutting the other. So it's best to think of them together.[3] We think the same way about the verbal and the nonverbal parts of communication; they're like the two sides of one sheet of paper.

This is actually the way they occur in human experience. For example, consider this conversation:

SCOTT: *(Smiling and nodding)* Hi, John Paul. Howzit goin'?

JOHN PAUL: *(Excited look)* Scott! *(Shaking hands)* It's good to see you! I heard you'd moved. Where've you *been?*

SCOTT: *(Smiling knowingly)* Nowhere, really. I've just been working and going to school. But Heather and I have been hangin' around together quite a bit.

JOHN PAUL: *(Teasing)* Yeah, I heard that. What's the story with you two anyway?

SCOTT: *(Playful but cagey)* What do you mean "What's the story"? We just like each other, and we spend a lot of time together.

JOHN PAUL: *(Still teasing)* Yeah, like all weekend. And every night. And most of the rest of the time.

SCOTT: *(Turning the tables)* Well, what about you and Bill? I've heard you two are a duo . . . partners . . . an item.

JOHN PAUL: *(A little shy)* Where'd you hear that? Yeah, it's pretty true. *(Brighter)* And it's kind of neat, actually. It's the first time I've felt like part of *a couple.* We might even get an apartment together. But he's got to get a job that pays more. I can't support both of us.

SCOTT: *(Friendly)* Sounds like you've got the same questions Heather and I have. But her folks are also a problem.

JOHN PAUL: *(Serious)* My mom and dad are fine. But Bill's parents don't know anything about us, and I'm trying to get him to change that. In fact, I was thinking that I'd like to talk to you about that. I also wonder how you and Heather plan to actually set up living together. But I've got to get to work now. Give me your new number so I can give you a call, Okay?

John Paul and Scott build this conversation together by using verbal and nonverbal aspects of language simultaneously. There is never a point in the talk where these two parts of communicating are separate. When Scott's intent is to be "playful," he communicates this verbally and nonverbally to John Paul. When the tone of the conversation turns "serious," John Paul communicates this through posture, facial expression, and tone of voice, as well as through the words he chooses.

This chapter emphasizes the fact that people engaged in conversation construct all verbal and nonverbal aspects of talk together. To put it in researchers' terms, utterance meaning and nonverbal meaning are not discrete and independent.[4] This is true even of words written on a page. What you might consider to be "purely verbal" written words appear in a designed typeface, on a certain weight and color of paper, and surrounded by more or less white space. All of these nonverbal elements affect how people interpret the written words of any language. Similarly, even purely nonverbal behaviors, such as gestures or eye behavior, occur in the context of some spoken or written words. One way to sort out the verbal and nonverbal aspects of language is to think in terms of a continuum or sliding scale like the following.

Primarily Verbal————————**Mixed**————————**Primarily Nonverbal**		
written words	vocal pacing, pause, loudness, pitch, silence	gestures, eye gaze, facial expression, touch, space

Written words are classified as primarily verbal for the reasons we just gave. They appear in a nonverbal typeface surrounded by nonverbal space, but readers interpret or make meaning primarily on the basis of the words' verbal content. To the degree that you can isolate the words speakers use, they might be considered primarily verbal, too. But spoken words always come with vocal pacing, pause, loudness, pitch, and silence, and as a result these are labeled mixed. Gestures, facial expression, and so on are labeled primarily nonverbal because they can occur without words, but they are usually interpreted in the context of spoken words.

It would be possible to highlight some of the verbal parts of Scott and John Paul's conversation. Scott says, "Howzit going'?" rather than "How is it going?" or the even more formal "It's good to see you again." He uses the general phrase "spending a lot of time together" rather than a more specific description of his and Heather's activities. For John Paul, the word "couple" is significant. The two share an understanding of what it means, in this context, to say that parents are a "problem."

We could also pinpoint some nonverbal aspects of the conversation. For example, Scott's initial tone of voice is pretty low-key, but John Paul sounds excited to see him. They touch briefly as they shake hands. Their smiles "say" several different things—"It's good to see you." "I like you." "I'm teasing." "I'm teasing back." "We've got something in common." Since they're friends, they stand fairly close together.

In order to focus on the exclusively verbal or exclusively nonverbal parts, however, we'd have to distort what actually happens in Scott and John Paul's conversation. As we've said, the verbal and nonverbal aspects of the conversation are as inseparable as the two sides of a piece of paper. So in this reading:

We describe three approaches to *primarily verbal* cues ("language") that help clarify our reasons for combining verbal and nonverbal communication.

We discuss how several *mixed* cues affect meaning-making and how facial expression and gestures work together with words.

We describe the five most influential *primarily nonverbal* cues—facial expression, eye contact and gaze, space, touch, and body movement and gesture.

THREE APPROACHES TO STUDYING PRIMARILY VERBAL CUES (LANGUAGE)

1. Language Is a System of Symbols

Historically, this is the oldest point of view. From this perspective, language is a system made up of different kinds of words and the rules governing their combinations. Your grade-school teachers emphasized the systematic features of language when they helped you learn the differences among nouns, verbs, adjectives, and adverbs and the rules for making grammatical sentences. When you think of German, Mandarin Chinese, or Spanish as a "language," you're thinking of it as a language *system*. Dictionaries record a part of a language system and provide a record of, for example, word histories and new words like ROM, uplink, and downsize.

Those who study language as a system emphasize that it is a system of symbols. They develop a point made about 2,500 years ago when the Greek philosopher Aristotle began one of his major works on language this way: "Spoken words are the symbols of mental experience and written words are the symbols of spoken words."[5] As a contemporary linguist explains, "This criterion implies that for anything to be a language it must function so as to *symbolize* (represent for the organism) the not-necessarily-*here* and not-necessarily-*now*."[6] In brief, since a symbol is something that stands for something else, this approach emphasizes that units of language—words, usually—represent, or stand for, chunks or pieces of nonlinguistic reality. In the simplest terms, the word "cat" stands for the furry, purring, tail-twitching animal sitting in the corner.

One of the features of symbols that this approach also highlights is that they're *arbitrary*. This means that there is no necessary relationship between the word and the thing it symbolizes. Even though the word *five* is physically smaller than the word *three*, the quantity that *five* symbolizes is larger. So there's no necessary relationship between word (in this case, its size) and meaning. Or consider the words that people from different language communities use to symbolize a dwelling where someone lives: *casa* in Spanish, *maison* in French, and *Haus* in German. This couldn't happen unless the relationship between the word and its meaning were arbitrary.

A classic book, first published in 1923, elaborated just this point. Its authors, C. K. Ogden and I. A. Richards, diagrammed this insight with their famous "triangle of meaning" (see Figure 1).[7] Ogden and Richards' triangle is meant to illustrate how words are related to both thoughts and things. The word-thought relationship is direct—that's why the line is solid. For Aristotle, words stood for thoughts. The relationship between thought and thing was also more or less

FIGURE 1 Ogden and Richards' triangle of meaning

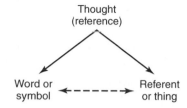

direct. But the word-thing relationship is arbitrary; there is no necessary relationship between the word and its referent. The dotted line across the bottom of the triangle emphasizes this point.

The main advantage of viewing language as a system of arbitrary symbols is that it alerts us to the dangers of abstractions and of the assumptions people make about what words mean by emphasizing that the *thought* or meaning associated with a word may or may not be directly related to the *thing* the word symbolizes. The clearest, most easily understood words are those that are easiest to connect with concrete reality: "this car," "my CD collection," "his blue hair." But from Ogden and Richards' point of view, people should be careful with abstract words like "safety," "style," "love," and "honesty," because the thoughts that they call up may or may not be linked to concrete realities that they symbolize. One person's writing or talk about safety may be connected with safety pins, bank vaults, or a seat belt, and because of the dotted-line relationship in the triangle, the individual to whom the person is writing or talking may not be able to tell the difference. We can also learn from this perspective that, since the relationship between words and meanings is arbitrary, we should never assume that another person means exactly what we do, even when he or she uses the same words. What does "early" mean, for example, when your mom or dad tells you to "get home early"? When your teacher says you should "get started early on your papers"? When the person you're dating feels it's too early in the relationship for sex? When you tell your roommate you want to get up early? Assumptions about identical word meaning often create communication problems.

This view of language is also drastically oversimplified, however. The triangle of meaning makes it appear that language is essentially made up of concrete nouns, labels for things in the world. It doesn't take much reflection to realize that language is much more complicated than that. Often the topic you're discussing and the ideas you want to express require abstract words, such as "love," "pride," and "homelessness." The advice to avoid these kinds of words because there are no "things" or "referents" to which they are even arbitrarily related is not very practical. And what about words like "and," "whether," "however," and "larger"? It can be really confusing to try to figure out what things these words symbolize. Even more important, we don't usually experience language as individual words, but as statements, utterances, messages, or parts of a conversation. So an approach that tries to explain living language by focusing on individual words has to be limited. All this is why it's partly true to say that language is a system of symbols, but there's much more to it than that.

2. Language Is an Activity

A second, more recent approach to the study of language views it as an activity. The most influential version of this approach began in the 1950s when several researchers showed how many utterances actually perform actions. They called these utterances "speech acts." For example, the words "I will" or "I do" in a marriage ceremony are not just symbolizing or referring to getting married. Rather, they are an important part of the activity of marrying itself. If they're not said at the right time by the right people, the marriage hasn't happened. Similarly, the words "I agree" or "Okay, it's a deal" can perform the activity of buying, selling, or contracting for work. And "Howzitgoin'?" is not about a greeting; it is the activity of greeting itself. A group of researchers called conversation analysts have shown how to extend and apply this insight about the action-performing function of language.

Conversation analysts, for instance, have identified the crucial features of many of the speech acts that people typically perform, such as promise, request, threat, offer, command, compliment, and greeting.[8] Each of these terms labels what certain utterances *do* rather than what they symbolize or say. And, these researchers point out, a given utterance won't perform this action unless it has certain features. For example, a *request* requires the speaker to ask for a preferred future behavior from the hearer, and the person who hasn't done this has not competently performed a request. A *promise* is also about a preferred future behavior, but it identifies what the speaker rather than the hearer will do.

If you understand the building blocks of each speech act, you can see why some *indirect* requests and promises will work and others won't. For example, "Are you taking your car to the game tonight?" could function as a *request* for a ride to the game, even though it does not actually identify a preferred future behavior. But it can only work as a request when the context allows both speaker and hearer to fill in the parts that the words themselves leave out. This explains how problems arise when one person fills in the blanks and another doesn't, or when one person means or hears a promise even though the crucial parts of the speech act are absent. For example, when Reggie and Kevin were discussing the game they both wanted to attend, Reggie heard Kevin's "Yeah, I'll be driving" as a *promise* to give him a ride. But Kevin meant it only as a response to Reggie's direct question. So he was surprised and a little angry when Reggie called to confirm the ride he'd "promised."

Conversation analysts have also studied several ways in which people collaborate to mutually construct some speech acts. For example, greetings, goodbyes, invitations, apologies, offers, and congratulations are all speech acts that almost always require two or more conversational moves rather than just one. If one conversation partner greets the other, the expectation is that the other will respond with another greeting. If this doesn't happen, the speech act of "greeting" has only partly occurred. The same thing happens with goodbyes; it takes both one person's "goodbye" *and* the other person's response. This requirement can create problems when one person means to be leaving and the other doesn't pick up on it. Similarly, an invitation is expected to be followed by an acceptance, questioning, or rejection of the invitation; an apology is expected to be followed by an acceptance or rejection, and so on. As one conversation analyst puts it:

> As we shall see, when one of these first actions has been produced, participants orient to the presence or absence of the relevant second action. There is an expectation by participants that the second action should be produced, and when it does not occur, participants behave as if it should have.[9]

Many insights into language use have been generated by people viewing it as an activity that people carry out by following certain sets of conversational rules. At the same time, the more researchers have studied communication as people actually experience it, the more they've recognized that although a great deal can be learned about the individual moves conversation partners make with their various speech acts, natural conversations almost always include unpredictable events or surprises. People improvise as much as they follow conversational rules. In other words, there is a structure to conversation, but it is less like the repetitive pattern followed by a supermarket checkout clerk and more like the loose and varied collaboration of five good musicians getting together to jam.

In summary, conversation analysts have demonstrated the value of studying language as an activity. They have shown that every time we say something, we're also doing something—that speech is a kind of action. They have catalogued many of the actions that people perform by talking and have also shown that some of these actions are produced collaboratively. But they have only been able to consider a few of the important nonverbal elements of conversation, and they have had to admit that there is almost as much improvisation as rule following. Every day people engage in greetings, goodbyes, promises, threats, compliments, offers, commands, requests, and dozens of other conversation acts. But we also improvise and modify expected patterns. Finally, conversation analysts have very little to say about the crucial identity-constructing function of communication. . . . We believe that the most helpful approach to language is the one that includes a focus on identities.

3. Language Is a Soup

This may sound a little weird, but stay with us for a few paragraphs. This approach does include identities.

Especially in the last 30 years, many scholars have recognized the limitations of both the system and action views of language. Both of these views treat language as a tool that humans manipulate, either to arbitrarily stand for some referent or to perform an action. As we have explained, there's some truth to these views, and they can teach us some important things about language. But language is more than a tool. If it were just a tool, we could lay it aside when we didn't need it and pick up some other tool, just as we can lay aside a screwdriver and pick up a hammer. But we can't do that. As humans, we're immersed in language, like a fish is immersed in water. And this quality is what the "soup" metaphor is meant to highlight. As one writer puts it:

> In all our knowledge of ourselves and in all knowledge of the world, we are always already encompassed by the language that is our own. We grow up, and we become acquainted with [people] and in the last analysis with ourselves when we learn to speak. Learning to speak does not mean learning to use a pre-existent tool for designating a world already somehow familiar to us; it means acquiring a familiarity and acquaintance with the world itself and how it confronts us.[10]

This is what it means to say that language is a soup. We're immersed in it from birth to death, just as a fish is immersed in the water in which it lives.

In fact, language experience may begin even before birth. As soon as 20 weeks after conception, the human fetus has functioning ears and is beginning to respond to sounds.[11] Its mother's voice is clearly one sound the fetus learns to identify.[12] Some pregnant couples talk to and play music for their unborn child. When the infant is born, it typically enters an environment of exclamations and greetings. Then verbal and nonverbal communication experiences fill the infant's life. Touch, eye contact, smiles, and a great deal of talk are directed to him or her. As infants develop, parents and other caregivers invite them into conversations or exclude them from conversations by providing a context for talk, by encouraging them with positive attitudes toward talk or discouraging them with negative attitudes, and by interpreting, modeling, and extending talk.[13] This process continues right up to the last tearful goodbyes a person hears at death. In between, humans live more or less like nutritious morsels in a broth of language. This soup includes all the verbal and nonverbal parts of our communicative life. In fact, the theorists and researchers who treat language as a soup have begun to mean by "language" what used to be called "communication"—all the verbal and nonverbal, oral and nonoral, ways that humans make meaning together. As you might be assuming, this view of language fits most comfortably with the approach to communication outlined in Chapter 1.

Language and Perception   If this notion of language as a soup sounds a little abstract, consider one important practical implication of the fact that language is all-encompassing: Because we are immersed in language all our lives, language and perception are thoroughly interrelated. . . . When we perceive, we select, organize, and make meaning out of the things and events we see, hear, touch, taste, and smell. The point that language and perception are thoroughly interrelated means that everything we perceive, all the things that make up our world, is affected by the language in which we live. In the early 20th century, one version of this insight about language and perception was called the Sapir-Whorf hypothesis, for the two people who originally wrote about it, Edward Sapir and Benjamin Lee Whorf. It was summarized by Whorf in these words:

> The background linguistic system (in other words, the grammar) of each language is not merely a reproducing instrument for voicing ideas but rather is itself the shaper of ideas, the program and guide for the individual's mental activity, for his [or her] analysis of impressions. . . . We dissect nature along lines laid down by our native language.[14]

Thus, if you have spent enough time on boats and around the water to learn a dozen different words for water conditions, you will perceive more differences in the water than will the person who was born and raised in Cheyenne, Oklahoma City, or Calgary. That person might distinguish between *waves* and *smooth water*, but you will see and feel differences between *cats' paws, ripples, chop*, and *swells* that he or she probably won't even notice.[15] Or if you have learned important meanings for *latex, natural, lubricated*, and *spermicidal*, you can make distinctions among condoms that were impossible for the high school graduate of the 1970s or early 1980s.

A Chinese-American woman, Mandy Lam, made the point that she felt "similar to the fish that lives in an area of water where the river mixes with the ocean. I have only to travel a little further in either direction to experience the extremes." Her grandparents speak only Chinese, and she relates to them, and often to her parents and other elders, in Chinese ways. But all her premed classes are in English, and she lives in an almost completely English world at school.

As the two of us try in this book to write about communication as a continuous, complex, collaborative meaning-making process, we especially notice two particular ways in which our native language limits our perceptions. The first has to do with the ways that the English language affects how people understand ongoing processes. Unlike some languages, English maintains clear distinctions between noun subjects and verb predicates, causes and effects, beginnings and ends, and this affects how native English speakers perceive communication. A surprising number of other language systems do not do this. According to one researcher, for example, Navajo speakers characteristically talk in terms of processes—uncaused, ongoing, incomplete, dynamic happenings. The word that Navajos use for wagon, for example, translates roughly as "wood rolls about hooplike."[16] The Navajo words that we would translate as "He begins to carry a stone" mean not that the actor produces an action, but that the person is simply linked with a given round object and with an already existing, continuous movement of all round objects in the universe. The English language, by contrast, requires its users to talk in terms of present, past, future, cause and effect, beginning and end. Problems arise when some things that English speakers would like to discuss just can't be expressed in these terms. To continue our example, we would like to be able to talk more clearly about the emergent, ongoing nature of communication. . . . But, especially since communication doesn't always obey the rules of cause and effect, the noun-plus-verb-plus-object structure of the English language makes it difficult to do this. For this topic, Navajo would probably work better than English.

The second way in which we notice that the English language affects our discussion of communication has to do with the ways English speakers perceive gender differences. One accomplishment of research encouraged by the feminist movement of the 1960s and 1970s is that people now recognize how the male bias of standard American English has contributed to the ways in which English-speaking cultures perceive women and men. The fact that, until recently, there were no female firefighters was not caused simply by the existence of the word fire*man.* It's not that simple. But research indicates that gender-biased words affect perceptions in at least three ways. They shape people's attitudes about careers that are "appropriate" for one sex but not for the other, they lead some women to believe that certain jobs and roles aren't attainable, and they contribute to the belief that men deserve higher status in society than do women.[17] This is why changes in job titles have helped open several occupations to more equal male-female participation. Consider, for example, *parking checker* instead of *metermaid, chair* or *chairperson* instead of *chairman, salesperson* instead of *salesman,* and *server* instead of *waiter* or *waitress.* We have also just about stopped referring to female physicians as woman doctors and female attorneys as lady lawyers, and it is more than a coincidence that these changes have been accompanied by significant increases in the numbers of women in these two professions.

Since the mid-1990s, both scholarly and popular books have emphasized this point about gender, language, and perception by highlighting the differences between the language worlds into which men and women are socialized in North America. Sociolinguist Deborah Tannen's book *You Just Don't Understand: Women and Men in Communication*[18] was on the best-seller list for months, and John Gray has sold millions of copies of *Men Are From Mars, Women Are From Venus*[19] and *Mars and Venus in Love.*[20] All of these books describe the ways in which women's communication differs from men's and explain how many problems between genders are influenced by these differences. Some people complain that the books reinforce the very stereotypes they're trying to reduce by generalizing about "women's communication" and "men's communication." Despite the very real danger of this oversimplification, however, there is considerable research evidence to indicate that most North American, English-speaking women and most of their male counterparts do communicate differently. In other words, carefully controlled observations of how these men and women actually talk found that there are important gender-linked patterns.

The women observed in these studies generally use communication as a primary way to establish and maintain relationships with others, whereas the men generally talk to exert control, preserve independence, and enhance status. More specifically, most of these women's communicating is characterized by seven features that are not generally found in the men's talk: an emphasis on equality, support, attention to the relationship, inclusivity, concreteness, and tentativeness, and a preference for collaborative meaning-making. Men's communicating is described in this same research as functioning to exhibit knowledge or skill, accomplish goals, assert dominance, avoid tentativeness, stay abstract rather than concrete, and minimize relationship responsiveness.[21] . . .

To summarize, from the point of view of this soup or fish-in-water idea, language is more than a *system* we use or an *activity* we perform. It is larger than any of us; it happens to us and we are subject to it as much as we manipulate or use it. . . . When studied from this third perspective, language has both verbal and nonverbal aspects. Language researchers and teachers have become increasingly aware that languaging as people actually live it is less of a system or action and more of a mutual event or collaborative process. "Language" is the term these researchers and teachers use for the communicating that, as [was] said in Chapter 1, makes us who we are.

MIXED CUES: VOICE, SILENCE, FACE AND WORDS, GESTURES AND WORDS

The first section of this reading was about the primarily verbal parts of communication—the parts that are often called "language." By now, you know that language includes both verbal and nonverbal elements, but that it can still be distinguished from the "mixed" parts, which include the rate, pitch, volume, and quality of the voice; silence; facial expressions accompanying words; and gestures that accompany words. Let's consider next how these mixed cues operate.

Voice

Sometimes people overlook the fact that spoken language includes many different nonverbal vocal elements. The technical term for these cues is *paralinguistics,* and they include rate of speech, pitch variation, volume, and vocal quality. If you think about your perceptions of someone who speaks reallyrapidly or v-e-r-r-r-y s-l-o-o-o-w-l-y, you have a sense of how rate affects communicating. Listeners and conversation partners also make inferences about how monotone or melodic speech is, how softly or loudly someone speaks, and whether a speaker's vocal quality is resonant, squeaky, nasal, or breathy. Sometimes people manipulate these four dimensions of their voice to assist listeners in interpreting what they're saying, whether they're emphasizing various words or phrases, expressing feelings, or indicating when they're serious and when they're sarcastic or joking. In other cases, speakers don't mean to manipulate any of the four; they're "just talking normally" when people hear them as too fast, as too soft, as a monotone, or as too loud.

As these examples suggest, one of the ways people interpret others' vocal cues is to make stereotyped judgments about the speakers' personalities. It's not a good idea, but we do it nonetheless. For example, a male with a breathy voice is likely to be stereotyped as gay, or at least as young and artistic, whereas a female with the same vocal quality is usually thought of as "more feminine, prettier, more petite, more effervescent, more high-strung, and shallower."[22] Nasal voices are heard as undesirable for both males and females, and low, deep voices are perceived as being more sophisticated, more appealing, and sexier than are higher-pitched voices. People also use vocal cues to draw conclusions about the age, sex, and ethnicity of speakers they hear. What can you conclude from the fact that we use voices this way? According to Mark Knapp:

> You should be quick to challenge the cliché that vocal cues only concern how something is said—frequently they are what is said. What is said might be an attitude ("I like you" or "I'm superior to you"), it might be an emotion . . . or it might be the presentation of some aspect of your personality, background, or

physical features. Vocal cues will, depending on the situation and the communicators, carry a great deal of information. . . . [23]

Silence

> With silence we express the most varied and conflicting states, sentiments, thoughts and desires. Silence is meaningful. There is the silence of fear and terror, of wonder and stupor, of pain and joy. . . . "Dumb silence" is a contradictory expression. Instead of describing the same thing the two terms exclude each other; silence is not dumb and whatever is dumb is not silent. Silence is a form of communication . . . dumbness, on the other hand, isolates and excludes us from all communication.[24]

The reason we classify silence as a mixed cue is that it most often becomes significant in the context of talk. As one author puts it, "A discourse without pauses [is] incomprehensible. Silence is not an interval . . . but the bridge that unites sounds."[25] In other words, silence is usually noticed because of the way it relates to speaking. Examples include the failure or refusal to respond to a question, and the pregnant pause. Even the silence of the forest, prairie, mountain, lake, or bayou is most meaningful because of the way it contrasts with the noises of city crowds.

Silence is one of the least understood nonverbal behaviors, partly because people use and interpret it in so many different ways. Silence can be interpreted to mean apathy, patience, boredom, fear, sadness, love, intimacy, anger, or intimidation. We have talked with married couples who use silence as a weapon. One husband, who knew his wife hated it when he didn't talk out a problem, sometimes would refuse to talk to her for two or three days. His wife said she found this "devastating." When there are prolonged silences in group meetings, people start shifting nervously and making inferences, such as "nobody is interested," "people don't like this group," and "nobody really cares what we're doing."

But silence also works in positive ways. Beginning teachers, for example, have to learn that the silence that sometimes comes after they ask their students a question can be very fruitful. A group's silence can mean that there's a lot of thinking going on. Two close friends may also say nothing to each other just so they can share the experience of the moment. Or in an interview, silence can be a welcome opportunity for the interviewee to elaborate, return to a topic discussed earlier, or simply reorganize her or his thoughts. A friend of ours reported that the long silences he and his mother shared during the last two days of her life were some of the richest times they had spent together. Love, warmth, and sympathy are sometimes best expressed through silent facial and body movements and touch.

Facial Expression and Words

[Later in] this reading, we'll discuss facial expression as a primarily nonverbal cue. But peoples' faces also connect with words when they help to regulate utterance "turns" in conversations, and when they do, they can be considered mixed cues. The next time you're in a conversation, notice how you know when it's your turn to talk. The other person's face and eyes will almost always "tell" you. People also use faces and eyes to tell someone who approaches them either that they are welcoming the person into conversation or that they would rather be left alone.

Eye behavior is an important part of facial expression, and people use specific forms of eye behavior to accomplish several general goals in most conversations. First, we look away when we're having difficulty putting our thoughts into words. The amount of information we seem to be getting from another's eyes can be intense enough to be distracting, so if we're having trouble saying what we want to say, we look away to reduce the amount of input.

We also use eye contact to monitor feedback, to check the other's responses to the conversation. If we notice that the person is looking at us, we infer that she or he is paying attention; if we see that the person is staring into space, or over our shoulder to something or someone behind us, we draw the opposite conclusion. This phenomenon often helps make "cocktail party" conversation uncomfortably superficial. Neither conversation partner wants to be left standing alone, so both are as concerned about the next conversation as they are about the current one. As a result, both divide their looking between eye contact with the other and the search for the next partner.

Visual contact is also a primary way to indicate whose turn it is to talk. When a person tries to "catch the eye" of a server in a restaurant, the point is to open the channel, to initiate talk. And the same thing happens in conversation; I can "tell" you that it's your turn to talk by making eye contact with you. One communication researcher summarizes the typical conversation pattern in this way: "As the speaker comes to the end of an utterance or thought unit, gazing at the listener will continue as the listener assumes the speaking role; the listener will maintain gaze until the speaking role is assumed when he or she will look away. When the speaker does not yield a speaking turn by glancing at the other, the listener will probably delay a response or fail to respond. . . . "[26] Of course, this description is accurate for some cultures and not for others. Like other nonverbal cues, the facial expressions that accompany words vary among ethnic groups, genders, social classes, and sexual preferences. Eye contact and facial expressions are so critical to regulating conversations that a speaker's elimination of either one will seriously affect the responses of the listener.

Gestures and Words

Researcher David McNeill emphasizes why gestures can be considered mixed cues by examining their connection to spoken words. In one of McNeill's articles, "So You Think Gestures Are Nonverbal?" he explains how they are not just nonverbal, because gestures and speech are part of the same language structure. As he puts it, certain "gestures are verbal. They are the overt products of the same internal processes that produce the other overt product, speech." He goes on to point out that this is another reason we have to change what we mean by "language." He writes, "We tend to consider linguistic what we can write down, and nonlinguistic, everything else . . ."[27] However, he says, we now know better. Language is made up of both verbal and nonverbal aspects. This is "contrary to the idea of body language, that is, a separate system of body movement and postural signals that is thought to obey its own laws and convey its own . . . meanings."[28] It's misleading to talk of body language, McNeill argues, because posture and gesture are too intimately connected with the other part of language—words. . . .

Communication researcher Janet Bavelas and her colleagues have extended McNeill's work by studying what they call interactive gestures. These are movements that are related not to the content of the conversation, but to the relationship between or among the people communicating. Interactive gestures include the listener and thus "act to maintain the conversation as a social system."[29] For example, Bavelas describes how one speaker was discussing the summer job options that would contribute the most to his career goal.

> The listener had suggested earlier that working for Canada Customs would be a good idea; the speaker, after listing several other possibilities, adds "and Customs is DEFINITELY career-oriented." As he said "Customs," the speaker moved his hand up and toward the other person (almost as if tossing something to him), with palm up, fingers slightly curled, and thumb pointing directly at the other at the peak of the movement. Our translation of this gesture is "which YOU suggested," that is, the speaker credits the other person with the idea.[30]

Other interactive gestures were translated as "Do you get what I mean?" "Would you give me the answer?" and "No, no, I'll get it myself." All of these gestures are connected not to the conversational topic, but to the other speaker. Thus, they add important social content to the conversation, content separate from what is contributed verbally. In this way, they take on part of the work of mutual meaning constructing that is normally thought to be done only by words. So these so-called nonverbal gestures are actually functioning exactly as words do to add substance to the conversation.

Bavelas and her colleagues explain the importance of this added substance when they write:

> An interesting, intrinsic problem in dialogue is that, while both partners must remain involved, only one person can talk at once. Whenever a speaker has the floor, there exists the possibility that the conversation could veer off into monologue. One solution to the problem . . . is for the speaker to involve the listener regularly. To a certain extent, the speaker can do this by verbal statements, such as "You know," "As you said," "As you know," "I'm sure you agree," etc. However, the frequent use of verbal interjections and addenda would constantly disrupt the flow of content, so nonverbal means of seeking or maintaining involvement are well suited to this function. . . .
>
> We propose that interactive gestures, for all their many specific forms and translations, form a class with the common function of including the listener and thereby counteracting the beginning of a drift toward monologue that is necessarily created every time one person has the floor.[31]

In summary, vocal rate, pitch, volume, and quality affect how people collaboratively construct meaning in communication; this is why they can be thought of as mixed cues. Silence is another influential mixed building block. In addition, many facial expressions, much eye behavior, and even many gestures work so intimately with spoken words that they should also be thought of as mixed.

PRIMARILY NONVERBAL CUES: FACE, EYE CONTACT AND GAZE, SPACE, TOUCH, MOVEMENT AND GESTURE

Although we're not going to present an exhaustive list of primarily nonverbal cues (for example, we omit appearance and dress, smells, time, and colors), we think that the following five categories will give you a broad sense of the most influential primarily nonverbal parts of your communicating.

Facial Expression

Your face is probably the most expressive part of your body and one of the most important focal points for nonverbal communicating. Most of the time, people are unaware of how much they rely on faces to give and get information. But a little reflection—or reading some of the research—can change your level of awareness. Consider, for example, how important the face is in expressing emotion. An extensive program of research has demonstrated that certain basic emotions are facially expressed in similar ways across cultures.[32] Every culture studied so far has been found to include some conventional facial expressions that people use to communicate joy or happiness, sadness, surprise, fear, anger, and disgust. There are some culture-specific rules for the display of these emotions, but they are expressed in very similar ways in most cultures.

Researchers have discovered these similarities by showing photographs of North American faces, for example, to Japanese or preliterate New Guinean observers, and then showing photographs of Japanese and New Guineans to North Americans. In most cases, members of one culture were able to identify accurately the emotions being expressed by the faces of persons from the other cultures.[33] They recognized, for example, that surprise is consistently communicated by a face with widened eyes, head tilted up, raised brow, and open mouth. Disgust is communicated with brows pulled down, wrinkled nose, and a mouth with raised upper lip and downturned corners.

Although the facial expression of emotions is similar across cultures, there are important differences in facial displays, for example, between Japanese and North Americans. Historically, Japanese have been taught to mask negative facial expressions with smiles and laughter and to display less facial emotion overall.[34] There are a number of competing ideas about why these differences exist, but regardless of the origins, differences in expression have contributed to misunderstandings between Japanese and North American businesspeople. Many

Japanese still appear to be some of the least facially expressive of all cultural groups, and persons from other cultures are learning to adapt to this difference.

Eye Contact and Gaze

Although eyes are obviously a part of facial expression, gaze and eye contact are important enough to discuss separately. Eye contact appears to be one of the first behaviors that infants develop. Within a few days of birth, infants seem to recognize and attend to the caregiver's eyes. In the weeks immediately after birth, researchers have observed that simply seeing the eyes of the caregiver is enough to produce a smiling reaction.[35] Eye contact also significantly affects development. Infants who lack mutual gaze do not appear to mature perceptually and socially as rapidly as those who experience regular eye contact.[36]

If you doubt the importance of eye contact, consider the inferences you make about someone who doesn't look you in the eye "enough." What "enough" means varies from person to person, and certainly from culture to culture, but most Caucasian Americans infer that the person with too little eye contact is insincere, is disinterested, lacks confidence, is trying to avoid contact, or is lying. There aren't many other possibilities. And all these inferences are negative. Generally, there are *no* positive messages conveyed by too little eye contact in white American cultures. . . .

One important function of eye gaze is to enhance the intimacy of the relationship. Especially when it is accompanied by forward lean, direct body orientation, and more gesturing, it can help promote closeness.[37] Some intimacy research has studied not sexual contact, but the kind of intimacy that increases the desire to help. Gaze has been found to increase the probability that a bystander will help a person with a medical problem or someone who has fallen.[38] But this phenomenon seems to characterize female-female contacts more than it does those involving males. As Judee Burgoon and her colleagues summarize, "Under some circumstances, prolonged gaze may serve as an affiliative cue in the form of a plea for help, while in other cases it may be seen as overly forward or aggressive behavior."[39]

Another primary function of eye behavior is to express emotions. Some of the same people who studied facial expressions have also researched how people use eyes and eyebrows to interpret the six common emotions. Generally eyes are used more than brows/forehead or lower face for the accurate perception of fear, but eyes help less for the accurate perception of anger and disgust.[40]

Feelings about others are also communicated visually. For example, if you perceive a person as being of significantly lower status than you are, the tendency will be for you to maintain considerable eye contact. On the other hand, communicators tend to look much less at high-status people. Generally, we also look more at people we like and at those who believe as we do. The obvious reason, as Albert Mehrabian explains, is that eye contact is a kind of approach behavior, and approach behaviors are connected with liking.[41] So one response to someone who is appealing is to approach by looking, and one way to avoid a person we dislike is to look away.

We also use gaze and eye behavior to make and influence credibility judgments. Several studies on persuasive effectiveness and willingness to hire a job applicant have underscored the importance of normal or nearly continuous gaze. It appears that gaze avoidance is interpreted negatively, as we mentioned above, and that it can significantly affect your chances of being perceived as credible.[42] This is why those who teach or coach people for public speaking or interview situations emphasize that speakers and interviewees should generally try to maintain eye contact 50 to 70 percent of the time. As we mentioned earlier, cultural identities affect this formula, but it is a reliable basic guideline for many North American communication situations.

The bottom line is that people give considerable weight to eye behavior and eye contact, because they apparently believe that the eyes are indeed the "windows of the soul." Especially in Western cultures, people are confident that they can spot even the most practiced liar if they can just "look the person in the eye"[43] (although detecting deception is more complicated than this, as we explain below). People are also generally impressed by the confidence and overall effectiveness of a speaker with good eye contact. But since different cultures have different estimates of what constitutes "good" eye contact, it's important not to oversimplify gaze and eye behavior and to remember that, especially because this category of nonverbal cues is given so much credence, it's important to become aware of and to learn to manage your own eye behavior.

Proximity or Space

You have probably noticed that you often feel possessive about some spaces—perhaps your room, yard, or car—and that you sometimes sit or stand very close to people with whom you're talking and at other times feel more comfortable several feet away. These feelings are related to what is known as *proxemics*, the study of the communicative effects of space or distance.

As [was] said in Chapter 1, space is one of the basic dimensions of every human's world, and the primary tension that describes this dimension is near-far. Because we all have basic human needs both for privacy (distance) and to be interdependent (nearness), one way we manage this tension is by defining and defending a *territory*. A territory is an identifiable geographic area that is occupied, controlled, and often defended by a person or group as an exclusive domain.[44] For example, for many North Americans, one's bedroom, or a particular space in a shared room, is yours whether you're in it or not, and one of the reasons you guard your right to keep it in your preferred state of neatness or disorder is to underscore the point that it's your territory. In a library, cafeteria, or other public space, people use overcoats, briefcases, newspapers, food trays, dishes, and utensils to establish a claim over "their" space, even though it's temporary.

A number of studies have identified differences between ways women and men use territory. For example, in most cultures, women are allowed less territory than are men. As Judy Pearson notes, "Few women have a particular and unviolated room in their homes while many men have dens, studies, or work areas which are off limits to others. Similarly, it appears that more men than women have particular chairs reserved for their use."[45]

Each of us also lives in our own personal space, a smaller, invisible, portable, and adjustable "bubble," which we maintain to protect ourselves from physical and emotional threats. The size of this bubble varies; how far away we sit or stand depends on our family and cultural memberships, the relationship we have with the other person, the situation or the context, and how we are feeling toward the other person at the time. Anthropologist Edward Hall says it this way:

> Some individuals never develop the public phase of their personalities and, therefore, cannot fill public spaces; they make very poor speakers or moderators. As many psychiatrists know, other people have trouble with the intimate and personal zones and cannot endure closeness to others.[46]

Within these limitations, Hall identifies four distances he observed among middle-class adults in the northeastern United States. Although the limits of each zone differ from culture to culture, something like these four types of space exist in many cultures.

Intimate Distance (Contact to 18 Inches)   This zone begins with skin contact and ranges to about a foot and a half. People usually reserve this distance for those to whom they feel emotionally close, and for comforting, protecting, caressing, or lovemaking. When forced into intimate distance with strangers—as on an elevator, for example—people tend to use other nonverbal cues to reestablish separateness. So we avoid eye contact, fold our arms, or perhaps hold a briefcase or purse in front of our body. Allowing someone to enter this zone is a sign of trust; it says we have willingly lowered our defenses. At this distance, not only touch, but also smells, body temperature, and the feel and smell of breath can be part of what we experience. Voices are usually kept at a low level to emphasize the "closed circle" established by intimates.

Personal Distance (1.5 to 4 Feet)   This is the distance preferred by most conversation partners in a public setting. Typically, subjects of personal interest and moderate involvement can be discussed at this distance. Touch is still possible, but it is limited to brief pats for emphasis and reassurance. Finer details of the other's skin, hair, eyes, and teeth are visible, but one can't discern body temperature or feel the breath.

The far range of this distance is just beyond where you can comfortably touch the other. Hall calls it the distance we can use to keep someone "at arm's length." John sometimes works as a communication consultant training people to do information-gathering interviews. In that context, he encourages the people he's training to try to work within this zone. It appears that three to four feet is far enough away not to threaten the other and yet close enough to encourage the kind of relatively candid responses that make the interviews most successful.

Social Distance (4 to 12 Feet)   More impersonal business generally is carried out at this distance. People who work together or who are attending a social gathering tend to use the closer ranges of social distance. Salespeople and customers typically are comfortable within the four- to seven-foot zone. Most people feel uncomfortable if a salesperson approaches within three feet, but five or six feet nonverbally "says," "I'm here to help but I don't want to be pushy."

At the farther ranges of this distance, eye contact becomes especially important. When a person is 10 or 11 feet away, it's easy to be uncertain about who the person is talking with until you can determine where the person is looking. This is also the distance we often use with people of significantly higher or lower status. Sitting at this distance from a superior will tend to create a much more formal conversation than might take place if one or both persons moved their chairs much closer. As a result, it can be more effective to reprimand using social distance and less effective to give praise in this zone.

Public Distance (12 to 25 Feet)   The closer range of this distance is the one commonly used by instructors and managers addressing work groups. The farthest end of this zone is usually reserved for public speeches. When communicating at this distance, voices need to be loud or electronically amplified. At the farther ranges of this distance, facial expression, movements, and gestures also need to be exaggerated in order to be meaningful.

Like many other general observations about human communication, these four distances need to be taken with a grain of salt. Several studies have shown, for example, that females sit and stand closer together than do males, and that mixed-sex pairs consistently adopt closer distances than do male-male pairs.[47] Interpersonal distance also generally increases with age from preschool and grade school through the teen years to adulthood, but this tendency is mitigated somewhat by the fact that people also tend to adopt closer distances with age peers than with those who are younger or older.[48] So people's interpretations of distance and closeness may depend not only on their cultural identity, but also on their gender and age and on the gender and age of the person with whom they're conversing.

Space is usually interpreted in the context of other nonverbal cues. For example, a Chinese-American student reported:

> [My grandfather] commands his presence with silence, limited facial expressions and lots of space between himself and others. I have never thought of jumping into his lap like Ol' St. Nick or even felt comfortable talking to him at any great length. When I do scrounge up the courage to speak to him, it is almost always to greet him or ask him to come to dinner. The speech used would have to be laden with respectful words.[49]

Touch

Touch is the most direct way that humans establish the contact that makes us who we are. "It is well documented that touch is essential to the physical, emotional, and psychological well-being of human infants and to their intellectual, social, and communication development."[50] Touch is equally important for adults, although taboos in many Western cultures make it much more difficult to accomplish. That's why some scholars believe that these cultures are "touch-starved."

Touch plays a part in just about every activity of our waking day—not just with other humans but also with objects. You may not be aware of the feel of your clothes; the chair, couch, or floor on which you're sitting, standing, or lying; or the feel of the book you're holding, the pencil or pen you're grasping, or the shoes you're wearing. But you couldn't write, walk, make a fist, smile, or comb your hair without the sense of touch. In addition, the ways in which we hold and handle such things as books, pencils, cups or glasses, and purses or briefcases can affect another person's responses to us.

Touch between persons is even more complex. Stan Jones and Elaine Yarbrough, two speech communication researchers, found that people touch to indicate positive feelings, to play, to control, as part of a greeting or departure ritual, to help accomplish a task, to combine greeting or departure with affection, and accidentally.[51] In their studies, control touches occurred most frequently, touches that were primarily interpreted to mean a request for compliance or attention getting. A spot touch with the hand to a nonvulnerable body part—hands, arms, shoulders, or upper back—frequently accompanies and emphasizes such statements as, "Move over," "Hurry up," "Stay here," "Be serious," and "Do it." A similar touch reinforces such messages as, "Listen to this," "Look at that," and "I want your attention." These touches are almost always accompanied by verbalization, and both sexes initiate these touches with almost equal frequency.

Positive affect touches were the second most frequent kind of touch Jones and Yarbrough observed. The highest number of these touches were expressions of affection. As you would expect, these occur predominantly in close relationships and include hugs, kisses, and often contacts with "vulnerable body parts"—head, neck, torso, lower back, buttocks, legs, or feet. But affection can also be communicated by touch in some business settings. Long-term work teams sometimes engage in spontaneous brief touches among team members that are interpreted as positive and supportive. On the other hand, . . . sexual harassment in the workplace often consists in part of inappropriate or manipulative positive affect touching.

Research such as that of Jones and Yarbrough is important because it helps us comprehend a poorly understood, and sometimes even feared, aspect of our communicating. As Mark Knapp says:

> Some people grow up learning "not to touch" a multitude of animate and inanimate objects; they are told not to touch their own body and later not to touch the body of their dating partner; care is taken so children do not see their parents "touch" one another intimately; some parents demonstrate a noncontact norm through the use of twin beds; touching is associated with admonitions of "not nice" or "bad" and is punished accordingly—and frequent touching between father and son is thought to be something less than masculine.[52]

We know that touch is an enormously powerful kind of nonverbal communication; a very small amount of it can say a great deal. We can harness this power by becoming aware of how touch affects where our communication is on the social-cultural-interpersonal scale.

Body Movement and Gestures

The technical term for the study of movement and gesture is *kinesics*, from the Greek word for "motion." Some kinesic behaviors mean virtually the same thing whether they're performed by men or women, young or old people, and in the United States, Latin America, Europe, Australia, or Japan. For example, the head nod for agreement, shaking a fist in anger, clapping hands for approval, raising a hand for attention, yawning in boredom, rubbing hands to indicate coldness, and the thumbs-down gesture for disapproval are all interpreted similarly in at least several western hemisphere cultures.

Movements and gestures can also reflect the type of relationship that exists between partners or spouses. Communication researcher Mary Anne Fitzpatrick has distinguished among three general couple types who are identifiable in part by their patterns of movement and gesture. Traditionals accept conventional beliefs about relational roles, for example, about which are "the husband's" duties and which are "the wife's."[53] They value stability over spontaneity and affirm the traditional community customs that a woman should take her husband's last name when she marries, and the belief that infidelity is always inexcusable. Independent couples are at the opposite end of the ideological scale. They believe that one's relationship should not limit her or his individual freedom in any way. "The independent maintains a high level of companionship and sharing in marriage, but . . . [he or she] maintains separate physical spaces to control accessibility." Separates are conventional regarding marital and family issues but also support independent values. "They may espouse one set [of values] publicly while believing another privately. The separates have significantly less companionship and sharing in their marriage."[54] One of the ways to distinguish among the three couple types is to observe their movements and gestures when they are together.

Traditionals engage in a high number of meshed movements and actions. Each partner facilitates the other partner's actions. If the woman moves toward the door, for example, the man will typically move to open it for her. Separates, on the other hand, engage in very few meshed action sequences. They are disengaged from one another. However, even though their gestures and movements don't interconnect, they are often parallel. For example, one may move toward the door while the other moves to get his or her coat. Finally, the gestures and movements of independents clash more often than they are parallel. If one moves toward the door, the other may sit down or even try to keep the door closed.

People also communicate dominance and submission posturally. A male may hook his thumbs in his belt and both females and males may stand with hands on hips in the akimbo position. When a seated person leans back with hands clasped behind her or his head, this is typically another dominance posture. When a conversational group of three is approached by a fourth person, they typically rotate their bodies out to encourage the fourth to join them or in to discourage him or her.

Forward lean is commonly interpreted as more involved and usually more positive, while "seated male and female communicators both perceived a person leaning backward and away from them as having a more negative attitude than one who was leaning forward."[55] A direct vis-à-vis posture, movement toward the other, affirmative head nods, expressive hand gestures, and stretching are all rated as "warm" behaviors, while moving away, picking one's teeth, shaking the head, and playing with hair are rated as "cold."[56] All of these descriptions illustrate how body movement and gesture make up still another important category of nonverbal behaviors.

REVIEW QUESTIONS

1. To check your understanding of the relationship between verbal and non-verbal cues, itemize six nonverbal features of the words you find in this book.
2. Explain what it means to say that words are "arbitrary symbols."
3. What's the problem with an explanation of language based on an analysis of concrete nouns?
4. What's missing, according to Stewart and Logan, from the account of language as an activity?
5. Explain the Sapir-Whorf hypothesis in your own words.
6. Give an example from your own experience of gendered (masculine/feminine) language affecting your perception of someone or something.
7. What are paralinguistics?
8. Especially in conversation, silence, this reading argues, is much more than the absence of noise. Explain.
9. Why is facial expression discussed in two separate places in this reading?
10. What are interactive gestures?
11. What makes eye behavior so important in conversations?
12. Stewart and Logan make the point that a very small amount of touch can "say" a great deal. Which other mixed and primarily nonverbal cues are similarly high in potency—where a little can go a long way?

PROBES

1. Stewart and Logan explain some disadvantages of separate discussions of verbal and nonverbal cues. What are some advantages?

2. When does it most seem as if language is a "system"? When does this label seem least appropriate?
3. One famous author expressed something very close to the "language is a soup" idea in these words: "The limits of my language are the limits of my world." With the "soup" metaphor in mind, explain what you believe that means.
4. Stewart and Logan repeat the claims about the differences between masculine and feminine communication styles that have been popularized by Deborah Tannen and John Gray. The first reading in Chapter 12 challenges these claims. Flip forward in the book to Chapter 12 and make a note there to discuss whether you agree with this reading or that one.
5. In your experience, which kinds of mixed and primarily nonverbal cues vary the most between or among cultures? Which kinds of cues from other cultures are the most different from your preferred patterns?
6. Give an example from your own experience of gender differences in spatial nonverbal cues.
7. Summarize three pieces of advice about your own verbal and nonverbal communicating that you drew from this reading. If you are to take seriously what's here, what three changes might you make?

NOTES

1. D.J. Higginbotham and D.E. Yoder, "Communication within Natural Conversational Interaction: Implications for Severe Communicatively Impaired Persons." *Topics in Language Disorders* 2 (1982): 4.
2. Wendy Leeds-Hurwitz, *Communication in Everyday Life* (Norwood, NJ: Ablex, 1989), p. 102.
3. Ferdinand de Saussure, *Course in General Linguistics*, ed. Charles Bally and Albert Sechehaye, trans. Roy Harris (LaSalle, IL: Open Court, 1986), pp. 66–70. After making this point, de Saussure focused his attention on the *system* of language, in order to make linguistics a "science."
4. Robert E. Sanders, "The Interconnection of Utterances and Nonverbal Displays." *Research on Language and Social Interaction* 20 (1987): 141.
5. Aristotle, *De Interpretatione*, trans. E.M. Edgehill in *The Basic Works of Aristotle*, ed. Richard McKeon (New York: Random House, 1941), p. 20.
6. Charles E. Osgood, "What Is a Language?" in I. Rauch and G.F. Carr (eds.), *The Signifying Animal* (Bloomington, IN: Indiana University Press, 1980), p. 12.
7. C.K. Ogden and I.A. Richards, *The Meaning of Meaning*, 8th ed. (New York: Harcourt Brace, 1986), p. 11. If you're interested in reading more about this view of language and its problems, see John Stewart, *Language as Articulate Contact: Toward a Post-Semiotic Philosophy of Communication* (Albany, NY: State University of New York Press, 1995); and John Stewart (ed.), *Beyond the Symbol Model: Reflections on the Representational Nature of Language* (Albany, NY: State University of New York Press, 1996).
8. Robert E. Nofsinger, *Everyday Conversation* (Newbury Park, CA: Sage, 1991), pp. 19–26.

9. Nofsinger, p. 51.

10. Hans-Georg Gadamer, "Man and Language," in David E. Linge (ed.), *Philosophical Hermeneutics* (Berkeley, CA: University of California Press, 1976), pp. 62–63.

11. D.B. Chamberlain, "Consciousness at Birth: The Range of Empirical Evidence," in T.R. Verney (ed.), *Pre- and Perinatal Psychology: An Introduction* (New York: Human Sciences, 1987), pp. 70–86.

12. A. Tomatis, "Ontogenesis of the Faculty of Listening," in Verney (ed.), pp. 23–35.

13. Beth Haslett, "Acquiring Conversational Competence." *Western Journal of Speech Communication* 48 (1984): 120.

14. John B. Carroll (ed.), *Language; Thought and Reality: Selected Writings of Benjamin Lee Whorf* (New York: Wiley, 1956), pp. 212–213.

15. For over 50 years, linguistics, anthropology, and communication textbooks have used the example of Eskimo words for snow to illustrate how language and perception are interrelated. According to this account, the importance of snow in Eskimo culture is reflected in the many terms they have for "falling snow," "drifting snow," "snow on the ground," "slushy snow," and so on. Earlier editions of this text repeated this myth. But we now know it isn't true. The myth began in 1911 when an anthropologist working in Alaska compared the different Eskimo root words for "snow on the ground," "falling snow," "drifting snow," and "a snow drift" with different English root words for a variety of forms of water (liquid, lake, river, brook, rain, dew, wave, foam, and so on). The anthropologist's comment was popularized in a 1940 article and then found its way into literally hundreds of publications that confidently asserted that Eskimos had 9, 23, 50, and even 100 words for snow. But they don't. The best available source, *A Dictionary of the West Greenlandic Eskimo Language,* gives just two: *quanik,* meaning "snow in the air," and *aput,* meaning "snow on the ground." So if you hear or read of the Eskimo-words-for-snow example, feel free to correct it. Or at least don't repeat it. See Geoffrey Pullum, "The Great Eskimo Vocabulary Hoax." *Lingua Franca* 14 (June 1990): 28–29.

16. Harry Hoijer, "Cultural Implications of Some Navajo Linguistic Categories." *Language* 27 (1951): 117.

17. J. Birere and C. Lanktree, "Sex-Role Related Effects of Sex Bias in Language." *Sex Roles* 9 (1980): 625–632; D.K. Ivy, "Who's the Boss? He, He/She, or They?" Unpubl paper, 1986; cited in D.K. Ivy and Phil Backlund, *Exploring Gender Speak: Personal Effectiveness in Gender Communication* (New York: McGraw-Hill, 1994), p. 75.

18. Deborah Tannen, *You Just Don't Understand: Women and Men in Communication* (New York: Morrow, 1990).

19. John Gray, *Men Are from Mars, Women Are from Venus* (New York: HarperCollins, 1992).

20. John Gray, *Mars and Venus in Love* (New York: HarperCollins, 1996).

21. Julia T. Wood reviews this research in *Gendered Lives: Communication, Gender, and Culture* (Belmont, CA: Wadsworth, 1994), pp. 141–145.

22. D.W. Addington, "The Relationship of Selected Vocal Characteristics to Personality Perception." *Speech Monographs* 35 (1968): 492–503.
23. Mark L. Knapp, *Essentials of Nonverbal Communication* (New York: Holt, 1980), p. 361.
24. M.F. Sciacca, *Come Si Vinci a Waterloo* (Milan: Marzorati, 1963), p. 129; quoted in Gemma Corradi Fiumara, *The Other Side of Language: A Philosophy of Listening* (London: Routledge, 1990), p. 101.
25. Sciacca, p. 26, quoted in Corradi Fiumara, p. 102.
26. Knapp, p. 298.
27. D. McNeill, "So You Think Gestures Are Nonverbal." *Psychological Review* 92 (1985): 350–371.
28. McNeill, p. 350.
29. Janet Beavin Bavelas, Nicole Chovil, Douglas A. Lawrie, and Allan Wade, "Interactive Gestures." Paper presented at the International Communication Association, Chicago, 1991, p. 2.
30. Bavelas, Chovil, Lawrie, and Wade, p. 7.
31. Bavelas, Chovil, Lawrie, and Wade, pp. 10–11.
32. See, for example, Paul Ekman, "Universal and Cultural Differences in Facial Expressions of Emotions," in *Nebraska Symposium on Motivation,* Vol. 19, ed. J.K. Cole (Lincoln, NE: University of Nebraska Press, 1971), pp. 207–283; C.E. Izard, *Human Emotions* (New York: Plenum, 1977).
33. Paul Ekman, W.V. Friesen, and S. Ancoli, "Facial Signs of Emotional Experience." *Journal of Personality and Social Psychology* 39 (1980): 1125–1134; Paul Ekman and W.V. Friesen, *Unmasking the Face* (Englewood Cliffs, NJ: Prentice-Hall, 1975).
34. R.A. Miller, *Japan's Modern Myth: The Language and Beyond* (Tokyo: Weatherhill, 1982).
35. Michael Argyle and M. Cook, *Gaze and Mutual Gaze* (Cambridge, England: Cambridge University Press, 1976).
36. Janis Andersen, Peter Andersen, and J. Landgraf, "The Development of Nonverbal Communication Competence in Childhood." Paper presented at the annual meeting of the International Communication Association, Honolulu, May 1985.
37. Judee K. Burgoon, David B. Buller, and W. Gill Woodall, *Nonverbal Communication: The Unspoken Dialogue* (New York: Harper & Row, 1989), p. 438.
38. R.L. Shotland and M.P. Johnson, "Bystander Behavior and Kinesics: The Interaction between the Helper and Victim." *Environmental Psychology and Nonverbal Behavior* 2 (1978): 181–190.
39. Burgoon, Buller, and Goodall, p. 438.
40. Ekman and Friesen, *Unmasking the Face,* pp. 40–46.
41. Albert Mehrabian, *Silent Messages: Implicit Communication of Emotion and Attitudes,* 2nd ed. (New York: Random House, 1981), pp. 23–25.
42. See, for example, J.K. Burgoon, V. Manusov, P. Mineo, and J.L. Hale, "Effects of Eye Gaze on Hiring Credibility, Attraction, and Relational Message Interpretation." *Journal of Nonverbal Behavior* 9 (1985): 133–146.

43. We elaborate on the process of deception in Chapter 8. Closely related to the work on deception is research on equivocal communication. See, for example, Janet Beavin Bavelas, Alex Black, Nicole Chovil, and Jennifer Mullet, "Truths, Lies, and Equivocation," in *Equivocal Communication* (Newbury Park, CA: Sage, 1990), pp. 170–207.
44. Burgoon, Buller, and Woodall, p. 81.
45. Judy C. Pearson, *Communication in the Family* (New York: Harper & Row, 1989), p. 78.
46. Edward T. Hall, *The Hidden Dimension* (Garden City, NY: Doubleday, 1966), p. 115.
47. For example, N.M. Sussman and H.M. Rosenfeld, "Influence of Culture, Language, and Sex on Conversational Distance." *Journal of Personality and Social Psychology* 42 (1982): 66–74.
48. Burgoon, Buller, and Woodall, p. 110.
49. Mandy Lam, *Interpersonal Communication Journal*, October 19, 1996. Used with permission.
50. Burgoon, Buller, and Woodall, p. 75.
51. Unless otherwise noted, the material on touch is from Stanley E. Jones and A. Elaine Yarbrough, "A Naturalistic Study of the Meanings of Touch." *Communication Monographs* 52 (1985): 19–56.
52. Knapp, pp. 108–109.
53. Mary Anne Fitzpatrick, *Between Husbands and Wives* (Newbury Park, CA: Sage, 1988), p. 76.
54. Fitzpatrick, pp. 218–219.
55. Knapp, p. 224.
56. G.L. Clore, N.H. Wiggins, and S. Itkin, "Judging Attraction from Nonverbal Behavior: The Gain Phenomenon." *Journal of Consulting and Clinical Psychology* 43 (1975): 491–497.

Virginia Satir was a family counselor who spent over 40 years helping parents and children communicate. Her small book, *Making Contact,* is her response to the many persons who asked her to write down the ideas and suggestions that she shared in workshops and seminars. As she said in the introduction, "The framework of this book is the BARE BONES of the possible, which I believe applies to *all* human beings. You, the reader, can flesh out the framework to fit you."

I like the simple, straightforward, no-nonsense way she talks about words, and I think that she's pinpointed several insights that can help all of us communicate better. If we did, as she suggests, pay more attention to the ways we use the 10 key words she discusses, I'm convinced that we'd experience considerably less conflict, misunderstanding, and frustration. See if you agree.

PAYING ATTENTION TO WORDS

Virginia Satir

Words are important tools for contact. They are used more consciously than any other form of contact. I think it is important to learn how to use words well in the service of our communication.

Words cannot be separated from sights, sounds, movements, and touch of the person using them. They are one package.

However, for the moment, let's consider only words. Using words is literally the outcome of a whole lot of processes that go on in the body. All the senses, the nervous system, brain, vocal chords, throat, lungs, and all parts of the mouth are involved. This means that physiologically, talking is a very complicated process. . . .

If you think of your brain as a computer, storing all your experiences on tapes, then the words you pick will have to come from those tapes. Those tapes represent all our past experiences, accumulated knowledge, rules, and guides. There is nothing else there until new tapes are added. I hope that what you are reading will help you to add new tapes out of getting new experiences.

The words we use have an effect on our health. They definitely influence emotional relationships between people and how people can work together.

WORDS HAVE POWER

Listen to what you say and see if you are really saying what you mean. Nine people out of ten can't remember what they said sixty seconds ago; others remember.

There are ten English words that it is well to pay close attention to, to use with caution and with loving care: *I, You, They, It, But, Yes, No, Always, Never, Should.*

If you were able to use these special words carefully it would already solve many contact problems created by misunderstanding.

I

Many people avoid the use of the word *I* because they feel they are trying to bring attention to themselves. They think they are being selfish. Shades of childhood, when you shouldn't show off, and who wants to be selfish? The most important thing is that using "I" clearly means that you are taking responsibility for what you say. Many people mix this up by starting off with saying "you." I

From *Making Contact* by Virginia Satir, (Millbrae, Calif.: Celestial Arts, 1976). The excerpt covers twelve pages in the text of Satir's book. Courtesy of Celestial Arts Pub. Co., 231 Adrian Rd., Millbrae, Calif. 94030.

have heard people say "You can't do that." This is often heard as a "put-down," whereas "I think you can't do that" makes a more equal relationship between the two. It gives the same information without the put-down.

"I" is the pronoun that clearly states "me" when I am talking so it is important to say it. If you want to be clear when you are talking, no matter what you say, it is important to state clearly your ownership of *your* statement.

"I am saying that the moon is made of red cheese."
(*This is clearly your picture*)

instead of saying . . .

"The moon is made of red cheese."
(*This is a new law*)

Being aware of your clear use of "I" is particularly crucial when people are already in crisis. It is more clear to say "It is my picture that . . . " (which is an ownership statement). Whoever has the presence of mind to do this can begin to alter an escalating situation. When "I" is not clear, it is easy for the hearer to get a "you" message, which very often is interpreted as a "put-down."

You

The use of the word *you* is also tricky. It can be felt as an accusation when only reporting or sharing is intended.

"You are making things worse" can sound quite different if the words "I think" are added. "I think you are making things worse. . . . "

When used in clear commands or directions, it is not so easily misunderstood. For example, "I want you to . . . " or "You are the one I wanted to speak to."

They

The use of *they* is often an indirect way of talking about "you." It is also often a loose way of spreading gossip.

"They say . . . "

"They" can also be some kind of smorgasbord that refers to our negative fantasies. This is especially true in a situation where people are assessing blame. If we know who "they" are we can say so.

How many times do we hear "They won't let me." "They will be upset." "They don't like what I am doing." "They say . . ."

If someone else uses it, we can ask "Who is your *they*?"

The important part of this is to have clear who "they" are so that inaccurate information is not passed on and it is clear exactly who is being referred to. Being clear in this way seems to add to everyone's security. Information becomes concrete which one can get hold of, instead of being nebulous and perhaps posing some kind of threat.

It

It is a word that can easily be misunderstood because it often isn't clear what "it" refers to. "It" is a word that has to be used with care.

The more clear your "it" is, the less the hearer fills it in with his [or her] own meaning. Sometimes "it" is related to a hidden "I" message. One way to better understand your "it" is to substitute "I" and see what happens. "It isn't clear" changed to "I am not clear" could make things more accurate and therefore easier to respond to.

"It often happens to people" is a statement that when said straight could be a comfort message that says, "The thing you are talking about has happened to me. I know how feeling humiliated feels."

To be more sure that we are understood, it might be wiser to fill in the details.

But

Next is the word *but*.

"But" is often a way of saying "yes" and "no" in the same sentence.

"I love you *but* I wish you would change your underwear more often."

This kind of use can easily end up with the other person feeling very uncomfortable, uneasy, and frequently confused.

Try substituting the word "and" for "but," which will clarify the situation. Your body will even feel different.

By using "but" the speaker is often linking two different thoughts together, which is what causes the difficulty.

Thus "I love you, but I wish you would change your underwear more often" could be two expressions.

"I love you," and "I wish you would change your underwear more often."

It could also represent someone's best, although fearful, attempt to make an uncomfortable demand by couching the demand in a love context, hoping the other person would not feel hurt.

If this is the case, what would happen if the person were to say "I want to ask something of you that I feel very uncomfortable about. I would like you to change your underwear more often."

Yes, No

A clear "yes" and "no" are important. Too many people say "yes, but" or "yes, maybe" or "no" just to be on the safe side, especially if they are in a position of power.

When "yes" or "no" are said clearly, and they mean NOW and not forever, and it is further clear "yes" and "no" relate to an issue rather than a person's value, then "yes" and "no" are very helpful words in making contact.

People can get away with much misuse of words when trust and good feeling have been established and when the freedom to comment is around. However, so often people feel so unsure about themselves that the lack of clarity leaves a lot of room for misunderstanding and consequent bad feelings. It is easy to build up these bad feelings once they are started.

"No" is a word that we all need and need to be able to use when it fits. So often when people feel "no," they say "maybe" or "yes" to avoid meeting the issue. This is justified on the basis of sparing the other's feelings. It is a form of lying and usually invites distrust, which, of course, is death to making contact.

When the "no" isn't clear, the "yes" can also be mistrusted. Have you ever heard "He said yes, but he doesn't really mean it"?

Always, Never

Always is the positive form of a global word. *Never* is the negative form. For example:

> *Always* clean up your plate.
> *Never* leave anything on your plate.

The literal meaning of these words is seldom accurate and the directions seldom applicable to life situations. There are few cases in life where something is always *or* never. Therefore to try to follow these demands in all situations will surely end up in failure like the rules I described earlier.

Often the use of these words is a way to make emotional emphasis, like . . .

> "You *always* make me mad."

meaning really . . .

> "I am NOW very mad at you."

If the situation were as the speaker states, the adrenals would wear out.

Sometimes the words *always* and *never* hide ignorance. For example, someone has spent just five minutes with a person and announces,

> "He is always bright."

In most cases the literal use of these two words could not be followed in all times, places and situations. Furthermore, they are frequently untrue. For the most part they become emotionally laden words that harm rather than nurture or enlighten the situation.

I find that these words are often used without any meaning in any literal sense. . . .

Should

"Ought" and "should" are other trap words from which it is easy to imply that there is something wrong with you—you have failed somehow to measure up.

Often the use of these words implies stupidity on someone's part . . .

"You should have known better."

This is frequently heard as an accusation. Sometimes it merely represents some friendly advice. When people use the words "ought" and "should," often they are trying to indicate a dilemma in which they have more than one direction to go at a time—one may be pulling harder than the rest although the others are equally important . . .

"I like this, but I should get that."

When your words are these, your body often feels tight. There are no easy answers to the pulls which "ought" and "should" represent. Biologically we really can go in only one direction at a time.

When your body feels tight your brain often freezes right along with your tight body, and so your thinking becomes limited as well.

Hearing yourself use the words "ought" and "should" can be a tip-off to you that you are engaged in a struggle. Perhaps instead of trying to deal with these opposing parts as one, you can separate them and make two parts.

"I like this . . . " (one part)
"But I should get that"

translated into . . .

"I also need that . . . " (a second part).

Such a separation may be helpful in considering each piece separately and then considering them together.

When you do this your body has a chance to become a little looser, thus freeing some energy to negotiate a bit better.

When I am in this spot, I can help myself by asking whether I will literally die in either situation. If the answer is *no,* then I have a different perspective, and I can more easily play around with alternatives, since I am now out of a win-loss feeling in myself. I won't die. I may be only a little deprived or inconvenienced at most.

Start paying attention to the words you use.

Who is your *they?*
What is your *it?*
What does your *no* mean?
What does your *yes* mean?
Is your *I* clear?

Are you saying *never* and *always* when you mean sometimes and when you want to make emotional emphasis?
How are you using *ought* and *should?*

REVIEW QUESTIONS

1. What reasons do people give for *not* using the word *I?*
2. What is similar about the problems Satir finds with the words *they* and *it?*
3. Does Satir suggest that we should not use the words *but, yes,* and *no?* What is she saying about these words?
4. How does a person's use of the words *ought* and *should* reflect that person's value system?

PROBES

1. When you're in a conversation, can you recall what you said 60 seconds earlier? Try it. What do you notice?
2. Notice how, as Virginia Satir says, *it* and *they* both often work to hide the fact that some I is actually talking. When do you hear yourself using *it* and *they* that way?
3. What happens when you substitute *and* for *but?*
4. Do you experience your body responding as Satir describes to the words *ought* and *should?*

*A*my Tan, a widely published Chinese-American author, is impatient with some popular assumptions about how Chinese people in the United States communicate. In this reading she pays special attention to the commonly held belief that Chinese people are unfailingly "discreet and modest," so much so that there aren't even words in the Chinese language for "yes" and "no." As she writes, "That's not true . . . although I can see why an outsider might think that."

Tan reports, "I find there was nothing discreet about the Chinese language I grew up with. My parents made everything abundantly clear. Nothing wishy-washy in their demands, no compromises accepted." She points out how direct and unambiguous demands and rejections can be clearly expressed in a language without a single term for "yes" or "no," and how euphemisms and indirect language can smooth relationships. Along the way, Tan raises some interesting questions about some aspects of the Sapir-Whorf hypothesis.

In addition to helping correct some cultural stereotypes, this reading also provides support for the usefulness of viewing language as a soup (see Carole's and my essay at the start of this chapter). The language Amy Tan's parents and family spoke helped construct a particular world, with values and ways of relating that helped its members feel "at home" in that world.

THE LANGUAGE OF DISCRETION

Amy Tan

At a recent family dinner in San Francisco, my mother whispered to me: "Sau-sau [Brother's wife] pretends too hard to be polite! Why bother? In the end, she always takes everything."

My mother thinks like a *waixiao*, an expatriate, temporarily away from China since 1949, no longer patient with ritual courtesies. As if to prove her point, she reached across the table to offer my elderly aunt from Beijing the last scallop from the Happy Family seafood dish.

Sau-sau scowled. *"B'yao, zhen b'yao!"* (I don't want it, really I don't!) she cried, patting her plump stomach.

"Take it! Take it!" scolded my mother in Chinese.

"Full, I'm already full," Sau-sau protested weakly, eyeing the beloved scallop.

"Ai!" exclaimed my mother, completely exasperated. "Nobody else wants it. If you don't take it, it will only rot!"

At this point, Sau-sau sighed, acting as if she were doing my mother a big favor by taking the wretched scrap off her hands.

My mother turned to her brother, a high-ranking communist official who was visiting her in California for the first time: "In America a Chinese person could starve to death. If you say you don't want it, they won't ask you again forever."

My uncle nodded and said he understood fully: Americans take things quickly because they have no time to be polite.

I thought about this misunderstanding again—of social contexts failing in translation—when a friend sent me an article from the *New York Times Magazine* (24 April 1988). The article, on changes in New York's Chinatown, made passing reference to the inherent ambivalence of the Chinese language.

Chinese people are so "discreet and modest," the article stated, there aren't even words for "yes" and "no."

That's not true, I thought, although I can see why an outsider might think that. I continued reading.

If one is Chinese, the article went on to say, "One compromises, one doesn't hazard a loss of face by an overemphatic response."

My throat seized. Why do people keep saying these things? As if we truly were those little dolls sold in Chinatown tourist shops, heads bobbing up and down in complacent agreement to anything said!

I worry about the effect of one dimensional statements on the unwary and guileless. When they read about this so-called vocabulary deficit, do they also conclude that Chinese people evolved into a mild-mannered lot because the language only allowed them to hobble forth with minced words?

Something enormous is always lost in translation. Something insidious seeps into the gaps, especially when amateur linguists continue to compare, one-for-one, language differences and then put forth notions wide open to misinterpretation: that Chinese people have no direct linguistic means to make decisions, assert or deny, affirm or negate, just say no to drug dealers, or behave properly on the witness stand when told, "Please answer yes or no."

Yet one can argue, with the help of renowned linguists, that the Chinese are indeed up a creek without "yes" and "no." Take any number of variations on the old language-and-reality theory stated years ago by Edward Sapir: "Human beings . . . are very much at the mercy of the particular language which has become the medium for their society. . . . The fact of the matter is that the 'real world' is to a large extent built up on the language habits of the group."

This notion was further bolstered by the famous Sapir-Whorf hypothesis, which roughly states that one's perception of the world and how one functions in it depends a great deal on the language used. As Sapir, Whorf, and new carriers of the banner would have us believe, language shapes our thinking, channels us along certain patterns embedded in words, syntactic structures, and intonation patterns. Language has become the peg and the shelf that enables us to sort out and categorize the world. In English, we see "cats" and "dogs"; what if the language had also specified *glatz,* meaning "animals that leave fur on the sofa," and *glotz,* meaning "animals that leave fur and drool on the sofa"? How would language, the enabler, have changed our perceptions with slight vocabulary variations?

And if this were the case—of language being the master of destined thought—think of the opportunities lost from failure to evolve two little words, *yes* and *no,* the simplest of opposites! Ghenghis Khan could have been sent back to Mongolia. Opium wars might have been averted. The Cultural Revolution could have been sidestepped.

There are still many, from serious linguists to pop psychology cultists, who view language and reality as inextricably tied, on being the consequence of the other. We have traversed the range from the Sapir-Whorf hypothesis to est and neurolinguistic programming, which tell us "you are what you say."

I too have been intrigued by the theories I can summarize, albeit badly, ages-old empirical evidence: of Eskimos and their infinite ways to say "snow," their ability to *see* the differences in snowflake configurations, thanks to the richness of their vocabulary, while non-Eskimo speakers like myself founder in "snow," "more snow," and "lots more where that came from."

I too have experienced dramatic cognitive awakenings via the word. Once I added "mauve" to my vocabulary I began to see it everywhere. When I learned how to pronounce *prix fixe,* I ate French food at prices better than the easier-to-say *à la carte* choices.

But just how seriously are we supposed to take this?

Sapir said something else about language and reality. It is the part that often gets left behind in the dot-dot-dots of quotes: " . . . No two languages are ever sufficiently similar to be considered as representing the same social reality. The worlds in which different societies live are distinct worlds, not merely the same world with different labels attached."

When I first read this, I thought, Here at last is validity for the dilemmas I felt growing up in a bicultural, bilingual family! As any child of immigrant parents knows, there's a special kind of double bind attached to knowing two languages. My parents, for example, spoke to me in both Chinese and English; I spoke back to them in English.

"Amy-ah!" they'd call to me.

"What?" I'd mumble back.

"Do not question us when we call," they scolded me in Chinese. "It is not respectful."

"What do you mean?"

"Ai! Didn't we just tell you not to question?"

To this day, I wonder which parts of my behavior were shaped by Chinese, which by English. I am tempted to think, for example, that if I am of two minds on some matter it is due to the richness of my linguistic experiences, not to any personal tendencies toward wishy-washiness. But which mind says what?

Was it perhaps patience—developed through years of deciphering my mother's fractured English—that had me listening politely while a woman announced over the phone that I had won one of five valuable prizes? Was it respect—pounded in by the Chinese imperative to accept convoluted explanations—that had me agreeing that I might find it worthwhile to drive seventy-five miles to view a time-share resort? Could I have been at a loss for words when asked, "Wouldn't you like to win a Hawaiian cruise or perhaps a fabulous Star of India designed exclusively by Carter and Van Arpels?"

And when this same woman called back a week later, this time complaining that I had missed my appointment, obviously it was my type A language that kicked into gear and interrupted her. Certainly, my blunt denial—"Frankly I'm not interested"—was as American as apple pie. And when she said, "But it's in Morgan Hill," and I shouted, "Read my lips, I don't care if it's Timbuktu," you can be sure I said it with the precise intonation expressing both cynicism and disgust.

It's dangerous business, this sorting out of language and behavior. Which one is English? Which is Chinese? The categories manifest themselves: passive and aggressive, tentative and assertive, indirect and direct. And I realize they are just variations of the same theme: that Chinese people are discreet and modest.

Reject them all!

If my reaction is overly strident, it is because I cannot come across as too emphatic. I grew up listening to the same lines over and over again, like so many rote expressions repeated in an English phrase-book. And I too almost came to believe them.

Yet if I consider my upbringing more carefully, I find there was nothing discreet about the Chinese language I grew up with. My parents made everything abundantly clear. Nothing wishy-washy in their demands, no compromises accepted: "Of course you will become a famous neurosurgeon," they told me. "And yes, a concert pianist on the side."

In fact, now that I remember, it seems that the more emphatic outbursts always spilled over into Chinese: "Not that way! You must wash rice so not a single grain spills out."

I do not believe that my parents—both immigrants from mainland China—are an exception to the modest-and-discreet rule. I have only to look at the number of Chinese engineering students skewing minority ratios at Berkeley, MIT, and Yale. Certainly they were not raised by passive mothers and fathers who said, "It is up to you, my daughter. Writer, welfare recipient, masseuse, or molecular engineer—you decide."

And my American mind says, See, those engineering students weren't able to say no to their parents' demands. But then my Chinese mind remembers: Ah, but those parents all wanted their sons and daughters to be *pre-med.*

Having listened to both Chinese and English, I also tend to be suspicious of any comparisons between the two languages. Typically, one language—that of the person doing the comparing—is often used as the standard, the benchmark for a logical form of expression. And so the language being compared is always in danger of being judged deficient or superfluous, simplistic or unnecessarily complex, melodious or cacophonous. English speakers point out that Chinese is extremely difficult because it relies on variations in tone barely discernible to the human ear. By the same token, Chinese speakers tell me English is extremely difficult because it is inconsistent, a language of too many broken rules, of Mickey Mice and Donald Ducks.

Even more dangerous to my mind is the temptation to compare both language and behavior *in translation.* To listen to my mother speak English, one might think she has no concept of past or future tense, that she doesn't see the difference between singular and plural, that she is gender blind because she calls my husband "she." If one were not careful, one might also generalize that, based on the way my mother talks, all Chinese people take a circumlocutory route to get to the point. It is, in fact, my mother's idiosyncratic behavior to ramble a bit. . . .

I worry that the dominant society may see Chinese people from a limited—and limiting—perspective. I worry that seemingly benign stereotypes may be part of the reason there are few Chinese in top management positions, in mainstream political roles. I worry about the power of language: that if one says anything enough times—in *any* language—it might become true.

Could this be why Chinese friends of my parents' generation are willing to accept the generalization?

"Why are you complaining?" one of them said to me. "If people think we are modest and polite, let them think that. Wouldn't Americans be pleased to admit they are thought of as polite?"

And I do believe anyone would take the description as a compliment—at first. But after a while, it annoys, as if the only things that people heard one say were phatic remarks: "I'm so pleased to meet you. I've heard many wonderful things about you. For me? You shouldn't have!"

These remarks are not representative of new ideas, honest emotions, or considered thought. They are what is said from the polite distance of social contexts: of greetings, farewells, wedding thank-you notes, convenient excuses, and the like.

It makes me wonder though. How many anthropologists, how many sociologists, how many travel journalists have documented so-called "natural interactions" in foreign lands, all observed with spiral notebook in hand? How many other cases are there of the long-lost primitive tribe, people who turned out to be sophisticated enough to put on the stone-age show that ethnologists had come to see?

And how many tourists fresh off the bus have wandered into Chinatown expecting the self-effacing shopkeeper to admit under duress that the goods are not worth the price asked? I have witnessed it.

"I don't know," the tourist said to the shopkeeper, a Cantonese woman in her fifties. "It doesn't look genuine to me. I'll give you three dollars."

"You don't like my price, go somewhere else," said the shopkeeper.

"You are not a nice person," cried the shocked tourist, "not a nice person at all!"

"Who say I have to be nice," snapped the shopkeeper.

"So how does one say 'yes' and 'no' in Chinese?" ask my friends a bit warily.

And here I do agree in part with the *New York Times Magazine* article. There is no one word for "yes" or "no"—but not out of necessity to be discreet. If anything, I would say the Chinese equivalent of answering "yes" or "no" is dis*crete*, that is, specific to what is asked.

Ask a Chinese person if he or she has eaten, and he or she might say *chrle* (eaten already) or perhaps *meiyou* (have not).

Ask, "So you had insurance at the time of the accident?" and the response would be *dwei* (correct) or *meiyou* (did not have).

Ask, "Have you stopped beating your wife?" and the answer refers directly to the proposition being asserted or denied: stopped already, still have not, never beat, have no wife.

What could be clearer?

As for those who are still wondering how to translate the language of discretion, I offer this personal example.

My aunt and uncle were about to return to Beijing after a three-month visit to the United States. On their last night I announced I wanted to take them out to dinner.

"Are you hungry?" I asked in Chinese.

"Not hungry," said my uncle promptly, the same response he once gave me ten minutes before he suffered a low-blood-sugar attack.

"Not too hungry," said my aunt. "Perhaps you're hungry?"

"A little," I admitted.

"We can eat, we can eat," they both consented.

"What kind of food?" I asked.

"Oh, doesn't matter. Anything will do. Nothing fancy, just some simple food is fine."

"Do you like Japanese food? We haven't had that yet," I suggested.

They looked at each other.

"We can eat it," said my uncle bravely, this survivor of the Long March.

"We have eaten it before," added my aunt. "Raw fish."

"Oh, you don't like it?" I said. "Don't be polite. We can go somewhere else."

"We are not being polite. We can eat it," my aunt insisted.

So I drove them to Japantown and we walked past several restaurants featuring colorful plastic displays of sushi.

"Not this one, not this one either," I continued to say, as if searching for a Japanese restaurant similar to the last. "Here it is," I finally said, turning into a restaurant famous for its Chinese fish dishes from Shandong.

"Oh, Chinese food!" cried my aunt, obviously relieved.

My uncle patted my arm. "You think Chinese."

"It's your last night here in America," I said. "So don't be polite. Act like an American."

And that night we ate a banquet.

REVIEW QUESTIONS

1. What does it mean to say that "social contexts" can "fail in translation"?
2. What is the Sapir-Whorf hypothesis? What does it say about interpersonal communication?
3. What point is Amy Tan making about "respect" when she uses the examples of telephone calls about a time-share resort or a Hawaiian cruise?
4. Amy Tan admits that the Chinese language does not have one word for "yes" or "no," but she insists that speakers of Chinese are *not* wishy-washy or noncommittal. As she explains it, how do they affirm or deny without these words?

PROBES

1. Amy Tan wants to correct a stereotype about Chinese communication. She makes the point of her first example in these words: "Americans take things quickly because they have no time to be polite." Is this a stereotype, too? Discuss.
2. As Carole and I explained in the first reading in this chapter, the Sapir-Whorf hypothesis says that language affects perception. On the one hand, Amy Tan rejects the idea that vocabulary determines behavior—that "Chinese people evolved into a mild-mannered lot because the language only allowed them to hobble forth with minced words." On the other hand, she says, "Sapir was right about differences between two languages and their realities." What do you understand her position to be on this idea about the relationship between language and perception?
3. If you know at least two languages, you can respond to this question on your own. If not, interview someone who does before you respond to it. Here's the question: What does it mean to say that the "worlds" inhabited by people who speak different languages "are distinct worlds, not merely the same world with different labels attached"?

NOTE

1. Edward Sapir, *Selected Writings,* ed. D. G. Mandelbaum (Berkeley and Los Angeles, 1949).

*T*his chapter from a recent interpersonal communication text begins with the same point we made at the start of "Verbal and Nonverbal Dimensions of Talk": In actual communicating, you can't really separate the verbal and the nonverbal. As Ted Grove puts it, in real life, "There are no separate chapters." Grove also emphasizes that another distinction we use for thinking and talking about communication is difficult to apply in practice—the distinction between the expression or production of cues ("exhaling") and the reception or experience of cues ("inhaling"). But this distinction can help organize some of what we know about nonverbal communicating into an understandable whole.

Under the heading "Expressive Functions" Grove talks about kinds or types of nonverbal communicating. He distinguishes among kinds of cues by the function they perform—illustrating, adapting, displaying emotions, and the like. He concludes the section with a discussion of five characteristics of nonverbal cues, which helps explain how they work.

Then he shifts perspective from the "exhaling" side to "inhaling" and talks about how nonverbal communicating gets interpreted. For example, we draw conclusions from nonverbal cues about how responsive a person is and about what the power balance is between us and them. We also use nonverbal cues to give us insights into how the other person is feeling. Grove talks about how "nonverbal leakage" works in communication, and how we interpret nonverbal cues to detect when someone is lying. He concludes by emphasizing that no nonverbal cue "means" anything by itself, because each has to be interpreted in relation to the context in which it's experienced.

This reading provides a general overview of the nonverbal cues that affect conversations the most.

NONVERBAL ELEMENTS OF INTERACTION

Theodore G. Grove

In ongoing dyadic interaction, verbal and nonverbal behavior occur together and influence one another. There are no separate chapters. Nonverbal and verbal behavior are *produced* concurrently as part of the holistic larger pattern of individuals' behavior and are *experienced* as integrated patterns by the actor and observer alike.

Similar to the verbal elements, nonverbal behavior forms part of both the *expressive* and *interpretive* domains of dyadic interaction. As such, nonverbal elements contribute in a powerful way to the course of interaction episodes and, thereby, to the texture of conversations and the definition of relationships. However, in many fundamental respects, the nonverbal codes differ greatly from the verbal. . . .

EXPRESSIVE FUNCTIONS OF NONVERBAL BEHAVIOR

. . . [One] well-known set of distinctions classifies nonverbal behavior on the basis of the kind of meanings it functions to create—what it *does* in the interaction (Ekman and Friesen 1969). The five categories in this scheme are *illustrators, regulators, emblems, adaptors,* and *affect displays. Illustrators* are those gestures that support or complement the meaning of the utterance. For example, one uses an illustrator when one points while saying, " . . . then you take a left. . . . " *Regulators* refer to the way we use the whole body, even the head, eyes, and voice, to regulate the flow of our interaction. For example, when we touch someone to get their attention, turn toward someone as we interrupt, or back away as we terminate a conversation, we are using regulators.

Emblems consist mainly of head, shoulder, arm, and hand signals that have precise, usually quite specific meanings, such as waving "good-bye," shrugging "I don't know," and nodding "yes." Emblems differ from the rest of interactive nonverbal behavior in that, like language symbols, they have a specific denotative value—a relatively stable designated meaning, regardless of context. More on this, later.

A fourth category in this functional classification scheme is *adaptors.* Adaptors bear little consistent relationship to the content of conversation; however, occasionally they have been observed being used to emphasize some point. Some adaptors are widely used. Examples are rubbing the back of one's neck while pondering a verbal response and touching one's chin or forehead during interaction. Other adaptors are idiosyncratic behaviors, perhaps habituated by the individual as nervous habits and eventually incorporated into their interactive behavior. [Former] television talk-show host Johnny Carson has offered a virtual encyclopedia of adaptors with his stylized, jerky, roosterlike head movements, tie-touching, pencil play, and other behaviors.

Finally, *affect displays* refers to nonverbal expression of emotions, utilizing primarily facial expressions (Ekman and Friesen 1975). Studying facial affect displays in several cultures, investigators have identified some universally observed patterns of facial movements during expression of the emotions of happiness, fear, surprise, sadness, anger, and disgust. While public facial displays of each of these emotions may vary across cultures, private expressions of each are quite similar. Four display rules that seem to govern when particular emotions are publicly displayed within specific cultures have been identified (Ekman and Friesen 1971).

One display rule is to *intensify*—make the emotional involvement bigger than it really is. For example, facial displays of pleasure as we greet invited guests in our own culture suggest the "intensify" rule. "We're just *sooo* happy you could come!" In contrast, we seem to *de-intensify* our public disappointment or sadness upon being passed over for some sought-after honor or prize and, in some situations, de-intensify our joy when we gain the honor. Some situations and some publicly visible roles prescribe that individuals *neutralize* their facial affect displays for certain emotions. For example, the behavior of judges in the courtroom and of referees at athletic contests rarely include expressions of glee at the outcomes of the trials and games over which they preside, even though privately they must be happier over some outcomes than others. Finally, some situations seem to call for suppressing displays of a particular emotion by *masking* it with a different one. Losers of Miss America "talent" contests smile brightly while the winner cries and, in the presence of a girlfriend or comrades, teenage American boys and "macho" men have been observed to mask fear with anger.

While many emotions are expressed as *full* facial displays, those rules sometimes influence the way emotions are displayed on the face. For example, de-intensification as well as inept attempts to neutralize sometimes lead to *partial* facial involvement. As a small boy I recall swinging furiously and futilely, trying to hit another in the stomach, while my much larger adversary calmly held me at bay at arm's length with one hand on the top of my head. To my humiliation, the teacher who broke up the "fight" ineptly neutralized her amusement, resulting in a partial facial display. In similar fashion, inept attempts at masking may lead to facial *blends,* a merging of the suppressed and the superimposed emotions. For example, part of the face may reflect surprise, while another part reveals the anger one is actually feeling.

Five Characteristics of Nonverbal Codes

Contrasting nonverbal behavior with our linguistic interactive behavior will illustrate several fundamental properties of how the nonverbal codes function. First, unlike verbal behavior, we engage in nonverbal action constantly throughout a conversation, when we are not talking as well as when we are talking. We wrinkle the nose, scratch, turn our head toward or away from the other person, nod, stop nodding, and the like. Therefore, each party to a conversation is *unceasingly engaged in nonverbal behavior,* regardless of whether one is talking or is listening to the utterances of the other person.

Second, except for some noninteractive aspect like physical appearance and artifacts, one's nonverbal behaviors are produced more thoughtlessly and, therefore, are largely *out of the behavior's awareness,* relative to the more consciously selected verbal behavior. This characteristic has a number of important implications for observing the partner's nonverbal behavior, discussed in a later section.

There is some indication that we are even less aware of some of our nonverbal behaviors than of others. We tend to be more aware of our face and head than of what we are doing with the rest of our body. For example, we are able to produce "social smiles" at appropriate times in the interaction. Moreover, generally low self-awareness seems to be even lower with respect to the lower regions of the body, being lower in the legs and extremities (feet and hands) than in the head and arms.

A third difference is that while our words bear an arbitrary relationship to what they are supposed to represent, with a few exceptions (like emblems) individual nonverbal behaviors do not have arbitrarily assigned denotative meanings. They are *iconic* (Burgoon 1985) representations of meaning and do not possess the designated character of spoken words. For example, the spoken word "chair" is a designated set of sounds and could be replaced by "spurk" or any other equally arbitrary set of sounds, as long as members of our language community all agreed upon that usage. The meaning is *outside of* the actual behavior. On the other hand, if I motion to a chair as you enter the room, the gesture I make literally models the action it represents.

Fourth, while the meanings elicited by spoken words and language utterances are dependent, to some extent, on the context in which they are uttered, the meaning of nonverbal behavior is *more exclusively a function of contextual factors* just because they do lack conventional definition. Even the variety of meanings associated with the simple act of touching or being touched are heavily dependent on the context, including the verbal and other nonverbal behaviors as well as relational and situational factors (Jones and Yarbrough 1985).

Regardless of the different connotations elicited in different listeners, the word "father" refers to a fixed biological relationship; that designated core of meaning is relatively stable irrespective of connotation or context. But a particular nonverbal act lacks such linguistically conferred stability—lacks a core of consistent meaning. The same behaviors are used in connection with quite different, sometimes opposite, meanings, and those meanings are rooted in the context where the behavior occurs. For example, given a slight shift in context, my pointing toward the door could convey, "Godspeed!" or, "Get out of my office!" With the exception of emblems, each little movement does *not* have a meaning of its own. For that and other reasons, scholars have little faith in the *body-language* view of nonverbal behavior (Burgoon and Saine 1978). This contextual feature of nonverbal behavior will be elaborated in the next section interpreting nonverbal behavior.

Fifth, specific nonverbal behaviors are always produced as one part of a larger pattern along with other nonverbal behaviors; that is, they are *integrated.* That means we tend to produce nonverbal behaviors in concurrent *sets* and coordinated *sequences* rather than as single isolated behaviors. For example, typical smiling behavior may involve, in addition to an upturned mouth, crinkling the skin at the temples, cheek movements, and the like. Laughing may be accompanied by total bodily involvement including postural changes and momentary withdrawal of eye contact. Although the words in our utterances also follow combinational patterns prescribed by rules of syntax, we are able to select and utter any given single word or verbal expression in isolation from all others. We can select language segments to include in our utterances. But we would have a hard time segmenting our muscles to produce only a "lip smile." Try as we might, our cheek, nose, jaw and chin muscles, perhaps our eyes, would join in. All of these ways in which nonverbal behavior differs from verbal behavior have important consequences for interpreting the nonverbal behavior of one's interactional partner.

THE INTERPRETIVE FUNCTIONS
OF NONVERBAL BEHAVIOR

As indicated in the introductory discussion of this chapter, nonverbal behavior may be viewed both in terms of its expressive role and its interpretive role in dyadic interaction. The immediately preceding material introduced nonverbal functioning from the perspective of the actor. Here, we shift gears to interpretive processes by exploring those important topics from the perspective of the observer. These explorations are organized into sections on strong nonverbal messages, nonverbal leakage, clues to deception, and the contextual interpretation of nonverbal behavior.

Strong Nonverbal Messages

Our interpretations of nonverbal behavior are certainly a crucial part of the interpersonal communication process. Based on an analysis of results from twenty-four studies comparing verbal and nonverbal behavior, Philpott found verbal interaction was associated with only 31 percent of elicited meaning, while nonverbal interaction, alone and coupled with verbal, accounted for the remaining 69 percent (Burgoon 1985). While the linguistic aspect of others' utterances can provide us with very precise information and distinctions not available through observation of nonverbal behavior alone, the latter seems to outstrip the contributions of verbal behavior with respect to a number of interpretive functions. Three of these include responsiveness, dominance relations, and expression of feelings.

Responsiveness Interpretations   "Responsiveness interpretations" refer to our sense of how engaged the partner is in our interaction—to what extent the other is *listening to* and *involved in* the give-and-take of our exchange. How do you know whether someone is listening carefully to what you are saying—listening at the very peak of their effort? There are several clues provided by your *own* listening function. For example, when your conversational partner asks a targeted question, one which required careful attention to your previous remarks, you know they have been listening attentively. Or if the partner paraphrases what you just said or asks you to elaborate on or repeat something you ineptly expressed, you know he or she has been attentive at some level. Certainly, numerous "yeah's," "I see's," and other verbal prompts and acknowledgments (or lack of them) add to one's sense of how well the other is listening. But more often and with great accuracy, we interpret how well someone is listening from our observation of their nonverbal behavior.

Behaviors called *backchanneling* (Duncan 1975) are indicative that one is continuing to listen. These may include head nods, eye contact, vocalic cues, leaning in, sitting close, standing close, direct shoulder and head orientation, alert body posture, and the like. People vary somewhat in their propensity to provide such backchannels when listening and to need them when talking. An acquaintance required constant and direct eye contact in all circumstances, whether talking or listening. Once, it was my misfortune to be in the backseat of his car as he chatted constantly, shooting frequent glances at me as we careened along at high speeds over narrow winding country roads. Despite my increasingly desperate "uh-huh's," "right's," and "yeah's," he seemed to need, above all else, the sign of responsiveness that only my eye contact could provide.

Unlike my friend, most of us are content to observe whatever nonverbal signs of responsiveness the situation permits. These interpretations of another's responsiveness pertain not only to the other's listening, but to whether the other is interested in continued interaction or even starting a conversation in the first place. We rarely need to talk about these things, because we usually can observe the partner's eye gaze, head orientation, body posture and movement, and vocalics, and draw our own fairly accurate conclusions at a given moment.

Interpretations of Dominance Relations "Dominance relations" refers to the power relationship between the partner and oneself. . . . One tends to convey a sense of being a subordinate, a peer, or one of superior status by eye behavior, postural attitude, use of space, and the like. For example, while speaking we tend to gaze most at partners with moderate positional power, somewhat less toward high-power partners, and least toward low-power partners (Knapp 1978).

One's nonverbal behavior may be *deference-demanding, deferential,* or *neutral* with respect to dominance relations (Dovidio and Ellyson 1982). Observing a conversation from afar, one obtains a pretty accurate idea of how the interacting parties perceive their own dominance pattern. For example, individuals who perceive themselves as lower status or subordinate to the interaction partner tend to maintain more tense musculature and more erect, less relaxed postural attitudes. This feature has been recognized for thousands of years in the military services and ritualized in the command of *"attention!"* and its historical precursors, directed at lower-ranking individuals and groups.

Gaze behavior also conveys different power impressions. Both large amounts of gaze while speaking and small amounts of gaze while listening convey the impression of high power (Dovidio and Ellyson 1982). With these and many more signs of dominance relations available, it is rarely necessary to be told, "I feel we are equals," or, "I am your boss," or even, "I feel that I am not in control here." Careful observation of the other's nonverbal behavior in a few seconds of interaction usually tells you all you need to know about deference and other trappings of dominance relations in a given dyad.

Interpretations of Feelings   Our judgments concerning the immediate feelings of the other party usually rely more on our observation of nonverbal behavior than on what the other is saying. We arrive at these judgments through observation of facial affect displays, postural cues, and the like. Words need to be decoded into symbolic meaning denoted in our language system. But, as discussed earlier, nonverbal signals do not require such processing. Our reactions to combinations of gestures, bodily posture, tones of voice, and facial expressions provide instantaneous clues to the feeling states of the partner (Burgoon 1985). As one begins to tell us how they feel about something, we most frequently have a pretty good idea of their emotional state, even before the utterance has been completed. Additional bases for the nonverbal contribution to our capacity to interpret one another's feelings are examined in the subsequent discussion of "nonverbal leakage."

Summary

Judee Burgoon (1985) characterizes the difference between how we use the verbal and nonverbal codes as follows. We place more importance on verbal cues for factual, abstract, and persuasive meanings, but place more importance on nonverbal cues for relational, attributional, emotional, and attitudinal meanings. In general, we are influenced more by our partner's language behavior with respect to *objective, denotative information,* and more by his or her nonverbal behavior with respect to *relational, connotative information.* In large part, that division of labor reflects the different limitations of the nonverbal and verbal codes.

Nonverbal Leakage

The spontaneous, out-of-awareness way in which nonverbal behavior is produced also provides a *direct* indicator of the other's feelings. This is in contrast to our interpretation of verbal behavior, which is dependent on the other's awareness of and willingness to verbally express his or her emotional states. Through such *nonverbal leakage,* subtle feelings may be accurately perceived and much faster than it takes to utter a short sentence (Ekman and Friesen 1969). Although we do talk about our feelings more than, for example, our dominance relations, by the time we say, "I'm happy" or, "I'm angry," those words are often unnecessary. The other often knows just how happy or angry we are through observation of our nonverbal behavior. Although the emotional states of some people are more guarded or impassive than others, at some level we all wear our spleens, as well as our hearts, on our sleeves.

    Nonverbal leakage is presented through those nonverbal signs which are outside of the awareness of the behavior and which may contain information about the internal state (thoughts, feelings, attitudes) of the one who exhibits the behavior. The professor who frequently misses or is late for student appointments but who is unceasingly punctual for meetings with the Dean of the College may be "leaking" his or her orientation about dominance relations and what he or she feels is appropriate behavior there. "Yeah, I'm listening" may be uttered in a tone of voice and with facial affect that suggests the opposite would be a more accurate statement.

This leakage exerts a strong influence on how we view the interacting partner. When what the other says is clearly discrepant with what he or she does and how he or she says it, the nonverbal interpretation is the more credible of the two interpretations. On those occasions when what the partner *says* seems disparate with what the partner *does* with body and voice, the observer trusts his or her nonverbal behavior interpretation over the verbal. However, as the correspondence between verbal and nonverbal behavior increases toward the point of no discrepancy, we give more and more weight to the verbal implications (Burgoon 1985).

Sometimes someone intentionally displays discrepant verbal/nonverbal behavior to achieve some effect. For example, old friends meeting after a long separation have been observed directing the most unflattering remarks at one another ("you old so-and-so") with voices and facial expressions that leave no doubt they are indeed good friends. In the other direction, coupling verbal expressions of positive evaluation with nonverbal behavior that suggests negative feeling is such a frequent occurrence that we have a special term for it—"sarcasm."

In instances where we observe discontinuity between verbal and nonverbal behavior, it is not certain why we place greater trust in our interpretations of the nonverbal. It may be we sense the difficulties we all have in monitoring our own nonverbal behavior and, therefore, find the nonverbal behavior of others more credible than their words. Perhaps, without even thinking about it in any orderly fashion, we register that nonverbal behavior is more automatic and out-of-awareness than one's language utterances and is, therefore, less subject to control.

Clues to Deception

Clues to deception are a special kind of nonverbal leakage. These are instances where observed discrepancies between utterance and nonverbal behavior or other observations suggest the speaker may be actively attempting to conceal or misrepresent something during interaction. Again these are instances where the words say one thing, but the nonverbal behavior does not seem to "fit." Some features that have been found to occasionally accompany deceitful utterances include shortened response latency to questions and increases in adaptor gestures and in foot, hand, and leg movement, and decreases in eye contact, in physical directness in head and shoulders, and in illustrator gestures (Knapp and others 1987).

Most investigators believe that the most reliable cues to deception exist in those nonverbal behaviors over which we have the least self-conscious control and which are therefore most subject to leakage. John Hocking and Dale Leathers' (1980) ideas have guided several recent efforts to isolate reliable clues to deceptive intent during interaction. They suggest that deceivers who are motivated to avoid detection 1) *suppress controllable behaviors* stereotypical of liars in an attempt to avoid appearing like liars, 2) while at the same time *increasing less controllable behaviors* that are also indicative of anxiety during lying. Controllable behaviors might include various head, foot, leg, and hand-to-face movements, and gaze avoidance. Liars have been observed exhibiting increased vocal nervousness and dysfluencies, shorter response latencies (pre-reply pauses), shorter hesitation pauses (within-turn pauses), and briefer answers than truth-tellers (Cody and O'Hair 1983). In addition, during falsification individuals have been observed to decrease the stereotyped and controllable liar behaviors such as postural shifts. Among other effects, such adjustments result in an abnormally still body during interaction.

It is likely that individuals who rely almost exclusively for their interpretations on the partner's utterances place themselves at a disadvantage in a few of their important encounters. At the same time, the reader needs to be aware that none of the above are infallible indicators of intentional deceit, for reasons discussed in the next section.

Contextual Interpretation of Nonverbal Behavior

Notwithstanding the immediately preceding discussions of leakage and clues to deception, *contextual* interpretations of another's nonverbal behavior are more likely to be valid than single-cue "body language" interpretations. Observers' judgments of what behaviors represent are more likely to be accurate when observers take into account the total context in which the behavior occurs and when those judgments are based on observation of whole sets or sequences of nonverbal behaviors. Stated another way, our judgments are likely to be wrong when they are based on interpretation of a single behavior in isolation from its context.

With few exceptions (like *emblems*), individual nonverbal acts do not have conventional assigned meanings. They are produced in combination with other nonverbal and verbal behaviors in holistic patterns. Some important contextual features include what has been and is being said in the interactional episode, the setting of the interaction, why it is taking place, the relationship between the parties, and how the partner usually behaves. Several reasons compel this emphasis on the wisdom of contextual interpretations of nonverbal behavior.

1. *First,* the same behavior supports very different interpretations in different contexts. For example, arm-stretching could be indicative of relaxation, of dominance, of boredom or even represent a nervous adaptor, given specific situations. There is ample evidence that the one-meaning-for-every-behavior fallacy is likely to mislead our attempts to interpret accurately. For example, among other things decreased eye gaze can represent dislike or submissiveness or rejection, and complete withdrawal of gaze can be associated with extreme anxiety. Heightened gaze can reflect liking or can intensify either the positive or the negative values of uttered sentiments (Bowers and others 1985). Steady eye gaze during a plea for help calls for a very different interpretation than a steady gaze accompanied by "Stop it!" As

indicated earlier, the simple act of touching the other person can represent a very large number of different meanings (Jones and Yarbrough 1985), all rooted in the specific interactional context in which the touching occurred.

A class of senior law students once sought support for the *body language* fallacy from a guest who had been invited to speak on nonverbal signs of deception in deposition-taking and witness-stand behavior. These future attorneys were understandably interested in learning about behaviors that could "tip off" a witness's deceptive utterances, and they were particularly interested in eye gaze behavior. But they learned that withdrawal of eye gaze is also frequently associated with stressful moments. Testifying in a legal proceeding would be very stressful for most people. Undoubtedly, observation of nonverbal leakage may provide information that enhances interactional effectiveness, but there are no shortcuts across the terrain of contextual interpretation.

2. *Second,* reasonably accurate interpretations must be based on several behaviors, because any single behavior occurs within a framework of many other behaviors. For example, the presence of any one of the behaviors associated with active listening does not automatically mean the partner is responsive to your comments. At one time or another all of us have faked attention by maintaining eye contact and throwing in an occasional head nod.

By the same reasoning, absence of a specific sign of responsivity does not necessarily indicate poor listening. The grade school student who is admonished to "sit up and listen" may actually have been listening very carefully. Some of us slouch our way through school. Because a friend stands farther away while talking to you does not mean he/she likes you any less at the moment. But, if the same friend simultaneously talks impersonally with lower-than-normal eye contact while facing less directly than usual and unexpectedly ends the conversation without explanation, one is probably justified in concluding that all is not well.

3. *Third,* even if you interpret the behavior correctly, you may be wrong in your inference about the implications of that interpretation, until you fully understand the context. For example, laughter ranks among the most unequivocal nonverbal behaviors one will ever observe; it usually means the laugher thinks something is funny. Yet, one still must infer the source of the laugher's amusement. On one occasion, a professor made what he thought was a witty remark before turning to the blackboard. Sensing something was amiss when the anticipated chuckle gave way to a roar, he turned to face the class, clearly puzzled. A sympathetic student pointed out the professor's V-neck sweater was on backwards.

Sometimes information required for accurate inferences is simply not available at the time the nonverbal behavior occurs. A graduate student and mother of two small children was taking an independent study from her professor/adviser. During one of their meetings, she was markedly more responsive and cheerful than usual. She smiled frequently, was more animated, and her voice conveyed pleasure and excitement throughout. At the end of the meeting the professor asked if she thought the material covered held promise for her dissertation topic. She replied she would "think about that later when I calm down." Just before the meeting, she had received a check for over a year of delinquent child support. When a behavior is viewed in isolation from the context in which it occurred, one's interpretations are more likely to be inaccurate. Sometimes one simply does not know enough about the context.

SUMMARY

Some nonverbal elements of interaction are described, first from the point of view of expressive behavior, then from the perspective of one who is interpreting the nonverbal expressions of the interactional partner. Several common classification schemes are used to describe the domain of nonverbal interactional behavior, and five interrelated characteristics of nonverbal behavior are discussed. During interaction nonverbal behaviors 1) are unceasingly produced, 2) are produced relatively out-of-awareness, 3) are nonarbitrary, 4) have contextually determined meanings, and 5) are produced in integrated sets.

REVIEW QUESTIONS

1. Explain the difference between the terms *expressive* and *interpretive* as used here.
2. Define the following jargon terms from this chapter: *illustrators, regulators, emblems, adaptors, affect displays, iconic cues, dominance relations, nonverbal leakage.*
3. What's the significance of Grove's point that nonverbal cues tend to be produced in "sets" or "sequences"?
4. Grove says that you can't rely on specific nonverbal cues to tell whether a person is lying. Why not?

PROBES

1. Sometimes people tell how someone "stopped communicating," or how a problem was caused by communication being "terminated." Does Ted Grove believe that people can "stop" communicating nonverbally? Explain.
2. Give an example from your own experience that illustrates how "strong" nonverbal messages can be.
3. Why do you believe nonverbal leakage can exert such a strong influence on how we view our interacting partner?
4. Grove discusses four ways context can affect the interpretation of nonverbal cues. What practical advice for your own communicating do you draw from this discussion?

REFERENCES

Bowers, J. W., Metts, S. M., and Duncanson, W. T. 1985. Emotion and interpersonal communication. In *Handbook of interpersonal communication*, eds. M. L. Knapp and G. R. Miller, 500–550. Beverly Hills, CA: Sage Publications.

Burgoon, J. K. 1985. Nonverbal signals. In *Handbook of interpersonal communication*, eds. M. L. Knapp and G. R. Miller, 344–390. Beverly Hills, CA: Sage Publications.

Burgoon, J. K., and Saine, T. 1978. *The unspoken dialogue: An introduction to nonverbal communication.* Boston: Houghton Mifflin Co.

Cody, M. J., and O'Hair, H. D. 1983. Nonverbal communication and deception: Differences in deception cues due to gender and communicator dominance. *Communication Monographs:* 176–192.

Dovidio, J. F., and Ellyson, S. L. 1982. Decoding visual dominance: Attributions of power based on relative percentages of looking while speaking and looking while listening. *Social Psychology Quarterly* 45: 106–113.

Duncan, S. 1975. Interaction units during speaking turns in dyadic, face-to-face conversations. In *Organization of behavior in face-to-face interaction*, eds. A. Kendon, R. M. Harris, and M. R. Key, 199–213. The Hague: Mouton.

Ekman, P., and Friesen, W. V. 1969. Nonverbal leakage and clues to deception. *Psychiatry* 32: 88–106.

Ekman, P., and Friesen, W. V. 1971. Constancy across cultures in the face and emotion. *Journal of Personality and Social Psychology* 17: 124–129.

Ekman, P., and Friesen, W. V. 1975. *Unmasking the face.* Englewood Cliffs, NJ: Prentice-Hall.

Hocking, J. E., and Leathers, D. 1980. Nonverbal indicators of deception: A new theoretical perspective. *Communication Monographs* 47: 119–131.

Jones, S. E., and Yarbrough, A. E. 1985. A naturalistic study of the meanings of touch. *Communication Monographs* 52: 19–56.

Knapp, M. L. 1978. *Nonverbal communication in human interaction.* New York: Holt, Rinehart, and Winston.

Knapp, M. L., Cody, M. J., and Reardon, K. K. 1987. Nonverbal signals. In *Handbook of communication science*, eds. C. R. Berger and S. H. Chaffee, 385–418. Beverly Hills, CA: Sage Publications.

Openness as Inhaling

CHAPTER 4

Self-Awareness

THE METAPHORS—"OPENNESS" AND "BREATHING"

*A*s I noted in the Preface, the next five chapters (those in Part Two and Part Three) are organized with the help of two metaphors. The first is "openness," which can mean both willing and able to perceive and listen fully *and* willing and able to disclose thoughts and feelings. As my introductions and the readings make clear, this book does not argue that it's always good to be completely welcoming (open to input) or transparent (ready to disclose). Common sense says that there needs to be limits on both. But when you want to move your communicating along the scale introduced in Chapter 2—from social toward interpersonal communicating—openness in both its senses is important. The materials in these chapters explain how.

The second metaphor is "breathing"; this inhaling–exhaling metaphor is a little more involved. At the most basic level, I use the terms *inhaling* and *exhaling* to begin to break down or organize the continuous, changing, multidimensional, often confusing processes called "communicating." One commonsense, close-to-experience way to organize this overall process is to divide it up into what people take in (inhaling) and what they give out (exhaling).

You can figure out my second and most important reason for choosing this metaphor if you try to inhale without exhaling, or vice versa. These labels allow me to separate communication into two of its important parts while still emphasizing that the parts happen together. As I noted in Chapter 2, communicators are always receiving and sending at the same time. *While we're talking,* we're noticing how people are responding, and *while we're listening,* we're giving off mixed and primarily nonverbal cues.

No metaphor is perfect, of course, and one problem with this one is that inhaling and exhaling happen *sequentially,* while perceiving and talking take place *simultaneously.* In this way, communication is even more dynamic than this metaphor suggests.

A third reason I'm using this metaphor is that it is organic. Breathing is a part of living for most of the organisms in the world. It's vital for humans and other animals, of course, but you can also think of the fish's intake and output of water and even the plant's intake of water and output of oxygen as forms of breathing.

The fourth reason is that this metaphor organizes breathing into a process that begins with input. If somebody asks, "What are the two parts of the breathing process?" the common answer is "inhaling and exhaling" not "exhaling and inhaling." So the metaphor allows me to focus *first* on perception and listening. This reverses the historical tendency to begin one's efforts to improve communication by focusing on what one *says.* I'm convinced that listening is the often neglected, but crucially important half of the listening–speaking pair, and this metaphor makes it easier to redress some of this imbalance.

So Chapter 4 highlights the inhaling processes of self-perception, and Chapter 5 shifts focus to how we perceive others. Then Chapter 6 treats listening as the main communication skill connected with perception. In Part Three, Chapter 7 discusses the exhaling processes that are connected to self-expression; then Chapter 8 focuses on hurtful and negative expressions.

"MEANING AND VALUES" BY GERALD COREY AND MARIANNE SCHNEIDER-COREY

*T*his first reading comes from a book written to help college students of all ages who want to expand their self-awareness and explore the choices available to them in significant areas of their lives. It is a personal reading, partly because it asks you to focus on yourself as you read it, and partly because its authors, Gerald Corey and Marianne Schneider-Corey, write about their personal experiences. This chapter encourages you to look critically at the *why* of your existence and to clarify the sources of your values. The authors emphasize the importance of listening to your own inner desires and feelings as you ask three key questions, "Who am I?" "Where am I going?" and "Why?" But they also make the point that "meaning in life is found through intense relationships with others, not through an exclusive and narrow pursuit of self-realization."

Jerry and Marianne encourage you to reflect on your philosophy of life, your response to religion, and your values. You might think a discussion of religion is out of place in a textbook, but, as they point out, religious faith can be a powerful source of meaning and purpose. Even reflection that begins with the question "Is there a God?" is religious, and as you extend your exploration of some of the related questions they suggest, you can often learn a great deal about your self. When I grew up, for example, church was just something the family automatically did on Sunday, and my responses were predictable. I didn't hate it, but I also didn't get much out of it. For a time I didn't have much connection with religion, but when I attended a church-sponsored college and developed some religious friends, I discovered some deep resonances between my fundamental values and those I saw being lived out by some of the religious people I knew. Since then I've profited a whole lot from the academic writings of some theologians and from friendships with people with a variety of religious commitments. My spiritual life is important to me, and I define myself in part as a "religious" person.

Your experience might be totally different. But the point these authors reinforce is that, as part of your study of interpersonal communication, it can be helpful to reflect on your own philosophy, values, and religious beliefs. Why? Because (a) they have been developed in your past communication experiences, (b) they will be changed by communication you experience in the future, and (c) your philosophy, values, and religious beliefs affect how you communicate with others today.

MEANING AND VALUES

Gerald Corey and Marianne Schneider-Corey

In this chapter we encourage you to look critically at the *why* of your existence, to clarify the sources of your values, and to reflect on questions such as these: In what direction am I moving in my life? What do I have to show for my years on this earth so far? Where have I been, where am I now, and where do I want to go? What steps can I take to make the changes I have decided on?

Many who are fortunate enough to achieve power, fame, success, and material comfort nevertheless experience a sense of emptiness. Although they may not be able to articulate what is lacking in their lives, they know that something is amiss. The astronomical number of pills and drugs consumed to allay the symptoms of this "existential vacuum"—depression and anxiety—is evidence of our failure to find values that allow us to make sense of our place in the world. In *Habits of the Heart,* Bellah and his colleagues (1985) found among the people they interviewed a growing interest in finding purpose in their lives. Although our achievements as a society are enormous, we seem to be hovering on the very brink of disaster, not only from internal conflict but also from societal incoherence. Bellah and his associates assert that the core problem with our society is that we have put our own good, as individuals and as groups, ahead of the common good.

The need for a sense of meaning is manifested by the increased interest in religion, especially among young people in college. A student told us recently that in her English class of twenty students, four of them had selected religion as a topic for a composition dealing with a conflict in their lives. Other signs of the search for meaning include the widespread interest in Eastern and other philosophies, the use of meditation, the number of self-help and inspirational books published each year, the experimentation with different lifestyles, and even the college courses in personal adjustment!

The paradox of our contemporary society is that although we have the benefits of technological progress, we are still not satisfied. We have become increasingly troubled about ourselves and our place in the world, we have less certainty about morality, and we are less sure that there is any meaning or purpose in the universe (Carr, 1988, p. 167). It seems fair to say that we are caught up in a crisis of meaning and values.

OUR SEARCH FOR IDENTITY

The discovery of meaning and values is essentially related to our achievement of identity as a person. The quest for identity involves a commitment to give birth to ourselves by exploring the meaning of our uniqueness and humanity. A major problem for many people is that they have lost a sense of self, because they have directed their search for identity outside themselves. In their attempt to be liked and accepted by everyone, they have become finely tuned to what *others* expect of them but alienated from their *own* inner desires and feelings. As Rollo May (1973) observes, they are able to *respond* but not to *choose.* Indeed, May sees inner emptiness as the chief problem in contemporary society; too many of us, he says, have become "hollow people" who have very little understanding of who we are and what we feel. He cites one person's succinct description: "I'm just a collection of mirrors, reflecting what everyone expects of me" (p. 15).

Moustakas (1975) describes the same alienation from self that May talks about. For Moustakas, alienation is "the developing of a life outlined and determined by others, rather than a life based on one's own inner experience" (p. 31). If we become alienated from ourselves, we don't trust our own feelings but respond automatically to others as we think they want us to respond. As a consequence, Moustakas writes, we live in a world devoid of excitement, risk, and meaning. . . .

Achieving identity doesn't necessarily mean stubbornly clinging to a certain way of thinking or behaving. Instead, it may involve trusting ourselves enough to become open to new possibilities. Nor is an identity something we achieve for all time; rather, we need to be continually willing to reexamine our patterns and our priorities, our habits and relationships. Above all, we need to develop the ability to listen to our inner selves and trust what we hear. To take just one example, some students for whom academic life has become stale and empty have chosen to leave it in response to their inner feelings. Some have opted to travel and live modestly for a time, taking in new cultures and even assimilating into them for a while. They may not be directly engaged in preparing for a career and, in that sense, "establishing" themselves, but they are achieving their own identities by being open to new experiences and ways of being. For some of them, it may take real courage to resist the pressure to settle down in a career or "complete" their education.

Our search for identity involves asking three key existential questions, none of which has easy or definite answers: Who am I? Where am I going? Why?

The question Who am I? is never settled once and for all, for it can be answered differently at different times in our life. We need to revise our life, especially when old identities no longer seem to supply a meaning or give us direction. As we have seen, we must decide whether to let others tell us who we are or to take a stand and define ourselves.

Where am I going? This issue relates to our plans for a lifetime and the means we expect to use in attaining our goals. Like the previous question, this one demands periodic review. Our life goals are not set once and for all. Again, do we show the courage it takes to decide for ourselves where we are going, or do we look for a guru to show us where to go?

Asking the question Why? and searching for reasons are characteristics of being human. We face a rapidly changing world in which old values give way to new ones or to none at all. Part of shaping an identity implies that we are actively searching for meaning, trying to make sense of the world in which we find ourselves. . . .

Finding Meaning by Transcending Personal Interests

Carr (1988) concludes that what most of us want is to make a difference in the world. The process of becoming self-actualizing begins as a personal search. Although self-acceptance is a prerequisite for meaningful interpersonal relationships, there is a quest to go beyond self-centered interests. Ultimately, we want to establish connections with others in society, and we want to make a contribution. Likewise, Bellah and his colleagues (1985) conclude that meaning in life is found through intense relationships with others, not through an exclusive and narrow pursuit of self-realization. In their interviews with many people they found a desire to move beyond the isolated self. Our common life requires more than an exclusive concern with material accumulation. These authors maintain that a reconstituting of the social world is required, involving a transformation of consciousness.

Developing a Philosophy of Life

A philosophy of life is made up of the fundamental beliefs, attitudes, and values that govern a person's behavior. Many students have said that they hadn't really thought much about their philosophy of life. However, the fact that we've never explicitly defined the components of our philosophy doesn't mean that we are completely without one. All of us do operate on the basis of general assumptions about ourselves, others, and the world. Thus, the first step in actively developing a philosophy of life is to formulate a clearer picture of our present attitudes and beliefs.

We have all been developing an implicit philosophy of life since we first began, as children, to wonder about life and death, love and hate, joy and fear, and the nature of the universe. We probably didn't need to be taught to be curious about such questions; raising them seems to be a natural part of human development. If we were fortunate, adults took the time to engage in dialogue with us, instead of discouraging us from asking questions and deadening some of our innate curiosity.

During the adolescent years the process of questioning usually assumes new dimensions. Adolescents who have been allowed to question and think for themselves as children begin to get involved in a more advanced set of issues. Many of the adolescents we've encountered in classes and workshops have at one time or another struggled with questions such as the following:

- Are the values that I've believed in for all these years the values I want to continue to live by?
- Where did I get my values? Are they still valid for me? Are there additional sources from which I can derive new values?
- Is there a God? What is the nature of the hereafter? What is my conception of a God? What does religion mean in my life? What kind of religion do I choose for myself? Does religion have any value for me?
- What do I base my ethical and moral decisions on? Peer-group standards? Parental standards? The normative values of my society?
- What explains the inhumanity I see in our world?
- What kind of future do I want? What can I do about actively creating this kind of future?

These are only a few of the questions that many adolescents think about and perhaps answer for themselves. However, a philosophy of life is not something we arrive at once and for all during our adolescent years. The development of a philosophy of life continues as long as we live. As long as we remain curious and open to new learning, we can revise and rebuild our conceptions of the world. Life may have a particular meaning for us during adolescence, a new meaning during adulthood, and still another meaning as we reach old age. Indeed, if we don't remain open to basic changes in our views of life, we may find it difficult to adjust to changed circumstances.

Keeping in mind that developing a philosophy of life is a continuing activity of examining and modifying the values we live by, you may find the following suggestions helpful as you go about formulating and reforming your own philosophy:

- Frequently create time to be alone in reflective thought.
- Consider what meaning the fact of your eventual death has for the present moment.
- Make use of significant contacts with others who are willing to challenge your beliefs and the degree to which you live by them.
- Adopt an accepting attitude toward those whose belief systems differ from yours, and develop a willingness to test your own beliefs. . . .

Religion and Meaning: A Personal View

Religious faith can be a powerful source of meaning and purpose. Religion helps many people make sense out of the universe and the mystery of our purpose in living. Like any other potential source of meaning, religious faith seems most authentic and valuable when it enables us to become as fully human as possible. This means that religion helps us get in touch with our own powers of thinking, feeling, deciding, willing, and acting. You might consider reflecting on the following questions about your religion to determine whether it is a constructive force in your life:

- Does my religion provide me with a set of values that is congruent with the way I live my life?
- Does my religion assist me in better understanding the meaning of life and death?
- Does my religion allow tolerance for others who see the world differently from me?
- Does my religion provide me with a sense of peace and serenity?
- Is my religious faith something that I actively choose or passively accept?
- Do my religious beliefs help me live life fully and treat others with respect and concern?
- Does my religion help me integrate my experience and make sense of the world?
- Does my religion encourage me to exercise my freedom and to assume the responsibility for the direction of my own life?
- Are my religious beliefs helping me become more of the person I'd like to become?
- Does my religion encourage me to question life and keep myself open to new learning?

As you take time for self-examination, how able are you to answer these questions in a way that is meaningful and satisfying to you? If you are honest with yourself, perhaps you will find that you have not really critically evaluated the sources of your spiritual and religious beliefs. Although you may hesitate to question your belief system out of a fear of weakening or undermining your faith, the opposite might well be true: demonstrating the courage to question your beliefs and values might strengthen them. As we have mentioned, increasing numbers of people seem to be deciding that a religious faith is necessary if they are to find an order and purpose in life. At the same time, many others insist that religion only impedes the quest for meaning or that it is incompatible with contemporary beliefs in other areas of life. What seems essential is that our acceptance or rejection of religious faith come authentically from within ourselves and that we remain open to new experience and learning, whatever points of view we decide on.

It is perhaps worth emphasizing that a "religion" may take the form of a system of beliefs and values concerning the ultimate questions in life rather than (or in addition to) membership in a church. People who belong to a church may not be "religious" in this sense, and others may consider themselves religious even though they are atheists or agnostics. Like almost anything else in human life, religion (or irreligion) can be bent to worthwhile or base purposes.

In my own experience, I (Jerry) have found religion most valuable when it is a challenge to broaden my choices and potential, rather than a restrictive influence. Until I was about 30, I tended to think of my religion as a package of ready-made answers for all the crises of life and was willing to let my church make many key decisions for me. I now think that I was experiencing too much anxiety in many areas of life to take full responsibility for my choices. My religious training had taught me that I should look to the authority of the church for ultimate answers in the areas of morality, value, and purpose. Like many other people I was encouraged to learn the "correct" answers and conform my thinking to them. Now, when I think of religion as a positive force, I think of it as being *freeing,* in the sense that it encourages me to trust myself, to discover the sources of strength and integrity within myself, and to assume responsibility for my own choices.

Although as an adult I've questioned and altered many of the religious teachings with which I was raised, I haven't discarded many of my past moral and religious values. Many of them served a purpose earlier in my life and, with modification, are still meaningful for me. However, whether or not I continue to hold the beliefs and values I've been taught, it seems crucial to me that I be willing to subject them to scrutiny. If they hold up under challenge, I can reincorporate them; by the same token, I can continue to examine the new beliefs and values I acquire.

My (Marianne's) religious faith has always been a positive force in my life. Sometimes people who are religious suffer from feelings of guilt and fears of damnation. This saddens me greatly, for if this is the case, religion ceases being a positive and powerful force in one's life. For me, religion helps me with an inner strength on which I can rely and that helps me to overcome difficulties that life presents. Although religion was encouraged in my childhood, it was never forced on me. It was a practice that I wanted to emulate because I saw the positive effects it had on the people in my life. Religion was practiced more than it was preached. The questions that we asked you to reflect on earlier are ones that I pose to myself as well. I want to be sure that I am aware of my beliefs and the necessity for making changes if I am not satisfied with my answers. . . .

Becoming Aware of How Your Values Operate

Your values influence what you do; your daily behavior is an expression of your basic values. We encourage you to make the time to continue examining the source of your values to determine if they are appropriate for you at this time in your life. Furthermore, it is essential that you be aware of the significant impact your value system has on your relationships with others. In our view, it is not appropriate for you to push your values on others, to assume a judgmental stance toward those who have a different world view, or to strive to convert others to adopt your perspective on life. Indeed, if you are secure in your values and basic beliefs, you will not be threatened by those who have a different set of beliefs and values.

In *God's Love Song,* Maier (1991) wonders how anyone can claim to have found the only way, not only for himself or herself but also for everyone else. We strongly agree with his view that there is a unique way for each person, however different that may be from the way of anyone else. As a minister, Sam Maier teaches that diversity shared not only is beautiful but also fosters understanding, caring, and the creation of community. He puts this message in a powerful and poetic way:

It is heartening to find communities where the emphasis is placed upon each person having the opportunity to:

- share what is vital and meaningful out of one's own experience;
- listen to what is vital and meaningful to others;
- not expect or demand that anyone else do it exactly the same way as oneself. (p. 3)

Reverend Maier's message is well worth contemplating. Although you might clarify a set of values that seem to work for you, we would hope that you respect the values of others that may be quite different from yours. It is not that one is right and the other is wrong. The diversity of cultures, religions, and world views implies a necessity not only to tolerate differences but also to embrace diverse paths toward meaning in life.

Whatever your own values are, they can be further clarified and strengthened if you entertain open discussion of various viewpoints and cultivate a nonjudgmental attitude toward diversity. You might raise questions such as:

- Where did I develop my values?
- Are my values open to modification?
- Have I challenged my values, and am I open to being challenged by others?
- Do I insist that the world remain the same now as it was earlier in my life?
- Do I feel so deeply committed to any of my values that I'm likely to push my friends and family members to accept them?
- How would I communicate my values to others without imposing those values?
- How do my own values and beliefs affect my behavior?
- Am I willing to accept people who hold different values?
- Do I avoid judging others if they think, feel, or act in different ways from myself? . . .

WHERE TO GO FROM HERE: CONTINUING YOUR PERSONAL GROWTH

. . . As you consider what experiences for continued personal growth you are likely to choose at this time, be aware that your meaning in life is not cast in concrete. As you change, you can expect that what brings meaning to your life will also change. The projects that you were deeply absorbed in as an adolescent may hold little meaning for you today. And where and how you discover meaning today may not be the pattern for some future period.

You can deliberately choose experiences that will help you actualize your potentials. Perhaps you remember reading a book or seeing a film that had a profound impact on you and really seemed to put things in perspective. Certainly, reading books that deal with significant issues in your life can be a growth experience in itself, as well as an encouragement to try new things.

Often, we make all sorts of resolutions about what we'd like to be doing in our life or about experiences we want to share with others, and then we fail to carry them out. Is this true of you? Are there activities you value yet rarely get around to doing? Perhaps you tell yourself that you prize making new friendships; yet you find that you do very little to actually initiate any contacts. Or perhaps you derive satisfaction from growing vegetables or puttering in your garden and yet find many reasons to neglect this activity. You might tell yourself that you'd love to take a day or two just to be alone and yet never get around to arranging it. When you stop to think about it, aren't there choices you could be making right now that would make your life a richer one? How would you really like to be spending your time? What changes are you willing to make today, this week, this month, this year?

In addition to activities that you enjoy but don't engage in as often as you'd like, there are undoubtedly many new things you might consider trying out as ways of adding meaning to your life and developing your potentials. You might consider making a contract with yourself to start now on a definite plan of action, instead of putting it off until next week or next year. Some of the ways in which many people choose to challenge themselves to grow include the following:

- finding hobbies that develop new sides of themselves
- going to plays, concerts, and museums
- taking courses in pottery making, wine tasting, guitar playing, and innumerable other special interests
- getting involved in exciting work projects or actively pursuing forms of work that will lead to the development of hidden talents
- spending time alone to reflect on the quality of their lives
- initiating contacts with others and perhaps developing an intimate relationship
- enrolling in continuing-education courses or earning a degree primarily for the satisfaction of learning
- doing volunteer work and helping to make others' lives better
- experiencing the mountains, the desert, and the ocean—by hiking, sailing, and so on
- becoming involved in religious activities or pursuing a spiritual path that is meaningful to them
- traveling to new places, especially to experience different cultures
- keeping a journal in which they record feelings and dreams
- sharing some of their dreams with a person they trust

Any list of ways of growing is only a sample, of course; the avenues to personal growth are as various as the people who choose them. Growth can occur in small ways, and there are many things that you can do on your own (or with friends or family) to continue your personal development. Perhaps the greatest hindrance to our growth as a person is our failure to allow ourselves to imagine all the possibilities that are open to us.

REVIEW QUESTIONS

1. What do these authors mean by "existential vacuum"?
2. What does it generally mean to "find meaning by transcending personal interests"?
3. According to these authors, how much of a person's philosophy of life is stable, and how much changes?
4. What rationale do the Coreys give for including the topic of religion in this chapter?
5. What's the difference between religious influences and values?
6. How do these authors view individual choice? How important is it?

PROBES

1. Do you agree that there is a widespread need for a sense of meaning among people you know, or do you think that these authors exaggerate the problem?
2. Before you read this essay, did you believe you had a "philosophy of life"? Do you now believe you do? What's it made up of?
3. What feelings are generated in you by this reading's discussion of religion? What experiences with others (family, friends, etc.) do those feelings grow out of?
4. How do you respond to Jerry's and Marianne's individual discussions of the roles of religion in their lives?
5. Do you agree that you can make conscious choices to change the directions of your personal growth? What examples from your own experience reinforce your view?

REFERENCES

Bellah, R. N., Madsen, R., Sullivan, W. M., Swidler, A., & Tipton, S. M. (1985). *Habits of the Heart: Individualism and Commitment in American Life.* New York: Harper & Row.

Carr, J. B. (1988). *Crisis In Intimacy: When Expectations Don't Meet Reality.* Pacific Grove, CA: Brooks/Cole.

Maier, S. (1991). *God's Love Song.* Corvallis, OR: Postal Instant Press.

May, R. (1973). *Man's Search for Himself.* New York: Dell.

Moustakas, C. (1975). *Finding Yourself, Finding Others.* Englewood Cliffs, NJ: Prentice-Hall.

*H*arold Barrett is an award-winning professor of communication at California State University, Hayward. This reading is taken from his book, which approaches interpersonal communication from what he argues is the normal, natural, and pervasive human tendency to protect the self. As he puts it early in the reading, "our persistent and compelling need in communication is to give an account of ourselves." Later, in Chapter 13 of *Bridges Not Walls*, Jack Gibb will call this phenomenon "defensiveness," and he will argue that it is the most important barrier to interpersonal communication. Barrett agrees, but he also offers some specific ways to overcome the detrimental effects of defensiveness.

Barrett begins from the idea that, whenever we communicate, we want to influence our listeners—he calls them "audiences"—favorably about ourselves. Yet we can never be sure of their attitude toward us or of our capability to relate to their attitude. So we adopt a more or less rigid posture of defensiveness. Barrett anchors his analysis in the neo-Freudian explanation of the human self put forward by a psychologist named Heinz Kohut. Kohut argued that unless a person has had just about completely perfect parents and has been raised in a perfect network of relationships, he or she carries some "shame," some feelings of "emptiness, unfulfillment, and deficiency." So from this perspective shame is not necessarily bad; it's just part of what each human experiences. And this experience leads us "to invent modes of maintaining the self," some of which work positively and some of which work negatively.

One tension that arises in this situation is that "rewards of individualism increasingly come into conflict with rewards of community affiliation." That is, people can get caught between the "rock" of individual integrity and the "hard place" of getting along with others. Culture, especially ethnicity, helps determine how we cope with these tensions. But regardless of culture or ethnicity, Barrett writes, we're all struggling with similar issues. In short, regardless of who you are, says Barrett, "the great commandment is to maintain the self." And interpersonal contacts are the ones that both pose the greatest threats to the self and provide the most maintenance of it. This means that selves are "in play" in every interpersonal encounter—as Barrett puts it, in "every conversation, public speech, interview, and discussion." But there are also at least eight specific self-maintenance resources available to every communicator, and the last major section of this reading explains these eight resources—Barrett uses the term *topoi*—that people use to maintain their threatened selves.

Barrett begins by talking about how control can help maintain your sense of self. Then he discusses achievement, which can also help, so long as you avoid its extreme, which is perfectionism. The third resource, or *topos*, is opposition, which means "standing up for oneself." The fourth is attribution, or identifying responsibility. Anger, denial, withdrawal, and lying are the final four resources, or *topoi*. The last page of the reading encourages you to reflect on which resources you draw on in various situations.

I put this reading into this chapter in order to offer the opportunity to reflect on how the natural tendency to "protect your own ego" affects your interpersonal communicating. If Barrett and the scholars he cites are right, defensiveness is a normal and always-present human tendency. It can be helpful to think and talk about how this dynamic operates in our own communicating.

MAINTAINING THE SELF IN COMMUNICATION

Harold Barrett

LOOKING AFTER THE SELF

Interpersonal security is currently a common topic in the media. An example is a recent interview with Harvard political scientist Robert D. Putnam. Putnam believes that Americans have lost much of their willingness to trust. A generation ago, when asked if they trusted other people, two-thirds said yes; now two-thirds say no. Americans are untrusting because they don't know each other, Putnam says. Today they are less connected to each other—and less happy.[1]

One result of this lack of connection and trust is a greater dedication to self-protection in communicating with others. Given a condition of insecurity, the solution is predictable: purposeful effort to look after and justify the self. Insecurity and protectiveness have always been a part of human interaction; the issue of the moment is about their increase. . . .

Self-maintenance behavior arises from some sense of uncertainty with others, from a perception of danger to the self—whether negligible or great, obscure or obvious. Thus we have defense mechanisms, as they are called. Theorist Karl E. Scheibe holds that *defense* mechanisms are so named in psychoanalytic theory because "the ego is considered to be under a more or less constant state of siege."[2] And, I would add, the communicator's response to the siege is *constant*.

It's easy to find testimony to the pervasiveness of insecurity and consequent safeguarding. Psychoanalytic theorist Marshall Edelson holds that defensiveness is "a ubiquitous aspect of human action." (Indeed, *any* use of language is defensive, he believes.)[3] Just yesterday I heard down at my little post office, "Why is everyone so damned defensive these days?"

From *Maintaining the Self in Communication: Concept and Guidebook* by Harold Barrett 1998. Reprinted by permission of Alpha & Omega Book Publishers.

A FUNCTION OF COMMUNICATION

Gregory Rochlin . . . offers this truth on the self (and self-esteem): "Its defense may bring the highest honors and justify the lowest violence."[4] Defending and thus maintaining the self, an ordinary function of communication, has both good and bad dimensions. Moreover, no mode of conduct is more fascinating in the drama of human interaction, as is apparent in the life stories of communicators, including those whose deeds we celebrate: Washington and Lincoln, Churchill and Roosevelt, Joan of Arc and Susan B. Anthony, Martin Luther and Martin Luther King, Jr.—as well as in those whose deeds we deplore: Joseph Stalin, Richard III, Adolf Hitler, and Joseph McCarthy. All of these notable figures were self-defenders in their communicating. Sigmund Freud said that defenses of the self direct the daily functioning of humankind. That's true, for better or worse.

There's high adventure and peril in communication, a fact that all of us seem to feel. Using athletic talk about teams playing defense ("D"), we can say that in the risky interactive game called communication, we play "D" at every moment. Knowing our ways, advisers urge, "Don't explain, don't complain!" ("Don't be defensive!") That's appealing advice, yet asking us not to look after ourselves is like asking us to give up being human.

Every Communicator's Story

Plots of every communicator's story are built around self-maintenance. Why so? Because self-worth is always at issue in communication; it hurts to be disrespected, dismissed, or disregarded. This may explain why **our persistent and compelling need in communication is to give an account of ourselves.** Intense or minimal, our motivation will never cease; protective messages will continue, whether as simple explanations, subtle excuses, hostile retorts, or anxious retreats. Such is our uneasiness about personal status and safety—apparent now more than ever before. A generation ago, Dean C. Barnlund saw signs of increasing interpersonal vulnerability—if not danger—and noted that a common use of communication is to act on our own behalf: "Communication arises out of the need to reduce uncertainty, to act effectively, to defend or strengthen the ego."[5] Thus, in studying the act of communication, we must include the fundamental needs of self as sources of motivation.

Now, before expanding the discussion, I want to present some concepts in communication that will be basic from this point on.

A Rhetorical Perspective

In this exploration of ordinary human interaction, I am guided by a rhetorical perspective on communication: that we *choose* ways to be with others, always with *purpose*, always seeking to be *effective* with them. That's what it means to be rhetorical in communication. Whether succeeding or failing, our aim is to use self-sustaining methods that will help us be effective. Psychologist Guy E.

Swanson, in his scientific study of defenses, holds that defensive strategies of daily life, grounded in social interaction and interdependence, "are justifications tailored to social relations that are in danger and need of preservation." In other words, the goal is to adapt to others and maintain connections to them. In this, the choices are "likely to be determined by the nature of the social relationship concerned."[6] What's useful in maintaining one relationship may not be useful in another.

Characterized by strategic choice in the exchange of messages, the interactive function of communication is rhetorical. **To be rhetorical is to make choices for success.** Consequently, I will always use the word *communication* in a rhetorical sense, i.e., to refer to the symbolic interactions of people *exercising options* in saying things and pursuing their respective *purposes.* The rhetorical function is at the heart of communication, for participants put messages together to secure responses from each other . . .

In terms of rhetorical theory, those with whom we relate and communicate are our "audiences." Moreover, as audience-conscious communicators, we're never innocent in our efforts to get a response, for our intent is to "get something"; most fundamentally, it is to secure confirmation of the person we believe we are—or want to be. That's why mindfulness of *self*-status is foremost in communication—*always,* regardless of the occasion or apparent meaning of the message. **We can never be sure of ourselves, especially of the other's attitude toward us or of our capability to relate to that.** Possessed of a vulnerable self and being rhetorically aware, we involve ourselves inventively with relevant ideas and feelings, dealing with issues of the moment, seeking to be successful: we want to identify with audiences and be confirmed by them. . . .

The Rhetorical Imperative   Our strategies of interaction arise from a powerful rhetorical imperative: to affect audiences favorably about ourselves. Most of our self-sustaining measures work fairly well most of the time and with most audiences. Swanson found that defenses "enable us to go on acting in a coherent fashion," promising to "afford us whatever gratification seems possible. In that sense they are adequate—sometimes ingeniously so."[7] Stories of brilliant accomplishment can be traced to this very ingenuity: for example, the eloquence of Winston Churchill.[8] Yet, other stories tell of inadequate self-maintenance strategy: stories of personal failure, strained relations, and communicative disaster.

And remember our internal messages, those we send to ourselves. In an *intra*personal sense, excuses, denials, rationalizations, and other kinds of validating messages to ourselves about ourselves can help us to feel good with ourselves and to accept ourselves. Being comfortable with ourselves is basic to acting comfortably with others.

SHAME

For a psychological grounding on the nature of the social threat to the self, we can do no better than to consult Heinz Kohut, founder of the school of self psychology. Kohut's study of human behavior led to an important challenge to classical Freudian psychoanalytic thought. Departing from classical theory on the conflict of drives as fundamental to human behavior, Kohut centered instead on humankind's sense of self-defectiveness. In arguing his theory, he contrasted the family environment of Freud's time with that of subsequent generations, finding great differences in influences on child development. He contrasted the close household involvements and constant family stimulation of Freud's Victorian era with conditions of more recent decades. Families now have looser ties. There's much greater emotional distance among members, and one result is understimulation.

In Freudian theory, the *neurosis* is the common psychological complaint; it's tied to guilt and overstimulation from the persistent presence of family members, particularly parents. Guilt results from felt transgression, e.g., in violation of parental or social rule. But more recently, reflecting shame from felt neglect or deprivation, particularly parental, it is *narcissism* that is the common condition.

Shame results from a sense of felt defectiveness. In the absence of optimal parental or social constraint, the self is inadequately responded to, resulting in the narcissistic feelings of emptiness, unfulfillment, and deficiency. Thus, Kohut concluded, this is "the era of the endangered self."[9] The prime motivator of our time is shame. As we strive to protect ourselves against shame, our communicating is affected. . . .

To counter the same of personal deficit (felt inadequacy), humans invent modes of maintaining the self: some facilitative, others maladaptive. Of course, shame has always been with us, and the response to it is not a new behavioral act. But now the incidence is much higher, leading to a higher incidence of corrective activity to protect and justify ourselves. Of course guilt continues, but given increased narcissistic injury, e.g., from neglect, shame has become the master emotion. We live in an age of diminished parental presence and authority and in a general culture marked by increased social disregard. Consequently, we are provided with less feedback on connectedness and worth—or less constructive feedback. We are more on our own and more likely to question our adequacy, experience social endangerment, and respond self-protectively. The results—good and bad, hardly noticeable or blatant—appear in all daily communication: at home, on the job, at school—everywhere. . . .

ON CULTURE AND SOCIALIZATION

Consider the following premise and implications for communication: **Rewards of individualism increasingly come into conflict with rewards of community affiliation.** "I want to be *me,* but I need *you*" expresses this personal-interpersonal conflict of our time: Or "It's great to be a person apart from others, but I need things from them." Issues of the conflict can be set out in various subjective terms:

- being gloriously alone and independent versus being safely associated and interdependent

- magnifying personal differences versus acknowledging kinship with others
- keeping distance versus seeking intimacy
- suffering the pain of separation versus enjoying the compensations of communication

The communicator's dilemma is about wanting to rely on self-confirmation versus needing the confirmation of others. It's a question of in*tra*personal (individual) versus in*ter*personal (social) satisfaction. It's an old story but with numerous postmodern twists and significant connections to other conditions of this age.[10] The dilemma is basic to the study of maintaining the self in communication.

East and West

At the outset, let's recognize the fact of cultural diversity in communication patterns. For example, in the United States, there is variance from culture to culture in strategies of self-maintenance—and from family to family, gender to gender, and from region to region. Communicators and students of communication should be aware that differences exist, and should be attentive to specific instances, some of which may influence the character of a moment of communication.

Thus we take the workings of socialization into account when studying variations in communication methods. And though anthropologists occasionally point to an isolated culture in which constraints on infant behavior appear to be minimal, apparently all cultures impose a socialization process on their children, one that moderates expression of their natural and normal narcissism. Certain differences in self-perception observed among Western and Eastern cultures can be traced to variations in the tightness of socialization processes that are imposed, primarily during the first two years or so of life. In some cultures, the social framing of the self is keen, and narcissism is actively suppressed, i.e., expressions of self and self-fulfillment are discouraged. The most familiar examples are collectivistic cultures like those of Asia. In others, such as the traditionally individualistic cultures of North America, greater encouragement is given to development of a self and related behaviors.

We know that in East Asian cultures, shame is a product of ardent socialization and group association. But in North American cultures . . . individuals value independence, and they feel shame when they sense personal inadequacy. Thus they seek some kind of exoneration or justification when they perceive themselves to be in violation of their self-concept. Pride, respect, trust, specific kinds of prowess, and other personal mandates are among the major issues. East Asians feel shame when they violate group norms, when their behavior hurts the group.

But note the common property. While forces of socialization differ in intensity, people of every culture and background possess a self that is subject to threat and injury. And all are influenced by a concept of self. For instance, the pain that East Asians feel in bringing discredit to the group comes from knowing that they have violated their concept on group allegiance. Defending against that shame—maintaining or saving face—is necessary because self-worth and continuation of benefits of membership are in the balance. . . .

When interpersonally uncertain or threatened, people on all continents respond protectively. Thus **the great commandment is to maintain the self. . . .**

Of the Highest Order

Self-maintenance activity is more than mere habit; it pursues a major goal and is carried on with structures that have become integral to one's total being. Looking after the self has a place of the highest order in everyone's life.

. . . First of all, each of us has a self-concept: a demanding and assertive personal view of who we are and how we want to be seen and taken, of the kind of person we feel ourselves to be or the kind of person we think we *ought* to be. Specific reflections of this insistent self-concept appear in our attitudes, values and ideals, ways of doing, and positions on just about anything that is important to us.

Second, each of us needs to be treated as a worthy person and cared about— at least, to be taken seriously and respected. We need others to support and confirm us in who we are. In a word, self-esteem is a critical personal factor in communicating; it has to do with how you pay attention to my *self* needs and I to yours. **Climates of mutual support—and nonsupport—are created by the two of us together, as we bring our needy and sensitive selves to each other.**

. . . Effort to uphold and justify the self arises from threat to individual well-being—and it appears most obviously in *interpersonal* communication, as we put ourselves in association with others. And the fear of being hurt, offended, disqualified, or diminished in some way can be very strong. . . .

The All-Powerful Self-Concept

What do the incidents below suggest about the self-concept and the need to be regarded well? Note the variety of motivating circumstances and how the individuals met ordinary human challenges. The circumstances are in italics.

Offended and wanting revenge, he vowed, "I'm gonna tell everyone what I know about her!"

Pleased with acknowledgment and praise, he modestly admitted, "Well, yes, I was the one who assisted him with CPR."

Unwilling to accept an almost unbearable feeling of defeat, she proclaimed, "I feel great! No problem! None whatever!"

Stinging from a felt attack on her religion, she never said another word during the entire evening.

Jolted by a sudden and loud command to leave the room, she cringed and murmured submissively, "Yes, ma'am."

Consumed with jealousy, he held her shoulders tightly and demanded, "Where in hell were you when I called seventeen times last night?"

Add to these instances all those messages communicated by persons who feel *slighted, put down, praised only faintly, unfairly compared, ridiculed,* or *passed over.* There's pain in *feeling unwanted and rejected, "out of one's element," unappreciated and misunderstood, incompetent*—and *believing oneself to be an imposter, a victim, weak link, traitor to the cause, ugly duckling,* or *an outsider.*

What about You?

Then there's you. Are you ever defensive or anxious to prove your worth? Say "Yes," because I know you are. Like the rest of us, you have a vulnerable self. It's disturbing to you to feel neglected or perceived as less than you think you ought to be. You have pride but also occasional feelings of inadequacy; you need recognition and approval. Feeling insecure at times about your place in life or your status at home, work, or school, you try harder—you're anxious to do better, to feel good about yourself or show that you're somebody. Much of such effort to achieve is beneficial, but it doesn't always come off smoothly. Sometimes there's distracting anger and hostility, criticism of self and others, backing off, and hiding out.

Try This   Recall a recent intense urge to protect yourself: when you felt that "call to action," to justify your background, explain your sexual orientation, stand behind your family, or vindicate your profession or political party or favorite music group. Or think back to how you felt down deep when you sensed that someone was trying to

- manipulate you or boss you around. What was your response to this felt abuse?
- lord it over you, acting in a superior manner. How did you handle that interpersonal wrong?
- impose on you a rigid and unacceptable point of view. What did you do about that?
- be noncommittal with you, remaining adamantly silent and evasive. How did you meet that?

On such occasions, how did you react? With a self-maintenance strategy? Quite likely. If so, what form did it take?

HOW PREVALENT IS THIS BEHAVIOR?

Self-maintenance strategies in communication appear in all relationships and interpersonal events: in friendships, romantic relationships, family systems, professional situations, church organizations, political entities, all school groups, and so forth. . . .

Who can begin to calculate the vast amount of communicative energy spent in ordinary self-maintenance by one ordinary person in one ordinary day? That's a good question, for it suggests a fact: **A degree of uncertainty about**

one's social safety or status operates in every message sent: in every conversation, public speech, interview, and discussion. And it's a part of every display of "attitude," as we call some kinds of scornful behavior or insolence.

Human uncertainty is one of the staple elements of television situation
comedies. It's prominent in the lives of characters in novels, stage plays, movies,
and comic strips. One of the most lovable insecure comic strip people is Cathy;
her self-maintenance strategies are quite true to life. Without conditions of self-
doubt and unpredictability on personal status, communication in the Doones-
bury and Dilbert strips would be literally unreal. The conditions of characters
would be false and the stories unappealing. Can you identify any important
character in any well-written piece of fiction who is fully secure? I can't. The
characters of *good* fiction are *real* in their self-maintenance activity.

Now, when talking about proving the self, justifying, and so forth, we must
acknowledge (and be grateful for) the good results that often occur. Worthy accomplishment, professional success, and good works all have beginnings related to self-maintenance needs, in that all are associated with requirements of
security and support—and of choices made to meet those requirements. Thus
there are two possible consequences: Our self-protective ways *do* find positive
and useful expression, but sometimes they function negatively against our best
interests: for example, when they take the shape of neglectfulness or some kind
of abuse. It follows that communicative interaction, energized with goals of
self-maintenance, ranges from stimulating and constructive dialogue and rewarding interpersonal communication to personal attack and counter-attack.
Whether obvious or indistinct, strategies of self-care are ever present in
communication. . . .

SELF-MAINTENANCE IN
COMMUNICATION: EIGHT *TOPOI*

Is there a useful way to categorize self-maintenance resources available for communication? Classically, we have the psychological nomenclature called "defense mechanisms." Remember those? They have names like rationalization, repression, regression, projection, introjection, sublimation, and so forth.

But rather than adopt a list of mental "mechanisms" and end up with nothing but an outline of abstractions, we must find categories that will reflect a
sense of the behavioral dynamics of communicative *interaction.* Any practical
study of self-maintenance strategies will take account of the potent energy involved, while emphasizing the interactive give-and-take and ever-present fact
of personal purpose. Consequently, we need action terms to depict what goes
on, to give meaning to the justifying, qualifying, rationalizing, asserting, confronting, bragging, avoiding, excusing, soft-pedaling, soothing, supporting, and
so forth of ordinary communicating. To this end, I have identified eight strategic groupings. They are expressed as common purposes: to control, achieve, oppose, attribute, express anger, deny, withdraw, and prevaricate.[11] Each of the
eight *topoi* is a package, a collection of related options. Incidentally, *topoi* is a

Greek word for topics. Aristotle used it. I like the word because it conveys the idea of *purposeful action* and connotes *strategic choice in interaction* and *variety of choice and opportunity in interaction.* . . . . As you look over the eight categories, note those that seem to have appeared in your recent communications with others. You hear and see them every day.

1. Control

Needs of security and certainty move communicators to regulate events, to find strategies for making things happen favorably. The need to control may be compelling or casual, and specific behaviors are numerous. Aims relate to ordinary communicative effectiveness, e.g., in being ready to handle unwelcome surprises or shocks as they might arise. But the goal may extend beyond seeking ordinary communicative control and effectiveness. For example, contrast the simple act of a person's choosing appropriate telephone language in placing a catalog order (necessarily exercising some control) to the extreme of a parent's determination to regulate an adult child's social activities. Likewise, at work, one employee may be rather easygoing, getting the routine communicative jobs done without excessive exertion (though there's always *some* management of events in communication), while another person will act to gain complete personal dominance of all functions related to on-the-job interactions. The latter mode might be considered "more defensive" than the former. Yet another example is the individualistic, iron-handed executive who seems unable to delegate authority to others or make use of cooperative problem-solving methods.

2. Achievement

Achievement needs frequently lie behind acts like self-justification. Related strategies often operate at a sensible and relaxed level: for example, that of doing a job adequately and feeling good about it. But contrast that with a level of functioning that is tremendously intense—when the communicator is determined to be absolutely right or brilliant or unchallengeable—anxious to stand out over others. Behavior of this extreme type is commonly called "perfectionism."

An example of the extreme is the vice president whose quarterly reports consistently and unnecessarily double the length of other vps' reports. This person's fervent drive to achieve—and get credit for it—requires great expenditure of time and energy.

3. Opposition

Protection of the self is a purpose of messages using the *topos* of *Opposition.* In this instance, a communicator assumes a contrary stance in communication with others, e.g., in "standing up for oneself." It may be expressed in some cases as disagreement or disapproval and in other cases as abject repugnance or contempt. *Opposition,* whether taken as ordinary dissent, rebuttal, stubbornness, resistance, challenge, nonconformity, derision, obstinacy, negativity, or scorn—

whether seen as spirited support of one's position or as fierce denunciation or counteraction—is prevalent in all quarters of daily life.

4. Attribution

Attribution is common in communication to maintain the self. Communicators frequently face "How did this happen?" issues and matters of cause, responsibility, fault, or blame. In "getting to the bottom of things," one may name someone responsible—or oneself. Whether the communicator's spirit is constructive or malicious, the motivation is often one of self-protection, from a need to ascribe blame or accountability, and so forth. In this way the communicator attempts to maintain personal equilibrium and satisfactory communication.

Examples include the employee who realizes his computation error and consequently accepts responsibility; an older brother who blames his little sister when he trips on the stairs; the baseball batter whose habit is to scowl at the umpire when he takes a called third strike; the well-intentioned soul who needs to know whom to *absolve*, and the person who is motivated to solve "Who dunnit?" puzzles of relationships, whether concerned with a minor disagreement or a serious interpersonal conflict. . . .

5. Anger

If or when one is inclined toward sustaining the self through *Anger,* one will express strong displeasure or perhaps resort to violent verbal attacks. Like all *topoi, Anger* may be either beneficial or harmful. Others may view the behavior as useful passion, righteous indignation, bad temper, sullenness, belligerence, wrath, resentment, or great furor.

One example is two drivers' heated exchange after racing to occupy that empty space in the parking lot. What's at the root of such expression? Fairness is an issue, as is self-worth. Thus do self-maintenance needs of these communicators enter in: They feel a need to stand up for themselves and protect their "rights." That's one reason why some businesses install a "Take-a-Number" system to facilitate fair turn-taking at the counter. Customers who become preoccupied with protecting themselves may be less likely to return than customers who feel secure.

6. Denial

When choosing *Denial* as a method of self-care, one seeks to dodge an unpleasant or threatening reality, whether with a customary strategy or a spur-of-the-moment choice. Such communication involves inventing a method to protect against facing the "truth" or the "facts." In refusing to perceive something that's psychologically menacing, the communicator attempts to insulate the self from it by negating reality.

For example, a person may deny the fact of someone's death and thus provide cushioning against loss. Another example is the middle-aged woman who prefers teenage-style clothes, thereby revealing both her self-perception and her protective regression. Then there's the father who, unwilling to accept his son's rather ordinary athletic ability, criticizes the coach for not nominating his boy to the all-star team.

7. Withdrawal

If maintaining the self through *Withdrawal,* one will shun a certain event or individual, retreat from a threatening scene, maintain silence and mental distance, assume a passive posture, repress thoughts or feelings, resist disclosure of feelings, or in any number of other ways protect against the dangers and discomforts of social participation or judgment.

8. Prevarication

Prevarication is self-protection involving falsehood, excuse-making, justification of personal beliefs or actions, inhibition, deceptive statement, evasion, and so forth. As with all *topoi,* the strategic aim is to uphold the self: the self-concept, self-esteem, or sense of worth. Other modes of *Prevarication* are equivocation, euphemizing, use of passive voice, and "waffling."

An example of *Prevarication* is the socially useful "white lie." Another is shown in the case of the project coordinator who when asked for a progress report responded evasively, "Everybody's working real hard on this one, Chief— yes sir. I'll have more to tell you at mid-week." In this case, what needs of the self is the communicator seeking to care for?

Selecting Useful *Topoi*

In the process of communication, one isn't restricted to drawing from only one of the eight *topoi.*[12] Some of us find ourselves using them all at various times. Also interesting is the view that choice of *topos* may depend on personality type. For instance, extroverts may favor expressions of *Anger,* while introverts may favor *Withdrawal.*[13] But our social consciousness dictates that our choice of *topos* will be influenced by our perception of the situation and conditions. Audience characteristics are particularly significant in communication. That is, we fashion our messages in accord with the likely reactions of others. Why? Because we humans are *rhetorical* creatures: practical, purposeful, and adaptable. That's a point not to be forgotten by communicators! . . .

Try This   From the twenty-five OCCASIONS FOR SELF-MAINTENANCE COMMUNICATION listed below, select one that relates to an experience you've had. Recall the occasion, and do the following:

1. Tell how in an insecure moment you came to perceive an exigence (some condition that required a response).
2. From which of the eight *topoi* did you draw for a strategic response? Was it one of the eight that I have discussed above? If not, what's your name for it?

3. Briefly stated, what message did you want to send? To whom did you send the message? What kinds of inward—intrapersonal—messages were a part of the process? Distinguish between verbal and nonverbal elements of the message. What result and feedback (response) did you want?

Occasions for Self-Maintenance Communication

When you . . .

- respond to the charge of damaging another's property
- are embarrassed after making a social error
- try to handle the boss's dissatisfaction with a job you've done
- seek satisfaction after an acquaintance spreads a false story
- feel hurt in not being invited to the party
- sense public criticism of your behavior
- take a comment as threatening to your self-image
- feel shunned by a friend
- feel slighted in a group activity
- don't want to face the facts or your true feelings
- hear a comment that seems to be critical of your race, religion, sex, family, or school
- are jolted by a loud command of a coach, parent, or other
- feel down deep that you do not believe yourself to be qualified, e.g., to be in college or a given profession ("I'm just an imposter.")
- feel apprehensive about a surprising change in company policy or a relationship
- have a feeling of not belonging in a certain group
- are jealous
- are unsure of your personal status with someone or some group
- feel socially awkward in a specific situation
- fear speaking up in class
- are denied an expected honor or reward
- sense diminishment of your reputation in the family or other group
- feel wronged by a boyfriend or girlfriend
- feel that you deserve better treatment from someone on whom you depend for confirmation
- feel incompetent as a writer, athlete, cook, mother, etc.
- feel lacking in good looks

REVIEW QUESTIONS

1. According to Barrett, what is a defense mechanism?
2. Barrett says he is "guided by a rhetorical perspective on communication." What does this mean?
3. Define *shame* as Barrett discusses it.
4. Explain the individual versus social cultural tension that Barrett describes.

5. What's the difference between an individualistic and a collectivistic culture?
6. What's narcissism?
7. What's the difference between the first two *topoi,* control and achievement?

PROBES

1. I can imagine people agreeing with Barrett about the significance of defensiveness and appreciating the increased self-awareness that comes from reading this selection. And I can also imagine some people rejecting Barrett's analysis as too obscurely Freudian, negative and pessimistic, and ultimately not very productive. If we imagine a sliding scale between these two positions, where on the scale would you put your response to this reading?
2. Barrett argues that every single time we communicate we are partly engaged in defending our selves. Do you agree or disagree? Explain.
3. Which type of culture that Barrett discusses do you identify with—individualistic or collectivistic? How does this affect your communicating?
4. "Are you ever defensive or anxious to prove your worth?" Barrett asks. "Say 'Yes,' because I know you are. Like the rest of us, you have a vulnerable self." How do you respond to that part of the reading?
5. Compare and contrast Barrett's discussion of attribution and my discussion of fault and blame in Chapter 2.
6. What did you learn from the list of "occasions for self-maintenance communication" at the end of this selection?

NOTES

1. "Social Insecurity," *America West Airlines Magazine,* April 1996: 74, 76–77, 79–80.
2. "Historical Perspectives on the Presented Self," *The Self and Social Life,* ed. Barry R. Schlenker (New York: McGraw-Hill, 1985) 33–64.
3. "Two Questions about Psychoanalysis and Poetry," *The Literary Freud: Mechanisms of Defense and the Poetic Will,* ed. Joseph H. Smith (New Haven: Yale UP, 1980) 113–18. To demonstrate the ubiquity or prevalence of the defensiveness that Edelson notes, I can't resist quoting a line from a recent film version of *Shadowlands* (a story about the relationship of C. S. Lewis and Joy Davidman): "People read to know they're not alone." The quotation suggests that to be alone is to be unprotected, an unacceptable condition, and to read is to guard against that.
4. *Man's Aggression: The Defense of the Self* (Boston: Gambit, 1973) 216.
5. "Toward a Meaning-Centered Philosophy of Communication," *Journal of Communication* 12 (1962): 197–211.
6. *Ego Defenses and the Legitimation of Behavior* (Cambridge: Cambridge UP, 1988) 2.
7. *Ego Defenses,* 24.

8. See Heinz Kohut, *The Analysis of the Self* (London: Hogarth Press, 1971) 108–9 and Kohut, *Self Psychology and the Humanities: Reflections on a New Psychoanalytic Approach*, ed. Charles B. Strozier (New York: Norton, 1985) 12–13, 110, 198–99.

9. *The Restoration of the Self* (New York: International Universities Press, 1977) 290. For an important comment on Kohut's belief on shame as the central affect in narcissism, see Andrew P. Morrison, "Shame and the Psychology of the Self," *Kohut's Legacy: Contributions to Self Psychology,* ed. Paul E. Stepansky and Arnold Goldberg (Hillsdale: The Analytic Press, 1984).

10. In this regard, I recommend David Zarefsky's thoughtful (and rhetorical) exploration of the problem relating to the current conflict in the United States on diversity and community interests: *The Roots of American Community* (Boston: Allyn and Bacon, 1996).

11. Besides relying on my catalogue of extensive observations of human interaction and responses of focus groups, I have found two books particularly useful as sources for developing the eight *topoi:* Merle A. Fossum and Marilyn J. Mason, *Facing Shame: Families in Recovery* (New York: Norton, 1986) and Gershen Kaufman, *Shame: The Power of Caring,* 2nd ed. rev. (Cambridge, MA: Schenkman, 1985).

12. On the topic of choice in selecting maintenance strategies, defenses in particular, turn to George Vaillant, *The Wisdom of the Ego* (Cambridge: Harvard UP, 1993).

13. See Gershen Kaufman, *Shame,* 71.

*J*ohn Welwood is a therapist and counselor whose writing and workshops focus on how to build intimate relationships. You'll find another reading by Welwood in the "Intimate Partners" chapter of *Bridges Not Walls* (Ch. 12). But I include some of Welwood's ideas in this chapter, because he believes that "we can know another, and be known, only as deeply as we know ourselves—and coming to know ourselves can be a long and arduous journey."

Welwood acknowledges that there is some value to books and articles that help people build relationships by developing strategies and techniques—how to have better sex, stop being codependent, handle gender differences, and so on. But he believes that these "fix-it" materials also can foster a mind-set in which people imagine that the answers to relationship problems can be found in some formula or procedure other than "in our own deepest resources." This reading directs your attention toward those resources as it guides your self-exploration of what Welwood calls "the genuine, powerful male and female" that is part of each of us.

He proposes that this exploration can move through three main stages, but because of space limitations, only the first two are covered in this excerpt. Stage one is to "wake up from" whatever stereotyped sex roles we are unreflectively acting out. The second stage is to discover how both sexes have access to both the masculine and the feminine, and to balance and blend these in ourselves. In the third step, men celebrate what is genuinely male in themselves, and women celebrate their own "genuine, powerful femaleness."

There are plenty of materials currently available that challenge older gender stereotypes, so the first stage mainly involves paying attention to them and relating them to our own lives. This can obviously be threatening for anyone who has been comfortably living one of the stereotypes that defines men as strong and protective and women as soft and compliant. But, says Welwood, "feeling the pain of these dead ends can provoke us to explore our masculinity or femininity in a deeper, more conscious way."

Stage two involves exploring and cultivating the qualities in ourselves that have previously been thought of as the property of the other gender. The Chinese view of yin and yang can help build a view of gender differences as *complementary* rather than oppositional. Welwood emphasizes that yin and yang do not label dichotomous, totally distinct qualities, but that they can be understood to highlight useful gender distinctions. He identifies several pitfalls that it's important to avoid in this reflecting. And he explains how, when you open to this mixture or balance in your own life, your awareness of yourself can become much richer and your interpersonal relationships can move in the same direction.

IN SEARCH OF THE GENUINE, POWERFUL MALE AND FEMALE

John Welwood

If we were men, if we were women, our individualities
would be lone and a bit mysterious, like tarns, and fed with
power, male power, female power, from underneath,
invisibly. And from us the streams of desire would flow out
in the eternal glimmering adventure. . . .
—D. H. Lawrence

For thousands of years the relations between men and women have been clouded and distorted by unrealistic fantasies. Projecting our hopes and fears, we have idealized each other as angels and saviors or maligned each other as monsters and demons. Rarely have we recognized each other as whole human beings.

Now, with all the traditional sex roles and stereotypes breaking down, even *our own* maleness or femaleness, which used to be taken for granted, has become a matter of uncertainty and doubt. Yet the current upheaval going on within men and women also provides a new opportunity—to uncover a more essential maleness or femaleness concealed beneath our old conventional roles. The present situation challenges us to dig deep and ask the most fundamental questions. How can we bring forth the authentic, powerful male or female energies from within us? How can we draw on these elemental energies to deepen our sense of who we are and what we have to give each other? How can men and women overcome the oppositional struggles that have plagued them for thousands of years and forge a new kind of creative alliance?

Since there are few sources of external guidance to draw on, we each have to undertake our own individual search to find out what it means to be an authentic, powerful man or woman. This search begins by digging down through conventional notions of manliness or womanliness and considering what is valid for ourselves as individuals. In doing this, we soon discover that masculine qualities do not belong to men alone, any more than feminine qualities belong only to women. Every individual has access to a whole range of masculine and feminine energies. As we cultivate this wider spectrum, our ways of expressing our manhood or womanhood become more flexible and dynamic, rather than stereotypical. This allows us to take a further step: discovering the essential male or female within.

So this search seems to have three main stages:*

1. Waking up from socially conditioned sex roles and stereotypes that we have unconsciously acted out.
2. Discovering that both sexes have access to both masculine and feminine energies, and blending and balancing these energies within ourselves.
3. For a man, celebrating the genuine, powerful maleness within him, and for a woman, celebrating her genuine, powerful femaleness. For both sexes, appreciating and living their differences consciously, and using them to help spark each other's growth.

STAGE ONE: RECOGNIZING UNCONSCIOUS SEX ROLES

Our identity as a male or female begins with imitation. From the earliest age, we seek a sexual identity, yet all we can do is imitate the models available to us—parents, older siblings, peers, or images in the media.

People in most cultures through the ages have related to their sexual identity in this unconscious, imitative way. Among traditional peoples, the tribe or social collective prescribed how men and women should interact. Since individuals did not have to question or even think about male/female roles in such cultures, the relations between the sexes were able to function smoothly and unconsciously.

---

*This excerpt describes the first two stages.

In our culture, the predominant stereotype portrays a strong, protective male and a soft, compliant female. Whether we regard these roles with nostalgia or with horror, they no longer seem to be viable models. Cut off from masculine strength, women often become passive, dependent types who desperately try to attach themselves to men. Cut off from their feminine sensitivity, men become brittle and overbearing, lacking in vision and depth. And couples who try to live out conventional stereotypes of domestic bliss often wind up sadly disillusioned. Nonetheless, feeling the pain of these dead ends can provoke us to explore our masculinity or femininity in a deeper, more conscious way.

STAGE TWO: DEVELOPING A BALANCE OF MASCULINE AND FEMININE WITHIN

To be individual is, literally, to be "undivided, whole." So to find an authentic individual style of being male or female, we need access to the whole spectrum of masculine and feminine energies moving in us, beneath any stereotypes of manliness or womanliness.

This means exploring and cultivating certain qualities previously considered the province of the other sex. When a woman, for instance, decides to face life as an individual, rather than as a man's appendage, she naturally begins to develop qualities once considered masculine—such as autonomy, independence, or assertiveness. When a man feels stifled by the conventional codes of manliness, he naturally becomes more curious about his gentle, intuitive, receptive side. Although it may seem risky to try out these new qualities, the potential reward is a more balanced expression of masculine and feminine energies within us.

Cultivating this wider spectrum of energies also expands our vision. We begin to see how masculine and feminine are part of a larger interplay of polar forces at work in everything, down to the very spin of the subatomic particles. The ancient Chinese view of yin and yang is particularly useful in revealing how these two energies interact in all phenomena. By helping us see how there are two sides to *everything,* it can change our view of masculine and feminine from *oppositional* to *complementary.*

Yin is the energy of centripetal force, associated with inwardness, gathering together, cohesion, and relatedness. It is associated with the elements earth—the abundant ground that connects and sustains us as human beings—and water—the fluid, graceful mother of life. Like the generous, accommodating earth, yin nurtures the ripening of individual beings. Whether we are male or female, we can find sustenance in this power of connectedness. Its mature expression is earth wisdom or "old yin"—a seasoned knowledge that comes from working with things from the ground up. When we are in touch with this quality, we are not afraid to be ourselves. We can take our seat on this earth without apology or pretense, drawing on a power that comes to us from the depths. If we ignore this deep earth-body-wisdom and live mainly in our busy minds, we tend to shrivel up.

Yang is the principle of centrifugal force, separation, and individuation. Like a rocket exerting tremendous force to break away from earth's gravity, yang is the power that propels our development as individuals. It is associated with the expansive elements, air and fire. Yang is the energy of fertilizing, initiating, and executing. It is piercing, penetrating, and arousing, like thunder and lightning. And its mature expression is heaven wisdom: the ability to expand beyond narrow viewpoints and to see one's life in larger cosmic perspective. While yin governs coming together, yang governs moving apart. These two poles of human relationships are the basic principles governing all interactions in the universe.

Yin and yang are not confined to any single form of expression. We can see this in polytheistic religions, like those of ancient Greece or India, whose pantheons of gods and goddesses embody these energies in many different ways. For example, a scientist (Apollo) and a warrior (Mars) express yang in very different ways, just as a mother (Demeter) and a sensual lover (Venus) express yin differently. Polytheistic religions also portray yang qualities in women (Artemis, Athena) and yin qualities in men (Adonis, Pan). They recognize earthy male gods (Dionysus, Vulcan, the Celtic horned gods) as well as heavenly female goddesses (Ishtar, the Queen of Heaven, and the skydancer dakinis in the Tibetan tradition).

So we cannot strictly associate yin and earth with women or yang and heaven with men. In the area of emotional expressiveness, for instance, women are often more yang—initiating, provoking, penetrating—than men, who are often more passive, shy, or hidden with their feelings. As an ancient Chinese medical text states, "Both man and woman are products of two primary elements, hence both qualities are contained in each sex."

Nonetheless, men generally contain a larger proportion of yang, and are said to "belong to yang." Women generally contain a larger proportion of yin, and are said to "belong to yin." In other words, yang is "home base" for men, and yin is "home base" for women. Thus a man could be earthy and sensitive, but unless he is also in touch with yang energy—his fiery initiative or expansive vision—his masculinity will be incomplete. And a woman could be a strong leader or a brilliant thinker, but unless she is in touch with her earthy receptive qualities or her watery intuitive side, something will be missing from her femininity.

Thus it becomes clear that men and women cannot ripen fully into themselves unless they develop both yin and yang within them. A woman who is yielding and nurturing, but cannot act on her own or think for herself, is not yet fully developed. She may have "young yin"—and be girlish, attractive, and sweet. Yet developing her yang side can help her tap a deeper kind of female power. When she can stand up as an individual, she can also sink deeper roots into her earth-wisdom, developing "old yin" sagacity and prowess.

Similarly, the classic macho male who has to prove that he is a "real man" is still unripe. As long as he fears opening to his softer yin side, he will never grow up. He has "young yang"—he can be bold and aggressive—but he has not yet ripened into "old yang," the real power and wisdom of manhood. Young yang is green and raw, very full of itself, like a new shoot pushing up through the earth. Yet if this shoot is to grow into a tree that can bear fruit, it must go through a yin stage of opening and receiving—light from the sun and nutrients from the earth.

Now that women are turning their energies outward, it is not surprising that many men have started turning inward, seeking new sources of guidance through meditation, psychotherapy, or just plain soul-searching. When a man becomes more receptive, rather than trying to control or manipulate, he develops a larger vision of life, which is the hallmark of old yang wisdom. A man becomes truly wise only when he has integrated his yin side.

Yet because oppositional mind runs so deep, we may find that in overthrowing the hold one side has over us, we become dominated by the other side instead. Thus, in cultivating gentleness and receptivity, and in reacting against old macho stereotypes, many modern men have turned against their male power altogether. As their newfound yin sensitivity takes them over, they are unable to take forceful stands or express strong convictions. Robert Bly has described such men as "soft males," who are lacking in energy, "life-preserving, but not exactly life-giving." There are times when a man must be able to bend and yield, but at other times he must be able to take charge. If a man's sensitivity undermines his yang strength, and he cannot express firmness or leadership, this only creates a new set of problems in his life and in his relationships.

A similar danger exists in reverse for many modern women. A woman's newfound yang power may attack or eclipse her feminine softness, making her brittle, hard, and inflexible. Taking on the brash quality of young yang, she adopts the same negative bias toward the feminine that has oppressed women throughout history, and so loses touch with her native feminine powers. This has a disruptive influence on her intimate relationships. And she misses the larger purpose of cultivating her yang power—which is to overcome one-sidedness and become a fuller, richer human being.

Another potential hazard in cultivating both yin and yang within ourselves would be to conclude that men and women are not really different. Couples who water down their differences, overemphasizing how they are both "just people" or "pals," create a unisex blandness that lacks passion and vigor. Androgyny—the complementary expression of masculine and feminine within each individual—can be an important stage. However, when used as a way to avoid the sharp edge where male and female differences rub up against each other, it can lead to a dry sort of companionship that lacks creative spark and sacred depth.

Finding a graceful balance between masculine and feminine ways of being is never easy. Just as a dancer has to work hard to develop spontaneity and grace, so learning to dance in a balanced way with the full spectrum of our sexual energies takes practice. We have been out of balance for so long that we can expect to fall into extremes along the way. In this light, the rigid man, the passive woman, the soft male, and the hard female *all* have further to go. They all manifest incomplete stages in a larger development.

In the end, a relationship can become richer, more spontaneous, and more adventurous when neither partner has a monopoly on either pole of tenderness or toughness, receptivity or power. Then not only can the masculine energies in the man dance with the feminine energies in the woman, but the feminine in the man can play with the masculine in the woman as well. A man might exert an earth influence on a woman through his steadiness or support, and help settle her down. And a woman might bring in a heaven influence, arousing and stimulating her man by providing a larger perspective in certain areas. When the young yin and yang are strong in a woman and a man, their energy as lovers will remain vital; no matter what their age, she can be the playful heroine/ maiden, and he the gallant hero. Yet at other times she might express young yang—by being boisterous or pursuing him sexually—while he might express the softer sensitivities of young yin. Finally, the interaction of their old yin and old yang would allow them to be parents or wise friends who can offer each other counsel and support.

In opening to this wider range of interactions, the play of man and woman develops a much richer texture and counterpoint than just two-part harmony. Men and women today can no longer afford to yield their "other half" to each other.

REVIEW QUESTIONS

1. Welwood says that stage one involves the action of "waking up," and stage two involves the action of "discovering," and "celebrating." What does he mean by "celebrating"?
2. The bad side of stereotyped female identity is passivity and overdependence. What is the bad side of stereotyped male identity?
3. Which (yin or yang) is the energy of inwardness, cohesion, relatedness, and the earth? Which (yin or yang) is the principle of separation, individuation, and initiation?
4. What distinction does Welwood make between "young" and "old" yin and yang?
5. How can an "oppositional mind" create problems as one attempts to explore the nondominant side of him- or herself?
6. What's Welwood's opinion about unisex identities?

PROBES

1. Which of the three stages is most difficult for you? Which do you think is most productive?
2. Welwood says that we develop sexual identity mainly by imitating. How has this been true in your life?
3. Welwood argues that in some arenas, women are more often yang—initiating, provoking, and penetrating—while men are more often passive or shy. In which arenas? How do you respond to this idea? Do you agree or disagree with Welwood?
4. What experiences in your life most helped your dominant gender energies grow from "young" yin or yang to "old" yin or yang?
5. What is suggested to you by Welwood's "dancing" metaphor? How is the dynamic he's encouraging us to get involved in much like dancing?

CHAPTER 5

Awareness of Others

*T*his reading surveys how people perceive persons, relationships, and social events. In the past couple of decades, research on what's often called "social cognition" has exploded. Increasing numbers of communication scholars have been figuring out how interpersonal communication is affected by such things as cognitive scripts, episodes, prototypes, and self-monitoring. But the authors of this selection don't bore you with the details of all this research. Instead, Sarah Trenholm and Arthur Jensen translate key findings into understandable principles and tell you how they can be applied to your communication.

They summarize the information into four processes that people engage in before, during, and after communicating: (1) identifying the situation, (2) defining the other person, (3) defining yourself and your relationship with the other, and (4) figuring out why things unfold the way they do. This reading discusses each of the four.

First, they describe how we orient ourselves to the situations we're in by defining what kind of *episode* it is. Definitions vary from culture to culture, of course. Examples of Western middle-class episodes include the big family dinner, the parent-teacher conference, TV viewing, and such less enjoyable episodes as avoiding dad or mom when he or she is drunk, and apologizing to the neighbor whose property you've damaged. Communication within various episodes often follows a script. The major way we make overall sense of the situations we're in is to define the episode, figure out the script, and then identify the *consequences* of being in the middle of this episode and following this script.

Second, we size up the people we're around. Again, we use several strategies, including personal constructs, implicit personality theory, self-fulfilling prophecies, and cognitive complexity. Trenholm and Jensen explain each of these jargon terms and give examples of them, so you can see how they operate in your own communication life. For example, they point out how people tend to group certain personality traits together, so if we perceive someone as "friendly" and "quiet," we may also believe them to be "intelligent," even though we have no evidence of how smart they are. This is how we apply an overall implicit personality theory as we perceive others.

Third, we size up relationships. We begin with perceptions of ourselves (as were discussed in the readings in Chapter 4), and then we develop perceptions of who we are in relation to the person or people we're communicating with. In this section, Trenholm and Jensen explain briefly the identity-negotiation process that is described much more completely in Chapter 9. They talk about how we label relationships and manage our responses to fit the labels.

Finally, these authors discuss how we use communication to answer the questions "Why did I do what I did?" and "Why did she or he do that?" under the heading *attribution theories.* These theories explain how we attribute reasons or causes to the events we experience. They distinguish between attributing events to surrounding situations (external) versus attributing them to somebody's personality traits (internal). They also describe some of the biases that affect peoples' attributions.

By the end of this reading you should have a pretty good overview of how perception processes affect your interpersonal communicating.

INTERPRETIVE COMPETENCE:

How We Perceive Individuals, Relationships, and Social Events

Sarah Trenholm and Arthur Jensen

To interact with others successfully requires a wealth of social knowledge. You must be able to perceive the information in your social environment accurately enough to know which of the hundreds of schemata in your memory bank are the best ones to pull out of the vault. This is, of course, a very complicated operation. Cognitive psychologists are just beginning to understand how we do it. We have tried to simplify the problem by highlighting four perceptual processes that people engage in before, during, and after social interaction. These include identifying (1) what the situation is, (2) who the other person is, (3) who you are and what kind of relationship between self and other is implied, and (4) why things unfold the way they do. Let's examine each of these processes more closely.

SIZING UP SITUATIONS

The more we know about the particular situations in which we interact with others, the more likely we are to produce effective messages. We propose three useful ways to manage situations: (1) identifying episodes, (2) knowing scripts, and (3) perceiving potential consequences of following scripts.

Orienting Ourselves: Episode Identification

At one time or another, we have all been in situations where we didn't know what was going on or what to do. Visiting a foreign culture or being initiated into a sorority or fraternity are examples of situations that are not very well defined for us. Knowing the situation can make interactions much easier. In its simplest form a situation is "a place plus a definition."[1] When we enter a place, our first task is to orient ourselves or get our bearings. One way to do this is to ask the simple question "Where am I?" We find ourselves in a variety of places

Excerpted from *Interpersonal Communication, 3rd ed. by Sarah Trenholm & Arthur Jensen.* Reprinted by permission of Wadsworth Publishing Co.

every day: in the car, at home or work, in the shopping mall, at the zoo, church, or bus station, and so on. Where we are determines to a large extent what we can do socially. But identifying the place alone is not enough. For instance, a church building can serve as a place for worship, weddings, ice cream socials, even bingo. To communicate appropriately requires that we recognize the physical and social cues that define the episode or activity that is taking place. Each culture has an array of social episodes or activities for its members to follow. For the individual, **social episodes** are "internal cognitive representations about common, recurring interaction routines within a defined cultural milieu."[2] Some typical social episodes? Having a big family dinner, attending a parent-teacher conference, planning a party, gossiping. How do we know which episodes to enact? Often we have a particular episode in mind when we initiate a conversation with someone. Perhaps you know someone who likes to "pick fights" or tease a brother or sister in order to get him or her riled up. Often enacting an episode is a process of negotiation—one person suggests an activity, only to have the other counter with another option, as in this conversation:

LAURA: I noticed that Kmart is having a sale on lawn mowers.

BUD: This is the only evening I'm free all week. I don't want to spend it shopping for a lawn mower. Besides, the Battle of the Mack Trucks is going on at the fairgrounds tonight.

Social interaction is a continuous dance in which participants accept and decline each other's invitations to enact different episodes. For instance, when two old friends have a chance meeting on the street, the question "Can I buy you a drink?" is an invitation to engage in the episode of "talking over old times." Refusing the drink because you are not thirsty would be missing the point—it would reflect a failure to recognize the other's definition of the situation.

Using Scripts to Guide Interaction:
Open, Closed, and Defined Episodes

When people play out an episode, they may also follow a script. As we have seen, a script is a highly predictable sequence of events. Some classroom learning episodes are highly scripted; others are not. For example, you may be able to predict (from experience) that every Wednesday morning your history professor will call the roll, hand out a quiz, collect the quizzes, lecture for 20 minutes, and end the class with a humorous anecdote. The more predictable the sequence of events, the more scripted the interaction is. Another class may be taught so differently that you never know for sure what will happen in a given class period. Both examples are classroom episodes, but only the first one follows a clearly identifiable script.

Scripts and episodes are useful guides to interaction. Identifying the episode narrows the range of possible actions and reactions. Knowing the script makes social life even more predictable. Michael Brenner has proposed that the vast majority of social episodes fall into one of three types: closed, open, and defined.[3]

Closed Episodes   When a situation is almost completely scripted, it is a **closed episode.** Rules for proper behavior are well known in advance and govern the flow of interaction. Rituals such as greetings and religious observances are closed episodes. Many business organizations tightly script interactions by training their personnel to follow carefully devised sets of procedures. If you've ever applied for a loan at a bank, you have probably participated in a closed episode. You have a standard set of questions you want answered (the loan rate, fixed or variable, length of repayment, and so on) and so does the loan officer (income, collateral, address, credit references, and so on). Other, less formal, interactions are also somewhat scripted. An episode of "small talk" has a limited range of topics, although the sequence in which these topics are discussed may vary.

Open Episodes   When participants enter a situation without any preconceived plan or with a very general one, they are involved in an **open episode.** In such situations there is greater freedom to create new forms of interaction and to change episodes midway through. Episodes such as "hanging out with friends" are sometimes scripted, but not always. When almost anything can be introduced as a topic of conversation or an activity to perform, the episode is an open one. An orchestra performing a John Philip Sousa march is clearly following a musical script, but a group of musicians having a "jam session" is not. The freedom to improvise or break the rules is typical of an open episode. Some open episodes may be unsettling, since there is no clear idea of what should be done next. Perhaps you have been in situations where nobody seemed to know what to do. We know of an instructor whose routine on the first day of class was to walk into the room, assume the lotus position on top of his desk, and say nothing for the first half of the class. His point was to show how communication is used to define ambiguous situations. Eventually, students would begin talking to one another, trying to figure out what he was doing. From the students' point of view, this was an open episode.

Defined Episodes   While closed episodes are known to be such in advance as a result of expectations, many situations are defined "in progress" as participants follow their own personal goals and plans to achieve a working consensus. Even so, the consensus is often temporary—definitions of the situation may fall apart as quickly as they develop. A **defined episode** is an open episode in which the participants are trying to negotiate some closure. The difference is that open episodes are experienced as creative and liberating; defined episodes are competitive attempts to control the activity. Brenner suggests that defined episodes are often ambiguous and unstructured interactions because each partner may be proposing alternative directions for the episode. For example, a not-very-good salesperson might initiate a "sales episode" but eventually succumb to a clever-but-unwilling-to-buy customer's definition of the situation as "shooting the breeze." A romantic evening can be spoiled quickly when a candlelight dinner becomes redefined as an episode of "stilted conversation" or "talking about the kids." In closed relationships people may spend a lot of time just deciding what episode to enact next. We know of four friends who, in the course of one evening, proposed over 20 different activities for that evening. Needless to say, they ended up doing nothing but talking about what they could be doing. Chances are none of the persons involved planned to spend the evening that way, but our observations lead us to believe that these two couples frequently end up playing this "what do you want to do tonight" episode.

Although we may think that closed episodes are too limiting and value open ones for the freedom they provide, stop and think how chaotic social life would be without any well-defined or scripted episodes. The important thing, of course, is that we recognize the types of episodes others propose so that we can accept the invitation or decline gracefully.

Identifying Consequences of Episodes and Scripts

Sometimes it is just as important to perceive the possible outcomes of a situation, like the chess player who sees several moves ahead, as it is to properly label that situation. We can avoid detrimental outcomes if we can see them coming. Salespeople often use the tried-and-true "yes technique" to set up unwitting customers. They ask questions that seem unrelated to selling their product, such as "Are those lovely photographs of *your* children?" or "I've had a hard time catching you at home. You must work awfully long hours." The customer's automatic "yes" in response to each question or comment establishes a habitual pattern that could cost a lot of money at the end of the episode.

Following a script can lead to positive or negative outcomes. Sometimes we know the script so well that we can tell our friends what they are going to say next. If we finish the sentence for them, they may be gratified that we understand them so well or offended that we cut them off. Another negative consequence is that scripted interactions can become boring or even damage a relationship if repeated too often. Researchers who study marital conflict patterns often comment that couples get caught up in "conflict scripts" that neither person intended to start but both felt compelled to see to the bitter end once the episode began. And as we have already seen, expecting the interaction to follow a script can prevent us from perceiving important messages the other may be sending our way. Following the script can also limit creativity, but only if we remain tied completely to the script. Minor alterations, improvisations, and other forms of playing with the script can add some spice to everyday interactions.

SIZING UP PEOPLE

As we interact, we come to an understanding of what other people are like. Knowing how to size up the individual is another way to reduce our uncertainty about communication. In studying the process of impression formation, researchers have discovered several factors that influence our judgment. We will discuss four of these factors: (1) the use of personal constructs, (2) implicit personality theory, (3) self-fulfilling prophecies, and (4) cognitive complexity.

The Use of Personal Constructs to Judge Others

. . . Personal constructs [are] mental yardsticks for evaluating objects, events, and people. . . . Since constructs are "personal," no two people will use them in exactly the same way. You and I may both observe Bill eating a sandwich in two bites, mustard dribbling down his chin. You may think he is "aggressive" while I argue that he is "messy" and "impolite." What we see in others is a combination of their actual behavior and our personal construct of their behavior. These constructs say as much about you and me as they do about Bill.

Even though we each use different constructs to judge others, we do use them in similar ways. Steven Duck has noted a typical pattern in the use of four different kinds of constructs.[4] The four types are:

- Physical constructs (tall-short, beautiful-ugly)
- Role constructs (buyer-seller, teacher-student)
- Interaction constructs (friendly-hostile, polite-rude)
- Psychological constructs (motivated-lazy, kind-cruel)

Our initial impressions are frequently based on physical attributes—we take stock of how people are dressed or how attractive they are. These are quickly followed by the formation of role constructs as we try to make sense out of each other's position in the social world. As we talk, we may focus attention on interaction constructs, or aspects of the other's style of communication. Finally, we use these observations to infer what makes the other tick (psychological constructs)—we begin to guess at motivations and build a personality for the other. When we reach this last stage, we have gone beyond simply interpreting what we see and hear; we've begun to assume that we know things about the person that we can't see.

Implicit Personality Theory: Organizing Trait Impressions

We don't simply form isolated opinions of other people; rather, we organize all of our individual perceptions into a more complete picture by filling in a lot of missing information. One of the ways we do this is through what is referred to as an **implicit personality theory.** This is the belief on our part that certain individual traits are related to other traits. If we observe a trait that we think is part of a cluster, we will assume that the person also has the rest of the traits in the cluster. Each of us has our own notions of what traits go together. For some, the traits (or constructs) "intelligent," "quiet," and "friendly" may cluster together.[5] If we observe behavior that we interpret as friendly and quiet, we may then attribute intelligence to that person without any firsthand evidence. . . .

Interpersonal Self-Fulfilling Prophecies

Another important perceptual tendency is the **self-fulfilling prophecy.** Unlike the more passive implicit personality theory (in which traits are associated in the mind), the self-fulfilling prophecy involves both perception *and* behavior. It starts when one person—the observer—believing something to be true about another person—the target—begins acting toward the target as if the belief were fact. This action prompts the target to behave in line with the observer's expectations. If you believe your friend is "touchy," you are likely to avoid sensitive topics and be more hesitant in what you say. The effect of your behavior? Your friend becomes oversensitive because *you* are acting oversolicitous. Unaware that you helped create the prickly atmosphere, you say to yourself, "My God, it's true. You can't say anything to him."

Cognitive Complexity: Factors Affecting Impression Formation

Not everyone forms impressions in the same way. Observers differ in the number and quality of personal constructs they use to evaluate others. A **cognitively complex** person's system is greater in number of personal constructs (*differentiation*), includes more abstract psychological categories (*abstraction*), and has more elaborate ways of relating various constructs (*integration*).[6] A cognitively simple person has fewer, less abstract constructs about people and views those constructs as relatively isolated impressions. Let's look at an example comparing the two extremes.

Suppose Pat and Chris observe Marvin on several occasions. They are both present when Marvin (1) cheats on an English test, (2) takes charge and gets everyone out of a burning building, (3) refuses to help with a charity car wash, (4) helps a friend study for a difficult math test, (5) embarrasses another friend by pointing out her faults in front of a large group of people, and (6) always gives blood when there is an opportunity.

If you want to test yourself, you might write down your own impression of Marvin before reading on. Then come back and read the impressions that Chris and Pat formed.

To Pat, Marvin is "tall and handsome, but extremely selfish, difficult to get along with, and not trustworthy." When reminded of some of the positive things Marvin has done, Pat shrugs and says, "It's just a front. The real Marvin is a cheat."

To Chris, "Marvin seems selfish when he is unsure of himself, but quite selfless when he knows he can help out. Marvin is also very outspoken and direct—he says what is on his mind. If he believes in a cause, he'll support it. If he doesn't think it's important he won't give it the time of day." Chris sums up Marvin's behavior as being motivated by his insecurity: "If he didn't worry so much about being noticed, he wouldn't make himself look so bad. He has real potential."

Why are these two impressions so different? Pat uses fewer, more concrete constructs (for example, "tall and handsome") and ignores much of the information that doesn't fit with the emerging impression. If this impression is typical of her reactions, Pat's construct system is a relatively undeveloped one. Contrast that with Chris, who demonstrates a fairly high level of cognitive complexity. By integrating the apparent contradictions in Marvin's behavior, Chris has arrived at a more subtle understanding of Marvin, recognizing situational constraints as well as psychological motivations.

Research has shown cognitively complex persons to be more accurate in processing information about others, better at placing themselves in the role of the other person, and more patient in weighing most of the evidence before formulating a complete impression.[7] Less complex individuals tend to either stick with their original impression and ignore contradictory information or to change the impression to fit the most recent information they have.[8] They lack the ability to integrate the constructs they use into a more complete image of others.

Considering the differences between more complex and less complex persons, you might get the impression that the more complex, the better. Actually, it depends on the situation and the other person. Imagine Pat and Chris talking to each other. They would probably drive each other crazy. Pat would claim that Chris thinks too much and analyzes everybody. Chris would charge Pat with making snap judgments. In general, complex persons are more versatile in social situations and better at cross-cultural adaptation. . . . But a cognitively complex person is not necessarily a "better" person. Like any of us, such a person can abuse his or her abilities by being unethical, insensitive, and so on.

SIZING UP RELATIONSHIPS

As we read the situation and form impressions of the other, we also face the perceptual task of determining what relevant aspects of self fit the situation and how the emerging relationship between self and other should be interpreted.

Self-Monitoring: Deciding Who to Be

. . . Just as we form impressions of others, we form and present images of ourselves to others. The awareness of images of self and the ability to adapt these images to the situation at hand has been referred to as **self-monitoring.**[9] A high self-monitor tends to read the social situation first and then present an appropriate face, as opposed to simply presenting a consistent image of self in every situation.

Mark Snyder characterizes the difference between a high and low self-monitor in the form of the question each might ask in defining the situation.

> The high self-monitor asks, "Who does this situation want me to be and how can I be that person?" In so doing, the high self-monitoring individual reads the character of the situation to identify the type of person called for by that type of situation, constructs a mental image or representation of a person who best exemplifies that type of person, and uses the prototypic person's self-presentation and expressive behavior as a set of guidelines for monitoring his or her own verbal and nonverbal actions. [The low self-monitor asks] "Who am I and how can I be me in this situation?"[10]

Instead of calling on a prototype to guide his or her actions, the low self-monitor behaves in accordance with an image of his or her "real" self.

To test yourself, make a short list of five or six very different social situations you frequently take part in. Write down how you typically behave in each situation, or better yet, have someone observe you in each of those situations and write down what you do. Then compare your actual behavior to Snyder's self-monitoring questions. Do you normally present a consistent self-image, or do you alter your self-presentation for each situation?

Our culture often sends us mixed messages. For instance, we are told to "be ourselves" and "remain true to self," messages that seem to endorse the low self-monitor's position. On the other hand, research demonstrates that being adaptable (being a high self-monitor) is one of the keys to social success. It is probably best to recognize that either extreme can be limiting. If we always try to maintain a consistent self-concept, we will be less versatile and probably less human because we won't experience the full range of human emotions and potentials. But if we are always changing to fit the situation or someone else's conception of us, we may compromise important standards and values. The best course is to ask ourselves which is more important in a given situation—being adaptable or being consistent. On one occasion it may be important for you to exert your individuality and violate the family rule that "everyone comes home for Christmas." The next year you might pass up a wonderful ski trip just to be home and fit in again.

Defining Relationships: Self in Relation to Others

When people interact, each presents an image of self to the other. These images are, however, usually quite fluid. We are responsive to the feedback of the other and begin quickly to negotiate a definition of the relationship between self and other. Thus, one important perceptual process is the identification of the type of relationship that applies in a given situation. Office workers at a company picnic may perceive that the superior-subordinate relationship with the boss no longer applies during a game of softball. As long as the boss sees things the same way, there is no problem. But what if the boss assumes he or she is still in charge and wants to pitch? The difference in perceptions may lead to negative feelings that were never intended.

A wide range of relationship labels are available to us. We can be casual or long-time acquaintances, friends, close friends, almost friends, just friends, coworkers, neighbors, bowling partners, platonic lovers, husbands and wives, ex-husbands and -wives, blood brothers or sisters, business associates, straight man and funnyman, roommates, counselor and advisee, master and slave, even student and teacher. The list could go on.

Once a relational label is firm in our mind, it tends to limit our perception of what we can do together. Most American couples who have just begun dating probably don't even think about drawing up and signing prenuptial agreements about finances, children, property, and so on. These actions are not perceived as having anything to do with "real" romantic relationships.

Several studies have demonstrated the existence of relational prototypes. In the same way that we have mental images of typical personalities, we also form cognitive models of the best example of a romantic relationship or a good friendship. Sally Planalp found that prototypes students held of the student-professor relationship seemed to be guided by their expectations about the respective rights and obligations that each party has in different situations. Planalp had students read three conversations between a professor and student: (1) a student asking to add the professor's class, (2) a student asking to make up an exam that had been missed, and (3) a student requesting a change of grade for the professor's class. Different students read different versions of the conversations, some in which the professor made dominant, neutral, or submissive statements and others in which the student's statements varied in terms of dominance or submissiveness. One week later, students were asked to identify whether the conversation they had read the week before contained the dominant, neutral, or submissive statements. As expected, students "remembered" (incorrectly) having read statements that were more in line with prototypical expectations than they were with the actual dialogues the students had read.[11]

Robert Carson has used the term **master contract** to refer to the worked-out definition of a relationship that guides the recurring interaction of any dyad.[12] This means that as relationships develop, perceptions that were originally guided by a prototype eventually give way to an understanding based on verbalized agreements or silent acceptance of established patterns of behavior. . . . It is important to recognize that identifying what type of relationship you're involved in may be just as crucial as knowing the situation or forming a useful impression of the other.

EXPLAINING BEHAVIOR: ATTRIBUTION THEORIES

When all is said and done, we are frequently left with the question "Why did he (or she) do that?" or "Why did I do that?" Most of the time we are quick to offer some type of explanation. If we think we understand what motivated our own or another's actions, we have reduced some uncertainty and made our world a little more predictable. Theories concerned with how the average person infers the cause(s) of social behavior have been called *attribution theories.* Before we examine some of these theories, let's look at a typical conversation and try to explain each person's behavior.

Imagine that you've been visiting your friends Angela and Howie for a few days. You are sitting at the kitchen table with Howie when Angela comes home from work. She looks very tired. The following conversation ensues:

HOWIE: *(looking up from the plastic model car kit he has been putting together)* Hi, honey. How was work?

ANGELA: *(after saying hello to you, she scans the room)* Howie! You haven't done the dishes yet? They're left over from last night. Can't you do anything you're asked to do?

HOWIE: It's been a busy morning. I just haven't had time.

ANGELA: No time! You don't have a job. You're not looking for work. And you can't find 15 minutes to do a dozen dishes?

HOWIE: I've been looking through the classifieds, for your information.

ANGELA: Did you send out any resumes?

HOWIE: No, not really . . .

ANGELA: Here we go again. Do I have to physically force you to sit down and write letters of application and send your resume out?

HOWIE: I'll do it. I'll do it.

ANGELA: You'll do what? The dishes or the resumes? . . .

How would you explain the communication behavior of your two friends? Is Angela the kind of person who constantly nags and belittles others? Or did Howie provoke this tirade? What other explanations could there be? . . .

Identifying Attributional Biases

If all the causes of behavior we attribute were clearly logical and made use of all the relevant information, our social lives would be much easier to manage. Unfortunately, we humans are notoriously irrational at times. A number of perceptual biases affect how we arrive at causal attributions. We rely on some of these biases when we have no prior knowledge of the persons being observed, and at other times the biases just override whatever knowledge we do have.

Personality Bias Toward Others   The most common bias is to explain other people's behavior in terms of their personality dispositions.[13] We are especially prone to this **personality bias** when we observe strangers. We just naturally assume that a stranger who throws a shoe at the television screen lacks self-control or is mentally unstable. The bias is even stronger if the person's behavior is contrary to our expectations.[14] Since we expect people in a restaurant to be eating or drinking, we probably think that only a buffoon would start singing in that setting. Rarely do we look for other explanations—such as the possibility that someone offered him $50 to do it or that the woman he was with accepted his proposal of marriage. Cognitively complex individuals may be less susceptible to this bias, perhaps because of their tendency to engage in role-taking. When we try to see a situation from the other person's point of view, we may see more situational or relational causes.

Situational Bias Toward Self   When we're asked to explain our own behavior, the story is somewhat different—we're more likely to rely on **situational bias.** If I throw a shoe at the television, I can explain that it was because of tension built up at the office, a stupid call by the referee, or the loose morals of television producers. There are several reasons why we tend to attribute our own behavior to situational factors. In the case of negative behavior, blaming it on the situation can serve as an excuse or justification for that behavior. Another reason is that we simply have more information about our own past and present experience than an observer would. We know if we've had a bad day; an observer probably doesn't. Finally, our visual vantage point makes a difference. When we behave, we don't see ourselves performing the action. What we do see is other people and external circumstances. It's much more likely that we will reference the situation as the cause of our behavior.

Bias Toward Groups   In addition to these two biases, perceived group membership also produces a bias. We explain the behavior of members of highly stereotyped *out-groups* (groups we do not belong to) differently than the behavior of *in-group* members (such as our own friends, associates, or ethnic group). In general, researchers have found that we attribute positive behavior by in-group members to their personal dispositions, while negative behavior is explained in terms of situational factors. We explain the behavior of out-group members in exactly the opposite manner. Positive behavior is explained away as situationally produced, while negative behavior is seen as the product of personality or group culture.[15] For example, suppose you are watching a close friend play in a tennis tournament when she screams at the referee for calling her shot out of bounds. You turn to the person next to you and say, "She's been under a lot of pressure lately. I think she just needed to blow off some steam." Moments later, her opponent (from an arch-rival institution) heatedly disputes another out-of-bounds call. "Why do they let people without manners play this game?" you think to yourself.

Why are we so prone to discriminate in favor of friends and against members of other social groups? We usually think of friends as being similar to us in many ways, but apparently perceive them to be even more similar when compared to an outsider. This in-group/out-group comparison seems to set in motion a role-taking process in which we identify closely with the in-group member and view things from his or her perspective. As a result, we often seek a situational account for the behavior. In contrast, we tend to view the out-group member with very little empathy or understanding. This makes it easier to assume the person would behave negatively regardless of the situation.

Bias Toward Cultures   Culture also plays a significant role in producing attributional bias. Our culture is a very individualistic one. As a result, we have a greater tendency to believe that the individual person is responsible for his or her behavior. In collectivist cultures such as Japan or India, situational attributions are more common.[16] A *collectivist culture* is one in which group goals have a higher priority than individual goals; loyalty to the group is usually expressed by behaving according to the rules in different situations. Thus, in collectivist cultures people are more aware of situational constraints and less aware of individual differences.

How can knowledge of these casual schemata and attributional biases help improve interpersonal communication? The first step is to realize that our past interactions with a person influence how we decide to communicate in the present. To a large extent, what we remember about past interactions is stored in the form of attributions. If you have a tendency to explain interactions in terms of single causes (such as personal or stimulus attributions), your communication may frequently take the form of complaining about or blaming the other. You may even do this without realizing it. It may be beneficial to sit down occasionally and evaluate how you've been explaining the events that have happened in your important relationships. . . .

CONCLUSION

This [reading] has provided you with a lot of information about the perceptual process and some of the cognitive schemata that people use to make sense of their social world. We have tried to simplify what you need to know by structuring this information around four cognitive processes that influence interpersonal communication: how we size up situations, people, and relationships and how we explain the causes of social interaction. . . . Understanding social cognition processes is the first step to improving interpersonal communication because so much of the meaning we assign to messages depends on our *perceptions* of the social context and the persons involved.

REVIEW QUESTIONS

1. List the four perception processes this reading explains.
2. How are scripts related to episodes?
3. What's the difference between closed episodes and defined episodes?
4. What's the relationship between personal constructs and implicit personality theory?
5. What's an *interpersonal* self-fulfilling prophecy?
6. Explain the difference between a high self-monitor and a low self-monitor.
7. People use attribution theories to infer the _____ of other people's behavior.

PROBES

1. Trenholm and Jensen say at one point that "social interaction is a continuous dance in which participants accept and decline each other's invitations to enact different episodes." Extend their metaphor of "dance" to explain your own experience. In what ways are your conversations, say at work, like a dance?
2. What principle is exemplified by the salesperson's "yes technique"? What do you hear Trenholm and Jensen saying about this technique? Do they think it's a good tactic to use?
3. Do you agree or disagree with the claim that first impressions are formed solidly within the first four minutes of interaction with a stranger, and that we use these hastily formed impressions to decide whether to continue conversing or not? Explain.
4. Do you tend to be a high self-monitor or a low self-monitor? How does your tendency affect your communicating?
5. Give an example of a bias toward groups and a bias toward cultures that affects how you perceive some of the people you're communicating with.

NOTES

1. Stanley Deetz and Sheryl Stevenson, *Managing Interpersonal Communication* (New York: Harper & Row, 1986), p. 58.
2. Joseph Forgas, "Affective and Emotional Influences on Episode Representations," in *Social Cognition: Perspectives on Everyday Understanding*, ed. Joseph Forgas (London: Academic Press, 1981), pp. 165–80.
3. Michael Brenner, "Actors' Powers," in *The Analysis of Action: Recent Theoretical and Empirical Advances*, ed. M. von Cranach and Rom Harre (Cambridge: Cambridge University Press, 1982), pp. 213–30.
4. Steven Duck, "Interpersonal Communication in Developing Acquaintances," in *Explorations in Interpersonal Communication*, ed. Gerald R. Miller (Beverly Hills, Calif.: Sage, 1976), pp. 127–47.
5. Seymour Rosenberg and Andrea Sedlak, "Structural Representations of Implicit Personality Theory," in *Advances in Experimental Social Psychology* 6, ed. Leonard Berkowitz (New York: Academic Press, 1972).
6. Walter Crockett, "Cognitive Complexity and Impression Formation," in *Progress in Experimental Personality Research* 2, ed. B. A. Maher (New York: Academic Press, 1965). See also Jesse Delia, "Constructivism and the Study of Human Communication," *Quarterly Journal of Speech* 63 (1977): 68–83.
7. Jesse Delia, Ruth Ann Clark, and David Switzer, "Cognitive Complexity and Impression Formation in Informal Social Interaction," *Speech Monographs* 41 (1974): 299–308. See also Claudia Hale and Jesse Delia, "Cognitive Complexity and Social Perspective-Taking," *Communication Monographs* 43 (1976): 195–203.
8. Crockett, "Cognitive Complexity."
9. Mark L. Snyder, "The Self-Monitoring of Expressive Behavior," *Journal of Personality and Social Psychology* 30 (1974): 526–37.
10. Mark L. Snyder, "Self-Monitoring Processes," in *Advances in Experimental Social Psychology* 12, ed. Leonard Berkowitz (New York: Academic Press, 1979), pp. 86–131.
11. Sally Planalp, "Relational Schemata: A Test of Alternative Forms of Relational Knowledge as Guides to Communication," *Human Communication Research* 12 (1985): 3–29.
12. Robert Carson, *Interaction Concepts of Personality* (Chicago: Aldine, 1969).
13. For a review, see Lee Ross, "The Intuitive Psychologist and His Shortcomings: Distortions in the Attribution Process," in *Advances in Experimental Social Psychology* 10, ed. Leonard Berkowitz (New York: Academic Press, 1977).
14. E. E. Jones and D. McGillis, "Correspondent Inferences and the Attribution Cube: A Comparative Reappraisal," in *New Directions in Attribution Research* 1, ed. J. H. Harvey, W. J. Ickes, and R. F. Kidd (Hillsdale, N.J.: Lawrence Erlbaum, 1976).
15. J. Jaspars and M. Hewstone, "Cross-Cultural Interaction, Social Attribution, and Intergroup Relations," in *Cultures in Contact*, ed. S. Bochner (Elmsford, N.Y.: Pergamon Press, 1982); B. Park and M. Rothbart, "Perceptions of Out-

group Homogeneity and Levels of Social Categorization: Memory for the Subordinate Attributes of In-Group and Out-Group Members," *Journal of Personality and Social Psychology* 42 (1982): 1051–68.
16. J. Miller, "Culture and the Development of Everyday Social Explanations," *Journal of Personality and Social Psychology* 46 (1984): 961–78.

*J*ulia Wood teaches in the department of communication studies at the University of North Carolina at Chapel Hill, does research on gender and communication, and has published several interpersonal communication texts. This chapter comes from a recent book that she dedicates to enhancing its reader's understanding of "different meanings that people may attribute to what they say and do." In her book, Wood emphasizes how diversity can contribute to misunderstanding and how awareness and acceptance of diversity can help improve understanding.

As the subtitle of this selection says, this is a discussion of stereotyping, one of the most familiar and unfortunate features of the way we perceive people. As the subtitle also suggests, the key concept in this chapter is "totalizing." Wood explains that this word describes "communication that emphasizes one aspect of a person above all others." Totalizing means thinking and acting as if a single aspect of a person is the totality of that person. So calling Spike Lee a "black filmmaker" spotlights his race in a way that makes it the dominant feature that's being noticed. The same thing happens when people talk of "that short guy you dated," "a Japanese friend of mine," and "his deaf sister."

Wood makes the obvious—though important—point that totalizing has negative effects on the people who are its target. But she also describes some of the effects of totalizing on the people who do it. Basically, when we engage in totalizing, we cripple our perceiving by forcing ourselves to look through blinders. As Wood puts it, "we tend to perceive others through the labels we use to describe them."

One reason people stereotype or totalize is that it's easier to deal with a one-dimensional person that someone with many different important qualities. Another reason is that several automatic human brain processes produce classifications and generalizations. It would be impossible for us constantly to notice every detail of everything available to our senses, so our brain automatically classifies what we perceive to help keep us from going nuts.

But when we perceive people, this natural process can lead us to operate on the basis of what are called "implicit personality theories" (this same idea was discussed by Trenholm and Jensen in the previous reading). As both readings note, these are generalizations about groups of qualities that seem "obviously" to go together—like being overweight, happy, lazy, and undisciplined. Problems arise when we perceive one of these features—that a person is overweight, for example—and our implicit theory about the rest of the personality fills in other features that may or may not be parts of who the person is.

Wood discusses some of Dawn Braithwaite's research about how totalizing applies to people with disabilities. Even that term—*disabled*—is often hurtful because it makes it easier for others to reduce the amputee or the deaf or partly sighted person to the negative status of being incomplete or flawed in some vital way.

Near the end of this short reading, Wood includes 10 examples of statements that often come from well-meaning people, but that are usually heard by the people they're directed to as totalizing or stereotyping. This list and the other ideas in this selection should help sensitize you to whatever tendencies you have to rely on stereotypes in your communication.

IT'S ONLY SKIN DEEP

Stereotyping and Totalizing Others

Julia T. Wood

I want to be known as a talented young filmmaker. That should be first. But the reality today is that no matter how successful you are, you're black first. (p. 92)

Those are Spike Lee's words. In an interview with Diane McDowell, reporter for *Time* magazine, the gifted filmmaker lamented the reality that most people see and respond to his blackness more than his other qualities and achievements. Sometimes, awareness of Lee's blackness overrides all other perceptions of him.

Distinguished historian John Hope Franklin made the same point in an interview with Mark McGurl, reporter for the *New York Times*. According to Franklin, many people assume that because he is an African American historian, he must study African Americans. He is often introduced as the author of 12 books on black history. In reality, Franklin points out, he is *not* a historian only of African Americans. His specialty is the history of the South and, as he notes, that history includes both whites and blacks. In fact, several of his books have focused primarily on whites in the South. Franklin has been elected president of the American Historical Association, the Organization of American Historians, and the Southern Historical Association—none of which is specifically an African American organization. Still, many people perceive his skin color above all else and they assume his ethnicity defines his work.

The misunderstanding of identity and achievement that Spike Lee and John Hope Franklin confront is not unique to people of minority races. Women report that they are often asked to serve on committees. Many times the person asking says, "We need a woman on the committee" or "We think you can provide the woman's perspective on the issues." Like Lee and Franklin, professional women may feel that all their accomplishments and abilities are erased by those who ask them to be "the woman on the committee." The language in the request communicates that all that is noticed is biological sex: She can fill the "woman slot" on the committee.

In this [reading], we focus on communication that highlights one aspect of a person—usually race, sex, sexual orientation, disability, or economic status. We discuss common instances of such communication and explore how it fosters misunderstandings and often offense.

UNDERSTANDING THE MISUNDERSTANDING

Scholars use the term *totalize* to describe communication that emphasizes one aspect of a person above all others. When someone totalizes, he or she acts as if a single facet of an individual is the totality of that person or as if that single aspect is all that's important about the person. For example, describing Spike Lee as a *black* filmmaker spotlights his race as what is worthy of attention. Calling John Hope Franklin a *black* historian emphasizes his race and obscures his professional expertise and accomplishments. Asking a professional to provide the *woman's* perspective highlights sex as the criterion for serving on committees. Referring to a person as *gay* stresses sexual orientation and obscures all the person's other qualities. Describing people as *blue collar* or *white collar* makes their class visible and everything else about them invisible.

Totalizing affects both those who do it and those who are its targets. When we feel that someone totalizes us, we are likely to be offended and resentful. We may also be hurt that we have been reduced to a single part of our identity— perhaps not the part most important to us in a particular context. These feelings create barriers to open, healthy communication and comfortable relationships.

Less obvious but no less important is the impact of totalizing on people who engage in it. Language shapes our perceptions by calling certain things to our attention. When we use language that focuses our attention on race, class, sex, or any [other] single aspect of another person, we limit our perception of that person. In other words, we tend to perceive others through the labels we use to describe them.

Kenneth Burke, a distinguished critic of language and literature, observes that language simultaneously reflects, selects, and deflects. In his book *Language as Symbolic Action*, Burke writes: "Any given terminology is a *reflection* of reality, by its very nature as a terminology it must be a *selection* of reality; and to this extent it must function also as a *deflection* of reality" (p. 45). Burke means that the words we use to reflect our perceptions select certain aspects of what we are describing while simultaneously deflecting, or neglecting, other aspects of what we are describing. When we select *woman, black, gay,* and so forth to describe people, other aspects of those people are deflected (neglected or added as an af-terthought). Consequently, we may not see in others whatever our labels deflect. Thus, we are unlikely to interact with those others in their wholeness.

Most of us wouldn't intentionally reduce another person to one aspect of who he or she is, but it happens. One motive for totalizing is the desire for re-ducing uncertainty. We tend to be uncomfortable when we are unsure about oth-ers and situations. To ease discomfort, we often attempt to reduce our uncer-tainty about others and circumstances. One way to do this is to define others as belonging to a group about which we have definite ideas (although the ideas may not be accurate). It is easier to think of Spike Lee as black than to try to per-ceive him as a unique individual who is—among other things—male, young, a filmmaker, educated, and African American.

In the classic book *The Nature of Prejudice,* psychologist Gordon Allport observed that stereotyping and prejudice grow out of normal—not deviant or unusual—cognitive activities. Specifically, Allport identified classification and generalization as commonplace mental activities that can foster stereotypes and prejudice. One reason we use stereotypes, then, is that they reduce our uncertainty by grouping people into broad classes that obscure individual characteristics.

A second reason we stereotype is that we rely on what psychologists call im-plicit personality theory. Most of us have certain unspoken and perhaps unrec-ognized assumptions about qualities that go together in personalities. Many people assume that attractive individuals are more extroverted, intelligent, and socially skilled than less attractive individuals. Another common implicit per-sonality theory (one that research does not support) is that people who are over-weight are also lazy, undisciplined, and happy. In both examples, we attribute to others a constellation of qualities that we associate with a particular quality we have noticed.

If we meet an individual who is overweight (in our judgment), we may as-sume that the person meets our implicit personality theory of overweight peo-ple and is happy, lazy, and undisciplined. Our implicit personality theories may also lead us to think that a nice-looking person must be intelligent, outgoing, and socially skilled. When we rely on our implicit personality theories, we latch onto one quality of another person—often a characteristic we can see, such as race, sex, or weight—and attribute to the person other qualities that we perceive as consistent with the quality we have identified. . . .

One form of totalizing . . . involves defining individuals by their member-ship in a specific group. Years ago sociologist Louis Wirth conducted classic studies of racial prejudice. One of his more important conclusions was that when we perceive people primarily in terms of their membership in a particu-lar racial or ethnic group, we tend to think about them and interact with them in terms of our stereotypes of race, regardless of their unique qualities, talents, and so forth. In other words, their individuality is lost, submerged in our pre-conceptions of the group to which we assign them.

A second form of totalizing reduces individuals to one quality or aspect of their identities. This type of totalizing is evident in some of the language used to describe persons who have disabilities. How we perceive and label people with disabilities is the research focus of Dawn Braithwaite, a communication scholar at Arizona State University West. From interviews with persons who have disabilities, Braithwaite learned that the term *disabled person* is likely to offend. The reason is that the term suggests that their personhood is disabled—that they are somehow inadequate or diminished as persons simply because they have disabilities. One of the people Braithwaite interviewed asserted, "I am a person like anyone else" (1994, p. 151). Another interviewee said, "If anyone refers to me as an amputee, that is guaranteed to get me madder than hell! I don't deny the leg amputation, but I am me. I am a whole person" (1994, p. 151).

Individuals who have disabilities have been vocal in resisting efforts to label them *disabled.* They point out that calling them disabled emphasizes their disabilities above all else. "We're people who have disabilities. People first," a deaf student explained to me. When someone with a disability is described as disabled, we highlight what they cannot do rather than all they can do. . . .

When we think stereotypically, we expect people to conform to our perceptions of the group to which we assign them. Sometimes, however, we meet someone who doesn't fit our stereotypes of the group to which we think he or she belongs. Have you ever said or heard the phrases "woman doctor," "male nurse," or "woman lawyer"? Notice how they call attention to the sex of the doctor, nurse, or lawyer. Have you ever heard or used the phrases "man doctor," "woman nurse," or "man lawyer"? Probably not—because it is considered normal for men to be doctors and lawyers and women to be nurses. Many people perceive it as unusual for women to practice law or medicine or men to be nurses. "Woman doctor," "male nurse," and "woman lawyer" spotlight the sex of individuals as the element worthy of notice. The phrases also reflect stereotyped views of the professional groups.

When we mark an individual as an exception to his or her group, we unknowingly reveal our own stereotypes. In fact, we may reinforce them because marking an individual who doesn't conform to the stereotype as unusual leaves our perceptions of the group unchanged. All we do is remove the "exceptional individual" from the group. Consider these statements:

White manager to black manager:	"You really are exceptional at your job."
	[*Translation:* Black women aren't usually successful.]
Male professional to female professional:	"You don't think like a woman."
	[*Translation:* Most women don't think like professionals.]
Able-bodied individual to person in wheelchair:	"I'm amazed at how well you get around."
	[*Translation:* I assume that people who use wheelchairs don't get out much.]

Upper-class person to working-class person:	"It's remarkable that you take college classes."
	[*Translation:* Most working-class people aren't interested in higher education.]
White person to African American:	"I can't believe you don't like to dance."
	[*Translation:* I think that all blacks dance, have rhythm.]
Heterosexual to lesbian:	"I think it's great that you have some male friends."
	[*Translation:* Most lesbians hate men.]
Homeowner to maid:	"You speak so articulately."
	[*Translation:* I assume most domestic workers don't speak well and/or aren't educated.]
White man to black man:	"I never think of you as black."
	[*Translation:* You don't fit my views of blacks; you're an exception to my (negative) stereotype of blacks.]
Christian to Jew:	"I'm surprised at how generous you are."
	[*Translation:* Most Jews are tight with money.]
African American to white person:	"You're not as stuffy as most of your people."
	[*Translation:* Most whites are stuffy, or up-tight, but you're not.]

Would any of the above statements be made to a member of the speaker's group? Would a heterosexual say to a heterosexual woman, "It's great that you have some male friends"? Would a white man say to another white man, "I never think of you as white"? Would a maid say to his or her employer, "You speak so articulately"? Would a white person say to another white person, "I can't believe you don't like to dance"? In each case, it's unlikely. By changing the speakers in the statements, we see how clearly the statements reflect stereotypes of groups.

Communicating that you perceive an individual as an exception to his or her group invites two dilemmas. First, it expresses your perception that the person belongs to a group about which you have preconceptions. Understandably, this may alienate the other person or make her or him defensive. The person may feel compelled to defend or redefine the group from which you have removed that individual. An African American might, for instance, say "Lots of blacks don't enjoy dancing." A working-class person might inform an upper-class person that "education has always been a priority in my family."

A second possible response to communication that marks an individual as an exception to her or his group is the effort to deny identification with the group. A professional woman may strive not to appear feminine to avoid being judged by her colleagues' negative perceptions of women. A white person may try to "talk black" or play music by black artists to prove he or she isn't like most whites. The group stereotypes—no matter how inaccurate—are left unchallenged.

Whether individuals defend or redefine their groups or separate themselves from the groups, one result is the same: The possibilities for open communication and honest relationships are compromised.

REVIEW QUESTIONS

1. Define *totalizing* in your own words, and give an example from your own experience of how totalizing can affect communication.
2. Specifically how does totalizing affect the person who *does* it?
3. Define and give an example of *implicit personality theory*.
4. My wife, Kris, is an attorney. Use Wood's article to explain why she does not like to be called a "woman lawyer."
5. Explain the point Wood is making when she asks, "Would a white man say to another white man, 'I never think of you as white'?"

PROBES

1. On the first day of class, the instructor says in a genuinely pleased way, "It's great to have so many persons of color in the class." Explain how this can be heard as a totalizing statement.
2. Wood quotes Gordon Allport to make the point that stereotyping is a normal, natural activity. But if it's normal and natural, then how much sense does it make to encourage people not to do it?
3. Privately, if you prefer, or with a classmate, if you're willing, explore some of your own implicit personality theories. For example, if you're not thinking carefully about it, what qualities do you presume a person has who is (a) a teenage African-American male, (b) a female athlete, (c) a 20-something gay male, (d) a middle-aged female nurse?
4. If it's obviously true that a person does not have normal sight, hearing, intelligence, or mobility, what is the problem with referring to that person as "disabled"?
5. What's the connection between the main point made in this reading and the social–cultural–interpersonal continuum discussed in Chapter 2?

REFERENCES

Allport, G. (1979). *The nature of prejudice*. Reading, MA: Addison-Wesley.
Braithwaite, D. (1994). Viewing persons with disabilities as a culture. In L. Samovar & R. Porter (Eds.), *Intercultural communication: A reader* (7th ed., pp. 148–154). Belmont, CA: Wadsworth.

Burke, K. (1966). *Language as symbolic action*. Berkeley, CA: University of California Press.

McDowell, D. (1989, July 17). He's got to have his way. *Time*, pp. 92–94.

McGurl, M. (1990, June 3). That's history, not black history. *The New York Times
Book Review*, 13.

Wirth, L. (1945). The problem of minority groups. In R. Linton (Ed.), *The science
of man* (pp. 347–372). New York: Columbia.

*T*his reading introduces a key idea from a book that's had a significant impact on our contemporary understanding of human intelligence. For a long time, at least in the Western world, people have given
considerable weight to IQ (Intelligence Quotient) as a measure of a person's "smarts." For many decades, IQ tests have been given to school
children, and IQ scores have been used to define people as "gifted,"
"special needs," or "genius." Daniel Goleman argues that these tests are
fatally flawed, because they measure only part of what it means to be
intelligent. There is a very important, complementary set of human
competencies that he calls "emotional intelligence," and these affect our
interpersonal communication at least as much as IQ, if not more so.

Goleman cites research done by several psychologists who identify
four abilities that make up emotional, or interpersonal, intelligence: organizing groups, negotiating solutions, personal connecting, and social
analysis. Each is significantly different from the kinds of intelligence
that standard IQ tests measure.

The first involves "initiating and coordinating the efforts of a network of people." The second is the talent of a mediator—resolving conflicts. The third kind of emotional intelligence is the capacity for empathy—reading emotions and responding appropriately to them. And the
fourth consists of being able to "detect and have insights about people's
feelings, motives, and concerns."

Goleman briefly describes how these abilities are related to other
kinds of emotional intelligence. For example, the person who is empathic is also able to notice his or her own emotions, to fine-tune them
to fit the situation, and to adjust them flexibly. He also cites the same research about self-monitoring that was discussed earlier in this chapter
by Trenholm and Jensen to make the point that it's important to have a
balance of the emotional capabilities of empathy and the awareness of
your *own* needs and feelings.

In a section of the reading called "The Making of a Social Incompetent," Goleman discusses some of the experiences that help shape individual emotional intelligence. He quotes a psychologist who emphasizes that children need to be taught "to speak directly to others when
spoken to; to initiate social contact, not always wait for others; to carry

on a conversation, not simply fall back on yes or no or other one-word replies; to express gratitude toward others, . . . to thank others, to say 'please,' to share," and so on. Young children learn these capabilities— or fail to learn them—in countless informal contacts with family members, schoolmates, and friends, and this fact underscores the significance, in the early years, of these everyday, mundane activities. Goleman notes that psychologists have coined the term *dyssemia* to label people who haven't learned to read the nonverbal messages that primarily communicate emotions. He also points out that this difficulty affects not only a child's interpersonal life but also his or her academic success.

One of the primary tests of a young child's emotional intelligence is being on the edge of a group that the child wants to join. Some research indicates that even popular second- and third-graders are rejected almost a quarter of the time they attempt to join in such groups. And as each of us can probably remember, young children can be brutally candid in this situation. Researchers observe these events in classrooms and on playgrounds in order to assess individual abilities and clarify the features of emotional intelligence.

The selection ends with a description of an event of "emotional brilliance" that a friend of Goleman's observed on a train outside Tokyo. This story, along with the rest of this reading, should enable you to evaluate your own emotional intelligence and to recognize how this kind of knowledge affects your perceptions of people, relationships, and social situations.

THE RUDIMENTS OF SOCIAL INTELLIGENCE

Daniel Goleman

It's recess at a preschool, and a band of boys is running across the grass. Reggie trips, hurts his knee, and starts crying, but the other boys keep right on running—save for Roger, who stops. As Reggie's sobs subside Roger reaches down and rubs his own knee, calling out, "I hurt my knee, too!"

Roger is cited as having exemplary interpersonal intelligence by Thomas Hatch, a colleague of Howard Gardner at Spectrum, the school based on the concept of multiple intelligences.[1] Roger, it seems, is unusually adept at recognizing the feelings of his playmates and making rapid, smooth connections with them. It was only Roger who noticed Reggie's plight and pain, and only Roger who tried to provide some solace, even if all he could offer was rubbing his own knee. This small gesture bespeaks a talent for rapport, an emotional skill essential for the preservation of close relationships, whether in a marriage, a friendship, or a business partnership. Such skills in preschoolers are the buds of talents that ripen through life.

Roger's talent represents one of four separate abilities that Hatch and Gardner identify as components of interpersonal intelligence:

- *Organizing groups*—the essential skill of the leader, this involves initiating and coordinating the efforts of a network of people. This is the talent seen in theater directors or producers, in military officers, and in effective heads of organizations and units of all kinds. On the playground, this is the child who takes the lead in deciding what everyone will play, or becomes team captain.
- *Negotiating solutions*—the talent of the mediator, preventing conflicts or resolving those that flare up. People who have this ability excel in deal-making, in arbitrating or mediating disputes; they might have a career in diplomacy, in arbitration or law, or as middlemen or managers of takeovers. These are the kids who settle arguments on the playing field.
- *Personal connection*—Roger's talent, that of empathy and connecting. This makes it easy to enter into an encounter or to recognize and respond fittingly to people's feelings and concerns—the art of relationship. Such people make good "team players," dependable spouses, good friends or business partners; in the business world they do well as salespeople or managers, or can be excellent teachers. Children like Roger get along well with virtually everyone else, easily enter into playing with them, and are happy doing so. These children tend to be best at reading emotions from facial expressions and are most liked by their classmates.
- *Social analysis*—being able to detect and have insights about people's feelings, motives, and concerns. This knowledge of how others feel can lead to an easy intimacy or sense of rapport. At its best, this ability makes one a competent therapist or counselor—or, if combined with some literary talent, a gifted novelist or dramatist.

Taken together, these skills are the stuff of interpersonal polish, the necessary ingredients for charm, social success, even charisma. Those who are adept in social intelligence can connect with people quite smoothly, be astute in reading their reactions and feelings, lead and organize, and handle the disputes that are bound to flare up in any human activity. They are the natural leaders, the people who can express the unspoken collective sentiment and articulate it so as to guide a group toward its goals. They are the kind of people others like to be with because they are emotionally nourishing—they leave other people in a good mood, and evoke the comment, "What a pleasure to be around someone like that."

These interpersonal abilities build on other emotional intelligences. People who make an excellent social impression, for example, are adept at monitoring their own expression of emotion, are keenly attuned to the ways others are reacting, and so are able to continually fine-tune their social performance, adjusting it to make sure they are having the desired effect. In that sense, they are like skilled actors.

However, if these interpersonal abilities are not balanced by an astute sense of one's own needs and feelings and how to fulfill them, they can lead to a hollow social success—a popularity won at the cost of one's true satisfaction. Such is the argument of Mark Snyder, a University of Minnesota psychologist who has studied people whose social skills make them first-rate social chameleons, champions at making a good impression.[2] Their psychological credo might well be a remark by W. H. Auden, who said that his private image of himself "is very different from the image which I try to create in the minds of others in order that they may love me." That trade-off can be made if social skills outstrip the ability to know and honor one's own feelings: in order to be loved—or at least liked—the social chameleon will seem to be whatever those he [or she] is with seem to want. The sign that someone falls into this pattern, Snyder finds, is that they make an excellent impression, yet have few stable or satisfying intimate relationships. A more healthy pattern, of course, is to balance being true to oneself with social skills, using them with integrity.

Social chameleons, though, don't mind in the least saying one thing and doing another, if that will win them social approval. They simply live with the discrepancy between their public face and their private reality. Helena Deutsch, a psychoanalyst, called such people the "as-if personality," shifting personas with remarkable plasticity as they pick up signals from those around them. "For some people," Snyder told me, "the public and private person meshes well, while for others there seems to be only a kaleidoscope of changing appearances. They are like Woody Allen's character Zelig, madly trying to fit in with whomever they are with."

Such people try to scan someone for a hint as to what is wanted from them before they make a response, rather than simply saying what they truly feel. To get along and be liked, they are willing to make people they dislike think they are friendly with them. And they use their social abilities to mold their actions as disparate social situations demand, so that they may act like very different people depending on whom they are with, swinging from bubbly sociability, say, to reserved withdrawal. To be sure, to the extent that these traits lead to effective impression management, they are highly prized in certain professions, notably acting, trial law, sales, diplomacy, and politics.

Another, perhaps more crucial kind of self-monitoring seems to make the difference between those who end up as anchorless social chameleons, trying to impress everyone, and those who can use their social polish more in keeping with their true feelings. That is the capacity to be true, as the saying has it, "to thine own self," which allows acting in accord with one's deepest feelings and values no matter what the social consequences. Such emotional integrity could well lead to, say, deliberately provoking a confrontation in order to cut through duplicity or denial—a clearing of the air that a social chameleon would never attempt.

THE MAKING OF A SOCIAL INCOMPETENT

There was no doubt Cecil was bright; he was a college-trained expert in foreign languages, superb at translating. But there were crucial ways in which he was completely inept. Cecil seemed to lack the simplest social skills. He would muff a casual conversation over coffee, and fumble when having to pass the time of day; in short, he seemed incapable of the most routine social exchange. Because his lack of social grace was most profound when he was around women, Cecil came to therapy wondering if perhaps he had "homosexual tendencies of an underlying nature," as he put it, though he had no such fantasies.

The real problem, Cecil confided to his therapist, was that he feared that nothing he could say would be of any interest to anybody. This underlying fear only compounded a profound paucity of social graces. His nervousness during encounters led him to snicker and laugh at the most awkward moments, even though he failed to laugh when someone said something genuinely funny. Cecil's awkwardness, he confided to his therapist, went back to childhood; all his life he had felt socially at ease only when he was with his older brother, who somehow helped ease things for him. But once he left home, his ineptitude was overwhelming; he was socially paralyzed.

The tale is told by Lakin Phillips, a psychologist at George Washington University, who proposes that Cecil's plight stems from a failure to learn in childhood the most elementary lessons of social interaction:

> What could Cecil have been taught earlier? To speak directly to others when spoken to; to initiate social contact, not always wait for others; to carry on a conversation, not simply fall back on yes or no or other one-word replies; to express gratitude toward others, to let another person walk before one in passing through a door; to wait until one is served something . . . to thank others, to say "please," to share, and all the other elementary interactions we begin to teach children from age 2 onward.[3]

Whether Cecil's deficiency was due to another's failure to teach him such rudiments of social civility or to his own inability to learn is unclear. But whatever its roots, Cecil's story is instructive because it points up the crucial nature of the countless lessons children get in interaction synchrony and the unspoken rules of social harmony. The net effect of failing to follow these rules is to create waves, to make those around us uncomfortable. The function of these rules, of course, is to keep everyone involved in a social exchange at ease; awkwardness spawns anxiety. People who lack these skills are inept not just at social niceties, but at handling the emotions of those they encounter; they inevitably leave disturbance in their wake.

We all have known Cecils, people with an annoying lack of social graces—people who don't seem to know when to end a conversation or phone call and who keep on talking, oblivious to all cues and hints to say good-bye; people whose conversation centers on themselves all the time, without the least interest in anyone else, and who ignore tentative attempts to refocus on another topic; people who intrude or ask "nosy" questions. These derailments of a smooth social trajectory all bespeak a deficit in the rudimentary building blocks of interaction.

Psychologists have coined the term *dyssemia* (from the Greek *dys-* for "difficulty" and *semes* for "signal") for what amounts to a learning disability in the realm of nonverbal messages; about one in ten children has one or more problems in this realm.[4] The problem can be in a poor sense of personal space, so that a child stands too close while talking or spreads their belongings into other people's territory; in interpreting or using body language poorly; in misinterpreting or misusing facial expressions by, say, failing to make eye contact; or in a poor sense of prosody, the emotional quality of speech, so that they talk too shrilly or flatly.

Much research has focused on spotting children who show signs of social deficiency, children whose awkwardness makes them neglected or rejected by their playmates. Apart from children who are spurned because they are bullies, those whom other children avoid are invariably deficient in the rudiments of face-to-face interaction, particularly the unspoken rules that govern encounters. If children do poorly in language, people assume they are not very bright or poorly educated; but when they do poorly in the nonverbal rules of interaction, people—especially playmates—see them as "strange," and avoid them. These are the children who don't know how to join a game gracefully, who touch others in ways that make for discomfort rather than camaraderie—in short, who are "off." They are children who have failed to master the silent language of emotion, and who unwittingly send messages that create uneasiness.

As Stephen Nowicki, an Emory University psychologist who studies children's nonverbal abilities, put it, "Children who can't read or express emotions well constantly feel frustrated. In essence, they don't understand what's going on. This kind of communication is a constant subtext of everything you do; you can't stop showing your facial expression or posture, or hide your tone of voice. If you make mistakes in what emotional messages you send, you constantly experience that people react to you in funny ways—you get rebuffed and don't know why. If you're thinking you're acting happy but actually seem too hyper or angry, you find other kids getting angry at you in turn, and you don't realize why. Such kids end up feeling no sense of control over how other people treat them, that their actions have no impact on what happens to them. It leaves them feeling powerless, depressed, and apathetic."

Apart from becoming social isolates, such children also suffer academically. The classroom, of course, is as much a social situation as an academic one; the socially awkward child is as likely to misread and misrespond to a teacher as to another child. The resulting anxiety and bewilderment can themselves interfere with their ability to learn effectively. Indeed, as tests of children's nonverbal sensitivity have shown, those who misread emotional cues tend to do poorly in school compared to their academic potential as reflected in IQ tests.[5]

"WE HATE YOU": AT THE THRESHOLD

Social ineptitude is perhaps most painful and explicit when it comes to one of the more perilous moments in the life of a young child: being on the edge of a group at play you want to join. It is a moment of peril, one when being liked or hated, belonging or not, is made all too public. For that reason that crucial moment has been the subject of intense scrutiny by students of child development, revealing a stark contrast in approach strategies used by popular children and by social outcasts. The findings highlight just how crucial it is for social competence to notice, interpret, and respond to emotional and interpersonal cues. While it is poignant to see a child hover on the edge of others at play, wanting to join in but being left out, it is a universal predicament. Even the most popular children are sometimes rejected—a study of second and third graders found that 26 percent of the time the most well liked children were rebuffed when they tried to enter a group already at play.

Young children are brutally candid about the emotional judgment implicit in such rejections. Witness the following dialogue from four-year-olds in a preschool.[6] Linda wants to join Barbara, Nancy, and Bill, who are playing with toy animals and building blocks. She watches for a minute, then makes her approach, sitting next to Barbara and starting to play with the animals. Barbara turns to her and says, "You can't play!"

"Yes, I can," Linda counters. "I can have some animals, too."

"No, you can't," Barbara says bluntly. "We don't like you today."

When Bill protests on Linda's behalf, Nancy joins the attack: "We hate her today."

Because of the danger of being told, either explicitly or implicitly, "We hate you," all children are understandably cautious on the threshold of approaching a group. That anxiety, of course, is probably not much different from that felt by a grown-up at a cocktail party with strangers who hangs back from a happily chatting group who seem to be intimate friends. Because this moment at the threshold of a group is so momentous for a child, it is also, as one researcher put it, "highly diagnostic . . . quickly revealing differences in social skillfulness."[7]

Typically, newcomers simply watch for a time, then join in very tentatively at first, being more assertive only in very cautious steps. What matters most for whether a child is accepted or not is how well he or she is able to enter into the group's frame of reference, sensing what kind of play is in flow, what out of place.

The two cardinal sins that almost always lead to rejection are trying to take the lead too soon and being out of synch with the frame of reference. But this is exactly what unpopular children tend to do: they push their way into a group, trying to change the subject too abruptly or too soon, or offering their own opinions, or simply disagreeing with the others right away—all apparent attempts to draw attention to themselves. Paradoxically, this results in their being ignored or rejected. By contrast, popular children spend time observing the group to understand what's going on before entering in, and then do something that shows they accept it; they wait to have their status in the group confirmed before taking initiative in suggesting what the group should do.

Let's return to Roger, the four-year-old whom Thomas Hatch spotted exhibiting a high level of interpersonal intelligence.[8] Roger's tactic for entering a group was first to observe, then to imitate what another child was doing, and finally to talk to the child and fully join the activity—a winning strategy. Roger's skill was shown, for instance, when he and Warren were playing at putting "bombs" (actually pebbles) in their socks. Warren asks Roger if he wants to be in a helicopter or an airplane. Roger asks, before committing himself, "Are you in a helicopter?"

This seemingly innocuous moment reveals sensitivity to others' concerns, and the ability to act on that knowledge in a way that maintains the connection. Hatch comments about Roger, "He 'checks in' with his playmate so that they and their play remain connected. I have watched many other children who simply get in their own helicopters or planes and, literally and figuratively, fly away from each other."

EMOTIONAL BRILLIANCE: A CASE REPORT

If the test of social skill is the ability to calm distressing emotions in others, then handling someone at the peak of rage is perhaps the ultimate measure of mastery. The data on self-regulation of anger and emotional contagion suggest that one effective strategy might be to distract the angry person, empathize with his feelings and perspective, and then draw him into an alternative focus, one that attunes him with a more positive range of feeling—a kind of emotional judo.

Such refined skill in the fine art of emotional influence is perhaps best exemplified by a story told by an old friend, the late Terry Dobson, who in the 1950s was one of the first Americans ever to study the martial art aikido in Japan. One afternoon he was riding home on a suburban Tokyo train when a huge, bellicose, and very drunk and begrimed laborer got on. The man, staggering, began terrorizing the passengers: screaming curses, he took a swing at a woman holding a baby, sending her sprawling in the laps of an elderly couple, who then jumped up and joined a stampede to the other end of the car. The drunk, taking a few other swings (and, in his rage, missing), grabbed the metal pole in the middle of the car with a roar and tried to tear it out of its socket.

At that point Terry, who was in peak physical condition from daily eighthour aikido workouts, felt called upon to intervene, lest someone get seriously hurt. But he recalled the words of his teacher: "Aikido is the art of reconciliation. Whoever has the mind to fight has broken his connection with the universe. If you try to dominate people you are already defeated. We study how to resolve conflict, not how to start it."

Indeed, Terry had agreed upon beginning lessons with his teacher never to pick a fight, and to use his martial-arts skills only in defense. Now, at last, he saw his chance to test his aikido abilities in real life, in what was clearly a legitimate opportunity. So, as all the other passengers sat frozen in their seats, Terry stood up, slowly and with deliberation.

Seeing him, the drunk roared, "Aha! A foreigner! You need a lesson in Japanese manners!" and began gathering himself to take on Terry.

But just as the drunk was on the verge of making his move, someone gave an earsplitting, oddly joyous shout: "Hey!"

The shout had the cheery tone of someone who has suddenly come upon a fond friend. The drunk, surprised, spun around to see a tiny Japanese man, probably in his seventies, sitting there in a kimono. The old man beamed with delight at the drunk, and beckoned him over with a light wave of his hand and a lilting "C'mere."

The drunk strode over with a belligerent, "Why the hell should I talk to you?" Meanwhile, Terry was ready to fell the drunk in a moment if he made the least violent move.

"What'cha been drinking?" the old man asked, his eyes beaming at the drunken laborer.

"I been drinking sake, and it's none of your business," the drunk bellowed.

"Oh, that's wonderful, absolutely wonderful," the old man replied in a warm tone. "You see, I love sake, too. Every night, me and my wife (she's seventy-six, you know), we warm up a little bottle of sake and take it out into the garden, and we sit on an old wooden bench . . ." He continued on about the persimmon tree in his backyard, the fortunes of his garden, enjoying sake in the evening.

The drunk's face began to soften as he listened to the old man; his fists un-clenched. "Yeah . . . I love persimmons, too . . . ," he said, his voice trailing off.

"Yes," the old man replied in a sprightly voice, "and I'm sure you have a wonderful wife."

"No," said the laborer. "My wife died. . . ." Sobbing, he launched into a sad tale of losing his wife, his home, his job, of being ashamed of himself.

Just then the train came to Terry's stop, and as he was getting off he turned to hear the old man invite the drunk to join him and tell him all about it, and to see the drunk sprawl along the seat, his head in the old man's lap.

That is emotional brilliance.

REVIEW QUESTIONS

1. What's the difference between ability 3, "personal connection," and ability 4, "social analysis"?
2. What does Goleman mean when he says that emotionally intelligent people are "nourishing" to others?
3. How is the discussion of self-monitoring in this reading similar to and dif-ferent from the discussion of the same construct in this chapter's first read-ing, by Trenholm and Jensen?
4. What's *dyssemia*, and how does it fit into this reading?
5. Goleman says that "the two cardinal sins that almost always lead to rejec-tion" are (a) trying to _____ too soon and (b) being _____ the frame of reference."
6. How did the old man on the train outside Tokyo demonstrate a key principle of aikido?

PROBES

1. Explain the balance that Goleman emphasizes is necessary between emotional intelligence and "an astute sense of one's own needs and feelings and how to fulfill them."
2. In this selection, Goleman does not describe in detail *how* emotional intelligence can result in using one's social polish in keeping with one's true feelings, rather than becoming an "anchorless social chameleon." What do you believe it takes to do this?
3. It's relatively easy to describe what Cecil in Goleman's example failed to learn—"to speak directly to others when spoken to; . . . to carry on a conversation, not simply fall back on yes or no . . . replies," and so on. But it's more difficult to describe what parents (and other caregivers) need *to do* to be sure their children learn all these things. What do you believe are the most important ways to help young children learn emotional intelligence?
4. How does Goleman's focus on *nonverbal* communication support or challenge what's said about nonverbal communication in the first and last readings in Chapter 3?
5. Young children can be brutally candid in their rejection of would-be playmates. Do adults communicate these same messages in other ways? Or is rejection less common among adults? Discuss.
6. Goleman discusses a child named Roger who shows his emotional intelligence by checking with his playmate before committing himself "to be in a helicopter or an airplane." Describe an adult version of this same communication move.

NOTES

1. Thomas Hatch, "Social Intelligence in Young Children," paper delivered at the annual meeting of the American Psychological Association (1990).
2. Social chameleons: Mark Snyder, "Impression Management: The Self in Social Interaction," in L. S. Wrightsman and K. Deaux, *Social Psychology in the '80s* (Monterey, CA: Brooks/Cole, 1981).
3. E. Lakin Phillips, *The Social Skills Basis of Psychopathology* (New York: Grune and Stratton, 1978), p. 140.
4. Nonverbal learning disorders: Stephen Nowicki and Marshall Duke, *Helping the Child Who Doesn't Fit In* (Atlanta: Peachtree Publishers, 1992). See also Byron Rourke, *Nonverbal Learning Disabilities* (New York: Guilford Press, 1989).
5. Nowicki and Duke, *Helping the Child Who Doesn't Fit In.*
6. This vignette, and the review of research on entering a group, is from Martha Putallaz and Aviva Wasserman, "Children's Entry Behavior," in Steven Asher and John Coie, eds., *Peer Rejection in Childhood* (New York: Cambridge University Press, 1990).
7. Putallaz and Wasserman, "Children's Entry Behavior."
8. Hatch, "Social Intelligence in Young Children."

*T*his chapter begins with Trenholm and Jensen's discussion of *individual* perception processes—how we perceive people and social situations. It concludes with this reading that discusses what David Bohm believes is a characteristic of *collective* perception that also significantly affects interpersonal communication.

In fact, this particular way of thinking contributes to all kinds of social problems, Bohm believes, from dirty tricks in politics, to the polarization between East and West and between North and South, to the threat of biological and chemical weapons, to the growth of crime and violence and the abuse of drugs.

What is the way of thinking that helps generate all these problems? *Fragmentation.* The tendency to "break things up into bits, as if they were independent." On the one hand, fragmentation is part of the process of *analysis,* which is one of the real powers of the human intellect. On the other hand, if things (the environment, people, human systems) are all as interconnected as contemporary science tells us they are, the tendency to treat them as if they were fragmented is a serious distortion. And Bohm argues that this distortion contributes in some significant ways to many of the social, cultural, and interpersonal problems that people currently experience.

Bohm acknowledges that problems like wars, crime, drugs, and economic chaos can seem hopelessly big, but he argues that fragmented ways of thinking contribute to all of them, and "each person can do something about that thought, because [he or she is] in it." This way of thinking is like a virus that is spreading all over the world.

Bohm believes that it's important to recognize this kind of thinking as problematic, but that isn't enough. Just becoming aware of the problem would be like telling someone, "Don't be sad." That advice just focuses you on your sadness. You need to get engaged with an *alternative,* a way of thinking that won't create the problems that sadness or fragmentation creates.

A first step is to notice how collective our seemingly "individual" thinking actually is. As Bohm reminds us, "We pick it up as children from parents, from friends, from school, from newspapers, from books, and so on." In other words, we're socialized into our ways of thinking by our culture. These general forces make up the "pool" that generates what we know as "knowledge." In this sense knowledge has a life of its own, it passes from one individual to another.

Much of this knowledge is what Michael Polyani calls "tacit." You can't state it in words, but you know it's there because you can ride a bike, hit a baseball, and flip a coin. It's the kind of knowledge that you might say your body "knows."

It's also possible to distinguish between "thinking" and "thoughts" and between "feeling" and what might be called "felts." But these distinctions can be very misleading when they encourage us to separate the parts of experience that they name. For example, as Bohm puts it, "thoughts and felts are one process; they are not two."

Finally, it can help to recognize how thought presents us with *representations* of what we experience. Like maps of some territory, representations are necessarily partial and presented from only one perspective. But problems arise because a representation always *"fuses with the actual perception or experience."* In other words, everything that is "presented" as perception—as something I see, hear, touch, taste, or smell—is actually made up of both what I sense *and* various thoughts I have about what I sense. So the sensing and the representations fuse to make what Bohm calls a "net presentation."

The important thing, says Bohm, is that we are often not aware of how much our perception is affected by various representations. We think that what we perceive is reality rather than our constructions. Bohm reminds us that the Latin root of the word *fact* means "what has been made" or "manufactured." And what we call "facts" are manufactured from the combination of what we sense and our thoughts about it. The thoughts, in turn, "arise collectively," from the individuals and groups we associate with.

This general process affects every communication experience we have. As Bohm puts it, "our relationship depends on how we present other people to ourselves, and how we present ourselves to other people. And all of that depends on the general collective representations." All this only becomes obvious when there's some misunderstanding. But the process is present in all of human life.

The bottom line is that the huge social, political, and cultural problems that Bohm starts by discussing can be understood in part to be constructions of (manufactured by) the very people they threaten. We are perceiving these situations through the lenses of the representations we use to understand them. And if we can shift those representations, we can shift the "actual" shape of the things we call "problems." As Bohm concludes, "many worlds are possible—it all depends on representation, especially the collective representation."

I hope you don't hear Bohm arguing for some naïve, pie-in-the-sky belief that "thinking makes it so." But I do hope you hear, and can respond to, his advice to pay attention to the representations that mold your thinking, and to recognize that your ways of understanding even difficult situations can be transformed by changing the representations that help shape them.

THE NATURE OF COLLECTIVE THOUGHT

David Bohm

What are the troubles of the world? They seem so many that we can hardly begin even to list them. We can see wars going on, starvation, torture, pillage, disease, all sorts of dirty tricks played in politics. We have a kind of polarization between East and West—the West professes the value of the individual and freedom, and the East professes the value of the collective society, with everybody being taken care of. We have the North/South polarization—the North is more wealthy and the South less so. There's tremendous trouble in Africa and South America and southern parts of Asia; there's very great poverty and indebtedness and a breakdown of the economy and general chaos in what's going on there.

With advancing technology you have the possibility that nuclear bombs will perhaps be available to all sorts of dictators, even in relatively small nations. There are biological and chemical weapons, and other kinds of weapons that have not yet been invented, but surely will. And we have the danger of ecological destruction—destruction of agricultural land and forests, pollution, the change of climate, and many other things. There could be a real ecological disaster within not too long a period of time if people keep doing whatever they're doing. Then we have the growth of crime and violence everywhere—drugs and so on—indicating that people are very unhappy and not satisfied. I don't need to multiply it. The list could be extended almost indefinitely.

Why have we accepted this state of affairs which is so destructive and so dangerous and so conducive to unhappiness? It seems we're mesmerized in some way. We go on with this insanity and nobody seems to know what to do or say. In the past people used to hope that some solution would appear, such as democracy or socialism or something else, perhaps religion; but this hopeful state of mind is very much weakened now because it has not worked out at all. I am suggesting that underneath it there's something we don't understand about how thought works.

In the beginning of the process of civilization, thought was regarded as a very valuable thing. And it still is. Thought has done all the things which we are proud of. It has built our cities (we shouldn't be so proud of them, I suppose). It has created science and technology, and has been very creative in medicine. Practically all of what has been called nature has been arranged by thought. Yet thought also goes wrong somehow, and produces destruction. This arises from a certain way of thinking, i.e., *fragmentation.* This is to break things up into bits, as if they were independent. It's not merely making divisions, but it is breaking things up which are not really separate. It's like taking a watch and smashing it into fragments, rather than taking it apart and finding its parts. The parts are parts of a *whole,* but the fragments are just arbitrarily broken off from each other. Things which really fit, and belong together, are treated as if they do not. That's one of the features of thought that's going wrong.

Excerpted from *On Dialogue* by David Bohm, 1996. Reprinted by permission of Routledge.

In the past, people may not have noticed this, and may have thought only that "knowledge is power" and ignorance is bad. But there's a certain danger in knowledge and in thought, which people haven't paid enough attention to. Thought may have started to go wrong thousands or tens of thousands of years ago—we don't know. But now technology has gone so far that it has really become deadly. If you imagine a thousand years of what's going on now, what will happen? Will there not be some catastrophe or another? Therefore, with the growth of technology the human race is faced with a tremendous crisis, or challenge. We have got to do something about this thought process—we can't just let it go on destroying us. But then, what do you do about it? You can't cut out thought—clearly we couldn't do without it. And you can't just select all the bad thoughts and cut them out. So we have to go into it more deeply. I say this is not an obvious thing—it's very subtle and it goes very deep. We want to get to the root of it, to the base, to the source of it. . . .

If you say, "This is too big for me," in one sense that's true. In another sense, I say it's not. If you say the crisis is only the external phenomenon—what's going on in the outside world—then it's very big. It's like this: suppose you have a dam which has not been constructed properly, and it slowly erodes away. Then it suddenly goes, and that wall of water is running down. Indeed, you're not going to be able to stop it at that moment. But the question is—what about the process which is constantly making the wrong kind of dam and letting it erode? What's going on deeper down?

The real crisis is not in these events which are confronting us, like wars and crime and drugs and economic chaos and pollution; it's really in the thought which is making it—all the time. Each person can do something about that thought, because [he or she is] in it. But one of the troubles we get into is to say, "It's they who are thinking all that, and I am thinking right." I say that's a mistake. I say thought *pervades* us. It's similar to a virus—somehow this is a disease of thought, of knowledge, of information, spreading all over the world. The more computers, radio, and television we have, the faster it spreads. So the kind of thought that's going on all around us begins to take over in every one of us, without our even noticing it. It's spreading like a virus and each one of us is nourishing that virus.

Do we have a kind of immune system that stops it? The only way to stop it is to recognize it, to acknowledge it, to see what it is. If any one of us starts to look at that, then we are looking at the source of the problem. It's the same in all of us. We may imagine that the source of the problem is that somebody "over there" is thinking these wrong thoughts—or that a lot of people are. But the source of the problem is much deeper. It is that something is going wrong in the whole process of thought, which is collective, which belongs to all of us.

A key assumption that we have to question is that our thought is our own individual thought. Now, to some extent it is. We have some independence. But we must look at it more carefully. It's more subtle than to say it's individual or it's not individual. We have to see what thought *really* is, without presuppositions. What is really going on when we're thinking? I'm trying to say that most of our thought in its general form is not individual. It originates in the whole culture and it pervades us. We pick it up as children from parents, from friends, from school, from newspapers, from books, and so on. We make a small change in it; we select certain parts of it which we like, and we may reject other parts. But still, it all comes from that pool. This deep structure of thought, which is the source, the constant source—timeless—is always there. It's not that we go back in time to find its origin, but rather that it's constantly working. This deep structure of thought is what is common, and this is what we have to get at. We will have to come to see that the content of thought and the deep structure are not really separate, because the way we think about thought has an effect on its structure. If we think, for example, that thought is coming from *me* individually, this will affect how thought works. So we have to look at both content and structure.

We have the sense that we "know" all sorts of things. But we could say that perhaps it is not "we," but *knowledge itself* which knows all sorts of things. The suggestion is that knowledge—which is thought—is moving autonomously: it passes from one person to another. There is a whole pool of knowledge for the whole human race, like different computers that share a pool of knowledge. This pool of thought has been developing for many thousands of years, and it is full of all sorts of content. This knowledge, or thought, knows all of that content, *but it doesn't know what it is doing.* This knowledge knows itself wrongly: it knows itself as doing nothing. It therefore says, "I am not responsible for any of these problems. I'm just here for you to use."

All of this thought, which is based on what one has been thinking, is clearly coming from memory. You build up knowledge through experience, through practice. You think about it, you organize it, it goes into memory and becomes knowledge. Part of that knowledge is skill, through practice—that too is a kind of memory, somewhere in the body or in the brain. It's all part of one system. In this connection, there is what Michael Polanyi has called *tacit knowledge*—the knowledge which you can't state in words, but which is there. You know how to ride a bicycle, but you can't state how. If a bicycle is falling, you have to turn it in the direction it's falling in order to make it come up. Mathematically, there is a formula that shows that the angle to which you turn is related in a certain way to the angle at which you're falling. This is what you'll actually do, *but you don't work out the formula.* Your whole body does countless movements that you can't describe, and it makes it all work. That's tacit knowledge. It's a kind of knowledge you've got, without which you could do nothing. It's a continuation from the past of something that you learned. So we have experience, knowledge, thought, emotion, practice—all one process.

Further, in our language we have a distinction between "thinking" and "thought." "Thinking" implies the present tense—some activity going on which may include critical sensitivity to what can go wrong. Also there may be new ideas, and perhaps occasionally perception of some kind inside. "Thought" is the past participle of that. We have the idea that after we have been thinking something, it just evaporates. But thinking doesn't disappear. It goes somehow into the brain and leaves something—a trace—which becomes thought. And thought then acts automatically. So thought is the response from memory— from the past, from what has been done. Thus we have thinking and thought.

We also have the word "feeling." Its present tense suggests the active present, that the feeling is directly in contact with reality. But it might be useful to introduce the word "felt," to say there are "feelings" and "felts." That is, "felts" are feelings which have been recorded. A traumatic experience in the past can make you feel very uncomfortable when remembered. Nostalgic feelings are also from the past. A lot of the feelings that come up are really from the past, they're "felts." But if they are just a recording being replayed, they don't have as much significance as if they were a response to the present immediate situation.

It's really very important to see that our culture gives us a wrong lead about thoughts and felts. It constantly tends to imply that they could be separated and that one could control the other. But thoughts and felts are one process; they are not two. They both come from the memory; in the memory they are probably all mixed. Memory also affects the physical body. It affects the sensations. You can produce states of stress in the body from memory of states of stress. Therefore, when memory acts you cannot separate the intellectual function, the emotional function, the chemical function, the muscular function—because this *tacit knowledge* is also a kind of memory—they're all there.

Neuroscientific studies of brain structure suggest that thought originates somewhere in the outer cortex of the brain—in the prefrontal lobes—and that the emotional center is deeper down. There is a very thick bundle of nerves connecting them, and in this way they should be closely related; there is a lot of evidence that they are. Consider the primitive reflex to fight or to run or to freeze. There was a nice example of how this works under modern conditions in a television program which, among other things, showed an airport controller who is angry at his boss. His boss is mistreating him. He can't run, because he has to stay there. He can't fight his boss. And he can't just stop and freeze and do nothing. Meanwhile, the brain is pouring neurochemicals into the system, *as if he were being attacked in the jungle.* This process is stirring up the body and making it all work rather badly, and also preventing rational thought because such thought requires a nice, quiet brain. The more he thinks, the worse it gets. He'll get thoughts which lead him further astray and make more trouble. . . .

You could ask, "Why don't people see this clearly? It seems a very present danger and yet it seems people can't see it." They don't see it because of this thought process, which is collective as well as individual. The thoughts, the fantasies, and the collective fantasies are entering perception. Myths are collective fantasies, and every culture has its myths. Many of them are entering perception as if they were perceived realities. Everybody has a somewhat different way in which this happens, and we don't actually see the fact. *That* is the fact: that we don't see the fact. There is a higher order of fact—which is that we are not seeing the direct fact. This is the fact from which we must start.

I think we can get a further insight into why concepts and images have such a powerful effect, if we more fully consider that thought is able to provide a *representation* of what we experience. "Representation" is a very appropriate word here, because it just says "re-present"—to present again. Thus, we may say that perception *presents* something, and that thought *re-presents* it in abstraction.

A map is a kind of representation. The map is obviously much less than the territory it represents. This abstraction is advantageous because it focuses on what may be important for our purposes, with all the unnecessary detail left out. It is structured and organized in a way which may be helpful and relevant. Therefore, a representation is not just *a* concept—it's really a number of concepts together.

Another example would be the case of someone giving a talk—there forms in the minds of those who listen a representation of whatever is meant. In listening to someone who is describing something, some sort of representation will form in your mind—in the imagination perhaps—as if it were perceived. It will not be the same as the thing itself—it will be very abstract compared with it. It will highlight certain points, which may be of interest compared to the original perception, and so on. We are constantly forming re-presentations in this way.

But the thing to notice—the key point—is that this representation is not only present in thought or in imagination, but *it fuses with the actual perception or experience*. In other words, the representation fuses with the "presentation," so that what is "presented" (as perception) is already in large part a re-presentation. So it "presents again." You then get what we might call a "net presentation," which is the result of the senses, of thought, and possibly some insight. It all comes together in one net presentation. The way you experience something, therefore, depends on how you represent it—or mis-represent it.

If you represent yourself to yourself as noble and capable and honest, that representation enters the perception of yourself. That's how you perceive yourself. Now, somebody else gives another representation—which is that you are dishonest and stupid—and this goes in, too, and affects your "perception" of yourself. And that shakes up the whole neurophysiological system in a very disturbing way. Thought is then under pressure to represent the situation in a better light—and there you see the beginning of self-deception.

We generally do not notice the connection between representation and presentation—the two-way connection. Thought seems to lack the ability to see that this is happening. The process is unconscious, implicit, tacit—we don't know exactly how it happens. But we can see that something happens in which thought mixes these up. Imagine the information coming in from the senses and being organized in the brain, but then another stream of information comes in from thought, and the two mix in the whole. The net presentation is a result of the two.

The important point is that we are not aware that this is happening. The human race by and large has seldom known this—if ever. Perhaps a few people have known it, but by and large we go ahead without being aware of it. We're not saying that this process is bad or good. What's wrong with it is not that it takes place, but rather that we are not aware of it. . . .

What is not represented as interesting generally does not hold your interest. If it is not represented as valuable and interesting, it is not presented in that way, and therefore it doesn't hold the interest. And in some cases you *should* represent it according to your interest. You may say, "I need to represent it in a certain way to do something." It will therefore hold your interest and attention while you're doing it. Now, none of this is wrong. In fact, all of it is absolutely necessary. Unless something is presented in that way, you can't take action. You can't just act from the abstract representation in the imagination. You have got to act from the concrete presentation.

But the lack of awareness of this process is crucial. If someone says, "People of this category are bad," and you accept that, then *the representation of thought enters the presentation of perception.* Once you've accepted that, it goes into implicit, tacit thought. The next moment, when you see a person of that kind, it comes up as a presentation. The "badness" is perceived as inhering in him. It is not that you say, "I know that somebody has *told* me that these people are bad, and they may be bad or they may be good. I'd better look and see." But rather, what they "are" is apparently right "there." From there on, you think about that as if it were entirely an independent fact—independent of thought.

Thought then begins apparently to *prove* itself, and to create "facts" which are not really facts. The Latin root of the word "fact" means "what has been made," as in "manufacture." In some sense we have to establish a fact, but this sort of fact is being made wrongly. This is a fact which is, so to speak, not being properly manufactured. It's being made in the wrong way because we are mixing up thought into that "fact," and not knowing that we are doing it. It's necessary to let thought enter the fact, but we fail to notice that this is happening. If we say it's a "pure" fact, which is just "there," we will give it tremendous value, and say, "How can you deny the fact? You can see what sort of people they are."

It is important to see that most of our representations arise collectively, and that gives them greater power. If everybody agrees on something, we take that as evidence that it's right, or that it could be right. This then creates a pressure on us—we don't want to get out of the consensus. This means that we are constantly under pressure to accept any particular representation, and to see it that way. . . .

But going further, getting more of a feeling for this notion, you begin to see how it works inside of us and between us—in communication and in dialogue. You see that this question of representation is crucial in our communication. Suppose people meet in a group, bringing certain representations about what other people are like, or what they themselves are like. As the group communicates, these representations may get shaken, and change; the presentation changes, and therefore the whole relationship changes. Our relationship depends on how we present other people to ourselves, and how we present ourselves to other people. And all of that depends on the general collective representations.

When things are going smoothly there is no way to know that there's anything wrong—we have already made the assumption that what's going on is independent of thought. When things are represented, and then presented in that way, there is no way for you to see what is happening—it's already excluded. You cannot pay attention to what is outside the representation. There's tremendous pressure not to; it's very hard. The only time you can pay attention to it is when you see there is trouble—when a surprise comes, when there's a contradiction, when things don't quite work.

However, we don't want to view this process as a "problem," because we have no idea how to *solve* it—we can't project a solution. One of our representations is that everything we do is in time. We project a goal and we find the means to achieve the end. Therefore everything in the world is presented that way—as something that could be handled in that way. We should, then, think of this as a question, or a difficulty—seeing that things are not working right. We're beginning to see where it's going wrong, though perhaps not yet being able to really change it. But we're starting to get some sort of feeling for where it's going wrong—namely, that a lot of what we take to be fact is not really fact.

This implies a different way of seeing the world—it implies that our whole way of seeing the world could change. We see the world according to the general collective representations circulating around our society and culture, and insofar as these could be dropped, then we may change, because the world is presented differently. If you are presented to me as a dangerous person, then I will shrink back—I can't help it. But if I represent you differently, then my whole approach is different. Further, we have to be careful about mis-representation. We could say, "We are all loving one another, everything is solved." That would then be presented, and we would get a nice glow; however, this would be based on a *mis*-representation. But this doesn't change the fact that any real change in presentation—any *genuine* change—is a change of being.

We could consider a representation which is current in our society, such as, "You have to take care of yourself first, you have to watch out—people are dangerous—you can't trust them," and so on. This will produce a response, not only outwardly but also inwardly. The entire neurochemistry develops accordingly, as does the tension in the body. Now, it's true that the world is dangerous, but we are looking at this wrongly. It's dangerous not because people are intrinsically dangerous, but because of mis-representation that has generally been accepted. We have to see the right reason. Therefore, we don't approach such people as intrinsically dangerous, but as people who are the victims of mis-representation.

Changing this representation then opens the way to further change. We don't say it's going to be easy, or hard—we don't know—but it opens up the way, it opens up a big perspective. If we could learn to see thought actually producing presentations from representations, we would no longer be fooled by it—it would be like seeing the trick of a magician. As long as you don't see what the magician is doing, it seems like magic. But if you had a direct insight into the trick, it could change everything.

Many worlds are possible—it all depends on representation, especially the collective representation. To make a "world" takes more than one person, and therefore the collective representation is the key. It's not enough merely for one person to change his [or her] representation. That's fine, but we're saying that the real change is the change of collective representations.

REVIEW QUESTIONS

1. Explain what Bohm means by the way of thinking called "fragmentation." What is powerful about this way of thinking? What is problematic about it?
2. What's the difference between "taking a watch and smashing it into fragments" and "taking it apart and finding its parts"?

3. What is "the deep structure of thought"?
4. What does Bohm mean when he says that *"knowledge itself* knows all sorts of things"?
5. Define *tacit knowledge* and give two examples from your own experience.
6. "Thoughts" and "felts" are *representations,* but "thinking" and "feeling" are not. Explain.
7. Explain what it means to say that representations "fuse with the actual perception or experience." How is this a "two-way connection"?
8. How do you respond to Bohm's explanation of "facts"?

PROBES

1. How would you label (represent) the *opposite* of what Bohm calls "fragmentation"? How would you describe this alternative way of thinking?
2. In what sense, according to Bohm, is thought individual? In what sense or to what degree is it collective? Explain whether you agree or disagree with Bohm on this point.
3. Bohm says that tacit knowledge involves "experience, knowledge, thought, emotion, practice—all one process" and that it is known, in an important sense, by your *body.* Explain.
4. Think about how you perceive your supervisor or boss at work. How are representations part of this perception? What specific representations commonly fuse with your actual experience of your boss?
5. Bohm claims that the problem is *not* that facts or reality are made up of representations plus perceptions or experiences, but that most people are not aware that they are. Explain.
6. Partly to guard against simplistic interpretations of what he's saying, Bohm emphasizes that "any real change in presentation—any *genuine* change—is a change of being." What does this mean? How does this guard against simplistic interpretations of his ideas?

CHAPTER 6

Listening

*A*s the authors of this reading point out, most treatments of listening begin by arguing for the importance of good listening and then try to convince you that you're probably not an effective listener. But if you're studying listening, chances are you already know it's important and believe you could do it better. So rather than telling you what you already know, these authors begin their book on listening by discussing three misconceptions people commonly have about the listening process. Their idea is that it will be easier to improve your listening if you begin with an accurate rather than a distorted understanding of what's involved.

The first misconception is that listening is natural. The authors explain that hearing is the natural process, and that listening takes some thought, training, and effort. I've always believed that one of the most ironic things about listening is that, according to several surveys, we spend much more time listening than we spend reading, writing, or speaking, but we get almost no organized training in listening. So we are taught the least about the communication activity we engage in the most! Roach and Wyatt discuss this phenomenon.

The second misconception they discuss is the belief that listening is a passive act, a process of simply being open to what's available. This misconception exists primarily because we associate "work" with *visible* effort, and the effort you invest in listening is sometimes not very visible. But every person who listens for a living—therapist, lawyer, doctor, accountant, business consultant—has personally experienced the crushing fatigue that can come from working hard at listening.

The third misconception is that "I'm a good listener when I try." Some early listening research indicated that the average white-collar worker remembers about 25 percent of what he or she hears. So most of us start with a pretty low efficiency rate. Raw effort can improve that number, but not very permanently. It's most effective to get some listening training aimed at both attitudes and skills and then to practice what you learn long enough to make it habitual.

My primary purpose for including this brief reading is to set up the more developed articles that follow. If you're well informed about misconceptions, you'll be prepared to take on some new understandings and skills.

LISTENING AND THE RHETORICAL PROCESS

Carol A. Roach and Nancy J. Wyatt

Most texts on listening begin by establishing that listening skills are important to you in school, on the job, and in your personal relationships. Then they go on to convince you that you're not a very good listener. While these two observations may be true, we believe that you already know you could benefit by improving your listening skills or you wouldn't be taking this course. We will not, therefore, bore you by telling you what you already know. Instead, we will introduce you to some common misconceptions about listening and refute those misconceptions. . . .

MISCONCEPTION NUMBER ONE: LISTENING IS NATURAL

The misconception that listening is natural arises partly because we confuse the process of listening with the process of hearing. Hearing is certainly a natural process. Unless you have organic damage to some part of your ear, you will have been hearing since before you were born. Hearing is a matter of perception of small changes in atmospheric pressure, which goes on continuously, even when you are sleeping. How else would the alarm wake you in the morning? . . .

Humans can "hear" changes in air pressure in an effective range of frequencies from 20 to 20,000 cycles per second. Changes in air pressure impact the eardrum and are transmitted through the middle ear to the inner ear, where they are transformed into electrochemical messages and sent to the hearing center in the brain. That process is natural and automatic and outside conscious control. Problems start when we confuse this purely automatic physical process with the consciously purposeful psychological process of listening.

Listening is largely a process of discriminating and identifying which sounds are meaningful or important to us and which aren't. We actually focus our hearing in the same way we focus our sight. You can probably remember a time when you didn't "see" something that was in plain sight. Maybe you even fell over it. You have probably also had the experience of talking to someone— a parent, a teacher, a colleague, even a friend—who was thinking about something else and didn't "hear" what you said. In fact, they did hear in the sense that the sounds reached their ears, but they didn't hear what you said because they were paying attention to something else at the time. If you're sufficiently candid, you may also remember some times when you didn't hear something that was said to you because you weren't paying attention. We are all guilty of thinking about other things sometimes. The point is, you did hear, but you weren't listening.

"Excuse me, Dr. Simpson, I'm having trouble thinking of a good attention getter for my speech."

"What's your topic?"

"I'm talking about Cambodia and the Khmer Rouge, all that killing."

"In that case why don't you use the technique I just illustrated in class, the one from the acid rain speech?"

"I didn't hear that one. I guess I wasn't listening."

The importance of distinguishing between hearing and listening is that we don't need training to hear well, but we do need training to listen well. In fact, if the hearing mechanism is damaged, no amount of training will improve its function. Real deafness can't be cured by trying harder. Faulty listening, on the other hand, can't be cured by medical science or by magic. To learn to listen more effectively, you have to try harder. You have to learn how to listen.

The idea that we learn to listen as children is partially true. Before they start to school, children learn many things by listening. But they only learn as well as they were trained. Unfortunately most of the training children receive in listening skills comes largely in the form of injunctions. "Now, you listen to me!" they are told, or "Listen carefully!" The usefulness of such training can be illustrated by comparing it to a similar injunction to a child to "Catch the ball!" Not very useful advice. It's more useful to show children how to hold their hands and tell them to keep their eyes on the ball. Then give them plenty of supervised practice and explain to them what they are doing right and what they're doing wrong, so they can improve. Without supervised practice, children can pick up bad habits of listening which serve them indifferently as they grow up. Learning to listen is a matter of training; it doesn't come naturally any more than playing ball does.

In one very interesting study, Nichols and Stevens (1957) found evidence that younger children listen better than older children. When the researchers stopped teachers in the middle of lectures and asked the students what the teachers were talking about, they found that 90 percent of the first graders could answer correctly, 80 percent of the second graders could answer correctly, but only 28 percent of the senior high school students could answer correctly. These results might even lead us to believe that we become worse listeners as we grow up. Far from being a natural process, listening is clearly a consciously purposive activity for which we need systematic training and supervision to learn to do well.

Another way to look at listening is as one part of the communication process, like speaking. While we could agree that speaking is a natural human function, no one could deny that children have to be taught how to speak. Certainly no one was born speaking standard English. If you have forgotten the process of learning to speak, spend a couple of hours in a supermarket listening to mothers talk to toddlers as they shop. You will hear careful and constant instruction, reiteration, correction, and reinforcement of correct language patterns and usage. Or, if you have studied a second language, remember how much time you had to spend memorizing, listening, and practicing to become fluent.

Listening and speaking are both consciously purposive activities for which we need training to do well. The idea that some people are born listeners or born speakers is a fiction. It's a copout for people who don't want to try harder.

MISCONCEPTION NUMBER TWO:
LISTENING IS PASSIVE

One of the most common misconceptions we have in our American way of life is the idea that work is always active. We seem to think that if we don't "see" something happening, work is not being done. So thinking is not often defined as work. Children are encouraged to "do something"—join the Little League, scouts, clubs. They are enrolled in camps, dancing lessons, junior business associations, and extracurricular activities. Students are encouraged to "get involved"—join the students' government, join a club or fraternity or association, contribute time to charities, and attend social events. Time spent "doing nothing" is assumed to be time wasted. In businesses and corporations people spend much of their working day going to meetings, having lunch, traveling, doing anything to look busy. Employees learn very quickly how to "look busy" when the boss comes around, even though no specific action is required at the moment. Also, scholars, whose business is thinking, have to list specific activities to their administrators to prove they really are working. In our culture, movement is equated with work.

This American orientation toward a definition of work with visible activity leads us to view listening as passive. After all, you can't see anyone listening, so they must not be "doing" anything. What we have done instead is to define the visible signs of listening as the activity itself. You will understand this statement if you think back to when you were in high school. Think about the most boring class you had in high school. You didn't want to be caught daydreaming, so what did you do! You perfected the "student's stare." You put your chin in your hand, opened your eyes real wide, and nodded periodically as though you were agreeing with what was being said. If you were clever, you remembered to throw in a frown once in a while to show you were trying to understand something particularly difficult. You smiled occasionally to show you were glad to have something so interesting to listen to in school. Meanwhile your mind went on vacation. It worked perfectly. You had learned that activity equates with work.

> When I began teaching I learned very quickly that I couldn't tell by looking who was listening and who wasn't. I had one student who always sat in the back, tilted his chair against the wall, and seemed to go to sleep. Finally one day I got fed up and challenged him. I told him that if he only meant to sleep, he could do it at home on his own time. He sat up, pushed his hat back, and recited to me the last ten minutes of my lecture. Boy, was I embarrassed.

One consequence of defining listening by its visible signs is to deny the active nature of real listening. When you are listening, your mind is extremely busy receiving and sorting out new ideas and relating them to what you already know and making new connections with old information. Real listening involves taking in new information and checking it against what you already know, selecting important ideas from unimportant ideas, searching for categories to store the information in (or creating new categories), and predicting what's coming next in order to be ready for it. . . . When you're listening, your brain is busy actively reconstructing what the speaker is saying into meaningful units in terms of your own experience. But all this activity takes place in your brain; none of it necessarily shows itself outwardly. So it often looks like nothing is being done.

> One of the things I found most frustrating about working in a group was that no one ever seemed to be listening to me. It was like I was always talking to myself. But then when it came time to prepare the final report, I discovered that the other group members knew a lot of the things I had been talking about. I was surprised to find out they had been listening after all. Especially John. I had thought he was a total deadhead.

MISCONCEPTION NUMBER THREE: I'M A GOOD LISTENER WHEN I TRY

Most people vastly overestimate their own listening skills. One clever educator illustrates this to people who take his workshop on listening skills by having each person introduce herself to the class. Then he asks each of them to name the person who is sitting to her left. Most people can't do it.

If you ask most people what their listening efficiency is, they will tell you that they remember about 75 to 80 percent of what they hear. Most people think they are good listeners. Research findings directly contradict this perception. The research finding most often cited to illustrate this poor listening efficiency comes from the work of Nichols (1957) who found that the average white-collar worker demonstrates only about 25 percent listening efficiency. This means that the average person only remembers about one-quarter of what he or she hears. Both these percentages are in comparison to the ideal of 100 percent recall, a feat only accomplished by fictional detectives and a few unusual persons who have perfect auditory recall (like some people have photographic memories).

The real test of listening skills is, of course, not what you can do on a listening test, but how well you understand and remember the things you have to understand and remember to get along in your daily life. When the television news broadcast is over, how much of what you heard do you remember? Can you pick out the main points when someone is giving a speech? Can you understand and remember oral instructions? How good are you at discovering people's feelings when they are talking to you? Can you distinguish between a genuinely good business deal and a scam? Can you pick out the arguments and evidence in a political speech? Can you pick out the different instruments in a band or identify the theme of a symphony? All these tasks are related to your ability to listen effectively, and skill at these tasks is important to your welfare. But most people are only partially successful at any of these tasks.

The fact is that most of us would like to think we are better listeners (more intelligent, more sensitive, more beautiful) than we really are. Listening is hard work, and we don't apply ourselves to the task unless there is a clear payoff. But unless we practice and sharpen our listening skills and develop good listening habits, it may be too late when opportunity knocks. When you're in the middle of a business deal or in the middle of a physics lecture is not the time to start practicing listening skills.

REVIEW QUESTIONS

1. What are the primary differences between hearing and listening?
2. What kind of listening training do we typically get as young children?
3. How is our attitude about listening affected by the typically North American belief that "movement is equated with work"?
4. What do your lecture notes say about your listening efficiency? Do they indicate that you're retaining more or less than 25 percent of what you hear in class?

PROBES

1. Assume for a minute that human activities can be divided into the physiological (nerve impulses, skin reactions to chemicals, bleeding, etc.), psychological (attitudes, beliefs, fears, etc.), and communicative (involving coordination with at least one other person). Which type or types of activity are involved in hearing? Which ones characterize listening?
2. How would you describe some of the "invisible" activities that are involved in effective listening? What specifically is going on that can't be seen?
3. Think about your own listening efficiency. Do you remember more than 25 percent of what you hear in class? At a party? Around the dinner table at home? When talking to your boss at work? In the past, what factors have increased or decreased your listening efficiency?

REFERENCES AND RECOMMENDED READING

Barbara, Dominick A. *How to Make People Listen to You.* Springfield, Ill.: Charles C. Thomas, 1971.

Barker, Larry L. *Listening Behavior.* Englewood Cliffs, N.J.: Prentice-Hall, 1971.

Hirsh, Robert O. *Listening: A Way to Process Information Aurally.* Dubuque, Iowa: Corsuch Scarisbrich, 1979.

Nichols, Ralph G. "Factors in Listening Comprehension." *Speech Monographs* 15 (1948): 154–163.

Nichols, Ralph G., and Leonard A. Stevens. *Are You Listening?* New York: McGraw-Hill, 1957, pp. 12–13.

Phillips, Gerald M., and Julia T. Wood. *Communication and Human Relations.* New
    York: Macmillan, 1983.
Steil, Lyman, Larry L. Barker, and Kittie W. Watson. *Effective Listening.* Reading,
    Mass.: Addison-Wesley, 1983.
Wolff, Florence I., Nadine C. Marsnik, William S. Tracy, and Ralph G. Nichols.
    Perceptive Listening. New York: Holt, Rinehart and Winston, 1983.

*T*his selection is taken from the "Listening" chapter of a book called
Messages: The Communication Skills Book, authored by two psy-
chotherapists and a professional writer. I include it because of the clear,
straightforward, concrete, and useful things it says about listening.

After underscoring the importance of listening to all interpersonal
communication, the authors note that "being quiet while someone talks
does not constitute real listening." They use this as a lead-in to their discussion of the differences between "real" and "pseudo-listening." They
list 10 typical needs that can be met by pseudo-listening, including
"making people think you're interested so they will like you," "buying
time to prepare your next comment," and "listening for the weak points
in an argument so you can always be right."

Then the authors review 12 blocks to effective listening. I won't review all of them here, but I hope you find them as familiar and insightful as I do. Even after studying listening and practicing it for years, I still
find myself falling into the traps that McKay, Davis, and Fanning call
"rehearsing," "identifying," "sparring," and "placating." If listening is
a real challenge for you, you might carry this list of blocks with you for
a time so you can remind yourself of some ways to improve this part of
your communicating.

The last part of this reading outlines four steps to effective listening.
The first is listening actively. McKay, Davis, and Fanning sketch three
activities that can especially help: paraphrasing, clarifying, and giving
feedback. They also encourage you to try to make your feedback immediate, honest, and as supportive as you can. The second step is to listen with empathy. The key to this step, the authors believe, is to remember that "everyone is trying to survive." Carole Logan and I will
discuss empathic listening again later in this chapter.

Step three is listening with openness, and this means reserving or
otherwise postponing judgments until after you've listened fully. These
authors admit that judgments and criticism can be personally gratifying in the short term, but they also discuss five ways you pay for the
judgments you pronounce on others. Step four is listening with awareness. One feature of this step is "to compare what's being said to your
own knowledge of history, people, and the way things are . . . without
judgment." A second part of this step is to track the congruence, or fit,
between the content of a person's communication and her or his tone of
voice, emphasis, facial expression, and posture.

The four steps and the authors' final six very concrete suggestions ("Maintain good eye contact. Lean slightly forward," etc.) sound fairly straightforward, but they're not easy to put into practice. Especially when you disagree, are impatient, or feel some tension, genuine listening can be a significant communication challenge. But this reading and the other ones in this chapter should enable you to become much better at it.

LISTENING

Matthew McKay, Martha Davis, and Patrick Fanning

You're at a dinner party. Someone is telling anecdotes, someone is complaining, someone is bragging about his promotion. Everyone there is anxious to talk, to tell his or her story. Suddenly you get the feeling that no one is listening. While the talk goes on you notice that people's eyes wander. They are perhaps rehearsing their own remarks. It's as if they have secretly agreed: "I'll be an audience for you if you'll be an audience for me." The party may be a success, but people go home without hearing or knowing each other.

Listening is an essential skill for making and keeping relationships. If you are a good listener, you'll notice that others are drawn to you. Friends confide in you and your friendships deepen. Success comes a little easier because you hear and understand people: you know what they want and what hurts or irritates them. You get "lucky" breaks because people appreciate you and want you around.

People who don't listen are bores. They don't seem interested in anyone but themselves. They turn off potential friends and lovers by giving the message: "What you have to say doesn't matter much to me." As a result, they often feel lonely and isolated. The tragedy is that people who don't listen rarely figure out what's wrong. They change their perfume or cologne, they get new clothes, they work at being funny, and they talk about "interesting" things. But the underlying problem remains. They aren't fun to talk to because the other person never feels satisfied that he or she has been heard.

It's dangerous not to listen! You miss important information and you don't see problems coming. When you try to understand why people do things, you have to mind-read and guess to fill in the gaps in your listening skills.

Listening is a commitment and a compliment. It's a commitment to understanding how other people feel, how they see their world. It means putting aside your own prejudices and beliefs, your anxieties and self-interest, so that you can step behind the other person's eyes. You try to look at things from his or her perspective. Listening is a compliment because it says to the other person: "I care about what's happening to you; your life and your experience are important." People usually respond to the compliment of listening by liking and appreciating you.

From *Messages: The Communication Skills Book* by Matthew McKay, Martha Davis, and Patrick Fanning. Published by New Harbinger Publications, Oakland, CA, www.newharbinger.com.

REAL VERSUS PSEUDO-LISTENING

Being quiet while someone talks does not constitute real listening. Real listening is based on the *intention* to do one of four things:

1. Understand someone
2. Enjoy someone
3. Learn something
4. Give help or solace

If you want to understand someone, you can't help but really listen to him/her. When you're enjoying a conversation or you intend to learn something, listening comes quite naturally. When you want to help someone express his or her feelings, you are involved, listening. The key to real listening is wanting and intending to do so.

Unfortunately, a lot of pseudo-listening masquerades as the real thing. The intention is not to listen, but to meet some other need. Some of the typical needs met by pseudo-listening are:

1. Making people think you're interested so they will like you
2. Being alert to see if you are in danger of getting rejected
3. Listening for one specific piece of information and ignoring everything else
4. Buying time to prepare your next comment
5. Half-listening so someone will listen to you
6. Listening to find someone's vulnerabilities or to take advantage
7. Looking for the weak points in an argument so you can always be right, listening to get ammunition for attack
8. Checking to see how people are reacting, making sure you produce the desired effect
9. Half-listening because a good, kind, or nice person would
10. Half-listening because you don't know how to get away without hurting or offending someone

BLOCKS TO LISTENING

There are 12 blocks to listening. You will find that some are old favorites that you use over and over. Others are held in reserve for certain types of people or situations. Everyone uses listening blocks, so you shouldn't worry if a lot of blocks are familiar. This is an opportunity for you to become more aware of your blocks at the time you actually use them.

1. Comparing

Comparing makes it hard to listen because you're always trying to assess who is smarter, more competent, more emotionally healthy—you or the other. Some people focus on who has suffered more, who's a bigger victim. While someone's talking, you think to yourself: "Could I do it that well? . . . I've had it harder, he doesn't

know what hard is. . . . I earn more than that. . . . My kids are so much brighter."
You can't let much in because you're too busy seeing if you measure up.

2. Mind Reading

The mind reader doesn't pay much attention to what people say. In fact, he often distrusts it. He's trying to figure out what the other person is *really* thinking
and feeling. "She says she wants to go to the show, but I'll bet she's tired and
wants to relax. She might be resentful if I pushed her when she doesn't want to
go." The mind reader pays less attention to words than to intonations and subtle cues in an effort to see through to the truth.

If you are a mind reader, you probably make assumptions about how people react to you. "I bet he's looking at my lousy skin. . . . She thinks I'm stupid.
. . . She's turned off by my shyness." These notions are born of intuition,
hunches, and vague misgivings, but have little to do with what the person actually says to you.

3. Rehearsing

You don't have time to listen when you're rehearsing what to say. Your whole
attention is on the preparation and crafting of your next comment. You have to
look interested, but your mind is going a mile a minute because you've got a
story to tell, or a point to make. Some people rehearse whole chains of responses:
"I'll say, then he'll say, then I'll say," and so on.

4. Filtering

When you filter, you listen to some things and not to others. You pay only
enough attention to see if somebody's angry, or unhappy, or if you're in emotional danger. Once assured that the communication contains none of those
things, you let your mind wander. One woman listens just enough to her son to
learn whether he is fighting again at school. Relieved to hear he isn't, she begins
thinking about her shopping list. A young man quickly ascertains what kind of
mood his girlfriend is in. If she seems happy as she describes her day, his
thoughts begin wandering.

Another way people filter is simply to avoid hearing certain things—
particularly anything threatening, negative, critical, or unpleasant. It's as if the
words were never said: You simply have no memory of them.

5. Judging

Negative labels have enormous power. If you prejudge someone as stupid or
nuts or unqualified, you don't pay much attention to what they say. You've already written them off. Hastily judging a statement as immoral, hypocritical,
fascist, pinko, or crazy means you've ceased to listen and have begun a "kneejerk" reaction. A basic rule of listening is that judgments should only be made
after you have heard and evaluated the content of the message.

6. Dreaming

You're half-listening, and something the person says suddenly triggers a chain of private associations. Your neighbor says she's been laid off, and in a flash you're back to the scene where you got fired for playing hearts on those long coffee breaks. Hearts is a great game; there were the great nights of hearts years ago on Sutter Street. And you're gone, only to return a few minutes later as your neighbor says, "I knew you'd understand, but don't tell my husband."

You are more prone to dreaming when you feel bored or anxious. Everybody dreams, and you sometimes need to make herculean efforts to stay tuned in. But if you dream a lot with certain people, it may indicate a lack of commitment to knowing or appreciating them. At the very least, it's a statement that you don't value what they have to say very much.

7. Identifying

In this block, you take everything a person tells you and refer it back to your own experience. They want to tell you about a toothache, but that reminds you of the time you had oral surgery for receding gums. You launch into your story before they can finish theirs. Everything you hear reminds you of something that you've felt, done, or suffered. You're so busy with these exciting tales of your life that there's no time to really hear or get to know the other person.

8. Advising

You are the great problem-solver, ready with help and suggestions. You don't have to hear more than a few sentences before you begin searching for the right advice. However, while you are cooking up suggestions and convincing someone to "just try it," you may miss what's most important. You didn't hear the feelings, and you didn't acknowledge the person's pain. He or she still feels basically alone because you couldn't listen and just *be* there.

9. Sparring

This block has you arguing and debating with people. The other person never feels heard because you're so quick to disagree. In fact, a lot of your focus is on finding things to disagree with. You take strong stands, are very clear about your beliefs and preferences. The way to avoid sparring is to repeat back and acknowledge what you've heard. Look for one thing you might agree with.

One subtype of sparring is the *put-down*. You use acerbic or sarcastic remarks to dismiss the other person's point of view. For example, Helen starts telling Arthur about her problems in a biology class. Arthur says: "When are you going to have brains enough to drop that class?" Al is feeling overwhelmed with the noise from the TV. When he tells Rebecca, she says, "Oh god, not the TV routine again." The put-down is the standard block to listening in many marriages. It quickly pushes the communication into stereotyped patterns where each person repeats a familiar hostile litany.

A second type of sparring is discounting. Discounting is for people who can't stand compliments. "Oh, I didn't do anything. . . . What do you mean, I was totally lame. . . . It's nice of you to say, but it's really a very poor attempt." The basic technique of discounting is to run yourself down when you get a compliment. The other person never feels satisfied that you really heard his appreciation. And he's right—you didn't.

10. Being Right

Being right means you will go to any lengths (twist the facts, start shouting, make excuses or accusations, call up past sins) to avoid being wrong. You can't listen to criticism, you can't be corrected, and you can't take suggestions to change. Your convictions are unshakable. And since you won't acknowledge that your mistakes are mistakes, you just keep making them.

11. Derailing

This listening block is accomplished by suddenly changing the subject. You derail the train of conversation when you get bored or uncomfortable with a topic. Another way of derailing is by *joking it off*. This means that you continually respond to whatever is said with a joke or quip in order to avoid the discomfort or anxiety in seriously listening to the other person.

12. Placating

"Right. . . . Right. . . . Absolutely. . . . I know. . . . Of course you are. . . . Incredible. . . . Yes. . . . Really?" You want to be nice, pleasant, supportive. You want people to like you, so you agree with everything. You may half-listen, just enough to get the drift, but you're not really involved. You are placating rather than tuning in and examining what's being said. . . .

FOUR STEPS TO EFFECTIVE LISTENING

1. Active Listening

Listening doesn't mean sitting still with your mouth shut. A corpse can do that. Listening is an active process that requires your participation. To fully understand the meaning of a communication, you usually have to ask questions and give feedback. Then, in the give and take that follows, you get a fuller appreciation of what's being said. You have gone beyond passively absorbing; you are a collaborator in the communication process. Here are the ways to listen actively.

Paraphrasing   To paraphrase means to state in your own words what you think someone just said. Paraphrasing is absolutely necessary to good listening.

It keeps you busy trying to understand and know what the other person means, rather than blocking. You can paraphrase by using such lead-ins as "What I hear you saying is. . . . In other words. . . . So basically how you felt was . . . Let me understand, what was going on for you was. . . . What happened was. . . . Do you mean . . .?" You should paraphrase every time someone says something of any importance to you. Try it and you will reap five big dividends:

1. People deeply appreciate feeling heard.
2. Paraphrasing stops escalating anger and cools down crisis.
3. Paraphrasing stops miscommunication. False assumptions, errors, and misinterpretations are corrected on the spot.
4. Paraphrasing helps you remember what was said.
5. When you paraphrase you'll find it much harder to compare, judge, rehearse, spar, advise, derail, dream, and so on. In fact, paraphrasing is the antidote to most listening blocks.

If it's so great and solves so many listening ills, why doesn't everybody do it? Everybody should. But schools rarely teach basic life skills, and most people learn their listening skills by example. There are a lot of bad examples. . . .

Clarifying   Clarifying often goes along with paraphrasing. It just means asking questions until you get more of the picture. Since your intention is to fully understand what's being said, you often have to ask for more information, more background. You have to know the circumstances. Clarifying helps you sharpen your listening focus so that you hear more than vague generalities. You hear events in the context of what someone thought and felt, the relevant history. Clarifying also lets the other person know that you're interested. It gives the message: "I'm willing to work at knowing and understanding you."

Feedback   Active listening depends on feedback. You've paraphrased and clarified what was said, and hopefully understand it. This is the point at which you can talk about your reactions. In a nonjudgmental way, you can share what you thought, felt, or sensed. This doesn't mean falling back into sparring or identifying as a reaction. It means sharing what happened inside you.

Now is a good time to check your perceptions. You watched the body language and listened to the tone of voice. You noticed things that seemed to betray what the other person felt. You may have also drawn conclusions about the content of the communication. To check perceptions, you transform what you saw and heard into a tentative description: "I want to understand your feelings—is this [*giving a description*] the way you feel?" "Listening to what you said, I wonder if [*your description*] is what's really happening in the situation." All this is done without approval or disapproval, with only a wish to see if your hunch is correct.

Feedback also helps the other person understand the effect of his or her communication. It's another chance to correct errors and misconceptions. It's also a chance for him or her to get a fresh and valuable point of view—yours.

There are three important rules for giving feedback. It has to be immediate, honest, and supportive. *Immediate* means as soon as you fully understand the communication (after paraphrasing and clarifying). Putting your feedback off, even a few hours, makes it much less valuable. *Honest* means your real reaction—not something out of *Who's Afraid of Virginia Woolf?* You don't have to cut somebody up to give your reaction. In fact, brutality is rarely honest. Your feedback should be honest *and* supportive. You can be gentle, saying what you need to say without causing damage or defensiveness. For example, "I get the feeling that there's something you're not telling me" is more supportive than "You're holding out on me." "I think there's a real possibility that you've made a mistake" is more supportive than "You've been a fool."

2. Listening With Empathy

There is only one requirement for listening with empathy: simply know that everyone is trying to survive. You don't have to like everyone or agree with them, but recognize that you do share the same struggle. Every second of the day you are trying to survive both physically and psychologically. Every thought, every choice, every movement is designed to preserve your existence.

The outrageous, the inconsiderate, the false, and the violent acts are all strategies to minimize pain (death) and hold on to life. Some people have better survival strategies than others. And some are plainly incompetent, making a mess of everything they touch. They don't live as long physically, and they die an early psychological death from chronic depression or anxiety.

Listening with empathy means saying to yourself, "This is hard to hear, but it's another human being trying to live." Ask yourself: "How did this belief or this decision, though it may ultimately fail, lower this person's anxiety or get some needs met?"

Your ability to listen naturally goes down when someone is angry, criticizes, or wallows in self-pity. If you find listening with empathy difficult, ask these questions:

1. What need is the [*anger, etc.*] coming from?
2. What danger is this person experiencing?
3. What is he or she asking for?

3. Listening With Openness

It's difficult to listen when you're judging and finding fault. All the information gets scrambled coming in, while you build a case to dismiss a person or his [or her] ideas. You have to listen selectively, filtering out everything that makes sense and pouncing on whatever seems false or silly. You collect and hoard the "stupidities" so you can share them later with a sympathetic audience.

Judgments can be very gratifying, but here's how you pay for them:

1. If your opinions have been proven false, you are the last to know.
2. You don't grow intellectually because you only listen to viewpoints you already hold.

3. You dismiss otherwise worthwhile people because you disagree with their ideas.
4. You turn people off because you spar and don't listen.
5. You miss important information.

Nearly everyone has trouble listening openly. You don't want to hear your sacred cows reduced to hamburger. You don't want to face certain facts about yourself. Nor do you want to believe that an unlikable person has said something worth thinking about. You naturally want to argue, to shout it down.

The fear of being wrong has vast proportions. That's because your opinions and beliefs are closely tied to self-esteem. Being wrong can equal being stupid, bad, or worthless. It would be a great step forward if beliefs and opinions could be seen as temporary hypotheses—held until disproved or modified. Rather than building your self-esteem on being right, you might reform your picture of yourself into that of one who, above all, wants to find the truth.

Listening with openness is a skill you can learn. The following exercise, called a *reversal*, should be tried with someone you trust. Select an old disagreement that isn't too explosive. Each of you state your side of the argument. Now reverse, and argue for the opposite position. Do it convincingly, really pushing the other person's point of view. Try to win the debate from the other side. Don't stop until you feel immersed in the viewpoint you once opposed. At the end, share with each other what you experienced.

Obviously, you can't practice reversals in most situations. What you can do, as an exercise in openness, is become an anthropologist. Imagine that the individuals that you're talking to hail from another planet or country. They have different customs, religion, ways of thinking. And you are an anthropologist trying to understand it all. Your job is to find out how their point of view makes sense, to see how it fits their world view, their history, their particular social system.

The most important rule for listening with openness is to hear the whole statement, the entire communication, before judging. Premature evaluations don't make sense because you don't have all the information.

4. Listening With Awareness

There are two components to listening with awareness. One is to compare what's being said to your own knowledge of history, people, and the way things are. You do this without judgment, simply making note of how a communication fits with known facts.

The second way you listen with awareness is to hear and observe congruence. Does the person's tone of voice, emphasis, facial expression, and posture fit with the content of his or her communication? If someone is telling you that his father has just died, but smiles and leans back comfortably with his hands laced behind his head, the message doesn't make sense. There is no congruence. If body, face, voice, and words don't fit, your job as a listener is to clarify and give feedback about the discrepancy. If you ignore it, you're settling for an incomplete or confusing message.

If you want to practice noticing incongruity, watch some TV comedies. Much of the humor is based on the mismatch of expression and content.

TOTAL LISTENING

People want you to listen, so they look for clues to prove that you are. Here's how to be a total listener:

1. Maintain good eye contact.
2. Lean slightly forward.
3. Reinforce the speaker by nodding or paraphrasing.
4. Clarify by asking questions.
5. Actively move away from distractions.
6. Be committed, even if you're angry or upset, to understanding what was said.

REVIEW QUESTIONS

1. The authors suggest that good listening can improve your "luck." How?
2. What is pseudo-listening? Why is it undesirable? Potentially dangerous?
3. How is filtering different from dreaming? How are they similar?
4. How does it feel to talk with someone whose listening is polluted by what these authors call "identifying"? What does this tell you about this listening block?
5. How is discounting a type of sparring? What are the similarities and differences between discounting and placating?
6. "Brutality is rarely honest," the authors write. Explain. Why is this point significant?
7. Which of the five "costs" of judgments have you had to pay in your relationships?
8. Explain what these authors mean when they encourage you to listen with openness by "becoming an anthropologist."

PROBES

1. Real listening, these authors believe, depends on the *intention* to understand, enjoy, learn, or give help or support. What do you believe they would advise you to do if you honestly do not want to do any of these four things?
2. Especially when you're being bombarded by advertisers or politicians, it can be helpful or even necessary to listen *critically*, so you don't get taken in by weak or invalid arguments. What do you believe these authors would say about critical listening?
3. A teacher I know enforces the rule during class discussions that you cannot raise your hand while someone else is talking, because if you have your hand

up, you're probably filtering or rehearsing, so you can't be listening effectively. What do you think of this rule?

4. "You should paraphrase," these authors write, "every time someone says something of any importance to you." I believe that paraphrasing is extremely important, but that if you follow their advice literally, your conversation partners will think you're trying to manipulate them with listening techniques you just learned in a self-help book. What do you think?

5. Paraphrase the following comment by McKay, Davis, and Fanning, and explain why it's important: "The outrageous, the inconsiderate, the false, and the violent acts are all strategies to minimize pain (death) and hold on to life."

This brief reading is here to underscore the "hard work" and "maturing" dimensions of listening. Its author, John Sanford, is a Jungian counselor in San Diego who helps people improve their skills at one-to-one communication. His discussion of listening does not so much add new ideas to what's been said in the other readings as it emphasizes parts of the listening process that the other readings only mention.

Like the other authors in this chapter, Sanford reminds us that "creative listening does not come naturally," but must be learned, and that the art of creative listening is different from lecturing, giving advice, making pronouncements, and judging. Listening creatively helps the person we're listening to work through his or her own agenda, and this means that as listeners, we need to "put aside our own agenda for the time being."

But then Sanford extends this point to emphasize that this kind of listening takes *discipline,* and requires *maturity.* It is not easy to set aside one's own agenda, and it is a measure of maturity to be able to put another's needs first for a time. This is part of the reason why listening is "simple, but it is also hard work." You don't have to be a genius to figure out how to do it , but it is still difficult. And this is one reason why it's often not done, or not done well.

At the end of this reading Sanford notes that discipline and maturity do not mean supporting another person's selfishness, inconsiderateness, or egocentric attitude. As he puts it, "it does not do anyone any good to listen to another person unless that person is talking responsibly." Counselors or parents may find it necessary or wise to listen even when they don't really want to, but this kind of selfless willingness cannot realistically be extended to everyone or at all times.

I'm not sure how you'll respond to these paragraphs, but when I read them I hear a voice like my father's. Sanford speaks about listening in the culturally typical tones of a male authority figure. He's gentle enough, but especially when he talks about discipline and maturity, he emphasizes some of the harder side of the "soft" art of listening. In this way, his words can usefully complement, I think, what's said in the rest of this chapter.

THE POWER OF CREATIVE LISTENING

John A. Sanford

Creative listening takes place when one person devotes her attention whole-heartedly to what another person is saying. Creative listening is receptive, but not passive. It is receptive because the listener is taking in what the other person is saying, feeling, and experiencing. It is active and not passive because the listener is actively seeking to understand what the other person is expressing.

There is healing power in creative listening because it develops a climate between two people in which relationship and understanding can grow. . . .

Creative listening is a fundamental and important part of all human relationships. It is essential for all of us to learn to listen creatively to others: friends listen to friends, employers to their employees and vice versa, parents to children, husbands and wives to each other. We even need to learn to listen to our enemies and those who oppose us in life. In this way we may turn a hostile relationship around, or, at least, learn something important.

There are many reasons why so many people lack the art of creative listening in our culture. First, because creative listening does not come naturally but is, for most people, a skill that must be acquired. We would like to think that the capacity to relate comes naturally, but to a great extent it is something that must be learned in life just as other abilities must be learned. It is something that requires work.

Second, many people lack the art of creative listening because of what it is not. It is not lecturing. It is not giving advice. It is not admonishing someone. It is not making pronouncements. It is not judging. All of these functions . . . may have their place in human communication, but they do not belong in creative listening. When we want to listen we must be careful to rule out that part of us that wants to lecture, admonish, advise or judge. But right here is where many people fail at listening, for the judging-lecturing-advising side of us wants to jump in and take over. To listen effectively we must be able to put aside these other functions, at least for the time being. This means that when we listen to someone we must reject the temptation to leap in and say, "Let me tell you what I would do . . ." or "I understand exactly what you are feeling . . ."

Listening creatively, and not jumping in with our advice, helps a person work through her agenda. We have already noted that when people want to communicate they have, as a rule, an agenda they must work through. When we listen it gives them the opportunity to work through all of their agenda. It gives them the satisfaction of having been able to express all of the things that were bothering them, all those matters and feelings that wanted to be shared.

But here we run into a problem, for the chances are that we have our agenda too. Especially in a close interpersonal relationship, both persons have their agendas, and when people start to talk with us about their feelings we naturally want to bring up our feelings as well. Nevertheless, if we wish to listen creatively we must learn to put aside our own agenda for the time being and listen to what the other person is saying. Perhaps the other person will then listen to us as well. If not, the relationship will become unequal and will lose its staying power, for to keep a relationship going both people must put energy into it. First we honor the other person's need to express himself, if he has been the one to begin the dialogue; then we should have our turn.

When our turn comes, and we have listened to the other person and heard what he is saying, we will find that our agenda is more likely to be heard than would have been possible if we had not listened first. For . . . when someone tries to express himself to another person, and that person refuses to listen, the first person feels frustrated and blocked and is not in a position to hear what is being said back. But if a person feels he has been heard, he is open to hearing someone else.

This is why I said that certain skills in relationship do not come naturally, for it takes discipline on our part to hear what another person is saying, and to listen until he is through. It takes discipline to hold back our own list of grievances or whatever else is on our mind. We can think of this devotion to listening as a sacrifice, for we sacrifice our own agenda for the time being, and devote our energy in a sacrificial way to the other person. This requires and develops maturity, for it takes maturity to be able to sacrifice in this way for the sake of communication.

Truly it has been said that we become what we do. Listening is a maturing activity. If we listen creatively it will not only help the other person, it will also help us to mature.

Creative listening is simple, but it is also hard work. It is like cutting down a tree with an axe. There are only a few basic principles to follow when cutting down a tree, but it is hard work. And listening is hard work, for it requires a concentration of energy on another person and what he is saying and feeling. In fact, it is usually more important to hear feelings than content.

Once we have heard what another person is saying it often helps to reflect that back to him. Let us take the situation in which a man has come home from work and has begun to complain about things around the house. His wife might say, "It sounds as if you are angry at me." This gives her husband a chance to clarify the situation. He might answer, "No, I am not angry at you. I am angry, but it is not at you, but at what happened at the office today." In this way a potentially serious misunderstanding can be resolved. Also, when we reflect back what we have heard the other person say, we are indicating to him that we have truly heard him. . . .

Simple, but hard work. That is creative listening. And precisely because it *is* hard work we do not listen to everyone, nor can we always be available to people who want us to listen to them. For instance, if a person has been drinking we may decline to listen to her. It does no good to listen to a person who is under the influence of alcohol; it drains us, without helping her. The situation is similar with regard to people under the influence of drugs. Sometimes it does not help people to listen to them on the telephone either (though not always). The reason for this is that when a person calls us on the phone it is at that person's convenience, but perhaps at our inconvenience. Many people call others and immediately start to talk out their agenda without inquiring if it is a good time for such a talk or not. This may reflect a manipulative or egocentric attitude on the part of that person, and if, through a false feeling of guilt, we feel compelled to listen to that person, we do not help her but only confirm her in her egocentric attitude.

In short, it does not do anyone any good to listen to another person unless that person is talking responsibly. To listen to someone is like giving him a gift. It does no good to give a gift unless we want to give it, or feel it is part of our integrity to give it. For instance, a counselor may listen to a client whether she wants to or not because the client is paying her to listen. Even if she is not in a mood to listen she is a professional who honors her obligation to her client and has carefully developed the ability to respond to a client's needs when called upon to do so at an appropriate time. A sensitive parent might also listen to a small child who has a sudden need to be heard, even though she might not want to listen at that moment. She listens when the child wants to be heard because she knows that the child's need is *now* and cannot be postponed; she wants to honor this in the child, and feels it is her appointed task to listen then if she possibly can. But this willingness to listen no matter how we feel at the time does not extend to everyone. In fact, even the counselor or parent might have to ask for a postponement of a listening situation if he or she is not able to do it at the time. There are times when we cannot listen to others because we do not have the energy; we may be fragmented, exhausted, or too absorbed with our own problems. In this case we might make an appointment at some definite future time to discuss the matter. This gives us the opportunity to become inwardly ready to listen and to have energy available for the other person.

REVIEW QUESTIONS

1. According to Sanford, what are the two main reasons why so many people lack the art of creative listening in our culture?
2. Explain the relationships Sanford describes between creative listening and the agendas of the speaker and the listener.
3. What does Sanford mean by "discipline"?
4. In what way is creative listening like cutting down a tree with an axe?
5. What is Sanford's advice about listening creatively to a person who is drunk or drugged?

PROBES

1. Sanford says that creative listening is not just desirable in a relationship but "essential." What makes it essential?
2. Other treatments of listening suggest that you paraphrase what you hear. Sanford says that it often helps to reflect back what you've heard. But he does not mean paraphrasing. What does he mean?

3. Unless you're a parent or a counselor, advises Sanford, don't listen when you really don't want to. How do you respond to this advice?

*T*his reading comes from the second of two chapters on listening in the basic interpersonal communication text that I coauthor with Carole Logan. In that book, the chapter before this one treats reflective listening—enjoying music, silence, or the sounds of nature—and analytic listening—critically evaluating what you hear from politicians or via the media. Then the chapter this reading is taken from discusses the other two important ways to listen.

Carole and I begin this reading with the point that people usually don't *talk* their way into good relationships, but *listen* their way into them. Then we distinguish the various kinds of listening by identifying whose goals each kind focuses on. Reflective and analytic listening are designed to meet the *listener's* goals to enjoy or to meditate (reflective) or to test incoming messages so as not to be taken advantage of (analytic). Empathic listening, on the other hand, focuses on the goals of the person being listened to. This is the kind of listening that the other authors in this chapter discuss most. Many people believe that empathic listening is the "highest form" of the art. But Carole and I believe that effective listening can move one more step, from a focus on "mine" (reflective and analytic listening) through a focus on "yours" (empathic listening) to a focus on *"ours,"* on the meanings that we construct together (dialogic listening).

After briefly introducing this idea, we spend some time explaining empathic listening. In that section of the reading you'll hear ideas that are discussed by other authors in this chapter. For example, like Sanford, we note that empathic listening requires you to postpone your own agendas. But unlike Sanford and the other authors in this chapter, we discuss some specific ways to engage in this kind of listening, under the headings of "focusing skills," "encouraging skills" and "reflecting skills."

Focusing skills help you orient your attention to the person you're listening to. Encouraging skills are designed to "pull" more talk from the person you're listening to. We suggest several, including the simple "Say more," "Keep talking," "Could you elaborate on that?" or "For example?" We also talk about how "mirroring" can encourage others to talk, and how open questions and clarifying questions can do the same. At the end of this section we underscore the usefulness of attentive silence and mention two kinds of questions to avoid.

Then we outline three reflecting skills. The first, paraphrasing, has been discussed in other readings in this chapter. But we also include the skills of "adding and example" and "gently pursuing verbal/nonverbal inconsistencies." After a summary with a concrete example of empathic listening in it, we move to a discussion of dialogic listening.

Dialogic listening is the fullest application in this book of the collaborative approach to communicating and interpersonal communicating that I lay out in Chapter 2. It's more than what people often think of as "listening." Dialogic listening involves a particular attitude or orientation to what it means to communicate and a group of skills that help you make meaning *together with* your conversation partner.

This section of the chapter begins with a couple of pages on what *dialogue* means. We emphasize, as David Bohm does in Chapter 1, that the Greek term *dia-logos* means not "two people talking" but "meaning-through," the process of people collaboratively figuring out what they mean together. We note communication teacher Bruce Hyde's very important point that if you're going to listen dialogically, you have to be more interested in collaborating on meanings than in being right. Unfortunately, as Bruce writes, "In my experience, this is the hardest single thing you can ask of anyone."

Our final effort to describe the basic mind-set of dialogic listening borrows Barnett Pearce's distinction between an "ethnocentric" and a "cosmopolitan" attitude. Dialogic listening, we emphasize, requires the latter, and we explain why.

Then we offer the metaphor of "sculpting mutual meanings" to clarify how dialogic listening works. Imagine that you and your conversation partner(s) are sitting around a potter's wheel. At various times someone puts some clay on the moving wheel, and then both or all of you mold it with wet fingers, palms, and thumbs into the meaning you're co-constructing.

The final part of the chapter describes some special kinds of focusing and encouraging and three specific sculpting skills. The focusing, as I've already noted, is on "ours" rather than on "mine" or "yours." Encouraging, in this kind of listening, resembles the "nexting" skill I introduced in Chapter 2. Then the first sculpting skill is what we call a "paraphrase plus"—a paraphrase plus your own view on the topic and an invitation for the other to respond to your view. The second sculpting skill is "asking for a paraphrase," and the final one is called "running with the metaphor."

This reading is definitely longer than most selections in this book, but it should give you a comprehensive grounding in the attitudes and skills that make up this most important part of the interpersonal communication process.

EMPATHIC AND DIALOGIC LISTENING

John Stewart and Carole Logan

At the beginning of our classes, we sometimes ask students to fill out a three-part questionnaire. The first part asks them to use a four-point scale to rate the importance of nine different relationships they're in—with a romantic partner, parent(s), sibling(s), other family members, close and best friends, other friends, supervisor at work, coworkers, and others (pastor/priest, mentor, etc.). The second part of the questionnaire asks them to rate the difficulty of managing these relationships, and the third asks, "In your three most difficult-to-manage relationships, what two things do you want to do more effectively?" We encourage them to use their responses to the third part when they set their own learning goals for the course. Then, at the end of the term, we ask them to review the course to compare what they learned with what they wanted to learn and to identify the topics or skills that the course did not cover as fully as they would have liked. In response to the "What wasn't covered enough?" question, many people write, "Focus on the building of relationships more," "Should go into more depth about building relationships," "How to initiate relationships," and "Relationship development.". . .

Ironically, when people ask how to build relationships better, they often expect to learn what they should *say*. As one person put it, "When I want to get closer to someone I like, I've heard I should compliment the person a lot. Does that work?" This way of thinking overlooks the fact that *most of the time you don't talk your way into good relationships, you listen your way into them.* Relationships usually grow more because of how people feel listened to than because of what is said to them.

In his recent book *The Lost Art of Listening*, family therapist Michael Nichols describes many instances in which friends, spouses, coworkers, parents and children, bosses, and acquaintances fail to listen to each other. He reminds his readers that when people aren't listened to, they come to feel that their ideas and emotions are not taken seriously and that what they have to say doesn't matter. Learning how to be an effective listener means becoming aware of and developing . . . interpersonal connections between ourselves and others. . . . As Nichols puts it . . . "our lives are coauthored in dialogue."[1]

. . . Reflective listening intensifies the perceptual processes of selecting, organizing, and inferring. It is a way to concentrate and focus your perception. Analytic listening, on the other hand, responds to several of the problems . . . of overload, stereotyping, and attribution errors by organizing what you hear, checking assumptions and asking the "How does this apply to me?" question.

These two kinds of listening emphasize the *listener's* agendas and goals. Reflective listening can enhance the listener's serenity, and bring more enjoyment

Excerpts from *Together: Communicating Interpersonally*, 5th ed. by John Stewart and Carole Logan, 1997. Reprinted by permission of The McGraw-Hill Companies.

into his or her life. Analytic listening can help protect the listener from weak arguments and faulty reasoning, and it can help the listener think through his or her own reasons for holding important beliefs and opinions.

This [reading] discusses two additional kinds of listening that shift the listener's focus away from his or her own agendas and goals. Empathic listening concentrates on the *other's* meanings. The goal of empathic listening is not to analyze or critique what the other person is saying, but to fully understand his or her thinking and feeling. Dialogic listening moves the listener's awareness one more step—from *me* (reflective and critical listening) and *you* (empathic listening) to *us*, to the meanings that listener and speaker construct together. As a result, dialogic listening is our label for a kind of involvement in the communication process that applies this entire book's approach to co-constructing meaning. . . .

EMPATHIC LISTENING

. . . Carl Rogers, the counselor who pioneered the technique of empathic listening, described it as "entering the private perceptual world of the other and becoming thoroughly at home in it." He continued:

> It involves being sensitive, moment by moment, to the changing felt meanings which flow in this other person. . . . To be with another in this way means that for the time being, you lay aside your own views and values in order to enter another's world without prejudice. In some sense it means that you lay aside yourself.[2]

This kind of listening is important, for example, when you are aware that your friend needs to vent and you are willing to listen without adding anything beyond your friend's point of view. In fact, if you respond in these situations by saying, "Well, if I were you . . .," your friend may insist, "I don't need your advice. I want you to just *listen* to me." It can also be important to listen empathically if you've been asked to mediate a dispute. You can't function very well as a mediator until you fully understand each person's point of view, and empathic listening can help you build this understanding.

Empathic listening is an important skill for parents, teachers, and managers, as well. Family communication research indicates, for example, that toddlers, children, and adolescents often feel as though their parents only listen from their own points of view, rather than taking the time and effort to fully understand the young person's thinking and feeling.[3] Books on *Parent Effectiveness Training*[4] and *How to Talk So Kids Will Listen and Listen So Kids Will Talk*[5] also emphasize how pity and advice can leave one feeling worse than before. "But let someone really listen [empathically], let someone acknowledge my inner pain and give me a chance to talk more about what's troubling me and I begin to feel less upset, less confused, more able to cope with my feelings and my problem." [p. 9] Managers and teachers often need to listen empathically in order to understand how to help their subordinates or students, and . . . counselors and doctors also routinely respond this way to their clients.

One danger of empathic listening is that it's possible to end up withdrawing. Sometimes an observer is most effective when he or she is attentive and silent. But silence can also signal that the listener has "checked out" and is no longer available to the other communicator. Another risk of empathic listening is that it can be used manipulatively. The person being listened to may begin to feel that, since there's so much concentration on *his* or *her* thoughts and feelings, he or she is the only one who's vulnerable. It's important to examine your motives for listening empathically and to recognize that you may want to move beyond it toward dialogic listening, in order to balance the amount of risk and vulnerability in the conversation.

In order to listen empathically, however, it's important to develop three sets of competencies: focusing skills, encouraging skills, and reflecting skills.[6] As with any complex process, it works best to select from among the various ways to focus, encourage, and reflect. Think of the specific skills as [foods on] a salad bar—put on your plate the ones that you're comfortable with and that fit the situation you're in.

Focusing Skills

As with analytic listening, the first step is to orient your attention to the person you're listening to. This begins with an internal decision about how you are going to invest your time and energy. It helps to recall the distinction between *spending* time and *investing* it and to realize that empathic listening can often pay the dividends of any good investment. Then you remember that listening takes effort, and you put aside the other things you're doing in order to concentrate on the other person. At this point, focusing surfaces in four skills.

The first is **aiming your posture.** Turn your body so that you're facing or nearly facing the person to whom you're listening, and if you're seated, lean toward your conversation partner. This is a simple thing to do, and yet a variety of studies have underscored its importance. According to one textbook for counselors: "Usually, the interested helper leans toward the helpee in a relaxed manner. Relaxation is important because tenseness tends to shift the focus from the helpee to the helper."[7] It's been demonstrated that when listeners focus their bodies this way, the people with whom they're talking perceive them as "warmer" and more accessible, and consequently they find it's easier to volunteer more information.[8]

A second part of focusing is making **natural and appropriate eye contact.** . . . In most Western cultures, when you look the other person in the eye, you not only are acutely aware of him or her, but you are also directly available to that person. Studies of nonverbal listening behavior in these cultures typically identify eye contact and forward body lean or movement toward the other as two of the most important indicators of attraction and contact.[9] If you cannot easily make eye contact with the other person, move to a position from which you can.

If you're talking with children, get down on the same level by kneeling or sitting, so that they can see you looking at them.

. . . What's appropriate eye contact depends partly on the cultural identities of the people involved. If you're talking with a person from a culture that proscribes eye contact except between intimates or a superior and an inferior, it's important to try to honor these limitations. If you're from one of these cultures and your conversation partner is not, it can help to alter your own behavior in the direction of the other person's expectations as far as you comfortably can. But so long as you are operating in a generally Western communication context, it's important to work toward making eye contact 50 to 70 percent of the time.

In cultures that value direct eye contact, breaking it while listening can create real problems. As one of our students put it, "Based on my own experience, and that of a few others I've talked with, when a listening partner suddenly breaks eye contact to focus on something else (say a friend who's walking by and waving), it can have an almost disconfirming effect on those of us who want to express ourselves."[10]

The third and fourth ways to "do" focusing are to **move responsively** and to **make responsive sounds.** We've known people who believed they were listening intently when they sat staring at the other person, completely immobile, and with unchanging, deadpan expressions. There are two problems with this habit. The most obvious one is that, even though you may think you're listening well, it doesn't look as though you are. Unless I see some response in your body and on your face, I'm not convinced that you're really being affected by what I'm saying. The second problem is more subtle: You are not actually fully involved in what you're hearing until your body begins to register your involvement. So even though you might think you're focused when you're immobile and silent, you are not as focused as you will be when you start moving responsively and making responsive sounds. Since everybody's mind and bodies are intimately connected, the kinesthetic sensations of your body's responsiveness will actually help your mind stay focused.

Moving responsively means smiling, nodding or shaking your head, moving your eyebrows, shrugging your shoulders, frowning, and so on. These actions should be prompted by, in response to, and linked up with what the other person says and does. An effective listener isn't nodding or smiling all the time; he or she nods or smiles when that is responsive to what the other person is saying, and frowns or shakes his or her head when that's responsive.

Responsive sounds include the "Mnnhuh," "Oh?," "Yeah . . .," "Ah?," "Sure!," "Really?," "Awww" utterances that audibly tell the other person that you're tuned in to what he or she is saying. If you doubt the importance of responsive sounds, try being completely silent the next time you're listening over the phone. After a very short time, the other person will ask "Are you still there?" We need sounds like these to reassure us that our hearer is actually listening.

These four skills may seem overly obvious or simplistic, but it is quite clear from a number of communication studies that people differ greatly in their ability to apply these behaviors. . . . Communicators who are perceived as more "immediate" are generally judged as more competent, attractive, and approachable than are those who are not. Teacher immediacy, for example, is repeatedly linked to perceived effectiveness, motivation, and learning.[11] Research indicates that there are definite benefits to learning to use these skills effectively.

"But . . .," a student responds. . . .

When I have a problem listening, it's usually because I'm thinking about something else—what to say next, how I'd answer the speaker's point, or some off-the-topic distraction. How can I pay more attention?

Sounds like a problem with your focusing. Try one or more of these suggestions. (1) When you're really seriously distracted, don't try to listen. Tell the other person you're too preoccupied to talk now, reschedule the meeting, or do whatever you can to give yourself the space to get in a more receptive frame of mind. (2) If you're distracted by "I just don't have the time" worries, try, as we suggested, thinking of the time it takes you to listen as an *investment* rather than as a *expenditure.* Just like money in a savings account or a mutual fund, time put into listening pays dividends. The minutes you invest now will double or triple in value, and the return could be a better working relationship, a much clearer understanding of where and why you disagree, less defensiveness, more intimacy, and/or more cooperative feelings. (3) Practice *presentness.* . . . Presentness means making a commitment to stay focused on the current situation. Resist the temptation to indulge in "what ifs" about the future or "if onlys" about the past. A friend of Martin Buber's described him as uniquely able to be present to the presentness of the other and able to call the other into presence with him.[12] Set that as a goal for yourself: to work with the other person(s) in the here-and-now to develop understandings together. Neither the future nor the past is irrelevant, but listening happens in the present. Stay focused there. (4) If you're worried about forgetting or losing your own point if you pay too close attention to the other person's, try jotting down a word or two to remind yourself of what you want to say.

Encouraging Skills

The second set of empathic listening skills is designed to "pull" more talk from the other person. More talk obviously is not always a good thing. But when you want to understand as completely as possible where another person is coming from, you need to have enough verbal and nonverbal talk to make the picture clear. Thus, we want to make seven specific suggestions about how to encourage.

The first is the most direct one: as a listener, respond when appropriate with "Say more," "Keep talking," "Could you elaborate on that?" or "For example?" One situation in which this response can help is when someone makes a comment that sounds fuzzy or incomplete. Frequently, the listener's inclination is to try to paraphrase what's been said or to act on the information even though it's uncertain whether he or she has the materials to do so. Of course, it would be pretty ridiculous to respond to "I wonder what time it is" with "Could you say more about that?" But each time you hear a new idea, a new topic, or an important point being made, we suggest you begin your empathic listening effort at that moment not by guessing what the other person means, but by asking her or him to tell you. "Say more," "Keep talking," or some similar encouragement can help.

A second encouraging skill is called **mirroring.** Mirroring means repeating a key word or phrase of the other person's with a question on your face and in your voice. Repeating? Yes, you just pick up on one term, for example, and feed it back with a questioning inflection and raised eyebrows, and the other person will elaborate on what he or she has just said. Elaborate? Yes—You know, he or she will give an example, or restate what was said in other terms, or make some such effort to clarify the point he or she is making. Just as we have been doing here.

A third encouraging response is the **clarifying question.** Often these take the form "Do you mean . . . ?" or "When you say . . ., do you mean . . .?" You might ask for an explanation of how the person is defining a word or phrase or for a clarification of the implications of what is being said. In a job interview, for example, the interviewer might comment, "Our company is interested only in assertive people." The candidate then could ask, "When you say 'assertive,' what do you mean?" Tone of voice is an important part of clarifying questions. Remember that your questions are motivated by a need to understand more clearly; they are not meant to force the other person into a corner with a demand to "define your terms!"

Open questions are a fourth way to encourage. Closed questions call for a yes/no, single-word, or simple-sentence answer. Open questions just identify a topic area and encourage the other person to talk about it. "Who was that person I saw you with last night?" is a closed question, and "How's your love life going?" is a more open one. Open questions often begin with "What do you think about . . .?" or "How do you feel about . . .?" A closed version of a similar question might begin "Do you think . . .?" "Do you like this chapter?" is a closed question; "Which parts of this chapter do you like best?" is more open. Both types of questions can be useful, but when you want to encourage, use open ones.

A fifth way to encourage is by using **attentive silence.** As we've said before, the point of empathic listening is to develop and understand the perspective of the speaker. Stay focused and give the other person plenty of room to talk. This is frequently all a person needs to be encouraged to contribute more.

Our final two suggestions about encouraging highlight what *not* to do. Encouraging obviously involves asking questions, but not just any question. We have already explained why using open questions is generally more effective than using closed questions. But there are also two types of questions to avoid. The first are what we call **pseudoquestions.** "Pseudo" means "pretended," "unreal," or "fake," and a pseudoquestion is a judgment or opinion pretending to be a question. "Where do you think you're going?" is not really a question, it's a pseudoquestion. In other words, if you think about how this question functions in actual conversation, you can hear how it's almost always a complaint or a judgment that one person is making about the other. "Where do you think you're going?" usually says something like "Get back here!" or "I don't want you to leave." "Is it safe to drive this fast?" is another pseudoquestion; here, the hidden statement is something like "I'm scared by your driving," or "I wish you'd slow down." At times, we may use pseudoquestions to soften a more directly negative evaluation of the other person.[13] However, such softening attempts can be confusing and can add more frustration than they're worth. Our point here is that if you use them in your efforts to encourage, they can backfire. Instead of pseudoquestions, try to ask only real ones, genuine requests for information or elaboration.

A second kind of question to avoid is the one that begins with the word **"Why,"** because these questions tend to promote defensiveness. When people hear "why" questions, they often think the questioner is asking them for a rationale or an excuse. "Why did you decide to bring him to this meeting?" "Why are you turning that in now?" "Why didn't you call me?" "Why did you decide to do it that way?" Do you hear the implicit demand in these questions? The problem is that "why" questions often put the person questioned on the spot. They seem to call for a moral or value justification. As a result, they don't work as encouragers. In their place, try asking exactly the same question, but begin it with different words. For example, try "How did you decide to . . .?" or "What are your reasons for . . .?" We believe that you will find it works better.

Reflecting Skills

This third set of skills will help you directly reflect the other person's perspective in the communication process. This is the central goal of empathic listening. There are three skills in this final set. The first is called **paraphrasing.** *A paraphrase is a restatement of the other's meaning in your own words followed by a verification check.* This means there are four important parts to a paraphrase: (1) It's a restatement, not a question. A paraphrase doesn't start out by asking, but by telling the other what you have heard. The first words of a paraphrase might be "So you believe that . . ." or "In other words, you're saying that . . ."(2) It's a restatement of the other's *meaning,* not a repetition of the other's words. Meanings include both ideas and feelings, and the fullest paraphrase captures some of both. Sometimes the feeling content is very important, and sometimes it is less so. But your paraphrase ought at least to suggest the emotion that's included in what the other person said. "So you're worried that . . ." or "It sounds like you are really upset, because you believe that . . ." are two examples of restating feelings. (3) A paraphrase has to be in your own words. . . . Translating the other's meaning into your words demonstrates that you've thought about it, that it's gone through your brain cells. (4) After the restatement, you finish a paraphrase with an opportunity for the other person to verify your understanding. You can do this very simply—just by pausing and raising your eyebrows, or asking, "Right?" or "Is that it?" Paraphrasing is such a powerful communication move that, if you follow these four steps periodically in your conversations, your empathic listening effectiveness will improve significantly.

The second reflective skill is **adding an example.** You can contribute to the listening process by asking the other person to respond to an example from your own experience that you believe illustrates his or her point. Remember that this is an effort to listen empathically, not to turn the conversation away from the other person's concerns and toward yours. The example clearly needs to be one that makes his or her main point. Here is part of a conversation that illustrates what we mean.

KAREN: I've had my share of problems with this TA position, but in some ways this job is actually rewarding.

(Clarifying question)

HABIB: Since it's payday, are you talking about your check?

KAREN: No, one of my students just wrote this note on her copy of the exam we were going over in class: "I liked the way you were willing to listen to our side and to consider giving back some points. I think it takes real confidence as a teacher to do that."

(Adds example)

HABIB: That's really great. But I got a comment like that from a student once, and it turned out that he was being sarcastic. He was really ticked off about the way I graded his exam, and he even complained to the department chair. Do you think she could be setting you up?

(Clarifies)

KAREN: I never thought about that. No, I don't think so. This is a returning student, and I think she appreciates it when she feels as though she's being treated as an adult.

Remember that understanding is different from agreement, and that neither the paraphrase nor adding an example requires you to agree with the other person. These listening responses are designed to promote the empathic listening process, to simply help you understand the other person's perspective.

The third and final reflecting skill also takes some finesse. The skill consists of **gently pursuing verbal/nonverbal inconsistencies.** The first step is to identify when you think they've occurred. You have to be sensitive enough to recognize when the words a person is speaking don't match the way he or she is saying them. A shouted, scowling "I'M NOT MAD!!" is an obvious example of an inconsistency between verbal and nonverbal cues. Most of the time, though, it's much more subtle. Carole has a friend who declared she was not going to waste any more time being angry at her boss, and then spent the next half hour complaining about his most recent actions. In other situations, facial expression and tone of voice accompanying a person's "Sure," "I don't care," "Go ahead with it," or "It doesn't make any difference to me," reveal that the words are thin masks for disappointment, concern, or hurt feelings.

As a listener, you can help move beyond surface-level meanings by gently pursuing the verbal/nonverbal inconsistencies you notice. We stress the word *gently.* When you notice an inconsistency, remember that it's your interpretation of what's going on; be willing to own it as your own. Remember, too, that if the other person also sees an inconsistency, there's a reason for its being there. He or she may not be ready or willing to admit the difference between cues at one level and cues at another. So don't use this skill as a license to clobber someone with a club made of sidewalk psychoanalysis. Instead, just describe the inconsistency you think is there and open the door for the other person to talk about it.

For example, one group of professionals with whom John worked were experiencing some conflict over a proposal their new manager had instituted. The manager decided that the group needed to be more cohesive, and so proposed that each Friday afternoon the office would close an hour early so that the workers could spend some time together informally chatting over wine and cheese. Most of the people welcomed the idea, but two resisted it. They didn't like what they saw as a "forced socializing," and they resented the fact that only alcoholic drinks were being served. They didn't think it was appropriate to "drink on the job." As part of their listening training, John asked the group to discuss this issue. Ann, the manager, turned to Gene, one of the two persons resisting the plan, and asked what he thought about these Friday afternoon get-togethers. Gene turned slightly away in his chair, folded his arms in front of him, looked down at the floor, and said, "Well . . . it's a pretty . . . good idea . . ." Ann smiled and softly said, "Gene, your words tell me one thing and your body says something else." Then she was silent. After a couple of seconds, Gene relaxed his body posture, smiled, and admitted that he actually didn't like the plan very much. This began a conversation that ended up redesigning the get-togethers to respond to Gene's concerns.

The primary reason why this listening response works is that many nonverbal cues "leak" implicit or hidden messages. . . . Some nonverbal behavior is very much under our conscious control, but much of it is not.[14] Thus, tone of voice, posture, eye behavior, and even facial expression often reveal levels of meaning that are obscured by choice of words. Sensitive listeners try to respond to such inconsistencies and, as we suggest, gently pursue them.

SUMMARY SO FAR

Mandy Lam, a student, provided the following example of empathic listening in a brief conversation she had with a friend.

MANDY: Oh Lily! Haven't seen you around for a while. How's it going?

LILY: Hi, Mandy. Yeah, I know. I've been so stressed out these last few weeks working on my medical school applications. As you probably know, I haven't been to biochem lectures lately.

MANDY: Yeah, I noticed. Medical school applications, huh? Have they been a pain in the butt?

LILY: Well, I'm finding that I have to juggle trying to put together 15 applications with schoolwork. It's stressing me big time! What's worse is that they often require a couple of pages of essay-type responses, and that just takes me a while.

MANDY: It sounds like you have your plate full this quarter with classes and
     your med school apps. So that's why I've missed you in class lately, huh?
LILY: Yup. Wish things could get back to some sense of normality.

As this example shows, empathic listening . . . happens when the listener focuses closely on the perspective of the speaker. The listener tries to "get inside"
the other person's thoughts or to "walk a mile in his moccasins." This is often
the goal of a counselor or therapist, but it's also an important thing for friends,
parents, and managers to be able to do. But if you want to make the most of each
person's contributions to the conversation, it's more effective to shift the focus
from the speaker to both participants. Then you move to what we call dialogic
listening.

DIALOGIC LISTENING

There is no simple recipe for dialogic listening—no six easy steps or five sure-
fire techniques. This is something that anybody who wants to do can do, but it
requires an overall approach to communicating that's different from the stance
most people ordinarily take when they listen or talk. You also need to maintain
a fairly challenging tension or balance . . . between holding your own ground
and being radically open to the person(s) with whom you're communicating.
The best way to get a sense of this approach and this tension is to understand a
little bit about the idea of "dialogue."

Ordinarily, dialogue just means conversation between two or more people,
or between the characters in a novel or play. But in two periods of recent history,
the term took on some special meanings. First, between about 1925 and the early
1960s, the philosopher and teacher Martin Buber and other writers used the
term "dialogue" to talk about a special kind of communication. In his book *I and
Thou* . . . and in many other books and articles, Buber tried to point toward a way
of communicating that he had noticed in some factories, family homes, schools,
political organizations, churches, and even on buses and trains, a way of communicating that accomplished genuine *interpersonal* contact. Buber readily admitted that people can't and don't communicate dialogically all the time, but he
maintained that we could do more of it, and if we did, we'd be better off. . . .

Buber's view of dialogue lost some credibility in the United States when it
became associated with the hippie movement of the 1960s and 1970s. But since
the early 1990s, the term and the ideas surrounding it have begun to become
prominent again. Today, . . . management theorists from the Massachusetts Institute of Technology, Harvard, and other prominent schools are arguing that in
this age of globalization and constant rapid change, the only way a company can
keep up is to constantly learn from its successes and mistakes. And the only way
to become "a learning organization" is to replace traditional hierarchical communication with dialogue. As we write this chapter in late 1996, Ford Motor
Company and Boeing are two of many U.S. companies that are spending millions of hours and dollars to help their people learn to open spaces in their organizations for dialogue.[15]

Dialogue is also being promoted as the best way to improve the quality of public discourse in the United States[16] and Great Britain,[17] and some psychologists are arguing that the focus of the entire discipline of psychology needs to shift from the individual psyche to the dialogic person-in-relation.[18] The concept is also being used more and more by communication researchers and teachers.[19] In short, increasing numbers of influential people are recognizing in the late 1990s that dialogue is a seriously beneficial phenomenon. We—John and Carole—believe that dialogic listening is the most direct way to promote dialogue. By "promote" we mean that dialogue can't be guaranteed, but it can be encouraged. And dialogic listening will help open up a space for the kind of person-to-person contact that . . . theorists and teachers call "dialogue."

Dia-logos as Meaning Through

The key to understanding how to open up this space is to recognize that the *logos* in " dia-logos" is the Greek word for *meaning* or *understanding*,[20] and that the *dia* in "dia-logos" means not "two" but "through."[21] So dialogue is not restricted to two-person communicating, and it is an event where meaning emerges *through* all the participants. This is another way of saying that meaning or understanding is collaboratively co-constructed. The important implication of this idea for each participant is that, when you're listening and talking dialogically, *you are not in control of what comes out of the communicating.* This is a point we've made in various ways before, and it's stated clearly by Abraham Kaplan:

> When people are in [dialogue], . . . the content of what is being communicated does not exist prior to and independently of that particular context. There is no message, except in a post-hoc reconstruction, which is fixed and complete beforehand. If I am really talking with you, I have nothing to say; what I say arises as you and I genuinely relate to one another. I do not know beforehand who I will be, because I am open to you just as you are open to me.[22]

As communication teacher Bruce Hyde points out, the main obstacle to dialogic listening is the kind of self or identity that replaces this openness to collaboration with the conviction that the ideas I utter are tightly connected with who I am. There's a big difference, Bruce notes, "between being right about something and being committed to something. Being right makes somebody else wrong; being committed has room to engage productively with other points of view." In other words, if you're committed, you might even welcome the chance to talk with someone who believes differently, but if you're committed to being *right*, there's not much room for people who don't share your position to be anything but wrong. The key difference has to do with identity. The person who's caught up in being right identifies himself or herself first as an advocate for a certain position. The person who's committed, on the other hand, identifies himself or herself first as a listener who's collaborating on, but not in control of, what comes out of the conversation. If you're going to listen dialogically, you have to be more interested in building-meaning-through than in being right. And this, Bruce writes, "in my experience is the hardest single thing you can ask of anyone."[23]

Communication theorist and teacher Barnett Pearce expresses basically this same idea but with a cultural slant when he contrasts an *ethnocentric* with a *cosmopolitan* approach to communication. Recall that the term "ethnocentric" means viewing other cultures from the perspective of one's own. When I communicate from an ethnocentric attitude, I begin with the assumption that my culture's way is normal, natural, preferred, and that, in these important senses, it is "right." Barnett argues that "ethnocentric communication is the norm in contemporary American society. It is, of course, the stuff of racism, sexism, and the like. It also structures domestic political discourse."[24] Ethnocentric communication also privileges *coherence*—the kind of sense that emerges when other ideas fit into a comfortable whole, in part by matching or echoing what's already there and hence what is normal and natural. A person who approaches communication with an ethnocentric attitude assumes that his or her ways of thinking and doing are normal and natural and that conversations ought to make the kind of sense that you get when feelings and ideas fit together into familiar patterns.

A cosmopolitan attitude, on the other hand, is one that embraces all the "politics" in the "cosmos." It is inclusive rather than exclusive. A person with a cosmopolitan attitude may be *committed* to an idea or position, but does not assume that it is absolutely right. As a result, cosmopolitan communication privileges *coordination* rather than *coherence*. There's no assumption that the only way to put ideas or people together is the logical way, or the way based on "what we've always believed and done." People with a cosmopolitan attitude are open toward all kinds of creative syntheses of ideas, procedures, and past experiences. The main goal is to work toward alignment, even when there is little or no agreement. As psychologist Gordon Allport is reported to have said, this kind of communicator is "half sure yet wholehearted."

Dialogic listening begins with a cosmopolitan rather than an ethnocentric attitude. . . . When you listen dialogically, you are acting on the conviction that communication really is the process of collaboratively making the meanings that constitute the worlds we inhabit. Some people might reject this idea. They might believe in the ultimate effectiveness and power of me-focused communicating and that one person alone can be responsible for the meanings that emerge from a communication event. They might believe that one person can completely control how and what other people understand. But just a little reflection will tell you that this isn't true. Beyond earliest childhood, no one person can unilaterally change or make up somebody else's mind. The me focus of reflective listening can definitely benefit the individual, and the me focus of analytic listening can protect the person practicing it. But the meanings that emerge out of reflective and analytic listening events are still collaborations. They are affected by all the people involved. The speaker being listened to analytically, for example, might think about the listener, "Why is she so interested in my assumptions? Why can't we just talk about outlawing abortion?" and this response will affect the understandings both speaker and listener construct together. Our point is that first step toward dialogic listening is to recognize that each communication event is a ride on a tandem bicycle, and you may or may not be in the front seat.

Sculpting Mutual Meanings

To shift from the bicycle metaphor, we've found that it helps to think and talk about the basics of dialogic listening with the help of the image of a potter's wheel.[25] The sculpting mutual meanings metaphor was created by our friend, communication teacher Milt Thomas, and he uses it to suggest a concrete, graphic image of what it means to listen dialogically.

Picture yourself sitting on one side of a potter's wheel with your conversation partner across from you. As you participate (talk) together, each of you adds clay to the form on the wheel, and each uses wet fingers, thumbs, and palms to shape the finished product. Like clay, verbal and nonverbal talk is tangible and malleable; it's out there between people to hear, to record, and to shape. If I am unclear or uncertain about what I am thinking or about what I want to say, I can put something out there and you can modify its shape, ask me to add more clay, or add some of your own. Your specific shaping, which you could only have done in response to the shape I formed, may move in a direction that I would never have envisioned. The clay you add may be an idea I've thought about before—although not here or in this form—or it may be completely new to me. Sometimes these cosculpting sessions will be mostly playful, with general notions tossed on the wheel, and the result will look like a vaguely shaped mass. At other times, the basic shape is well defined and we spend our time on detail and refinement. Our efforts, though, always produce some kind of result, and it can be very gratifying. Sometimes I feel that our talk helps me understand myself better than I could have alone. At other times, we produce something that transcends anything either of us could have conceived of separately. This is so because the figure we sculpt is not mine or yours, but ours, the outcome of both of our active shapings.

Thus, in order to enter into the sculpting process effectively, you need to remember, as we have said many times before, that the meanings that count between people are not just the ones inside somebody's head, but the ones that are constructed in conversations. With this understanding, you will be willing to sit down at the potter's wheel, throw your clay on the wheel, and encourage the other person to add clay, too. Then you need to be willing to get your hands dirty, to participate in the collaborative process of molding meanings together.

As you might be guessing, in order to put this basic attitude into action, you need to practice some special kinds of focusing and encouraging.

Focus on "Ours"   We mentioned before that dialogic listening involves a crucial change from a focus on *me* or a focus on the *other* to a focus on *ours*, on what's *between* speaker(s) and listener(s). Contrast this with empathic listening, which requires you to try to experience what is behind another's outward communication. When you focus on "ours," you don't look "behind" the verbal and nonverbal cues. You don't try to deduce or guess what internal state the other is experiencing. Instead, you concentrate on the meanings you and the other person are mutually creating between yourselves. Empathic listening can be helpful, as we said, but dialogic listening requires a move beyond empathy to a focus on "ours."

It can make a big difference whether you are trying to identify what's going on inside the other person or are focusing on building-meaning-between. When your focus is on the other's thoughts and feelings behind their words, you spend your time and mental energy searching for possible links between what you're seeing and hearing and what the other "must be" meaning. "Look at those crossed arms. She must be feeling angry and defensive." Or, "He said he'd 'never' pay all the money back. That means it's hopeless to try to get him to change his mind." When you think in this way, you're moving back and forth between what's outside, in the verbal and nonverbal talk, and what's inside the person's head. From this position, it's easy to believe that what's inside is more reliable, more important, more true, and hence more interesting than the talk on the surface.

When you're focusing on "ours," however, you concentrate on what's outside, not what's supposedly inside. We don't mean that you should be insensitive to the other person's feelings. In fact, you will be even more sensitive when you are focused on what's between you here and now. You concentrate on the verbal and nonverbal talk that the two (or more) of you are building together. In a sense, you take the conversation at face value; you never stop attending to it instead of trying to infer what is behind it. This doesn't mean that you uncritically accept everything that's said as "the whole truth and nothing but the truth." But you do realize that meaning is not just what's inside one person's head. Focusing on "ours" prepares you to respond and inquire in ways that make it clear that getting to the meaning is a mutual process.

Encouraging . . .   Dialogic listening also requires a special form of encouraging. Basically, instead of encouraging the other person(s) to say more, you're encouraging them to respond to something you've just put on the potter's wheel in response to something they said. So your encouraging . . . actively and relevantly keeps the collaborative co-construction process going.

One specific way to do this is with a **paraphrase plus.** We've already said that a paraphrase consists of (1) a restatement, (2) of the other's meaning, (3) in your own verbal and nonverbal talk, (4) concluded with an opportunity for the other person to verify your understanding. The paraphrase plus includes all of these elements *plus* a small but important addition.

The plus is your own response to the question, "What's next?" or "Now what?" You start by remembering that the meanings you are developing are created between the two of you, and individual perspectives are only a part of that. If you stopped with just the paraphrase, you would be focusing on the other person exclusively instead of keeping the focus on what is happening between you. So, you follow your verifying or perception-checking paraphrase with whatever your good judgment tells you is your response to what the person said, and you conclude your paraphrase plus by inviting the person to respond to your synthesis of his or her meaning and yours. The spirit of the paraphrase plus is that each individual perspective is a building block for the team effort. For example, notice the three possible responses to Rita's comments.

RITA: I like having an "exclusive" relationship, and I want you to be committed to me. But I still sometimes want to go out with other people.

(Paraphrase)

1. MUNEO: So even though part of you agrees with me about our plan not to date others, you're still a little uncertain about it. Right?

(Attack)

2. TIM: Oh, so you want me to hang around like an idiot while you go out and play social butterfly! Talk about a double standard!

(Paraphrase plus)

3. SCOTT: It sounds like you think there are some pluses and minuses in the kind of relationship we have now. I like it the way it is, but I don't like knowing that you aren't sure. I guess I want you to tell me some more about why you're questioning it.

Muneo responds to Rita's comment with a paraphrase. This tells us that Muneo listened to Rita, but not much more. Tim makes a caricature of Rita's comment; his interpretation reflects his own uncertainty, anger, and fear. His comment is more a condemnation than a paraphrase. Scott offers a paraphrase plus. After explaining his interpretation of what Rita was saying, he says briefly how he *responds* to her point, and then moves the focus back between the two of them, back to the middle where both persons are present in the conversation and can work on the problem together. He does this by adding some of his own clay to the potter's wheel. He paraphrases, but he also addresses the "What's next?" question as he interprets and responds to her comments. Then he concludes the paraphrase plus with encouragement rather than simply verifying the accuracy of his paraphrase. When all this happens, both the paraphrase and the plus keep understanding growing between the individuals instead of just within them.

Another way to think about the paraphrase plus is that you're broadening your goal beyond listening for "fidelity" or "correspondence." If you're paraphrasing for fidelity or correspondence, you're satisfied and "finished" with the task as soon as you've successfully *reproduced* "what she means." Your paraphrase is a success if it corresponds accurately to the other person's intent. We're suggesting that you go beyond correspondence to creativity, beyond reproducing to producing, to mutually constructing meanings or understandings between you.

Because paraphrasing is so potentially helpful, another sculpting skill is to **ask for a paraphrase.** Whenever you're uncertain about the extent of the other person's involvement or whether the two of you share an understanding, you can ask the person for his or her version of the point you're making. It is difficult to do this well. Often a request for a paraphrase sounds like an accusation: "Okay, stupid, why don't you try telling me what I just said." This obviously is not going to contribute much to the cosculpting process. The idea is to ask for a paraphrase without demanding a response and without setting the person up so that you can play "Gotcha!" if she or he doesn't get it right. You can try putting it this way: "Just to make sure we're going in the same direction, could you tell me what you think we've agreed to so far?" Or you might say, "I'm not sure I've been clear—what do you hear me saying?" The point is, if it's done with an eye toward nexting, a paraphrase can promote collaborating whether it comes from your side or the other person's side. You sometimes can help that happen by asking for one.

Another skill you can use in the sculpting process is to **run with the metaphor.** You can build meaning into the conversation by extending whatever metaphors the other person has used to express his or her ideas, developing your own metaphors, and encouraging the other person to extend yours. Metaphors, of course, are figures of speech that link two dissimilar objects or ideas in order to make a point. "Communication is made up of inhaling and exhaling," "Conversation is a ride on a tandem bicycle," and "Dialogic listening is sculpting mutual meanings," all are metaphors, as are "This place is a zoo," "My vacation was a circus," and "She's as nervous as a flea on a griddle." As these examples illustrate, metaphors don't appear only in poetry or other literature; they are a major part of most everyday conversation. In fact, it's becoming increasingly clear that virtually all language is metaphoric.[26] In our label for this skill, "run with the metaphor," for example, the term "run" itself is metaphoric.

This skill consists of listening for both subtle and obvious metaphors and then weaving them into your responses. We have found that when other people hear their metaphor coming back to them, they can get a very quick and clear sense of how they're being heard, and they typically can develop the thought along the lines sketched by the metaphor. For example, in a workshop he was leading, John was listening to an engineer describe part of his job, which involved going before regulatory boards and municipal committees to answer questions and make arguments for various construction projects. Part of what Phil said about his job was that it was a "game." John tried to run with the metaphor by asking, "What's the name of the game?" "Winning," Phil responded. John recognized that his question had been ambiguous, so he continued: "Okay, but what kind of game is it—is it baseball, football, soccer, chess, or what?" "It's football," Phil replied. "What position do you play?" "Fullback." "And who's the offensive line?" "All the people in the office who give me the information I take to the meetings." "Who's the coach?" "We don't have one. That's the major problem." This was a telling response. In fact, from that point on, the workshop was focused on one of the major management problems that engineering firm was having.

Here's another example of how running with the metaphor can work in conversation:

TANYA: You look a lot less happy than when I saw you this morning. What's happening?

ANN: I just got out of my second two-hour class today, and I can't believe how much I have to do. I'm really feeling squashed.

TANYA: Squashed like you can't come up for air, or squashed as in you have to
    do what everybody else wants and you can't pursue your own ideas?
ANN: More like I can't come up for air. Every professor seems to think that this
    is the only class I'm taking.

Again, the purpose of running with the metaphor is to . . . build the conversation between the two of you in order to produce as full as possible a response to the issues you're talking about. In addition, the metaphors themselves
reframe or provide a new perspective on the topic of your conversation. A project manager who sees himself or herself as a "fullback" is going to think and behave differently from one who thinks in other metaphorical terms, such as "general," "Joan of Arc," "guide," or "mother hen." And the work stress that
"squashes" you is different from the pressure that "keeps you jumping like a
flea on a griddle." Listen for metaphors and take advantage of their power to
shape and extend ideas. . . .

Remember our point that all these specific listening skills are like foods on
a salad bar: You don't eat everything, and at different times, you select different
dishes. Let's look at an extended example of a conversation that illustrates some
of the listening attitudes and skills we've discussed. Sally and Julio start out at
opposite sides in their opinions about the class. But first Julio, and then both he
and Sally, dialogically listen to each other. As a result, their interpretations of the
class and the teacher change; they build together a meaning that neither of them
had at the beginning of the conversation. In the margins, we've labeled some of
the specific empathic and dialogic listening skills they're using.

SALLY: That class drives me up a wall.

(Open question)
JULIO: I thought it was going pretty well. What happened?
SALLY: She's so strict! We can't miss more than five hours of class, everything
    has to be typed, she won't take late papers. I'll bet she wouldn't even allow
    a makeup exam if I was in the hospital!

(Say more)
JULIO: I didn't know she wouldn't take late papers. Where did you hear that?
SALLY: Alaysha told me that on Tuesday she tried to hand in the article analy-
    sis that was due on Monday and Dr. Clinton wouldn't accept it.

(Clarifying question)
JULIO: Was there anything else going on? Hilary and I both turned in our jour-
    nals late and she took them. I also thought the five-hour restriction and the
    typing requirement were pretty standard at this school.

(Say more)
SALLY: Do you have them in other classes?
JULIO: Yeah. My geology prof only allows two days' absence and won't accept
    hardly any excuses.

(Say more)

SALLY: Are your other profs so stiff and formal in class?

JULIO: Some are and some aren't. Clinton is a lot looser in her office. Have you ever talked to her there?

SALLY: No, I don't like the way she treated Alaysha.

(Paraphrase)

JULIO: So Alaysha did the assignment like she was supposed to and Clinton wouldn't take it even though it was only one day late?

SALLY: Well, it wasn't typed, but I still think it's pretty unreasonable. I haven't started the paper that's due this Friday, and I'll bet there's no way she'd accept it Monday.

(Paraphrase plus)

JULIO: I know how that feels. But if you've got a good reason, I'll bet she would. She told me last term that most of her rules come from what other profs tell her are the "standards" here. This school is really into "developing responsibility" and "treating everybody like an adult"; that's why I thought they required attendance and typed papers. But I think Clinton is willing to listen, and she's bent the rules for me a couple of times. You've been doing fine in class, and I'd really be surprised if she turned you down.

SALLY: I didn't know that about this school; this is my first term here.

JULIO: Well, I didn't know about Alaysha, but she probably should have typed it.

SALLY: Yeah. Well, thanks for listening—and for the information.

We do not mean to present these skills as a guaranteed step-by-step way to instant success. They are suggestions, guidelines, examples of ways you can behaviorally work on the focusing, encouraging, and sculpting processes of dialogic listening. They won't work if you apply them woodenly or mechanically; you have to use them with sensitivity to the relationship and the situation.

As you begin applying these skills—and this also applies to all the skills we have discussed—you may feel awkward and even phony. This is natural. It is part of learning any new skill, whether it's skiing, tennis, aerobics, or listening. Remember that the better you get with practice, the less awkward you will feel. Try not to let any initial feelings of discomfort distract you from working on specific ways to improve.

REVIEW QUESTIONS

1. Early in this reading we argue that people usually don't _____ their way into good relationships; they _____ their way into them.
2. What are two dangers or risks of empathic listening?
3. Some listeners nod their heads constantly or say something like "Yeah . . . yeah . . . yeah" to everything. How is this different from moving responsively and making responsive sounds?

4. How is mirroring different from asking a clarifying question?
5. What is a pseudoquestion?
6. What's the problem with a question that begins with "Why"?
7. List the four parts of a paraphrase.
8. Explain what it means to say that *dialogue* means "dia-logos" or "meaning-through."
9. Explain the difference between an ethnocentric attitude toward communication and a cosmopolitan one.
10. How is the skill called "nexting" in Chapter 2 related to this chapter's discussion of dialogic listening?
11. What do Stewart and Logan mean when they say that these skills are like foods on a salad bar?

PROBES

1. Explain the difference between thinking about the time you spend listening as an expenditure and thinking of it as an investment.
2. What are some cultural differences in eye contact that you've noticed? (Remember that culture includes not only ethnicity but also age, gender, social class, sexual orientation, etc.)
3. When would encouraging be inappropriate?
4. The discussion of open, closed, clarifying, pseudo-, and "why" questions emphasizes how the type of question you ask can significantly affect your listening. Describe the three most important things you know about how to use questions to listen effectively.
5. It can be tricky to gently pursue verbal/nonverbal inconsistencies. How might you actually respond to a good friend who shouts, "I'M NOT MAD!!"?
6. What evidence do you see in the world around you of the growing interest in dialogue? (Consider the growing efforts to replace litigation with mediation, public forums on racism, management seminars on dialogue, etc.)
7. How does the difference between a paraphrase and a paraphrase plus capture or embody the distinction between empathic and dialogic listening?
8. If you and I were talking right now, and you wanted to encourage me to run with the metaphor of "sculpting mutual meanings," what would you ask me?
9. *Why* can there not be any series of steps or techniques that can be guaranteed to produce dialogue?

NOTES

1. M. Nichols, *The Lost Art of Listening* (New York: Guilford, 1995), p. 6.
2. Carl Rogers, *A Way of Being* (Boston: Houghton Mifflin, 1980), pp. 142–143.
3. Steven A. Beebe & John T. Masterson, "Listening to Each Other," *Family Talk: Interpersonal Communication in the Family* (New York: Random House, 1986),

pp. 203–223; Judy C. Pearson, *Communication in the Family: Seeking Satisfac-tion in Changing Times* (New York: Harper & Row, 1989), pp. 260–281.

4. Thomas Gordon, *PET In Action* (New York: Wyden, 1976).

5. Adele Faber and Elaine Mazlish, *How to Talk So Kids Will Listen and Listen So Kids Will Talk* (New York: Avon, 1980).

6. These three skill sets are adapted from Robert Bolton, "Listening Is More Than Merely Hearing," in J. Stewart (ed.), *Bridges Not Walls,* 5th ed. (New York: McGraw-Hill, 1990), pp. 175–191.

7. Lawrence M. Brammer, *The Helping Relationship: Process and Skills,* 2nd ed. (Englewood Cliffs, NJ: Prentice-Hall, 1979), p. 70.

8. M. Reece and R. Whitman, "Expressive Movements, Warmth and Nonver-bal Reinforcement." *Journal of Abnormal and Social Psychology* 64 (1962): 234–236.

9. For example, see G. L. Clore, N. H. Wiggins, and S. Itkin, "Judging Attrac-tion from Nonverbal Behavior: The Gait Phenomenon." *Journal of Counsel-ing and Clinical Psychology* 43 (1975): 491–497.

10. Jay Adams, journal entry in Speech Communication 103, Autumn 1996, Uni-versity of Washington. Used by permission.

11. For general readings in this area, see Judith A. Sanders and Richard L. Wise-man, "The Effects of Verbal and Nonverbal Teacher Immediacy on Per-ceived Cognitive, Affective, and Behavioral Learning in the Multicultural Classroom." *Communication Education,* 39 (1990): 341–353; Joan Gorham and Walter R. Zakahi, "A Comparison of Teacher and Student Perceptions of Im-mediacy and Learning: Monitoring Process and Product." *Communication Education* 39 (1990): 354–368; Diane M. Christophel, "The Relationship Among Teacher Immediacy Behaviors, Student Motivation, and Learning." *Communication Education* 39 (1990): 323–340.

12. Maurice Friedman, quoted in Stewart and Thomas, "Dialogic Listening," in J. Stewart (ed.), *Bridges Not Walls,* 6th ed. (New York: McGraw Hill, 1995) p. 193.

13. Gerald Goodman and Glen Esterly, "Questions—The Most Popular Piece of Language," in J. Stewart (ed.), *Bridges Not Walls,* 6th ed. p. 76.

14. See, for example, Judee K. Burgoon, "Nonverbal Signals," in Mark L. Knapp and Gerald R. Miller (eds.), *Handbook of Interpersonal Communication.* (Beverly Hills, CA: Sage, 1985), pp. 377–378.

15. For example, see Peter Senge, *The Fifth Discipline: The Art and Practice of the Learning Organization* (New York: Doubleday, 1990).

16. See, for example, S. Roth, L. Chasin, R. Chasin, C. Becker, and M. Herzig, "From Debate to Dialogue: A Facilitating Role for Family Therapists in the Public Forum." *Dulwich Centre Newsletter,* no. 2, 1992: 41–48.

17. In 1995 and 1996, British Telecommunications was engaged in a nationwide project to enhance the quality of interpersonal communication. Several U.S. interpersonal communication scholars contributed to this effort.

18. Edward E. Sampson, *Celebrating the Other: A Dialogic Account of Human Na-ture* (Boulder, CO: Westview Press, 1993).

19. Leslie A. Baxter and Barbara M. Montgomery, *Relating: Dialogue and Dialectics* (New York: Guilford, 1996); John Shotter, *Conversational Realities: Constructing Life Through Language* (London: Sage, 1993).

20. The Greek term *logos* has other meanings, too. Sometimes it is translated "logic," and at other times it comes into English as "language." But its most fundamental meaning is "meaning."

21. We get this idea from British theoretical physicist David Bohm, whose books and seminars introduce people to dialogue. See, for example, David Bohm, *On Dialogue* (Ojai, CA: David Bohm Seminars, 1990).

22. *The Preach of Dialogue: Confirmation, Voice and Community,* Rob Anderson, Kenneth N. Cissna, & Ronald C. Arnett (eds.) (Cresskill, NJ: Hampton Press, 1994).

23. Bruce Hyde, "E-mail Contribution to Redwood Forest Dialogue," August 29, 1996. A contribution to the same E-mail conversation by Kimberly Walters on September 3, 1996, was crucial in sharpening what Hyde wrote.

24. Barnett Pearce, *Communication and the Human Condition* (Carbondale, IL: Southern Illinois University Press, 1989), p. 120.

25. The metaphor was first developed in John Stewart and Milt Thomas, "Dialogic Listening: Sculpting Mutual Meanings," in John Stewart (ed.), *Bridges Not Walls,* 6th ed. pp. 184–202.

26. George Lakoff and Mark Johnson, *Metaphors We Live By* (Chicago: University of Chicago Press, 1980); Paul Ricoeur, *The Rule of Metaphor,* trans. Robert Czerny with Kathleen McLaughlin and John Costello, S. J. (London: Routledge & Kegon Paul, 1978).

PART THREE

Openness as Exhaling

CHAPTER 7

Expressing Yourself

As I explained at the beginning of Part Two, we move now from discussions of the input, or inhaling, parts of communicating to the output, or "exhaling," parts. In the next two chapters you will find discussions of self-expression, self-disclosure, and negative and hurtful messages.

*T*his reading, as the authors note in their introduction, "is about ex-pressing yourself when it counts and to the people who matter to you. It tells you how to make clear and complete statements about your inner experience."

McKay, Davis, and Fanning identify four kinds of expression: ob-servations, thoughts, feelings, and needs. Even though in actual experi-ence you can't separate the four, these distinctions can help you recog-nize whether you're trying to express something about what you've seen, heard, read, or experienced, something you've concluded or in-ferred, something you are feeling, or something you want.

There are various kinds of thoughts, including beliefs, opinions, and theories about what should, or will, happen. Expressions of thoughts are different from feeling statements, even though they some-times sound similar. As the authors point out, "Sometimes I feel that you are very rigid" expresses an opinion or belief, *not* a feeling. Feeling statements label part of a person's visceral, affective experience—"I miss her," "I'm really excited," "I feel stunned and a little angry." Espe-cially in close relationships it is important to learn to express needs rather than to expect the other person to read your mind. As the authors put it, "Trying to have a close relationship in which you don't express your needs is like driving a car without a steering wheel."

Whole messages, they note, include all four kinds of expression, and intimate relationships thrive on whole messages. Contaminated messages are mixed or mislabeled. As the authors' examples of conta-minated messages illustrate, they create problems because they can be understood in more than one way and they don't tell the listener how to interpret them correctly.

The final section of this reading offers five rules for effective expres-sion: Be direct, immediate, clear, straight and supportive. Directness re-quires knowing when something needs to be said—rather than assumed or implied—and the willingness and ability to talk about it. Immediacy means not putting off discussions, either by avoiding them or by "gun-nysacking." The authors identify two concrete benefits of immediacy.

They also provide six ways to enhance the clarity of your messages. The first echoes the discussion of pseudoquestions in Chapter 6—as McKay, Davis, and Fanning put it, "Don't ask questions when you need to make a statement." The second is to keep your messages congruent, which means to match, so far as you can, the external message and your internal experience. The third is to avoid double messages, and the fourth is to be as clear as you can about your wants and feelings. The final two suggestions for clarity are to distinguish between observations and feelings and to focus on one thing at a time.

The fourth rule for effective expression states that messages should be straight. Straight messages are those "in which the stated purpose is identical with the real purpose of the communication." In other words, the authors are suggesting that you avoid communication based on disguised intentions and hidden agendas. Examples of hidden agendas include "I'm helpless," "I'm fragile," "I'm tough," and "I know it all," any of which can be behind ambiguous talk. Being straight also means that you tell the truth. For example, "You don't say you're tired and want to go home if you're really angry and want more attention."

The final rule is that messages should be supportive, and the authors contrast supportive statements with six hurtful tactics. These include global labels, sarcasm, threats, and dragging up the past. The authors conclude by urging you to avoid communicating from a win/lose mind-set.

There are important cultural limitations of this reading. McKay, Davis, and Fanning do a very good job of articulating a Western, white, middle-class perspective that helps define effective communicating in many U.S. and Canadian contexts, and in some contexts in Western Europe, Australia, and New Zealand—*but not all cultures in these countries.* And their perspective certainly does not apply in some other cultures. For example, the kind of directness they urge would be considered very inappropriate in Japan and in parts of Britain. People in some blue-collar cultures in the United States would also ridicule the advice to "be supportive." So this reading can definitely sharpen your communication skills in some cultural contexts, but I believe that it would be a mistake to apply all these rules in every situation. Use the information to hone your knowledge about communication in the cultures that the authors belong to.

EXPRESSING

Matthew McKay, Martha Davis, and Patrick Fanning

SAM: "Do we have to go down to the P.T.A. meeting tonight?"

JANE: "Why, does it bother you?"

SAM: "It's just the same old thing. I don't know."

JANE: "Did something happen last time?"

SAM: "It's nothing. Sometimes the speakers are interesting, but I don't know . . . and Mrs. Williams is running it now."

Excerpts from *Messages: The Communication Skills Book* by Matthew McKay, Martha Davis and Patrick Fanning. Published by New Harbinger Publication, Oakland, CA, www.newharbinger.com.

JANE: "You don't like how she's handling it?"

SAM: "She's all right. She's so . . . organized. Forget it, let's get a move on if we're going."

Sam is in for another deadly evening. Mrs. Williams will carry on like General Patton. A speaker will drone about "multicultural awareness." If Sam had been able to express himself, he might have persuaded Jane to skip a night, or to help him push for changes in the meeting format. As it is, Jane has no idea what's irking him and can't respond to his needs.

This [reading] is about expressing yourself when it counts and to the people who matter to you. It doesn't tell you how to assertively ask your butcher for a good cut of meat. But it does tell you how to make clear and complete statements about your inner experience.

THE FOUR KINDS OF EXPRESSION

Your communications to other people can be broken down into four categories: expressing your observations, thoughts, feelings, and needs. Each category requires a different style of expression, and often a very different vocabulary.

Observations

This is the language of the scientist, the detective, the TV repairman. It means reporting what your senses tell you. There are no speculations, inferences, or conclusions. Everything is simple fact. Here are some examples of observations:

1. "I read in the *Enquirer* that an ice age is due to start within five hundred years."
2. "My old address was 1996 Fell Street."
3. "She plans to wear a chiffon dress with white ruffled collar."
4. "I broke the toaster this morning."
5. "It was a very hot day when I left Kansas. A slight wind riffled the fields and a thunderhead was beginning to form up north."

All of these statements adhere strictly to what the person has heard, read, or personally experienced. If Sam had been able to talk about his observations at the P.T.A. meeting, he might have pointed out that the meetings invariably went overtime, that the speakers were selected by Mrs. Williams without consulting the group, and that certain parent-teacher problems were never discussed.

Thoughts

Your thoughts are conclusions, inferences drawn from what you have heard, read, and observed. They are attempts to synthesize your observations so you can see what's really going on and understand why and how events occur. They may also incorporate value judgments in which you decide that something is good or bad, wrong or right. Beliefs, opinions, and theories are all varieties of conclusions. Here are some examples:

1. "Unselfishness is essential for a successful marriage." (*belief*)
2. "I think the universe will keep exploding and collapsing, exploding and collapsing, forever." (*theory*)
3. "He must be afraid of his wife; he always seems nervous around her." (*theory*)
4. "Log Cabin is the only syrup worth buying." (*theory*)
5. "You were wrong to just stop seeing her." (*value judgment*)

If Sam had been able to express his thoughts about the P.T.A. meeting, he might have said that Mrs. Williams was dominating and grandiose. He might have suggested that she was deliberately squelching conflicts because she was friendly with the school administration.

Feelings

Probably the most difficult part of communication is expressing your feelings. Some people don't want to hear what you feel. They get bored or upset when feelings come up. Some people are selectively receptive. They can hear about your post-divorce melancholy, but not about your fear of death. Anger is the most discouraged feeling because it's threatening to the listener's self-esteem.

Since people are often threatened or frightened by emotion, you may have decided to keep many feelings to yourself. Yet how you feel is a large part of what makes you unique and special. Shared feelings are the building blocks of intimacy. When others are allowed to know what angers, frightens, and pleases you, two things happen: They have greater empathy and understanding and are better able to modify their behavior to meet your needs.

Examples of some feeling statements are:

1. "I missed Al and felt a real loss when he left for Europe."
2. "I feel like I let you down, and it really gnaws at me."
3. "I sit alone in the house, feel this tingling going up and down my spine, and get this wave of anxiety."
4. "I light up with joy when I see you. I feel this incredible rush of affection."
5. "I'm checking my reactions, and I feel stunned and a little angry."

Note that feeling statements are not observations, value judgments or opinions. For example, "Sometimes I feel that you are very rigid," has nothing to do with feelings. It's just a slightly buffered judgment.

If Sam had expressed his feelings to Jane, he might have told her that he felt bored at the meetings and that he was angry at Mrs. Williams. He also might have discussed his worries that the school has serious curriculum inadequacies and his frustration that nothing was being done about it.

Needs

No one knows what you want, except you. You are the expert, the highest authority on yourself. However, you may have a heavy injunction against expressing needs. You hope friends and family will be sensitive or clairvoyant enough to know what you want. "If you loved me, you'd know what's wrong" is a common assumption. Since you feel it's bad to ask for anything, your needs are often expressed with a head of anger or resentment. The anger says "I'm wrong to ask, and you're wrong to make me have to."

Trying to have a close relationship in which you don't express your needs is like driving a car without a steering wheel. You can go fast, but you can't change directions or steer around chuckholes. Relationships change, accommodate, and grow when both people can clearly and supportively express what they need. Some typical need statements are:

1. "Can you be home before seven? I'd love to go to a movie."
2. "I'm exhausted. Will you do the dishes and see that the kids are in bed?"
3. "I need a day to myself this weekend. Can we get together Sunday night?"
4. "I need to reserve time with you so we can sit down and work this out."
5. "Could you just hug me for a while?"

Needs are not pejorative or judgmental. They don't blame or assign fault. They are simple statements about what would help or please you. . . .

WHOLE MESSAGES

Whole messages include all four kinds of expressions: what you see, think, feel, and need. Intimate relationships thrive on whole messages. Your closest friends, your mate, and your family can't know the real you unless you share all of your experiences. That means not leaving things out, not covering up your anger, not squelching your wants. It means giving accurate feedback about what you observe, clearly stating your inferences and conclusions, saying how it all makes you feel, and if you need something or see possibilities for change, making straightforward requests or suggestions.

When you leave something out, it's called a *partial message*. Partial messages create confusion and distrust. People sense something is missing, but they don't know what. They're turned off when they hear judgments untempered by your feelings and hopes. They resist hearing anger that doesn't include the story of your frustration or hurt. They are suspicious of conclusions without supporting observations. They are uncomfortable with demands growing from unexpressed feelings and assumptions.

Not every relationship or situation requires whole messages. Effective communication with your garage mechanic probably won't involve a lot of deep feeling or discussion of your emotional needs. Even with intimates, the majority of messages are just informational. But partial messages, with something important left out or obscured, are always dangerous. They become relational boobytraps when used to express the complex issues that are an inevitable part of closeness.

You can test whether you are giving whole or partial messages by asking the following questions:

1. Have I expressed what I actually know to be fact? Is it based on what I've observed, read, or heard?

2. Have I expressed and clearly labeled my inferences and conclusions?
3. Have I expressed my feelings without blame or judgment?
4. Have I shared my needs without blame or judgment?

CONTAMINATED MESSAGES

Contamination takes place when your messages are mixed or mislabeled. For example, you might be contaminating feelings, thoughts, and observations if you said to your daughter, "I see you're wearing that old dress again." What you really needed to say were three very distinct things:

1. "That dress is a little frayed and still has the ink spot we were never able to get out." (*observation*)
2. "I don't think it's nice enough for a Sunday visit to Grandpa's." (*thought*)
3. "I feel anxious that your grandfather will think I'm not a very good parent if I let you wear a dress like that." (*feeling*)

Contaminated messages are at best confusing and at worst deeply alienating. The message "I see your wife gave you two juicy oranges for lunch" is confusing because the observation is contaminated by need. The need is only hinted at, and the listener has to decide if what he heard was really a covert appeal. The message "While you were feeding your dog, my dinner got cold" is alienating because what appears to be a simple observation contains undercurrents of anger and judgment ("You care more about your dog than me").

Contaminated messages differ from partial messages in that the problem is not merely one of omission. You haven't left the anger, the conclusion, or the need out of it. It's there all right, but in a disguised and covert form. The following are some examples of contaminated messages:

1. "Why don't you act a little human for a change?" In this message need is contaminated with a value judgment (*thought*). A whole message might have been, "You say very little, and when you do it's in a soft, flat voice (*observation*). It makes me think that you don't care, that you have no emotions (*thought*). I feel hurt (*emotion*), but what I really want is for you to talk to me (*need*)."
2. "Every year you come home to visit with a different man. I don't know how you move from one to another like that." Said in an acid tone, this would be an observation contaminated with a value judgment (*thought*). The whole message might be "Each year you come home with someone else (*observation*). I wonder if it creates a sort of callousness, a shallow affection (*thought*). I worry, and also feel disappointed when I start liking your friend and never see him again (*feeling*). I hope you'll make a commitment to a life partner (*need*)."
3. "I know what your problem is, you like to get paid but you don't like to work." This is an example of feeling contaminated with a value judgment (*thought*). The whole statement might be "You've been late six times in the last two weeks (*observation*). It makes me think that you're trying to work as

little as possible (*thought*). The lateness irritates me (*feeling*) and I want you to be late no more than once a month (*need*)."

4. "I need to go home . . . another one of those headaches." Said in an angry voice at a party, this is an example of feelings contaminated with need. The person really wants to say "I've been standing by myself (*observation*). You don't seem to care or draw me into conversation (*thought*). I get to feeling hurt and angry (*feeling*). I want you to involve me in things or I don't want to be here (*need*)."

5. "You eat your breakfast without a word, you get your hat, you leave, you get home, you mix a drink, you read the paper, you talk about golf and your secretary's legs at dinner, you fall asleep in front of the TV, and that's the way it is." In this case observation is contaminated with feelings. It seems like a straightforward recital of events, but the speaker really wants to say "I'm lonely and angry, please pay attention to me."

The easiest way to contaminate your messages is to make the content simple and straightforward, but say it in a tone of voice that betrays your feelings. "I want to stop interviewing people, we have enough already" can be said in a matter-of-fact or very annoyed voice. In one case it's a clear statement of need. In the other, need is contaminated with unacknowledged anger. The secret of avoiding contaminated messages is to separate out and express each part of the communication. . . .

RULES FOR EFFECTIVE EXPRESSION

Messages Should Be Direct

The first requirement for effective self-expression is knowing when something needs to be said. This means that you don't assume people know what you think or want.

Indirectness can be emotionally costly. Here are a few examples. One man whose wife divorced him after fifteen years complained that she had no right to call him undemonstrative. "She knew I loved her. I didn't have to say it in so many words. A thing like that is obvious." But it wasn't obvious. His wife withered emotionally without direct expression of his affection. A woman who had been distressed by her child's performance in school stopped nagging when his grades went up. She was surprised to learn that her son felt unappreciated and wanted some direct approval. A man who had developed a chronic back problem was afraid to ask for help with gardening and household maintenance. He suffered through these tasks in pain and experienced a growing irritation and resentment toward his family. A fifteen-year-old retreated to her room when her divorced mother became interested in a new man. She complained of headaches and excused herself whenever the boyfriend arrived. Her mother, who once told the children they would always come first, assumed that her daughter was just embarrassed and would soon get over it.

These are all examples of people who have something important to communicate. But they don't know it. They assume others realize how they feel. Communicating directly means you don't make any assumptions. In fact, you should assume that people are poor mind readers and haven't the faintest idea what goes on inside you.

Some people are aware of the times when they need to communicate, but are afraid to do so. Instead they try hinting, or telling third parties in hope that the target person will eventually hear. This indirectness is risky. Hints are often misinterpreted or ignored. One woman kept turning the sound down on the TV during commercials. She hoped her husband would take the hint and converse a little at the breaks. Instead he read the sports page until she finally blew up at him. Third-party communications are extremely dangerous because of the likelihood that your message will be distorted. Even if the message is accurately delivered, no one wants to hear about your anger, disappointment, or even your love secondhand.

Messages Should Be Immediate

If you're hurt or angry, or needing to change something, delaying communication will often exacerbate your feelings. Your anger may smoulder, your frustrated need become a chronic irritant. What you couldn't express at the moment will be communicated later in subtle or passive-aggressive ways. One woman was quite hurt at the thought of not being invited to Thanksgiving at her sister's house. She said nothing, but broke a date they had to go to the planetarium and "forgot" to send a Christmas card.

Sometimes unexpressed feeling is gunnysacked to the point where a small transgression triggers a major dumping of the accumulated rage and hurt. These dumping episodes alienate family and friends. A hospital ward secretary had a reputation with peers for being dangerous and volatile. For months she would be sweet, considerate, and accommodating. But sooner or later the explosion came. A slight criticism would be answered with megatons of gripes and resentments.

There are two main advantages to immediate communication: (1) Immediate feedback increases the likelihood that people will learn what you need and adjust their behavior accordingly. This is because a clear relationship is established between what they do (for example, driving too fast) and the consequences (your expressed anxiety). (2) Immediate communication increases intimacy because you share your responses now. You don't wait three weeks for things to get stale. Here-and-now communications are more exciting and serve to intensify your relationships.

Messages Should Be Clear

A clear message is a complete and accurate reflection of your thoughts, feelings, needs, and observations. You don't leave things out. You don't fudge by being vague or abstract. Some people are afraid to say what they really mean. They talk in muddy, theoretical jargon. Everything is explained by "vibes" or by psychological interpretations. One woman who was afraid to tell her boyfriend she was turned off by public petting said that she felt "a little strange" that day and thought that her parents' upcoming visit was "repressing her sexuality." This ambiguous message allowed her boyfriend to interpret her discomfort as a temporary condition. He never learned her true needs.

Keeping your messages clear depends on awareness. You have to know what you've observed, and then how you reacted to it. What you see and hear in the outside world is so easily confused with what you think and feel inside. Separating these elements will go a long way toward helping you express yourself clearly.

Here are some tips for staying clear:

1. Don't ask questions when you need to make a statement. Husband to wife: "Why do you have to go back to school? You have plenty of things to keep you busy." The statement hidden in the question is "I'm afraid if you go back to school I won't see you enough, I'll feel lonely. As you grow in independence I'll feel less control over the direction of our lives."

Wife to husband: "Do you think we need to make an appearance at your boss's barbeque today?" Imbedded in the question is the unexpressed need to relax and putter in the garden. By failing to plead her case clearly, her husband can either miss or safely ignore her needs.

Daughter to father: "Are we going to have a little three-foot tree this year?" What she thinks but doesn't say is that she likes the big trees seen at friends' houses—the ones full of lights and tinsel around which the family gathers. She wishes that her family did more things together, and thinks Christmas decorating would be a good place to start.

Father to son: "How much did that paint job cost?" He really wants to talk about the fact that his son lives above his means, and then borrows from Mom without any intention of paying back. He's worried about his son's relationship to money and angry because he feels circumvented.

2. Keep your messages congruent. The content, your tone of voice, and your body language should all fit together. If you congratulate someone on getting a fellowship, his response is congruent if the voice, facial gestures, and spoken messages all reflect pleasure. Incongruence is apparent if he thanks you with a frown, suggesting that he doesn't really want the compliment.

Incongruence confuses communication. Congruence promotes clarity and understanding. A man who spent the day in his delivery truck arrived home to a request that he make a run to the supermarket. His response was, "Sure, whatever you want." But his tone was sarcastic and his body slumped. His wife got the message and went herself. But she was irritated by the sarcastic tone and later started a fight about the dishes. A model asked soothingly to hear about her roommate's "boyfriend in trouble." But while the story unfolded, her eyes flitted always to the mirror and she sat on the edge of her chair. Her voice said, "I care," but her body said, "I'm bored, hurry up."

3. Avoid double messages. Double messages are like kicking a dog and petting it at the same time. They occur when you say two contradictory things at once. Husband to wife: "I want to take you, I do. I'll be lonely without you. But I don't think the convention will be much fun. Really, you'd be bored to death." This is a double message, because on the surface the husband seems to want his wife's company. But when you read between the lines, it's evident that he's trying to discourage her from coming.

Father to son: "Go ahead, have a good time. By the way, I noticed your report card has some real goof-off grades. What are you doing about them?" This is a rather obvious double message, but the effect is confusing. One message undercuts the other, and the son is left unclear about his father's real position. The most malignant double messages are the "come close, go away" and "I love you, I hate you" messages. These communications are found in parent-child and lover relationships, and inflict heavy psychological damage.

4. Be clear about your wants and feelings. Hinting around about your feelings and needs may seem safer than stating them clearly. But you end up confusing the listener. Friend to friend: "Why don't you quit volunteering at that crazy free clinic?" The clear message would be: "I'm afraid for you struggling in that conflict-ridden place. I think you are exhausting yourself, and I miss the days when we have time to spend an afternoon together. I want you to protect your health and have more time for me."

Husband to wife: "I see the professors and their wives at the faculty party, and I shudder at some of the grotesque relationships." The real message that couldn't be said was "When I see that terrible unhappiness, I realize what a fine life we have and how much I love you."

Mother to daughter: "I hope you visit Grandma this week." On the surface this seems straightforward, but underneath lurks the guilt and anxiety she feels about Grandma's loneliness. She worries about the old woman's health and, without explaining any of this, badgers her daughter to make frequent visits.

Two lovers: "I waited while you were on the phone and now our dinners are cold." The underlying statement is "I wonder how much you care about me when you take a phone call in the middle of dinner. I'm feeling hurt and angry."

5. Distinguish between observations and thoughts. You have to separate what you see and hear from your judgments, theories, beliefs, and opinions. "I see you've been fishing with Joe again" could be a straightforward observation. But in the context of a longstanding conflict about Joe, it becomes a barbed conclusion. Review the section on contaminated messages for more discussion of this issue.

6. Focus on one thing at a time. This means that you don't start complaining about your daughter's Spanish grades in the middle of a discussion about her boyfriend's marijuana habits. Stick with the topic at hand until both parties have made clear, whole messages. If you get unfocused, try using one of the following statements to clarify the message: "I'm feeling lost . . . what are we really talking about?" or "What do you hear me saying? I sense we've gotten off the track."

Messages Should Be Straight

A straight message is one in which the stated purpose is identical with the real purpose of the communication. Disguised intentions and hidden agendas destroy intimacy because they put you in a position of manipulating rather than relating to people. You can check if your messages are straight by asking these two questions: (1) Why am I saying this to this person? (2) Do I want him or her to hear it, or something else?

Hidden agendas . . . are usually necessitated by feelings of inadequacy and poor self-worth. You have to protect yourself, and that means creating a certain image. Some people take the *I'm good* position. Most of their communications are subtle opportunities to boast. Others play the *I'm good but you aren't* game. They are very busy putting everyone down and presenting themselves, by implication, as smarter, stronger, more successful. Agendas such as *I'm helpless, I'm fragile, I'm tough,* and *I know it all* are good defensive maneuvers to keep you from getting hurt. But the stated purpose of your communication is always different from your real purpose. While you are ostensibly discoursing on intricate Middle East politics, the real purpose is to show how knowledgeable you are. We all succumb to little vanities, but when your communications are dominated by one such agenda, you aren't being straight.

Being straight also means that you tell the truth. You state your real needs and feelings. You don't say you're tired and want to go home if you're really angry and want more attention. You don't angle for compliments or reassurance by putting yourself down. You don't say you're anxious about going to a couples therapist when actually you feel angry about being pushed to go. You don't describe your feelings as depression because your mate prefers that to irritation. You don't say you enjoy visiting your girlfriend's brother when the experience is one step below fingernails scraping on the chalkboard. Lies cut you off from others. Lies keep them from knowing what you need or feel. You lie to be nice, you lie to protect yourself, but you end up feeling alone with your closest friends.

Messages Should Be Supportive

Being supportive means you want the other person to be able to hear you without getting blown away. Ask yourself, "Do I want my message to be heard defensively or accurately? Is my purpose to hurt someone, to aggrandize myself, or to communicate?"

If you prefer to hurt your listener with your messages, use these six tactics:

1. Global labels. Stupid, ugly, selfish, evil, assinine, mean, disgusting, worthless, and lazy are a few of the huge list of hurtful words. . . . Making your point that way creates a total indictment of the person, instead of just a commentary on some specific behavior.

2. Sarcasm. This form of humor very clearly tells the listener that you have contempt for him. It's often a cover for feelings of anger and hurt. The effect on the listener is to push him away or make him angry.

3. Dragging up the past. This destroys any chance of clarifying how each of you feels about a present situation. You rake over old wounds and betrayals instead of examining your current dilemma.

4. Negative comparisons. "Why aren't you generous like your brother?" "Why don't you come home at six like other men?" "Sarah's getting A's and you can't even get a B in music appreciation." Comparisons are deadly because they not only contain "you're bad" messages, but they make people feel inferior to friends and family.

5. Judgmental "you messages." These are attacks that use an accusing form. "You don't love me anymore." "You're never here when I need you." "You never help around the house." "You turn me on about as much as a 1964 Plymouth."

6. Threats. If you want to bring meaningful communication to a halt, get out the big guns. Threaten to move out, threaten to quit, threaten violence. Threats are good topic changers, because instead of talking about uncomfortable issues, you can talk about the hostile things you plan to do.

Communicating supportively means that you avoid "win/lose" and "right/wrong" games. These are interactions in which the intention of one or both players is "winning" or proving the other person "wrong" rather than sharing and understanding. Your intention in communication will guide you toward a predictable result. Real communication produces understanding and closeness, while "win/lose" games produce warfare and distance. Ask yourself, "Do I want to win or do I want to communicate? Do I want to be right or do I want mutual understanding?" If you find yourself feeling defensive and wanting to criticize the other person, that's a clue that you're playing "win/lose."

Win/lose interactions can be avoided by sticking rigidly to the whole-message structure. You can also get around the win/lose pattern by making clear observations on your process. "I'm feeling pretty defensive and angry right now, and it looks like I've fallen into the old win/lose syndrome."

REVIEW QUESTIONS

1. What kinds of fear can make it difficult to express feelings?
2. How are feelings different from and similar to needs?
3. "Not every relationship or situation requires whole messages," the authors note. So why do they discuss them? When and where *are* they required?
4. How do contaminated messages differ from partial messages?
5. What do you believe might be some of the emotional cost of indirect messages?
6. What is "gunnysacking"? How can you avoid it?
7. What is a double message?
8. These authors encourage you to communicate "straight" messages. What is a "crooked" one?

PROBES

1. On the one hand, the distinction between observations and thoughts makes clear sense and is useful. But how many of your actual communicating consists mainly of pure observations? How commonly are thoughts and feelings mixed into your messages?
2. One reason why it's difficult to express feelings is the feelings people experience *about* feelings. What is an example of this?
3. How effectively do you believe you express your needs? When is it easiest to do this? When is it most difficult?
4. What are some of the reasons why it is difficult to be direct? What gets in the way of directness?
5. You could argue that sometimes it's helpful to be indirect rather than direct, that questions can soften otherwise hard statements, and that it's not always wise to express your wants and needs. How do you believe McKay, Davis, and Fanning would respond to these reservations?
6. When, if any time, might you argue that messages should be, or could usefully be, nonsupportive?

S teve Duck is a highly respected interpersonal communication teacher and researcher from Iowa (via England). In this reading he contributes a very important idea to the understanding of "expression"—"expressing yourself," or "self-disclosure." With the help of Kathryn Dindia, Barbara Montgomery, and other communication researchers, Duck emphasizes the limitations of treating expression as a one-way communication phenomenon. Disclosures about one's self and expressions of opinions and feelings are *interpreted* by others in some physical and psychological *context*. So if you want to understand these expressions, you need to pay attention not only to what is said, but also to how *responses* to what is said help determine what it *means*.

Early in the reading, Duck notes that some authors have treated expression as if it were synonymous with communication, but that more recent writing demonstrates the oversimplification in this view. Simplistic definitions of disclosure overlook, for example, the fact that some declarations "serve to keep the conversation going rather than offering much information," and that others can be "used to control conversation or manage identity." It can be misleading, in other words, to treat expressiveness as an individual rather than a "dyadic [two-person] or relationship characteristic."

Self-disclosure can be more clearly understood when it is recognized to be not just information about one's self that one expresses, but also information that the expresser knows or expects will be *treated as revealing by his or her listeners*. Ambiguity also makes self-disclosure more complicated than it may first appear. Just as a bucket dipped into a pool brings up only part of the water, a disclosing statement only samples what a person could say. As a result *listeners* are always contributing to the meaning of what's said. This is another way that communication is collaborative, as I said in Chapter 2.

In the final section of the reading, Duck notes how self-disclosure can be used to interrogate people. Here, I'm reminded of a friend of mine who used to say he knew a person who "could self-disclose the shirt right off your back." Disclosure can also be used to educate another person, as it is when a parent discloses how he or she handled a challenge that is being faced by his or her child. Duck concludes with an example of disclosure that was meant to convey not the literal meaning of the information disclosed but a broader point about the significance of the friend in forming the discloser's view of herself as a teenager.

The readings in this chapter are designed to give you an overview of the exhaling part of communicating and some specific guidelines for your own disclosure. It's my hope that they also underscore once again how completely, as is pointed out in Chapter 2, the meanings of communicative events are *collaboratively constructed* by all the people involved.

EXPRESSING MEANING TO OTHERS

Steve Duck

Alternative constructions of reality are the basis for individuality, but do not exist only in some abstracted personal black hole. They have social force as soon as people open their mouths. As people behave, talk, and use symbols, they declare their constructions of experience in all manner of ways, whether through content and/or through style of talk. In talk, people do not only do big things, such as offer opinions or take formal positions on debatable matters. They also declare or "leak" their constructions and interpretations of events in many ways both verbal and nonverbal (Goffman, 1959). Such "leakages" form the basis of the polygraph lie detector test, for example, and are familiar to a host of researchers into nonverbal behavior, speech patterns, power, status, liking, self-disclosure, and clinical psychology (Keeley & Hart, 1994, review these implications for relationships). In such research it has been established that nonverbal communication conveys intimations of attitudes about self, attitudes about others, and attitudes about degree of comfort with the interaction itself, while small features of language style themselves convey liking, intimacy, and status (Duck, 1992). In everyday real life, however, such cues are also readily available through the normal discourse of life and relationships.

Excerpts from *Meaningful Relationships* by Steve Duck, pp. 58–62 & 166–168. Reprinted by permission of Sage Publications, Inc.

COMMUNICATION IS MORE THAN JUST EXPRESSION

Cues to a person's thinking are, however, evident even if we look only at an expressive function of language—"communication *at*" rather than "communication *with*." Expressiveness is not really "communication" between two people but is like two people holding up advertising billboards in one another's presence, each declaring their internal states, view of the world, attitudes, and so forth. Such a view of communication is not as simpleminded as it first sounds. Indeed, several people who use the word *communication* actually mean little more than this expressive function ("You should communicate your feelings"). Such academic writers as Jourard (1971) focused on self-disclosure as the opening up of oneself to others to create a transparent self. Jourard (1971) regarded such open expressiveness as a sign of mental health. For some later writers self-disclosure came to be nothing more interactive than a simple declaration of feelings (see Hendrick, 1987, for a discussion). These one-sided, billboarding ways in which self-disclosure is frequently operationalized in research often lead reviewers to see the whole "self-disclosure" process as no more than the expression of feelings and experiences that characterize the discloser's inner self. In reality, self-disclosure is a much more complex process (Dindia, 1994; Spencer, 1994). It involves many declarations that in truth serve to keep the conversation going rather than offering much information per se (Planalp & Garvin-Doxas, 1994) but can also be used to control conversation or manage identity (e.g., when parents confront adolescents and require them to disclose things about their habits and behavior—Spencer, 1994).

The depiction of disclosure as declaration naturally, even if unintentionally, channels us to see self-disclosure as an essentially individual characteristic rather than an interactive or communicative one (Duck & Pittman, 1996). The representation of self-disclosure as a personality trait or an individual characteristic is not itself a problem for some purposes (e.g., clinical work or the enhancement of the conversation skills of lonely persons; Jones, Hansson, & Cutrona, 1984). Yet such representation of self-disclosure becomes misleading, when other scholars treat such declarations of the self as being the same thing as self-disclosure as an *inter*action, or when scholars use it as a criterion for "good communication" in relationships or as a predictor of relationship intimacy (e.g., Berg & McQuinn, 1986). The intention of such research is to treat self-disclosure as a dyadic or relationship characteristic, but "expressiveness" is not dyadic, and such mistaken equation of self-disclosure misrepresents its contribution to the intimacy level in the relationship (Acitelli & Duck, 1987).

Simple billboarding and expressiveness probably do have important roles to play in relationships and in relationship development (e.g., in creating opportunities for reciprocity of disclosure between two interactants or making the expresser feel relaxed in the presence of the other person or providing information). However, this fact exemplifies the problem of assuming that "expression" is also "communication." For example, reciprocity of self-disclosure is not necessarily valuable (Fitzpatrick, 1988). If Person A says "I have a medical problem" and Person B responds "So do I," then the reciprocity may not be very useful on its own. The usefulness of a reciprocal self-disclosure or its importance instead depends on how each listener reacts to the expression and whether the reciprocator then launches off into a catalogue of sores, pustules, and malodorous symptoms. (There are some interesting sex differences on this where females are more likely to find a "So do I" supportive because it is communal; Wood, 1993, for example).

Several writers (e.g., Montgomery, 1984) have pointed out that what is intimate for a speaker may not seem intimate to a listener and so may not have any effective influence on the listener's urges to reciprocate or to develop a relationship. Rather, scholars must change focus and see that it is the *perception* of a statement *as* intimate self-disclosure that creates in the listener a likelihood of reciprocity, and not the expression of a statement on its own, nor the content of the statement itself that does so. The background and social context for a behavior (such as self-disclosure)—including the role of the perceptive listener (Harris & Sadeghi, 1987)—is at least as important to its social impact as is the behavior itself.

Recent work increasingly recognizes that, to a significant degree, the meaning and impact of self-disclosure comes not from itself but partly from its impact on, and involvement of, the listener (Hendrick, 1987). To make such a claim is to note that self-disclosure is a relational force *when* it is communication between two people that is based on the use of messages that *one knows or expects will be understood* by someone else.

How might a sender come to believe that a listener will "get it" when he or she expresses something? One fair assumption is that a listener may understand simply because members of the same culture recognize the symbols and language being used. However, there is no guarantee. A sender may also help the listener by disambiguating the expression or clarifying the choice that has been made and thus the possibilities that are excluded. "I mean these, not those; she is indicating here, not there; your meaning is this, not that." Very little can be said that cannot be challenged, negated, or placed in the context of an alternative interpretation or an extended way of viewing it. Such implications and clarifications through contrast are the baggage, the threads and ropes, of meaning that senders need in order to be able to express things in a way compatible with their partner's style of looking at the world.

SPEECH AS A SAMPLER OF MEANING

Ambiguity of language is important because it again emphasizes the inadequacies of treating expression as all there is to communication. Not only do some things have personal meaning to an expresser but words, places, and suggestions are often ambiguous for a listener within a relational context or can mean different things simultaneously depending on how a partner chooses to take them. For example, "Why don't we both go back to my place for some coffee" *could* just mean what it says on its face, or it could be a sexual proposition, or it could be an invitation that expresses interest in seeing what possibilities arise.

The listener will have to decide what the implications of acceptance are to be in the face of such possible ambiguity. Much of relational and social life is similarly ambiguous, and the interactants' task is precisely that of determining what it is that the speaker intends (Shotter, 1987).

As the true currency of the interchanges of relational life, meaning (like talk) is much more complex than simple declaration of feelings or expression of what is in one's mind. Individual statements are always incomplete in the sense that they could be revised during the unfinished business of thinking. Individual statements do not always state clearly and exhaustively what it is with which they contrast themselves. Furthermore, few people can express the complete essence of all that they know about a given topic in a single sentence. Perhaps one should see meaning not as a single thing but rather as a well into which a given piece of speech throws a bucket. The bucket samples the water but does not bring it all up at once. Likewise, different buckets bring up different volumes, have different shapes, and sample different parts of the well. Thus a single statement samples what a person could say about a given object and thus represents a momentary choice made from all the things that a person could say about something. Such statements may or may not give an adequate picture for observers to comprehend the full significance of something. So here, too, we see that our metaphors influence our thought and action. If we believe that talk is meaning (or identity) we behave differently than if we believe talk is a sample of meaning or identity. It is through extended interaction and talk with a partner that the detail can be understood and the representativeness of any particular sample becomes more apparent. . . .

Because most statements made by persons are indicators of choice, are less than all of what they could say, and are rarely fully elaborated every time the person speaks, *listeners* must themselves devise ways to interpret and complete the statements that they hear in order to divine the speaker's meaning. Initially, the listener presumably attributes significance in terms of his or her own system of thought, projects intentions, and does a lot else besides just being a receptacle for sound waves. Thus "communication" involves not only the expression of personal values and meanings by a speaker but also their interpretation by a listener. Such interpretation could transform a speaker's meaning or locate it in some way or associate/transfer/extend it. . . .

SELF-DISCLOSURE

I have said quite a lot about self-disclosure as I have gone along, so it should be clear why I believe that the meaning of a disclosure is not necessarily the same for speaker and listener, as has all too often been assumed. Perhaps because of implicit awareness of this fact, persons who wish to make a disclosure make strategic preparations to manipulate context so that the listener's response becomes somewhat more predictable. Miell and Duck (1986) have shown that people lead up slowly to the disclosure on intimate topics in real encounters, first testing the ground by mentioning the topic in a joking or slighting way in order to see the general reaction of the listener to the topic as a whole. If the response is safe (i.e., if it appears that the listener is not hostile to the topic), then the speaker will go ahead and make a self-disclosing statement about the topic. Thus the risk of intimacy that is often discussed in research reports about self-disclosure, and is sometimes seen to give self-disclosure its intimate meaning and force, is in fact strategically reduced beforehand by manipulation of *the meaning of the situation* where the disclosure is about to be made.

Furthermore, Miell (1984) reasoned that other meanings can be constructed for apparently self-disclosing statements. Self-disclosure can be used in order to interrogate other people! Miell argued that people are aware that a norm of reciprocity exists in respect of disclosure and that if a person discloses to us we are implicitly pressured to disclose in return. Given such knowledge, then, it is possible to ask another person questions in a very subtle manner. Miell showed that speakers would declare their own experience with a topic and then sit back and wait for the listener to feel the pressure of a norm to reciprocate equally disclosing information.

Equally, Spencer (1993) has noted that self-disclosure has other more complex meanings than those that researchers assume. In many circumstances, especially in mentor or parent-child relationships, the disclosure often has an educative purpose. The disclosure is not intended to tell the listener about the speaker's personal life nor to increase relational intimacy so much as to provide guidance based on the speaker's experience. For example, Spencer (1993) found that parents would declare to adolescents statements of the form: "When I was your age I used to feel terribly shy too, but I overcame it by. . . ."

In these cases, the meaning of the act of disclosure is rather similar to the advice-giving strategies used by teachers (Glidewell, Tucker, Todt, & Cox, 1982). In the latter study, inexperienced teachers told stories about problems they had encountered, yet they did not ask directly for advice about how to solve those problems. Experienced teachers did not respond with advice as such either, but instead told stories about situations where they had solved a similar problem. Thus the disclosure of both predicaments and possible solutions was handled indirectly without one side having to lose face by a direct request for help or a direct acknowledgment of the one-down position of being advised. These examples again suggest that the meaning of a situation is a guide to the interpretation and understanding of what people do in it, more so than is the absolute value of the behavior per se. In the everyday discourses of life, then, the revelation of a speaker's feelings may be oblique to self-disclosure in the traditional sense. The nature of a disclosure takes its meaning from the speaker's purposes in the encounter, and the response of the listener to that meaning.

Finally, in everyday life, statements that would be rated as disclosures may in fact be used to share broad experiences rather than literal and specific content. For example, my wife Joanna recently told me about a friend she had during teenage years and some of the unconventional things that they did. Joanna disclosed many memories and feelings about the friend during this conversation. It was also clear to me, however, that these details were essentially irrelevant to her purposes. The point of describing them was to convey to me the significance of the friend in forming Joanna's view of herself as a teenager and *that* was what was really being disclosed. The fuller experience—not the specific details or emotions—was the essence of the act of disclosure that had meaning to her and to me.

In all of the above instances, some drawn from research and some from life, there is evidence that an utterance can be designated as a true self-disclosure in the sense assumed in research only after careful consideration of the relational and interactional context in which it occurs. The literal meaning of the utterance itself is therefore less important for relational research than the social meaning and significance of the fact of its utterance. This can be determined only after careful consideration of the interpersonal meaning that it has for the relationship rather than only from the personal significance or literal meaning of the statement.

REVIEW QUESTIONS

1. How important is what Duck calls "leakage" in your communication experience (see the first paragraph of this reading)?
2. What's the difference between communication *at* and communication *with*?
3. Paraphrase Duck's statement and explain its significance: "Individual statements are always incomplete in the sense that they could be revised during the unfinished business of thinking."
4. Some authors would define *self-disclosure* as simply revealing something personal about yourself. Duck would not define it this way. How would he define it?

PROBES

1. Duck briefly mentions gender differences in expressiveness or self-disclosure. What gender patterns do you notice? What exceptions to these patterns have you experienced?
2. Duck emphasizes that self-disclosure is not just information about your self, but information that you predict will be heard by the other person as (a) about your self *and* (b) significant in some way. Give an example from your own experience that supports this point.
3. What's the main point of Duck's "bucket of water" analogy?

REFERENCES

Acitelli, L. K., & Duck, S. W. (1987). Intimacy as the proverbial elephant. In D. Perlman & S. W. Duck (Eds.), *Intimate relationships: Development, dynamics and deterioration* (pp. 297–308). Newbury Park, CA: Sage.

Berg, J. H., & McQuinn, R. D. (1986). Attraction and exchange in continuing and noncontinuing dating relationships. *Journal of Personality and Social Psychology, 50*, 942–952.

Dindia, K. (1994). The intrapersonal-interpersonal dialectical process of self-disclosure. In S. W. Duck (Ed.), *Dynamics of relationships* (Understanding Relationship Processes Series, Vol. 4, pp. 27–57). Thousand Oaks, CA: Sage.

Duck, S. W. (1992). *Human relationships* (2nd ed.). London: Sage.

Duck, S. W. (1994). Attaching meaning to attachment. *Psychological Inquiry, 5*, 34–38.

Duck, S. W., & Pittman, G. (1996). Social and personal relationships. In M. L. Knapp & G. R. Miller (Eds.), *Handbook of interpersonal communication* (2nd ed.). Thousand Oaks, CA: Sage.

Fitzpatrick, M. A. (1988). *Between husbands and wives: Communication in marriage.* Newbury Park, CA: Sage.

Glidewell, J. C., Tucker, S., Todt, M., & Cox, S. (1982). Professional support systems—The teaching profession. In A. Nadler, J. D. Fisher, & B. M. De Paulo (Eds.), *Applied research in help-seeking and reactions to aid* (pp. 163–184). New York: Academic Press.

Goffman, E. (1959). *Behavior in public places.* Harmondsworth, UK: Penguin.

Harris, L. M., & Sadeghi, A. (1987). Realizing: How facts are created in human interaction. *Journal of Social and Personal Relationships, 4*, 480–495.

Hendrick, S. S. (1987). Self disclosure and marital satisfaction. *Journal of Social and Personal Relationships, 10*, 459–466.

Jones, W. H., Hansson, R. O., & Cutrona, C. E. (1984). Helping the lonely: Issues of intervention with young and older adults. In S. W. Duck (Ed.), *Personal relationships 5: Repairing personal relationships* (pp. 143–162). London: Academic Press.

Jourard, S. (1971). *Self-disclosure.* New York: John Wiley.

Keeley, M., & Hart, A. (1994). Nonverbal behavior in interaction. In S. W. Duck (Ed.), *Dynamics of interactions* (Understanding Relationship Processes Series, Vol. 4, pp. 135–162). Thousand Oaks, CA: Sage.

Miell, D. E. (1984). *Cognitive and communicative strategies in developing relationships: Converging and diverging social environments.* Unpublished doctoral dissertation, University of Lancaster, UK.

Miell, D. E., & Duck, S. W. (1986). Strategies in developing friendship. In V. J. Derlega & B. A. Winstead (Eds.), *Friendship and social interaction* (pp. 129–143). New York: Springer.

Montgomery, B. M. (1984). Behavioral characteristics predicting self and peer perception of open communication. *Communication Quarterly, 32*, 233–240.

Planalp, S., & Garvin-Doxas, K. (1994). Using mutual knowledge in conversation: Friends as experts in each other. In S. W. Duck (Ed.), *Dynamics of interactions* (Understanding Relationship Processes Series, Vol. 4, pp. 1–26). Thousand Oaks, CA: Sage.

Shotter, J. (1987). The social construction of an "us": Problems of accountability and narratology. In R. Burnett, P. McGhee, & D. D. Clarke (Eds.), *Accounting for relationships* (pp. 225–247). London: Methuen.

Spencer, E. E. (1993). *New approaches to assessing self-disclosure in conversation*. Paper presented to the Western Speech Communication Association, Albuquerque, NM.

Spencer, E. E. (1994). Transforming relationships through ordinary talk. In S. W. Duck (Ed.), *Dynamics of relationships* (Understanding Relationship Processes Series, Vol. 4, pp. 58–86). Thousand Oaks, CA: Sage.

Wood, J. T. (1993). Engendered relations: Interaction, caring, power and responsibility in intimacy. In S. W. Duck (Ed.), *Social contexts and relationships* (Understanding Relationship Processes Series, Vol. 3, pp. 26–54). Newbury Park, CA: Sage.

CHAPTER 8

Hurtful and Negative Communicating

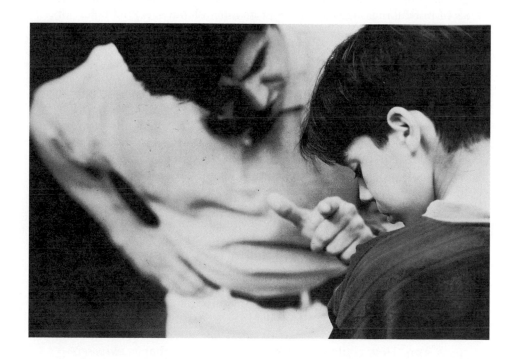

The previous chapter discussed exhaling in general by focusing on expressive and disclosive messages. Now this chapter narrows the focus to some particular kind of messages, those that generate relational problems or pollute the interpersonal water.

I remember when Anita Vangelisti was an undergraduate student in my interpersonal communication class. Now she is a respected researcher and a professor in one of the best communication departments in the United States at the University of Texas. This reading, which I excerpted from a considerably longer chapter in a recent book, summarizes some of Anita's work on hurtful messages.

This selection reviews work done by others and reports on some studies Anita and her colleagues have done. As she reports, one of her early moves was to ask several hundred college students to recall a situation in which someone said something to them that hurt their feelings. From these data she was able to identify *categories* of hurtful messages. They are summarized in Table 1 and include accusations, evaluations, threats, lies, and six other types. She also identified nine *topics* of hurtful messages, including romantic relations, sexual behavior, physical appearance, personality traits, and so on. This early research gave Anita an overall view of the phenomenon she was studying.

One of her next moves was to explore why some messages hurt more than others. She found that informative messages hurt the worst, primarily because there seems to be little opportunity to defend oneself or repair the damage created by comments like, "You aren't a priority in my life," "I decided we can only be friends," or "I'm really attracted to Julie." As you might expect, messages centering on romantic relationships were also perceived as extremely hurtful. And again, their hurtfulness is partly a function of how much the recipient can do about the message. The most hurtful messages tend to be those that we can do the least to respond to. This is one of the reasons why recipients in at least one study responded to extremely hurtful messages by withdrawing—either by crying or by verbally complying.

Anita extends her discussion of these most hurtful messages by reviewing some attributions that people make to help them cope. (For a review of attributions, look back at the reading by Trenholm and Jensen in Chapter 5.) Sometimes people cope by providing a generous attribution about intent—"After all, she didn't *mean* to hurt my feelings." In other situations intent is clearer and the person receiving the message focuses on "How could anyone say something like that *on purpose?*"

The mental effort expended to make sense of hurtful messages varies, as you might expect, with the closeness of the relationship. Few people invest much effort in a hurtful message from a store clerk, but a comment from one's spouse might provoke considerable work. There are exceptions to this rule, however, including the son who excuses his father's put-downs with "I guess that's what fathers are supposed to do" and the abused wife who minimizes the negative messages received from her husband.

The final section of this reading focuses on how hurtful messages affect relationships. When the message is perceived to be unintentional, the impact on the relationship tends to be negligible. When the hurt is perceived to be intentional, there is a greater impact, but this tendency is balanced by the tendency to excuse intimates. In both family and dating relationships, hurtful messages are often forgiven.

Anita's research clearly demonstrates the inaccuracy of the old adage, "Sticks and stones can break my bones, but names can never hurt me." Hurt is a relational phenomenon that depends not only on what is said but when, by whom, to whom, and how seriously. But the potential of destructive words is clearly great. "Names" and other hurtful messages can cut deep.

MESSAGES THAT HURT

Anita L. Vangelisti

After my parents got divorced, my father sat down and had a long talk with me. He told me a lot of things that my mom did to hurt him and tried to explain his side of the story. I already knew most of what he said, but there was one thing that really surprised me. He said, "Your mother never really loved you as much as she did your brother or sister. . . . It was obvious from the start. You looked like me and she couldn't hide her feelings." He probably didn't mean this the way I took it, but it has bothered me ever since. I wish now he wouldn't have said it. I'm not sure why he did. I guess he was just expressing his anger.

Although most of us have used the old adage "sticks and stones may break my bones,"[1] few who study communication would argue that the impact of words on people and relationships is less than that of physical objects—whether those objects be sticks, stones, bats, or fists. Words not only "do" things when uttered (Austin, 1975), but they have the ability to hurt or harm in every bit as real a way as physical objects. A few ill-spoken words (e.g., "You're worthless," "You'll never amount to anything," "I don't love you anymore") can strongly affect individuals, interactions, and relationships.

Feeling hurt, by its nature, is a social phenomenon. Except in relatively rare circumstances, people feel hurt as a result of some interpersonal event—

Excerpts from "Messages That Hurt," by Anita Vangelisti from *The Dark Side of Interpersonal Communication*, Ed. William R. Cupach et al., 1994. Reprinted by permission of Lawrence Erlbaum Associates, Inc. and the author.

something they perceive was said or done by another individual. The hurtful utterance may be spoken with the best of intentions or it may be overtly aggressive. It may occur as a one-time event or it may be embedded in a long history
of verbal abuse. It may be spoken by a complete stranger or by a life-long friend.
Regardless of intentionality, context, or source, feelings of hurt are evoked by
and expressed through communication. Although theorists of emotion and of
communication have acknowledged the potential association between social interaction and the elicitation of emotions such as hurt, theoretical work has only
recently begun to explain the processes that link communication and emotion
(Averill, 1980; Bowers, Metts, & Duncanson, 1985; de Rivera & Grinkis, 1986;
Shimanoff, 1985, 1987; Weiner, 1986).

Weiner (1986) suggested that emotions are determined, in part, by attributions. He and his colleagues have found, for example, that the attributions people make about interpersonal events distinguish whether individuals feel anger,
guilt, or pity (Weiner, Graham, & Chandler, 1982). Given this, when people feel
hurt, their attributions concerning the messages that initially evoked their feelings should distinguish those (hurt) feelings from other similarly "negative"
emotions. Although researchers have begun to study the association between attribution and emotion, they have largely neglected the relationship between
communication and attribution. Because attributions are based, in part, on individuals' observations of interpersonal events, the messages that people believe
evoked their feelings of hurt are central to understanding how hurt is elicited.

The purpose of this reading is to begin to describe the social interactions that
people define as hurtful. . . .

EXAMINING MESSAGES THAT HURT

To begin to describe hurtful messages, data collected from two groups of undergraduate students were examined. The first set of data was collected from
students ($N = 179$) enrolled in a large, introductory communication course. The
second data set was collected approximately 1 year later and consisted of responses from individuals ($N = 183$) enrolled in one of several introductory communication courses.

Respondents were instructed to recall a situation in which someone said
something to them that hurt their feelings. Then they were asked to write a
"script" of the interaction as they remembered it. They were told to include what
was said before the hurtful comment was made, what the comment was, and
how they reacted to the comment.[2] After completing their script, participants
were asked to look back on the conversation they described and to rate how
hurtful it was (a high score indicated that it was "Extremely Hurtful" and a low
score that it was "Not At All Hurtful").[3]

Inductive analysis (Bulmer, 1979) was used to develop a category scheme to
describe the acts of speech that characterize hurtful messages.[4] With the exception of the data from five respondents (who could not recall any particularly hurtful messages), over 96% of the messages were codable into the typology. Defini-

tions and examples of the categories are provided in Table 1. . . . The most commonly perceived hurtful messages across both data sets were accusations, evaluations, and informative messages, whereas the least common were lies and threats.

A brief perusal of these data suggested that the messages varied in terms of how hurtful they were to respondents. Interactions ranged from a former coach telling a respondent, "My, you seem to have put on a few pounds" to a physical education teacher exclaiming, "You are the worse [*sic*] player I've ever seen in my life!" In one case, a peer asked a respondent who was mourning her father's death, "When are you going to get over this?" In another, a respondents' stepmother told her, "You caused your grandmother's death. She died of a broken heart because you didn't show her how much you loved her." Although all of these examples were rated above the midpoint in terms of how hurtful they were to respondents, some were rated as more hurtful than others. . . .

The topics addressed by hurtful messages were coded using a procedure identical to the one outlined for the coding of message type. Initial categories were generated, the data were coded, the categories were refined, and the data were recoded. Table 2 provides a list of topic categories as well as examples of each topic. Over 93% of the messages reported were codable into the typology. . . .

TABLE 1 Typology of Hurtful Message Speech Acts

Definition	Examples
Accusation: A charge of fault or offense.	"You are a liar." "You're such a hypocrite."
Evaluation: A description of value, worth, or quality.	"Well, if I met him and liked him, I would have remembered him." "Going out with you was the biggest mistake of my life."
Directive: An order, set of directions, or a command.	"Just get off my back." "Just leave me alone, why don't you!"
Advice: A suggestion for a course of action.	"Break up with her so you can have some fun." "I think we should see other people."
Expression of Desire: A statement of preference.	"I don't want him to be like you." "I don't ever want to have anything to do with you."
Information: A disclosure of information.	"You aren't a priority in my life." "Well, I'm really attracted to Julie."
Question: An inquiry or interrogation.	"Why aren't you over this [a family death] yet?"
Threat: An expression of intention to inflict some sort of punishment under certain conditions.	"If I find out you are ever with that person, *never* come home again."
Joke: A witticism or prank.	"The statement was really an ethnic joke against my ethnicity."
Lie: An untrue, deceptive statement or question.	"The worst part was when he lied about something. . ."

TABLE 2 Examples of Hurtful Message Topics

Topic	Example
Romantic Relations	"He never liked you anyway. He just used you to get back at me."
Nonromantic Relations	"You're trying too hard to be popular. . . you're ignoring your 'real' friends."
Sexual Behavior	"Why? Do you still want to sleep around?"
Physical Appearance	"God almighty you're fat!"
Abilities/Intelligence	"I guess it's hard for you teenage illiterates to write that stuff."
Personality Traits	"Well, I think you're selfish and spoiled!"
Self-Worth	"I don't need you anymore."
Time	"We don't do things together like we used to."
Ethnicity/Religion	"You're a stupid Jew!"

WHY SOME MESSAGES HURT MORE THAN OTHERS

Of the hurtful messages described, informative statements were the only speech acts that were rated extremely hurtful more often than they were rated low in hurtfulness. Informative statements, in short, were most typically seen as highly hurtful messages. Although potential explanations for this finding vary, the ability of recipients to "repair" or offer alternatives to the content of the message seems a particularly likely contributor. Whereas listeners are less likely than speakers to initiate repair (Schegloff, Jefferson, & Sacks, 1977), when accused or evaluated, recipients have the control to either overtly or covertly "defend" themselves against hurt. If the speaker does not initiate repair, the recipient may do so by offering alternatives to the accusation (e.g., accounts, excuses, justifications) and even verifying those alternatives with examples from his or her own experiences.[5] On the other hand, when informed of something, there are few such arguments available. The opportunities for recipients to repair any damage to their own face are severely limited. If, for example, a person is accused of being selfish and inconsiderate, that person can point out instances in which that has not been the case. However, if the same person is informed by a lover that the lover is "seeing someone else," there is little the person can say to counter the statement.

Like informative statements, hurtful messages (in the second data set) centering on romantic relationships were, more often than not, perceived as extremely hurtful (although this difference was significant only for the second data set, messages in the first data set were similarly distributed). Given that over 54.5% of the informative messages concerned romantic relationships (i.e., "I don't love you anymore," "I've been sleeping with someone else," "I decided we can only be friends"), this finding is not surprising. It is interesting, however, that participants tended to rate these relational hurts as more hurtful, whereas they tended to rate some personal or individual hurts (i.e., statements regarding self-worth) as less hurtful. One explanation for this contrast involves the potential recency of the messages concerning romantic relationships. Because the sample for this study was college students, events centering on romantic relationships may have been more recent and therefore more salient in the minds of respondents. However, this was not the case ($F(1,283) = 1.76$, ns). Furthermore, participants' ratings of hurtfulness were positively correlated with the amount of time that had passed since the hurtful event. . . .

A second explanation is that hurtful messages focusing on relational issues, like those comprised of informative statements, may be more difficult for recipients to repair than messages that emphasize nonrelational issues. This explanation is supported by the finding (in the first data set) that hurtful messages concerning nonromantic relationships were seen as extremely hurtful more often than not. (In the second data set this difference was not significant, but the data were distributed in a similar pattern.) Because relationships involve two people, they are at once controllable and uncontrollable. Each individual has the power to influence, but neither has complete reign. In contrast, many nonrelational issues such as time management are more controllable. Recipients may repair by excusing, justifying, or apologizing for their behavior or choices (McLaughlin, 1984). Further, because recipients have access to a great deal of information concerning their own behavior (e.g., the situational parameters they face), they may be able to rationalize their limitations by adjusting their own criteria for evaluating the behavior. Other nonrelational issues such as physical appearance and intelligence are relatively uncontrollable. Recipients therefore need not take responsibility for evaluative remarks or questions from others.

In comparison to nonrelational issues, relational issues present both recipients and speakers with a unique situation. Neither has complete control or responsibility for relational outcomes. As a result, when one partner evaluates ("You aren't going to make a very good husband") or makes an accusation ("You don't care about our friendship at all") concerning the relationship, the other is faced with a dilemma. He or she must seek a repair strategy that addresses the (relational) issue at hand without threatening the face of either partner. In many cases, these two goals are incompatible. The difficulties of dealing with such incompatible goals are reflected by the findings of a pilot study that suggest that recipients tend to react to extremely hurtful messages by withdrawing—either by crying or verbally acquiescing to their conversational partner (Vangelisti, 1989).

In addition to presenting participants with potentially difficult behavioral choices, extremely hurtful messages may also create some difficult cognitive tasks. When a loved one says something that hurts, participants may make one of at least two attributional choices. First, they may reason that the person did not intend to hurt their feelings. If this choice is made, the message may evoke feelings of hurt, but might not have a major effect on the relationship ("After all, she didn't *mean* to hurt my feelings"). Second, participants may believe that the message was intentionally hurtful. If so, they will likely have more difficulty discounting the impact of the message on the relationship ("How could anyone say something like that *on purpose?*"). In some cases, people may examine the available data to determine whether or not a message was intended to hurt. In others, the need or desire to maintain a close relationship may encourage participants to make attributions that minimize the intentionality they attach to hurtful messages.

The cognitive "effort" that individuals expend to make sense of hurtful messages should depend, in part, on the individuals' relationship with the person who uttered the message. For example, if a clerk in a department store hurts a person's feelings, that person is probably less likely to spend time contemplating the clerk's motives than if the same person was treated badly by a friend, parent, or spouse. Why? In part because people expect to be treated by intimate relational partners in relatively positive ways.

Obviously, there are exceptions to this rule. For instance, when explaining why his father said something hurtful to him, one respondent noted, "I don't understand why he always puts me down. I guess that's what fathers are supposed to do." Clearly this respondent did not expect positive feedback from his father. The rather bewildered account of his father's behavior suggests that the hurtful message described by the respondent may have been one of many—that it was contextualized in an ongoing stream of verbal abuse (Leffler, 1988; Vissing, Straus, Gelles, & Harrop, 1991; Yelsma, 1992) and/or intentional verbal aggression (Infante, Riddle, Horvath, & Tumlin, 1992; Martin & Horvath, 1992). Another example would be a physically abused wife who comes to expect negative behavior from her spouse. Even in such extreme cases, however, researchers have found that both the abused and the abuser use cognitive strategies to minimize the control and intentionality associated with abusive acts (Andrews, 1992; Herbert, Silver, & Ellard, 1991; Holtzworth-Munroe, 1992). In the context of close relationships, acts of violence are often interpreted as representing "love" rather than more obvious emotions such as anger or rage (Cate, Henton, Koval, Christopher, & Lloyd, 1982; Henton, Cate, Koval, Lloyd, & Christopher, 1983; Roscoe & Kelsey, 1986). In short, relational intimacy, the type of relationship people have with those who utter hurtful messages, and the intentionality attributed to the message should affect the impact of hurtful messages on relationships. . . .

DISCUSSING THE IMPACT OF HURTFUL
MESSAGES ON RELATIONSHIPS

Although the vast majority (64.8%) of hurtful messages were perceived to be unintentional, those that were seen as intentional had a significantly greater distancing effect on the relationship. Recipients' remarks regarding intentionality reflected their willingness to make allowances for a variety of speaker difficulties. When asked whether the speaker intended to hurt them, recipients often made comments such as "she was mad at someone else," "he just doesn't know how to fight," "he has a personal problem with alcohol," or "he said it because he loves me." If speakers seemed to regret the hurtful message (Knapp et al., 1986), or if the message was offered for the good of the recipient (Weber & Vangelisti, 1991), the message did not have as strong an effect on the relationship. In contrast, when recipients perceived that the message was intentionally hurtful, their remarks frequently focused on stable personality traits of the speaker: "She's just that sort of person," "he is very cruel and unforgiving," "he doesn't care about anyone except himself." . . .

The impact of hurtful messages on relational intimacy was also affected by ratings of relational closeness at the time the message was uttered. Ratings of relational closeness were negatively associated with the distancing effect of hurtful messages. Because there was not a similarly negative association between closeness and message hurtfulness, the apparent lack of distancing in more intimate relationships was not due to the fact that the messages hurt less. Instead, those who were involved in intimate relationships may be more willing to offer interpretations of the hurtful messages that are less harmful to the relationship. It is also possible that intimates have developed idiosyncratic patterns to deal with hurtful events (Montgomery, 1988), or that they have developed enough of a positive regard for one another that a single hurtful message does not affect relational intimacy (Knapp, 1984).

Similar explanations may be offered for the findings concerning family relationships. Although intimacy did not significantly differentiate between family and nonfamily relationships, results indicated that hurtful messages occurring in the context of the family had less of an effect on the relationship than did those occurring in nonfamily contexts. In contrast to intimate nonfamily relationships, family associations may encourage people to deal with hurtful messages by relying on the assumption that the relationships are involuntary and therefore virtually impossible to dissolve. One respondent noted in the margin of his questionnaire that "It seems if something happens with your family . . . [you are] a lot more apt to forgive them." Because family members are, for all practical purposes, irreplaceable, recipients of hurtful messages may feel more obligated to absorb the blow of a hurtful message without allowing it to impact the family relationship. In addition, the variety of circumstances family members have experienced together may create a sort of "immunity" to the impact of hurtful messages. Family members' experience with other negative interpersonal events may better prepare them for the feelings of hurt that can be elicited by other members. . . .

In sum, the findings of this research suggest that the old adage concerning "sticks and stones" requires, at the very least, a lengthy addendum. Hurt is a socially elicited emotion (de Rivera, 1977)—people feel hurt because of the interpersonal behavior of others. Because feelings of hurt are elicited through social interaction, words can "hurt"—both individuals and relationships.

REVIEW QUESTIONS

1. Paraphrase the relationship between attributions and hurtfulness that Anita outlines in the third paragraph of this reading.
2. What is the main characteristic of a hurtful message that informs?
3. Why does Anita believe that informative hurtful messages are so painful?
4. What is Anita's theoretical explanation for the finding that recipients tend to react to extremely hurtful messages by withdrawing?
5. How does the desire to maintain a close relationship sometimes affect attributions about a hurtful message?
6. What do you make out of the finding that almost 65 percent of hurtful messages were perceived to be unintentional?

PROBES

1. If you were a participant in Anita's first study, what two examples of hurtful messages would you first recall? Label them using the categories in Table 1. Then identify the topics of these messages, as in Table 2.
2. What is the frequency of hurtful messages in your life by topic type? Which topic in Table 2 do you hear the most hurtful messages about? What is ranked second and third?
3. "Time heals all wounds," the saying goes. Yet Anita found that "participants' ratings of hurtfulness were positively correlated with the amount of time that had passed since the hurtful event." Comment on this finding.
4. Explain how, in the context of close relationships, "acts of violence are often interpreted as representing 'love.'"
5. Anita found in her research that the distancing effects of hurtful messages in intimate relationships was less than she expected. How does she explain this finding?

NOTES

1. Steve Duck has informed me of a German proverb that provides a more accurate representation of the association between words and feelings of hurt: "Böse Disteln stechen sehr, böse Zungen stechen mehr." A colleague from Germany, Jurgen Streeck, confirmed the translation: "Nasty thistles hurt/stick a great deal, but nasty words hurt/stick more."
2. Respondents participating in the second data collection session were also asked to indicate how long ago the hurtful message occurred.
3. To reduce demand characteristics, participants were also informed that some people may not have experienced (or may not be able to remember) the type of conversations called for by the questionnaire and that part of the research project was to assess the percentage of people who could and could not do so. Subjects were further reminded that they would receive extra credit regardless of whether or not they completed the questionnaire (see Planalp & Honeycutt, 1985).
4. Because the data were collected approximately 1 year apart, the analyses were conducted separately (also approximately 1 year apart). The initial category scheme, therefore, was primarily developed using the first data set. The second set of data was collected, in part, to demonstrate the applicability of the category scheme and to replicate the frequencies found using the first data set.
5. Work on accounts, blaming, excuses, and attributions (e.g., Cody & McLaughlin, 1988; Fincham, Beach, & Nelson, 1987; Fincham & Jaspers, 1980; Harvey, Weber, & Orbuch, 1990; Hilton, 1990; McLaughlin, Cody, & French, 1990; Weber & Vangelisti, 1991; Weiner, Amirkhan, Folkes, & Verette, 1987) certainly supports the notion that people generate such alternatives to explain unexpected social circumstances, potentially negative behavior, or broken social contracts.

REFERENCES

Andrews, B. (1992). Attribution processes in victims of marital violence: Who do women blame and why? In J. H. Harvey, T. L. Orbuch, & A. L. Weber (Eds.), *Attributions, accounts, and close relationships* (pp. 176–193). New York: Springer-Verlag.

Austin, J. L. (1975). *How to do things with words* (2nd ed., J. O. Urmson & M. Sbisa, Eds.). Cambridge, MA: Harvard University Press.

Averill, J. R. (1980). A constructivist view of emotion. In R. Plutchik & K. Kellerman (Eds.), *Theories of emotion* (Vol. 1, pp. 305–339). New York: Academic Press.

Bowers, J. W., Metts, S. M., & Duncanson, W. T. (1985). Emotion and interpersonal communication. In M. L. Knapp & G. R. Miller (Eds.), *Handbook of interpersonal communication* (pp. 500–550). Beverly Hills, CA: Sage.

Bulmer, M. (1979). Concepts in the analysis of qualitative data. *Sociological Review, 27,* 651–677.

Cate, R. M., Henton, J. M., Koval, J., Christopher, F. S., & Lloyd, S. (1982). Premarital abuse: A social psychological perspective. *Journal of Family Issues, 3,* 79–90.

Cody, M. J., & McLaughlin, M. L. (1988). Accounts on trial: Oral arguments in traffic court. In C. Antake (Ed.), *Analyzing everyday explanation: A casebook of methods* (pp. 113–126). London: Sage.

de Rivera, J. (1977). *A structural theory of the emotions.* New York: International Universities Press.

de Rivera, J., & Grinkis, C. (1986). Emotions in social relationships. *Motivation and Emotion, 10,* 351–369.

Fincham, F. D., Beach, S., & Nelson, G. (1987). Attribution processes in distressed and nondistressed couples: III. Casual and responsibility attributions for spouse behavior. *Cognitive Therapy and Research, 11,* 77–86.

Fincham, F. D., & Jaspers, J. M. (1980). Attribution of responsibility: From man the scientist to man as lawyer. In L. Berkowitz (Ed.), *Advances in experimental social psychology* (Vol. 13, pp. 82–139). New York: Academic Press.

Harvery, J. H., Weber, A. L., & Orbuch, T. L. (1990). *Interpersonal accounts.* Oxford: Blackwell.

Henton, J. M., Cate, R. M., Koval, J., Lloyd, S., & Christopher, F. S. (1983). Romance and violence in dating relationships. *Journal of Family Issues, 4,* 467–482.

Herbert, T. B., Silver, R. C., & Ellard, J. H. (1991). Coping with an abusive relationship: I. How and why do women stay? *Journal of Marriage and the Family, 53,* 311–325.

Hilton, D. J. (1990). Conversational processes and causal explanation. *Psychological Bulletin, 107,* 65–81.

Holtzworth-Munroe, A. (1992). Attributions and martially violent men: The role of cognitions in marital violence. In J. H. Harvery, T. L. Orbuch, & A. L. Weber (Eds.), *Attributions, accounts, and close relationships* (pp. 165–175). New York: Springer-Verlag.

Infante, D. A., Riddle, B. L., Horvath, C. L., & Tumlin, S. A. (1992). Verbal aggressiveness: Messages and reasons. *Communication Quarterly, 40,* 116–126.

Knapp, M. L. (1984). *Interpersonal communication and human relationships.* Boston: Allyn & Bacon.

Knapp, M. L., Stafford, L., & Daly, J. A. (1986). Regrettable messages: Things people wish they hadn't said. *Journal of Communication, 36,* 40–58.

Leffler, A. (1988). *Verbal abuse and psychological unavailability scales and relationship to self-esteem.* Paper presented at the annual meeting of the American Psychological Association, Atlanta, GA.

Martin, M. M., & Horvath, C. L. (1992, November). *Messages that hurt: What people think and feel about verbally aggressive messages.* Paper presented at the annual meeting of the Speech Communication Association, Chicago, IL.

McLaughlin, M. L. (1984). *Conversation: How talk is organized.* Beverly Hills, CA: Sage.

McLaughlin, M. L., Cody, M. J., & French, K. (1990). Account-giving and the attribution of responsibility: Impressions of traffic offenders. In M. J. Cody & M. L. McLaughlin (Eds.), *The psychology of tactical communication* (pp. 244–267). Clevedon, England: Multilingual Maters.

Montgomery, B. M. (1988). Quality communication in personal relationships. In S. W. Duck (Ed.), *Handbook of personal relationships* (pp. 343–359). New York: Wiley.

Planalp, S., & Honeycutt, J. M. (1985). Events that increase uncertainty in personal relationships. *Human Communication Research, 11,* 593–604.

Schegloff, E. A., Jefferson, G., & Sacks, H. (1977). The preference for self-correction in the organization of repair in conversation. *Language, 53,* 361–382.

Shimanoff, S. B. (1985). Rules governing the verbal expression of emotion between married couples. *Western Journal of Speech Communication, 49,* 147–165.

Shimanoff, S. B. (1987). Types of emotional disclosures and request compliance between spouses. *Communication Monographs, 54,* 85–100.

Vangelisti, A. L. (1989, November). *Messages that hurt: Perceptions of and reactions to hurtful messages in relationships.* Paper presented at the meeting of the Speech Communication Association, San Francisco, CA.

Vissing, Y. M., Straus, M. A., Gelles, R. J., & Harrop, J. W. (1991). Verbal aggression by parents and psychosocial problems of children. *Child Abuse and Neglect, 15,* 223–238.

Weber, D. J., & Vangelisti, A. L. (1991). "Because I love you": The use of tactical attributions in conversation. *Human Communication Research, 17,* 606–624.

Weiner, B. (1986). *An attributional theory of motivation and emotion.* New York: Springer-Verlag.

Weiner, B., Amirkhan, J., Folkes, V. S., & Verette, J. A. (1987). An attributional analysis of excuse giving: Studies of a naïve theory of emotion. *Journal of Personality and Social Psychology, 52,* 316–324.

Weiner, B., Graham, S., & Chandler, C. C. (1982). Pity, anger, and guilt: An attributional analysis. *Personality and Social Psychology Bulletin, 8,* 225–232.

Yelsma, P. (1992, July). *Affective orientations associated with couples' verbal abusiveness.* Paper presented at the bi-annual meeting of the International Society for the Study of Personal Relationships, Orono, ME.

"*L*ead into Gold" is the title of this next reading. "Lead" is negativity in a relationship—whatever contaminates the communication. "Gold" is its opposite. Therapist John Welwood believes that lead can be turned into gold, that hurtful messages and events can be transformed into experiences that actually contribute to the richness of the relationship.

The first step is to avoid what Welwood calls "negative negativity," which is basically fear of negative thoughts or feelings or blame for bringing them up. As he puts it, "censuring our anger . . . is a further act of aggression. Denying our fear is a further expression of fear." The problem, as he sees it, is that humans inevitably experience negativity about the people close to them, and then we also often fear being judged harshly for these negative experiences. It's important to try to move beyond this stage.

A crucial step toward working this problem is to distinguish between what Welwood calls "discernment" and "condemnation." It's useful to develop the ability to discern whatever truth there might be in the negative criticism aimed at us without getting caught in the trap of condemning ourselves for our failings.

Another way to work the problem is with what might be called "emotional judo." Judo teachers train their pupils to exploit the energy of their opponent to increase their own strength. A version of this approach can work with negativity. The key is that, just as resisting negativity creates more of the same, acknowledging it diminishes its power. In other words, you can best deal with negativity by going through it rather than around it. First own and even honor the negativity and then it will be easier to cope with.

In a long-term relationship, negativity can get blown out of proportion by what Welwood calls the "relationship shadow." This is the baggage of dark thoughts, feelings, and comments that a couple or work group can drag around with itself. As the baggage accumulates, the people involved get increasingly afraid to discuss it for fear that the relationship will be swept away by its power. It works best to stay current so that the baggage doesn't accumulate. But if you're in a relationship with an already sizeable shadow, the only way to cope with it is to begin talking it through. Again, it can help to recognize what Welwood calls "the principle of coemergence," which means that all forms of negativity contain some intelligence. So each party can learn from the particles of truth, accuracy, and insight that are wedged into the corners of the negativity.

Perhaps the biggest challenge to a long-term relationship is the place where the partners' rough edges rub up against each other. This might mean that one person's habit of lying rubs up against the other person's judgmentalness, or that one person's rigidity rubs up against another's depression. Again, the partners do not have to focus exclusively on these negativities, but if they can acknowledge and discuss them, they can substantially increase their intimacy.

Finally, Welwood urges those in close relationships to be each other's teacher. Each can ask him- or herself, "Am I willing to receive help from my partner with this part of myself that I have a hard time with?" And when asked for help, each can treat the request as an opportunity, as Welwood puts it, "to relate to this part of them in a more conscious, empowered way, instead of just putting up with it."

LEAD INTO GOLD

John Welwood

Negativity clearly seen becomes intelligence.
—Chögyam Trungpa

As two people's love for each other penetrates their hardened defenses, it brings to light hidden negativities—raw edges in themselves and in their relationship that they would rather keep hidden away in the dark. When we live alone, we develop strategies for ignoring these raw edges. But when we live with someone we love, we can no longer hide from ourselves like this.

It is important to let these negativities come out into the open, where we can work with them in the light of awareness and compassion. Only then can they relax their anxious grip, yielding access to hidden resources they have been blocking. If we always try to avoid the darker aspects of ourselves, they remain underground, and never evolve in a more positive direction. Even worse, they start to fester and spread, eventually contaminating our whole relationship or our whole life, like poison seeping into groundwater. Learning to work directly with negativity is an essential step on the path of conscious relationship.

NEGATIVE NEGATIVITY

Often when our shadow side comes to light, we criticize ourselves or our partner for bringing out the worst in us. Yet blame is just another form of negativity, which only aggravates the situation.

Whenever we turn against something negative in ourselves or our partner, we are essentially contracting against a contraction, effectively tightening the knot rather than letting it unravel. In fact, our aversion to a negative feeling often contains, and thus intensifies, the very quality we are trying to push away. Censuring our anger, for instance, is a further act of aggression. Denying our fear is a further expression of fear. Blaming ourselves for being stingy is ungenerous and only makes us hold on more tightly. Like Brer Rabbit's attacks on the Tar-Baby in the Uncle Remus story, our aversive reactions to our dark side keep us stuck in the very tendencies that cause us the most pain. That is why Chö-gyam Trungpa once called this kind of reaction "negative negativity."

WORKING WITH NEGATIVITY

Often what keeps us from acknowledging our negative tendencies is a fear of being judged for them. Perhaps we imagine our partner will no longer respect us if we reveal our flaws or limitations. But this is usually a projection: We are seeing our own critic—the part of ourselves that condemns us for being human, all too human—in our partner's eyes. Before we can work creatively with negativity, we must first learn to neutralize the attacks of our inner critic.

As a step in this direction, it is important to make a crucial distinction—between *discernment* and *condemnation*. We need to be able to *discern* whatever truth there is in the critic's message—which may be trying to tell us where we are off the mark—while putting aside the tendency to *condemn* ourselves for our failings. This means learning to stand up to the critic's attack—firmly saying "no" to its censure—while at the same time recognizing what it is trying to bring to our attention: "Yes, it's true . . . I am often lost and out of touch . . . I try to use my partner to fill up my holes and shore up my ego . . . I have a hard time really listening . . . when I give, I am often looking for something in return . . ." When we can gently admit to ourselves where we are off track, we take away the critic's ammunition.

If contracting against negativity only creates more negativity, the opposite is also true—acknowledging it diminishes its power, revealing positive impulses concealed within it. For example, perhaps your relationship brings to light your tendency to be selfish. If you attack yourself for this, then it only goes underground, becoming more furtive and entrenched. What's needed instead is a deeper understanding of the selfishness—what it consists of and where it comes from. In truth, you probably don't know why you are selfish, or even what this "selfishness" really is. You may have theories about it, but you have probably never looked into it that deeply. And it will never really change or evolve until you do.

The key, once again, lies in allowing and inquiry. Allowing does not mean acting out impulses. Instead, it means letting your experience be there, just as it is, and touching it directly. Both the allowing and the touch should be gentle. This takes practice, steadfastness, and courage.

When you let yourself experience the selfish impulse as it arises—noticing how it feels in your body—you may find a certain sensation connected with it, perhaps a tightness in the belly or chest. Looking further, you see that this contraction indicates something inside you desperately trying to hold on; and that underneath this grasping there is a tremendous hunger. In acknowledging this, you may find the tightness starting to ease. Then if you explore the underlying sense of hunger, to see where it's coming from, you may realize that you are not very generous with yourself—which creates an inner sense of poverty. As a result, you always try to "get what's coming to you."

In recognizing your grasping as an attempt to remedy a sense of poverty, you start to bring compassionate understanding to what is going on inside you, instead of simply condemning it and remaining divided against yourself. Then you can also address the real issue—the need to be more generous with yourself—instead of unconsciously acting it out through selfish behavior.

Even though negative tendencies do not always open up like this right away, they eventually will if we keep inquiring into them, without blame. All negativity is the result of some loss of being. When we discover how we are disconnected from ourselves, we see our negativity for what it really is—a cry for attention from some part of us we've forgotten, which we can only recover once we recognize it's been lost.

BRINGING THE RELATIONSHIP
SHADOW OUT INTO THE OPEN

. . . Every couple develops a relationship shadow. Robert Bly once likened the shadow to a long bag, stuffed with unwanted experiences, that weighs us down as we drag it around with us. Relationships also become weighed down by their shadow—all the denials, evasions, resentments, and grievances that a couple have stuffed away over many months or years.

As two partners' grievances accumulate, they become increasingly afraid to open up the bag, for fear that their relationship will be swept away in a torrent of negativity. As a result, the bag grows heavier and the distance between them increases, while symptoms of their accumulated bad feelings—distrust and resentment, withdrawal and distancing, loss of sexual interest, excessive harshness and lack of forgiveness—start poisoning the atmosphere.

Couples can never entirely avoid accumulating this kind of shadow. Even in the most conscious of relationships, tensions and frictions are bound to build up. Often the more loving two people feel, the less inclined they are to focus on areas of conflict. Therefore couples need to practice consciously emptying the bag on occasion, by setting aside special times to explore grievances and resentments that have been building under the surface.

According to the principle of coemergence . . . all forms of negativity contain a certain intelligence. So if two people can talk over their negative feelings in a spirit of openness and caring, they will also uncover important messages that need to be communicated, for their own well-being and for the good of their relationship. And when they realize that it is possible to reveal what they thought they had to hide, this builds trust and strengthens the relationship as a container or "holding environment" where all the different parts of themselves can be included.

This kind of airing, which seems so threatening at first, revives the spark that was dampened by denial and evasion, freeing up a flow of positive energy between them. And as their love comes back, it feels especially sweet, like fresh air after a storm.

TURNING A WEAK LINK INTO A STRONG LINK

In addition to working with negativity in ourselves and our relationships, we need to learn how to relate to the less evolved parts of our partner as well. How do we deal with what we most dislike in those we love—their fear, their rigidities, their low self-esteem, their depression, their anger, their blind spots? Often we try to wage a crusade against these negative elements. Or we ignore them and hope for the best. Or else we resign ourselves, suffer in silence, and think about leaving.

The place where lovers rub up against each other's rough edges is usually the weak link in their relationship. Here is where their bond most easily starts to fray and unravel. Yet this is also where their love is really put to the test. If they can learn to relate more consciously to each other's negative tendencies, they may find themselves reaping unexpected benefits.

For one person, this might involve standing up and saying no to a judgmental tendency in her partner—which may help her find hidden strength in herself. This leads to greater self-respect, which may in turn help her partner respect her more as well. For another person, it may be important to learn to treat her partner's inner conflicts with loving kindness—which expands her own capacity for love, while also developing a deeper level of trust and friendship between them. And for another, relating to what troubles him in his partner may force him to come to terms with parts of himself he has never acknowledged before. For instance, if his partner has a tendency to feel sad or depressed, this may threaten him because he has always run away from his own weightier feelings. Learning to relate to this side of his partner helps him connect with his own darker, deeper soul qualities, bringing him down to earth from his boyish illusions of life as an eternal, Icarus-like ascent.

BEING EACH OTHER'S TEACHER

No friend, therapist, or spiritual teacher could ever feel the impact of my negative tendencies as vividly as my partner does. And no one else could ever have as much interest in seeing her open or expand in places where she is contracted as I do. So if we both want to grow in these areas, it would be wise to enlist each other's aid. Having a soul connection means that each can ask the other for support or guidance in areas where the other is stronger or more evolved.

A couple wanting to explore this might start by asking themselves, "Am I willing to receive help from my partner with this part of myself that I have a hard time with? And am I willing to extend the same kind of help to her (him)?" If they have this willingness, they could then formally ask each other for support or guidance in an area of difficulty, and let each other know what would be most helpful.

For example, a man who has difficulty residing in his heart or revealing his feelings might ask his partner for help with this, if this is one of her strengths.

He might also let her know what would help him most; for instance: "It's not helpful if you lecture me or become disapproving when my heart is closed. It would help me most if you could hear my struggle with this, share your knowledge or understanding in this area, and provide encouragement."

Conversely, when those we love ask for our help with one of their weak points, this provides an opportunity to relate to this part of them in a more conscious, empowered way, instead of just putting up with it. Here we will find that our work on learning to be present with our own raw edges is the best practice we could have for helping those we love. What will help them most is no different from what we ourselves need when we feel stuck: Instead of trying to fix them, we can give them space, let them have their experience, and be there for them, maintaining presence and friendly contact.

As two partners learn to be there for each other in this way, their soul connection deepens, and their areas of weakness become a source of unexpected strength.

REVIEW QUESTIONS

1. What's "negative negativity"?
2. Explain the point of Welwood's distinction between discernment and condemnation.
3. What does Welwood mean by "allowing and inquiry"?
4. What is a relationship shadow?
5. What are the main challenges for a couple in each being the other's teacher, in the sense that Welwood urges?

PROBES

1. Recall a time when you felt something strongly negative in a relationship and forced yourself not to talk about it. This is an example of what Welwood calls "negative negativity." What negative evaluations kept you from discussing your feelings?
2. One idea behind a lot of what Welwood writes is that negativity is inevitable. Every long-term relationship, whether at work, among family members, or elsewhere naturally includes some dark-side elements. How do you respond to this claim? Do you agree or disagree? Do you accept Welwood's corollary conclusion that these negative elements need somehow to be surfaced and discussed in order for the relationship to thrive? Explain.
3. Think about one close relationship you're in. What are the main weak links or less evolved parts of your partner in this relationship? What are the corresponding less evolved parts you bring to the relationship?

*T*his next reading is a discussion of three more of what some authors call the "dark" elements of interpersonal communicating: lying, betrayal, and aggression. This reading combines insights from recent research into these phenomena with some practical suggestions about how to cope with them.

Carole and I begin by arguing that, like all communicating, these elements are collaboratively constructed. This is an especially difficult point to make about deception. If there is any kind of communication that seems to be one person's fault, it has to be lying. But we believe that if you look closely at deception as it actually occurs between people, you'll find collaboration. Not only do both gullible and overly demanding people tend to "pull" deception from others, but people who are doing their best to resist being lied to are often unwittingly contributing to the problem. As we emphasize, this does not mean that we're blaming the victim of deception. In fact, we want to move beyond blaming of any kind to recognize how the problem is co-constructed.

We also review some of the research that identifies reasons people give for lying and some of the consequences of deception. We note that there is a "truth bias" in most relationships that quickly changes to a "lie bias" once deception is revealed. It appears unfortunately to be true that "trust is a precious commodity that, once lost, is very difficult to regain."

All deception researchers agree that there is lying of some kind in *every* relationship. They disagree about whether it can ever be positive. Some believe that lies to protect the other person can be beneficial, and some believe that even the most well-meaning lies damage the relationship.

It is not possible, we believe, to be completely truthful all the time, and we do not urge you to be brutally honest with those around you. But it is important to be aware of patterns of deception in your relationships and to work to eliminate them.

Betrayal is closely related to deception, partly because it is similarly widespread. In one study, over 90 percent of the participants were able to discuss examples of both being the betrayer and being the one betrayed. Examples range from the quite common occurrence of sexual activity inconsistent with the definition of a relationship, through lack of support from a partner, criticism, and gossip, to being abandoned by a parent.

Some research indicates that there are gender differences in betrayal. For example, women are more likely to betray and to be betrayed by other women, whereas men report betraying their wives or dating partners most. Betrayal is also part of the cycle that often characterizes life in a family with a member addicted to alcohol or drugs. As we note, it can help to become aware of the frequency and shape of betrayal, and it is often a stubborn and serious enough problem to warrant help from a third party—a therapist or counselor.

Part of our discussion of aggression reviews the treatment of hurt-ful messages reprinted earlier in this chapter. But we also discuss ver-bal aggressiveness and sexual harassment in this section. We want to alert you to the patterned nature of verbal aggressiveness so that, if you experience it, you can examine what you might be contributing to its oc-currence (again, *without* falling into blaming the victim). Verbal aggres-sion is especially important to identify and change because it is often followed by physical violence.

Our brief discussion of sexual harassment emphasizes, once again, how widespread it is. Estimates vary, but it appears that more than two-thirds of the women involved in various studies have experienced some harassment. After discussing some examples, we try to clarify the different fears that tend to promote this kind of communicating. It would help for men to understand the fear of violence that many women experience, and the tendency among many women not to want to offend by calling attention to something that makes them uncom-fortable. It would also help for women to understand many men's fears of being falsely accused and of having a woman they believe they are complimenting or protecting turn on them and destroy them. Each gender should move beyond the easy dodge that the other's fears are unwarranted.

The two final sections of this reading briefly discuss psychological abuse and physical violence. The target of psychological abuse is usu-ally the other person's identity—the sense of who she or he is as a per-son. This is what can make it so devastating. The only way we know to counter this phenomenon is with the help of a trained outsider. Physi-cal violence is also more widespread than one might want to believe, since it probably occurs in something like one-third of the couples in the United States. As with these other phenomena, it can help to view vio-lence as a pattern that often begins relatively weakly and grows into a serious problem. Communication training can sometimes help rela-tional partners cope with physical violence, but, again, outside help is often very useful.

This discussion is certainly not designed to solve or even to fully an-alyze these very important and very damaging patterns of interper-sonal communicating. But we hope that these paragraphs might sensi-tize you to the pervasiveness of these problems and the extent to which they are collaboratively constructed.

DECEPTION, BETRAYAL, AND AGGRESSION

John Stewart and Carole Logan

DECEPTION

> He told me he was all through with his old girlfriend. We started sleeping to-
> gether, spending three or four nights a week at each other's place. I have a
> friend in one of my classes that's in the same sorority as his ex-girlfriend. A cou-
> ple of days ago, my friend told me she saw them together, and that it didn't look
> to my friend like she was an "ex." She said that they seemed pretty intensely in-
> volved with each other. I saw my boyfriend last night, and he didn't act differ-
> ent in any way then he normally does. I don't believe anything he tells me now.[1]

We probably all have heard stories like the one this student tells about her
boyfriend. . . . In the next several paragraphs, we explore the motives or reasons
for deception in interpersonal communication and identify potential consequences for the relationship.

Motives for Deception

Deception can range . . . from very direct lies to "softer," more indirect actions,
such as exaggerations and false implications.[2] Deception can also be unintentional, as when someone mis-remembers or mistakenly forgets or omits information. Like all other communication phenomena, deception is a joint action,
the outcome of a collaboration between or among communicators. For example,
some people make it relatively easy for others to lie to them. Both gullible and
overly demanding people are often targets for deception. You could say that
naivete and authoritarianism both help "pull" lying from others. Similarly, people considering whether to tell lies can be either encouraged or discouraged by
the danger of getting caught. Occasionally, couples even collaborate on lies, and
this is called collusion.[3] One partner may routinely deceive the other about infidelities, for example, and although the other suspects the truth, he or she
agrees to look the other way. In short, like all other kinds of communication, deception is strongly affected by its context.

Communication researchers Dan O'Hair and Michael Cody identify six motives or reasons people give for lying to their relational partners. Three of the
motives—**egoism, benevolence,** and **utility**—are labeled positive because they
generally have positive consequences for at least one individual and appear
to O'Hair and Cody to do no harm to the relationship. The other three—
exploitation, malevolence, and **regress**—are labeled negative because their
consequences include harm to at least one person in the relationship. Egoism
and exploitation are the positive and negative *self*-related motives, benevolence

Excerpt from *Together: Communicating Interpersonally,* 5th ed. by John Stewart and Carole Logan,
1997. Reprinted by permission of The McGraw-Hill Companies.

and malevolence are related to the *other* person, and utility and regress have to do with the *relationship*.[4]

When egoism is the motive, deception works as a way of protecting or promoting the deceiver's positive self-concept. A person might respond to a question with a half-truth, for example, in order to avoid embarrassment. Exploitation is an entirely selfish motive. For instance, if one person pretends to be interested in another solely for the purpose of gaining some useful information, the deceiver has exploited the deceived. Benevolence as a deception motive is an attempt of the deceiver to protect the self-esteem, safety, and general well-being of the other person(s). For example, when neighbors who hid Jews from the Nazis lied to army officers, their lies were motivated by benevolence. Malevolence, which means intentionally trying to hurt others, is cited in at least one study as a more frequent motive for deception.[5] O'Hair and Cody list revenge, vindictiveness, retaliation, sadism, sabotage, and hatefulness as examples of malevolent lies.[6]

The last two motives focus on outcomes for the relationship. A utility motive for deception means that the deceiver wants to improve, enhance, escalate, or repair the relationship with the other person. For example, one person could pretend to a relational partner not to know how an important friend voted on an issue if that information was likely to lead to a conflict. This would be an example of using a lie to help keep the peace. Regress means using deception as a means to stymie, damage, or terminate the relationship. For instance, one person might tell the other that they should go back to being "just friends" after becoming romantically intimate, knowing that this option would be unacceptable to the other person. In this case, the deceiver has manipulated the relational partner to end the relationship.[7]

Consequences of Deception

Most acts of deception have consequences that people don't fully consider when justifying their reasons for lying. For one thing, when deception is undetected, its burden often stays with the deceiver. In some cases, a deceiver experiences a greater sense of autonomy, privacy, or control, but such emotions are often compromised by feelings of shame or guilt for deceiving the other, and perhaps even anger at or contempt for the deceived person. Frequently, one lie requires many subsequent supporting lies. If, for instance, a person decides to have an extramarital affair and to lie about it, it will also be necessary to lie about times, dates, locations, the basis on which one knows the other person, and so forth. Any deception requires that the deceiver pay greater attention to verbal and nonverbal cues, and this increased attention usually generates stress. Once the deception is detected by a relational partner, the consequences expand accordingly and are largely negative. Until people discover that someone has lied to them, they generally operate from a "truth bias," that is, a basic belief that the other communicator is telling the truth. This state quickly changes to a " lie bias" once deception is revealed.[8] At this point, the deceived person is likely to assume that the communicator is always lying. This change in a relationship is one way in which many people discover that trust is a precious commodity that, once lost, is very difficult to regain.

The deceived person must also decide whether to expose the lie or suppress it. Suppression may require increasingly monumental efforts at denial over time ("She/he couldn't possibly be lying to me!"), while exposure means admitting to the deceiver one's hurt, loss of esteem, anger, and increased uncertainty about the relationship. The deceiver who is caught and confronted by the deceived partner frequently also suffers embarrassment, increased guilt, and loss of credibility. Usually, deception increases tension, conflict, and even aggression in a relationship.

These are many of the reasons why communication researcher and teacher Bill Wilmot argues that deception is always damaging to the other person and to the relationship. Wilmot contends that deception is by its very nature a self-centered act. Unlike O'Hair and Cody, Wilmot does not believe that any motives for deception are positive. Relational partners might justify a deceptive act on the grounds that it will help the other person or the relationship, but, Wilmot maintains, "the recipient of deception has no hand in deciding if it is 'good' for the relationship or not—he or she is out of the loop. . . . Deception, even in its most benign forms, is a form of information control that one exercises; you want to be the one determining the course of the relationship, so you withhold information from the partner."[9] This is what makes even so-called benevolent lies damaging.

Wilmot also points out how easily relationship partners can get into a spiral of truth telling or deception. As we mentioned previously, one deceptive act has a way of snowballing into a number of deceptive acts. Then, the more lies that are told, the greater is the need for more deception. In general, we agree with Wilmot that it is not a good idea to get into the habit of lying in one's intimate relationships. In these cases, deception is almost always toxic.

If you discover a pattern of deception in an intimate relationship, then we think it is useful to consider the motives for the deception and the consequences for yourself, your partner, and the relationship. It may be that the deception is a way of establishing more personal privacy in order to balance the intrusiveness that is being experienced by one or both partners. Or perhaps deception points toward areas of the relationship where the deceiver feels the need to establish greater control over the other person and the relationship. Whether you are the deceiver or the person being lied to, you can start to reverse the pattern by interjecting more honesty whenever possible. Sometimes detecting a lie and working through its aftermath can also lead to relationship development and growth.

We hope it is obvious that we are not advising you to be brutally honest in all your relationships, whether or not others will be hurt. Telling your boss that you think she has a big nose, for example, is irrelevant and unnecessarily hurtful, to say nothing of being foolish if you want to keep your job. But when a pattern of deception has developed between you and the people closest to you, it's important to identify what's going on and to restore as much of the truth bias as possible in the relationship.

"But . . . ," a student responds. . . .

I have a hard time agreeing that betrayal, aggression, and deception are a result of collaboration. That is like shifting the fault and blame away from the betrayer, the aggressor, and the liar, and saying, "Well, it was the victim's fault also." How can one blame a person who is very trusting of their partner for believing lies told to them? Just because they trusted what was told them doesn't mean they're 'gullible' or that they collaborated in making the lie.

This is an important issue, one that we discussed a great deal while writing this chapter. Notice first how the concepts of fault and blame don't work well here. When someone lies by exaggerating and I don't question them, is the lie their fault because they exaggerated, my fault because I learned in my family of origin not to confront others, my parents' fault because they taught me to be nonconfrontational, my grandparents' fault because they taught my mom and dad nonassertiveness, or what? Or is it most accurate to blame the parents of the exaggerator because they contributed to the low self-esteem that may have led him or her to lie? Which generation should take the blame? Which culture? Is it always completely the liar's fault, because, even if their choice was affected by culture and socialization, it *shouldn't* have been? How much of a lie can be blamed directly on the liar, and how much is due to external forces he or she might not even be aware of? These questions don't have any clear answers, which is one reason why we suggest giving up fault and blame when talking about human problems.

But this does *not* mean that we are "blaming the victim." From our perspective, the victim is no more to be blamed than is the liar, or, as we discuss later in this chapter, the betrayer or aggressor. We are working to understand these problems for the collaborative patterns they are, mainly so we can help do something effective to change them. Blaming almost never promotes meaningful *change*.

On the one hand, every time a person communicates, he or she becomes at least minimally vulnerable to deception, betrayal, or aggression, but this doesn't mean you're asking to be lied to or attacked. On the other hand, when someone consciously and reflectively lies to, betrays, or attacks another, these actions are a *response* to the context, and they are also an important part of what will be responded to next. It is completely legitimate to expect the person tempted to lie or attack to be *response-able:* to respond thoughtfully to the temptation, and to respond humanely to the results. People who yield to these temptations make choices that they are accountable for. The liar or aggressor should not be excused from the outcomes of his or her choices any more than the victim should be blamed.

Lying sometimes works so well that the person lied to doesn't even know it's happened. But he or she can still respond rather than react to whatever happens next, including effects of the lies. One response can be to radically change his or her relationship with the liar. Another can be to understand more about why the lying happened. Persons who lie should also notice the outcomes of their responses and reflect about their response-ability.

But our main point is that things are not as simple as fault-and-blame analysis tries to make them. With respect to lying, the research—and your own experience—demonstrate that no relationship is completely free of deception. Every day people exaggerate or minimize, try to spare another's feelings, or strategically leave out part of the story, and some of the time the relationship is undamaged, or even helped. Still, we agree with Wilmot that a pattern of deception is just about always toxic. Humans never achieve perfect anything, including perfect honesty. But if you want to make changes to improve a pattern of deception, we believe it's important to begin by recognizing the degree to which lying is collaborative. The following sections of this [reading] show how betrayal, aggression, and harassment are also collaborative.

BETRAYAL

> I thought I had a really good friend at work. I told her a secret. Even though I was embarrassed while I was telling her, I let her know I had lost my virginity the night before. I had to tell somebody. I thought she would be a good person to tell because she was like a sister to me. I made her promise not to tell anyone! This is a secret I wasn't even going to tell my best friend. Three days later, my other coworkers came up to me and asked me how my "first night" was. I was livid.[10]

Deception and betrayal are closely related; in fact, some researchers see them as almost synonymous.[11] The difference is that betrayal violates the betrayed person's expectations, and may even do so by being the truth. Several studies indicate that the term "betrayal" labels some experiences that most people have had in at least one of their interpersonal relationships. For example, when Warren Jones and Marsha Parsons Burdette asked their research participants to write narrative accounts of betrayal episodes, over 90 percent were able to discuss examples both of being the betrayer and of being the betrayed.[12] Based on their findings, Jones and Burdette define betrayals as "violations of trust or expectations on which the relationship is based."[13] As people become more intimate, they tend to develop a sense of trust and commitment that grows out of consistently meeting mutual expectations. Thus, it's very possible that any violation of expectations can be viewed as a betrayal by at least one of the people involved.

The types of betrayal people have described include extramarital affairs or affairs outside of a sexually exclusive relationship, lies, betrayed confidences, jilting a romantic partner, lack of support from a partner, ignoring or avoiding a partner or friend, criticism, and gossip. There are also the infrequent but most severe forms of betrayal, such as being abused or abandoned by a parent.[14] Unfortunately, the most hurtful kinds of betrayal happen in the most important relationships. One of Carole's students said he wondered how his father could have betrayed him by cutting ties to him after his parents' divorce. People relate stories about betrayal by spouses, romantic partners, friends, coworkers, mothers, fathers, daughters, bosses, sisters, brothers, and sons, among others.

Jones and Burdette draw five conclusions from their studies of betrayal. First, as we have indicated, events defined as betrayals appear to be a common occurrence in interpersonal relationships. A second finding is that the consequences of the betrayal incident depend on whether one is the betrayer or the betrayed. In one study, most betrayers reported that the relationship had improved, or at least had stayed the same since the event, whereas nearly all of those who had been betrayed said they felt that the relationship had worsened. In fact, a third discovery of these studies was that many friendships and romantic relationships were terminated by the victims of the betrayal. Even involuntary relationships (family of origin and coworkers) suffered serious decline following incidents of betrayal. This relational outcome may be attributable to the disconfirming effects of any betrayal. As Jones and Burdette explain, "The treachery is not just in the actual harm done to another, but also in the fact that betrayals threaten a major source of one's feelings of identity and well-being."[15] The effects can be so devastating that they persist for a long time, and outside help from a counselor, religious advisor, or a trusted friend may be required.

A fourth finding of betrayal studies is that there is a gender difference. Women are more likely to betray and to be betrayed by other women. The type of betrayal described most frequently in this regard is revealing a confidence or telling a secret. Men report betraying their wives or girlfriends more than a partner in any other type of relationship, and the betrayal most often is sexual. However, men describe themselves as being betrayed most frequently by coworkers for some competitive reason. Women and men also see different incidents as betrayals. Women are more likely to describe a general lack of emotional support as a betrayal of the relationship, whereas men are more likely to see only overt events or acts as betrayals.

Jones and Burdette's fifth conclusion is that some studies identify personality correlates of betrayal behavior. People who are likely to betray others also appear to be more jealous, suspicious, envious, and resentful of others generally, and seem to have more personal problems, such as alcoholism or other addictions, depression, or a self-reported inability to sustain intimate relationships. These characteristics are also likely to be true of victims of betrayal, but they do not distinguish females from males.

No one has determined a set of reasons why people betray those who are closest to them. One story that was told to Carole revealed an interesting pattern, however. A married man had been accused of repeated infidelities. His wife was very jealous and constantly suspected him of having affairs behind her back. He became angrier and angrier as time went on. He decided finally to have an affair to spite his wife. In this particular case, the pattern was clearly a degenerative spiral. The wife expected him to be unfaithful and looked for clues that he was. He eventually betrayed her, partly in compliance with her expectations.

Another type of pattern that involves betrayal often is seen in the family of an addict. . . . Briefly, the cycle of addiction often includes the following stages. The family of the addict sees that the addict is not taking drugs, drinking, or engaging in other addictive behaviors. This reminds the family of what things were like before the person became addicted. The family wants and expects this behavior, and feels betrayed when, after a short period of abstinence, the addict again uses drugs or drinks. After the addictive behavior, the addict usually expresses remorse and resolves "never to do it again." In the period of sobriety, the tension builds, the addict slips, and the family feels betrayed once again.[16] We explore a similar kind of cycle in the next section on aggression and physical violence.

Whether having an affair, succumbing to an addiction, or divulging a secret for "someone's own good," the betrayer is overemphasizing independent and controlling actions. Just as we described regarding deception, when one person in the relationship acts in a way that damages the relationship, the one who is hurt has a difficult time trusting again. The betrayer is acting in a way that disconfirms the partner, because he or she did not include the partner in the decision that led to the betrayal. This makes the decision independently the betrayer's, and this disconfirming independence has consequences for both people. The betrayer tries to control the situation by deciding to act without consulting the partner, knowing that the behavior will violate some relational expectation.

Because victims of betrayal rarely report any gain from the act, and often the betrayal itself can help end the relationship, betrayal of any kind is a difficult problem to surmount in any relationship. If you notice that you or members of your family are experiencing repeated feelings of betrayal, then it is time to consider what kinds of communication patterns continue to allow it to occur. In order to break such complex family patterns, it may be necessary to seek outside intervention. It may also help to remember that if you think you might need third-party support, researchers have found betrayals of all types to be common events in interpersonal relationships. As we mentioned earlier, you are not alone!

AGGRESSION

We were in the process of a divorce. It was hard because we were really angry and our two-year-old son got caught in the middle of our fights sometimes. One of the last things she said to me was that she figured if she left now, my son would have a better chance of learning not to be like me. This was like a dagger in my heart.[17]

There is a lot of ideological pressure to stay in the marriage; you have to stay married. My parents applied it, and my husband said, "You can't break your covenant." The argument is, of course, fallacious. By hitting me, I could argue that he broke his covenants, but there was all that pressure and just people wanting us to stay married. They didn't want to see another relationship crumble, but I realize there was nothing real, there was no material support for doing that. There hasn't been any material support since I've been single and raising the five kids by myself. There is no material help. . . . No one really helps out. They just don't want you to upset the apples. I think I felt that as a real heavy burden, that I needed not to blow my marriage. I had to keep up the picture even though mine was in pieces.[18]

When communication exhibits imbalances in power and a concern for self at the expense of another, the patterns sometimes include aggression, or even physical violence. These two narratives show a range of aggression, extending from hurtful messages to physical violence. Hurtful messages are the more frequent and milder form of aggression, but they can escalate through sexual harassment and psychological abuse to physical violence at the more extreme end of the scale.

Hurtful Messages

[As the first reading in this chapter explains,] communication teacher and researcher Anita Vangelisti identified 10 types of hurtful messages that people experience in their relationships with partners, friends, or family members. These included **accusations** about the other's negative behavior ("You are a liar"), **evaluations** of the other's value ("Going out with you was the biggest mistake of my life."), **directives** or commands ("Just get off my back"), **advice** ("I think we should start seeing other people"), **expression of desire** ("I don't ever want to have anything to do with you"), **information disclosure** ("Well, I'm really attracted to Julie"), **questions** used like interrogation ("Why aren't you over this [family death] yet?"), **threats** ("If I find out you slept with that person, never come home again"), **jokes** ("You are such a dumb blond—it's a good thing I'm around"), and **lies** ("No, really, I am not seeing him anymore [when the opposite is true]").[19] Vangelisti found that people usually reported information disclosures as more hurtful than accusations, and some topics, such as personality traits and romantic relationships, arose more often than others (e.g., ethnicity and religion). As you can easily see, there are many ways in which people can wound each other , and the extent of the hurt depends to a considerable degree on the relationship.

In fact, since the experience of hurt is a relational phenomenon, messages experienced as hurtful in one relationship might be ignored or discounted in another. Three factors seem to affect how hurtful the messages that Vangelisti studied were: (1) the intent of the person communicating the hurtful message, (2) whether the parties shared a family or a nonfamily relationship, and (3) the level of intimacy in the relationship.[20] Hurtful messages are found most frequently in families, partly because it can be difficult to escape them and almost impossible to terminate the relationship. People in family relationships, however, are also more likely to soften or excuse a hurtful message. Sometimes, the more intimate two people are, the easier it is for one to justify the other's action ("He wasn't trying to hurt me; he was just trying to get me to pay attention"). But if the relationship is not very satisfying, people are more likely to perceive hurt because they come to expect it. These messages add to increasing levels of dissatisfaction, and this experience can begin another kind of degenerative spiral.

Many hurtful messages are also difficult to repair. Although those in intimate or family relationships may be more forgiving, Vangelisti's study participants reported that they had real difficulties forgetting the hurtful events. Often they remembered the specific hurtful words, even if they had been said years earlier. Sometimes, several hurtful statements were reported to be the culminating actions that helped a person decide to terminate a relationship. Almost never did intentionally hurtful messages actually help a relationship to develop.

Verbal Aggressiveness and Sexual Harassment

When hurtful messages are evident in most of the conflicts or arguments in a relationship, they usually signal the presence of a communication pattern called verbal aggressiveness.[21] Communication that is verbally aggressive attacks the personality or character of the other person. In other words, it focuses negatively on identity rather than on content. In a recent study, Teresa Sabourin found that verbally aggressive partners would attack each other in escalating verbal exchanges by using one-up moves to gain control over the other person.[22] This escalation was part of a domineering pattern in which both partners make accusations and assertions, but neither accepts the other's attempt at control. As Sabourin describes it, this kind of power struggle can create a pattern that traps both people involved in it. She writes, "The boundaries between individuals and the potential for empathy are lost. The partner is no longer experienced as a distinct individual deserving of respect but instead, as an extension of [the aggressive person]. In the process of escalating aggression, paradoxically, the power of both partners is lost to the pattern between them."[23]

Sabourin also found that couples who were verbally aggressive in this kind of power struggle were also likely to become physically violent. Often a major part of the problem is that those trapped in this pattern lack the specific communication skills necessary effectively to avoid violence. Intervention from an outside party, such as a teacher or counselor, she suggested, could focus on "changing communication patterns between relational partners rather than on changing individual partners."[24]

One of the more common and damaging forms of verbal aggressiveness is sexual harassment. It is also one of the most difficult communication phenomena to deal with, partly because it is such a clear example of collaborative meaning-making. As Deborah Tannen notes, everything we say is, in the words of Spanish philosopher Ortega y Gasset, "exuberant and deficient." Speech is exuberant because people can take away more than we mean, and it is deficient because others necessarily miss some of the associations and connotations that are, for us, part of our talk. "Nowhere are these ambiguities as palpable," Tannen writes, "as in matters of sex, including what has come to be called sexual harassment."[25] Sexual harassment is difficult to define, prevent, and cope with, partly because one person's friendly gesture or expression of support can be experienced by another as an unwanted sexual advance.

However, the clearest conclusion that has emerged from the study of sexual harassment since the Anita Hill–Clarence Thomas hearings[26] is that it is undeniably widespread, especially, although not exclusively, with women as the target. Some men do report instances of this behavior, but very high percentages of women say that they have been sexually harassed in schools or at the workplace, even when they fill such socially powerful roles as those of physicians and legislators. A 1993 study, for example, found that 73 percent of female medical residents said that they had been sexually harassed, primarily by male physicians, and congresswomen Marjorie Margolies-Mezvinsky and Karen Shepherd described several experiences of inappropriate sexually oriented communication, including one that took place during a meeting held for beginning national legislators by the Motion Picture Association of America.[27]

There are significant gender differences in the ways sexually oriented talk and behavior are interpreted. In most cases, women primarily fear being verbally or physically assaulted by a man who is bigger and stronger than they are, and whose social and physical power they cannot easily escape. Often men, on the other hand, fear the loss of control that comes from a strong attraction to an alluring woman who can be impervious to losing her control as a result of sexual attraction. So although both genders fear the power that is connected with sexual talk and behavior, their fears are often very different. Many women fear violence, and many men fear manipulation and ridicule.

The most common kind of sexual harassment is the sexually oriented verbal or nonverbal message that is just ambiguous enough that it could be taken as a compliment. For example, as one woman reported:

> Most women recognize the experience of having a man's eyes continually drift to her chest. Although it might be a sign of interest, admiration, or invitation, most women take it as a fleeting but irritating reminder, "You're a woman, and I'm thinking about your sex rather than your brains, your authority, the words you are saying to me."[28]

A male manager's frequent comments about his female subordinate's attractive appearance also fall into this category, as do such patterns as telling obscene jokes and leaving pornographic magazines lying around. Both the popular media and research reports are also filled with explicit, and even violent, instances of harassment, such as ex-U.S. Senator Packwood's tongue-thrusting kisses of unsuspecting female visitors and some executives' patterns of hiring and firing subordinates because of their willingness or unwillingness to join in sexual talk and behaviors.

Sexual harassment could be reduced if more men and women clearly recognized how differently the genders often interpret verbal and nonverbal cues. . . . It would help for men to remember how many positions of social power are still filled mainly by males, and to try to understand women's abiding fear of male violence and the tendency among women not to want to offend by calling attention to something that makes them uncomfortable. Women can help by trying to understand men's fears of being falsely accused and of having a woman they believe they are complimenting or protecting turn on them and destroy them.[29] When both genders better understand the ways in which their counterparts often interpret cues, it can be easier to accept the idea that sexual harassment is defined by the person experiencing it, not by the one who believes that he or she is "just joking around."

There are also ways in which the person being harassed can defend against it. Because of the inherent ambiguity of this kind of communication, it is important for the person being victimized to be explicit and clear about his or her interpretation of what's happening: "I find that kind of talk offensive," or "You are touching me inappropriately and I want you to stop it now." It's also important to be clear about what will happen if the behavior doesn't stop. Federal legislation makes sexual harassment illegal in virtually all organizations, and those being harassed should be encouraged to take full advantage of the reporting systems and grievance processes available to them. If you've been criticized or warned about communication behavior that others may find inappropriate, it's also important to take these reminders seriously. Often sexual harassers mistakenly believe their behavior is "not that offensive" or that accusations are "blown all out of proportion." They need to remember that meaning-making is a *joint* process and that they are response-able for cues that others interpret as harassing. . . .

Psychological Abuse

Like harassment, forms of psychological abuse can be difficult to identify and define. Types of abuse include "the creation of fear, isolation, economic abuse, monopolization, degradation, rigid sex-role expectations, withdrawal, contingent expressions of love, and psychological destabilization which occurs when men's behavior challenges women's perceptions of reality."[30] These events are widespread enough to lead at least one researcher to conclude that some psychological abuse occurs in all close relationships.[31]

In many cases, psychological abuse, like physical violence, is a way of expressing dominance and control. As its label indicates, the impact of psychological abuse comes from its effects on identity; in fact, a psychological abuser can be defined as someone who effectively undermines a partner's sense of self.[32] In other words, this kind of abuse is defined by the fact that it challenges a person's personal or social competence. The abuse can be overt and dominating, or it can undermine a relational partner's self-concept in subtle and covert ways. Overt abuse often follows the failure of more covert attempts to influence. That is, it's usually associated with a pattern of communicating that develops over time. In order to intervene successfully in a relationship characterized by psychological abuse, a person needs to be trained to help communicators learn to influence their relational partners in ways that do not undermine the partner's self-concept or self-esteem through psychological abuse, and that do not resort to physical violence.[33]

Physical Violence

You might wonder why anyone would stay in a relationship that is physically violent. Part of the answer is that, like abuse, violence is part of a pattern that develops over time, sometimes without the participants' fully realizing what's happening. Recent studies indicate that relationships can become violent during the courtship period and that established patterns of interacting can form before the couple marries. Relational violence includes "the use or threat of physical force or restraint carried out with the intent of causing pain or injury to another" and can consist of "pushing, shoving, slapping, kicking, biting, hitting with fists, hitting or trying to hit with an object, beatings, and threats/use of a weapon."[34] In dating couples, estimates of the frequency of violence vary, but they range from about 30 to 40 percent of study samples. In other words, violence appears to occur in more than one out of three intimate relationships. These estimates vary partly because different researchers define violence differently and research participants often underreport its incidence in order to present a more socially desirable profile to the researcher. But the frequency of physical violence is high enough to make it the leading cause of death in the United States for women between the ages of 24 and 49.[35]

Although both men and women use physical violence as a tactic with their relationship partners, women are more likely to be harmed by such attacks.[36] Studies of violence have focused primarily on the woman as victim because of the debilitating effects of repeated physically violent acts. And, according to James West, married women are more likely to experience pressure from their social networks and institutional authorities to stay with their spouses.[37]

Most of the research on physical violence shows that it is used as a means of gaining power and control in the relationship and as a way of expressing anger toward one's partner. There is no typical profile of violent personality characteristics. However, some patterns emerge when researchers correlate violence with communication attitudes and skills. One study of patterns developed from six weeks before to 30 months after marriage found that violent couples showed a greater number of general speech problems and fewer communication skills overall. Women in this study were described as more compliant than were women in nonviolent relationships, and males were found to be less verbally positive or praising. Violent couples used fewer negotiation tactics in arguing with each other, all reported verbal attacks, and almost all reported anger. In other words, violent couples appeared not to have many of the tools for managing conflict. . . . Women are affected by violence the most, in that their "mental and physical health suffers in violent relationships where they are in more danger of killing or being killed by their partners."[38] In many instances of physical violence, women report a cycle characterized by increasing tension in the relationship, some precipitating event, a physically violent act, followed by remorse, and often some form of restitution (such as bringing flowers). However, many victims also reported that they were unable to predict when their partners were likely to become violent. Linda Marshall believes that the key to changing violent patterns to nonviolent ones is to focus on the communication that occurs between partners. She suggests that teaching specific skills, such as negotiation, may help to de-escalate conflicts and keep partners from resorting to physical violence.[39] As long as one person is physically violent with another, the relationship will be characterized by imbalances in power and control.[40]

If you or someone you know is in an abusive or violent relationship, as either abuser or victim, we hope that the information we sketched can help you understand what's happening. Of course, this understanding usually won't solve such serious problems. But four main points do emerge from recent studies: (1) Abuse and violence are pervasive, even common, in intimate relationships. (2) These overt actions and reactions are part of larger overall patterns that emerge over time. (3) Some [conflict management] skills . . . can help relational partners change the patterns and reduce the abuse and violence. (4) Often, as with the other kinds of communication discussed in this [reading], the best idea is to get help from a third party—a competent friend, counselor, therapist, member of the clergy, mediator, or specially trained law enforcement officer.

REVIEW QUESTIONS

1. Explain the difference between positive and negative motives for deception.
2. Explain "truth bias" and "lie bias."
3. Describe what some research has suggested are the personality features of frequent betrayers.
4. How does betrayal fit into the common pattern of communication in the family of an addicted person?
5. What relationship has been found between verbal aggression and physical violence? Does verbal aggression perform a "venting" function, or does it tend to lead to violence?
6. Research indicates that both genders fear sexual harassment, but for different reasons. Explain the fear that is experienced by many members of the gender other than yours.
7. Explain how some people contribute to the aggression or violence that they are subject to.
8. What specific communication skills may help reduce aggression and violence?

PROBES

1. O'Hair and Cody would probably view the lies told to Nazi soldiers to protect Jews in hiding as "benevolent" and therefore positive. But Wilmot does not believe that any motives for deception can be completely positive, and he briefly explains why in this reading. What do you believe? Explain.
2. How do you respond to Stewart and Logan's claim that deception is collaborative?
3. What is your response to the gender differences in betrayal behavior that are reported in some research?
4. What do you believe is the best way to minimize sexual harassment? What can you personally do to reduce the frequency of its occurrence in your own communication?
5. What resources are available in your community for people who are experiencing physical violence in a close relationship?

NOTES

1. This is a synopsis of a story related to Carole during a pilot research study in the spring of 1995.
2. R. Hopper & R. A. Bell, "Broadening the Deception Construct," *Quarterly Journal of Speech 70* (1984), 288–300.
3. Peter Andersen, *Beside Language: Nonverbal Communication in Interpersonal Interaction,* as cited in H. Dan O'Hair & Michael J. Cody, "Deception," In *The Dark Side of Interpersonal Communication,* ed. Wm. R. Cupach & Brian H. Spitzberg (Hillsdale, NJ: Lawrence Erlbaum, 1994), pp. 181–214.
4. O'Hair & Cody, p. 195.
5. G. Shippee, "Perceived Deception in Everyday Social Relationships," *Psychology 14* (1977), 57–62, cited in O'Hair & Cody, p. 195.
6. O'Hair & Cody, p. 195.
7. O'Hair & Cody, p. 196.
8. O'Hair & Cody, p. 197.
9. Wm W. Wilmot, *Relational Communication* (New York: McGraw-Hill, 1995), pp. 107–108.
10. This story is a synopsis of one related to Carole during a pilot study in the spring of 1995.
11. Warren H. Jones & Marsha P. Burdette, "Betrayal in Relationships," in A. L. Weber & J. H. Harvey (eds.), *Perspectives on Close Relationships* (Boston: Allyn & Bacon, 1994), p. 245.
12. Jones & Burdette, p. 260.
13. Jones & Burdette, p. 245.
14. Jones & Burdette, pp. 255–256.
15. Jones & Burdette, p. 245.
16. This type of cycle comes from a description in Paul and Katherine Wright, "Codependency: Personality Syndrome or Relational Process?" in Steve Duck and Julia Wood (eds.), *Confronting Relationship Challenges* (Thousand Oaks, CA: Sage, 1995), pp. 109–128.
17. This narrative is adapted from a student journal in one of Carole's classes.
18. This narrative is from an interview in a study of violence in relationships. James T. West, "Understanding How the Dynamics of Ideology Influence Violence between Intimates," in Duck and Wood (eds.), p. 130.
19. Anita Vangelisti, "Messages that Hurt," in Cupach and Spitzberg (eds.), p. 61.
20. Vangelisti, pp. 67–68.
21. See for example, D. A. Infante, T. C. Sabourin, JH. E. Rudd, and E. A. Shannon, "Verbal Aggression in Violent and Nonviolent Marital Disputes," *Communication Quarterly, 38* (1990): 361–371.
22. Teresa C. Sabourin, "The Role of Negative Reciprocity in Spouse Abuse: A Relational Control Analysis," *Journal of Applied Communication Research, 23* (1995): 271–283.
23. Sabourin, p. 281.

24. Sabourin, p. 281.
25. Deborah Tannen, *Talking from 9 to 5: How Women's and Men's Conversational Styles Affect What Gets Heard, Who Gets Credit, and What Gets Done at Work* (New York: Morrow, 1994), pp. 242–243.
26. In 1990, law professor Anita Hill accused U.S. Supreme Court nominee Clarence Thomas of sexual harassment in hearings before the U.S. Senate. This was the first time that sexual harassment gained national, and even international publicity. Thomas was confirmed by the Senate despite Hill's allegations.
27. Tannen, pp. 258–260.
28. Tannen, p. 261.
29. Tannen, p. 273.
30. Linda L. Marshall, "Physical and Psychological Abuse," in Cupach & Spitzberg (eds.), p. 294.
31. Marshall, p. 292.
32. Marshall, p. 298.
33. Marshall, pp. 296–297.
34. Rodney M. Cate & Sally A. Lloyd, *Courtship* (Thousand Oaks, CA: Sage, 1992), p. 97.
35. West, in Duck & Wood, p. 149.
36. Marshall, in Cupach & Spitzberg (eds.), p. 287; M. Cascardi, J. Langhinrichsen, & D. Vivian, "Marital Aggression: Impact, Injury and Health Correlates for Husbands and Wives," *Archives of Internal Medicine 152* (1992), 1178–1184; J. E. Stets & M. A. Straus, "Gender Differences in Reporting Marital Violence and Its Medical and Psychological Consequences," in M. A. Straus & R. J. Gelles (eds.), *Physical Violence in American Families: Risk Factors and Adaptations to Violence in 8,145 Families* (New Brunswick, N.J.: Transaction Books, 1992), pp. 151–165.
37. West, in Duck & Wood (eds.), pp. 142–145.
38. Marshall, in Cupach & Spitzberg (eds.), p. 292.
39. Marshall, in Cupach & Spitzberg (eds.), pp. 291–292.
40. Wilmot, pp. 111–112.

PART FOUR

Relationships

CHAPTER 9

Negotiating Relationships

*I*n Chapter 2, I said that one characteristic or feature of all communicating (it was number three in the list of five) is that it always involves negotiating identities, or selves. In other words, every time you or I communicate with anybody, one thing we're doing is mutually working out who we are for and with each other. This certainly isn't *all* we're doing. Most of the time we're also working with some *content*—anything from directions to the gym, to the best piece of new music, to the differences between our positions on abortion. But identities are always also in play. And this is one reason why there's such a direct connection between quality of communication and quality of life.

One way to talk about this identity-negotiation or identity-management part of communication is to use the vocabulary of "co-constructing selves." This way of talking describes how, in every relationship, the people involved directly and indirectly jockey for position with each other, sometimes competitively, but most of the time collaboratively. This process of co-constructing selves happens when employees meet their bosses for the first few times, when couples work through the early stages of a dating relationship, when teachers and students first get together, and in all other relationships. In addition, after the relationship has been established, the people involved still engage in identity management, but they do it more subtly and indirectly.

This next reading explains how this process happens. It's taken from the basic interpersonal communication text that I coauthored with Carole Logan. We begin with some examples of how this process operates to demonstrate that it's going on all the time. We point out that, since it is continuous, nobody always does it "perfectly or poorly, 'right' or 'wrong.' " As we emphasize, there is no one best or worst way to participate in this process. There are just outcomes of how you do it, results that people may or may not want. We also make the point that this process goes on in every culture, wherever humans communicate. And the reason it's important to understand this process is that when you want to influence where your communication is on the social–cultural–interpersonal continuum explained in Chapter 2, you need to pay attention to how you're co-constructing selves.

Then the reading moves into some more specific topics. We explain what the term *constructing* means in this context by identifying five key features: (a) The process is collaborative, which guarantees that (b) its outcomes are not predetermined, and that (c) it's made up of both reactions and responses, which (d) appear in what communicators give out and take in, and (e) that sometimes people realize they're doing it and sometimes they don't.

Then we talk about old and new views of identities or selves (we're using the terms synonymously here). We point out that for many years people thought of identities as individual, as if each human self existed within clear boundaries. But it turns out that the English term *self* is only about 300 years old, and the individualistic meaning for it is not widely shared across time (historically) or space (in other cultures). For years, in fact, anthropologists have been pointing out that the common individualistic view is an unusual—some even say a "peculiar"—way to think about human selves. The chapter uses examples from several countries to illustrate that many people, especially those in some Eastern cultures, have for centuries viewed the human self as a relational, joint, co-constructed being.

Then we explain what it means to say that selves are responders, not just reactors. Here our point is that people *choose*, more or less consciously, how to respond to the events and structures that confront them.

A third feature of selves is that they are complex—multidimensional and changing all the time. If you took an inventory of all the dimensions of your self, in fact, you'd undoubtedly find some internal inconsistencies. But this is to be expected. Our selves change over time, various qualities or features are in tension with their opposites, and different dimensions surface in different situations.

Our final point in this reading is that selves are developed in present and past relationships. Some of the most important parts of our identities are established in our families of origin—the caregivers with whom we spend at least the earliest years of our lives. But present relationships are also important. Genetic makeup has some influence on who you are, but the primary forces that define the self are communication forces in the past and present. This is why cultural and gender identity can be fluid and even troublesome. This part of the process is most obvious, perhaps, among gay and lesbian people who discover their sexuality and struggle with the process of "coming out," or with African Americans, Latinos, or other ethnically identifiable people who have questions about their cultural identity. But even when the features are much more subtle, all of us are continually growing and changing in our relationships.

The purpose of this reading is to introduce the idea that relationships involve continual processes of identity negotiation. Then the other readings in this chapter explain some of the intricacies of this overall process.

CO-CONSTRUCTING SELVES

John Stewart and Carole Logan

Notice the differences between the following two short conversations.

Conversation 1

RICARDO: I've got some ideas about Sunday afternoon.

CHERYL: What do you want to do?

RICARDO: I'd like to find that new park I read about. I heard it has some biking trails and not very many people. Why don't you pack a lunch, and we'll spend the afternoon there?

CHERYL: Sounds great. When will you pick me up?

RICARDO: I'll be by about one.

Conversation 2

DERECK: I have some ideas about what we could do Sunday afternoon.

MARIA: Good. I want to spend it together, but I'd rather not hang out with your friends. Let's just the two of us do something.

DERECK: Okay. Why don't we go down to the mall for a while and then see a movie? They just opened that place with 10 screens.

MARIA: Well . . . , there are usually lots of little kids there. Let's do something more active.

DERECK: Okay, you want to walk or bike around the lake?

MARIA: Sure! What time can I pick you up?

DERECK: Like, one? Did you get your bike rack back on your car?

MARIA: Yeah. No problem.

How would you describe Ricardo in conversation 1? As active? Assertive? Creative? A leader? Decision maker? Or as passive? Agreeable? Accepting? A follower? How about Cheryl? Which of these labels fit her? What are the differences between Cheryl's identity in conversation 1 and Maria's identity in conversation 2? And what kind of person is Dereck in relation to Maria?

The answers are pretty obvious. In conversation 1, Ricardo comes across as active, assertive, and the primary decision maker ("I'd like to find that new park. . . ." "Why don't you pack a lunch . . . ?" "I'll be by about one."), whereas Cheryl is more passive, accepting, and agreeable ("What do you want to do?" "Sounds great."). In this conversation, Ricardo defines himself as "leader," Cheryl accepts this identity, and she defines herself as "follower." These may be the typical selves or identities for Cheryl and Ricardo in this relationship, or there very well may be other times when Cheryl is the leader and Ricardo is the follower.

Excerpt from *Together: Communicating Interpersonally,* 5th ed. by John Stewart and Carole Logan, 1997. Reprinted by permission of The McGraw-Hill Companies.

In the second example, Maria comes across as much more of a decision maker than Cheryl. She wants to have an equal say in the plan for Sunday afternoon, rather than let Dereck make all the decisions. And in conversation 2, Dereck appears to be comfortable with this equality. He accepts Maria's way of defining herself and identifies himself as agreeable and cooperative. Again, these may or may not be the typical selves that these two people negotiate in their relationship.

The reason why these four persons' identities are fairly obvious is that their selves are present *in their talk*. When Cheryl asks Ricardo, "What do you want to do?" her words, tone of voice, and other nonverbal cues identify her as, at this moment, a follower, and her verbal and nonverbal talk encourages Ricardo to lead their decision making. On the other hand, when Maria says, "I want to spend it together, but I'd rather not hang out with your friends," she defines herself as an equal participant in the process of deciding what to do on Sunday. Then when Dereck responds, "Okay, Why don't we go down to the mall . . . ?" this comment verbally and nonverbally shows his acceptance of Maria's identity as an equal.

The conversations also show how each couple works out their identities *together*. Cheryl could have resisted Ricardo's definition of himself as leader, and Dereck could have identified himself as superior or inferior to Maria—rather than as her equal. But they didn't; in these particular exchanges, each cooperates with the other on their identities. If one would have resisted the other's definition of himself or herself as "equal," for example, the situation would have become more complicated. But however it worked out, the conversation partners would have collaborated on their respective definitions of each other's selves. This is so because identities aren't just individual creations, and they don't just exist inside people's heads or deep within their personalities. **Identities appear and are constructed or worked out in verbal and nonverbal talk.**

We want to emphasize that nobody in these two conversations is constructing identities perfectly or poorly, "right" or "wrong." In one sense, there is no right or wrong way to participate in this process. There are just *outcomes* of how you do it, *results* that people may or may not want. In these two brief conversations, it appears that the results are all positive. Ricardo and Cheryl seem to be perfectly satisfied with the identities of each other that they're constructing, and Maria and Dereck are as well. However, sometimes this process doesn't go so smoothly.

Conversation 3

CHAD: Have you got your tennis shoes?
JOSH: Yeah.
CHAD: Hey, are you gonna pay the money you owe the house?
JOSH: Yeah, sometime, but I'm a little short now, okay?
CHAD: Well, the pot needs the money and Mickelson is hitting everyone up for old bills.
JOSH: Hey, well, listen. Just get off my ass.
CHAD: I'm not on your ass. There are just a lot of outstanding bills, and yours is the biggest.

JOSH: Well, who made you enforcer? Back off!
CHAD: Right.

The basketball game Chad and Josh are about to play is liable to be pretty aggressive. In this conversation, Chad identifies himself as a concerned member of the group of housemates, who is trying to get his friend to be responsible for his debts. Josh rejects this identity; he may feel embarrassed and even a little guilty that he hasn't paid up, but he doesn't want his friend to set himself up as bill collector. Chad decides not to push the point, but at the end of this exchange, the problem is unresolved. This disagreement over identities—"Stop being a deadbeat!" "Stop being a cop!"—probably won't be fatal to their friendship, but it's an issue in the relationship that might very well come up again. If either Chad or Josh wants to change the way he's being defined in relation to the other person, it might help both of them to know more about how the process of constructing selves works.

We also want to note that none of the people in these conversations could avoid constructing selves. It's a process that happens whenever people communicate. . . . Some of the most important meanings people collaboratively create are their identities, and all communicating involves constructing identities or selves. No matter how brief or extended the contact, whether it's written or oral, mediated or face-to-face, impersonal or interpersonal, the people involved will be directly or indirectly constructing definitions of themselves and responding to the definitions offered by others. Hosts of radio talk shows and television newscasters are continually building identities. The person who writes a letter in longhand on colorful stationery is defining himself or herself in a different way than the person who writes the same letter on a word processor. The person who answers the telephone with "Yeah?" is defining himself or herself differently from the one who answers, "Good morning. May I help you?" In fact, this process goes on even when there seems to be no topic or subject matter.

Conversation 4

JAN: Hey, how's it goin'?
HEATHER: *(Silence and a scowl)*
JAN: What's the matter?
HEATHER: Nothing. Forget it.
JAN: What are you so pissed about?
HEATHER: Forget it! Just drop it.
JAN: Well, all right! Pout! I don't give a damn!

Here, even though Jan and Heather are not talking about any object, issue, or event, they are definitely constructing selves together. In this conversation, Heather's definitions of herself and of Jan go something like this:

> Right now I identify myself as independent of you (Silence. "Nothing. Forget it"). You're butting into my space, and you probably think I'm antisocial. But I've got good reasons for my anger.

On the other hand, Jan's definitions of herself and of Heather are something like this:

Right now I identify myself as friendly and concerned ("Hey, how's it goin'?" "What's the matter?"). I'm willing to stick my neck out a little, but you're obviously not interested in being civil. So there's a limit to how long I'll *stay* friendly and concerned. ("Well, all right! Pout! I don't give a damn!").

Research on intercultural communication shows how identity construction occurs all over the world. For example, in a bar in Nairobi, Kenya, a researcher observed three trilingual middle-class Kenyans constructing selves in part by switching among the three languages each of them knew—English, Swahili, and Luyia, a native dialect. Two of the speakers used Swahili for "How did things go today?" "Things went well for me," and "I'm waiting for you to order me a bottle of [beer]." But then one switched to Swahili/English to say, "Forget it, *bwana*," and into Luyia to add, "I found you here, so you're the one to buy for me first." This speaker used a language switch to help identify himself as a guest rather than as the buyer of the drinks. After a response from the other, which also relied on Luyia, the third man offered in English to mediate their argument over who would buy. The researcher points out that one of the main ways he defined himself as mediator was to use English.[1] So these three people used language choice as one of their ways to construct identities.

A similar process often happens in the United States when African-Americans switch between black English and standard American English to define themselves differently in informal versus official communication contexts. This process operates in other cross-cultural situations, too. For example, according to one researcher, "Much of the Spanish-English code switching by [Latino] bilinguals" functions to change self-definitions.[2] In various cultural contexts, speakers use language choices "imaginatively, . . . a range of options is open to them within a normative framework, and . . . taking one option rather than another is the *negotiation of identities.*"[3]

So two reasons why it's important to understand the process of identity construction are (1) that you're doing it whenever you communicate—and everybody else is, too; and (2) that the process affects who you are in relation to others. The third reason why it's important is that *your negotiation responses also affect where your communication is on the social–cultural–interpersonal continuum. . . .* Some responses just about guarantee that your communication will be social. Others lead to more interpersonal communicating. So if you want to help change the quality of your contacts with your dating partner, employer, roommate, sibling, or parent in either direction on the continuum, you'll want to learn as much as you can about this process.

UNDERSTANDING THE TERMS

Constructing

[Earlier treatments of this topic were called] "Negotiating Selves" rather than "Constructing Identities," even though [both terms] described the same process. Some students told us that the word "negotiation" sounded too much like a process whereby you end up winning, losing, or compromising on a final outcome—as you do when you negotiate a price to pay a friend for a used book. So that term may be a little misleading. On the other hand, you may prefer "negotiating" to "constructing." But whichever word is used, it's important to recognize that the process of identity construction is

- collaborative, which guarantees that
- its outcomes are not predetermined or static, and that
- it's made up of both reactions and responses,
- which appear in what communicators give out and take in,
- and that sometimes people realize they're doing it and sometimes they don't.

Collaborative As we've said before, when we say "construction," we mean "co-construction." You can't do it by yourself. It takes at least two. It happens between people. And as was also noted, "collaborate" doesn't mean "agree." It just means "labor together." Think of the difference between *alignment* and *agreement*. Two individuals or groups can be *aligned* (collaborating) in that they are moving in a similar direction, even though they *disagree* about how to get there or who should get there first. Even countries that are at war collaborate or are aligned, because they show up at the same place to fight and follow a general set of rules.[4] People and countries that are not officially at war collaborate much more obviously and directly. One implication of the fact that the process of constructing selves is collaborative is that you cannot control it yourself. Your responses make up no more than one half of the process.

Emergent Outcomes It's almost impossible to predict the results of any identity-construction process. If someone you know well is pretty predictable, you can probably guess how he or she will respond to some routine or common situations. However, that person may surprise you by, for example, not getting as defensive as he or she normally would, or by saying "No" when you fully expect the person to say "Yes." Since the identity-construction process is collaborative, its outcomes depend on both (or all) persons' responses. You have to "stay tuned" to see what the outcomes are going to be (remember "nexting". . . ?), and whatever they are, it's likely that they'll change. This is what it means to say that the outcomes are emergent. Identity construction is a fluid process.

Reactions and Responses As the examples above showed, some parts of the identity-construction process can also be almost automatic. Others are fairly subtle. Some people almost always react to a power move by making a power move of their own. Some consistently react to a person in need with an offer of help, and others react to the same situation by ignoring the person. But . . . people also respond rather than simply react. We do things that are out of character, especially when we want to change the situation. When people realize what's at stake—selves—and how fluid the process is, most want to make some choices or decisions about how to participate in it. In this [reading] we describe these four main choices, so you can either react or respond.

Give Out and Take In   Identities are constructed out of what communicators give out and take in. People are doing both of these things all the time, and identities emerge from this two-part, or bidirectional, process. In fact, as [was] said in the introduction to this section . . ., this process is as continuous, natural, and (often) unnoticed as is another bidirectional process, breathing. Because of these similarities between breathing and identity construction, we want to use the inhaling–exhaling metaphor to talk about the bidirectionality of this process. The *inhaling* parts of this process include what you perceive, how completely and carefully you listen, how much you are distracted by your own agendas, the extent to which you stereotype the people with whom you're communicating, and so on. What we call the *exhaling* parts include all the cues or messages you give out, such as your appearance and dress, tone of voice, facial expression, word choice, eye behavior, and amount of talk.

In and Out of Awareness   Many communicators don't even realize that this process is going on all the time. They think that communication only deals with information or content, and they don't notice the selves and relationships that are constantly being constructed. One main goal of this book is to reduce the number of these people. We believe strongly that everyone should know about identity construction. But this doesn't mean that you need to focus on it all the time. In many situations, people aren't aware of the identity-construction process because it's not creating any problems. If everybody agrees about who they are to each other, as in conversation 1, there's no reason to pay much attention to how selves are being collaboratively defined.

Effective communicators, however, are aware of the process when they need to be. They realize how the process works, and are flexible enough to adapt the ways they participate in it. They understand what's happening in a situation like conversation 3, and they know what they can do about it. . . .

"But . . . ," a student responds. . . .

Are people really defining themselves and responding to others' self-definitions all the time? Why?

When you're completely alone, the construction-of-selves process slows to a stop. But the process is active whenever you are in contact with someone else, whether you're just avoiding bumping into a stranger while crossing a street, writing a business letter, or proposing marriage to someone you've known since childhood. Identity construction is one of a human's basic sense-making or information-processing activities. Of course, a great deal of the time it is unproblematic, and it usually goes on outside our awareness—at least until you start studying interpersonal communication. You won't very often hear someone say, "No, I won't do that because I identify myself as superior to you," or "I see you seeing me as afraid of you." In addition, we often don't notice the process because it's working just fine. Everybody agrees on how each person defines the other, and we just go about our business. But even when we are unaware of identity construction, it's still operating.

But why do we construct definitions of, or selves for, each other?

Fundamentally, we do so to make sense out of the human parts of our world. As [was] said [earlier], communication is basically the process of collaboratively constructing meaning. There are literally millions of stimuli available to each of us all the time, and if we had to deal with all of them, the disorganization and sheer number would drive us crazy. So we organize the chaos, we structure our world. We put things and people into categories so that we can, for example, distinguish between what's important and what's unimportant. Part of this process involves constructing definitions to help make sense of ourselves and others.

In addition, part of what it means to be a human being is to reflect on who we are. Our own identity is important to us, and early on, we learn that who we are grows out of the contacts we have with others. So the other main reason why we engage in identity construction is that it's important to us, it's significant in our lives.

Identities

Old Versus Current Views   As you have noticed by now, we're using "selves" and "identities" synonymously. To say that selves are co-constructed in communicators' verbal and nonverbal talk is to say that this is where and how we negotiate who we are to each other.

This may sound weird to you. You might think of your *self* as a fairly stable, identifiable, clearly bounded person. If so, you're not alone. Most people in Western cultures have been taught to think of their "selves" as bounded, individual containers that enclose their unique essence. As described in one book:

> There is an individualist mode of thought, distinctive of modern Western cultures, which, though we may criticize it in part or in whole, we cannot escape . . . . This inescapable cultural vise has given us—or, at least, the dominant social groups in the West[5]—a sense of themselves as distinctive, independent agents who own themselves and have relatively clear boundaries to protect in order to ensure their integrity and permit them to function more effectively in the world.[6]

Most members of dominant social groups in the Western world think of the boundary of the individual as the same as the boundary of the body, and that the body houses or contains the "self." Common metaphors reflect this view, as when people say that a person is *"filled* with anger," "unable to *contain* her joy," *"brimming* with laughter," or trying to get anger *out of her system.*"[7] Some theories of psychology reinforce this view of identity or the self. Psychologists influenced by Sigmund Freud, for example, think of society as made up of individual selves who are each working out inner tensions. One Freudian insisted that a student revolt against university administrators was caused by the students' unresolved conflicts with their fathers. In his view, "Protestors were taking out their inner conflicts with parental authority by acting against the authority represented by the University. It was as though there were no legitimate problems with the University; it only symbolized protestors' unresolved Oedipal conflicts with the real source of their troubles, their fathers."[8] For this psychologist, selves were individual and internal.

In these last decades of the 20th century, the development of space travel, satellite television, and the World Wide Web; the globalization of music and business; and the end of the Cold War have all helped Westerners understand that this view of the person as a bounded individual is, as one anthropologist puts it, rather "peculiar."[9] For centuries, people in many cultures outside the West have not been thinking in this way. For example, if a North American is asked to explain why one person cheated another person financially, the North American's tendency will be to locate the cause in "the kind of person she is." A Hindu, by contrast, is more likely to offer a social explanation: "The man is unemployed. He is not in a position to give that money."[10] This interpretation indicates that many members of the Hindu culture don't think of identity or the self as individual, but as social or communal. For them, identity is a function of cultural or group memberships. Or, to take another example, in a study of U.S. and Samoan child-care workers, U.S. preschool teachers tended to help children socialize by developing their individuality, whereas Samoan caregivers' efforts "were directed towards helping the children learn how better to fit into their in-group."[11] In their broader culture, Samoans in this study also recognized the central role of other people in events that were deemed worthy of praise or compliments. One researcher reported that when a Samoan passenger complimented a driver in language that translates as "Well done the driving," the driver typically responded, "Well done the support." "In this Samoan view, if a performance went well, it is the supporters' merit as much as the performers'."[12] Japanese understanding of the person is similar. In Japan, one author notes, "The concept of a self completely independent from the environment is very foreign."[13] Rather, Japanese think of individuals in terms of the social context they fit into—their family, work group, and so on. The United States, Canada, Australia, Great Britain, and some other Western cultures have a strong belief in the individual self, but many European countries (e.g., Spain, Austria, and Finland) and most Asian and Latin American cultures understand selves as social, relational, or collective.[14]

It's easier to understand how identity construction works—and how to manage your own identity constructing—if you adopt what has historically been a more Eastern perspective. This obviously doesn't mean that you have to change cultures or religions, or pretend to be somebody you're not. In fact, this understanding is being accepted by communication scholars, psychologists, anthropologists, and other students of human behavior all over the world. Especially in the final decade of the 20th century, many of these scholars and teachers are recognizing that selves or identities are relational from birth, or perhaps even before. They are reconsidering what Lev Vygotsky and George Herbert Mead, two very influential human development researchers, said several decades ago; namely, that infants are first *social* beings and only later in life learn to see themselves as *individuals*. Psychologist Robert Sampson explains:

> Both Vygotsky and Mead clearly emphasize the necessary social bases of hu-
> man thinking, cognition, and mindedness. Indeed, rather than viewing the in-
> dividual's mind as setting forth the terms for the social order, the reverse de-
> scribes the actual event: the social process—namely, dialogue and
> conversation—precedes, and is the foundation for, any subsequent psycholog-
> ical processes that emerge.[15]

Here Sampson reinforces what [was] said about the importance of everyday conversation. . . . It's a basic social process that constructs selves and is the foundation for any subsequent psychological processes that emerge. Infants are born into a social world, and at first they are totally dependent on it. For example, a baby only a few weeks old may make grasping movements toward some object. When the caretaker notices the action and infers that the child wants the object, the caretaker may respond by offering or withholding it. From the point of view of the child, the *meaning* of the gesture is linked to the caregiver's response. In this basic way, the infant's primitive sense-making is relational, social, or fundamentally linked to others (Sampson indicates that it's "dialogic or conversational").

Even such seemingly private actions as memory have been demonstrated to be more social than individual. For example, consider how you'd respond if someone asked you to remember an important event from your childhood. If you view your "self" as simply a container, you might think that you would just pull out of your memory bank a trace that was stored there, like a computer pulls a file from its hard disk. But is this what would happen? Or would your response depend on who asked you the question and in what context? Would your answer be the same, for example, if the question were asked by a prospective employer or by your counselor or therapist? Would you recall the same event if you were in a group of six coworkers or alone with your best friend? As Sampson concludes, memory "may not simply involve calling forth a pure trace of the past or be entirely located inside the individual. It may be better to speak of a dynamic process located between person and other (including the context) rather than within the person."[16]

In short, the English term "self" and its meaning are only about 300 years old. Studies of history and of other cultures illustrate that the Western definition developed over the last 275 of these 300 years is very narrow. Today, this idea that selves are individual containers is being revised as communication scholars and psychologists are recognizing how much our selves are developed in, and show themselves in, communicative relations with others, and as historians and anthropologists are learning how many cultures have understood this point for a long time. Westerners increasingly recognize that identities or selves are multidimensional and changing, in response to the people and institutions with which we connect. Each of our identities has athletic, artistic, ethnic, gendered, occupational, scientific, political, economic, and religious dimensions, and all of these shift in content and importance as we move from situation to situation. One author names this condition "multiphrenia," and contrasts it with "schizophrenia."[17] Schizophrenia means having multiple personalities, and it is considered to be pathological, a disorder that needs to be cured. Multiphrenia means many-selved, and it is today considered to be a normal condition, the outcome of recognizing diversity and globalization, being a part of many different social institutions (family, school, workplace, spiritual or religious group, etc.), and understanding the important ways in which *who I am* grows out of how I talk and listen to and with others.

Selves Are Responders   Another way to see how selves are relational or social rather than individual is to understand what it means to say that selves are *responders.* . . . Responsiveness is one of the five features that makes each of us a person. [The] main point . . . [is] to contrast responding with simply reacting. Now we want to build the meaning of this idea by noting that responding implies both *choice* (not just reacting) and *connection* with what's already happened.

To say that selves are responders is to say that people grow out of and fit into a context of actions and events that they behave-in-relation-to. On the one hand, this is just another way of saying that selves are relational or social. On the other hand, this means that all human action is joint action. No human starts behaving from ground zero, so that everything we do, from the very beginning, is in answer to something else.

Humans begin responding from the first moment they develop any awareness, which, as noted earlier, probably happens before birth. Every baby is born into a world of verbal and nonverbal talk, family relationships, gender patterns, ongoing activities, and social and political events. This is the sense in which no person is, "after all, the first speaker, the one who disturbs the eternal silence of the universe."[18]

This isn't to say that all of what we do is completely *determined* or *caused* by the contexts we're in. People do more than just *react* to all these influences. We *choose* whether to try broccoli or clams for the first time, how to spend part of our allowance, what to wear, and what excuse to give for getting in trouble. These choices are not simply independent actions, however; they are *responses* to both global forces (how we've been raised, cultural influences, family value systems) and local ones (the mood we're in, whom we're talking to, how hurried we feel right now, and so on). Thus, our actions are *joint* actions.

We also sometimes think of our own or other people's actions as "starting" something—the argument, the meeting, the conversation, the sales pitch. But it's also true that none of *these* actions "disturbed the eternal silence of the universe." If you think about the broader, more inclusive context, all the actions we experience are responsive to the events that preceded them. . . .

Selves Are Multidimensional and Changing   A third feature of selves is that we're complex. On the one hand, each of us is characterized by some stabilities or patterns. Your genetic makeup is stable, and your gender and ethnic identity also probably haven't changed, and probably won't. In addition, you've developed some deeply ingrained habits. Someone who's known you all your life can probably identify some features you had when you were four or five years old and that you still have, and as you look at old photographs of yourself, you might recognize how the identity of the person in the picture is in some ways "the same" as who you are today.

On the other hand, you are different in at least as many ways as you are the same. Think, for example, of who you were at age 9 or 10 and who you were at age 14 or 15. Adolescence is a time of *significant* change in our selves. Or think of your self before you were married and after, or your identity before and after you had children. . . . Our point is that the human self is not simply a unified chunk of unchanging traits, beliefs, and values. One of John's friends, for example, has all of the following characteristics.

athletically active	mechanically awkward	impatient listener
high energy	extremely well read	ambitious
deeply religious	happily childless	cares about others
loves dark beer	protective of his wife	loves to perform
eloquent	tight-fisted with money	concerned about health

This list could include hundreds of entries, all of which help make up this person's "self." And even though some of John's friend's characteristics seem contradictory (for example, "impatient listener" and "cares about others"), they are all part of who this person is *in different situations and different relationships*. . . . When he's with people who let him decide the topic of conversation, he'll focus almost exclusively on his own concerns, but when he's working with the people from his church, he's very concerned about their well-being. Some version of the same thing is true of us and of you. Selves are multidimensional and *living*, and to be alive means to change. Our selves change over time, various qualities or features are in tension with their opposites, and different dimensions surface in different situations.

Selves Are Developed in Past and Present Relationships   The reason selves change over time is that we develop who we are in relationships with the people around us. Some of the most important parts of your identity are established in your family of origin, the people with whom you spend the first five to seven years of your life. For example, one of your parents may have consistently introduced you to new people from the time you were old enough to talk, and today you may still find it easy to make acquaintances. Or you may have moved around a lot when you were young, and today you feel most secure when you have your own "place" and you prefer to spend holidays close to home. You may remember always hearing that you were physically attractive, and you still enjoy having your picture taken. You may treasure a wonderful relationship with your dad, or you may have had the opposite experience.

> My father is an alcoholic. He has never admitted to that fact. He and my mom used to get in lots of fights when I lived at home. The six of us kids were used as pawns in their war games. I always wondered whether or not I was responsible for his drinking. When the fights were going on, I always retreated to my room. There I felt secure. Now, I am 22, and have been married for two years. I have this affliction that, whenever the slightest thing happens, I always say I am

so sorry. I am sorry when the milk is not cold, sorry that the wet towel was left in the gym bag. I just want to take the blame for everything, even things I have no control over.[19]

Many current studies about dysfunctional families emphasize how people with addictions to alcohol, cocaine, prescription drugs, or other chemicals develop the communication patterns that reinforced these addictions in their families of origin.[20] Other research focuses on how addictions affect the children or other family members of addicted persons. . . .[21] Our main point here is that past relationships contribute a great deal to the patterns that help make up our present selves.

Present relationships are also important. When you realize that a new friend really likes you, it can do great things for your self-definition. Getting an A from a teacher you respect can affect how you see yourself. At work, a positive performance evaluation from your supervisor or a raise can improve not only your mood and your bank account, but also your perception of yourself. And again, the reverse obviously can also happen. The point is, genetic makeup has some influence on who you are, but the primary forces that define the self are communication forces, and the communication process that produces these identities is called identity construction.

"But . . . ," a student responds. . . .

You are ignoring individual integrity. The most important parts of who I am are determined individually, not between me and someone else. In fact, it's not good for one person to let somebody else define who he or she is. Only weak people with low self-esteem let themselves be affected by others that much.

We also believe that individual integrity is important. This is why we emphasize how important your individual responses are. Human identity is not just a kneejerk reaction to surrounding forces. But it's also true that no person is an island. No humans determine who they are entirely on their own.

For example, although your racial identity is genetically determined, your ethnicity grows out of the relationships you have with others. Two college students might both be racially Chinese, but one might be ethnically more Caucasian—relating to his parents and family as Caucasians do, preferring Western food, attending a Western Christian church—while the other is ethnically more Chinese—relating to her parents in appropriately Chinese ways, preferring Chinese food, attending a Buddhist church. Each developed his or her ethnicity in contacts with other people. Similarly, some people who are born African-Americans learn pride, strength, and self-respect from the African-Americans in their family of origin and the Latinos, whites, and others they relate with. Other African-American children grow up without strong role models, experience continual racism, and develop weaker or angrier self-definitions. Still others are raised to be at home in a dominant power structure and develop identities almost indistinguishable from those of their Caucasian and Asian colleagues and friends. Even more important, many African-Americans in each of these groups *change* their self-definitions at some points in their lives. How? By changing the ways they relate to others.

The same can be said about sex and gender identity. Genetic makeup determines one's sex, but gender identity is affected more by the patterns we learn in our relationships with others.[22] A dozen males may all have the required X chromosome, but their self-definitions may vary widely, depending on who raised them, who their mentors were, and how they have been treated by women and by other men. All of this illustrates how identity is significantly affected by relationships, not only for "weak" people, but for everyone.

At the same time, deep-rooted habits and patterns that have become part of your "core self" certainly don't change every time you talk with someone new. In fact, even when you want to alter them, they can be incredibly resistant. But each of us is so multidimensional that important parts of who we actually are can and do change from one communication situation to the other.

REVIEW QUESTIONS

1. Fill in the blank: "_____ appear and are constructed or worked out in verbal and non-verbal talk."
2. Identify three plausible features of the identity being offered by the person who answers the telephone, "Yeah?" What are three plausible features of the identity of the person who answers the telephone, "Good morning. May I help you?"
3. Explain the difference between "alignment" and "agreement." Why is this important?
4. What's the difference between a reaction and a response?
5. Explain Sampson's point that memory is not an individual, private action.
6. What is "multiphrenia?"

PROBES

1. Think about the culture other than your own that you know the most about. What are two differences between the ways identities are negotiated in that culture and the ways identities are negotiated in your own?
2. It may well be that the most important single feature of the identities that are constructed in relationships is that they are *emergent*. Explain what it means to say that they are "emergent," and tell why this is such an important characteristic. Which basic communication skill from Chapter 2 does this feature foreground? (Hint: It begins with "n".)
3. Explain one specific and significant way that your "self" is not completely individualistic, but co-constructed. For me, it might be that my self is *younger*

than many 57 year olds, mostly because I'm continually relating to our 5-year old son and college-age students. What about you?

4. Does the culture you primarily identify with generally view selves as individualistic or relational? How does this affect your own sense of your self?

5. What past relationships most affected the development of your self? Which present relationships are having the most impact on the current development of your self?

6. If you are mainly a product of your relationships, what happens to your individual integrity?

NOTES

1. Carol Myers Scotton, "The Negotiation of Identities in Conversation: A Theory of Markedness and Code Choice." *International Journal of Sociological Linguistics* 44 (1983): 119–125.

2. Scotton, pp. 122–123.

3. Scotton, p. 133.

4. Does it sound strange to say that warring nations are collaborating or aligned? Modern warfare obviously does involve treachery, covert operations, disinformation, and even attempts at genocide. But warring nations still don't attack neutral or uninvolved countries or begin the fighting with their most horrendous weapon (nuclear bombs, biological warfare). And war-crimes trials indicate that some international laws are still operating, even in the Mideast and the Balkans. There is also some truth suggested by a challenge from the 1960s: "What if they gave a war and nobody came?"

5. . . . Here is a situation in which, as this clause suggests, we are going to advocate a way of thinking about selves that is different from the understanding of many members of [the] white, middle-class, U.S. culture. In other words, as this quotation says, most "dominant social groups in the West" see selves as individual containers, and we are going to suggest that another view is preferable.

6. Edward E. Sampson, *Celebrating the Other: A Dialogic Account of Human Nature* (Boulder, CO: Westview Press, 1993), p. 31, citing S. Lukes, "Conclusion," in M. Carrithers, S. Collins, and S. Lukes (eds.), *The Category of the Person: Anthropology, Philosophy, History* (Cambridge, England: Cambridge University Press, 1985), p. 298.

7. George Lakoff, *Women, Fire, and Dangerous Things* (Chicago: University of Chicago Press, 1987), p. 383.

8. Sampson, p. 44.

9. Clifford Geertz, "From the Native's Point of View: On the Nature of Anthropological Understanding," in P. Rabinow and W.M. Sullivan (eds.), *Interpretive Social Science* (Berkeley, CA: University of California Press, 1979), p. 229.

10. Sampson, p. 67, citing J.G. Miller, "The Development of Women's Sense of Self," in *Work in Progress. No. 12* (Wellesley, MA: Stone Center Working Papers Series, 1984), p. 968.

11. Sampson, p. 68, citing E. Ochs, *Culture and Language Development: Language Acquisition and Language Socialization in a Samoan Village* (Cambridge, England: Cambridge University Press, 1988),p. 199.
12. Sampson, p. 68, citing Ochs, p. 200.
13. Hideo Kojima, "A Significant Stride Toward the Comparative Study of Control." *American Psychologist*, 39 (1984): 972–973, cited in Sampson, pp. 70–71.
14. G. Hofstede, *Culture's Consequences: International Differences in Work-Related Values* (Beverly Hills, CA: Sage, 1980).
15. Sampson, p. 103.
16. Sampson, pp. 129–130.
17. Kenneth J. Gergen, *The Saturated Self: Dilemmas of Identity in Contemporary Life* (New York: Basic Books, 1991).
18. Mikhail Bakhtin, "The Problem of Speech Genres," in *Speech Genres and Other Late Essays*, trans. Vern W. McGee (Austin, TX: University of Texas Press, 1986), p. 69.
19. "Sharon R.," quoted in Claudia Black, *It Will Never Happen to Me! Children of Alcoholics as Youngsters–Adolescents–Adults* (Denver: M.A.C., 1982), p. 9.
20. J.R. Milam and K. Ketcham, *Under the Influence: A Guide to the Myths and Realities of Alcoholism* (Seattle: Madrona, 1981); Donald Goodwin, *Is Alcoholism Hereditary?* (New York: Oxford, 1976).
21. Janet Geringer Woititz, *Adult Children of Alcoholics* (Pompano Beach, FL: Health Communications, 1983). Also see Melody Beattie, *Codependent No More* (New York: Harper/Hazelden, 1984); Beattie, *Beyond Codependency* (New York: Harper/Hazelden, 1989); Anne Wilson Schaef, *Co-Dependence: Misunderstood-Mistreated* (New York: Harper & Row, 1986).
22. We do not mean to suggest that sexual preference is a matter of choice, or that it can be changed by simply selecting different identity-construction responses. The gay and lesbian people we know tell us that they knew that they weren't heterosexual early on, and even though several married and a couple of them even had families, their sexual preference persisted. We're not geneticists, but the research we're aware of and our personal experience both lead us to believe that sexual preference may be genetically determined.

*B*ill Wilmot is an interpersonal communication and conflict management researcher and teacher at the University of Montana. As these excerpts from his book, *Relational Communication* illustrate, Bill has an unusually acute sense of the complexities of interpersonal relationships. This next reading combines Bill's discussion of communication spirals and his ideas about paradoxes and conundrums (relationship puzzles).

The first section begins by explaining that a "communication spiral" happens when "the actions of each person in a relationship magnify those of the other." Bill gives several examples of both positive and negative spirals that can happen in family, work, and dating relationships. He emphasizes that spirals can be powerful because they pick up a momentum that feeds back on itself. This means that closeness and harmony can create more of the same, and that bitterness and hostility can operate the same way. He lists seven features of a communication spiral and then goes into some detail about generative spirals and degenerative ones.

An example of a generative spiral is the teacher who searches for the positive in a student and rewards it appropriately. As Bill summarizes it, "the more genuinely the teacher relates to the student, the better the student performs; the higher the quality of his or her performance, the more positive the teacher becomes."

Degenerative spirals are the mirror images of generative ones. Discord leads to more discord and the spiral intensifies. So, for example, if a person is hesitant to relate to others, he or she shuns contacts, which in turn make it more difficult to overcome the hesitancy. Some research that Bill cites shows that one of the most common degenerative spirals in a marriage occurs when the husband withdraws emotionally, the wife expresses dissatisfaction to her husband, and the husband then withdraws even more.

Bill follows this analysis of spirals with five concrete suggestions about how to alter degenerative ones. The first is deceptively simple-sounding: "Do what comes unnaturally." Spirals are relational phenomena, which is to say that they are fed by both (or all) the parties in a relationship. Change is impossible so long as things continue as they have. At least one party has to "do what comes unnaturally."

A second suggestion is to use third parties—friends, counselors, relatives, clergy, or others whom you trust. A specific suggestion for breaking the toxic pattern can often come from an informed but not intimately-involved outsider. A third suggestion is to reaffirm your relational goals. It can often help for people in a spiral to remind themselves and each other about the commitment they have to the relationship. This is a form of suggestion number four, "metacommunicating." This just means that you communicate about your communicating. You talk about the relationship and whatever has led to the degenerating series of actions.

The final two suggestions are that you try spending less time with the person and consider changing the external situation. Sometimes these moves will also break troublesome patterns.

The section of this reading on paradoxes and conundrums consists of brief discussions of twelve two-directional pulls that many people experience in their relationships. It can be reassuring to read that others feel some of the same tensions you do, and Bill also includes some suggestions about how to cope with these relational puzzles.

The first is that people want contradictory things in relationships: freedom and closeness, stability and excitement. It can be helpful to recognize that this is normal, and not necessarily problematic. A second is that both "objective" third-person observations and "subjective," insider observations about a relationship are fraught with errors. It's important to get both perspectives, and not to believe that either provides "the Truth" about the relationship.

Paradox #3 is that if you leave relationships completely alone they'll probably dissolve, and if you try to force them to happen, you can destroy them. This is a tension that it works best to stay in the middle of. Number four is the tension between expecting a relationship to generate happiness when its purpose may be the sense of wholeness that comes from the inherently unstable dialectical encounter between two people. The fifth paradox is that we get the most pleasure *and* the most pain from our closest relationships.

Bill also discusses some paradoxes about the connection between "the self" and "the relationship" and the fact that "relationships can serve as springboards for growth or just toss you higher so you land harder." Number nine reminds us how changes in any part or level of a relationship reverberate to other levels, number ten sketches the power inherent in and the problems created by relationship labels. And the last two emphasize the ever-changing, emergent quality of relationships.

By the time you've completed this reading you should have an appreciation for the sometimes startling complexity of the relationships you are a part of.

COMMUNICATION SPIRALS, PARADOXES, AND CONUNDRUMS

William W. Wilmot

A communication spiral occurs when the actions of each person in a relationship magnify those of the other. Communication spirals are evident almost everywhere, happening between humans, between us and other species, and among other species as well. A human–animal illustration should clarify the essential nature of spirals. My son Jason at age 3 saw a sleek, shiny cat. With the reckless abandonment of a child his age, he rushed at the cat to pet it. The wise cat, seeing potential death, moved out of Jason's reach. Not to be outdone, Jason tried harder. The cat moved farther away. Jason started running after the cat. The cat, no dummy about life, ran too. In a short 10 seconds from the initial lunge at the cat, Jason and the cat were running at full tilt. Luckily, the cat was faster and survived to run another day. Similarly, spirals occurs in many contexts:

- A child disobeys the parent, the parent acts more punitively and harshly, and the child becomes even more unruly.

Excerpts from *Relational Communication* 4th ed. by William W. Wilmot, 1995. Reprinted by permission of The McGraw-Hill Companies.

- A parent and 22-year-old son embark on a foreign adventure for 2 months—just the two of them. As the trip draws to a close, they both note on the plane ride home how close they feel to one another, and how easy their communication has become.
- An employee may be quiet and not forthcoming to the supervisor, the supervisor puts pressure on him to talk, and he becomes even more silent.
- Two guys are sitting in a bar; one accidentally touches the other, the first pushes him, an insult is uttered, and within a minute the two are fighting in the street.
- A supervisor is dissatisfied with an employee's performance but doesn't tell the employee. The employee is complaining to others about the supervisor. Both the employee and supervisor keep doing more of the same—the employee withdrawing and talking to others, the supervisor getting more annoyed and not telling the employee. Then 6 months later during the performance appraisal, the supervisor says, "We are reorganizing the office, and you won't be needed anymore."
- Two close friends buy a cabin midway between their two towns. Each time they go to the cabin, their relationship is reinforced, and not only do they ski better, they enjoy one another's company more.
- Two romantic partners feel that the other is pulling away. So each shares less, harbors grudges, and spends less time with the other, until there is a fight during which they end the relationship.
- Two opposite-sex friends spend a lot of time with one another. As they spend more time, they exclude others and feel closer and closer. It gets to the point that they don't want to begin other friendships because this one is so fulfilling.

All spirals, whether building in a positive or negative direction, tend to pick up a momentum that feeds back on itself—closeness and harmony builds more closeness and harmony; misunderstanding and dissatisfaction creates more misunderstanding and dissatisfaction. The responses produce a lock-step effect in relationships (Leary, 1955; Kurdek, 1991). Quality relationships, like close friendships, develop an "end in themselves"—quality—and become self-sustaining (Rose & Serafica, 1986).

Communication spirals, whether they head in positive or negative directions, are characterized by these elements:

1. The participants' meanings intertwine in such a way that each person's behavior accelerates the dynamism of the relationship. The relational synergy builds upon itself in a continuously accelerating manner.
2. *Each* person's actions contribute to the overall dynamic. Whether you talk, retreat, engage, reinvest, or disinvest in the relationship, your communication (or lack of communication) directly impacts the other person, and vice versa. Each person reacts to the other (Kurdek, 1991).
3. Bateson (1972, 1979) noted long ago that spirals manifest either (1) *symmetrical* communication moves or (2) *complementary* communication moves. In

symmetrical spirals, as Person One does "more of the same" Person Two also does "more of the same"—for example, two people shouting at each other. In complementary spirals, as Person One does "more of the same" Person Two does "more of the opposite"—Person A shouts and Person B withdraws in silence (Wilden, 1980).

4. At any given period of time, a spiral is contributing to the relationship in either generative or degenerative ways. Generative spirals promote positive feelings about the relationship and more closeness; degenerative spirals induce negative feelings about the relationship and more distance.

5. Both generative and degenerative spirals tend to continue accelerating until the participants check the movement by some action.

6. Spirals can be changed, their pace quickened or slowed, or the direction reversed by the participants' actions.

7. Based on the communication spirals that unfold, relationships expand, wither, and repeat patterns of close–far.

A diagram of the nature of spirals in Figure 1 shows how the dynamics of the communication for both persons tend to increase over time. Notice how the cycles get larger and larger across time—which is the nature of all communication spirals.

Generative Spirals

When communicative behaviors interlock to produce more positive feelings about the relationship, the participants are in a *generative spiral*. For instance, the teacher who can be open and accepting of students often experiences such spirals. Searching for the positive in a student and rewarding him or her appropriately can open a student up for teacher influence. The more genuinely the teacher relates to the student, the better the student performs; the higher the quality of his or her performance, the more positive the teacher becomes.

Generative spirals are obviously not limited to teacher–student relationships. A highly motivated worker illustrates the same ever-widening nature of spirals. As one improves working conditions, the worker's motivation increases, which cycles back and makes for an even better climate, which increases . . .

In generative spirals, the perceptions of the partners become more productive and their mutual adjustments continue to build. In romantic couples, "love generates more love, growth more growth, and knowledge more knowledge" (O'Neill & O'Neill, 1972). The favorableness builds upon itself. Trust and understanding cycle back to create more trust and understanding. The relationship is precisely like a spiral—ever-widening.

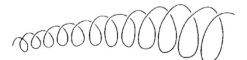

FIGURE 1 A communication spiral.

We all experience generative spirals. The student who begins doing work of a high caliber earns better grades, becomes self-motivated, and enters a generative spiral. Each piece of work brings a reward (good grades or praise) that further encourages him or her to feats of excellence. And if conditions are favorable, the spiral can continue. Teachers who retrain and become more knowledgeable discover that they have more to offer students. The excited students, in turn, reinforce the teachers' desire to work hard so they can feel even better about their profession. In generative spirals, the actions of each individual [supply] a multiplier effect in reinforcement. The better you do, the more worthwhile you feel; the more worthwhile you feel, the better you do. The effects of a simple action reverberate throughout the system. An unexpected tenderness from your loved one, for instance, will not stop there. It will recycle back to you and probably come from you again in increased dosage. A good relationship with your supervisor promotes you to want to please more, and the supervisor seeing your increased involvement, gives even more recognition to you.

Degenerative Spirals

Degenerative spirals are mirror images of generative spirals; the process is identical, but the results are opposite. In a degenerative spiral misunderstanding and discord create more and more relationship damage. As with generative spirals, degenerative spirals take many forms.

The inability to reach out and develop meaningful relationships is often compounded. The person who has reduced interest in others and does not form effective relationships suffers a lower self-esteem (because self-esteem is socially derived), which in turn cycles back and produces less interest in others. "The process is cyclical and degenerative" (Ziller, 1973). Or if one is afraid to love others, he or she shuns people, which in turn makes it more difficult to love. Also, such degenerative spirals often happen to people with regard to their sense of worth concerning work. People who have not established themselves in their profession but have been in the profession for a number of years may get caught in a spiral. They may spend time trying to appear busy, talking about others, or using various techniques to establish some sense of worth. Behavior that can change the spiral—working hard or retraining—are those least likely to occur. It is a self-fulfilling prophecy with a boost—it gets worse and worse. With each new gamut or ploy perfected (acquiring a new hobby, joining numerous social gatherings, etc.), the performance issues become further submerged.

A simple example of a degenerative spiral is the case of a lonely person. Lonely people tend to be less involved, less expressive, and less motivated in interactions. As a result, their partners in the conversation see the lonely person as uninvolved and less competent, and are less likely to initiate and maintain conversations with them. As a result, lonely people become further isolated from the social networks needed to break the cycle (Spitzberg & Canary, 1985).

Degenerative cycles are readily apparent when a relationship begins disintegrating. When distrust feeds distrust, defensiveness soars and the relationship worsens, and such "runaway relationships" become destructive for all concerned. In a "gruesome twosome," for instance, the two participants maintain a close, negative relationship. Each person receives fewer gratifications from the relationship, yet they maintain the attachment by mutual exploitation (Scheflen, 1960). When the relationship prevents one or both partners from gratifying normal needs, but the relationship is maintained, the twosome is caught in a degenerative spiral. Recent marital research demonstrates that, as love declines, negative conflict increases—a clear degenerative spiral (Lloyd & Cate, 1985).

Degenerative spirals, like generative spirals, occur in a variety of forms. A typical case involves the breakup of a significant relationship such as marriage. During a quarreling session one evening the husband says to the wife, "If you had not gone and gotten involved in an outside relationship with another man, our marriage could have made it. You just drained too much energy from us for our marriage to work." The wife responds by saying, "Yes, and had you given me the attention and care I longed for, I wouldn't have had an outside relationship." The infinite regress continues, each of them finding fault with why the other caused the termination of the marriage. The spiraling nature is clear. The more the wife retreats to an outside relationship, the less chance she has of having her needs met in the marriage. And the more the husband avoids giving her what she wants in the relationship, the more she will be influenced to seek outside relationships. One of the most common negative spirals between wives and husbands occurs when (1) the husband withdraws emotionally and (2) the wife expresses dissatisfaction to the husband (Segrin & Fitzpatrick, 1992).

Degenerative spirals are not limited to romantic relationships—they occur in all types. Parents and children often get caught up in spirals that create a dysfunctional system. The more dependent the child is on the parent, the more responsible and overburdened the parent is. And the more the parent takes responsibility for the child, the more this promotes dependence on the part of the child. It works like this: "One's actions toward other people generally effect a mirror duplication or a counter-measure from the other. This in turn tends to strengthen one's original action" (Leary, 1955). . . .

Altering Degenerative Spirals

Spirals, obviously, do change, with people going in and out of generative and degenerative spirals over the course of a relationship. And, as a relationship participant, you can have impact on the nature of the spirals—even altering degenerative spirals once they start. There are specific choices you can make that can alter the direction a relationship is flowing.

First, alter your usual response—do what comes unnaturally. For example, if you are in a relationship where you and the other tend to escalate, call each other names, you can stop the spiral by simply not allowing yourself to use negative language. Or, you can say, "This will just lead to a shouting match. I'm going to take a walk and talk with you when I come back," then exit from the normally hostile situation. Or say you have a roommate who is not very talkative and over the past 2 months you have tried to draw him out. You see that the more you talk, the more he retreats and the less he talks. Doing "more of the same" does not work, so do "less of the same." Don't act on the natural inclination to talk when he is silent; in fact, talk less and outwait him. Similarly, if you are often quiet in a group of four friends, people adapt to that by sometimes leaving you out of the decisions. Then, for the first time, begin to tell them what you would like to do. Change the patterns, and you change the spiral.

Wilmot and Stevens (1994) interviewed over 100 people who had "gone through a period of decline," and then improved their romantic, friendship, and family relationships—basically pulling out of a degenerative spiral. When asked what they did to "turn it around," it was found that a potent way of altering the patterns was to change behavior. The changes of behavior, of course, took many forms, given the particular type of relationship spiral that had occurred. Some people became more independent, some gave more "space" to the other, others changed locations or moved, and still others sacrificed for the partner or spent more time together. But the basic principle is the same—when in a degenerating or escalating set of communication patterns, change!

One last anecdote about changing patterns. I know one parent whose 11-year-old daughter was getting low grades in school. The parent had been a superb student, and the daughter, in the past, had done well. But, in the middle of the school year, the daughter started getting lower and lower grades. As the grades went down, the parent's criticism went up. Pretty soon, both the girl's grades and the mother-daughter relationship were in the cellar! After some help from an outsider, the mother took a vow to *not* talk anymore about grades, regardless of what happened. It was very difficult, for each evening the two had been arguing about grades; grades had become the focal point of the entire relationship. It only took 2 weeks, and the daughter's grades made dramatic jumps. The mother, who found "giving up" very difficult, had taken her negative part out of the communication system—and it changed.

One final note on changing your behavior. The people in the Wilmot and Stevens (1994) study noted that "persistence" was one important key to bringing about a change in the relationship. If the parent above had only stopped her criticism for one night, as soon as she resumed it, off the spiral would have gone again. The other person will be suspicious of your change at first, probably question your motives and other negative interpretations. But if you are persistent in bringing the change, it will have effects on the other person, for his or her communication patterns are interlocked with yours.

Second, you can use third parties constructively. Friends, counselors, relatives, clergy, and others can sometimes provide a different perspective for you to begin to open up a degenerative system for change. Third parties can often make specific suggestions that will break the pattern of interlocking, mutually destructive behaviors that keep adding fuel to the degenerating relationship. In one case, a husband and wife went to a marriage counselor because they had come to a standoff. He was tired of her demands to always talk to her and pay attention. She was tired of his demands for more frequent sexual activity. As result, they became entrapped in a degenerative spiral—he talked less, and she avoided situations of physical intimacy. Upon seeing the counselor, they both realized that they were getting nowhere fast. Each was trying to get the other to change first. With the help of the counselor, they renegotiated their relationship, and each began giving a little bit. Over a period of a few days they found themselves coming out of the degenerating patterns.

Third, you can reaffirm your relational goals. Often when people get stuck in negative patterns of interaction, the other automatically assumes you want to "jump ship." If you are in a downward spiral, whether with your parents, boss, lover, child, or friend, reaffirming what you each have to gain from the relationship can promote efforts to get it back. The couple who saw the counselor found that they both had an important goal to stay together—for if either one had "won" the fight and lost the relationship, neither would have gotten what he or she wanted. Relational reaffirmation can help you focus on all the things you can do to get the relationship back to a more positive phase. Good relationships take energy to sustain; similarly, making a commitment to the relationship obvious to the other will help pull you out of the debilitating negative patterns.

Fourth, you can alter a spiral by metacommunicating. Wilmot and Stevens' (1994) respondents reported having a "Big Relationship Talk"— talking about the relationship and what had led to the degenerating series of actions. When you comment on what you see happening, it can open up the spiral itself for discussion. One can say, "Our relationship seems to be slipping—I find myself criticizing you, and you seem to be avoiding me, and it looks like it is getting worse. What can we do to turn it around?" Such metacommunication, whether pointed to the conversational episodes or the overall relationship patterns, can set the stage for productive conflict management and give participants a sense of a control over the relationship dynamics. Metacommunication, especially when coupled with a reaffirmation of your relational goals ("I don't want us to be unhappy, I want us to both like being together, but we seem to . . ."), can alter the destructive forces in a relationship. And, of course, you can use metacommunication in any type of relationship, such as on the job. J.P., for example, says, "Sally, it seems to me like our work enthusiasm is slipping away. What might we do to get that sense of fun back like we had about 6 months ago?"

Fifth, try to spend more or less time with the person. If you are on the "outs" with your co-workers, you could begin to spend more time with them—go to lunch, have coffee, take short strolls together. It is amazing what kinds of large changes can be purchased with just a small amount of time. Likewise, relationships often suffer because the people spend more time together than they can productively handle. So Tom always goes on a 3-day fishing trip with me in the summer as a way to both get more distance and independence in his marriage (and, coincidentally, to reaffirm our relationship with one another). Getting more distance and independence can bring you back refreshed and ready to relate again. Interestingly, Wilmot and Stevens (1994) found such "independence" moves as an important way to alter a degenerating spiral.

Finally, we all recognize that changing an external situation can alter a degenerating relationship. One parent has a son who got into an ongoing battle with the principal of the junior high school. The feud went on for months, with the principal (according to the mother) tormenting her boy and the boy retaliating by being mischievous. The mutually destructive actions were arrested only when the boy switched schools. He (and the principal) had a chance to start over, not contaminated by the previous interlocking patterns.

Another way to change the external situation is to stay in the presence of the other person but move to a new environment. Many married couples have gone for extended vacations in order to give themselves time to work out new solutions to relationship problems. If the relationship is important to you and you want to preserve it, effort expended to help the relationship reach productive periods is time well spent. Retreats, for business partners, romantic partners, and friends, can allow an infusion of fresh energy into a declining relationship. Because once the degenerative phases are reached, the behaviors of each person tend to be mutually reinforcing and damaging. Each person can blame the other and claim his or her own innocence, but that will not alter the degeneration. It sometimes takes long hard work to alter a negative spiral, and it may be successful if both put in some effort. But as every counselor knows from experience, one person alone can usually not change the relationship. If that person makes changes, and the other reciprocates, you have a chance to turn the spiral around.

Woody Allen captured the essence of relational change when he said, "Relationships are like a shark. They either move forward, or they die." Our relationships are dynamic, always moving and changing either toward or away from improvement. Participants' behaviors interlock so that each one's behavior influences the others, and the mutually conjoined behaviors intensify the other's reactions.

People look at their relationships using different time frames. Some people tend to only look at the macro perspective, charting the changes in yearly units such as "do I feel as good about my job today as I did a year ago." A relationship may not look any different today than it did yesterday, but over a year's time, you can see either overall improvement or disintegration. The long-term spirals are identified by comparing the relationship to a much earlier state.

Other times one may process and categorize a relationship on an hour-by-hour basis. For example, when Jan's romantic partner announced that she wanted to "call it off," Jan spent the next 2 weeks thinking about the relationship, talking to her partner, and doing endless processing of all the changes coming her way. Rapid relational change, especially if it is unexpected, can cause intense processing of the relationship, sometimes to the point of overload. Those who suffer from an unexpected firing, termination of a romance, or disinheritance from the family find themselves processing at a depth they didn't think possible.

What is important, is to begin to sensitize yourself to the ebbs and flows inherent in all relationships, so you can make informed choices. Becoming attuned to the nature of communication spirals can increase your understanding of these processes.

TANGLES IN THE WEB:
PARADOXES AND CONUNDRUMS

As you go through life, whether you are 18 or 80, the experience and under-standing of your relationships is not a linear, step-by-step process. Like rela-tionships themselves, our understanding is imperfect, and it is easy to overesti-mate how much we know. Relationships are elusive.

There are some relational paradoxes (statements that are both true but con-tradict one another) (Wilmot, 1987) and conundrums—puzzlements and ele-ments that are inherently unsolvable. Here are a few of them.

1. We want contradictory things in relationships: freedom and closeness, openness to talk yet protection, stability and excitement. These dialectic ten-sions seem to be present in all relationships.

In many romantic relationships we want both freedom and connection, excite-ment and stability. In the family context we often want the others to accept who we are, yet we spend inordinate amounts of time centering on how we can change them. We talk openly about the importance of "communication" in re-lationships, but it appears to be more of a cultural belief than an actual fact (Wilmot & Stevens, 1994; Parks, 1982). Maybe we can begin to celebrate the ten-sion inherent in all relationships rather than trying to solve the contradictory needs, flowing with the needs as they change back and forth.

2. Both insider and outsider views of relationships are fraught with errors.

Outsiders to relationships can more accurately observe our actual communica-tion behavior but are less accurate than we are at specifying the *meaning* of those behaviors within this particular relationship. When you, as an outsider, look at someone else's relationship, your judgments can be a good projective test for what you personally believe is the "key" to success. Think of a marriage you know that you would describe as high quality. To what would you attribute it?

- hard work
- good match on background characteristics
- being raised in non-dysfunctional families
- luck
- how well they communicate with one another
- a fine match on introversion/extroversion
- similar religious affiliations
- the support of their networks of family and friends
- both being raised in the same part of the country
- the length of time they have been together
- their ability to raise children successfully
- their mutual respect and compassion
- their intelligence

- their warmth and expressiveness
- their similar life struggles
- their commitment to one another
- their clarity about how to perform their roles
- their overriding love of one another
- their supportive friends
- similar hobbies and pastimes
- being at the same level of attractiveness

Outsiders, looking at someone else's relationship, tend to rely on external or situational factors in making their guesses (Burgoon & Newton, 1991). And we tend to evaluate others a bit more harshly than they do themselves, with us seeing the limitations of one or both of the partners: "I can't believe she stays married to him—he is so boring in public." When looking at someone's communication behavior, outsiders judge conversations less favorably than do those on the inside (Street, Mulac, & Wiemann, 1988). Outsiders generate faulty hypotheses about the intentions of the communicators—"she did that because she wants to control him" (Stafford, Waldron, & Infield, 1989). When we observe others' communication, we compensate for lack of information about their internal states by using our own personal theories—our "implicit personality theories" (Stafford, Waldron, & Infield, 1989). As an outsider, our observations are fraught with errors and overinterpretations, sort of "what we get is what we see," with most of it coming from us.

As insiders, our views aren't any less biased; we just tend to focus on different aspects (Dillard, 1987; Sillars & Scott, 1983). For example, insiders to marital relationships tend to overestimate their similarity and act with confidence on their views of the other. Yet the perceptions are not objectively accurate. Therefore, *all* views of relationships are inherently distorted—outsiders and insiders alike. Researchers and book writers (including this one) are themselves influenced by their own needs and perspectives, often looking for some order in the midst of considerable chaos.

3. Relationships are problematic—if we don't do anything about their natural dynamic, they may atrophy. If we try to force them, to "make them happen," we may destroy their essential nature.

The natural forces on relationships, marriage partners having to earn a living and nurture children, friends moving away from one another, tend to move most in the direction of decreased quality over time. In a sense, it is as if there is an energy in relationships that, if you don't continually reinvest in it, will cause the relationship to atrophy. Yet, on the other hand, we need to not try to "force" relationships. It is a rare individual in this culture who can command himself or herself to "love" someone else. The question of how to enhance a long-term relationship—whether family, romantic, or friend—looms large for all of us. . . . It is clear that, so far, there are no guarantees in relationships.

4. Committed relationships, such as marriage, may bring us much unhappiness because we think their purpose is happiness generation. Maybe their purpose is wholeness, grounded in the dialectical encounter between mates (Guggenbuhl-Craig, 1977).

In North America and most western cultures, people choose marriage partners and friends for what they do for us—make us happy, excite us sexually, provide a sense of fun and connection. Yet . . . , maybe this "what does it do for me" sets us up for disappointment and failure. From a spiritual perspective, one could say that our relationships, while started to "make us happy," have a more difficult and nobler purpose—to allow us to be challenged, to grow, and to change. Lifetime friends, for example, may serve the function of helping us correct ourselves when we get out of line in public. Romantic partners will set the stage for our unresolved issues of life and eccentricity to flourish, and see their downside. Family members will test our commitment, resilience and love, and if we move through that test we can emerge on a higher plane of relatedness.

5. The more intimacy and closeness we want, the more risk we face in the relationship. The greatest pleasure *and* pain come from those to whom we are the closest. Relationships bring both joy and suffering.

The very relationships people spend so much time processing—romantic, family, and friendships—are the ones to bring both the extremes of joy and pain. The less close relationships, while they can bring stability and meaning into life, may not address some of our deepest needs. Risk and reward seem to be opposite sides of the same coin.

6. We often see the "self" as concrete and findable. Yet relationships are no less "real" than an individual self is.

In our culture, we take, as has been noted many times, the "self" as individual, disconnected, separate, and findable. We put the locus of most things into the self—discussing "self-esteem" and "personality" as if they were real things and not abstract concepts. Relationships are neither more nor less figments of our concepts than are our selves—but we don't tend to see it that way in this culture. It is important to note that our selves do have a conventional reality—there is a person standing there. Yet upon close examination, the "self" cannot be found. Is your brain yourself? Your torso? Your legs? Your emotions? We impose the concept of "self" onto the physical and emotional aspects and stop our analysis. Relationships, while not physically represented, are no less real than are our selves. We talk about relationships, and their "reality," upon examination, is just as findable (and no less so) than that of the self.

7. Self is produced in relationship to others; relationships are produced from two selves.

. . . It has been argued that we originate and live in-relation; we co-create our selves in relation to one another. And relationships are produced from the two persons who have a communication connection. Self and other produce, and are produced by, relationship. And self is more fruitfully viewed as "with the eco-logical system" rather than as the center of one's world (Broome, 1991, p. 375).

8. The greatest individual growth, and the greatest derailment of individ-ual growth, come from the hurt and disappointment of relationships gone awry. Relationships can serve as springboards for growth or just toss you higher so you land harder.

When we face the natural traumas of life, our response determines the outcome. Trauma can bring transformation or derailment. Some people are broken when a relationship terminates, for example, or when an important person dies. Oth-ers, through grieving and slowly transforming themselves, reopen to relation-ships and life, reconnecting anew and building better relationships in the future.

9. We can solve problems in relationships by (1) internal, personal change; and (2) changing the external, communication connection between the two. Change at any one level reverberates to the other level, for both us and the other person.

Like the chicken and the egg, which comes first—you or relationship? And if you have difficulties, do you "get your stuff together" and then reenter other re-lationships, or do you begin other relationships so you can become stronger? Both routes are used, and both can work. If you undergo change, it will rever-berate in all your relationships: the boundaries are permeable. If your relation-ship changes, it will alter you; the influence always flows both ways.

10. We can't fully understand our relationships without concepts, and as soon as we use an abstract notion we impose its limitations on what we are see-ing. Labels are essential and limiting, and cannot capture an ever-changing re-ality. As Wilden says, "all theories of relationship require a certain artificial clo-sure" (Wilden, 1980, p. 114).

We can't really proceed with understanding without labels, and when you in-troduce your "boyfriend" to your family, it gives them a clue about the rela-tionship. Yet when you use the label, it restricts both your and the other's views of that relationship. Each relationship contains many complex and contradic-tory elements, and it cannot be accurately captured by "boyfriend." Further, there is always "label lag"—the relationship changes, and the label stays the same. A "married couple" of 6 months will be very different than that very same couple at 6 years or 6 decades, yet they are still referred to as married. All con-cepts and labels are limiting and constricting—and essential.

11. General conclusions about gender, culture, and relationships may not apply at all to your particular relationships.

One of the problems in talking about "gender" or "cultural" effects is that we are always talking about groupings that help us "understand" on an abstract level. But your particular relationship may not reflect the general norms at all.

Just like a theory of gravity cannot tell you about when a particular apple will fall from a tree, studying relational dynamics will not tell you about what will happen in your relationship. When studies on gender, for example, show that females are more expressive than males, what do you do if the woman in a cross-sex romantic relationship is the less expressive of the two? It is probably better to focus on the central issue—expressiveness, and the match or mismatch between the partners—rather than trying to reflect the general norm. Similarly, the finding that gay males have more partners than lesbians or heterosexuals does not mean that a gay man cannot live a life of commitment to another.

12. Learning about relationships occurs before, during, and after the relationship is a findable event.

Our perspectives on our relationships do not end—they only change. Just think for a moment about how you interpret events that happened to you in your childhood. As you move through time you will reinterpret them many times, focusing on different aspects, and seeing them in a different light. Likewise, the friendship that you used to see as a barometer of yourself may be later seen as not helping you at all at a stage of life. A devastating romantic termination may be seen later as the "best thing that ever happened to me." While many of us do not seek difficulties, most of us say, in retrospect, that it is what produced the learning so essential to the next stage of our life. I was once talking to a fellow on a flight from Helsinki, Finland, to Boston. He was in a long-distance relationship with a Finnish woman, and he lived in Boston, and here is what he said. "I did fatherhood and marriage, so I guess I'm doing this for awhile"—making retrospective sense of his relationship that was allowing him to collect considerable frequent flyer miles!

REVIEW QUESTIONS

1. Define *communication spiral.*
2. According to this reading, what is necessary in order to stop a spiral?
3. What's the difference between a generative and a degenerative spiral?
4. What does Wilmot and Stevens's research indicate about the role of persistence in altering a degenerative spiral?
5. What is metacommunicating?
6. What is a dialectic tension in a relationship?
7. What are the specific problems Wilmot identifies with both insider and outsider views of a relationship?

PROBES

1. Explain what Bill means when he says that, in a spiral, "each person's behavior accelerates the dynamism of the relationship." Give an example that includes a positive dynamism and one that includes a negative dynamism.

2. Could a spiral that appears to be generative to some member(s) of a relationship appear to be degenerative to others? Explain.

3. What is one generative spiral in your communication experience that you could *enhance?* What is one degenerative spiral in your communication experience that you could *break?*

4. Wilmot suggests that one of the ways you can "do what comes unnaturally" is to stop trying to make things better. Explain why this might work.

5. Wilmot suggests that you might change an external situation in order to alter a degenerating spiral. This could include changing locations—moving your home, work, or school. But some people also emphasize that, "Wherever you go, there you are," which is to say that you need to change your attitude or approach, not your location. What do you think works best?

6. Do you believe that the main purpose of a long-term relationship like a marriage is happiness generation or what Bill calls "wholeness, grounded in the dialectical encounter between mates"?

7. What is the relationship between Bill's brief discussion of the self in paradoxes 6 and 7 and Stewart and Logan's discussion of the self in this chapter's first reading?

8. Identify one general conclusion about gender, culture, and relationships that does *not* apply to one of your relationships.

REFERENCES

Bateson, G. (1972). *Steps to an Ecology of Mind.* New York: Ballentine Books.

Bateson, G. (1979). *Mind and Nature: A Necessary Unity.* New York: Bantam Books.

Broome, B. J. (1991). Building shared meaning: Implications of a relational approach to empathy for teaching intercultural communication. *Communication Education, 40,* 235–249.

Burgoon, J. K., & Newton, D. A. (1991). Applying a social meaning model to relational message interpretations of conversational involvement: Comparing observer and participant perspectives. *The Southern Communication Journal, 56,* 96–113.

Dillard, J. P. (1987). Close relationships at work: Perceptions of the motives and performance of relational participants. *Journal of Social and Personal Relationships, 4,* 179–193.

Guggenbuhl-Craig, A. (1977). *Marriage Dead or Alive.* Murray Stein (trans.). Dallas, TX: Spring Publication.

Kurdek, L. A. (1991). Marital stability and changes in marital quality in newly wed couples: A test of the contextual model. *Journal of Social and Personal Relationships, 5,* 201–221.

Leary, T. (1955). The theory and measurement methodology of interpersonal communication. *Psychiatry, 18,* 147–161.

Lloyd, S. A., & Cate, R. M. (1985). The developmental course of conflict in dissolution of premarital relationships. *Journal of Social and Personal Relationships, 2,* 179–194.

O'Neill, N., & O'Neill, G. (1972). *Open Marriage*. New York: M. Evans.

Parks, M. R. (1982). Ideology in interpersonal communication: Off the couch and into the world. In Burgoon, M. (Ed.), *Communication Yearbook 5*. New Brunswick, NJ: International Communication Association/Transaction Books, pp. 79–107.

Rose, S., & Serafica, F. C. (1986). Keeping and ending casual, close and best friendships. *Journal of Social and Personal Relationships, 3*, 275–288.

Scheflen, A. (1960). Communication and Regulation in Psychotherapy, *Psychiatry, 26*, 126–136.

Segrin, C., & Fitzpatrick M. A. (1992). Depression and verbal aggressiveness in different marital types. *Communication Studies, 43*, 79–91.

Sillars, A. L., & Scott, M. D. (1983). Interpersonal perception between intimates: An integrative review. *Human Communication Research, 10*, 153–176.

Spitzberg, B. H., & Canary, D. J. (1985). Loneliness and relationally competent communication. *Journal of Social and Personal Relationships, 2*, 387–402.

Stafford, L., Waldron, V. R., & Infield, L. L. (1989). Actor-observer differences in conversational memory. *Human Communication Research, 15*, 590–611.

Street, R. L., Jr., Mulac, A., & Wiemann, J. M. (1988). Speech evaluation differences as a function of perspective (participant versus observer) and presentational medium. *Human Communication Research, 14*, 333–363.

Wilden, A. (1980). *System and Structure: Essays on Communication and Exchange, 2nd ed.* London: Tavistock Publication.

Wilmot, W. W. (1987). *Dyadic Communication*. New York: Random House.

Wilmot, W. W., & Stevens, D. C. (1994). Relationship rejuvenation: Arresting decline in personal relationships. In Conville, R. (Ed.), *Communication and Structure*. Philadelphia, PA: Ablex, pp. 103–124.

Ziller, R. C. (1973). *The Social Self*. New York: Pergamon Press.

The human person needs confirmation. . . . An animal does not need to be confirmed, for it is what it is unquestionably. It is different with [the person]. Sent forth from the natural domain of species into the hazard of the solitary category, surrounded by the air of a chaos which came into being with him, secretly and bashfully he watches for a Yes which allows him to be and which can come to him only from one human person to another. It is from one [person] to another that the heavenly bread of self-being is passed.*

—Martin Buber

---

*"Distance and Relation" by Martin Buber from *The Knowledge of Man*, edited by Maurice Friedman and translated by Maurice Friedman and Ronald Gregor Smith. (New York & Row, 1965), p. 71.

C onfirmation and its opposite—disconfirmation—are important elements of the process of negotiating selves. As the quotation by Martin Buber suggests, confirmation or disconfirmation exists to some degree or another in *every* relationship, and they distinguish the most positive relationships from the most toxic ones.

Confirmation means actively acknowledging a person as a person, recognizing him or her as a subject, a unique, unmeasurable, choosing, reflective, and addressable human. The authors of this next reading point out that Buber was the first to use the term in this interpersonal sense. In the words quoted above, Buber identifies confirmation as a phenomenon that distinguishes the human world from the nonhuman. His point is that we discover our personhood or humanness as we make contact with others. I learn that I am a person when I experience confirmation from another person. This is one of the crucial functions of communication: to confirm others and experience confirmation myself.

Ken Cissna and Evelyn Sieburg are two speech communication teachers who studied confirmation for several years. This essay is nicely organized into a section that defines and describes confirmation, a section that identifies its four main dimensions, and then a longer section that talks systematically about confirming and disconfirming behaviors.

The authors describe and illustrate how what they call indifferent responses, impervious responses, and disqualifying responses are all disconfirming. Indifference denies the other's existence, while imperviousness means responding only to my image of you, even if it contradicts your perception of yourself. We communicate indifference, for example, by avoiding eye contact or physical contact or by ignoring topics the other person brings up. Imperviousness can be communicated, for example, with "Don't be silly—of course you're not afraid," or, "Stop crying, there's nothing the matter with you!" Disqualification is the technique of denying without really saying "no," as we do when, for example, we utter the "sigh of martyrdom," respond tangentially to the other person, or say something like, "If I were going to criticize, I'd say your haircut looks awful, but I wouldn't say that."

Responses that confirm, the authors point out, are less clearly defined than disconfirming ones. However, they identify three clusters of confirmation: recognition, acknowledgment, and endorsement. They also emphasize that "confirming response is dialogic in structure; it is a reciprocal activity involving shared talk and sometimes shared silence." This echoes the points about contact and the between that I've made and that have been made by several other contributors to this book.

PATTERNS OF INTERACTIONAL
CONFIRMATION AND DISCONFIRMATION

Kenneth N. Cissna and Evelyn Sieburg

The term "confirmation" was first used in an interpersonal sense by Martin Buber (1957), who attributed broad existential significance to confirmation, describing it as basic to humanness and as providing the test of the degree of humanity present in any society. Although Buber did not explicitly define confirmation, he consistently stressed its importance to human intercourse:

> The basis of man's life with man is twofold, and it is one—the wish of every man to be *confirmed* as what he is, even as what he can become, by men; and the innate capacity in man to confirm his fellow men in this way. . . . Actual humanity exists only where this capacity unfolds. [p. 102]

R. D. Laing (1961) quoted extensively from Buber in his description of confirmation and disconfirmation as communicated qualities which exist in the relationship between two or more persons. Confirmation is the process through which individuals are "endorsed" by others, which, as Laing described it, implies recognition and acknowledgment of them. Though Laing developed confirmation at a conceptual level more thoroughly than anyone prior to him, his focus remained psychiatric: he was concerned with the effects of pervasive disconfirmation within the families of patients who had come to be diagnosed as schizophrenic. In such families, Laing noted, one child is frequently singled out as the recipient of especially destructive communicative acts by the other members. As Laing explained it, the behavior of the family "does not so much involve a child who has been subjected to outright neglect or even to obvious trauma, but a child who has been subjected to subtle but persistent *disconfirmation,* usually unwittingly" (1961:83). Laing further equated confirmation with a special kind of love, which "lets the other be, but with affection and concern," as contrasted with disconfirmation (or violence), which "attempts to constrain the other's freedom, to force him to act in the way we desire, but with ultimate lack of concern, with indifference to the other's own existence or destiny" (1967:58). This theme of showing concern while relinquishing control is common in psychiatric writing and is an important element in confirmation as we understand it. Although Laing stressed the significance of confirmation, he made no attempt to define it in terms of specific behaviors, noting only its variety of modes:

> Modes of confirmation or disconfirmation vary. Confirmation could be through a responsive smile (visual), a handshake (tactile), an expression of sympathy (auditory). A confirmatory response is *relevant* to the evocative action, it accords

recognition to the evocatory act, and accepts its significance for the other, if not for the respondent. A confirmatory reaction is a direct response, it is "to the point," "on the same wavelength," as the initiatory or evocatory action. [1961:82]

In 1967, Watzlawick, Beavin, and Jackson located confirmation within a more general framework of human communication and developed it as a necessary element of all human interaction, involving a subtle but powerful validation of the other's self-image. In addition to its content, they said each unit of interaction also contains relational information, offering first, a self-definition by a person (P) and then a response from the other (O) to that self-definition. According to Watzlawick *et al.,* this response may take any of three possible forms: it may confirm, it may reject, or it may disconfirm. The last, disconfirmation, implies the relational message, "You do not exist," and negates the other as a valid message source. Confirmation implies acceptance of the speaker's self-definition. "As far as we can see, this confirmation of *P's* view of himself by O is probably the greatest single factor ensuring mental development and stability that has so far emerged from our study of communication" (p. 84). The descriptive material provided by Watzlawick *et al.* to illustrate disconfirmation includes instances of total unawareness of the person, lack of accurate perception of the other's point of view, and deliberate distortion or denial of the other's self-attributes.

Sieburg (1969) used the structure provided by Watzlawick as well as the concept of confirmation/disconfirmation to begin distinguishing between human communication which is growthful, productive, effective, functional, or "therapeutic," and communication which is not. She developed measurement systems for systematically observing confirming and disconfirming communication (1969, 1972); she devised the first scale which allowed for measurement of an individual's feeling of being confirmed by another person (1972). She has continued to refine the basic theory of confirmation (1975), and has recently used the concepts to describe both organizational (1976) and family communication systems. During this time, a growing body of theoretical development and empirical research has attempted to explore these important concerns (cf. Cissna, 1976a, 1976b). . . .

DIMENSIONS OF CONFIRMATION

In the few direct allusions in the literature to confirmation and disconfirmation, several different elements are suggested. Confirmation is, of course, tied by definition to self-experience; our first problem, therefore, was to identify the specific aspects of self-experience that could be influenced positively or negatively in interaction with others. Four such elements seemed significant for our purpose:

1. The element of existence (the individual sees self as existing)
2. The element of relating (the individual sees self as a being-in-relation with others)

3. The element of significance, or worth
4. The element of validity of experience

Thus, it was assumed that the behavior of one person toward another is confirming to the extent that it performs the following functions in regard to the other's self-experience:

1. It expresses recognition of the other's existence
2. It acknowledges a relationship of affiliation with the other
3. It expresses awareness of the significance or worth of the other
4. It accepts or "endorses" the other's self-experience (particularly emotional experience)

Each unit of response is assumed to evoke relational metamessages with regard to each of the above functions, which can identify it as either confirming or disconfirming:

Confirming	Disconfirming
"To me, you exist."	"To me, you do not exist."
"We are relating."	"We are not relating."
"To me, you are significant."	"To me, you are not significant."
"Your way of experiencing your world is valid."	"Your way of experiencing your world is invalid."

In attempting to find behavioral correlates of these functions, we acknowledge that it is not possible to point with certainty to particular behaviors that universally perform these confirming functions for all persons, since individuals differ in the way they interpret the same acts; that is, they interpret the stimuli and assign their own meaning to them. Despite this reservation about making firm causal connections between the behavior of one person and the internal experience of another, we have followed the symbolic interactionist view that certain symbolic cues *do* acquire consensual validation and therefore are consistently interpreted by most persons as reflecting certain attitudes toward them on the part of others. Such cues thus have message value and are capable of arousing in the receiver feelings of being recognized or ignored, accepted or rejected, understood or misunderstood, humanized or "thingified," valued or devalued. This assumption was borne out in a very general way by our research to date (Sieburg & Larson, 1971). . . .

SYSTEMATIZING DISCONFIRMING BEHAVIOR

A variety of specific acts and omissions have been noted by clinicians and theoreticians as being damaging to some aspect of the receiver's self-view. We have arranged these behaviors into three general groupings, or clusters, each representing a somewhat different style of response:

1. Indifferent response (denying existence or relation)

2. Impervious response (denying self-experience of the other)
3. Disqualifying response (denying the other's significance)

These clusters include verbal/nonverbal and vocal/nonvocal behaviors. Since they encompass both content and process features of interaction, scorers must be trained to evaluate each scoring unit in terms of its manifest content, its transactional features, and its underlying structure. In either case, no single utterance stands alone since it is always in response to some behavior or another, and is so experienced by the other as having implications about his or her self.

Disconfirmation by Indifference

To deny another's existence is to deny the most fundamental aspect of self-experience. Indifference may be total, as when presence is denied; it may imply rejection of relatedness with the other; or it may only deny the other's attempt to communicate.

Denial of Presence   The absence of even a minimal show of recognition has been associated with alienation, self-destructiveness, violence against others, and with psychosis. Laing used the case of "Peter," a psychotic patient of 25 to illustrate the possible long-term effects of chronic indifference toward a child who may, as a consequence, come to believe that he has no presence at all—or to feel guilty that he *does*, feeling that he has no right even to occupy space.

> Peter . . . was a young man who was preoccupied with guilt *because* he occupied a place in the world, even in a physical sense. He could not realize . . . that he had a right to have any presence for others . . . A peculiar aspect of his childhood was that his presence in the world was largely ignored. No weight was given to the fact that he was in the same room while his parents had intercourse. He had been physically cared for in that he had been well fed and kept warm, and underwent no physical separation from his parents during his earlier years. Yet he had been consistently treated as though he did not "really" exist. Perhaps worse than the experience of physical separation was to be in the same room as his parents and ignored, not malevolently, but through sheer indifference. [Laing, 1961:119]

That such extreme indifference is also devastating to an adult is evident in the following excerpt from a marriage counseling session (Sieburg, personal audiotape). It is perhaps significant that throughout his wife's outburst, the husband sat silent and remote:

THERAPIST: . . . and is it okay to express emotion?
WIFE: Not in my house.
THERAPIST: Has he [the husband] ever *said* it's not okay to talk about feelings?
WIFE: But he never *says* anything!
THERAPIST: But he has ways of sending you messages?
WIFE: [loudly] Yes! And the message is *shut out*—no matter what I say, no matter what I do, I get no response—zero—shut out!

THERAPIST: And does that somehow make you feel you are wrong?

WIFE: Oh, of course not wrong—just *nothing!*

THERAPIST: Then what is it that makes you feel he disapproves of you?

WIFE: Because I get nothing! [tears] If I feel discouraged—like looking for a job all day and being turned down—and I cry—zero! No touching, no patting, no "Maybe tomorrow"—just *shut out.* And if I get angry at him, instead of getting angry back, he just walks away—just nothing! All the time I'm feeling shut out and shut off!

THERAPIST: And what is it you want from him?

WIFE: [quietly] Maybe sometimes just a pat on the back would be enough. But, no!—he just shrugs me off. Where am I supposed to go to feel real? [tears]

Avoiding Involvement   Extreme instances of indifference like those above are presumed to be rare because even the slightest attention at least confirms one's presence. Lesser shows of indifference, however, still create feelings of alienation, frustration, and lowered self-worth. Although recognition is a necessary first step in confirming another, it is not in itself sufficient unless accompanied by some further indication of a willingness to be involved.

The precise ways in which one person indicates to another that he or she is interested in relating (intimacy) are not fully known, but several clear indications of *unwillingness* to relate or to become more than minimally involved have emerged from research and have been included in our systemization of disconfirming behaviors. Of particular significance are the use of:

- Impersonal language—the avoidance of first person references (I, me, my, mine) in favor of a collective "we" or "one," or the tendency to begin sentences with "there" when making what amounts to a personal statement (as, "there seems to be . . .")
- Avoidance of eye contact
- Avoidance of physical contact except in ritualized situations such as handshaking
- Other nonverbal "distancing" cues

Rejecting Communication   A third way of suggesting indifference to another is to respond in a way that is unrelated, or only minimally related, to what he or she has just said, thus creating a break or disjunction in the flow of interaction.

Totally irrelevant response is, of course, much like denial of presence in that the person whose topic is repeatedly ignored may soon come to doubt his or her very existence, and at best will feel that he or she is not heard, attended to, or regarded as significant. Perhaps for this reason Laing called relevance the "crux of confirmation," noting that only by responding relevantly can one lend significance to another's communication and accord recognition (Laing, 1961:87).

The most extreme form of communication rejection is monologue, in which one speaker continues on and on, neither hearing nor acknowledging anything the other says. It reflects unawareness and lack of concern about the other person except as a socially acceptable audience for the speaker's own self-listening.

A less severe communication rejection occurs when the responder makes a connection, however slight, with what the other has said, but immediately shifts into something quite different of his or her own choosing.

Disconfirming by Imperviousness

The term "imperviousness" as used here follows Laing's usage and refers to a lack of accurate awareness of another's perceptions (Watzlawick *et al.*, 1967:91). Imperviousness is disconfirming because it denies or distorts another's self-expression and fosters dehumanized relationships in which one person perceives another as a pseudoimage rather than as what that person really is. Behaviorally, the impervious responder engages in various tactics that tend to negate or discredit the other's feeling expression. These may take the form of a flat denial that the other *has* such a feeling ("You don't really mean that"), or it may be handled more indirectly by reinterpreting the feeling in a more acceptable way, ("You're only saying that because . . ."), substituting some experience or feeling of the *listener* ("What you're trying to say is . . ."), challenging the speaker's right to have such a feeling ("How can you *possibly* feel that way after all that's been done for you?"), or some similar device intended to alter the feeling expressed. . . .

A slightly different form of imperviousness occurs when a responder creates and bestows on another an inaccurate identity, and then confirms the false identity, although it is not a part of the other's self-experience at all. Laing calls this pseudoconfirmation (1961:83). Thus a mother who insists that her daughter is always obedient and "never any trouble at all" may be able to interpret her daughter's most rebellious aggression in a way that fits the placid image she holds of her daughter, and the parents of even a murderous psychopath may be able to describe their son as a "good boy." Such a false confirmation frequently endorses the fiction of what the other is *wished* to be, without any real recognition of what the other is or how he/she feels. As noted earlier, this form of disconfirmation also appears as simply a well-meaning attempt to reassure another who is distressed, which too is usually motivated by the speaker's need to reduce his or her own discomfort.

> "Don't be silly—of course you're not afraid!"
>
> "You may think you feel that way now, but I know better."
>
> "Stop crying—there's nothing the matter with you!"
>
> "How can you possibly worry about a little thing like that?"
>
> "No matter what you say, I know you still love me."

Such responses constitute a rejection of the other person's expression and often identity, raising doubts about the validity of his/her way of experiencing by suggesting, "You don't really feel as you say you do; you are only imagining that you do."

A subtle variation of the same tactic occurs when the speaker responds in a selective way, rewarding the other with attention and relevant response *only* when he or she communicates in an approved fashion, and becoming silent or indifferent if the other's speech or behavior does not meet with the responder's approval. This may mean that the speaker limits response to those topics initiated by self, ignoring any topic initiated by the other person.

Imperviousness is considered disconfirming because it contributes to a feeling of uncertainty about self or uncertainty about the validity of personal experiencing. Imperviousness occurs when a person is told how he or she feels, regardless of how he or she experiences self, when a person's talents and abilities are described without any data to support such a description, when motives are ascribed to another without any reference to the other's own experience, or when one's own efforts at self-expression are ignored or discounted unless they match the false image held by some other person. . . .

Disconfirmation by Disqualification

According to Watzlawick (1964) disqualification is a technique which enables one to say something without really saying it, to deny without really saying "no," and to disagree without really disagreeing. Certain messages, verbal and nonverbal, are included in this group because they (a) disqualify the other speaker, (b) disqualify another message, or (c) disqualify themselves.

Speaker Disqualification   This may include such direct disparagement of the other as name-calling, criticism, blame, and hostile attack, but may also take the indirect form of the sigh of martyrdom, the muttered expletive, addressing an adult in a tone of voice usually reserved for a backward child, joking "on the square," sarcasm, or any of the other numerous tactics to make the other appear and feel too incompetent or unreliable for his message to have validity. This creates a particularly unanswerable put-down by evoking strong metamessages of insignificance or worthlessness. The following examples are spouses' responses from conjoint counseling sessions:

- "Can't you ever do anything right?"
- "Here we go again!" [sigh]
- "We heard you the first time—why do you always keep repeating yourself?"
- "It's no wonder the rear axle broke, with you in the back seat!" [laughter]
- "Why do you always have to get your mouth open when you don't know what you're talking about?"

Message Disqualification   Without regard to their content, some messages tend to discredit the other person because of their irrelevance—that is, they do not "follow" the other's prior utterance in a transactional sense. (This is also a tactic of indifference and may serve a dual disconfirming purpose.) Such disjunctive responses were studied by Sluzki, Beavin, Tarnopolski, and Veron (1967) who used the term "transactional disqualification" to mean any incongruity in the response of the speaker in relation to the context of the previous message of the other. A relationship between two successive messages exists, they noted, on two possible levels: (a) continuity between the content of the two messages (are both persons talking about the same subject?), and (b) indication of reception of the prior message (what cues does the speaker give of receiving and understanding the previous message?). If a message is disjunctive at either of these levels, transactional disqualification of the prior message is said to have occurred.

A similar form of message disqualification occurs when a speaker reacts selectively to some incidental clue in another's speech, but ignores the primary theme. Thus the responder may acknowledge the other's attempt to communicate, but still appears to miss the point. This "tangential response" was identified and studied by Jurgen Ruesch (1958), who noted that a speaker often picks up on a topic presented, but then continues to spin a yarn in a different direction. The response is not totally irrelevant because it has made some connection, although perhaps slight, with the prior utterance. Because it causes the first speaker to question the value or importance of what he or she was trying to say, the tangential response is reported to affect adversely a speaker's feeling of self-significance, and is therefore included as a form of disconfirmation.

Message Disqualifying Itself

A third way in which a speaker can use disqualification to "say something without really saying it," is by sending messages that disqualify themselves. There are many ways in which this may be done, the commonest devices being lack of clarity, ambiguity, and incongruity of mode. These forms of response are grouped together here because they have all been interpreted as devices for avoiding involvement with another by generating the metamessage "I am not communicating," hence "We are not relating."

SYSTEMATIZING CONFIRMING BEHAVIORS

Responses that confirm are less clearly defined than disconfirming behaviors because there has been less motivation to study them. In fact, identification of specific acts that are generally confirming is difficult unless we simply identify confirmation as the absence of disconfirming behaviors. More research in this area is clearly needed, but, in general, confirming behaviors are those which permit people to experience their own being and significance as well as their interconnectedness with others. Following Laing (1961), these have been arranged into three clusters: recognition, acknowledgment, and endorsement.

The Recognition Cluster   Recognition is expressed by looking at the other, making frequent eye contact, touching, speaking directly to the person, and allowing the other the opportunity to respond without being interrupted or having to force his or her way into an ongoing monologue. In the case of an infant, recognition means holding and cuddling beyond basic survival functions; in the case of an adult, it may still mean physical contact (touching), but it also means psychological contact in the form of personal language, clarity, congruence of mode, and authentic self-expression. In other words, confirmation requires that a person treat the other with respect, acknowledging his or her attempt to relate, and need to have a presence in the world.

The Acknowledgment Cluster   Acknowledgment of another is demonstrated by a relevant and direct response to his or her communication. This does not require praise or even agreement, but simple conjunction. Buber (Friedman, 1960) recognized this aspect when he wrote that mutually confirming partners can still "struggle together in direct opposition," and Laing (1961) made a similar point when he said that even rejection can be confirming if it is direct, not tangential, and if it grants significance and validity to what the other says. To hear, attend, and take note of the other and to acknowledge the other by responding directly is probably the most valued form of confirmation—and possibly the most rare. It means that the other's expression is furthered, facilitated, and encouraged.

The Endorsement Cluster   This cluster includes any responses that express acceptance of the other's feelings as being true, accurate, and "okay." In general, it means simply letting the other *be*, without blame, praise, analysis, justification, modification, or denial.

   Confirming response is dialogic in structure; it is a reciprocal activity involving shared talk and sometimes shared silence. It is interactional in the broadest sense of the word. It is not a one-way flow of talk; it is not a trade-off in which each speaker pauses and appears to listen only in order to get a chance to speak again. It is a complex affair in which each participates as both subject and object, cause and effect, of the other's talk. In short, confirming response, like all communication, is not something one does, it is a process in which one shares.

REVIEW QUESTIONS

1. Give a one-sentence definition of the term *confirmation*.
2. Discuss the distinctions among the four elements of confirmation that Cissna and Sieburg outline—existence, relating, significance, and validity of experience.
3. According to these authors, which are more important in the confirmation/disconfirmation process, verbal cues or nonverbal cues?
4. "The most extreme form of communication rejection is _____."
5. Which kind of disconfirmation is happening in the following example: Rae: "Damn! I wish that test wasn't tomorrow! That really ticks me off!" Kris: "You aren't mad, you're just scared because you haven't studied enough."
6. Give an example of a person "saying something without really saying it."
7. Explain the distinction between recognition and acknowledgment.

PROBES

1. What makes the term *confirmation* appropriate for what's being discussed here? You can confirm an airplane reservation and in some churches young people are confirmed. How do those meanings echo the meaning of confirmation that's developed here?
2. Notice how, in the first paragraph under the heading "Dimensions of Confirmation," the authors emphasize the transactional or relational quality of the phenomenon. Paraphrase what you hear them saying there.
3. All of us experience disconfirmation, sometimes with destructive regularity. Give an example where you have given an *indifferent* response. Give an example where you've received one. Do the same for *imperviousness* and *disqualification*.
4. When a person is impervious, what is he or she impervious *to?* Discuss.
5. Create an example of well-meant imperviousness, that is, imperviousness motivated by a genuine desire to comfort or to protect the other person. Do the same with a disqualifying response.
6. Identify five specific confirming communication events that you experienced in the last four hours.

REFERENCES

Buber, M. "Distance and Relation," *Psychiatry* 20 (1957): 97–104.

Cissna, K. N. L. "Interpersonal Confirmation: A Review of Current/Recent Theory and Research." Paper presented at the Central States Speech Association Convention, Chicago, 1976, and the International Communication Association Convention, Portland, Oregon, 1976.

Cissna, K. N. L. *Interpersonal Confirmation: A Review of Current Theory, Measurement, and Research.* Saint Louis: Saint Louis University, 1976.

Friedman, M. S. "Dialogue and the 'Essential We': The Bases of Values in the Philosophy of Martin Buber," *American Journal of Psychoanalysis* 20 (1960): 26–34.

Laing, R. D. *The Self and Others.* New York: Pantheon, 1961.

Laing, R. D. *The Politics of Experience.* New York: Ballantine, 1967.

Ruesch, J. "The Tangential Response," in *Psychopathology of Communication*, ed. P. H. Toch and J. Zuben. New York: Grune & Stratton, 1958.

Sieburg, E. "Dysfunctional Communication and Interpersonal Responsiveness in Small Groups." Doctoral dissertation, University of Denver, 1969.

Sieburg, E. "Toward a Theory of Interpersonal Confirmation," Unpublished manuscript, University of Denver, 1972.

Sieburg, E. *Interpersonal Confirmation: A Paradigm for Conceptualization and Measurement.* San Diego: United States International University, 1975.

Sieburg, E. "Confirming and Disconfirming Organizational Communication," in *Communication in Organizations*, eds. J. L. Owen, P. A. Page, and G. I. Zimmerman. St. Paul: West Publishing, 1976.

Sieburg, E., and C. E. Larson. "Dimensions of Interpersonal Response." Paper presented at the annual convention of the International Communication Association, Phoenix, 1971.

Sluzki, Carlos E., Janet Beavin, Alejandro Tarnopolsky, and Eliseo Veron. "Transactional Disqualification: Research on the Double Bind." Archives of General Psychiatry, April, 1967, 16(4), pp. 494–504.

Watzlawick, P. *An Anthology of Human Communication*. Palo Alto: Science and Behavior Books, 1964.

Watzlawick, P., J. Beavin, and D. D. Jackson. *Pragmatics of Human Communication: A Study of Interactional Patterns, Pathologies, and Paradoxes*. New York: Norton, 1967.

CHAPTER 10

Friendship

S teve Duck, an interpersonal communication professor at the University of Iowa, has written a number of books about how to understand and improve personal relationships. He begins this reading by explaining how "relationshipping" is a skill that each of us is taught—more or less effectively—and that we can learn to do better. He doesn't believe that building friendships is *nothing but* a mechanical process of applying certain skills, but he is convinced that skills are part of this process, just like they're part of the process of painting the Mona Lisa. As he suggests, the main advantage of treating relationshipping this way is that it can give you confidence in your ability to improve the ways you make and keep friends.

Duck talks about the general features that people expect friends to have and the friendship rules that people generally expect to be observed. Then he dedicates the bulk of this reading to a discussion of what he calls the "provisions" of friendships, that is, what they "provide" or do for us. He explains six reasons why we need friends: belonging and sense of reliable alliance; emotional integration and stability; opportunities for communication about ourselves; assistance and physical support; reassurance of our worth and value and opportunity to help others; and personality support.

His discussion helps me understand important features of the friendships I enjoy. For example, as I write these words, Stephanie Seideman, a family friend, is picking Lincoln up from preschool—a clear example of Stephanie giving us "assistance and physical support." During the times Kris and I are around Stephanie, our friendship with her also gives both of us opportunities for communication about ourselves as we discuss how we share or differ with his priorities and values. Our friendship with her also provides us opportunities to help, which feel good because they provide reassurance of our worth and value. I can also sense some of what our friendship provides Stephanie, how we might change things to make our relationships even better. It's clear from just this brief example that the ideas in this reading can help you understand your friendships and even improve them.

OUR FRIENDS, OURSELVES

Steve Duck

. . . "Relationshipping" is actually a very complicated and prolonged process with many pitfalls and challenges. Relationships do not just happen; they have to be made—made to start, made to work, made to develop, kept in good work-

Excerpted from *Understanding Relationships* by Steve Duck. Reprinted by permission of The Guilford Press.

ing order and preserved from going sour. To do all this we need to be active, thoughtful and skilled. To suggest that one simply starts a friendship, courtship, romantic partnership or marriage and "off it goes" is simple-minded. It is like believing that one can drive down the street merely by turning the ignition key, sitting back and letting the car take care of itself.

On the contrary, to develop a close personal relationship (with someone who was, after all, at first a stranger to us) careful adjustment and continuous monitoring are required, along with several very sophisticated skills. Some of these are: assessing the other person's needs accurately; adopting appropriate styles of communication; indicating liking and interest by means of minute bodily activities, like eye movements and postural shifts; finding out how to satisfy mutual personality needs; adjusting our behaviour to the relationship "tango" with the other person; selecting and revealing the right sorts of information or opinion in an inviting, encouraging way in the appropriate style and circumstances; building up trust, making suitable demands; and building up commitment. In short, one must perform many complex behaviours. These necessitate proficiency in presenting ourselves efficiently, attending to the right features of the other person at the right time, and pacing the friendship properly.

Rather as learning to drive a car does, learning to steer a relationship involves a range of different abilities and these must be co-ordinated. Just as when, even after we have learned to drive, we need to concentrate harder each time we get into a new model, drive in an unfamiliar country or travel through unknown streets, so when entering unfamiliar relationships we have to relearn, modify or re-concentrate on the things that we do. All of us have pet stories about the strain, embarrassment and awkwardness that occurred in a first meeting with a new neighbour or a "friend of a friend": some clumsy silence, an ill-judged phrase, a difficult situation. It is in such situations that the skills of friendship are bared and tested to the limits, and where intuition is so clearly not enough.

Because it is a skill, relationshipping—even in these novel situations—is something that can be improved, refined, polished (even coached and practised) like any other skill, trained like any other, and made more fluent. It can be taken right up to the level of expertise where it all flows so skillfully and automatically that we can metaphorically focus away from the position of the relational brakes or accelerator and devise ways to drive (the relationship) courteously, skillfully, carefully, or enjoyably, so that the others in it can have a smoother ride!

Since we are not usually disposed to think of friendship and close relationships in this new kind of way, people sometimes feel irrationally resistant to doing so. "How can you represent a close personal relationship as a simple mechanical skill?", they ask. "Isn't it more mystical, more magical, more moral, less manipulative than you make it sound?" Such people seem happy to see relationships merely as pleasant, passive states: relationships just happen to us and we don't have to do anything particular—let alone do anything properly.

My answer is clear: I am not saying that friendship is all mechanical, any more than making a beautiful piece of furniture or playing an enchanting piano rhapsody or winning a sports championship is simply a mechanical exercise. But each of these activities has some mechanical elements that must be mastered before the higher-level aspects of skill can be attempted. You can't paint the Mona Lisa until you know something about painting figures, using a canvas, holding a brush, mixing paints, and so on. Furthermore, research backs this up. Scholars now regard "relationship work" as a process that continues right through the life of the relationship, with a constant and perpetual need for the right actions and activities at the right time to keep it all alive (for example, Baxter and Dindia, 1990). . . .

There are many advantages to this way of looking at relationships. It leads to a direct and useful form of practical advice for people who are unhappy with one or more of their relationships, or who are lonely or frustrated. It focuses on the things that one can do to improve relationships. It also runs counter to the common, but rather simplistic, assumption that relationships are based only on the matching of two individuals' personalities. This pervasive myth says that there is a Mr or a Ms Right for everyone or that friends can be defined in advance. If this were true, then we could all list the characteristics of our perfect partner—looking for a partner or being attractive to one would be like shopping for or making a checklist of things we liked. By contrast, the new approach adopted here will focus on performance, on behaviour, on the simple mistakes that people make at the various stages of friendship development.

Is it such a strange and unacceptable idea that people can be trained to adopt more satisfactory styles in relationships? Not really. Therapists, social workers, doctors and dentists nowadays receive instruction on the ways to establish rapport with patients and how to develop a reassuring and constructive "bedside manner." We know also that insurance or car sales staff are trained in how to relate to possible customers, that airline cabin crew and the police alike receive instruction on relating to the public, and that managers are now encouraged to spend time building up good personal relationships with employees. Such emphasis on skills takes us beyond the trite commonsense advice for lonely persons to "go out and meet more people." It focuses us on the fact that relationship problems derive in part, if not on the whole, from people "doing relationships" wrongly rather than simply not getting enough opportunities to be in them.

The evidence suggests that all of us are probably missing out and not maximizing our potential for relationships. American research (Reisman, 1981) shows that people claim to have about fifteen "friends" on average, although the numbers change with age (17-year olds claim about nineteen, while 28-year olds have only twelve; 45-year olds have acquired sixteen, while people in their sixties enjoy an average of fifteen). When people are asked to focus only on the relationships that are most satisfying, intimate and close, however, the number drops dramatically to around six (5.6 to be precise). . . .

THE NATURE OF FRIENDSHIP

A friend of mine once defined a "friend" as someone who, seeing you drunk and about to stand up on a table and sing, would quietly take you aside to prevent you[r] doing it. This definition actually embodies quite a few of the important aspects of friendship: caring, support, loyalty and putting high priority on the other person's interests. We shall see later in the [reading] why these are important. However, when researchers have taken a more precise look at the meaning of friendship, they have focused on two specific things: the general *features* that humans expect friends to have and the *rules* of friendship that humans expect to be observed.

There are certain features that we find particularly desirable in friends and certain characteristics that everyone believes that being a friend demands. K. E. Davis and Todd (1985) found that we regularly expect a friend to be someone who is honest and open, shows affection, tells us his or her secrets and problems, gives us help when we need it, trusts us and is also trustworthy, shares time and activities with us, treats us with respect and obviously values us, and is prepared to work through disagreements. These are things that people *expect* a friend to do for them and expect to do for the friend in return. These features constitute a quite complex picture. However, when one looks at the *rules* of friendship that people actually adhere to, then the strongest ones are rather simple (Argyle & Henderson, 1985): hold conversations; do not disclose confidences to other people; refrain from public criticism; repay debts and favours. These researchers also demonstrate that emotional support, trust and confiding are among the rules that distinguish high-quality friendships from less close ones.

In ideal circumstances, then, a friend is an open, affectionate, trusting, helpful, reliable companion who respects our privacy, carries out interactions with all due respect to the norms of behaviour and ourselves, does not criticize us in public, and both does us favours and returns those that we do. In the real world, friendship is unlikely to live up to this ideal and we all have some range of tolerance. However, it is a *voluntary* bond between two people and the above ideals can be seen as part of an unwritten contract between them, whose violation can become the grounds for the dissolution of the relationship (Wiseman, 1986).

Another important view of friendship has been offered by Wright (1984). He too stresses the "voluntary interdependence" of friendship: it is important that people freely choose to be intertwined together in the relationship. He also places emphasis on the "person qua person" element, or the extent to which we enjoy the person for his or her own sake, rather than for the things that he or she does for us. More recent research on this idea (Lea, 1989) finds indeed that "self-referent rewards," or the way the other person makes us feel about ourselves, are just as important as these other things. The way in which the relationship helps us to feel about ourselves, and its voluntary nature, are crucial to the nature of friendship. There are good reasons why this is the case.

THE "PROVISIONS" OF FRIENDSHIP

There are several ways to start answering the large question: "Why do we need friends?" We could just decide that everyone needs intimacy, possibly as a result of dependency needs formed in childhood, just as the psychoanalysts tell us.

There may be something to this, as we shall see, but there is more to the need for friendships than a need for intimacy—and there is more to the need for intimacy than we may suppose, anyway. For instance, we might want to ask how intimacy develops, how it is expressed, what else changes when it grows, and so on. We might also note the curious finding (Wheeler *et al.*, 1983; R. B. Hays, 1989) that both men and women prefer intimate partners who are women! Indeed, Arkin and Grove (1990) show that shy men prefer to talk to women even when they are not in an intimate encounter. Not only this, but those people who talk to more women during the day have better health than those who talk to fewer women (Reis, 1986). Clearly the nature of needs for intimacy and friendship is rather intriguing and may be mediated by gender and other social contexts. . . .

Belonging and a Sense of Reliable Alliance

In writing about loneliness and the "provisions" of relationships—what it is that they do for us—Weiss (1974) proposed that a major consequence of being in relationships is a sense of belonging and of "reliable alliance." He is touching on something very important about human experience. We all like to belong or to be accepted; even those who choose solitude want it to be the result of their own choice, not someone else's. No one wants to be an outcast, a pariah or a social reject. Indeed, the powerful effects of being made *not* to belong were long recognized as a severe punishment in Ancient Greece, where people could be ostracized and formally exiled or banished. The modern equivalent is found in the British trade union practice of "sending someone to Coventry" when they break the union rules: the person's workmates, colleagues, neighbours and associates are instructed to refuse to speak to the person about anything. . . .

By contrast, relationships give us a sense of inclusion, a sense of being a member of a group—and, as the advertisers keep emphasizing, membership has its privileges. One of these privileges is "reliable alliance"; that is to say, the existence of a bond that can be trusted to be there for you when you need it. To [quote] a phrase, "A friend in need is a friend indeed"—or in our terms, the existence of a friendship creates a reliable alliance: one of the signs that someone is a true friend is when they help you in times of trouble.

Emotional Integration and Stability

Importantly, communities of friends provide a lot more than just a sense of belonging and reliable alliance (Weiss, 1974). They also provide necessary anchor points for opinions, beliefs, and emotional responses. Friends are benchmarks that tell us how we should react appropriately, and they correct or guide our attitudes and beliefs in both obvious and subtle ways. As an example, consider how different cultures express grief differently. In some countries it is acceptable to fall to the ground, cover oneself with dust and wail loudly; in other cultures it is completely unacceptable to show such emotion, and the emphasis falls on dignified public composure. Imagine the reaction in Britain if the Queen were to roll on the ground as a way of demonstrating grief, or in the United States if the

President and First Lady attended military funerals with their faces blacked and tearing their clothes. Humans have available many different ways of demonstrating grief but they typically cope with this strong emotion in a way particularly acceptable to their own culture.

Like cultures, friends and intimates develop their own sets of shared concerns, common interests and collective problems, as well as shared meanings, common responses to life and communal emotions. Friends are often appreciated exactly because they share private understandings, private jokes, or private language. Indeed, communication researchers (Hopper *et al.*, 1981; Bell *et al.*, 1987) have shown that friends and lovers develop their own "personal idioms" or ways of talking about such things as feelings, sex and bodily parts, so that they are obscure to third parties. By using a phrase with secret meaning, couples can communicate in public places about things that are private. Good examples are to be found in newspaper columns on St. Valentine's Day. What, for example, are we to make of a message I found in the local student newspaper: "Dinglet, All my dinkery forever, Love, Scrunnett"? Presumably it meant something both to the person who placed the advertisement and to the person who was the intended object of it. Be alert: the couple who announce that "We are going home to make some pancakes" may in fact be planning to have a night of passion!

Such language is just a localized version of the fact that different cultures use different dialects or languages. Equally, friends have routines of behaving or beliefs that are not shared by everyone in a particular country or culture, but for that reason they are more important in daily life. Loneliness is, and isolation can be, wretched precisely because it deprives people of such psychological benchmarks and anchor points. Lonely people lose the stability provided by the chance to compare their own reactions to life with the reactions of other people that they know, like and respect. . . .

So loneliness and isolation are disruptive because they deprive the person of the opportunity for comfortable comparison of opinions and attitudes with other people—of close friends. People who are parted from friends become anxious, disoriented, unhappy and even severely destabilized emotionally; they may become still more anxious just because they feel themselves behaving erratically, or they may experience unusual mood swings. They often report sudden changes of temper and loss of control, sometimes resulting in violent outbursts; but in any case their judgment becomes erratic and unreliable, and they may become unusually vigilant, suspicious or jumpy in the presence of other unfamiliar people.

Another function of friendship, then, a reason why we need friends, is to keep us emotionally stable and to help us see where we stand *vis-à-vis* other people and whether we are "doing OK." It is particularly noticeable in times of stress and crisis. I remember an occasion when all the lights [went out] in a student residence block where I was a [residence advisor]. The rational thing to do was to find a flashlight and await the restoration of power. What we all actually did was to stumble down to the common-room and chatter amongst ourselves: the need to compare our reactions to the emergency was so powerful and so universal that even the warden, a medical researcher who had doctoral degrees from both Oxford and Cambridge, did the same. Such behaviour often happens after any kind of stress or crisis, from the crowd of people who gather to swap stories after a fire or a car accident, to the nervous chatter that schoolchildren perform when the doctor comes to inject them against measles or TB. . . .

Opportunities for Communication about Ourselves

There is a third reason why we need friends (Weiss, 1974). A centrally important need is for communication. This particular wheel was strikingly reinvented by the Quaker prison reformers several generations ago, who attempted to cut down communication between criminals in prison in order to stop them educating one another about ways of committing crime. Accordingly, one of their proposals was that prisoners should be isolated from one another. What occurred was very instructive: the prisoners spent much of their time tapping out coded messages on walls and pipes, devising means of passing information to one another, and working out other clever ways of communicating. Evidently, people who are involuntarily isolated feel a need to communicate. One additional function that healthy friendships provide, then, is a place for such communication to occur—communication about anything, not just important events but also trivial stuff as well as personal, intimate details about oneself. In a study at the University of Iowa, I and my students (S. W. Duck, *et al.*, 1991) have found that most conversations with friends last very short periods of time (about three minutes on average) and deal with trivialities. They are nonetheless rated as extremely significant. They revitalize the relationship, reaffirm it and celebrate its existence, through the medium of conversation.

A mild form of this overwhelming need to communicate is to be found on railway trains, planes and long-distance buses. Here many lonely people strike up conversations—but usually monologues—which allow them to communicate to someone or to tell someone about themselves and their opinions. A striking thing about this is the intimacy of the stories that are often told. Perfect strangers can often be regaled with the life history, family details, and personal opinions of someone they have not seen before and will probably never see again. Indeed, that is probably a key part of it, for the listener who will not be seen again cannot divulge the "confession" to friends or colleagues and so damage the confessor's reputation. (In cases where it is known that the listener and confessor will meet again, as in the case of doctors and patients, priests and parishioners, counsellors and clients, or lawyers and consultants, the listeners are bound by strict professional ethical codes not to reveal what they have been told. On the train, the "ethics" are simply left to statistical chance, and the extreme improbability of the two strangers meeting one another's friends is a comfort in itself.) . . .

Provision of Assistance and Physical Support

Another "provision" of relationships is simply that they offer us support, whether physical, psychological or emotional (Hobfoll and Stokes, 1988). This section focuses on physical support and assistance, which are often as significant to us as is any other sort of support.

For example, when people lose a friend or a spouse through bereavement, they report a lack of support—they are cut off from someone who has helped them to cope with life and to adjust to its problems, tasks, and changing uncertainties. This can take one of two forms: physical support (such as help with day-to-day tasks) and psychological support (such as when someone shows that we are appreciated, or lets us know that our opinions are valued). Human beings need both of these types of support, but the types are significantly different.

This is very simply illustrated. When your friend gives you a birthday present you are supposed to accept it in a way that indicates your own unworthiness to receive it and also the kindness of the friend ("Oh you shouldn't have bothered. It really is very good of you"). In short, you repay your friend by accepting the gift as a token of friendship and by praising the friend. You "exchange" the gift for love and respect, as it were. Imagine what would happen if you repaid by giving the friend the exact value of the gift in money. The friend would certainly be insulted by the ineptness: you would have altered the nature of the social exchange and also, in so doing, the nature of the relationship, by focusing on money rather than the gift as a symbol for friendship. Indeed, Cheal (1986) has shown that gift-giving as a one-way donation is rare and gift *reciprocity* is the norm, indicating that it serves an important relational function. Gift exchange serves the symbolic function of cementing and celebrating the relationship.

There are other clear examples of this point—that the nature of the exchange or support helps to define the degree and type of relationship. For instance, many elderly people get resentful of the fact that they gradually become more and more physically dependent on other people for help in conducting the daily business of their lives. The elderly cannot reach things so easily, cannot look after themselves and are more dependent physically, while at the same time they are less able to repay their friends by doing services in return. This, then, is one reason why many people dislike or feel uneasy with old age: they resent the feeling of helpless dependency coupled with the feeling of perpetual indebtedness that can never be paid off. For many elderly people, then, the mending of a piece of furniture, the making of a fruit pie, or the knitting of a sweater can be traded off against dependency: elderly people *need to be allowed* to do things for other people as a way of demonstrating to themselves and to everyone else that they are valuable to others and can still make useful contributions to the world. . . .

Reassurance of Our Worth and Value, and Opportunity to Help Others

People who are lonely characteristically say that no-one cares about them, that they are useless, uninteresting, of low value and good for nothing. Studies of the conversation of severely depressed people invariably reveal indications that they have lost their self-respect or self-esteem (Gotlib and Hooley, 1988). In other words, they have come to see themselves as valueless, worthless and insignificant, often because that is how they feel that everyone else sees them.

Furthermore, analysis of suicide notes shows that many suicide attempts are carried out as a way of forcing some particular friend to re-evaluate the person, or to shock the friend into realizing just how much he or she really does esteem the person making the attempt. For this reason, Alfred Adler (1929) has claimed, with characteristic insight, that every suicide is always a reproach or a revenge.

One reason, then, that we appreciate friends is because of their contribution to our self-evaluation and self-esteem. Friends can do this both directly and indirectly: they may compliment us or tell us about other people's good opinions of us. Dale Carnegie's multimillion-seller book on *How to Win Friends and Influence People* stressed the positive consequences of doing this. Friends can also increase our self-esteem in other ways: by attending to what we do, listening, asking our advice, and generally acting in ways that indicate the value that they place on our opinions. However, there are less obvious and more indirect ways in which they can communicate this estimation of our value. For one thing, the fact that they choose to spend time with us rather than with someone else must show that they value our company more than the alternatives.

There is a subtler version of these points too. Just as we look to friends to provide us with all of these things, so we can get from friendship one other key benefit. Because friends trust us and depend on us, they give us the chance to help them. That gives us the opportunity to take responsibility for them, to see ourselves helping them with their lives, to give them our measured advice and consequently to feel good. Friends provide us with these possibilities of taking responsibility and nurturing other people.

Undoubtedly, these things are important in the conduct of relationships and in making them satisfactory for both partners, and it is critical that we learn to evince them effectively. However, one important point to note is that those people who are poor at doing this (e.g., people who are poor at indicating interest, or who seem to have little time for other people, or never let them help or let them give advice) will find that other people are unattracted to relationships with them. All people need indications of their estimability and need chances to nurture just as we do, and if we do not adequately provide such signs then these people will reject us—just as we would do in their position. . . .

Personality Support

Yet there is something even more fundamental to close relationships than this. Recent research indicates that each feature mentioned above—sense of community, emotional stability, communication, provision of help, maintenance of self-esteem—in its own way serves to support and integrate the person's personality (S. W. Duck and Lea, 1982). Each of us is characterized by many thoughts, doubts, beliefs, attitudes, questions, hopes, expectations and opinions about recurrent patterns in life. Our personalities are composed not only of our behavioural style (for example, our introversion or extraversion) but also of our thoughts, doubts and beliefs. It is a place full of symbols, a space where we are ourselves, a system of interlocking thoughts, experiences, interpretations, expectancies and personal meanings. Our personality would be useless to us if all of these opinions and meanings were not, by and large, supported. We would simply stop behaving if we had no trust in our thoughts or beliefs about why we should behave or how we should behave, just as we stop doing other things that we are convinced are wrong. Some schizophrenics and depressives actually do stop behaving when their thought-world falls apart: they just sit and stare.

Each of us needs to be assured regularly that our thought-worlds or symbolic spaces are sound and reliable. A friend can help us to see that we are wrong and how we can change, or that we are right about some part of our thinking. We may have vigorous discussions about different attitudes that we hold—but our friends are likely to be very similar to us in many of our attitudes and interests, so that these discussions are more probably supportive than destructive. However, we all know the anger and pain that follow a really serious disagreement with a close friend—much more unpleasant than a disagreement with an enemy. What we should deduce from all this is that we seek out as friends those people who help to support our thought-world-personality, and we feel chastened, sapped or undermined when they do not provide this support.

What sorts of person best gives us the kind of personality support that I have described here? In the first instance, it is provided by people who share our way of thinking. The more of these "thought-ways" that we share with someone, the easier it is to communicate with that person: we can assume that our words and presumptions will be understood more easily by someone who is "our type" than by someone who is not—we shall not have the repetitious discomfort of perpetually explaining ourselves, our meanings and our jokes.

Yet there is much more to it than this, although it has taken researchers a long time to sort out the confusing detail of the picture. For one thing, the type of similarity that we need to share with someone in order to communicate effectively depends on the stage that the relationship has reached. At early stages it is quite enough that acquaintances are broadly similar, but at later stages the similarity must be more intricate, precise, refined, and detailed. One of the skills of friend-making is to know what sorts of similarity to look for at which times as the relationship proceeds. General similarity of attitudes is fine at the early to middle stages, but matters much less later if the partners do not work at discovering similarities at the deeper level of the ways in which they view other people and understand their characters. Very close friends must share the same specific sorts of framework for understanding the actions, dispositions and characters of other people in general, and in specific instances of mutual acquaintance. Such similarity is rare and prized. For that reason, if for no other, it is painful and extremely significant to lose the persons who offer it.

Loss or absence of particular intimates or friends deprives us of some measure of support for our personality, and it is essential to our psychological health that we have the skill to avoid this. Losing an intimate partner or friend not only makes us die a little, it leaves floating in the air those bits of our personality that the person used to support, and can make people fall apart psychologically. Of course, this will depend on how much our personality has been supported by that partner, which particular parts are involved, how readily these parts are supported by others, how much time we have had to anticipate and adjust to the loss, and so on. But essentially the loss or absence of friends and of close, satisfying relationships does not merely cause anxiety, grief or depression; it can cause other, more severe, forms of psychological disintegration or deterioration, often with the physical and mental side-effects noted earlier. Many of the well-known psychosomatic illnesses and hysterical states are actually caused by relationship problems, although this has not been realized by as many doctors as one might expect (see Lynch, 1977). For too long the accepted medical folklore has assumed that the person's inner mental state is a given, and that it causes psychosomatic effects when it gets out of balance. It is now quite clear that the surest way to upset people's mental balance is to disturb their close relationships (Gerstein and Tesser, 1987). We need friends to keep us healthy both physically and mentally: therefore it is doubly important that we perfect the ways of gaining and keeping friends. An important first step is to recognize the different needs that each relationship can fulfill for us, and the means by which this can be achieved.

REVIEW QUESTIONS

1. Define *relationshipping*.
2. How many "satisfying, intimate, and close" relationships does the research say that people of your age typically have?
3. Duck lists four main rules that characterize friendship, according to the research. What are they?
4. Fill in the blank, explain, and tell whether you agree or disagree and why: "Both men and women prefer intimate partners who are_____."
5. What does it mean to have "a sense of reliable alliance"?
6. Paraphrase and give an example from your own experience of the reality-checking function of friendships.
7. Explain what Duck means when he says that sometimes elderly people need to be allowed to do things for others.
8. According to Duck, what is the relationship between friendship networks and personal mental health? Do you agree or disagree with this claim?

PROBES

1. In what ways does Steve Duck's example of learning to drive a car fit your experience of learning how to "do" relationships? In what ways does it not fit?
2. Test Duck's claim about the average number of "friends" reported by people of your age and the average number of "satisfying, intimate, and close" relationships. Do you find any differences among the people you know?
3. What is the function in intimate relationships of private language and personal idioms? What does the presence of these private modes of expression suggest about the similarities between friendships and cultures?

4. What explanation does Duck give for the "stranger on the train (bus, plane)" phenomenon, where your seatmate, whom you don't know, tells you intimate details of his or her life? Why does this happen?
5. How do you respond to Duck's claim that, in some important ways, birthdays are times when many people give gifts *in exchange for* respect and love?
6. Paraphrase and respond to Duck's explanation of the role of similarities in friendship relationships.

REFERENCES

Adler, A. (1929). *What Your Life Should Mean to You*. New York: Bantam.

Argyle, M., & Henderson, M. (1985). *The Anatomy of Relationships*. London: Methuen.

Arkin, R., & Grove, T. (1990). Shyness, sociability and patterns of everyday affiliation. *Journal of Social and Personal Relationships* (7), 273–281.

Baxter, L. A., & Dindia, K. (1990). Marital partners' perceptions of marital maintenance strategies. *Journal of Social and Personal Relationships* (7), 187–208.

Bell, R. A., Buerkel-Rothfuss, N., & Gore, K. (1987). "Did you bring the yarmulke for the cabbage patch kid?": The idiomatic communication of young lovers. *Human Communication Research* (14), 47–67.

Cheal, D. J. (1986). The social dimensions of gift behaviour. *Journal of Social and Personal Relationships* (3), 423–39.

Davis, K. E., & Todd, M. (1985). Assessing friendship: Prototypes, paradigm cases, and relationship description, in S. W. Duck & D. Perlman (eds.), *Understanding Personal Relationships*. London: Sage.

Duck, S. W., & Lea, M. (1982). Breakdown of relationships as a threat to personal identity, in G. Breakwell (ed.), *Threatened Identities*. Chichester: Wiley.

Duck, S. W., Rutt, D. J., Hurst, M., & Strejc, H. (1991). Some evident truths about communication in everyday relationships: All communication is not created equal. *Human Communication Research* (18), 114–29.

Gerstein, I. H., & Tesser, A. (1987). Antecedents and responses associated with loneliness. *Journal of Social and Personal Relationships* (4), 329–63.

Gotlib, I. H., & Hooley, J. M. (1988). Depression and marital distress: Current and future directions, in S. W. Duck (ed.) with D. F. Hay, S. E. Hobfoll, W. Ickes, & B. Montgomery, *Handbook of Personal Relationships*. Chichester: Wiley.

Hays, R. B. (1989). The day-to-day functioning of close versus casual friendship. *Journal of Social and Personal Relationships* (1), 75–98.

Hobfoll, S. E., & Stokes, J. P. (1988). The process and mechanics of social support, in S. W. Duck (ed.) with D. F. Hay, S. E. Hobfoll, W. Ickes, & B. Montgomery, *Handbook of Personal Relationships* (Chichester, UK: Wiley).

Hopper, R., Knapp, M. L., & Scott, L. (1981). Couples' personal idioms: Exploring intimate talk. *Journal of Communication* (31), 23–33.

Lea, M. (1989). Factors underlying friendship: An analysis of responses on the acquaintance description form in relation to Wright's friendship model. *Journal of Social and Personal Relationships* (6), 275–92.

Lynch, J. J. (1977). *The Broken Heart: The Medical Consequences of Loneliness.* New York: Basic Books.

Reis, H. T. (1986). Gender effects in social participation: Intimacy, loneliness, and the conduct of social interaction, in R. Gilmour & S. W. Duck (eds.), *The Emerging Field of Personal Relationships.* Hillsdale, NJ: Lawrence Erlbaum.

Reisman, J. (1981). Adult friendships, in S. W. Duck & R. Gilmour (eds.), *Personal Relationships 2: Developing Personal Relationships.* London: Academic Press.

Weiss, R. S. (1974). The provisions of social relationships, in Z. Rubin (ed.), *Doing Unto Others.* Englewood Cliffs, NJ: Prentice-Hall.

Wheeler, L., Reis, H. T., & Nezelek, J. (1983). Loneliness, social interaction and sex roles. *Journal of Personality and Social Psychology* (35), 742–54.

Wiseman, J. P. (1986). Friendship: Bonds and binds in a voluntary relationship. *Journal of Social and Personal Relationships* (3), 191–211.

Wright, P. H. (1984). Self referent motivation and the intrinsic quality of friendship. *Journal of Social and Personal Relationships* (1), 114–30.

*T*he author of this essay has been a philosophy teacher at East Tennessee State University. The paper appeared in an unusual collection of readings that discusses several *philosophical* aspects of interpersonal relationships. As you'll see, John Hardwig's concern is that interpersonal contacts often raise important ethical issues, but that few people have thought or written about how ethics work in these situations. One of the reasons he offers for this neglect is that most philosophy has been written by men, and men typically favor impersonal topics over personal ones.

Whether or not you agree with this reason, notice how Hardwig outlines his ethics. He defines a *personal*, as contrasted with a quasi-personal or impersonal, relationship as one in which I want you as an end, not as a means to an end, as one in which I see "you and the realization of your goals as part of me and the realization of my goals." A personal relationship also involves wanting to be in relation with precisely you, not just wanting something that could be provided by you or somebody else. He contrasts this kind of relationship with a *quasi-personal* one in which I want to have "the kind of friend" or "the kind of wife" or husband that you might be. These relationships may appear to be personal, but they're actually not, because I've chosen the person who fits into a *category* of desire, rather than choosing the person because of who he or she is as an individual. Hardwig also says that hatred can define a truly personal relationship when I hate you, not just some of the things you are, do, or stand for.

This analysis makes it easier to understand the kind of relationship where I want precisely *you*, but "you simply want to be loved and protected or to have a certain kind of marriage." As Hardwig points out, "relationships are often made or broken by the issue of whether I want you or 'someone who. . . .' "

The main principle of Hardwig's ethics of personal relationships is that when attitudes or actions depersonalize personal relationships, they do violence to what these relationships are, and this kind of violence ought to be avoided. This principle heightens the importance of motives in personal relationships. Motives that are completely acceptable in some impersonal relationships—duty, obligation, and pity, for example—are often inappropriate in personal relationships. As he explains, "While it might be nice to feel yourself to be charitable, benevolent, or compassionate, who could endure being emotionally involved with someone who saw you essentially or even very often as an appropriate object of benevolence, charity, or pity?"

It follows that personal relationships between adults ought to be entered into and continued out of a shared sense of vitality and strength rather than weakness and need. I'm reminded of the person who said that, whenever I try to feed my friends from a cup that is anything other than overflowing, I feed them poison.

Another implication of Hardwig's central ethical principle is that people in personal relationships should act toward each other as purely as possible because they *want* to, not out of a sense of duty, obligation, or *quid pro quo* (you did it for me, so now I owe you). All this doesn't mean that motives such as duty, pity, and sympathy are *always* inappropriate in personal relationships, but only that they should be fallback positions, not the main focus of the relationship.

A third implication is that in personal relationships you can't really separate egoism and altruism—self-interest and interest in the other. This is because if the relationship is personal, "your ends are my ends too." So "the distinction between giving and receiving thus collapses." This is an important claim, and it's one I encourage you to try applying to your own personal relationships. It doesn't mean that there are *never* conflicts or that *all* interests are shared, but that mutuality is primary.

A fourth implication is that personal relationships can't and don't have to be justified by an appeal to some higher value such as love, pleasure, or social utility. They are ends in themselves, justified by their own existence. If you try to make them dependent on another value, you depersonalize them.

The final implication is that this ethics of personal relationships sees people not as individuals but as relational beings, intimately tied in with others. This doesn't make me *dependent* on your friendship or even your presence. But it does mean that if our relationship ends, I change—just as you do.

Hardwig concludes with an argument that when it's necessary to end a relationship, it is both possible and desirable to do so without depersonalizing it. Spouses and attorneys involved in divorces could usefully reflect on this claim.

I find this a thought-provoking essay, and I hope you do too. It raises some important questions about friendships and other relationships that aren't often discussed but that can provide helpful guidance when you are faced with a hard decision.

IN SEARCH OF AN ETHICS OF PERSONAL RELATIONSHIPS

John Hardwig

Although it's been ten years, I can still see the student, hands on her hips, as she brought my beautiful lecture on Kant's ethics to a grinding halt: "Is Kant saying," she demanded, "that if I sleep with my boyfriend, I should sleep with him out of a sense of duty?" My response: "And when you're through, you should tell him that you would have done the same for anyone in his situation." What could I say?

We do not search for what we already have. Thus my title commits me to the thesis that we do not have an ethics of personal relationships. And that is in fact my view, a view grown out of incidents like this one.

More specifically, I believe that for at least the past 300 years or so, philosophers thinking about ethics have tacitly presupposed a very impersonal context. They have unconsciously assumed a context in which we mean little or nothing to each other and have then asked themselves what principles could be invoked to keep us from trampling each other in the pursuit of our separate and often conflicting interests. Consequently, I contend, what we now study and teach under the rubric of ethics is almost entirely the ethics of impersonal relationships.

Various explanations might be offered as to why philosophers have thought in terms of impersonal relationships. Philosophers have historically been almost exclusively males, and males have generally believed that the public realm where impersonal relationships predominate is much more important and worthy of study than the private and personal dimensions of life. Or perhaps the assumption that we are talking about impersonal relationships reflects the growing impersonality of modern society or an awareness of the increasing ability given us by our technology to affect the lives of people quite remote from us.

However, even if philosophers were not thinking about personal relationships when developing their ethics, it might seem that an ethics adequate to impersonal relationships should work at least as well in personal contexts. For in personal relationships there would be less temptation to callously ignore or to ride roughshod over each other's interests, owing to the greater meaning each has for the other. Thus it seems reasonable to assume that the principles constituting the ethics of impersonal relationships will work satisfactorily in personal contexts as well.

But this assumption is false. An ethics of personal relationships must, I try to show, be quite different from the ethics of impersonal relationships. Traditional ethics is, at best, significantly incomplete, only a small part of the story of the ethics of personal relationships. Often it is much worse: basically misguided or wrong-headed and thus inapplicable in the context of personal relationships. In fact, much of traditional ethics urges us to act in ways that would be inappropriate in personal contexts; and thus traditional ethics would often be dangerous and destructive in those contexts.

We do not search for what we already have. I do not have an ethics of personal relationships, though I offer some suggestions about what such an ethics would and would *not* look like. Since my views about the ethics of personal relationships depend, naturally enough, on what I take a personal relationship to be, I begin with a brief discussion of the nature and structure of personal relationships.

But I'm going to cheat some: Throughout, I speak of personal relationships as if they were static. Although this is obviously a gross oversimplification, limitations of space and understanding preclude a discussion of the beginnings and endings and dynamics of personal relationships.

I

So what's a personal relationship? Personal relationships, as opposed to impersonal relationships, are of course relationships such as love, being lovers, friends, spouses, parents, and so on. But these sorts of relationships aren't always very *personal*, since there are all sorts of marriages of convenience, Aristotle's "friendships of utility," Hobbesian power alliances, and many varieties of quite impersonal sexual relationships. Consequently, we need to distinguish what are commonly *called* personal relationships (love, friendship, marriage) from personal relationships in a deeper sense. Even when they are not *personal* in the deeper sense, relationships like love, friendship, and marriage are not exactly impersonal relationships either. So I use the phrase "quasi-personal relationships" to cover such cases, reserving the term "personal relationships" for those relationships which are personal in the deeper sense I hope to explicate. I thus work with a threefold distinction between personal, quasi-personal, and impersonal relationships.

Let us begin with the distinction between personal and impersonal relationships. I want to say two things by way of characterizing personal relationships: (1) If I have a personal relationship with you, I want you. You (and your well-being) are then one of my *ends*. This would seem to be part of what it means to care for or care about another person. (2) If my relationship to you is to be personal, this end must be *you*—precisely you and not any other person. The persons in personal relationships are not substitutable. . . .

First, then, the idea of having you as one of my ends is to be contrasted with both sides of the Kantian dichotomy between respecting you as an end in yourself and treating you as a means to my ends. Kant would have me respect you as a person, just as I would respect any person, simply because you (all) are persons. To respect you as an end in yourself is to recognize that you have value apart from whatever use I might be able to make of you. It is, moreover, to recognize that your goals and purposes have validity independent of whatever goals and purposes I may have and to acknowledge in my action that your goals and purposes have an equal claim to realization. Although respect for you and your goals is a part of a personal relationship, it is not what makes a personal relationship *personal*, valuable, or even a relationship. Instead, having you as one of my ends is valuing you in *relation* to me; it is seeing you and the realization of your goals as part of me and the realization of my goals. This is not, of course, to reduce you to a means to my ends. On the contrary, I want you. You are one of my *ends*.

The second characteristic of a personal relationship—that I want precisely *you*—serves to highlight the difference between this kind of relationship and impersonal relationships, and also to further elucidate the difference between seeing you as one of my ends and seeing you either as an end in yourself or as a means to my ends. The characteristic intentions in personal relationships are different from those in impersonal relationships. It is the difference between:

wanting *to get* something *T* and wanting to get *T from you*.
wanting *to give T* and wanting to give *T to you*.
wanting *to do T* and wanting to do *T with you*.

The first set of intentions or desires structures impersonal relationships; the second, personal relationships. There is a big difference between wanting to be loved, for example, and wanting to be loved *by you*; a crucial difference between wanting to go to bed (with someone) and wanting to go to bed *with you*. This difference seems to retain its significance whether "*T*" ranges over relatively insignificant things like taking a walk, having your breakfast made, sharing a ride to a party, and going to a movie, or over crucially important things like baring your soul, receiving love and emotional support, sharing your living space, and having children.

If I want *something* (as opposed to wanting something *from you*), I depersonalize you, reducing you (in my eyes) to an *X* who is a possessor or producer of certain goods. For it's these good things I want, not you; anyone who could and would deliver these goods would do as well. The language captures the depersonalization nicely: I want "someone who. . . ." It is when I want *something* and you become for me a "someone who" is the possessor or producer of this good that I reduce you to a means to my ends. This kind of desire and the intentions it gives rise to structure an impersonal relationship, though many of what are usually called "personal relationships" are structured by precisely this sort of impersonal desire. . . .

Let us now turn to quasi-personal relationships. These are the relationships that are commonly *called* personal, but that are not personal relationships in the deeper sense I have discussed. Quasi-personal relationships can be analyzed along similar lines. Suppose that it's important to me to have *the kind of friend* or *the kind of wife* who will help me with my work. In such cases, my desire or our relationship is not simply impersonal, for it won't do for me just to get help with my work— I want help from a friend or from a wife. In this intermediate case, the kind of relationship you have to me (wife, lover, loved one, friend, child) is essential to the structure of my desire; a certain kind of relationship is one of my ends.

But our relationship is still abstract or impersonal in a sense. I want something from you *because you are my wife* (lover, friend, child). I'd want the same from *any* wife (lover, friend, kid). Thus *you* are not important to the structure of my desire, *you* are not one of my ends. In such cases, the relationship I want must be defined (by me) in terms of roles and rules for those roles. I call these relationships quasi-personal. They are important for an ethics of personal relationships, for we often get hurt in precisely these sorts of relationships, especially when we believe we are involved in a personal relationship.

Two additional points about personal relationships are important for the ethics of personal relationships. First, although I talk mainly about positive, healthy personal relationships, it is important to recognize that *hatred*, as well as love, can be a personal relationship. As can resentment, anger, contempt. Hatred is personal if I hate *you*, not just some of the things you are or do or stand for, not just "anyone who. . . ." In cases of personal hatred, I may well desire your overall ill-being. Hatred that is personal rather than impersonal is much more thoroughgoing and often more vicious. Good sense suggests that we should get out of or depersonalize relationships dominated by intractable hatred, anger, or resentment. Interestingly, however, haters often don't get out of personal relationships with those they hate. And this calls for explanation. Such explanation must acknowledge that if I continue to hate *you* and to have your ill-being as one of my ends, there must be some sort of bond between you and me. *You* are important to me or I wouldn't devote my life to making *you* miserable. The opposite of love is not hatred; the opposite of love is indifference.

A second point important for the ethics of personal relationships is the possibility of one-sided personal relationships. Suppose I want *you* and you simply want to be loved and protected or to have a certain kind of marriage. Do I then have a personal relationship with you while you have an impersonal or quasi-personal relationship with me? Perhaps. But this surely is not the kind of relationship I will normally want. Such relationships are ripe for exploitation and tragedy. They are, in any case, almost always deeply disappointing, for we usually want *mutually* personal relationships. This means that not only do I want *you* and not just some producer of certain goods and services, but I want you to want *me*, not "someone who. . . ."

Although the logical structure of personal, quasi-personal, and impersonal relationships seems quite distinct, there can be tremendous . . . difficulties facing those of us who would know what kinds of relationships we have. Do I want *you* or do I want *something* (from you)? Do I want a relationship *with you* or do I want a *kind* of relationship with "someone who . . ."? Even if I think I want you, is it because I'm picking up on something that is *you*, or is it because you happen to resemble my childhood sweetheart, perhaps, or because you are so successful? If I cannot fathom my desires and intentions enough to make these discriminations accurately, it would be possible for me not to know whether I have a personal relationship with you, much less whether you have a personal relationship with me. These . . . difficulties notwithstanding, it may be *critically important*—both ethically and psychologically—to know what kinds of relationships we actually do have. Relationships are often made or broken by the issue of whether I want you or "someone who. . . ."

. . . Obviously, these characterizations of personal and quasi-personal relationships are based on my own intuitions, with which others may not agree. Fortunately, my argument does not require that my characterizations be accepted as necessary conditions, much less as necessary and sufficient conditions, for a personal relationship. It is enough for my purposes if it is admitted that many very healthy and beautiful personal relationships have the structure I have ascribed to them and that the reasons we often have for wanting personal relationships are expressed in my formulations.

II

Now for the ethics of personal relationships. My main contention and basic principle is that ethics must not depersonalize personal relationships, for doing so does violence to what these relationship are; to what is characteristically and normatively going on in them; and to the intentions, desires, and hopes we have in becoming involved in them. Particular persons figure essentially in personal relationships. But most ways of thinking about ethics invite or require us to treat ourselves or our loved ones as a "someone who. . . ." And this leads to many difficulties, both on the level of metaethical theory and on the practical level of ethical or moral prescription. . . .

III

"I don't want you to take me out," my wife exploded. "I just want you to want to go out with me. If you don't want to go out, let's just forget it." Motives, intentions, and reasons for acting play a *much* larger role in the ethics of personal relationships than they do in the ethics of impersonal relationships. In fact, the motivation of those who are close to us is often more important than the things which result from it. And even when actions are important in personal relationships, it is often because they are seen as symbols or symptoms of underlying feelings, desires, or commitments. Thus actions often seem worthless or even perverse if the motivation behind them is inappropriate.

In impersonal situations and relationships, on the other hand, we are much more content to allow people to do the right thing for the wrong reason and we are often even willing to provide incentives (for example, legal and financial) to increase the chances that they will do the right thing and also that they will do it for the wrong reason. I wouldn't, for example, be very much concerned about the motives of my congressman if I could be sure that he would always vote right. I believe that he should be well paid to increase the chances that he will vote right. But I would be deeply upset to learn that my wife is staying with me primarily for financial reasons. And I might be even more upset if her actions all along had been scrupulously wifelike. An ethics of personal relationships must, then, place more emphasis on motives and intentions, less on actions and consequences than most ethical theories have.

However, the motives that ethicists have found praiseworthy in impersonal contexts are usually inappropriate and unacceptable in personal contexts. Actions motivated by duty, a sense of obligation, or even a sense of responsibility are often unacceptable in personal relationships. A healthy personal relationship cannot be based on this sort of motivation; indeed, it cannot even come into play very often. . . . [It would be] devastating . . . to learn that your spouse of thirty-seven years had stayed in your marriage purely or even primarily out of a sense of obligation stemming from the marriage contract.

For similar reasons, motives of benevolence, pity, or compassion are also not acceptable as the characteristic or dominant motives in personal relationships. Acts of charity, altruism, and mercy are also, in general, out. As are sacrifices of important interests or a sense of self-sacrifice. Paternalism and maternalism are also generally unacceptable among adults in personal relationships. While it might be nice to feel yourself to be charitable, benevolent, or compassionate, who could endure being emotionally involved with someone who saw you essentially or even very often as an appropriate object of benevolence, charity, or pity? Of course, there always will be some occasions when you *are* an appropriate object of these attitudes, and it's desirable that they then be forthcoming . . . so long as they are viewed as exceptions. And yet, even in cases of great misfortune—if I contracted a debilitating disease, for example—I don't think I'd want my wife or friends to stay with me if they were motivated predominantly by pity or benevolence.

If even this much is correct, I think we can draw several lessons that point toward a deeper understanding of ethics in personal relationships. First, personal relationships between adults (and perhaps also between adults and children) are to be entered into and continued out of a sense of strength, fullness, and vitality, both in yourself and in the other, not out of a sense of weakness, need, emptiness, or incapacity.

Anything other than a shared sense of vitality and strength would lead to the unacceptable motives already discussed. Moreover, if I see myself primarily as a being in need, I will be too focused on myself and my needs. I will then tend to depersonalize you into a someone who can meet my needs. And I will also be generally unable to freely and joyously give: Since I see myself as not having enough as it is, my giving will seem to me a giving up. (Does this mean that those who most need a first-rate personal relationship will be unable to have one? I'm afraid that this might be true.)

The fact that giving characteristically must be free and joyous points to a second lesson about the ethics of personal relationships: Characteristically and normatively, the appropriate motive for action in personal relationships is simply that we want to do these things. Persons pursue whatever *ends* they have simply because they want to (that's what it means to say that something is an *end*, of course). And in a personal relationship, I and my well-being are ends of yours. From this vantage point it is easy to see why motives should play such a central role in personal relationships and also why *wanting* to do the things we do together is often the only acceptable motivation: That motivation is the touchstone of whether or not we have a personal relationship.

Of course, this is not to imply that personal relationships must rest simply on untutored feelings, taken as brute givens in the personalities of the participants. Indeed, it makes sense to talk about doing things, even for the wrong reasons, in order that doing those things will in time change you, your feelings, and your reasons. But it may be even more important to point out that continual attempts to create the right feelings in oneself are also not acceptable or satisfactory. If you must continually try to get yourself to want to do things with me, or for me, or for our relationship, we must at some point admit that I and my well-being are not among your ends and that we do not, therefore, have a personal relationship.

Nor am I claiming that actions motivated by a sense of duty or obligation, by altruism or self-sacrifice, by benevolence, pity, charity, sympathy, and so on *never* have a place in personal relationships. They may be appropriate in unusual circumstances. But such motives and actions are a fall-back mechanism which I compare to the safety net beneath a high wire act. We may be safer with a net, but the act is no good if the net actually comes into play very often. Similarly, the fall-back mechanisms may, in times of crisis, protect us and *some* of what we want, but they do not and cannot safeguard what is central to personal relationships. Thus when we find ourselves thinking characteristically or even very often in terms of the motives and concepts I have claimed are generally inappropriate in personal relationships, this is a symptom that our relationships are unsound, unhealthy, jeopardized, decayed, or that they never did become the personal relationships we wanted and hoped for. (Compare Hardwig, 1984.)

A third lesson about the ethics of personal relationships can be drawn from these reflections: The distinction between egoism and altruism is not characteristically applicable to personal relationships. Neither party magnanimously or ignominiously sacrifices personal interests, but the two interests are not independent, not really even two. For your ends are my ends too. The distinction between giving and receiving thus collapses. In impersonal contexts, if I respect your (independent) interests, that may be all you want of me. But in a personal context, you will want me to be interested in your interests. For if I am not interested in your interests, your well-being is not one of my ends.

This does not, of course, mean that all interests will be shared, but it means I am interested even in those of your interests I do not share. (I may have no appreciation of operas, but knowing how much they mean to you, it is important to me that your life include them. Operas for you are important to me in a way that operas for others who may love them just as much simply are not.) Nor, of course, am I claiming that there are *never* conflicts of interest in personal relationships. But such conflicts are set within the context of the meaning each has for the other and are therefore seen and handled differently. In personal relationships, conflicts of interest are conflicts within myself, a very different thing from a conflict of interest with someone separate from me.

A fourth lesson about ethics and personal relationships is this: Because personal relationships are ends—indeed, ultimate and incommensurable ends—they cannot and need not be justified by an appeal to some higher value such as love, pleasure, utility, or social utility. Any ethics that attempts to justify personal relationships in terms of more ultimate goods depersonalizes personal relationships. It construes us as wanting these higher goods, not each other.

Nor can the relative merits of personal relationships be adequately assessed in terms of abstract values. Each personal relationship is a good *sui generis.* Irreducibly involving the specific persons that they do, personal relationships cannot be reduced to common denominators that would permit comparison without depersonalizing them. Although persons caught in situations requiring choices between different personal relationships sometimes talk (and probably think) about comparing them in terms of abstract common denominators, evaluating relationships in this way Platonistically reduces our loved ones to mere instantiations of forms, thus depersonalizing them and our relationships to them.

A fifth and final lesson serves to summarize and conclude these reflections. The ethics of personal relationships must see persons in nonatomic terms; it must be based on a doctrine of internal relations. People see themselves in nonatomic terms if they see at least some other individuals not just as means to their well-being, but as part of their well-being. As I suggested earlier, there is no way to explain why I value a relationship with *you* (over and above the goods I desire from you and from this kind of relationship) except by saying that I feel a bond between us. I have come to see myself as a self that can only be fulfilled by a life that includes a relationship with you. Thus I see myself, in part, as part of a larger whole that is *us.* This does not mean that I see you as either a necessary or a sufficient condition for my well-being. If our relationship ends, my world will not fall apart and I may know that it won't. But if our relationship does end, I will have to alter my conception of myself and my well-being. . . .

Granted, we must remember that relationships can be viciously personal as well as gloriously personal. And it does seem plausible to maintain that we don't need an ethics for times when relationships are healthy and going smoothly. But again, I believe that the plausibility of this view reflects the limitations of the ways in which we have thought about ethics. I would contend, instead, that we *do* need an ethics for good times and for healthy, beautiful relationships—an ethics of *aspiration* that would serve to clarify what we aim for in personal relationships and to remind us of how they are best done.

Moreover, even when personal relationships become troubled, strained, or even vicious, it is not always possible or desirable to depersonalize the relationship. And an ethics must not tacitly urge or require us to depersonalize our relationships whenever serious conflicts arise. Within a personal relationship, the depersonalizing stance will often distort the issue beyond recognition. If we leave out my love for you, my turmoil over how often you drink yourself into oblivion vanishes, and with it, the issue that arises between us. For I can acknowledge with equanimity the drinking of others who are not personally related to me. My concern is simply not an impersonal concern that ranges indifferently over many possible objects of concern.

Depersonalizing (or ending) a relationship *may* be the appropriate final step in the face of intractable difficulties. But I would deny that depersonalizing is always the best course even here. For I think we should aspire to learn how to end relationships without depersonalizing them. If we can learn to continue to care and to care personally for our past loves, friends, and partners, we can be left happier, less bitter, wiser about the causes of the difficulties, and better able to go on to other relationships than if we end our relationships in hostility, anger, rejection, or even the kind of indifference characteristic of an impersonal stance.

What, then, is to be done? If we accept my position that we need an ethics of personal relationships and that such an ethics will have to be different from an ethics of impersonal relationships, the field of ethics opens up and ethical theory turns out to be a much less thoroughly explored domain than we might have thought. For my view implies that there are vast, largely uncharted regions beyond what we have come to know as ethics. I have tried to point to this region, but I have hardly begun to explore it.

1. We need to consider whether personal relationships are always better. If that view is correct, impersonal relationships would be only the result of the limitations of our sense of relatedness, and there would be a constant ethical imperative to personalize social contexts whenever possible and to expand our sense of connectedness. I suspect, however, that some relationships are better left impersonal and also that, because enmity, resentment, disgust, and many forms of conflict are much more bitter and intractable when they are personal, there are situations where depersonalizing is a good strategy. We must also understand more clearly exactly what depersonalizing a relationship involves.

2. We need an ethics for quasi-personal relationships (love, marriage, friendship) when these relationships are not also *personal* (in the sense I have been trying to explicate). For it is perhaps in such contexts that people are most devastatingly used, abused, and mistreated. Still, quasi-personal relationships have important roles to play, both when they do and when they do not involve a personal relationship: Marriage is also a financial institution; our concept of a parent seeks to insure that children will be protected and raised, even if not loved; even living together is in part an arrangement for sharing the chores of daily life.

3. We need some way to deal with the conflicts and tensions arising in situations involving both personal and impersonal relationships. Is it moral, for

example, for me to buy computer games and gold chains for my son while other children are starving, simply because he is *my son* and I have a personal relationship with him? The issues about the extent to which one can legitimately favor those to whom one is personally related are, for me, deeply troubling and almost impenetrable to my ethical insight. . . .

4. Then, when we have all this in view, we should perhaps reexamine our "stranger ethics" to see if we need to revise our ethics of impersonal relationships in light of the ethics of personal and quasi-personal relationships.

5. Finally, we undoubtedly need a more precise understanding of what makes relationships personal, a better grasp on the values of such relationships, and a much more rigorous and developed account of the ethics of personal relationships. For even if the present paper succeeds beyond my wildest dreams, it has only scratched the surface.

Until we have done all these things, it will be premature to make pronouncements about what constitutes "the moral point of view."

Note

Acknowledgments: This paper was begun in 1978 at a National Endowment for the Humanities Summer Seminar directed by Amelie Rorty. It has, in various versions, benefited from many helpful criticisms and suggestions from the members of that NEH seminar, from the Philosophy Departments at East Tennessee State University and Virginia Commonwealth University, from the members of Kathy Emmett's seminar on personal relationships, from the editors of the present volume, and especially from Amelie Rorty and Mary Read English. My many benefactors have left me with a whole sheaf of powerful and important ideas for revising, amending, and qualifying what I've said, but unfortunately too often without the wit and wisdom needed to incorporate their suggestions into this paper.

REVIEW QUESTIONS

1. Why does Hardwig believe that we don't yet have an ethics of personal relationships?
2. Paraphrase Hardwig's two main characteristics of personal relationships.
3. What does the "quasi" mean in quasi-personal relationships?
4. State and explain the basic principle of Hardwig's ethics of personal relationships.
5. Fill in the blanks and explain: "First, personal relationships between adults (and perhaps also between adults and children) are to be entered into and continued out of a sense of _____ , _____ and _____ , both in _____ and in the _____. . . ."
6. Explain what Hardwig means by his fifth lesson about the ethics of personal relationships; namely, that it's necessary to "see persons in nonatomic terms." Since this is such an important point, give a couple of examples of what it means to see persons as nonatomic.

PROBES

1. Explain the difference between treating a person as a means to an end and treating the person as an end in him- or herself. Give an example to illustrate your explanation.
2. What is the link between Hardwig's second main characteristics of a personal relationship and my discussion of uniqueness, or noninterchangeability, in Chapter 2?
3. Why does Hardwig believe that a one-sided personal relationship is "ripe for exploitation and tragedy"?
4. Why do motives and intentions play so much larger a role in personal relationships than in impersonal relationships?
5. Why does Hardwig discourage—but not completely reject—the motives of duty, altruism, pity, and sympathy in personal relationships?
6. Hardwig claims that the distinction between egoism and altruism is not normally applicable to personal relationships. Paraphrase the argument he makes to support this claim, and tell whether you agree or disagree.
7. Hardwig says that we should learn to end a relationship without depersonalizing it. Think back to the last time you ended a relationship. Did either of you depersonalize it? What effects did that have? How might you have kept it personal and yet ended it?

CHAPTER 11

Families

O ver the past five years, Julia Wood has written several well-received interpersonal communication books. This reading comes from a 1998 book designed to raise students' awareness of misunderstandings in human communication without analyzing them in great depth. This means that chapters are short and written in a conversational tone. All these features make this reading fit comfortably into *Bridges Not Walls*.

Julia Wood is a distinguished professor of communication studies at the University of North Carolina at Chapel Hill, recipient of four Outstanding Teacher awards, and author of more than 40 research articles and over a dozen books. These qualifications give her comments more credibility than some of what you'll find in popularized, self-help books.

I chose this selection because it offers an up-to-date and realistic description of the contemporary family, especially in the United States. Wood begins by contrasting the actual status of U.S. families with the myth of the traditional nuclear family—children living with a married mother and father. As she points out, the traditional picture excludes *the majority* of people living in the United States and much of the rest of the world.

Several examples illustrate her point. She describes how many African-American people understand "immediate family" to include many more people—for example, grandparents—than do some Caucasians. She also describes how lesbian and gay families are frequently misunderstood. She discusses some of the communication challenges faced by interracial families. And she outlines some ways members of divorced and blended families are often stereotyped. In this section, I'm reminded of the point I read that being a stepparent is probably *the* most difficult family role in Western culture today. Given the fact that around 50 percent of all marriages end in divorce and that many divorced people remarry, there are increasing numbers of women and men functioning as stepmothers and stepfathers. As Wood notes, children in blended families relate in different ways to their stepparents. But this often means that stepparents are caught between wanting to be full-fledged members of the family unit and being excluded by the natural parent and his or her offspring. This can be a recipe for anything from difficulty to disaster.

As a member of a childless couple, Wood also talks briefly about misunderstandings that occur around families without children. She often has to field the question, "Why don't you have a family?" with something like, "I *do* have a family—I have a husband, a sister, three nephews, and a niece." The final section in this part of the reading talks about *families of choice*. These are the family circles created by many gays, lesbians, and others "bound together by commitment, regardless of whether there are biological or legal ties."

The second major part of this reading directly addresses the discomfort some people have about discussions of family diversity because, for example, "My church says that homosexuality is immoral [and] I can't approve of that," or "It's wrong for members of one race to adopt children of a different race." Wood argues that you can respect a family form as a legitimate choice for others without embracing the choice for yourself. She also describes how family forms change over time in any culture, and she underscores the reality of family diversity today. Wood concludes with the suggestion that you can learn from observing and interacting with families different from your own. She gives an example of her own experience of learning about the relative lack of playfulness in her relationship with her partner by experiencing a family with young children.

Some of Wood's ideas are provocative. You may find yourself or some classmates resisting what she says. I hope that the group you're in will be able to discuss these responses as openly and productively as possible. I believe that the perspective on families that is offered here can provide a starting place for some fruitful thinking and feeling about family communication.

WHAT'S A FAMILY, ANYWAY?

Different Views of What Family Means

Julia T. Wood

In the autumn of 1992, the United States was engaged in its once-every-four-year ritual of presidential campaigning. One of the more memorable moments in the 1992 presidential race was when then–Vice President Dan Quayle castigated sitcom star Murphy Brown for choosing to be a single parent. Murphy Brown represents the decline of family values in America, proclaimed the vice president who, it turned out, was not to be reelected to a second term.

Who is Murphy Brown, and what did she do to earn such a chewing out from Dan Quayle? She was the female lead in a successful television situation comedy. Murphy was an accomplished professional, long parted from her former husband. She wanted a child and so she deliberately became pregnant (for the record, the father was her former husband) and gave birth to "baby Brown," who had to wait through several episodes to acquire a more personal name.

What's wrong with this picture? According to Dan Quayle, her choice to be a single mother was emblematic of the degeneration of morals and family values in America. Quayle spoke of the "right" kind of family as the traditional nuclear one—children who live with a married mother and father, who live together (that is, not separated or divorced and certainly not cohabiting without benefit of marriage). This is how the American family *should be,* insisted Dan Quayle. This kind of family is the only one that reflects "family values."

The problem with Quayle's definition of family is that it excludes the majority—yes, the *majority*—of people living in the United States as well as in the world. Instead of the singular model of family that Quayle championed, we have a cornucopia of different forms that are considered families by those who create and live in them. The family form Quayle endorsed, in fact, represents only a small portion of current U.S. families.

In the following pages, we consider the smorgasbord of families in the United States today. We also explore the ways in which failing to recognize multiple family forms can limit our personal growth and lead to misunderstandings and hurtful communication.

UNDERSTANDING THE MISUNDERSTANDING

There are several reasons that we may not wish to join Quayle in insisting there is one and only one "right" or "normal" family form. First, doing so limits our personal horizons and our opportunities to expand and enrich our own families. Second, recognizing only one form of family as legitimate disrespects the commitments of people whose families are unlike our own. Third, insisting that there is only one kind of "real," "moral," or "legitimate" family disregards the fact that society is always evolving, always in process. What family means, like the meanings of other things in the social world, changes over time. Finally, failure to recognize and respect different family forms can lead to misunderstandings in communication.

What Is Immediate Family?

One of the students I advise is an African American man who is preparing for a career in marketing. Franklin is an ideal student—smart, curious about ideas, responsible in getting his work done, and serious about his studies. Not long ago, Franklin came to me visibly upset, so I invited him to sit down and tell me what was bothering him.

"My grandmother had to go in the hospital for heart surgery, so I went home to be with her." I nodded. "I missed an exam in my history class. When I got back to school, I went to see Dr. Raymond to schedule a make up and he says he won't excuse my absence."

"Why not?" I asked. "Did he want some assurance that your grandmother really was in the hospital?"

Franklin shook his head. "No, I brought a copy of her admission form as proof. That's not the problem. He says he only excuses absences for medical problems in the student's *immediate* family."

Dr. Don Raymond, like many middle-class white people, thought of family as a mother, father (or stepmother or stepfather), and children. After all, when he was growing up, Don lived with his parents and two sisters. His other relatives did not live nearby and he saw them only once or twice a year, if that often. Now 48 years old, Don lives with his second wife and their two children, ages 12 and 15. He seldom sees his sisters and visits with his parents and in-laws only over Christmas. Aunts, uncles, and grandparents are not part of the immediate family that Don Raymond knows.

It wasn't difficult to resolve Franklin's situation. I simply called Don Raymond and talked with him about some of the typical differences between white and black family structures, and I emphasized that many African American families are more extended than those of most European Americans. Large, extended families are also common among second-generation Americans of many ethnic origins. Once Don understood that grandparents were immediate family to Franklin, he was more than willing to schedule a make-up examination.

There was nothing mean spirited or intentionally discriminatory in Don's initial refusal to schedule a make-up exam for Franklin. The problem was that he assumed—without even knowing he was making an assumption—that his definition of family was everyone's definition of family. He simply didn't understand that Franklin considered his grandmother immediate family. After all, she had raised him for the first seven years of his life, a situation not uncommon in African American families. She was more like a mother (in white terms) than a grandmother to him.

Lesbian and Gay Families

Lesbian and gay families are also frequently misunderstood. Not long ago I was having lunch with Jean and Arlene, who have been in a committed relationship for 15 years. With us were their two children, Michael and Arthur, age 6 and 8, respectively. A colleague of mine saw us in the restaurant and came over to our table to engage in small talk for a few minutes.

I offered the standard introduction: "Chuck Morris, I'd like you to meet Jean Thompson and Arlene Ross. And these are their sons, Michael and Arthur."

"Good to meet you," Chuck said. "Do you live here?"

"Yes, our home is just off Lystra Road," Arlene said. "And what about you?" Chuck asked Jean.

"Same place. The four of us are a family," she replied.

Chuck had made the mistake of assuming that the two women and the two sons constituted separate families. Once Jean clarified the relationship, Chuck understood and was not taken aback by the fact that Jean and Arlene were lesbians. Yet he was confused about the boys. "So how old were they when you got them?" he asked, assuming the boys were adopted.

"Depends on whether you count the gestation period," Jean said with a smile. She had run into this assumption before. "I carried Michael and Arlene carried Arthur."

"Oh, so they're your biological children?" he asked.

Arlene and Jean nodded.

Chuck made the mistake of assuming that lesbians (and gay men, too) can't be biological parents. Obviously they can, because sexual orientation has no bearing on a man's ability to produce viable sperm or a woman's ability to produce fertile eggs and carry a child in her womb. When we assume gay men and lesbians cannot have biological children, we conflate sexual orientation with reproductive ability.

Interracial Families

Misunderstandings also surround many interracial families. Matt and Vicky had been married for six years when they realized they weren't able to have biological children. They decided to adopt, first, James, and three years later, Sheryl. They love their son and daughter and consider themselves a close family. But, whenever they go out as a family, others subject them to stares and sometimes thoughtless comments.

"Are you baby-sitting?"

"Whose children are these?"

If you guessed that James and Sheryl are not the same race as Matt and Vicky, you're correct. The children are African American, and Matt and Vicky are European American. In recent years, two of my white friends have adopted children of other races—a young girl from China for one and a Native American girl for another. Like Matt and Vicky, they are hurt when people assume their children are not their children. Comments such as "Are you baby-sitting?" deny the families they have created.

Divorced and Blended Families

You have probably read the statistic that half of first marriages end in divorce. In addition, even more than half of second and subsequent marriages end in divorce. Divorce may end a marriage, but it doesn't end family. Instead, it changes the character and dynamics of family life.

If the former spouses had children, they are still parents, but how they parent changes. In some cases, one parent has sole custody of children and the other parent may have visiting rights. In other cases, parents agree to joint custody with each parent providing a home to children part of the time. Children experience two homes and two sets of rules, which may be inconsistent. One parent may have rigid requirements about dating, curfews, and household chores while the other parent is more relaxed.

If one or both parents remarry, families combine to create what are called blended families. Years ago *The Brady Bunch* was a popular television situation comedy. In it, two parents, each with several children, married and became a blended family. Among the Bradys, liking and comfort seemed effortless. Unlike the Bradys, many blended families find it difficult to reorganize into a functional, comfortable unit. Children may have to accommodate other children, from both former marriages and the current one, so jealousy and conflict often surface. New household rules may cause confusion, resentment, and resistance. Parents may have to accept the children's other parents and grandparents. And people outside the family may have to recognize multiple parents of children and both former and current spouses of parents.

Some children in blended families call their stepparent mother or father; other children reject that term. Similarly, some children in blended families consider their step-siblings and half-siblings brothers and sisters whereas other children don't accept those labels. When communicating with people who belong to divorced or blended families, we should be sensitive to how they perceive and name their family ties.

Families Without Children

My partner and I have been married for 23 years, and we have no children. We are a family without children. I am annoyed and hurt when people ask me, as they frequently do, "Why don't you have a family?" Sometimes I reply with a question: "What do *you* mean by family?" On other occasions, I respond by saying, "I *do* have a family—I have a husband, a sister, three nephews, and a niece." I consider all six of these people my immediate family. Like other people who don't have children, I resent it when others assume that I don't have a family just because Robbie and I don't have children.

What's a Family, Anyway?

Yet another kind of family was introduced by Kath Weston in her book, *Families We Choose*. Weston describes close friendship circles of gays and lesbians as the families they choose. For Weston, families are people who are bound together by commitment, regardless of whether there are biological or legal ties. Some biologically related people may have no commitment to each other and may refuse to interact. Siblings sometimes feel such animosity toward each other that they decide not to visit, write, call, or otherwise have contact. Some parents and children are estranged, and in extreme cases parents sometimes disown children. Biology, then, doesn't guarantee commitment.

Legal and religious procedures are also insufficient to ensure the level of commitment and caring most of us consider the crux of what a good family is. As noted earlier, current statistics indicate that approximately one-half of marriages in the United States will end in divorce. Laws that define marriage can be negated by laws that grant divorce. In a 1993 poll of the baby boom generation, only 58% of respondents said they considered it likely they would stay married to the same person for life. Pledging "until death do us part" before a magistrate or member of the clergy may create a legal marriage. It does not, however, guarantee that the people making the pledge will, in fact, be able or willing to stay together for life. These statistics show that the nature of family is neither as fixed nor as uniform as Dan Quayle suggested.

Thus, concludes Weston, it's reasonable to define family as people who elect to commit to each other in a sustained way—to have a family we choose. Their commitments may or may not be recognized by current laws or religious practices; but they are families, if by family we mean people who care about one another, organize their lives together, take care of one another, and intend to continue being together and caring for one another. This enlarged view of family pivots on the idea that people can commit to casting their fates together.

IMPROVING COMMUNICATION

When I teach about family diversity at my university, some of my students are uncomfortable. "I understand what you're saying," they often tell me, "but my church says that homosexuality is immoral. I can't approve of that." Others say, "It's wrong for members of one race to adopt children of a different race. The children will never understand their ethnic heritage. I just can't agree with interracial adoptions."

Distinguish Between Personal Choice and Respect for Others' Choices

What I try to show my students is that they don't have to embrace various family forms for themselves in order to respect them as legitimate choices for other people. In other words, there's a big difference between deciding what you personally want in a family (or career or spiritual practice or education or home life) and deciding to honor the choices that others make.

We already recognize and respect varied choices in many aspects of family life. For example, some parents believe that physically punishing children is wrong; other parents believe that if you spare the rod, you spoil the child. Some parents bring up children within strong religious traditions; other parents don't introduce children to any religious or spiritual path. In some families, children have to do chores and sometimes take on jobs outside the home to earn money; children in other families get automatic allowances. Few of us would label any of these choices wrong, deviant, or antifamily. Yet we sometimes find it difficult to accept other variations among families.

Recognize That Views of Family Change

Recently I collaborated with Steve Duck, who conducts research on communication and personal relationships, to co-edit a book. It includes chapters on different kinds of families, such as cohabiting couples, long-distance relationships, gay and lesbian commitments, and African-American and Hispanic families. The chapters in this book document the diversity of family forms in the United States today.

Family historian Stephanie Coontz points out that during the 300 years since Columbus landed in this hemisphere, families in the United States have taken many forms. The Iroquois lived with extended and matriarchal families, whereas the more nomadic Indian groups had small families. African-American slaves saw their nuclear families wrenched apart, so they developed extended communal networks, routinely engaged in co-parenting, and took orphaned children into their homes and raised them as their own, usually without formally adopting them.

The family form idealized by Dan Quayle came late in U.S. history and sustained its status as the dominant family form for only a short period. According to Coontz, only beginning in the 1920s did the majority of working-class white

people in the United States live in families that had male breadwinners and female homemakers. Today, by contrast, the majority of women work outside the
home, and approximately one-half of wives who work outside the home have
salaries equal to or greater than those of their husbands. The male breadwinner/
female homemaker model simply doesn't describe the majority of U.S. families
today.

Intact families, also part of Quayle's model, are more the exception than the
rule in this country. . . . Nearly half of first marriages (and an even greater percentage of second marriages) end in divorce. Only 50% of children live with
both their biological parents, and nearly one-quarter live with single parents,
usually their mothers.

The Census Bureau's 1996 survey of 60,000 U.S. households noted several
trends in families. The greatest shift is in the number of single-parent households.
Between 1990 and 1995, the number of single-parent families rose by a scant 3%.
In the single year 1995–1996, families headed by single mothers rose 12% as did
families headed by single fathers. Some single-parent households, such as Murphy Brown's, represent choices. In other cases, single parenting is not desired or
anticipated, but it becomes the only or the most acceptable option.

Recognize Diversity in Family Forms

Demographic trends in the United States clearly challenge the accuracy of any
singular view of what a family is. Effective participation in current society requires us to understand that people have diverse ideas about what counts as a
family and they have equally diverse ways of structuring family life. As one gay
man said to me, "I don't care if straights like me and my partner or not, but I do
care that they recognize I have rights to love a person and have a family just like
they do." Understanding this point can help us interact effectively in two ways.

First, when we recognize the normal diversity of family forms, we can
communicate more respectfully with people who have varying family structures. No longer is there a universal definition of family. Dan Quayle says single mothers are an affront to family values, but single mothers are no more or
less successful in parenting than married women. Just like mothers who are
married, some single mothers are devoted and effective parents, and some are
not. Just like married mothers, single mothers' effectiveness depends on a variety of factors including support networks, income, education, and employment.

Most states do not recognize gay and lesbian commitments, yet the evidence suggests they can be as healthy, stable, and enduring as heterosexual
unions. Even if gay and lesbian families do break up, that doesn't mean they
weren't families at one time. After all, if a heterosexual couple divorces, we
don't assume they were never married. Like heterosexuals, gays and lesbians
can pledge a lifetime of love and loyalty; like some heterosexuals, some gays
and lesbians will not realize that promise.

And what about the children of lesbian and gay parents? Child development
specialist Charlotte Patterson reports that there are currently between 1 million
and 5 million lesbian mothers and 1 million and 3 million gay fathers in the

United States and between 6 million and 14 million children who have a gay or lesbian parent. Many states don't allow gay or lesbian partners to be legal parents, even if one partner is the biological parent. These states argue that lesbians and gays cannot raise healthy children, but this argument isn't justified, according to *New York Times* columnist Jane Gross. Based on reviewing 35 studies of children who have gay or lesbian parents, Gross concluded that these children are as well adjusted as children of heterosexual parents and that they are no more or less likely to become gay or lesbian than the children of heterosexual parents. In a separate review of research, Charlotte Patterson found that children of gay and lesbian parents and children of heterosexual parents are no different in terms of intelligence, self-concept, and moral judgment. Existing evidence shows that both heterosexuals and gays and lesbians can raise children who are healthy and happy—and both can raise poorly adjusted children who have low self-concepts.

Learn from Differences

Diverse family forms also offer an opportunity for us to consider how we form our own families and live in them. Martha Barrett interviewed same-sex couples and concluded that they tend to relate to each other on equal terms more than do heterosexual couples. Barrett suggests that gays and lesbians have something to teach the heterosexual community about equality in rights and responsibilities in intimate relationships. Similarly, interracial families may discourage us from overemphasizing race in our thinking about personal identity and family. And families in which there are children may learn from child-free families about ways to keep couple communication alive and intimate.

We can learn about others and ourselves if we are open to differences in how people form and live in families. As long as we interact only with people whose families are like ours, it's hard for us to see some of the patterns and choices we've made in our own relationships. The particular ways that we charter our families remain invisible, unseen and unseeable because they seem "normal," "the only way to be a family." Yet when we consider some of the contrasts provided by interacting with people who have families different from ours, what was invisible and taken for granted in our own relationships becomes more visible. This realization allows us to reflect on the way we've created our families. In turn, this knowledge enables us to make more informed, more thoughtful choices about the kind of family we want to have.

In other words, heterosexuals don't have to change their sexual orientation to gain insight into their own relationships by observing gay and lesbian families. A heterosexual friend of mine once told me that only through her friendship with a lesbian couple had she realized how fully she centered her life around her male partner. She chose to stay married, but she and her husband communicated about ways they could be less centered on each other and enlarge their circle of friends.

A child-free family doesn't need to have children to learn something about their own relationship from interacting with families in which children are present. I've learned a lot about my relationship with Robbie by spending time with my sister Carolyn and her husband, Leigh, and their children, Michelle and Daniel. One of the insights I've gained from visiting them is that Robbie and I didn't include much play and frolic in our relationship.

Notice I used the past tense (didn't). Watching Carolyn and Leigh play with Michelle and Daniel and then blend into playfulness with each other allowed Robbie and me to notice that the playful dimension of relating was largely missing in our interaction. When Robbie and I played with Michelle and Daniel and then with them and their parents, we revived our dormant sense of how to be playful. Since learning this, Robbie and I have become more playful, even silly at times, with each other, and this enriches our marriage. Opening ourselves to various ways of being a family allows us to enlarge our personal identities and our relationships, including our own families.

REVIEW QUESTIONS

1. What is a nuclear family? How many nuclear families do you contact regularly? How many non-nuclear families do you contact regularly?
2. Who would you say makes up your immediate family?
3. What is a blended family?
4. Given all the different kinds of family forms Wood discusses, how do you believe she would define *family*? How do you define it? What does it take, in your opinion, to have a family?
5. Fill in the blanks and discuss the significance: Between 1990 and 1995, the number of single-parent families rose by _____ percent. In the single year 1995–1996, the number of single-parent families rose by _____ percent.
6. What does the initial research indicate about children raised by gay or lesbian parents?

PROBES

1. If you feel accepting of gay and lesbian couples being parents, what do you believe are the two or three strongest arguments against or challenges to those family configurations? If you have trouble accepting gay and lesbian couples being parents, what do you believe are the two or three strongest arguments in support of those family configurations?
2. A great deal of contemporary evidence indicates that globalization is a fact of life in business, music, banking, and academia. How is globalization related to interracial families?
3. What makes stepparenting such a difficult role to perform satisfactorily?
4. Wood argues that since we already respect considerable diversity in parenting styles, it should be possible to extend this respect to nontraditional family forms. How do you respond to this argument?
5. How diverse is your experience of other families? What is one way you might be able to increase the diversity of this part of your communication experience?

REFERENCES

Barrett, M. B. (1989). *Invisible lives: The truth about millions of women-loving women.* New York: Morrow.

Card, C. (1995). *Lesbian choices.* New York: Columbia University Press.

Changes in families reach plateau, study says. (1996, November 27). *Raleigh News and Observer,* pp. 1-A and 10-A.

Coontz, S. (1992). *The way we never were: American families and the nostalgia trap.* New York: Basic Books.

Coontz, S. (1996, May–June). Where are the good old days? *Modern Maturity,* pp. 36–43.

Ferrante, J. (1995). *Sociology: A global perspective* (2nd ed.). Belmont, CA: Wadsworth.

Goodman, E. (1997, January 17). Adopting across racial lines. *Raleigh News and Observer,* p. 13A.

Gross, J. (1991, February 11). New challenge of youth growing up in a gay home. *New York Times,* pp. 2B, 6B.

Guttmann, J. (1993). *Divorce in psychosocial perspective: Theory and research.* Hillsdale, NJ: Lawrence Erlbaum.

Indulgent "boomers" bring an unraveling of society. (1993, October 17). *Raleigh News and Observer,* p. 6E.

Marciano, T., & Sussman, M. B. (Eds.). (1991). *Wider families.* New York: Haworth Press.

Patterson, C. (1992). Children of lesbian and gay parents. *Child Development, 63,* 83–96.

Salter, S. (1996, April 7). With this ring I thee wed, or whatever. *San Francisco Examiner,* p. B-11.

Singer, B. L., & Deschamps, D. (Eds.). (1994). *Gay and lesbian stats: A pocket guide of facts and figures.* New York: The New Press.

Weston, K. (1991). *Families we choose.* New York: Columbia University Press.

Wood, J. T., & Duck, S. (Eds.). (1995). *Understanding relationship processes, 6: Understudied relationships: Off the beaten track.* Thousand Oaks, CA: Sage.

*A*s I said in Chapter 3, Virginia Satir was a family therapist who always emphasized the crucial importance of effective communication. Besides writing several influential books and offering dozens of workshops and seminars, she helped hundreds of families improve their communication. This reading is taken from her book *The New Peoplemaking.* In it, she explains what a family network is and how making a map of your family network can help reveal a great deal about how the family communicates.

Like most of her work, this essay is practical and applied. Satir asks you to actually draw a map of your family network as you read the selection. When you get to the point of specifying links between family pairs and role names for individuals, you'll begin to see how you can learn from this process. Then when you go to the next step—triangles— I suspect that additional insights will emerge. For example, I've often made one of Satir's points by noting that, although a triangle is the strongest geometric shape—it's widely used in bridges, house framing, cranes, and other structures—it is the weakest interpersonal shape. Why? Because, as Satir puts it, "A triangle is always a pair plus one and, since only two people can relate at one time, someone in the triangle is always the odd one out." This was a challenge for me to face when Kris's father died, leaving the triangle of me, Kris, and her mom; and the issue arose again 14 years later when Lincoln was born, creating a household of Kris, me, and Lincoln.

Satir offers several suggestions about how to handle the inevitable problems that arise from the triangles in a family. First, you need to understand that "no one can give equal attention to two people at the same time," but that if you are patient, the communication dynamic, like Texas weather, will change. A second step is to verbalize whatever concerns you have and to recognize that when you're the odd one out, it's because of the structure of the triangle, not because you are, or did something, wrong.

In the case of the family Satir uses as an example—the Lintons—the network includes 45 different units—five individuals, 10 pairs, and 30 triangles. No wonder family communication can be frustrating!

In this reading Satir does not explain specifically how to deal with all the family communication problems you might face. But she does provide a way to begin to understand what's going on, and this is a major contribution.

YOUR FAMILY MAP

Virginia Satir

When I first started working with entire families, I was struck by the tremendous unrelated activity that went on in all directions: physically through bodily movement and psychologically through double messages, unfinished sentences, and so on. More than anything else I was reminded of the can of angleworms my father used to take as bait on fishing trips. The worms were all entangled, constantly writhing and moving. I couldn't tell where one ended and the other began. They really couldn't go anywhere except up, and down, around, and sideways, but they certainly gave the impression of aliveness and purpose. Had I been able to talk to one of those worms to see how he felt, it is my feeling that

Reprinted by permission of the author and publisher, Virginia Satir, *The New Peoplemaking* available by contacting Science and Behavior Books, Inc., Palo Alto, California 800/547-9982.

he would have told me the same kinds of things I have heard from family members over the years: *Where am I going? What am I doing? Who am I?*

The comparison between the way many families conduct themselves and the purposeless, tangled writhing of these worms seemed so apt that I termed the network that exists among family members a *can of worms.*

To show you what your family network is and how to map it will be the goal of this [reading]. I think the best way to go about it is to take an imaginary family, the Lintons, and show you how their network works for and against them. No one can ever actually see this network, incidentally, but you can certainly feel it, as the exercises outlined in this [reading] will amply demonstrate to you.

All right. Here are the Lintons as individuals and as their family is today.

THE LINTON FAMILY NOW

ALICE
Adult Female
age 38

JOHN
Adult Male
age 40

JOE
Male Child
age 17

BOB
Male Child
age 16

TRUDY
Female Child
age 12

Tack a large sheet of paper to the wall where all of you can see it clearly. Begin the map of your family by drawing circles for each person, using a felt-tipped pen. Your family may now include a grandparent or other person as part of your household. If so, add a circle for that person on the row with the other adults.

If someone was once a part of your family but is gone now, represent her or him with a filled-in circle. If the husband or father is dead, has deserted the family or divorced his wife, and his wife has not remarried, your map would show it as follows:

If the woman has remarried, it would be shown thus:

If the second child died or was institutionalized, your map would look this way:

I believe that anyone who has ever been part of a family leaves a definite impact. A departed person is often very much alive in the memories of those left behind. Frequently, too, these memories play an important role—often a negative one—in what is going on in the present. This doesn't have to happen. If the departure has not been accepted, for whatever reason, the ghost is still very much around and often can disrupt the current scene. If, on the other hand, the departure has been accepted, then the present is clear as far as the departed one is concerned.

Each person is a separate self who can be described by name, physical characteristics, interests, tastes, talents, habits—all the qualities that relate to him or her as an individual.

So far our map shows the family members as islands, but anyone who has lived in a family knows that no one can remain an island for long. The various family members are connected by a whole network of ties. These links may be invisible, but they are there, as solid and firm as if they were woven of steel.

Let's add another strand to our network: pairs. Pairs have specific role names in a family. The illustration that follows shows the pairs in the Linton family with their *role names*.

Roles and pairs in the family fall into three major categories: marital, having the labels of husband and wife; parental-filial, having the labels of father-daughter, mother-daughter, father-son and mother-son; and sibling, having the labels of brother-brother, sister-sister, and brother-sister. Family roles always mean pairs. You can't take the role of a wife without a husband, nor father or mother without a son or daughter, and so on.

Beliefs about what different roles mean can differ. Each role evokes different expectations. It's important to find out what the various roles mean to each family member.

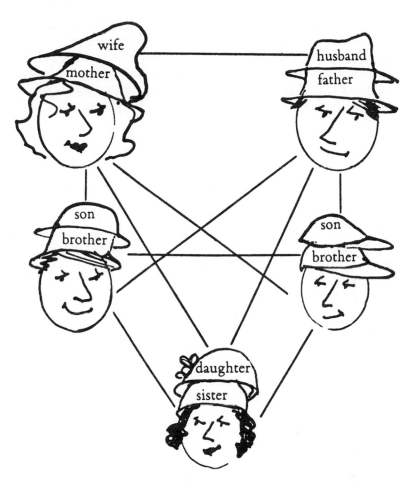

When families come to me a little mixed up, one of the first things I do is ask for each member's ideas about what his or her role means. I remember one couple very vividly. She said, "I think being a wife means always having the meals on time, seeing that my husband's clothes are in order, and keeping the unpleasant things about the children and the day from him. I think the husband should provide a good living. He should not give the wife any trouble."

He said, "I think a husband means being the head of the house, providing income, and sharing his problems with his wife. I think a wife ought to tell her husband what's going on. She ought to be a pussycat in bed."

You can see that both were practicing what they thought the roles were; they didn't know how far apart they actually were in these important areas. Never having spoken about it, they had just assumed their views on their respective roles were the same. When they shared their ideas, some new understanding developed between them, and they achieved a much more satisfying relationship. I have seen this particular couple's experience over and over again in troubled families that come to me for help.

What about your family and your respective role expectations and definitions? Why not all sit down and share what you think your role is, and those of your spouse and your offspring as well? I think you'll be in for some surprises.

Now let's examine another facet of this role business. Alice Linton is a person who lives and breathes and wears a certain dress size. She is also a wife when she is with John, and a mother when she is with Joe, Bob, or Trudy. It might be helpful if we think of her roles as different hats she puts on when the occasion demands. Aside from her self-role, which she wears all the time, Alice uses a particular hat only when she is with the person who corresponds to the role-hat. So she is constantly putting on and taking off hats as she goes through her day. If she or John were to wear all their role-hats at once, they would look like this, and it could get a little top-heavy.

Now add the network lines to your family map, linking every member with every other member. As you draw each line, think for a moment about that particular relationship. Imagine how each of those two people involved feels about that connection. All of the family should share in this exercise, so each can try to feel what the different relationships are like.

So far I have presented the Lintons to you as selves and pairs—five selves and ten pairs. If this were all there were to the map, living in a family would be quite an easy matter. When Joe arrived, however, a triangle came into being. Here the plot begins to thicken, for the triangle is the trap in which most families get caught. I'll talk more about triangles later, but first let's add the network of triangles to the Linton family map.

Now the Lintons' network looks like this. It's pretty hard to see any one part of it clearly, isn't it? You can see how the triangles obscure and complicate things. In families we don't live in pairs; we live in triangles.

When Joe was born, not one, but three triangles were formed. A triangle is always a pair plus one and, since only two people can relate at one time, someone in the triangle is always the odd one out. The whole nature of the triangle changes depending on who is odd one out, so what looks like one triangle actually is three (at different times).

Three [of the] triangles above [focus on] John, Alice, and Joe. In the first, John is the odd one, watching the relationship of his wife and son. In the second, Alice watches her husband and son together. In the third, little Joe watches his father and mother together. How troublesome any particular triangle is may depend on who is the odd one out at the moment and whether he or she feels bad about being left out.

There is truth to the old saying, "Two's company, three's a crowd." The odd person in a triangle always has a choice between breaking up the relationship between the other two, withdrawing from it, or supporting it by being an interested observer. The odd person's choice is crucial to the functioning of the whole family network.

All kinds of games go on among people in triangles. When a pair is talking, the third may interrupt or try to draw their attention. If the pair disagrees about something, one may invite the third to become an ally; this changes the triangle by making one of the original pair the odd one out.

Can you remember a time recently when you were with two other people? How did you handle that triangle? How did you feel? How are triangles handled in your family?

Families are full of triangles. The Linton family of five has thirty triangles:

John/his wife/his first son

John/his wife/his second son

John/his wife/his daughter

John/his first son/his second son

John/his first son/his daughter

John/his second son/his daughter

Alice/her husband/her first son
and so on.

Triangles are extremely important because the family's operation depends in large part on how triangles are handled.

The first step toward making a triangle bearable is to understand very clearly that no one can give equal attention to two people at the same time. Maybe the best idea is to approach the inevitable triangle as people do with Texas weather: stick around awhile, and it will change.

The second step, when you are the odd person, is to put your dilemma into words so that everyone can hear. The third step is to show by your own actions that being the odd one out isn't a cause for anger or hurt or shame. Problems arise when people feel that being on the outside means they are no good. Low self-worth!

To live comfortably in a triangle, it seems to me that one needs certain feelings about oneself. An individual has to feel good about him- or herself and be able to stand on two feet without leaning on someone else. He or she can be the odd one temporarily without feeling bad or rejected. She or he needs to be able to wait without feeling abused, talk straight and clearly, let the others know what she or he is feeling and thinking, and not brood or store up bad feelings.

If you glance again at the Lintons' family map and triangles, you can appreciate how complex family networks are. The concept of the can of worms may be more understandable to you, too.

Draw your family's can of worms by adding all the triangles to your family map. Using a different colored pencil or ink may help distinguish the triangles from the pairs. Again, as you draw, think of the relationship that each line represents. Among any three people you will be drawing only one triangle, although three actually exist. Think of how that triangle looks from each person's point of view.

The Lintons' network did not develop overnight. It took six years to gather the people now represented in the network—possibly eight years, if you consider the two years John and Alice courted. Some families take fifteen or twenty years to assemble their casts. Others take one or two years, and some never finish because the core (the couple in charge) keeps changing.

Whenever the Lintons are all together, forty-five different units are operating: five individuals, ten pairs, and thirty triangles. Similar elements exist in your family. Each person has his or her own mental picture of what each of these units is like. John may look very different to his wife Alice than to his son Bob. Alice may see her relationship to Bob one way; Bob would see it differently. John's picture is probably quite different from either of theirs. All these varying pictures are supposed to fit together in the family, whether or not the individuals are aware of them. In nurturing families, all of these elements and everyone's interpretation of them are out in the open and can easily be talked about. On the other hand, troubled families are either not aware of their family pictures or are unwilling or unable to talk about them.

Many families have told me they feel frustrated, physically tight, and uncomfortable when the whole family is assembled. Everyone feels constant movement, being pulled in many directions. If family members could be made aware of the can of worms in which they are trying to function, they wouldn't be so puzzled and uncomfortable.

When families see their network for the first time and fully realize how tremendously complicated family living really is, they often tell me they feel great relief. They realize they don't need to be on top of everything all the time. Who can keep track or control of forty-five units at once? Individual members can have a much easier time together because they didn't feel the necessity to control things; they became more interested in observing what is happening and in planning creative ways to make the family function better.

The challenge in family living is to find ways each individual can participate or be an observer of others without feeling he or she doesn't count. Meeting this challenge involves not being a victim of our old villain: low self-esteem.

A family's can of worms exerts tremendous push-pull pressures on the individual. It puts great demand on each one. In some families it is difficult to be an individual at all. The larger the family, the more units to be dealt with, the more difficult it is for each family member to get a share of the action. I certainly don't mean to imply that big families are always failures. On the contrary, some of the most nurturing families I know have large numbers of children.

Even so, the more children that come into the family, the more pressure on the marital relationship. A family of three has only three self-pair triangles; a family of four has twelve; a family of five has thirty; and a family of ten has 280 triangles! Each time a new person is added, the family's limited time and other resources have to be divided into smaller portions. A larger house and more money may be found, but the parents still have only two arms and two ears. And the airwaves can still carry only one set of words at a time without total bedlam.

What often happens is that the pressure of parenting gets so overwhelming that very little of the self of either parent finds expression, and the marital relationship grows weak with neglect. At this point many couples break up, give up, and run away. They have starved as individuals, failed as mates, and probably aren't doing very well as parents, either. Frustrated, turned off, emotionally dying adults don't make good family leaders.

Unless the marital relationship is protected and given a chance to flower and unless each partner has a chance to develop the family system becomes crooked and the children are bound to be lopsided in their growth.

Being good, balanced parents is not impossible. It is just that parents must be particularly skillful and aware to maintain their selfhood and keep their marriage partnership alive when the can of worms is so full. Such parents will be in charge of nurturing families. They are living examples of the kind of family functioning that channels pressures in the family network into creative, growth-producing directions.

REVIEW QUESTIONS

1. What are Satir's three major categories of roles and pairs in the family?
2. What's the relationship between family roles and expectations?
3. Satir's family (the Lintons) is made up of five people who comprise 30 triangles. How many triangles are there in your family?
4. What main points does Satir make about the tremendous complexity of family relationships?

PROBES

1. Why does Satir suggest that you include family members who have died or been institutionalized on your family map?
2. Why does Satir say that "family roles always mean pairs"?
3. What important feature is added to your family map when you move from pairs to triangles (besides the obvious additional person)?
4. Satir's map shows pairs and triangles linking *all* the members of a family. Do you think this is always true of family networks? Are there ever family members who are *not* connected as a pair or as part of a triangle?
5. Paraphrase Satir's main piece of advice to parents.

CHAPTER 12

Intimate Partners

O ne of the most dominant ideas in the late 1990s has been that, as author John Gray put it, "men are from Mars and women are from Venus." According to a considerable amount of scholarly research and several popular accounts of this research in Gray's hugely successful book and several best-sellers by Deborah Tannen, men and women have significantly different communication styles. This literature argues that a great deal of the misunderstanding between men and women is due to these differences, and that it can help for both genders to learn to accept these differences, and even to communicate using the other gender's preferred style.

This excerpt from the 1997 book *Sex and Gender Differences in Personal Relationships* challenges almost every claim that Gray and Tannen make. Communication researcher and teacher Daniel Canary and his coauthors claim that most of the research on gender and communication, when it is examined carefully, "does *not* support the view that men and women come from separate cultures, let alone separate worlds." They argue that these "long-presumed differences in men's and women's interpersonal behavior simply do not reflect in the empirical research literature." In other words, this reading claims that, if you examine studies of what actually happens when men and women communicate, you will not find support for the "two cultures," "Mars and Venus" view.

Instead, there is evidence for much more similarity than difference. For example, a review of some 1,200 studies regarding sex differences in social behavior found that only about 1 percent of the variance in people's social behavior is attributable to sex or gender. "If men and women do originate from different cultures or worlds, " these authors conclude, "they at least speak the same language about 99% of the time."

A major part of the problem, these authors argue, is that some of the people who contend that there are vast differences have stereotyped the women and men they have studied. Once these stereotypes are in the literature, they influence the studies that come after them. Canary, Emmers-Sommer, and Faulkner argue that, even though gender stereotypes offer simple answers to complex and troubling questions, there is in the end little to be gained by polarizing men and women in these ways. The serious problem, as these authors put it, is that "if one holds that men are from Mars and women are from Venus, then it follows that Earth provides no home for either sex."

This reading unpacks this problem, first, by defining *sex* and *gender* in order to clarify what's being studied in these articles and books. Then the authors analyze the presumption of differences between the genders. They acknowledge that there are obviously important distinctions in both sex and gender. But when one asks about whether there are consistent and important sex and gender differences in personal relationships, things are not so clear-cut.

One claim in the popular books is that women tend to be communal and men tend to be instrumental. But if one looks at much of the evidence, it is difficult to find these simple and clear differences. As this reading puts it, "expressive and instrumental characteristics are about equally prominent aspects of a strong friendship for both women and men." Another researcher concluded that "similarities between men and women [are] far greater than the differences, and that knowledge about a person's [sex] will give us little ability to accurately predict how a person will behave in many situations."

In place of the simplified stereotype, Canary and his colleagues propose what they call a "flowchart model" for predicting stereotypic interaction behavior. The model, which is presented in Figure 1 in this reading, indicates that sex-stereotyped behavior is liable to occur only when several of five conditions are present: (1) The people involved are focusing on gender, (2) their beliefs are consistent with stereotypes, (3) the context or situation is not one where men and women fill similar roles (e.g., managers or teachers), (4) the participants don't expect nonstereotyped behaviors, and (5) the partner's behavior promotes sexual stereotypes. When *these* conditions exist, then you're likely to observe "Mars vs. Venus" phenomena. But in the overwhelming percentage of the time when these conditions do not exist—for example, when the men and women are of similar role or status, when nobody is expecting sex-stereotyped behavior, and when sex or gender is irrelevant to the communicators—then there will be many more similarities than differences between women and men.

I chose this reading to challenge a currently popular set of beliefs about gender and communication, and to warn readers about the dangers of believing everything that's written in best-selling books. I hope these pages will encourage you to think again about the whole "Mars–Venus" hypothesis.

At the same time, I also hope you won't just accept *this* reading at face value. One of the reasons the "Mars–Venus" hypothesis is so popular is that *it resonates with many peoples' experiences.* Here, Canary and his colleagues argue that ordinary people have been misled, and that social science can free them from their confusion. Sometimes this is called the "cultural dopes" argument. It says that you can't trust laypeople to get it right, but that experts—usually some kind of scientists—can be trusted to have insight into the Truth. But does this idea make sense to you? Are laypeople this gullible? Or does the incredibly widespread acceptance of the "Mars–Venus" idea argue for its validity? I hope you'll think about these questions and discuss them in class.

MOVING BEYOND SEX AND GENDER STEREOTYPES

Daniel J. Canary and Tara M. Emmers-Sommer, with Sandra Faulkner

> *There are two types of people in this world—those who*
> *categorize people into one of two groups and those who*
> *do not.*
>
> —Popular paradox

How men and women communicate in their personal relationships has become a "hot" topic in both academic and popular discussions. A common assumption stresses differences between men and women that might explain problems between the sexes, which is conveyed in generalizations that take the form "Women want this, whereas men want that." Such views also suggest that people have only one brand of each sex to choose from; that is, all men are alike and all women resemble each other. . . . We attempt to counter the prevailing notion that differences between the sexes are constant and reveal separate molds, and we present an alternative to categorical thinking about men and women in their personal relationships. . . .

One relevant influence [on us as authors] is the recent popular portrayal of men and women. In 1990, Deborah Tannen published her widely accepted quasi-academic book, *You Just Don't Understand,* wherein men and women were cast as though they come from different cultures. Academics and lay people alike read Tannen's accounts of various "composite" couples and appreciated the nuance that Tannen offered. In addition, the two-cultures approach offered an alternative, though not necessarily an opposite point of view, to the dominance perspective that was popular in the 1970s and 1980s. Then John Gray (1992) exaggerated sex differences even further with the analogy that men are from Mars and women are from Venus, a thought that was inspired by the film *E.T.* (Gleick, 1997). The "nonfiction" portrayals by Tannen and Gray of men's and women's communication remained best sellers for years.

[But] most of the research does *not* support the view that men and women come from separate cultures, let alone separate worlds. Long-presumed differences in men's and women's interpersonal behavior simply do not reflect in the empirical research literature. Sex differences do not emerge because many researchers (like lay individuals) rely on traditional sex stereotypes when constructing the difference argument (i.e., men are instrumental, assertive, insensitive, and dominant, whereas women are communal, passive, sensitive, and subordinate), and the research shows that sex stereotypes poorly predict interpersonal communication behaviors.

Indeed, research suggests far more similarity than differences in men's and women's communication. For example, Canary and Hause (1993) reviewed 15

Excerpts from *Sex and Gender Differences in Personal Relationships* by Daniel J. Canary, Tara M. Emmers-Sommer, with Sandra Faulkner. Reprinted by permission of The Guilford Press.

meta-analyses (representing some 1,200 studies) regarding sex differences in social behavior and found that about only 1% of the variance in people's social behavior derives from sex differences. Likewise, in the area of organizational communication, Wilkins and Andersen's (1991) meta-analysis (which was missed by
Canary & Hause) found only one-half of 1% variance in behavior that was due
to sex differences. According to these objective summaries, men and women are
much more similar than different. If men and women do originate from different
cultures or worlds, they at least speak the same language about 99% of the time.

Yet no one can deny that men and women are different. The issue is to provide some account of sex or gender that provides more insights than stereotypes
can offer. Recently, scholars in psychology, communication, sociology, and related fields have offered theoretical models regarding men's and women's interaction in general that do not rely on stereotypic beliefs (e.g., Deaux & Major,
1987). . . .

How scholars and lay people conceptualize sex and/or gender differences
varies radically. Accordingly, we do not anticipate widespread agreement with
the points we make. We do hope for continued discussion about how men and
women do, in fact, communicate and create expectations.

Many people still rely on stereotypes for their judgments on the issue of sex
differences. But such a reliance on stereotypes only serves to perpetuate them
among students and lay persons. In our view, the perpetuation of stereotypes
constitutes the most disheartening outcome of books that distort and emphasize
sex differences. If people come to believe that they are from separate cultures or
worlds and that their social behavior is cast from separate molds, then they may
never accept the idea that they can create their own gendered identities. As a result, advances in social, political, and economic equity might be handicapped by
outdated notions of what men and women are capable of doing. [Here, we at-
tempt] to correct an antiquated, unfair portrayal of women and men. Many people still measure a man by his career advancement and intelligence and a woman
by her looks and spending habits. In light of widespread acceptance of such notions, our goal is to examine men and women in close relationships without assuming one sex is attracted to the mall, and the other a "cave" (Gray, 1992).

DO MEN AND WOMEN
INHABIT DIFFERENT WORLDS?

John Gray's *Men Are from Mars, Women Are from Venus* (1992) has sold over 6 million copies—more than any other nonfiction hardcover book (Gleick, 1997,
p. 69). Gray argues that men and women are so entirely different that it appears
they come from different planets. And these planets have alternative meanings
for the same language. But somewhere along the way, we have forgotten that
men and women originated in different worlds and that we need an interpreter
(John Gray?) to help us understand each other. This analogy not only provides
the foundation for Gray's portrayal of personal relationships between men and
women, it also serves as the premise for the entire book (and several other books

Gray has written). Gray's success in using this figurative analogy as a premise for understanding men and women cannot be denied in a social or monetary sense—Gray enjoys thousands of loyal followers and has earned approximately $18 million from book sales alone (i.e., not counting money he gets from seminars [$35,000 per engagement], Mars and Venus Counseling Centers, or multimedia [videos, CDs, etc.]; Gleick, 1997).

Of course, Gray's figurative analogy presents a polarized view of men and women communicating with each other. For example, consider the following passage about how one sex difference hurts relationships:

> Women generally do not understand how Martians [men] cope with stress. They expect men to open up and talk about all their problems the way Venusians [women] do. When a man is stuck in his cave, a woman resents his not being more open. She feels hurt when he turns on the news or goes outside to play some basketball and ignores her.
>
> To expect a man who is in his cave instantly to become open, responsive, and loving is as unrealistic as expecting a woman who is upset immediately to calm down and make complete sense. It is a mistake to expect a man to always be in touch with his loving feelings just as it is a mistake to expect a woman's feelings to always be rational and logical. (p. 33)

To the extent one accepts the premise that men and women are so different they seem to come from different social and psychological worlds, Gray's many prescriptions regarding communication make sense. However, to the extent one finds the premise grossly exaggerated (and it is), then such a polarizing and stereotypic presentation of men and women appears fictional and offensive (see Crawford, 1995, for other examples regarding Gray's extreme position).

Although polarized portrayals of men and women may be entertaining (see also Tannen, 1990), one must wonder at their effect on people's understanding of sex and gender roles and how men and women *should* act in their close relationships. Geis (1993), for example, has provided evidence that at a general social level stereotypes act as value-laden, self-fulfilling prophecies. In other words, stereotypes about men and women become standards for behavior. Moreover, people have a tendency to create bipolar constructs, and thereby they essentialize the "male" and "female" qualities (Thorne, 1990). The question then is whether such polarized views function for the social good, for scientific purposes, or whether they have little social or scientific payoff.

Putnam (1982) argued that nothing can be gained by polarizing men and women through reliance on stereotypes. More specifically, she pointed out that understanding sex/gender differences in social interaction behavior requires more than an affirmation of sex stereotypes that portray women as communal (i.e., primarily concerned with relational welfare) and men as instrumental (i.e., primarily concerned with task-related resources). She described the landscape of scientific theory on the issue as "barren," largely due to the polarizations of men and women that reside in traditional stereotypes.

Of course, many scholars have invested considerable effort in delineating the structure and content of sex stereotypes (e.g., Eagly & Steffen, 1984). Deaux and Lewis (1984) reported that the stereotypical man is instrumental, assertive, competitive, dynamic, and task-competent, whereas the stereotypical woman is kind, nurturing, sensitive, relationally oriented, and expressive. These authors found that their participants rely on such labels until they learn more specific information about one another, as partners do in close relationships.

Stereotypes can offer a means to explain sex and gender differences on at least two levels: (1) as a way to predict men's and women's behavioral differences; and (2) as a way that people establish baselines for expectations about other people's behavior. In the former case, researchers adopt sex role stereotypes to construct their own concepts and measures (e.g., Bem, 1974); in the latter case, researchers hold that participants rely on stereotypes to know how to behave or to judge behavior (e.g., Geis, 1993).

The problem does not reside in the theoretical construction and explanation of the understanding of the nature and function of stereotypes in interaction behavior; rather, the problem arises when researchers uncritically—and perhaps without realizing they do so—adopt stereotypes as a means for scientifically explaining and predicting sex and gender differences. Adopting stereotypic thinking represents a rather simple solution to the sex difference issues, although as a solution it is inadequate because people do not reliably conform in their interaction behavior to conventional sex stereotypes (Aries, 1996). Although we concur with Deaux (1984) and others who claim that sex stereotypes are pervasive, we also contend that they appear baldly essentializing in their portrayals of men's and women's behavior. In particular, we contend that stereotypes do not adequately or accurately represent men's and women's interactions in personal relationships.

We acknowledge that men and women sometimes differ in their interaction behavior and they sometimes rely on stereotypes as guidelines for interaction behavior (Deaux & Major, 1987). However, such stereotypes present an outdated view of men and women that distorts scientific understandings of male and female interaction, *especially in the context of personal relationships.* If one holds that men are from Mars and women are from Venus, then it follows that Earth provides no home for either sex.

INVESTIGATING SEX AND GENDER DIFFERENCES IN PERSONAL RELATIONSHIPS

Defining Sex and Gender

Defining terms is an important obligation because definitions establish the boundaries of a phenomenon and indicate one's understanding of it. We have considered several issues in the debate over the definition of the terms *sex* and *gender.* For instance, some scholars hold that gender is partially composed of one's biological sex, but that gender also entails "the psychological, social, and cultural features and characteristics strongly associated with the biological categories of male and female" (Gilbert, 1993, p. 11). Likewise, Moore (1994) has argued that the construct of sex entails both a reference to objective differences in the genetic/biological composition of men and women and to people's beliefs accompanying the term "sex"; gender refers to the cultural understandings and explanations that people have for sex. Accordingly, "sex" is partially socially constructed, is sometimes conflated with *sexuality*, and connotes sexual intercourse. In the scholarly debate about the term "gender," some argue that gender refers to cultural differences between men and women, whereas others argue that gender is a grammatical device (as in "masculine" nouns), and still others argue that gender refers exclusively to "women" and women's attitudes and behaviors (Scott, 1996).

Despite the definitional debates on the topic, which can appear quite nuanced, we opt for a clear distinction. More precisely, we adopt the advice set forth in the *Journal of Social and Personal Relationships (JSPR)* and define *sex* as the biological distinctions between men and women and *gender* as the social, psychological, and cultural differentiations between men and women (see also Deaux, 1985). This convention allows us to be clear about our terms, and this distinction appears to be gaining support among those who define *sex* versus *gender*. . . .

Assessing the Presumption of Differences

One does not need supporting research to claim that sex differences exist. Men and women obviously differ. Men's genetic code differs from women's, men have historically enjoyed greater sociopolitical power and status, and women have been conferred greater prestige in relationship matters. Yet precisely *how* men and women differ in their personal relationships remains quite a mystery, especially in comparison to sex differences on display in physical and sociopolitical realms of behavior. Sex and gender differences in personal relationships emerge in minute interaction behaviors, often in private contexts, and within different subcultures that defy sweeping, categorical generalizations about men's and women's behaviors in "society at large."

The issue of whether or not pervasive sex/gender differences exist in personal relationships is addressed variously and often inferred from research involving acquaintances or strangers. For example, Henley (1977) focused on how women suffer power deficits in the context of cross-sex interaction, arguing that men's greater occupational status affords them more power and freedom in several behavioral categories: space (e.g., women use less space in interactions with men), time (e.g., women wait on men), environment (e.g., women have less freedom to arrange their environment), language (e.g., men talk longer), demeanor (e.g., men act more relaxed), touch (men can, women cannot), eye contact (men stare, have higher visual dominance scores), and facial expression (e.g., women must offer a pleasant smile). Henley's review strongly supported the contention that men consistently dominate women through communication behavior.

More recently, scholars in the fields of communication, psychology, and family studies (among others) have begun to doubt findings regarding sex/gender differences that reflect the traditional women-as-communal and men-as-instrumental categories (e.g., various views by authors in Canary & Dindia, in press). Ragan (1989) observed that the study of sex differences in communication presents no single consistent finding. In a noteworthy paper, Duck and Wright (1993) reversed their own earlier interpretations of two sets of data to conclude that, within the sexes, the friendships of men and women were more similar than different: "Within sexes, characteristics that are important in friendship do not fit readily into expressive vs. instrumental categories for either women or men. That is, according to our factor analyses, expressive and instrumental characteristics are about equally prominent aspects of a strong friendship for both women and men" (p. 724). Analyzing the research on group interaction using Interaction Process Analysis (IPA), Aries (1996) also reversed an earlier claim she made that supported the stereotype of men as instrumental and women as communal:

> . . . While the case has been made that men are instrumental and women expressive, a closer examination of these studies suggests that this stereotyped description of men and women is an exaggeration of the data, that the differences are small to moderate in magnitude, and that role differentiation along instrumental–expressive lines by males and females does not appear consistently in all group situations. (p. 27)

Aries (1996) proceeded to review, in detail, interaction differences between men and women in a variety of behavioral domains (i.e., self-disclosure, leadership behaviors, interruptions, conversational management, etc.), and she concluded, "I have gone back through the research literature to demonstrate that the data reveal similarities between men and women to be far greater than the differences, and that knowledge about a person's [sex] will give us little ability to accurately predict how a person will behave in many situations" (p. 189). . . .

A FLOWCHART MODEL PREDICTING STEREOTYPIC INTERACTION BEHAVIOR

We believe that sex differences exist, but the manner in which they emerge in interaction behavior between partners remains opaque. As indicated above, the primary culprit for the fuzzy picture appears to be researchers' reliance on and perpetuation of exaggerated, "main effect" polarization arising from stereotypes (see also Aries, 1996; Putnam, 1982; Ragan, 1989). If we consider various models for sex-linked behavior (i.e., that within-group differences exist for men and women), and if we allow for various countervailing influences on one's communication behavior, then we should find as invalid studies presuming that stereotypes are powerful influences. Figure 1 presents what researchers and readers need to address when presupposing stereotypic behavior.

The model we offer in Figure 1 indicates how sex-relevant beliefs affect interaction (see also Deaux & Major, 1987). The flowchart in Figure 1 offers five questions that people should consider regarding behavior between close relationship partners (e.g., self-disclosure, touch, conflict). Our objective in this exercise is to show some of the pitfalls contained in the presumption of stereotypic sex differences in personal relationships. We assume that the mediating factors

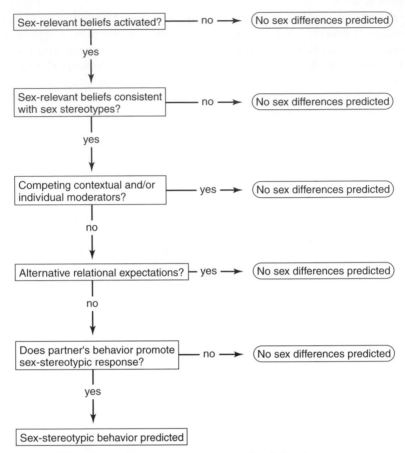

FIGURE 1 Model predicting sex-stereotypic interaction behaviors.

listed in Figure 1 are most often significant in personal relationships. In addition, we assume that during interaction two people are communicating, although this model might apply to other contexts (e.g., small groups, organizations). Finally, we focus on the sex-relevant behaviors of one person at a time (i.e., the *actor*), which reflects other researchers' view of sex as an individual, structural variable. The same questions addressed at the dyadic level would double and become more difficult to answer. Nevertheless, the search for stereotypic sex differences progresses as one answers each of the questions [in Figure 1].

    . . . Some authors argue that stereotypes are widely held and prompt people to conform to expectations implied by the stereotype in a self-fulfilling manner (Geis, 1993). At a social level, interactions exist wherein stereotypic responses may prevail and reinforce gender stereotypes (Deaux & Major, 1987). But the extent to which the self-fulfilling nature of stereotypes extends into personal relationships remains unclear, though we acknowledge that it happens. Geis (1993) noted that education about stereotypes and currently shifting occupational roles of men and women can counterbalance the self-fulfilling nature of stereotypes. One should be able to locate where the enactment and perception of stereotypic behavior occur in interaction that might prompt a stereotypic response. Whereas the data appear to support a few *general* trends among acquaintances regarding stereotyping and self-fulfilling behavior, the literature does not reveal specific stereotypic communication behaviors in close involvements. We question the assumption that stereotypic responses typify interaction in close, personal relationships (see also Duck & Wright, 1993).

CONCLUSION

Many social scientific researchers have examined sex and gender differences in interaction behavior for the past 50 years, though much of this research perpetuates stereotypic thinking of how men and women communicate in their personal relationships. Feminist reactions to sex differences have generally taken two routes, to deny difference or to celebrate women's differences. The meaning of difference has been problematic at best, restricting opportunities for both men and women and ignoring their experiences (Rhode, 1990).

Some people assume that differences between men and women reflect stable predispositions, leaving out potentially more important aspects of individuals and culture. In addition, as Deaux and Major (1990) stated, "Dualistic assumptions about gender may also preclude other relevant categories—race, class, age—from entering the analysis" (p. 89). We hope to locate places when difference should be questioned and when it should be celebrated. In our view, the quality of our close relationships depends on increased understanding of sex differences and similarities as well as the activities that reflect people's gender.

REVIEW QUESTIONS

1. The authors say that the "Mars–Venus" hypothesis is not supported by "the empirical research literature." What do they mean by "the empirical research literature"?
2. Explain the "Mars–Venus" hypothesis. According to this view, how do men generally communicate? How do women generally communicate?
3. Canary and his coauthors cite research that says that relational partners rely on stereotypes only until what happens?
4. Explain the difference between sex and gender.
5. What do you understand to be the basic message or insight of the flowchart model in Figure 1?
6. What do the authors mean in the conclusion when they agree with Deaux and Major, who wrote, "Dualistic assumptions about gender may also preclude other relevant categories—race, class, age—from entering the analysis"?

PROBES

1. You would certainly assume that authors like John Gray and Deborah Tannen, who support the "Mars–Venus" hypothesis do not *mean* to be reinforcing sex stereotypes. And yet Canary and his colleagues say that they are. How does this literature end up doing what it doesn't appear to mean to be doing?

2. How do you respond to the quotation from Gray's "Mars–Venus" book [p. 400] that begins, "Women generally do not understand how Martians [men] cope with stress" and ends "just as it is a mistake to expect a woman's feelings to always be rational and logical"? Do you sense stereotyping in these two paragraphs?

3. Explain how the distinction between sex and gender can complicate the answer to the question, "How do men and women actually communicate in close, personal relationships?"

4. The flowchart model in Figure 1 says that sex-stereotyped communication behavior is likely to happen *only* when at least several of five conditions are present. The first is "sex-relevant beliefs activated." This means that in order to have "Mars–Venus" behavior, one thing the parties have to be doing is consciously thinking about some sex-relevant beliefs ("Is she likely to be feeling differently because she's a woman?" "Is this a guy thing?"). Explain the other four conditions.

REFERENCES

Aries, E. (1996). *Men and women in interaction: Reconsidering the differences.* New York: Oxford University Press.

Bem, S. L. (1974). The measurement of psychological androgyny. *Journal of Consulting and Clinical Psychology, 42,* 155–162.

Canary, D. J., & Dindia, K. (Eds.). (in press). *Sex differences in communication.* Mahwah, NJ: Erlbaum.

Canary, D. J., & Hause, I. S. (1993). Is there any reason to research sex differences in communication? *Communication Quarterly, 41,* 129–141.

Crawford, M. (1995). *Talking difference: On gender and language.* Thousand Oaks, CA: Sage.

Deaux, K. (1984). From individual differences to social categories: Analysis of a decade's research on gender. *American Psychologist, 39,* 105–116.

Deaux, K. (1985). Sex and gender. *Annual Review of Psychology, 36,* 49–81.

Deaux, K., & Lewis, L. L. (1984). The structure of gender stereotypes: Interrelationships among components and gender label. *Journal of Personality and Social Psychology, 46,* 991–1004.

Deaux, K., & Major, B. (1987). Putting gender into context: An interactive model of gender related behavior. *Psychological Review, 94,* 369–389.

Deaux, K., & Major. B. (1990). A social-psychological model of gender. In D. L. Rhode (Ed.), *Theoretical perspectives on sexual difference* (pp. 89–99). New Haven, CT: Yale University Press.

Duck, S., & Wright, P. (1993). Reexamining gender differences in same-gender friendships: A close look at two kinds of data. *Sex Roles, 28,* 709–727.

Eagly, A. H., & Steffen, V. (1984). Gender stereotypes stem from the distribution of women and men into social roles. *Journal of Personality and Social Psychology, 46,* 735–754.

Geis, F. L. (1993). Self-fulfilling prophecies: A social psychological view of gender. In A. E. Beall & R. U. Sternberg (Eds.), *The psychology of gender* (pp. 9–54). New York: Guilford Press.

Gilbert, L. A. (1993). *Two careers/one family: The promise of gender equality.* Newbury Park, CA: Sage.

Gleick, E. (1997). Tower of psychobabble. *Time, 149,* 69–70, 72.

Gray, J. (1992). *Men are from Mars, women are from Venus.* New York: HarperCollins.

Henley, N. (1977). *Body politics: Power, sex, and non-verbal communication.* Englewood Cliffs, NJ: Prentice Hall.

Moore, H. L. (1994). Understanding sex and gender. In T. Ingold (Ed.), *Companion encyclopedia of anthropology* (pp. 813–830). New York: Routledge.

Putnam, L. L. (1982). In search of gender: A critique of communication and sex roles research. *Women's Studies in Communication, 5,* 1–9.

Ragan, S. L. (1989). Communication between the sexes: A consideration of differences in adult communication. In J. F. Nussbaum (Ed.), *Life-span communication: Normative processes* (pp. 179–193). Hillsdale, NJ: Erlbaum.

Rhode, D. L. (1990). Theoretical perspectives on sexual difference. In D. L. Rhode (Ed.), *Theoretical perspectives on sexual difference* (pp. 1–19). New Haven, CT: Yale University Press.

Scott, J. W. (1996). Gender: A useful category of historical analysis. In J. W. Scott (Ed.), *Feminism and history* (pp. 152–180). New York: Oxford University Press.

Tannen, D. (1990). *You just don't understand: Women and men in conversation.* New York: William Morrow.

Thorne, B. (1990). Children and gender: Construction of difference. In D. L. Rhode (Ed.), *Theoretical perspectives on sexual difference* (pp. 100–113). New Haven, CT: Yale University Press.

Wilkins, B. M., & Andersen, P. A. (1991). Gender differences and similarities in management communication: A meta-analysis. *Management Communication Quarterly, 5,* 6–35.

This next excerpt comes from the fifth edition of an unusual book designed to help people of any age expand their self-awareness and explore the choices available to them in significant areas of their lives. I've included it because it focuses on some of the most difficult and important topics to discuss—for example, what does it mean to be in an "intimate" relationship or to "love" someone—and it addresses these topics personally rather than impersonally. One author—Jerry—is a professor of human services and counseling, and the other—Marianne—is a marriage and family therapist.

One of the first really important points they make is that "we have the power to bring about change [in our relationships] if we ourselves change and do not insist that the other person make quick and total changes." This means that the rule of quid pro quo (I only give something when I get something in return) should *not* be applied in personal relationships. The only part of the relationship that I have any control over is my own part. And, although changes by one person almost always precede changes in the other (just because a relationship is a system in which everything affects everything else), it doesn't work to focus your change efforts on anyone but yourself. With this in mind, the authors emphasize, "you can choose the kinds of relationships you want to experience."

This selection discusses 19 characteristics of a meaningful relationship. I won't repeat the whole list here, but I think several are worth paying close attention to. For example, the Coreys emphasize that intimacy doesn't mean losing your sense of self; people in healthy close relationships maintain their own separate identities. This is often experienced and discussed as the difference between "wanting" the other person and "needing" him or her. Another is that, as Steve Duck emphasizes in Chapter 10, each person in a healthy relationship is willing to work at keeping the relationship alive. If the relationship includes a sexual component, this also means that each person also makes some attempt to keep the romance alive. Another feature is that each person finds meaning and nourishment outside the relationship, rather than being totally dependent on the other, and both avoid manipulating, exploiting, or using each other. Healthy relationships are also marked by the partners' abilities to deal with the anger that inevitably surfaces. And, perhaps most fundamentally, in a healthy intimate relationship, each person has a commitment to the other, an investment in their future together which can tide them over in times of conflict and crisis.

The second major section of the reading discusses how to deal with barriers to effective communication that inhibit the developing and maintaining of intimate relationships. Poor listening is one of the major barriers, which means that the materials in Chapter 6 apply to this chapter, too. Awareness of different gender styles is also important. The Coreys acknowledge that there are important cultural differences in what makes personal communication "effective," and they list 11 characteristics of this kind of communication in Euro-American cultures.

The Coreys conclude by encouraging you to apply what they discuss to improve some of your most important relationships. As they put it, "it will be helpful to begin by working on one of these skills at a time."

INTIMATE RELATIONSHIPS

Gerald Corey and Marianne Schneider-Corey

INTRODUCTION

Although this [reading] focuses mainly on the role that relationships play in our lives, we deal with relationships from a broad perspective, and also with a range of lifestyles. The [reading] deals with friendships, marital relationships, intimacy between people who are not married, dating relationships, relationships between parents and children, same-gender relationships as well as opposite-gender relationships, alternative lifestyles, and other meaningful personal relationships.

Marriage is still the dominant relationship in our society, particularly if the term *marriage* is construed broadly to include the many couples who consider themselves committed to each other even though they are not legally married as well as those who are creating relationships that are different in many respects from the traditional marriage. Bellah and his colleagues (1985) found that in today's society most people still want to marry, even though many of them no longer see it as a life requirement. For increasing numbers of people it is not considered disgraceful to be unmarried, and more people are remaining single by choice. There is less pressure to have children, and starting a family tends to be more of a conscious decision than was true in the past. Most of those interviewed believe in love as a basis for an enduring relationship. Love and commitment appear to be highly valued, although maintaining these qualities is difficult. Most people value spontaneity and solidity, freedom and intimacy, and the sharing of thoughts, feelings, values, and life goals. They feel freer than in the past to leave a marriage that is not working, and divorce is seen as one (but not the only) solution to an unhappy marriage.

Whether you choose to marry or not, or whether your preference is a same-gender or an opposite-gender primary relationship, you probably have many different types of relationships. What is true for marriage is largely true for these other relationships as well. Allowing for the differences in relationships, the signs of growth and meaningfulness are much the same, and so are the problems. Consequently, whatever lifestyle you choose, you can use the ideas in this [reading] as a basis for thinking about the role relationships play in your life. [Our] aim is to stimulate your reflection on what you want from all of your special relationships, and also to invite you to take an honest look at the quality of these relationships.

TYPES OF INTIMACY

[Psychologist Erik] Erikson maintains that the challenge of forming intimate relationships is the major task of early adulthood. Intimacy implies that we are able to share significant aspects of ourselves with others. The issues we raise concerning barriers to intimacy and ways of enhancing intimacy can help you better understand the many different types of relationships in your life. The ideas in this [reading] are useful tools in rethinking what kind of relationships you want, as well as in clarifying some new choices that you may want to make. You can take a fresh look at these relationships, including both their frustrations and their delights, and you can think about initiating some changes.

Consider the case of Donald, who told us about how little closeness he had experienced with his father. He saw his father as uncaring, aloof, and preoccupied with his own concerns. Yet Donald deeply wished that he could be physically and emotionally closer to him, and he had no idea how to bring this about. He made the difficult decision to talk to his father and tell him how he felt and what he wanted. His father appeared to listen, and his eyes moistened, but then without saying much he quickly left the room. Donald reported how hurt and disappointed he was that his father had not been as responsive as he had hoped he would be. What Donald was missing were subtle, yet significant, signs that his father had been touched and was not as uncaring as he had imagined. That his father listened to him, that he responded with even a few clumsy words, that he touched Donald on the shoulder, and that he became emotional were all manifestations that Donald's overtures had been received. Donald needs to understand that his father is probably very uncomfortable in talking personally. His father may well be every bit as afraid of his son's rejection as Donald is of his father's rebuffs. Donald will need to show patience and continue "hanging in there" with his father if he is really interested in changing the ways they relate to each other.

The experience Donald had with his father could have occurred in any intimate relationship. We can experience feelings of awkwardness, unexpressed desires, and fears of rejection with our friends, lovers, spouses, parents, or children. A key point is that we have the power to bring about change if we ourselves change and do not insist that the other person make quick and total changes. It is up to us to teach others specific ways of becoming more personal. It does little good to invest our energy in lamenting all the ways in which the other person is not fulfilling our expectations, nor is it helpful to focus on remaking others. . . . When you take a passive stance and simply hope the other person will change in the ways that you would like, you are giving away a sense of your power.

The intimacy we share with another person can be emotional, intellectual, physical, spiritual, or any combination of these. It can be exclusive or nonexclusive, long-term or brief. . . .

When we avoid intimacy, we only rob ourselves. We may pass up the chance to really get to know neighbors and new acquaintances, because we fear that either we or our new friends will move and that the friendship will come to an end. Similarly, we may not want to open ourselves to intimacy with sick or dying persons, because we fear the pain of losing them. Although such fears may be natural ones, too often we allow them to cheat us of the uniquely rich experience of being truly close to another person. We can enhance our life greatly by daring to care about others and fully savoring the time we can share with them now.

The idea that we most want to stress is that you can choose the kinds of relationships you want to experience. Often, we fail to make our own choices and instead fall into a certain type of relationship because we think "This is the way it's *supposed* to be." For example, some people marry who in reality might prefer to remain single—particularly women who often feel the pressure to have a family because it's "natural" for them to do so. Sometimes people choose a heterosexual relationship because they think that it is what is expected of them, when they would really prefer a homosexual relationship. Instead of blindly accepting that relationships must be a certain way or that only one type of lifestyle is possible, you have the choice of giving real thought to the question of what types of intimacy have meaning for you.

MEANINGFUL RELATIONSHIPS: A PERSONAL VIEW

In this section we share some of our ideas about the characteristics of a meaningful relationship. Although these guidelines pertain to couples, they are also relevant to other personal relationships, such as those between parent and child and between friends of the same or opposite gender. Take, for example, the guideline "The persons involved are willing to work at keeping their relationship alive." Sometimes parents and children take each other for granted and rarely spend time talking about how they are getting along. Either parent or child may expect the other to assume the major responsibility for their relationship. The same principle applies to friends or to partners in a primary relationship. As you look over our list, adapt it to your own relationships, keeping in mind your particular cultural values. Since the values that are a part of your cultural background play an influential role in your relationships, you will need to adapt them in appropriate ways. As you review our list, ask yourself what qualities you think are most important in your relationships.

We see relationships as most meaningful when they are dynamic and evolving rather than fixed or final. Thus, there may be periods of joy and excitement followed by times of struggle, pain, and distance. As long as the persons in a relationship are growing and changing, their relationship is bound to change as well. The following are some of the qualities of a relationship that seem most important to us.

- *Each person in the relationship has a separate identity.* Kahlil Gibran (1923) expresses this thought in *The Prophet:* "But let there be spaces in your togetherness, and let the winds of the heavens dance between you" (p. 16). In *The Dance of Anger,* Harriet Goldhor Lerner (1985) says that making long-term relationships work is difficult because it is necessary to create and maintain a balance between separateness and togetherness. If there is not enough togetherness in a relationship, people in it typically feel isolated and do not share feelings and experiences. If there is not enough separateness, they give up a sense of their own identity and control. They also devote much effort to becoming what the other person expects.
- *Although each person desires the other, each can survive without the other.* This characteristic is an extension of the prior one, and it implies that people are in a relationship by choice. They are not so tightly bound together that if they are separated, one or the other becomes lost and empty. Thus, if a young man says "I simply can't live without my girlfriend," he is indeed in trouble. His dependency should not be interpreted as love but as the seeking of an object to make him feel complete.
- *Each is able to talk openly with the other about matters of significance to the relationship.* The two persons can openly express grievances and let each other know the changes they desire. They can ask for what they want, rather than expecting the other to intuitively know what they want and give it to them. For example, assume that you are not satisfied with how you and your mother spend time together. You can take the first step by letting her know, in a nonjudgmental way, that you would like to talk more personally. Rather than telling her how she is, you can focus more on telling her how you feel in your relationship with her.
- *Each person assumes responsibility for his or her own level of happiness and refrains from blaming the other if he or she is unhappy.* Of course, in a close relationship or friendship the unhappiness of the other person is bound to affect you, but you should not expect another person to *make* you happy, fulfilled, or excited. Although the way others feel will influence your life, they do not create or cause your feelings. Ultimately, you are responsible for defining your goals and your life, and you can take actions to change what *you* are doing if you are unhappy with a situation.
- *The persons involved are willing to work at keeping their relationship alive.* If we hope to keep a relationship vital, we must reevaluate and revise our way of being with each other from time to time. Consider how this guideline fits for your friendships. If you take a good friend for granted and show little interest in doing what is necessary to maintain your friendship, she may soon grow disenchanted and wonder what kind of friend you are.
- *The persons are able to have fun and to play together; they enjoy doing things with each other.* It is easy to become so serious that we forget to take the time to

enjoy those we love. One way of changing drab relationships is to become aware of the infrequency of playful moments and then determine what things are getting in the way of enjoying life. Again, think of this guideline as it applies to your close friends.

- *Each person is growing, changing, and opening up to new experiences.* When you rely on others for your personal fulfillment and confirmation as a person, you are in trouble. The best way to build solid relationships with others is to work on developing your own personality. But do not be surprised if you encounter resistance to your growth and change. This resistance can come from within yourself as well as from others.

- *If the relationship contains a sexual component, each person makes some attempt to keep the romance alive.* The two persons may not always experience the intensity and novelty of the early period of their relationship, but they can devise ways of creating a climate of romance and closeness. They may go places they haven't been to before or otherwise vary their routine in some ways. They recognize when their life is getting dull and look for ways to eliminate its boring aspects. In their lovemaking they are sensitive to each other's needs and desires; at the same time, they are able to ask each other for what they want and need.

- *The two persons are equal in the relationship.* People who feel that they are typically the "givers" and that their partner is usually unavailable when they need him or her might question the balance in their relationship. In some relationships one person may feel compelled to assume a superior position relative to the other—for example, to be very willing to listen and give advice yet unwilling to go to the other person and show any vulnerability or need. Lerner (1985) says that women often define their own wishes and preferences as being the same as those of their partner. In this case there surely is no equality in the relationship. Both parties need to be willing to look at aspects of inequality and demonstrate a willingness to negotiate changes.

- *Each person actively demonstrates concern for the other.* In a vital relationship the participants do more than just talk about how much they value each other. Their actions show their care and concern more eloquently than any words. Each person has a desire to give to the other. They have an interest in each other's welfare and a desire to see that the other person is fulfilled.

- *Each person finds meaning and sources of nourishment outside the relationship.* Sometimes people become very possessive in their friendships. A sign of a healthy relationship is that each avoids assuming an attitude of ownership toward the other. Although they may experience jealousy at times, they do not demand that the other person deaden his or her feelings for others. Their lives did not begin when they met each other, nor would their lives end if they should part.

- *Each avoids manipulating, exploiting, and using the other.* Each respects and cares for the other and is willing to see the world through the other's eyes. At times parent-child relationships are strained because either or both parties attempt to manipulate the other. Consider the father who brags about his son, Roger, to others and whose affection is based on Roger's being an outstanding athlete. Roger may feel used if his father is able to talk only of sports. What if he were to decide to quit playing sports? Would he still be earning his father's approval?

- *Each person is moving in a direction in life that is personally meaningful.* They are both excited about the quality of their lives and their projects. Applied to couples, this guideline implies that both individuals feel that their needs are being met within the relationship, but they also feel a sense of engagement in their work, play, and relationships with other friends and family members. Goldberg (1987) makes some excellent points pertaining to these issues:

> Probably the best or healthiest relationships begin without intensely romantic feelings, but where there is a genuine basis for being with each other on a friendship level and where there is enjoyment of each other's company without concern over commitment or future. Add to that a balanced flow of power, healthy conflict resolution free of blaming guilt, a sense of being known for who you are and knowing your partner, and a relaxed desire to be fully present with little need to escape or avoid through distraction, and you have a fine potential for growth in a good relationship. (p. 89). . .

- *If they are in a committed relationship, they maintain this relationship by choice, not simply for the sake of any children involved, out of duty, or because of convenience.* They choose to keep their ties with each other even if things get rough or if they sometimes experience emptiness in their relationship. They share some common purposes and values, and therefore, they are willing to look at what is lacking in their relationship and to work on changing undesirable situations.

- *They are able to cope with anger in their relationship.* Couples often seek relationship counseling with the expectation that they will learn to stop fighting and that conflict will end. This is not a realistic goal. More important than the absence of fighting is learning how to fight cleanly and constructively, which entails an ongoing process of expressing anger and frustrations. It is the buildup of these emotions that creates trouble. If anger is not expressed and dealt with constructively, it will sour a relationship. Stored-up anger usually results in the target person's getting more than his or her share of deserved anger. At other times bottled-up anger is let out in indirect ways such as sarcasm and hostility. If the parties in a relationship are angry, they should try to express it in a direct way.

- *Each person recognizes the need for solitude and is willing to create the time in which to be alone.* Each allows the other a sense of privacy. Because they recognize each other's individual integrity, they avoid prying into every thought or manipulating the other to disclose what he or she wants to keep private. Sometimes parents are guilty of not respecting the privacy of their children. A father may be hurt if his daughter does not want to talk with him at any time that he feels like talking. He needs to realize that she is a separate person with her own needs and that she may need time alone at certain times when he wants to talk.

- *They do not expect the other to do for them what they are capable of doing for themselves.* They don't expect the other person to make them feel alive, take away their boredom, assume their risks, or make them feel valued and important. Each is working toward creating his or her own autonomous identity. Consequently, neither person depends on the other for confirmation of his or her personal worth; nor does one walk in the shadow of the other.

- *They encourage each other to become all that they are capable of becoming.* Unfortunately, people often have an investment in keeping those with whom they are intimately involved from changing. Their expectations and needs may lead them to resist changes in their partner and thus make it difficult for their partner to grow. If they recognize their fears, however, they can challenge their need to block their partner's progress.

- *Each has a commitment to the other.* Commitment is a vital part of an intimate relationship. It means that the people involved have an investment in their future together and that they are willing to stay with each other in times of crisis and conflict. Although many people express an aversion to any long-term commitment in a relationship, how deeply will they allow themselves to be loved if they believe that the relationship can be dissolved on a whim when things look bleak? Perhaps, for some people, a fear of intimacy gets in the way of developing a sense of commitment. Loving and being loved is both exciting and frightening, and we may have to struggle with the issue of how much anxiety we want to tolerate. Commitment to another person involves risks and carries a price, but it is an essential part of an intimate relationship.

DEALING WITH COMMUNICATION BLOCKS

A number of barriers to effective communication can inhibit the developing and maintaining of intimate relationships. Some of these barriers are failing to really listen to another person; selective listening—that is, hearing only what you want to hear; being overly concerned with getting your point across without considering the other's views; silently rehearsing what you will say next as you are"listening"; becoming defensive, with self-protection your primary concern; attempting to change others rather than first attempting to understand them; telling others how they are, rather than telling them how they affect you; bringing old patterns into the present and not allowing the other person to change; overreacting to a person; failing to state what your needs are and expecting others to know intuitively; making assumptions about another person without checking them out; using sarcasm and hostility instead of being direct; and speaking in vague terms such as "You manipulate me!"

In most of these cases you tend to be so concerned with getting your point across, defending your view of yourself, or changing another person that you cannot appreciate what the other person is thinking and feeling. These blocks make it very difficult to have what are called I-Thou encounters, in which two persons are open with themselves and each other, expressing what they think and feel and making genuine contact. Instead, the persons who are attempting to communicate typically feel distant from each other.

Deborah Tannen has written two best-selling books on the subject of communication between women and men. In *That's Not What I Meant* (1987), Tannen focuses on how conversational styles can make or break a relationship. She maintains that male-female communication can be considered cross-cultural. The language we use as we are growing up is influenced by our gender, ethnicity, class and cultural background, and location. Boys and girls grow up in different worlds, even if they are part of the same family. Furthermore, they carry many of the patterns they established in childhood into their transactions as adults. For Tannen, these cultural differences include different expectations about the role of communication in relationships. These factors make up our conversational style, and the subtle differences in this style can lead to overwhelming misunderstandings and disappointments. In her other book, *You Just Don't Understand* (1991), Tannen develops the idea that conversational style differences do not explain all the conflicts in relationships between women and men, but many problems result because partners are expressing their thoughts and feelings in different ways. She believes that if we can sort out these differences based on conversational style, then we are better able to confront real conflicts and find a form of communication that will allow for a negotiation of these differences.

[Carl R.] Rogers (1961) has written extensively on ways to improve personal relationships. For him, the main block to effective communication is our tendency to evaluate and judge the statements of others. He believes that what gets in the way of understanding another is the tendency to approve or disapprove, the unwillingness to put ourselves in the other's frame of reference, and the fear of being changed ourselves if we really listen to and understand a person with a viewpoint different from our own.

One of Rogers's suggestions for testing the quality of our understanding of someone is as follows: The next time you get into an argument with your partner, your friend, or a small group of friends, just stop the discussion for a moment and, for an experiment, institute this rule: "Each person can speak up for himself only after he has restated the ideas and feelings of the previous speaker accurately, and to that speaker's satisfaction" (p. 332). Carrying out this experiment implies that you must strive to genuinely understand another person and achieve his or her perspective. Although this may sound simple, it can be extremely difficult to put into practice. It involves challenging yourself to go beyond what you find convenient to hear, examining your assumptions and prejudices, not attributing to statements meanings that were not intended, and not coming to quick conclusions based on superficial listening. If you are successful in challenging yourself in these ways, you can enter the subjective world of the significant person in your life; that is, you can acquire empathy, which is the necessary foundation for all intimate relationships. Rogers (1980) contends that the sensitive companionship offered by an empathic person is healing and that such a deep understanding is a precious gift to another.

Effective Personal Communication

Your culture influences both the content and the process of your communication. Some cultures prize direct communication, while other cultures see this behavior as rude and insensitive. In certain cultures direct eye contact is as insulting as the avoidance of eye contact is in other cultures. Harmony within the family is a cardinal value in certain cultures, and it may be inappropriate for adult children to confront their parents. As you read the following discussion, recognize that variations do exist among cultures. Our discussion has a Euro-American slant, which makes it essential that you adapt the principles we present to your own cultural framework. You need to examine the ways that your communication style has been influenced by your culture and then decide if you want to modify certain patterns that you have learned. For example, your culture might have taught you to control your feelings. You might decide to become more emotionally expressive if you discover that this pattern is restricting you in areas of your life where you would like to be freer.

From our perspective, when two persons are communicating meaningfully, they are involved in many of the following processes:

- They are facing each other and making eye contact, and one is listening while the other speaks.
- They do not rehearse their response while the other is speaking. The listener is able to summarize accurately what the speaker has said. ("So you're hurt when I don't call to tell you that I'll be late.")
- The language is specific and concrete. (A vague statement is "I feel manip ulated. " A concrete statement is "I don't like it when you bring me flowers and then expect me to do something for you that I already told you I didn't want to do.")
- The speaker makes personal statements instead of bombarding the other with impersonal questions. (A questioning statement is "Where were you last night, and why did you come home so late?" A personal statement is "I was worried and scared because I didn't know where you were last night.")
- The listener takes a moment before responding to reflect on what was said and on how he or she is affected. There is a sincere effort to walk in the shoes of the other person. ("It must have been very hard for you when you didn't know where I was last night and thought I might have been in an accident.")
- Although each has reactions to what the other is saying, there is an absence of critical judgment. (A critical judgment is "You never think about anybody but yourself, and you're totally irresponsible." A more appropriate reaction would be "I appreciate it when you think to call me, knowing that I may be worried.")
- Each of the parties can be honest and direct without insensitively damaging the other's dignity. Each makes "I" statements, rather than second-guessing and speaking for the other. ("Sometimes I worry that you don't care about me, and I want to check that out with you, rather than assuming that it's true.")
- There is a respect for each other's differences and an avoidance of pressuring each other to accept a point of view. ("I look at this matter very differently than you do, but I understand that you have your own opinion.")

- There is a congruency (or a matching) between the verbal and nonverbal messages. (If she is expressing anger, she is not smiling.)
- Each person is open about how he or she is affected by the other. (An ineffective response is "You have no right to criticize me." An effective response is "I'm very disappointed that you don't like the work I've done.")
- Neither person is being mysterious, expecting the other to decode his or her messages.

These processes are essential for fostering any meaningful relationship. You might try observing yourself while you are communicating, and take note of the degree to which you practice these principles. Decide if the quality of your relationships is satisfying to you. If you determine that you want to improve certain relationships, it will be helpful to begin by working on one of these skills at a time.

REVIEW QUESTIONS

1. Give an example from your own experience of a relationship where the persons involved do not have very strong individual identities. Give an example of another relationship where they do.
2. What do the Coreys say about faultfinding and blaming in relationships?
3. Explain the conflict-management suggestion by Carl Rogers that the Coreys include in their discussion about communication blocks.
4. What do the Coreys mean when they say that effective communication involves "specific and concrete" language and "personal statements instead of impersonal questions"?

PROBES

1. How do you respond to these authors' comments about same-gender relationships? How might your response be reflected in your own communication with lesbian and homosexual individuals?
2. The Coreys say that in a meaningful relationship "each is able to talk openly with the other about matters of significance to the relationship." Are they suggesting that you need to be *completely* open and honest? What are some important limitations on this feature?
3. What might be the Coreys' rationale for beginning their discussion of "communication blocks" with a comment about *listening?* Why do they start at this end of the communication process?
4. Review the Coreys' 11 suggestions about effective communication from the perspective of a non-Euro-American culture. What differences do you believe characterize effective communication in another culture?

REFERENCES

Bellah, R. N., Madsen, R., Sullivan, W. M., Swidler, A., & Tipton, S. M. (1985). *Habits of the Heart: Individualism and Commitment in American Life.* New York: Harper & Row.

Gibran, K. (1923). *The Prophet.* New York: Knopf.

Goldberg, H. (1987). *The Inner Male: Overcoming Roadblocks to Intimacy.* New York: New American Library.

Lerner, H. G. (1985). *The Dance of Anger: A Woman's Guide to Changing the Patterns of Intimate Relationships.* New York: Harper & Row.

Rogers, C. R. (1961). *On Becoming a Person.* Boston: Houghton Mifflin.

Rogers, C. R. (1980). *A Way of Being.* Boston: Houghton Mifflin.

Tannen, D. (1987). *That's Not What I Meant: How Conversational Style Makes or Breaks Relationships.* New York: Ballantine.

Tannen, D. (1991). *You Just Don't Understand: Women and Men in Conversation.* New York: Ballantine.

I put this reading at the end of this chapter because it talks about the ultimate goal or the main point of all intimate partnerships: love. On the one hand, most people realize that love is the one thing *every* human desires to have in his or her life. On the other hand, we also realize that love is very difficult to talk about and impossible to capture fully in words. When you first began dating, you may have been frustrated by the older person who responded to your questions with, "I can't tell you what love is, but I can guarantee that when it happens, you'll know it." Something this universal and this important, you might have thought, ought to be easier to talk about.

John Welwood is one of the few authors I know who has partly solved this problem. In the next few pages he explains some things about love that can contribute significantly to your understanding of your intimate relationships with dating partners, family members, close friends, and, if you have them, your spouse and children. In addition, one of the special strengths of Welwood's approach is that he includes an understanding of some of the spiritual dimensions of love.

First Welwood describes the context of love by identifying the five "levels of connection" that humans experience in intimate relationships. The first is "fusion," the experience some people call being "joined at the hip." This is often an observable stage in a young dating relationship where the two people spend every available moment focused exclusively on each other. It's an important stage, Welwood notes, but only the beginning of a fully intimate relationship.

A second level is "companionship," which is rooted mainly in the desire not to be alone, to have the other person around. In some unfortunate cases, intimate partnerships don't progress much beyond this stage. Most others, though, move to the level of "community," where a couple co-creates a shared world of concrete existence—places they identify as theirs, activities and events they do together. The next stage is "communication," where each party is able to share some of what is going on inside him or her. Communication then opens the door to what Welwood calls "communion." This is a stage of connection beyond communication, where each person has "a deep recognition of another person's being." It can take place in silence, sometimes while looking into a partner's eyes. Both communication and communion are deeper and more subtle forms of intimacy than companionship and community.

Problems can arise, Welwood reminds us, when the intimacy of communion may generate a longing for "total union" with someone we love. Although this longing expresses a genuine human need, Welwood writes, "it is more appropriately directed to the divine, the absolute, the infinite." As a result, if it is attached to a specific intimate relationship, it can lead to idealization and addiction. The most appropriate way to address the natural longing for union is with some spiritual practice— religious involvement, meditation, or something similar.

In the next section of this reading Welwood explains how conditional and unconditional love relate to these five relationship stages. He begins this section by noting that, although unconditional love is mysterious, it is also common and readily available to all of us. People often glimpse unconditional love in experiences of birth or death. The basic quality is being fully open to reality. Welwood writes, "This openness of the heart, which is born tender, responsive, and eager to reach out and touch the larger life around us, is not something we have to manufacture. It simply *is*." Even if your history is painful and your present is cluttered, you can experience this simple, unconditional acceptance-and-connection with another being—a kitten or puppy, a newborn child, or an intimate partner. This is the most basic experience of unconditional love.

Conditional love happens when we overlay on this basic experience our likes and dislikes, personal needs and concerns. This kind of attraction can fade away if the other person no longer meets these needs.

Welwood emphasizes that intimate relationships "always contain both kinds of loving." And the mixture can sometimes be confusing in some ways that Welwood discusses. Love can also be confused by fear as we sometimes wonder, for example, "Can I let myself be this open? Can I trust this person? Can I live with what I don't like about her?"

But the key is to live in these tensions rather than trying to eliminate them. And this, I think, is the most important part of Welwood's message. There is almost always a desire to eliminate any risk—and the fear that goes with it—and to completely lose ourselves by merging with the other. But both these options undermine love because "they destroy the tension between self and other, known and unknown, that love actually thrives on." Especially if you're in a turbulent intimate relationship, it might be difficult to hear the idea that fears will continue and that a complete love cannot be "blind." But, for whatever it's worth, my experience is that Welwood is right on this one. If love's going to last, the tensions will definitely remain.

I hope this reading can prompt some fruitful discussion about the challenges and benefits of your intimate partnerships.

LOVE: CONSCIOUS, CONDITIONAL, UNCONDITIONAL

John Welwood

People generally consider an intimate relationship successful if it provides basic fulfillment in such areas as companionship, security, sex, and self-esteem. Describing such an arrangement, one of the characters in Woody Allen's film *Manhattan* provided what *Time* magazine called a "reasonable definition of modern love": "We have laughs together. I care about you. Your concerns are my concerns. We have great sex." Yet in regarding relationship as path, especially as a sacred path, we hold a larger vision, one that includes these needs, but is not limited to them. Our central concern is with cultivating a conscious love, which can inspire the development of greater awareness and the evolution of two people's beings.

Yet we should not be too idealistic about this, for intimate relationships never function entirely on a conscious level. We live on many levels simultaneously, all with different needs. The tender child, the adventurous youth, the seasoned adult, and the spiritual seeker are all simultaneously present in us. Intimate relationships reflect this multilevel quality of our existence and therefore never involve just one single kind of relatedness. To clarify the part that conscious love can play in a relationship, it helps to consider it in the context of the many different levels of connection that can exist between two people.

Levels of Connection

The most primitive bond that may form between intimate partners is the urge for symbiotic *fusion*, born out of a desire to obtain emotional nurturance that was lacking in childhood. Of course, it is common for many couples, when they first get together, to go through a temporary symbiotic phase, when they cut out other activities or friends and spend most of their free time together. This stage in a relationship may help two people establish close emotional bonding. Yet if symbiosis becomes the primary dynamic in a relationship or goes on for too long, it will become increasingly confining. It sets up a parent-child dynamic that limits two people's range of expression and interaction, undermining the male–female charge between them and creating addictive patterns.

Beyond the primitive need for symbiotic fusion, the most basic desire in an intimate relationship is for *companionship*. This can take more or less sophisticated forms. On a crude level, we might just want another body around, almost like a pet, to share our bed or keep us company. On a more sophisticated level, the child in us wants a playmate, someone we can laugh and romp with, and the adult in us enjoys sharing activities such as cooking or attending cultural events together. Basic companionship plays a part in all relationships, although some people do not seem to want anything more than this from an intimate partner.

A further level of connectedness can happen when two people share not only activities and each other's company, but also common interests, goals, or values. We could call this level, where a couple begins to create a shared world, *community*. Like companionship, community is a concrete, earthy form of relatedness.

Beyond sharing values and interests lies *communication*. On this level, we share what is going on inside us—our thoughts, visions, experiences, and feelings. Establishing good communication is much more arduous than simply creating companionship and community. It requires that a couple be honest and courageous enough to expose what is going on inside them, and be willing to work on the inevitable obstacles in the way of sharing their different truths with each other. Good communication is probably the most important ingredient in the everyday health of a relationship.

A further extension of communication is *communion*. Beyond just sharing thoughts and feelings, this is a deep recognition of another person's being. This often takes place in silence—perhaps while looking into our partner's eyes, making love, walking in the woods, or listening to music together. Suddenly we feel touched and seen, not as a personality, but in the depth of our being. We are fully ourselves and fully in touch with our partner at the same time. This kind of connection is so rare and striking that it is usually unmistakable when it comes along. While two people can work on communication, communion is more spontaneous, beyond the will. Communication and communion are deeper, more subtle forms of intimacy than companionship and community, taking place at the level of mind and heart.

The deeper intimacy of communion may stir up a longing to overcome our separateness altogether, a longing for total *union* with someone we love. Yet though this longing expresses a genuine human need, it is more appropriately directed to the divine, the absolute, the infinite. When attached to an intimate relationship, it often creates problems. Putting our whole longing for spiritual realization onto a finite relationship can lead to idealization, inflation, addiction, and death. . . . The most appropriate way to address our longing for union is through a genuine spiritual practice, such as meditation, that teaches us how to go beyond oppositional mind altogether, in every area of our life. By pointing us in this direction, intimate relationship may inspire this kind of practice, but it can never be a complete substitute for it.

Every relationship will have different areas of strength along this continuum of connectedness. Some couples may share companionship and common interests, but have little real communication or communion; and some may have occasional moments of communion, but still find their strongest link at more basic levels. Others may share a deep soul-communion, yet have little in common on the earthly plane of community and companionship. Such couples might have a hard time creating a life together because they would lack simpler forms of relatedness to fall back on when the intensity of their communion wanes. Couples who share a deep being-connection, good communication, common interests and values, and a simple enjoyment of each other's company will have an ideal balance of heaven and earth connectedness. (Sexuality can operate at any of these levels—as a form of symbiotic fusion, as a body-companionship, as a shared sport, as a form of communication, or as a deeper communion.). . .

CONDITIONAL AND UNCONDITIONAL LOVE

I falter before the task of finding the language to express the incalculable paradoxes of love. Here is the greatest and the smallest, the remotest and nearest, the highest and lowest, and we cannot discuss one side of it without also discussing the other. Whatever one can say, no words express the whole.
—C. G. Jung

Whenever our heart opens to another person, we experience a moment of unconditional love. People commonly imagine that unconditional love is a high or distant ideal, one that is difficult, if not impossible, to realize. Yet though it may be hard to put into everyday practice, its nature is quite simple and ordinary: opening and responding to another person's being without reservation.

We often glimpse this quality of love most vividly in beginnings and endings—at birth, at death, or when first falling in love—when we are least under the influence of conditioned, habitual patterns of perception. At such times, something vast inside us connects with something vast in another. The other person's sheer existence awakens us to the ordinary magic of life. When our child is born, we do not have to decide to love this infant—the feeling is choiceless, and flows forth freely. When someone close to us is dying, we feel touched and present in an all-pervasive way that goes beyond all the little pros and cons of our relationship.

This unconditional quality of love arises from that which is unconditioned in us and responds to that which is unconditioned in another—the heart, that is, *our basic openness to reality.* This openness of the heart, which is born tender, responsive, and eager to reach out and touch the larger life around us, is not something we have to manufacture. It simply *is.*

It is the heart's desire to circulate human warmth freely back and forth, without putting limits or conditions on that exchange. When we love in this way, it alters our perceptions—everything in our world seems more colorful, vivid, and penetrating. When we are loved in this way, we feel acknowledged, seen, nourished, held. Moments of unconditional love allow us to touch the vastness and depth of human experience altogether.

And yet, as we know, this is not all there is to love. Because we are not just pure heart, but also live in an earthly form, we bring to relationships a collection of conditioned likes and dislikes, personal needs, cautions, and concerns that influence how deeply we can become involved with a particular person. When someone fits our personal needs and preferences, we feel pleasure and liking. This kind of attraction—which we could call conditional love—is a lesser form of love, in that it can fade away if the other person no longer continues to meet our needs.

Confusing the Two Orders of Love

Relationships always contain both kinds of loving. Attraction to another person is usually most intense, and everything proceeds most smoothly, when they are in accord: The one we feel attracted to not only touches our heart, but also fits our personal conditions. Yet when these two orders of love do not mesh, it can be quite confusing. Someone may meet our conditions, yet somehow not move us very deeply. Or else someone may touch our heart, so that we want to say yes, while our personal criteria and considerations may lead us to say no. At the same time, our heart may look right past those things that jar our personal sensibilities, and rejoice in another person's very existence, despite all our reasonable intentions to maintain distance or play it safe. For in its deepest essence the heart knows nothing of conditions and is quite unreasonable. How then to proceed?

One common confusion at this point is to impose our conditional no on the yes of the heart: "I can only let myself feel this open *if* . . . she meets my needs . . . he loves me as much as I love him . . . she doesn't hurt me . . ." Yet our heart, whose nature is to say yes, only suffers when we try to constrict its openness by placing conditions on it. Although we may have to end or change the form of a relationship that does not meet our needs, we do not have to close down our heart. Trying to kill off the love that still wants to flow toward another human being constricts the very source of joy and aliveness inside us.

Another common confusion is to try to impose the yes of the heart on the no of our personal considerations. People often think that unconditional love means setting aside all their conditions and going along with whatever the person they love does. However, imagining that we should tolerate unconditionally anything our partner does can have devastating consequences. Unconditional love does not mean having to like something we in fact dislike or saying yes when we need to say no. Unconditional love arises from an entirely different place in us than conditional like and dislike, attraction and aversion. It is a

being-to-being acknowledgement. And it responds to that which is unconditioned—the intrinsic goodness of another's open heart, beyond everything we
may like or dislike about him or her. It is saying yes to another's being, but it
does not mean always saying yes to *how* they are or *what* they do.

So just because our heart is open does not mean we must set aside all caution. Nor does setting conditions about what we want from a relationship have
to negate the genuine openness we feel. Because relationships bring together
heaven and earth, they always involve connecting from our deeper being *and*
from our conditioned personality. While part of us might like to invite another
person into our heart without reservation, another part or us wants to avoid being hurt, trapped, or abandoned. This is not a problem unless we become caught
in a struggle between these two sides, feeling torn between unconditional love
and our personal considerations. How then can we include both these sides of
us in a relationship?

Love and Fear

Consider the kind of situation we find ourselves in when we are suddenly
drawn to a new lover with tremendous force and intensity. This can be so exhil-
arating that we want to open without reservation. Yet at the same time we come
up against inner cautions about letting our love flow so freely: "Can I let myself
be this open? Will I lose myself or be swept away? Can I trust this person? Will
she meet my needs? If so, will I become too dependent on her? Can I live with
what I don't like about her? Can she accept me as I am and really be there for
me? If not, could I be too badly hurt?"

If we listen to our heart, we may feel no reservations at all about becoming
involved with this person. Yet as soon as we begin to consider what kind of relationship we want, we find ourselves in the realm of conditions. Feeling pulled
in opposite directions—wanting to give ourselves freely while also honoring
our considerations—may leave us uncertain about how to proceed.

At first we may imagine that this uncertainty is a sign that something is
wrong. Yet it is natural to feel these opposite pulls. After all, we probably *have*
been hurt before, so it is intelligent to exercise some caution this time. If we simply let our passion override our caution, we could be asking for trouble. But if
we just let our fear close down our heart, we will never find out what a new relationship has to offer. Since there are no insurance policies in these matters,
love, or risking the heart, and fear, or safeguarding the heart, arise together as
intimate companions.

Here in the co-emergence of love and fear we feel the paradox of being human in a most poignant way. It would be so much easier if we could just remain
self-contained and establish an impeccable set of conditions to protect us from
risk. Or if we could simply open to someone without question, let ourselves go,
and completely lose ourselves in merging together. Yet both these alternatives
undermine love, *for they destroy the tension between self and other, known and unknown, that love actually thrives on.*

The key to finding our way in such situations lies in learning to allow opposite sides of our nature—unconditional and conditional love, passion and fear—to coexist, side by side, without letting one negate the other. When we do this, we become more fully present to our own experience and consequently to another person as well. We can let ourselves open and expand while still keeping our feet on the ground. In becoming more aware of the dynamic play and tension between the two sides of our nature, we begin to bring the whole of ourselves into a relationship.

Thus, some of the most powerful and penetrating moments in a relationship are those that bring us to an edge—where heaven and earth begin to connect with each other inside us. Here is where love leads into unknown territory and brings us most fully alive.

REVIEW QUESTIONS

1. What's the basic difference between companionship and community?
2. What's the main difference between communication and communion?
3. Explain what Welwood means when he says that sexuality can operate at any of the five levels—fusion, companionship, community, communication, and communion.
4. How is conditional love different from unconditional love? What are the "conditions"?
5. What does Welwood mean when he says that it doesn't work to "try to impose the yes of the heart on the no of our personal considerations"?

PROBES

1. As John Welwood notes, Woody Allen's reasonable definition of modern love is this: "We have laughs together. I care about you. Your concerns are my concerns. We have great sex." How does this definition fit your experience?
2. How do you respond to Welwood's point that your intimate relationships are related to your relationship with "the divine, the absolute, the infinite"? What connections do you believe there are between the spiritual parts of human beings and their intimate relationships?
3. *Why* do you suppose that people often experience unconditional love most vividly in beginnings and endings—"at birth, at death, or when first falling in love"?
4. Welwood includes a quotation from Carl Jung to the effect that words can never capture the whole of love. How does this point apply to Welwood's discussion of unconditional love?
5. Explain what Welwood means by "the tension between self and other, known and unknown."

PART FIVE

Bridging Differences

CHAPTER 13

Managing Conflict

This reading comes from the first chapter of the 1997 edition of a conflict management textbook written by three speech communication teachers. It lays out some of the basic ideas that I think it's important to understand if you're going to approach conflict constructively and effectively.

The authors begin with a "textbook case" that illustrates both the bad side and the potentially good side of conflict. Although they don't emphasize this point, the case shows how your view of conflict can strongly affect the ways you deal with it. For example, many people view conflict as always painful. From this point of view, unless you enjoy being blamed, put down, and shouted at, it's hard to be positive about conflicts. But if you see conflict as something entirely negative, you'll behave accordingly and will probably help create a self-fulfilling prophecy—the more you believe it's awful, the worse it will get. As the case study shows, there are actually some benefits to conflict. Feelings get out in the open where they can be dealt with, and often people discover creative solutions to problems that had stumped them. So the first step toward handling conflict effectively is to be open to the positive values of conflict so you can, as these authors suggest, analyze "both the specific behaviors and interaction patterns involved in conflict and the forces that influence these patterns."

Folger, Poole, and Stutman define *conflict* as "the interaction of interdependent people who perceive incompatible goals and interference from each other in achieving those goals." This means that struggles inside one person's head are not "conflict" as it's defined here. Conflict always involves communication. The definition also emphasizes that conflict doesn't happen unless the people involved are interdependent. It only happens when one person's beliefs or actions have some impact on the other's. Otherwise the parties could just ignore each other.

The central section of this chapter distinguishes productive from destructive conflict interaction. One difference is that productive conflicts are *realistic*, which means that they focus on substantive problems the parties can potentially solve, while *nonrealistic* conflicts are mainly expressions of aggression designed to defeat or hurt the other. Productive conflict attitudes and behaviors are also *flexible*, while destructive ones are *inflexible*. In addition, productive conflict management is grounded in the belief that all parties can realize at least some of their goals, while destructive conflict is thoroughly win/lose. Finally, productive conflict happens when the parties are committed to working through their differences, rather than either avoiding them or simply favoring one position over the other.

In the final section the authors develop the idea that every move made in a conflict has impact on the other parties, and that this is why conflicts often degenerate into destructive cycles or patterns. These cycles can only be understood as unified wholes, and they can often be self-reinforcing. This means that, if you want to manage conflict effectively, you have to (a) look for the cycles, and (b) be willing and able to take unilateral action to break the destructive pattern. Subsequent readings in this chapter suggest what you can do *after* this to handle conflicts more effectively.

CONFLICT AND INTERACTION

Joseph P. Folger, Marshall Scott Poole, and Randall K. Stutman

THE POTENTIAL OF CONFLICT INTERACTION

It is often said that conflict can be beneficial. Trainers, counselors, consultants, and authors of conflict textbooks point to the potential positive functions of conflict: conflicts allow important issues to be aired; they produce new and creative ideas; they release built-up tension; they can strengthen relationships; they can cause groups and organizations to re-evaluate and clarify goals and missions; and they can also stimulate social change to eliminate inequities and injustice. These advantages, and others, are raised to justify conflict as a normal, healthy occurrence and to stress the importance of understanding and handling it properly.

But why must such an argument be made? Everyone has been in conflicts, and almost everyone would readily acknowledge at least some benefits. Why then do social scientists, popular authors, and consultants persist in attempting to persuade us of something we already know? Perhaps the answer can be found by studying an actual conflict. The twists and turns of a specific case often reveal why negative views of conflict persist. Consider the fairly typical case study of a conflict in a small work group in Case I.

CASE I   THE WOMEN'S HOTLINE CASE

Women's Hotline is a rape and domestic crisis center in a medium-sized city; the center employs seven full- and part-time workers. The workers, all women, formed a cohesive unit and made all important decisions as a group; there were no formal supervisors. The hotline had started as a voluntary organization and had grown by capturing local and federal funds. The group remained proud of its roots in a democratic, feminist tradition.

The atmosphere at the hotline was rather informal. The staff saw each other as friends, but there was an implicit understanding that people should not have to take responsibility for each other's cases. Since the hotline's work was draining, having to handle each other's worries could create an unbearable strain.

This norm encouraged workers to work on their own and keep problems to themselves.

The conflict arose when Diane, a new counselor who had only six months' experience, was involved in a very disturbing incident. One of her clients was killed by a man who had previously raped her. Diane had trouble dealing with this incident. She felt guilty about it; she questioned her own ability and asked herself whether she might have been able to prevent this tragedy. In the months following, Diane had increasing difficulty in coping with her feelings and began to feel that her co-workers were not giving her the support she needed. Diane had no supervisor to turn to, and, although her friends outside the hotline were helpful, she did not believe they could understand the pressure as well as her co-workers.

Since the murder, Diane had not been able to work to full capacity, and she began to notice some resentment from the other counselors. She felt the other staff were more concerned about whether she was adding to their work loads than whether she was recovering from the traumatic incident. Although Diane did not realize it at the time, most of the staff felt she had been slow to take on responsibilities even before her client was killed. They thought Diane had generally asked for more help than other staff members and that these requests were adding to their own responsibilities. No one was willing to tell Diane about these feelings after the incident, because they realized she was very disturbed. After six months, Diane believed she could no longer continue to work effectively. She felt pressure from the others at the center, and she was still shaken by the tragedy. She requested two weeks off with pay to get away from the work situation for a while, to reduce the stress she felt, and to come back with renewed energy. The staff, feeling that Diane was slacking off, denied this request. They responded by outlining, in writing, what they saw as the responsibilities of a full-time staff worker. Diane was angry when she realized her request had been denied, and she decided to file a formal work grievance.

Diane and the staff felt bad about having to resort to such a formal, adversarial procedure. No staff member had ever filed a work grievance, and the group was embarrassed by its inability to deal with the problem on a more informal basis. These feelings created additional tension between Diane and the staff.

DISCUSSION QUESTIONS

- *Can you foresee any benefits to this conflict?*
- *Is it possible to foresee whether a conflict will move in a constructive or destructive direction?*
- *What cues would lead you to believe that conflict is going to be productive?*

The situation at the Women's Hotline has several features in common with destructive conflicts, and might easily turn in a destructive direction. **First, the situation is tense and threatening.** The weeks during which the incident evolved were an extremely difficult time for the workers. Even for "old hands" at negotiation, conflicts are often unpleasant and frightening. **Second, participants are experiencing a great deal of uncertainty.** They are unable to understand many aspects of the conflict and how their behavior affects it. Conflicts are confusing; actions can have consequences quite different from those intended because the situation is more complicated than assumed. Diane did not know her co-workers thought she was slacking even before the tragedy. When she asked for time off, she was therefore surprised at their refusal, and her own angry reaction nearly started a major battle. **Third, the situation is extremely fragile.** The conflict may evolve in very different ways depending on the behavior of just a single worker. If, for example, the staff chooses to fire Diane, the conflict might be squelched, or it might fester and undermine relationships among the remaining members. If, on the other hand, Diane wins allies, the staff might split over the issue and ultimately dissolve the hotline. As the case continues below, observe staff members' behavior and their method of dealing with this tense and unfamiliar situation.

CASE I THE WOMEN'S HOTLINE CASE, Continued

The staff committee who received Diane's grievance suggested that they could handle the problem in a less formal way if both Diane and the staff agreed to accept a neutral third-party mediator. Everyone agreed that this suggestion had promise, and a third party was invited to a meeting where the entire staff would address the issue.

At this meeting, the group faced a difficult task. Each member offered reactions they had been unwilling to express previously. The staff made several pointed criticisms of Diane's overall performance. Diane expressed doubts about the staff's willingness to help new workers or to give support when it was requested. Although this discussion was often tense, it was well directed. At the outset of the meeting, Diane withdrew her formal complaint. This action changed the definition of the problem from the immediate work grievance to the question of what levels of support were required for various people to work effectively in this difficult and emotionally draining setting. Staff members shared doubts and fears about their own inadequacies as counselors and agreed that something less than perfection was acceptable. The group recognized that a collective inertia had developed and that they had consistently avoided giving others the support needed to deal with difficult rape cases. They acknowledged, however, the constraints on each woman's time; each worker could handle only a limited amount of stress. The group recognized that some level of mutual support was essential and felt they had fallen below that level over the past year and a half. One member suggested that any staff person should be able to ask for a "debriefing contract" whenever they felt they needed help or support. These contracts would allow someone to ask for ten minutes of another person's time to hear about a particularly disturbing issue or case. The group members adopted this suggestion because they saw it could allow members to seek help without overburdening each other. The person who was asked to listen could assist and give needed support without feeling that she had to "fix" another worker's problem. Diane continued to work at the center and found that her abilities and confidence increased as the group provided the support she needed.

DISCUSSION QUESTIONS

- *In what ways did the parties in this conflict show "good faith"?*
- *Is "good faith" participation a necessary prerequisite to constructive conflict resolution?*

This is a "textbook" case in effective conflict management because it resulted in a solution that all parties accepted. The members of this group walked a tightrope throughout the conflict, yet they managed to avoid a fall. The tension, unpleasantness, uncertainty, and fragility of conflict situations make them hard to face. Because these problems make it difficult to deal with issues in a constructive way, conflicts are often terminated by force, by uncomfortable suppression of the issues, or by exhaustion after a prolonged fight—all outcomes that leave at least one party dissatisfied. Entering a conflict is often like making a bet against the odds: you can win big if it turns out well, but so many things can go wrong that few people are willing to chance it. It is no wonder that many writers feel a need to reassure us. They feel compelled to remind us of the positive outcomes of conflict because all too often the destructive results are all that people remember.

The key to working through conflict is not to minimize its disadvantages, or even to emphasize its positive functions, but to accept both and to try to understand how conflicts move in destructive or productive directions. Such an understanding requires a conception of conflict that calls for a careful **analysis of both the specific behaviors and interaction patterns involved in conflict and the forces that influence these patterns.** Moreover, we can only grasp the fragility of conflicts and the effects that tension and misunderstandings have in their development if we work at the level at which conflicts unfold—specific interactions among the parties.

DEFINITION OF CONFLICT

Conflict is the interaction of interdependent people who perceive incompatible goals and interference from each other in achieving those goals (Hocker and Wilmot 1985). This definition has the advantage of providing a much clearer focus than definitions that view conflict simply as disagreement, as competition, or as the presence of incompatible interests (Fink 1968). **The most important**

feature of conflict is that it is based in interaction. Conflicts are constituted and sustained by the behaviors of the parties involved and their reactions to one another. Conflict interaction takes many forms, and each form presents special problems and requires special handling. The most familiar type of conflict interaction is marked by shouting matches or open competition in which each party tries to defeat the other. But conflicts can also be more subtle. Often people react to conflict by suppressing it. They interact in ways that allow them to avoid confrontation, either because they are afraid of possible changes the conflict may bring about or because the issue "isn't worth fighting over." This response is as much a part of the conflict process as the open struggles commonly associated with conflict. This [reading] deals with the whole range of responses to conflict and how those responses affect the development of conflicts. Conflicts can best be understood and managed by concentrating on specific behavioral patterns and the forces shaping them.

People in conflict perceive that they have incompatible goals or interests and that others are a source of interference in achieving their goals. The key word here is "perceive." Regardless of whether goals are actually incompatible or if the parties believe them to be incompatible, conditions are ripe for conflict. Regardless of whether an employee really stands in the way of a co-worker or whether the co-worker interprets the employee's behavior as interference, the co-worker may move against the employee or feel compelled to skirt certain issues. Thus, the parties' interpretations and beliefs play a key role in conflicts. This does not mean that goals are always conscious as conflict develops. People can act without a clear sense of what their goals or interests are (Coser 1961). Sometimes people find themselves in strained interactions but are unsure how they got there. They realize afterward what their implicit goals were and how their goals were incompatible with those held by others (Hawes and Smith 1973). Communication looms large because of its importance in shaping and maintaining the perceptions that guide conflict behavior.

Indeed, communication problems are sometimes the cause of conflicts. Tension or irritation can result from misunderstandings that occur when people interact with very different communication styles (Tannen 1986, Grimshaw 1990). One person's inquisitive style may be perceived by someone else as intrusive and rude. One person's attempt to avoid stepping on another's toes may be perceived by someone else as distant and cold. Style differences create difficult problems that are often related to differences in cultural backgrounds (Kochman 1981, Dubinskas 1992). However, the old adage "most conflicts are actually communication problems" is not always true. The vast majority of conflicts would not exist without some real difference of interest. This difference may be hard to uncover, it may be redefined over time, and occasionally it may be trivial, but it is there nonetheless. Communication processes can cause conflicts and can easily exacerbate them, but they are rarely the sole source of the difficulty.

Conflict interaction is colored by the interdependence of the parties. For a conflict to arise, the behavior of one or both parties must have consequences for the other. Therefore, by definition, the parties involved in conflict are interdependent. The conflict at the hotline would not have occurred if Diane's behavior had not irritated the other workers and if their response had not threatened Diane's position. Furthermore, any action taken in response to the conflict affects both sides. The decision to institute a "debriefing contract" required considerable change by everyone. If Diane had been fired, that too would have affected the other workers; they would have had to "cover" Diane's cases and come to terms with themselves as co-workers who could be accused of being unresponsive or insensitive.

But interdependence implies more than this: when parties are interdependent they can potentially aid or interfere with each other. **For this reason, conflicts are always characterized by a mixture of incentives to cooperate and to compete.** Any comment during conflict interaction can be seen either as an attempt to advance the speaker's own interest or as an attempt to promote a good outcome for all involved. A party may believe that having their own point accepted is more important, at least for the moment, than proposing a mutually beneficial outcome. When Diane asked for two weeks off, she was probably thinking not of the group's best interest but of her own needs. In other cases, a participant may advance a proposal designed to benefit everyone, as when the staff member suggested the "debriefing contract." In still other instances, a participant may offer a comment with a cooperative intent, but others may interpret it as one that advances individual interests. Regardless of whether the competitive motive is intended by the speaker or assigned by other members, the interaction unfolds from that point under the assumption that the speaker may value only his or her own interests. Subsequent interaction is further likely to undermine incentives to cooperate and is also likely to weaken members' recognition of their own interdependence. The balance of incentives to compete or cooperate is important in determining the direction the conflict interaction takes.

ARENAS OF CONFLICT INTERACTION

Conflict occurs in almost all social settings. Most people learn at a very young age that conflicts arise in families, playgrounds, classrooms, Little League fields, ballet centers, scout troops, and cheerleading teams. Even as relationships become more complex and people become involved in more diverse and public settings, conflicts remain remarkably similar to those experienced in childhood. (Indeed, some argue that early experiences shape involvement in conflict throughout our lives.) Adults encounter conflict in casual work relationships and emotionally intense, intimate relationships as well as in close friendships or in political rivalries. Conflict is encountered in decision-making groups, small businesses, large corporations, church organizations, and doctors' offices. Given the diversity of conflicts typically encountered, what often is of most concern is how much is at stake in any conflict. Conflicts are assessed as pedestrian or profound, trivial or tremendous, or as major or minor maelstroms. The estimate of the significance of any conflict often influences the time and effort invested in strategizing or in developing safeguards or fallbacks. . . .

PRODUCTIVE AND DESTRUCTIVE
CONFLICT INTERACTION

As previously noted, people often associate conflict with negative outcomes. However, there are times when conflicts must be addressed regardless of the apprehension they create. When differences exist and the issues are important, suppression of conflict is often more dangerous than facing it. The psychologist Irving Janis points to a number of famous political disasters, such as the Bay of Pigs invasion and the failure to anticipate the Japanese attack on Pearl Harbor, where poor decisions can be traced to the repression of conflict by key decision-making groups (Janis 1972). The critical question is: what forms of conflict interaction will yield the obvious benefits without tearing a relationship, a group, or an organization apart?

Years ago the sociologist Lewis Coser (1956) distinguished realistic from nonrealistic conflicts. **Realistic conflicts are conflicts based in disagreements over the means to an end or over the ends themselves.** In realistic conflicts, the interaction focuses on the substantive issues the participants must address to resolve their underlying incompatibilities. **Nonrealistic conflicts are expressions of aggression in which the sole end is to defeat or hurt the other.** Participants in nonrealistic conflicts serve their own interests by undercutting those of the other party. Coser argues that because nonrealistic conflicts are oriented toward the expression of aggression, force and coercion are the means for resolving these disputes. Realistic conflicts, on the other hand, foster a wide range of resolution techniques—force, negotiation, persuasion, even voting—because they are oriented toward the resolution of some substantive problem. Although Coser's analysis is somewhat of an oversimplification, it is insightful and suggests important contrasts between productive and destructive conflict interaction (Deutsch 1973). What criteria could be used to evaluate whether a conflict is productive? **In large part, productive conflict interaction depends on flexibility.** In constructive conflicts, members engage in a wide variety of behaviors ranging from coercion and threat to negotiation, joking, and relaxation to reach an acceptable solution. **In contrast, parties in destructive conflicts are likely to be much less flexible because their goal is more narrowly defined: they are trying to defeat each other.** Destructive conflict interaction is likely to have protracted, uncontrolled escalation cycles or prolonged attempts to avoid issues. In productive conflict, on the other hand, the interaction in the group will change direction often. Short cycles of escalation, de-escalation, avoidance, and constructive work on the issue are likely to occur as the participants attempt to manage the conflict.

Consider the hotline case. The group exhibited a wide range of interaction styles, from the threat of a grievance to the cooperative attempt to reach a mutually satisfactory solution. Even though Diane and the members engaged in hostile or threatening interaction, they did not persist in this mode, and when the conflict threatened to escalate, they called in a third party. The conflict showed all the hallmarks of productive interaction. In a destructive conflict the members might have responded to Diane's grievance by suspending her, and

Diane might have retaliated by suing or by attempting to discredit the center in the local newspaper. Her retaliation would have hardened others' positions and they might have fired her, leading to further retaliation. Alternatively, the hotline conflict might have ended in destructive avoidance. Diane might have hidden her problem, and the other members might have consciously or unconsciously abetted her by changing the subject when the murder came up or by avoiding talking to her at all. Diane's problem would probably have grown worse, and she might have had to quit. The center would then revert . . . to "normal" until the same problem surfaced again. While the damage done by destructive avoidance is much less serious in this case than that done by destructive escalation, it is still considerable: the hotline loses a good worker, and the seeds of future losses remain. In both cases, it is not the behaviors themselves that are destructive—neither avoidance nor hostile arguments are harmful in themselves—but rather the inflexibility of the parties that locks them into escalation or avoidance cycles.

In productive conflicts, interaction is guided by the belief that all factions can attain important goals (Deutsch 1973). The interaction reflects a sustained effort to bridge the apparent incompatibility of positions. This effort is in marked contrast to destructive conflicts where the interaction is premised on participants' belief that one side must win and the other must lose. **Productive conflict interaction results in a solution satisfactory to all and produces a general feeling that the parties have gained something** (for example, a new idea, greater clarity of others' positions, or a stronger sense of solidarity). In some cases, the win-lose orientation of destructive conflict stems from fear of losing. People attempt to defeat alternative proposals because they believe that if their positions are not accepted they will lose resources, self-esteem, or the respect of others. In other cases, win-lose interaction is sparked, not by competitive motives, but by the parties' fear of working through a difficult conflict. Groups that rely on voting to reach decisions often call for a vote when discussion becomes heated and the members do not see any other immediate way out of a hostile and threatening situation. Any further attempt to discuss the alternatives or to pursue the reasons behind people's positions seems risky. A vote can put a quick end to threatening interaction, but it also induces a win-lose orientation that can easily trigger destructive cycles. Members whose proposal is rejected must resist a natural tendency to be less committed to the chosen solution and may try to "even the score" in future conflicts. **Productive conflict interaction is sometimes competitive; both parties must stand up for their own positions and strive for perceived understanding if a representative outcome is to be attained** (Cahn 1990). A great deal of tension and hostility may result as people struggle with the conflict. Although parties in productive conflicts hold strongly to their positions, they are also open to movement when convinced that such movement will result in the best decision. The need to preserve power, save face, or make the opponent look bad does not stand in the way of change. In destructive conflict, parties often become polarized, and the defense of a nonnegotiable position becomes more important than working out a viable solution. This description of productive and destructive conflict interaction is obviously an idealization. It is rare that a conflict exhibits all the constructive or destructive qualities just mentioned; indeed, many conflicts exhibit both productive and destructive interaction. However, better conflict management will result if parties can sustain productive conflict interaction patterns.

CONFLICT AS INTERACTIVE BEHAVIOR

Conflict is, by nature, interactive. It is never wholly under one person's control (Kriesberg 1973). The other party's reactions and the person's anticipation of the other's response are extremely important. **Any comment made during a conflict is made with some awareness or prediction about the likely response it will elicit.** This predictive basis for any move in interaction creates a strong tendency for conflict interaction to become cyclic or repetitive. Suppose Robert criticizes Susan, an employee under his supervision, for her decreasing productivity. Susan may accept the criticism and explain why her production is down, thus reducing the conflict and moving toward a solution. Susan may also shout back and sulk, inviting escalation, or she may choose to say nothing and avoid the conflict, resulting in no improvement in the situation. Once Robert has spoken to Susan and she has responded, the situation is no longer totally under Robert's control: his next behavior will be a response to Susan's reaction. Robert's behavior, and its subsequent meaning to Susan, is dependent on the interchange between them. **A behavioral cycle of initiation-response—counter-response results from the conflict interchange. This cycle cannot be understood by breaking it into its parts, into the individual behaviors of Robert and Susan.** It is more complex than the individual behaviors and, in a real sense, has a "life" of its own. The cycle can be self-reinforcing, if, for example, Susan shouts back at Robert, Robert tries to discipline her, Susan becomes more recalcitrant, and so on, in an escalating spiral. The cycle could also limit itself if Robert responds to Susan's shouting with an attempt to calm her and listen to her side of the story. Conflict interaction cycles acquire a momentum of their own. They tend in a definite direction—toward escalation, toward avoidance and suppression, or toward productive work on the conflict. The situation becomes even more complex when we remember that Robert formulated his criticism on the basis of his previous experience with Susan. That is, Robert's move is based on his perception of Susan's likely response. In the same way, Susan's response is based not only on Robert's criticism, but on her estimate of Robert's likely reaction to her response. Usually such estimations are "intuitive"—that is, they are not conscious—but sometimes parties do plot them out ("If I shout at Robert, he'll back down and maybe I won't have to deal with this"). They are always based on the parties' perceptions of each other, on whatever theories or beliefs each holds about the other's reactions. Because these estimates are only intuitive predictions, they may be wrong to some extent. The estimates will be revised as the conflict unfolds, and this revision will largely determine what direction the conflict takes. The most striking thing about this predictive process is the extraordinary difficulties it poses for attempts to understand the parties' thinking.

When Susan responds to Robert on the basis of her prediction of Robert's answer, from the outside we see Susan making an estimate of Robert's estimate of what she means by her response. If Robert reflects on Susan's intention before answering, we observe Robert's estimate of Susan's estimate of his estimate of what Susan meant. This string of estimates can increase without bounds if one tries to pin down the originating point, and after a while the prospect is just as dizzying as a hall of mirrors.

Several studies of arms races (Richardson 1960, North, Brody, and Holsti 1963) and of marital relations (Watzlawick, Beavin, and Jackson 1967; Rubin 1983; Scarf 1987) and employee-supervisor interactions (Brown 1983) have shown how this spiral of predictions poses a critical problem in conflicts. If the parties do not take the spiral into account, they run the risk of miscalculation. However, it is impossible to calculate all the possibilities. At best, people have extremely limited knowledge of the implications their actions hold for others, and their ability to manage conflicts is therefore severely curtailed. Not only are parties' behaviors inherently interwoven in conflicts, but their thinking and anticipations are as well. The key question . . . is: **how does conflict interaction develop destructive patterns—radical escalation, prolonged or inappropriate avoidance of conflict issues, inflexibility—rather than constructive patterns leading to productive conflict management?**

REVIEW QUESTIONS

1. Describe what the authors mean when they say that the case study about Diane and her co-workers shows how conflict situations are tense and threatening, uncertain, and fragile.
2. Explain what is significant about each of the following terms in the authors' definition of conflict: *interaction, interdependent, incompatible goals, interference.*
3. Why do the authors disagree with the old adage, "most conflicts are actually communication problems"?
4. Distinguish between realistic and nonrealistic conflict.

PROBES

1. As you read the case study about Diane and her co-workers, what single feature of the situation strikes you as the most important positive move that was made? In other words, what one thing most helped resolve this conflict productively?
2. Give an example from your own experience of the difference between a realistic and a nonrealistic conflict.
3. At one point the authors argue about the wisdom of resolving a conflict by voting. (a) What is their rationale for discouraging voting? (b) How do you respond; that is, do you agree or disagree, and why?

4. The authors end this excerpt with "the key question" about how conflicts develop destructive patterns. After you've read the other four readings in this chapter, what is your response to this key question?

REFERENCES

Brown, L. D. 1983. *Managing conflict at organizational interfaces.* Reading, MA: Addison-Wesley.

Cahn, D. 1990. *Intimates in conflict: A communication perspective.* Hillsdale, NJ: Lawrence Erlbaum.

Coser, L. 1956. *The functions of social conflict.* New York: Free Press.

Coser, L. 1961. The termination of conflict. *Journal of Conflict Resolution, 5:* 347–353.

Deutsch, M. 1973. *The resolution of conflict.* New Haven, CT: Yale University Press.

Dubinskas, F. 1992. Culture and conflict: The cultural roots of discord. In D. M. Kolb and J. M. Bartunek, Eds., *Hidden conflict in organizations:* 187–208. Newbury Park, CA: Sage.

Fink, C. F. 1968. Some conceptual difficulties in the theory of social conflict. *Journal of Conflict Resolution, 12:* 412–460.

Grimshaw, A. D., Ed. 1990. *Conflict talk: Sociolinguistic investigations of arguments in conversations.* Cambridge: Cambridge University Press.

Hawes, L., and Smith, D. H. 1973. A critique of assumptions underlying the study of communication in conflict. *Quarterly Journal of Speech, 59:* 423–435.

Hocker, J. L., and Wilmot, W. W. 1985. *Interpersonal conflict.* Dubuque, IA: Wm. C. Brown.

Janis, I. 1972. *Victims of groupthink.* Boston: Houghton Mifflin.

Kochman, T. 1981. *Black and white styles in conflict.* Chicago: The University of Chicago Press.

Kriesberg, L. 1973. *The sociology of social conflicts.* Englewood Cliffs, NJ: Prentice-Hall.

North, R. C., Brody, R. A., and Holsti, O. 1963. Some empirical data on the conflict spiral. *Peace Research Society: Papers I.* Chicago Conference: 1–14.

Richardson, L. F. 1960. *Arms and insecurity.* Pittsburgh: The Boxwood Press.

Rubin, L. 1983. *Intimate strangers.* New York: Harper and Row.

Scarf, M. 1987. *Intimate partners: Patterns in love and marriage.* New York: Ballantine.

Tannen, D. 1986. *That's not what I meant.* New York: William Morrow.

Watzlawick, P., Beavin, J. H., and Jackson, D. D. 1967. *Pragmatics of Human Communication.* New York: Norton.

*I*n the next selection, Jack Gibb shares some insights about how conflict happens and what you can do to promote a supportive rather
than a defensive climate for communication.

As Gibb points out, when you anticipate or perceive that you are
threatened by a person or a situation, you will usually react defensively
and so will the other persons involved. When any combination of the
six "defensiveness-producing" elements is present, a spiral usually begins, a spiral that starts with a little discomfort and often escalates into
all-out conflict.

But, Gibb notes, you can also start a spiral in the other direction.
The more supportive you can be, the less other people are likely to read
into the situation distorted reactions created by their own defensiveness. So when you can manifest any combination of the six alternative
attitudes and skills, you can help reduce the defensiveness that's present. You don't have to give up or give in. You just have to stop trying so
hard to demean, control, and impose your hard-and-fast superiority on
the others.

Most of the people I work with find this article very useful. They
discover that they can apply Gibb's analysis of the six characteristics of
defensive and supportive communication climates to their own experience. They also find that Gibb is right when he says that most people are
much more aware of being manipulated or deceived than the manipu-
lators or deceivers think and that such awareness creates defensiveness.
They are usually able to perceive quite accurately another's communication strategy or gimmicks. When they learn that sometimes it's their
own transparently manipulative behavior that creates defensiveness in
others, they get one step closer to communicating interpersonally.

This is a "classic" essay, written before authors understood that it's
inappropriate to refer to people in general as "he" and "him." I hope
you'll be able to read beyond this feature of the language for Gibb's excellent ideas.

DEFENSIVE COMMUNICATION

Jack R. Gibb

One way to understand communication is to view it as a people process rather
than as a language process. If one is to make fundamental improvement in communication, he must make changes in interpersonal relationships. One possible
type of alteration—and the one with which this paper is concerned—is that of
reducing the degree of defensiveness.

From "Defensive Communication," *Journal of Communication 11*, no. 3 (September 1961): 141–148.
Reprinted by permission of the *Journal of Communication* and the author.

DEFINITION AND SIGNIFICANCE

Defensive behavior is defined as that behavior which occurs when an individual perceives threat or anticipates threat in the group. The person who behaves defensively, even though he also gives some attention to the common task, devotes an appreciable portion of his energy to defending himself. Besides talking about the topic, he thinks about how he appears to others, how he may be seen more favorably, how he may win, dominate, impress, or escape punishment, and/or how he may avoid or mitigate a perceived or an anticipated attack.

Such inner feelings and outward acts tend to create similarly defensive postures in others; and, if unchecked, the ensuing circular response becomes increasingly destructive. Defensive behavior, in short, engenders defensive listening, and this in turn produces postural, facial, and verbal cues which raise the defense level of the original communicator.

Defense arousal prevents the listener from concentrating upon the message. Not only do defensive communicators send off multiple value, motive, and affect cues, but also defensive recipients distort what they receive. As a person becomes more and more defensive, he becomes less and less able to perceive accurately the motives, the values, and the emotions of the sender. The writer's analyses of tape recorded discussions revealed that increases in defensive behavior were correlated positively with losses in efficiency in communication.[1] Specifically, distortions became greater when defensive states existed in the groups.

The converse, moreover, also is true. The more "supportive" or defense reductive the climate the less the receiver reads into the communication distorted loadings which arise from projections of his own anxieties, motives, and concerns. As defenses are reduced, the receivers become better able to concentrate upon the structure, the content, and the cognitive meanings of the message.

CATEGORIES OF DEFENSIVE
AND SUPPORTIVE COMMUNICATION

In working over an eight-year period with recordings of discussions occurring in varied settings, the writer developed the six pairs of defensive and supportive categories presented in Table 1. Behavior which a listener perceives as possessing any of the characteristics listed in the left-hand column arouses defensiveness, whereas that which he interprets as having any of the qualities designated as supportive reduces defensive feelings. The degree to which these reactions occur depends upon the personal level of defensiveness and upon the general climate in the group at the time.[2]

Evaluation and Description

Speech or other behavior which appears evaluative increases defensiveness. If by expression, manner of speech, tone of voice, or verbal content the sender seems to be evaluating or judging the listener, then the receiver goes on guard.

TABLE 1 Categories of Behavior Characteristic of
Supportive and Defensive Climates in Small Groups

Defensive Climates	Supportive Climates
1. Evaluation	1. Description
2. Control	2. Problem orientation
3. Strategy	3. Spontaneity
4. Neutrality	4. Empathy
5. Superiority	5. Equality
6. Certainty	6. Provisionalism

Of course, other factors may inhibit the reaction. If the listener thought that the speaker regarded him as an equal and was being open and spontaneous, for example, the evaluativeness in a message would be neutralized and perhaps not even perceived. This same principle applies equally to the other five categories of potentially defense-producing climates. The six sets are interactive.

Because our attitudes toward other persons are frequently, and often necessarily, evaluative, expressions which the defensive person will regard as non-judgmental are hard to frame. Even the simplest question usually conveys the answer that the sender wishes or implies the response that would fit into his value system. A mother, for example, immediately following an earth tremor that shook the house, sought for her small son with the question: "Bobby, where are you?" The timid and plaintive "Mommy, I didn't do it" indicated how Bobby's chronic mild defensiveness predisposed him to react with a projection of his own guilt and in the context of his chronic assumption that questions are full of accusation.

Anyone who has attempted to train professionals to use information-seeking speech with neutral affect appreciates how difficult it is to teach a person to say even the simple "who did that?" without being seen as accusing. Speech is so frequently judgmental that there is a reality base for the defensive interpretations which are so common.

When insecure, group members are particularly likely to place blame, to see others as fitting into categories of good or bad, to make moral judgments of their colleagues, and to question the value, motive, and affect loadings of the speech which they hear. Since value loadings imply a judgment of others, a belief that the standards of the speaker differ from his own causes the listener to become defensive.

Descriptive speech, in contrast to that which is evaluative, tends to arouse a minimum of uneasiness. Speech acts which the listener perceives as genuine requests for information or as material with neutral loadings is descriptive. Specifically, presentations of feelings, events, perceptions, or processes which do not ask or imply that the receiver change behavior or attitude are minimally defense producing. The difficulty in avoiding overtone is illustrated by the problems of news reporters in writing stories about unions, communists, Blacks, and religious activities without tipping off the "party" line of the newspaper. One can often tell from the opening words in a news article which side the newspaper's editorial policy favors.

Control and Problem Orientation

Speech which is used to control the listener evokes resistance. In most of our social intercourse someone is trying to do something to someone else—to change an attitude, to influence behavior, or to restrict the field of activity. The degree to which attempts to control produce defensiveness depends upon the openness of the effort, for a suspicion that hidden motives exist heightens resistance. For this reason attempts of nondirective therapists and progressive educators to refrain from imposing a set of values, a point of view, or a problem solution upon the receivers meet with many barriers. Since the norm is control, noncontrollers must earn the perceptions that their efforts have no hidden motives. A bombardment of persuasive "messages" in the fields of politics, education, special causes, advertising, religion, medicine, industrial relations, and guidance has bred cynical and paranoidal responses in listeners.

Implicit in all attempts to alter another person is the assumption by the change agent that the person to be altered is inadequate. That the speaker secretly views the listener as ignorant, unable to make his own decisions, uninformed, immature, unwise, or possessed of wrong or inadequate attitudes is a subconscious perception which gives the latter a valid base for defensive reactions.

Methods of control are many and varied. Legalistic insistence on detail, restrictive regulations and policies, conformity norms, and all laws are among the methods. Gestures, facial expressions, other forms of nonverbal communication, and even such simple acts as holding a door open in a particular manner are means of imposing one's will upon another and hence are potential sources of resistance.

Problem orientation, on the other hand, is the antithesis of persuasion. When the sender communicates a desire to collaborate in defining a mutual problem and in seeking its solution, he tends to create the same problem orientation in the listener; and, of greater importance, he implies that he has no predetermined solution, attitude, or method to impose. Such behavior is permissive in that it allows the receiver to set his own goals, make his own decisions, and evaluate his own progress—or to share with the sender in doing so. The exact methods of attaining permissiveness are not known, but they must involve a constellation of cues and they certainly go beyond mere verbal assurances that the communicator has no hidden desires to exercise control.

Strategy and Spontaneity

When the sender is perceived as engaged in a stratagem involving ambiguous and multiple motivations, the receiver becomes defensive. No one wishes to be a guinea pig, a role player, or an impressed actor, and no one likes to be the victim of some hidden motivation. That which is concealed, also, may appear larger than it really is with the degree of defensiveness of the listener determining the perceived size of the suppressed element. The intense reaction of the reading audience to the material in *Hidden Persuaders* indicates the prevalence of defensive reactions to multiple motivations behind strategy. Group members who are seen as "taking a role," as feigning emotion, as toying with their colleagues, as withholding information, or as having special sources of data are especially resented. One participant once complained that another was "using a listening technique" on him!

A large part of the adverse reaction to much of the so-called human relations training is a feeling against what are perceived as gimmicks and tricks to fool or to "involve" people, to make a person think he is making his own decision, or to make the listener feel that the sender is genuinely interested in him as a person. Particularly violent reactions occur when it appears that someone is trying to make a stratagem appear spontaneous. One person has reported a boss who incurred resentment by habitually using the gimmick of "spontaneously" looking at his watch and saying, "My gosh, look at the time—I must run to an appointment." The belief was that the boss would create less irritation by honestly asking to be excused.

Similarly, the deliberate assumption of guilelessness and natural simplicity is especially resented. Monitoring the tapes of feedback and evaluation sessions in training groups indicates the surprising extent to which members perceive the strategies of their colleagues. This perceptual clarity may be quite shocking to the strategist, who usually feels that he had cleverly hidden the motivational aura around the "gimmick."

This aversion to deceit may account for one's resistance to politicians who are suspected of behind-the-scenes planning to get his vote, to psychologists whose listening apparently is motivated by more than the manifest or content-level interest in his behavior, or to the sophisticated, smooth, or clever person whose "oneupmanship" is marked with guile. In training groups the role-flexible person frequently is resented because his changes in behavior are perceived as strategic maneuvers.

In contrast, behavior which appears to be spontaneous and free of deception is defense reductive. If the communicator is seen as having a clean id, as having uncomplicated motivations, as being straightforward and honest, and as behaving spontaneously in response to the situation, he is likely to arouse minimal defense.

Neutrality and Empathy

When neutrality in speech appears to the listener to indicate a lack of concern for his welfare, he becomes defensive. Group members usually desire to be perceived as valued persons, as individuals of special worth, and as objects of concern and affection. The clinical, detached, person-is-an-object-of-study attitude on the part of many psychologist-trainers is resented by group members. Speech with low affect that communicates little warmth or caring is in such contrast with the affect-laden speech in social situations that it sometimes communicates rejection.

Communication that conveys empathy for the feelings and respect for the worth of the listener, however, is particularly supportive and defense reductive. Reassurance results when a message indicates that the speaker identifies himself with the listener's problems, shares his feelings, and accepts his emotional reactions at face value. Abortive efforts to deny the legitimacy of the receiver's emotions by assuring the receiver that he need not feel bad, that he should not feel rejected, or that he is overly anxious, though often intended as support giving, may impress the listener as lack of acceptance. The combination of understanding and empathizing with the other person's emotions with no accompanying effort to change him apparently is supportive at a high level.

The importance of gestural behavioral cues in communicating empathy should be mentioned. Apparently spontaneous facial and bodily evidences of concern are often interpreted as especially valid evidence of deep-level acceptance.

Superiority and Equality

When a person communicates to another that he feels superior in position, power, wealth, intellectual ability, physical characteristics, or other ways, he arouses defensiveness. Here, as with the other sources of disturbance, whatever arouses feelings of inadequacy causes the listener to center upon the affect loading of the statement rather than upon the cognitive elements. The receiver then reacts by not hearing the message, by forgetting it, by competing with the sender, or by becoming jealous of him.

The person who is perceived as feeling superior communicates that he is not willing to enter into a shared problem-solving relationship, that he probably does not desire feedback, that he does not require help, and/or that he will be likely to try to reduce the power, the status, or the worth of the receiver.

Many ways exist for creating the atmosphere that the sender feels himself equal to the listener. Defenses are reduced when one perceives the sender as being willing to enter into participative planning with mutual trust and respect. Differences in talent, ability, worth, appearance, status, and power often exist, but the low defense communicator seems to attach little importance to these distinctions.

Certainty and Provisionalism

The effects of dogmatism in producing defensiveness are well known. Those who seem to know the answers, to require no additional data, and to regard themselves as teachers rather than as co-workers tend to put others on guard. Moreover, in the writer's experiment, listeners often perceived manifest expressions of certainty as connoting inward feelings of inferiority. They saw the dogmatic individual as needing to be right, as wanting to win an argument rather than solve a problem, and as seeing his ideas as truths to be defended. This kind of behavior often was associated with acts which others regarded as attempts to exercise control. People who were right seemed to have low tolerance for members who were "wrong"—i.e., who did not agree with the sender.

One reduces the defensiveness of the listener when he communicates that he is willing to experiment with his own behavior, attitudes, and ideas. The person who appears to be taking provisional attitudes, to be investigating issues rather than taking sides on them, to be problem solving rather than debating, and to be willing to experiment and explore tends to communicate that the listener may have some control over the shared quest or the investigation of the ideas. If a person is genuinely searching for information and data, he does not resent help or company along the way.

CONCLUSION

The implications of the above material for the parent, the teacher, the manager, the administrator, or the therapist are fairly obvious. Arousing defensiveness interferes with communication and thus makes it difficult—and sometimes impossible—for anyone to convey ideas clearly and to move effectively toward the solution of therapeutic, educational, or managerial problems.

REVIEW QUESTIONS

1. How does Gibb define *defensiveness?*
2. What does defensiveness defend? What does supportiveness support?
3. How can description accomplish the same purpose as evaluation?
4. Based on what you've already read about empathy in Chapter 6, how is neutrality the opposite of empathy?

PROBES

1. Does Gibb see defensiveness as a relational thing—something that's created *between* persons—or does he see it as something one person or group creates and forces on another person or a group?
2. Gibb cautions us about the negative effects of evaluation. But is it possible actually to be nonevaluative? Or is that what Gibb is asking us to do?
3. Although most of Gibb's examples use verbal cues, each of the categories of defensiveness and supportiveness is also communicated nonverbally. Can you identify how you nonverbally communicate evaluation? Control? Strategy? Superiority? Spontaneity? Empathy? Equality?
4. Self-disclosing is one way to communicate spontaneity. Can you identify communication behaviors that help create the other kinds of supportive climate?
5. Which categories of defensive behavior are most present in your relationship with your lover or spouse? Your employer? Your parents? Which categories of supportive behavior characterize those relationships?

NOTES

1. J. R. Gibb, "Defense Level and Influence Potential in Small Groups," *Leadership and Interpersonal Behavior,* ed. L. Petrullo and B. M. Bass (New York: Holt, Rinehart and Winston, 1961), pp. 66–81.

2. J. R. Gibb, "Sociopsychological Processes of Group Instruction," *The Dynamics of Instructional Groups,* ed. N. B. Henry (Fifty-ninth Yearbook of the National Society of the Study of Education, Part II, 1960), pp. 115–135.

*T*his reading offers a fairly complete outline of how to think about and prepare for a productive, rather than a destructive, conflict. The authors have a long connection with *Bridges Not Walls.* When I was working on the first edition of this book, I wrote Hugh Prather asking for permission to reprint excerpts from his book *Notes to Myself.* I was struck by how his brief, journal-like notations captured several of the central points I wanted this book to make. He generously agreed to let me use some of his material, and his selections have appeared prominently in this book ever since. Now Hugh and his wife Gayle have written *A Book for Couples,* and I believe their discussion of conflict is among the best I've read.

They begin with an example of a typical everyday conflict that reveals how many issues are often buried in an argument between friends or intimates. It starts as an argument about the cat window and lasts only a couple of minutes, but the Prathers identify 17 separate issues that get raised. No wonder arguments like this create more problems than they solve!

The next important point that's made in this reading is that discussions like the one about the cat window "create the relationship's terrain." In other words, the way these discussions are carried out defines the quality of the couple's relationship. This means that *process* is vital. *How* an argument happens is more important than the outcome that emerges. Process is literally more important than product.

With their tongues firmly planted in their cheeks, the Prathers then offer seven "magic rules for ruining any discussion." You can probably recognize some of your favorite fighting moves in this list—I know I do. The point of the list is to contrast the main features of productive and destructive conflict.

Then the authors explicitly highlight the point about process that they introduced earlier. They urge you to recognize that when you are in a conflict with a person you're close to, "to agree is not the purpose." Rather, "the only allowable purpose" for this kind of discussion "is to bring you and your partner closer." This, it seems to me, is a profoundly simple but important idea. It challenges one primary assumption most of us carry into our conflicts with people we care about: that the point is to get my way, be sure the other knows how I feel, or make the other feel bad. What might happen if couples could actually internalize this idea: that the real point of our argument is to get closer?

The rest of this reading builds on this foundation. The Prathers offer five steps for preparing to argue. All these guidelines make good sense and, taken together, as I mentioned earlier, they provide a fairly comprehensive outline of how to prepare to "do" conflict well. I won't repeat what they say here, but I do want to highlight some points.

Preparation step 2 is to "try to let go" of the issue you're thinking of raising. Although I don't think it's good to suppress genuinely felt emotions, I do believe that couples could frequently profit from applying this suggestion. I've found that it can frequently be relaxing, freeing, and empowering simply to let an irritation go.

Preparation steps 4 and 5 operationalize the Prathers' point about the only allowable purpose for a conflict. It's revealing to ask about a conflict whether "communication is your aim" rather than winning or venting. It is also helpful for me to try to be clear that "the problem is the relationship's and not your partner's."

As I read some sections of their essay I am a little frustrated by what can sound like oversimplification and naïveté. The real tough arguments are much more intense and difficult than these two authors seem to realize. But when I look again at their advice, I recognize that they understand well enough how gut-wrenching a fight with a loved one can be. They are simply convinced, as have been a great many wise people over the ages, that returning anger for anger doesn't help. Ultimately, love, which in this case means the often unromantic commitment to a relationship, is stronger than defensiveness and bitterness.

HOW TO RESOLVE ISSUES UNMEMORABLY

Hugh and Gayle Prather

UNFINISHED ARGUMENTS ACCUMULATE

It's not that issues don't get resolved. Indeed they are settled but settled like ketchup settles into a carpet. An uncleaned carpet can triple in weight within five years, and most relationships get so laden with undigested arguments that they collapse into a dull, angry stupor and cease to move toward their original goal.

"Albert, you've just got to install the cat window. I woke up again at 3 A.M. with Runnymede standing on my chest staring at me. I'm not getting enough alpha sleep."

"Sorry about that, Paula. I'll get to it this weekend."

"But Albert, you've been saying that for a month."

"Well, you know, honey, we could just put the cat out at night like everyone else."

"Oh, sure, and then what if he needed to get in? What if something was after him? What then?"

"What difference will the cat window make? He can still stay out all night if he wants to."

"Yes, Albert, but he can *also* get in if he *needs* to. You know, if you're not going to be a responsible pet owner, you shouldn't have a pet."

"Now there's a thought."

"I see. And I guess you don't mind breaking Gigi's heart."

"That's another thing, Paula, her name is Virginia, not Gigi. Why do we have to have a cat named Runnymede and a daughter named Gigi? Besides, I'll buy her a nice stuffed Garfield after the cat is comfortably settled in at the animal shelter."

"You know, Albert, this conversation is opening my eyes to something I've felt for a very long time."

"What's that, Paula?"

"You only care about mixed soccer. Since joining that team with the silly name you haven't been playing horsey with Gigi and you haven't been scratching Runnymede under the chin where he can't lick. You certainly pretended to like Runnymede well enough when we were dating."

"You were the one who insisted I join the team. You were the one who said it would be good for me to 'get out of the house for a change.' I like the cat. I love my daughter. But I don't want to spend my Saturdays ruining a window with a perfectly good view."

"I guess you don't really care about me either, Albert. And you can stand there calmly peeling your Snickers while wanting Runnymede to be gassed. If I didn't know how much emotion you devote to *mixed* soccer I would say you have become psychotically insensitive and unfeeling. Perhaps you should seek help."

Here Albert, proving that he is neither insensitive nor unfeeling, flings his Snickers at the window in question, grabs his soccer gear, and storms from the house, where in an afternoon match playing goalie for the Yuma Yuccas he fractures the middle three phalanges in his right hand, thus ending the question of installing anything.

EACH NEW ISSUE RESURRECTS THE OLD

We wish we could say that this dialogue was a transcript but it is a composite. If we reprinted verbatim some of the typical arguments we have heard during counseling, they would be dismissed as overwrought fiction. The large number of digressions seen here is actually commonplace and illustrates the typical residue of unsettled questions found in most long-term relationships. The difference between this and the average disagreement is that some of these words might have been thought but left unspoken. Yet the feeling of estrangement by the end of the argument would have been the same.

On this Saturday morning Paula is upset because her sleep continues to be interrupted by the cat asking to be put out. That is the sum of the issue. If the couple had sat down together instead of using the problem as a means of separating still further, they could easily have solved this one difficulty in any of a hundred different mutually acceptable ways. But a hive of older discord lies just beneath their awareness, and therefore settling just one problem in peace is harder than it would seem.

The cry of unresolved issues is strong and persistent. Any couple will feel their failure to have joined. They yearn to bridge the old gaps and fear the potential of further separation more than they welcome the opportunity to reverse the process. To bring up former differences during a discussion is not blameworthy, it is in fact a call for help, but it is mistimed.

Without realizing it—because most arguments are conducted with no deep awareness—Albert and Paula allude to seventeen other issues, none of which had to be brought up to solve *this* problem. In the order they appear, here are the questions they have left unanswered in the past, a small fraction of the total residue if you consider all the others that will be mentioned in future arguments: (1) Why has Albert's promise gone unfulfilled for a month? (2) Should the cat be left out overnight? (3) Is Albert irresponsible? (4) Should the family continue having this pet? (5) Is Albert insensitive to his daughter? (6) Should Paula continue calling Virginia "Gigi"? (7) Should the cat be renamed? (8) Would a stuffed animal sufficiently compensate? (9) Is mixed soccer affecting Albert's attitude toward his daughter and pet? (10) Does the team have a silly name? (11) Is Albert being sufficiently attentive to Paula or has he changed in some fundamental way? (12) Does Paula want Albert around the house? (13) How important is the window view to Albert's happiness? (14) Does Albert still love Paula? (15) Should Albert eat Snickers? (16) Is Albert's contact with other women on Saturdays the root cause of his, in Paula's view, wavering commitment to his family? (17) Does Albert have serious psychological problems?

As can be seen here, it is not easy for most couples to concentrate on a single issue. Nevertheless it is certainly possible and, in itself, to practice doing so will begin giving them a new kind of evidence: that within this relationship there are still grounds for unity and happiness. If one of the partners deviates from this guideline, the other should not make still another issue of this or get caught up in the irrelevant point raised, but should see instead the real desire behind the digression and treat it gently and answer it with love.

DISCUSSIONS CREATE THE RELATIONSHIP'S TERRAIN

. . . To resolve issues in the usual way is as damaging to a relationship as not resolving them at all, because the gap is not truly bridged and the unsuccessful attempt merely adds more weight to the couple's doubts about each other. In the argument over the cat window, Paula's concern about the health of her marriage surfaces, a question of far greater importance to her than how she will manage to get more sleep, and yet without fully realizing it she exacerbates this larger problem and works against her own interests. By arguing in the manner they did, this couple, as do most, merely manufactured new issues between them. Albert probably did not mean to take that hard a stand on getting rid of the cat—he may actually have wanted to keep it. And Paula did not have real doubts about Albert's mental health.

The past that drives so many relationships into the ground is built piece by piece, smallness fitted to smallness, selfishness answered with selfishness. Yet the process is largely unconscious. Each couple quickly settles into a few sad methods of conducting arguments, but seldom is the means they use thought through or the results closely examined. One person nags, the other relents. One person reasons, the other becomes silent. One person flares, the other backs down. One person cajoles, the other gives in. But where are the joy and grandeur, where is the friendship that was supposed to flourish, the companionship that through the years was to fuse an invulnerable bond, a solace and a blessing at the close of life? Instead there is a bitter and widening wedge between the two, and even the briefest of discussions contains a hundred dark echoes from the past.

No matter how entrenched are our patterns of problem solving, they can be stepped away from easily once we see that they do not serve our interests. The only interest served in most discussions is to be right. But, truly, how deep is this? Do we actually want to make our partner wrong, to defeat a friend, and slowly to defeat a friendship? It certainly may feel that way. Caught up once again in the emotions of a disagreement, we stride doggedly toward our usual means of concluding every argument: adamant silence, crushing logic, patronizing practicality, collapsed crying, quelling anger, martyred acquiescence, loveless humor, sulking retreat.

These postures and a thousand more are attempts to prove a point other than love, and as with all endeavors to show up one's partner, the friendship itself is the victim, because the friendship becomes a mere tool, a means of making the other person feel guilty. The love our partner has for us is now seen as leverage, and in our quiet or noisy way we set about making the relationship a shambles, not realizing that we ourselves are part of the wreckage.

THE MAGIC RULES FOR RUINING ANY DISCUSSION

. . . The dialogue with which we began this [reading] incorporates a few of but not all the rules for disastrous communication—yet only one or two are needed to neutralize the best of intentions. Follow these guidelines, even a little sloppily, and you are guaranteed a miserable time:

1. *Bring the matter up when at least one of you is angry.*

   Variations: Bring it up when nothing can be done about it (in the middle of the night; right before guests are due; when one of you is in the shower). Bring it up when concentration is impossible (while driving to a meeting with the IRS; while watching the one TV program you both agree on; while your spouse is balancing the checkbook).

2. *Be as personal as possible when setting forth the problem.*

   Variations: Know the answer before you ask the question. While describing the issue, use an accusatory tone. Begin by implying who, as usual, is to blame.

3. *Concentrate on getting what you want.*

   Variations: Overwhelm your partner's position before he or she can muster a defense (be very emotional; call in past favors; be impeccably reasonable). Impress on your partner what you need and what he or she must do without. If you begin losing ground, jockey for position.

4. *Instead of listening, think only of what you will say next.*

   Variations: Do other things while your partner is talking. Forget where your partner left off. In other words, listen with all the interest you would give a bathroom exhaust fan.

5. *Correct anything your partner says about you.*

   Variations: Each time your partner gives an example of your behavior, cite a worse example of his or hers. Repeat "That's not what I said" often. Do not accept anything your partner says at face value (point out exceptions; point out inaccuracies in facts and in grammar).

6. *Mention anything from the past that has a chance of making your partner defensive.*

   Variations: Make allusions to your partner's sexual performance. Remind your husband of his mother's faults. Compare what your wife does to what other women do, and after she complains, say, "I didn't mean it that way."

7. *End by saying something that will never be forgotten.*

   Variations: Do something that proves you are a madman. Let your parting display proclaim that no exposure of your partner could be amply revealing, no characterization too profane, no consequence sufficiently wretched. At least leave the impression you are a little put out.

TO AGREE IS NOT THE PURPOSE

All couples believe they know how to hold a discussion, and yet it is not an exaggeration to say that in most long-term relationships there has rarely been one wholly successful argument. Obviously they are filled with disagreements that end in agreements, but when these are examined, it can be seen that at least a small patch of reservation had to be overlooked in order for accord to be reached.

We believe this is simply how differences are settled, and so even though we sense that our partner is still in conflict, we barge ahead with our newly won concession, thinking the bad moment will pass. Later it becomes painfully clear that it has not and we judge our partner irresolute. Or if we are the one who complied, we count our little sacrifice dear and wait for reparation—which never comes or is never quite adequate, and we cannot understand why our partner feels such little gratitude.

The aim of most arguments is to reach outward agreement. Until that is replaced with a desire for friendship, varying degrees of alienation will be the only lasting outcome. Couples quickly develop a sense of helplessness over the pattern that their discussions have fallen into. They believe they are sincerely attempting to break out of it and are simply failing. They try different responses, going from shouting to silence, from interminable talking to walking out of the room, from considering each point raised to sticking tenaciously to one point, but nothing they do seems to alter the usual unhappy ending.

There is no behavioral formula to reversing the habitual course of an argument. It requires a shift in attitude, not in actions, even though actions will modify in the process. No more is needed than one partner's absolute clarity about the purpose of the argument. This is not easy but it is simple. Therefore let us look again at what the aim should be. . . .

The only allowable purpose for a discussion is to bring you and your partner closer. Minds must come together to decide instead of backing away in order to apply pressure. How is this possible, given the fact that you and your partner are deeply selfish! Fortunately, the selfishness is compartmentalized and your hearts remain unaffected. You need not eliminate it; merely bypass it because you recognize that it is not in your interests to be selfish. To the ego, this concept is insane because it sees no value in love. But love is in your interests because you *are* love, or at least part of you is, and thus each discussion is a way of moving into your real self.

A little time is obviously needed to see one's true interests. If you rush into a discussion you will operate from your insensitivity by habit and aim for a prize your heart cares nothing about. Do not kid yourself. You *do* know whether the discussion is ending with the two of you feeling closer. The selfish part of your mind will tell you that the little sadness and sense of distance you may now feel was a small price to pay for the concession you won or the point you made. Or it will argue that it was all unavoidable. This may happen many times before you begin reversing your ordinary way of participating. This transition is an important stage of growth and entails looking more and more carefully at selfish impulses and their aftermath. Is how you feel really worth it? Was the way it went truly unavoidable?

Thus you will come to see the result you want, and this deeper recognition will begin to eclipse your pettiness in the midst of an argument. Gradually you will catch the mistakes sooner, and eventually you will learn to avoid them from the start. For you *do* want these times of deciding to warm your hearts and lighten your steps. So persist in the guidelines we will give, and these little defeats to your relationship will slowly give way to friendship.

We are so used to thinking of a discussion as a symbol of separation that it can often be helpful to change its form enough that something new will appear to be happening and thus the old mind set is undercut. To take the usual process, break it into steps and put them in order is usually all that is needed to accomplish this.

An issue could be said to pass through five stages in reaching resolution. First, it must be thought of by at least one of the partners as an issue. Second, a moment is chosen to bring the matter up. Third, a decision is made as to the manner in which it will be presented. Fourth, there is an exchange of thoughts and feelings. And fifth, the discussion is concluded.

Most couples give very little thought to the first three stages. They simply find themselves in the thick of a so-called spontaneous argument and no one is certain at what point it began. Obviously you must become more conscious of the subjects you bring up so carelessly. Any sign of fear over what you are about to say is a very useful indicator. If you see you have a question about whether to say it, let this be your cue to break these preliminary choices into conscious steps. Do not begrudge the time, remember instead how strongly you want to begin building a real friendship.

FIVE STEPS IN PREPARING TO ARGUE

First, you might ask yourself if the issue you are thinking of is actually a present issue or merely one you have been reminded of. In other words, be certain this is currently a problem and not one the relationship may already be on its way to solving. Many people habitually rake over their marriage for signs of imperfection and naturally they find a great many, but it can be far more disrupting to friendship to be constantly questioning and comparing than to wait to see if the problem continues in any severe way. Meanwhile, enjoy what is already between you without telling yourself what this is. . . .

If the issue is unquestionably a present one, the second step you might try is to let go of it. Letting go is not "better," but it is an option that current values tend to underrate. However, it must be accomplished thoroughly and honestly or the issue will grow like mold in a dark unseen place. If it is done consciously dismissal is not denial. Essentially it entails examining in detail what you do not like and then making a deliberate effort to identify with another part of you that never "takes issue" with any living thing, that is still and at ease, that acts only from peace. . . .

If a couple espouses world energy consciousness or is on a tight budget, for one of the partners to habitually leave the hot water running, not turn off lights, or keep the refrigerator door open may be grating or even shocking to the other partner. Yet the spectacle of someone wasting energy and money is *not* grating or shocking. The interpretation we assign it, and not the act itself, determines the emotions we feel. Jordan, age two, is "shockingly irresponsible." He has even been known (yesterday, in fact) to flush a toilet five times in a row and then run to tell his big brother about the accomplishment. "John, I flush, I flush!" "That's nice." said John, blatantly contributing to the delinquency of a minor. The reason Jordan didn't tell his father (who is the family's conscience in these matters) was that he was the very one who kept showing him how it was done, thereby encouraging him to waste over fifteen gallons of water (plus six more his father used researching that figure). . . .

So here we have four reactions issuing from four interpretations: pride from the father, support from the seven-year-old, excitement from the two-year-old and, having no originality, curiosity from the cat. Clearly no uniform effect was produced by an external and unreachable cause. How then might you let go of your reaction to your spouse's wasteful habits in lieu of bringing it up one more time? Certainly you would not try dishonestly to convince yourself that the practice was not costing money or energy. Or that it did not really matter to you. Neither would you attempt to assign some motive to your partner's acts that you did not believe, such as not knowing any better or really trying hard but being unable to stop. Dishonesty does not end an unhappy line of thought. That is why reinterpretation is generally not effective. . . .

If in your moment of consideration you are able to see these facts deeply enough, you may open your eyes to your partner's innocence and no longer feel compelled to understand why he or she does these things. But if after making the attempt to free your mind you see that you have not let the issue go, then perhaps to bring it up would be the preferable course, for undoubtedly that is better than storing anger or fear. . . .

The third step is to consider if this is the time. If you feel an urge to bring it up quickly, be very alert to anger. Your heart is willing to wait but your ego is not, especially if it senses an opportunity to strike back. The ego is merely our love of misery, of withdrawal and loneliness, and it can feel like our own deep impulse even though it exists on the most superficial level of the mind.

For too long now our relationships have been jerked around by our own lack of awareness. There is more to your mind than selfishness. So be still a moment and let peace arise from you. Is this the time? A simple question. There need not be great soul-searching and hand-wringing over it. If your partner has just done something and this is the issue, clearly he or she is likely to be more defensive if instantly called on it. If your partner is not in a particularly happy frame of mind, is hostile, worried or depressed, a more receptive state will surely come and nothing is lost by waiting. Is this the time? Merely look and know the answer. The urge to attack when you are angry is very strong, but if you will allow yourself time to reflect on your genuine feelings, this will do more to relieve your frustration.

The fourth step is to be certain that communication is your aim. Trying to get someone to change is not communication because you have already decided what change is needed. Your partner is therefore left with nothing to say and will definitely feel your unwillingness to consider, to listen, to appreciate. So before you speak take time to hear your heart.

You are not two advocates arguing a case. You are interested in joining, not in prevailing. You are like the directors of a business you both love coming together to help it over a difficult situation. You don't care from whose lips the solution comes. You welcome the *answer*. To this end what are you willing to do if your partner becomes defensive? Are you prepared, and have you prepared, to carry through your love of the relationship? . . .

The final point to consider is whether you are clear that the problem is the relationship's and not your partner's. In our example the problem was not Paula's, because her lack of sleep was affecting Albert also. One person's jealousy, appetite, hypersensitivity, frigidity, phobia or any other characteristic that has become an issue cannot successfully be viewed as more one's responsibility than the other's because friendship is always a mutual sharing of all burdens. . . .

You must understand that unless you make a specific effort to see through the fallacy, you *will* go into a discussion thinking one of you is more to blame than the other, and this will make it very hard to listen and be open. Learn to treat every issue as an impersonal and neutral enemy and to close ranks against it. An addiction, for example, can be viewed as you would a hurricane or a deluge—you need each other's help to survive the storm. Our dog, Sunny Sunshine Pumpkin Prather (whose very name is a masterpiece of family compromise), gets sprayed by a skunk about once a month and the smell is everyone's problem. What good would it do to blame the dog? And yet we have seen other families get angry at their dog "for being so stupid." . . .

These preliminary steps, which should only take an instant or two to complete, will at least make it possible for a discussion to begin with some chance of success. Now you are ready for a *real* argument, one in which your minds can join rather than separate.

REVIEW QUESTIONS

1. What point are the Prathers making by listing 17 issues that were brought up in the argument between Albert and Paula?
2. What do the authors mean when they say that discussions "create the relationship's terrain"?
3. Paraphrase this statement: "The only allowable purpose for a discussion is to bring you and your partner closer." Do you agree or disagree with it? Explain.
4. What do the authors mean when they say that you should "learn to treat every issue as an impersonal and neutral enemy and to close ranks against it"?
5. What keeps the "protect your gains" step from being selfish?

PROBES

1. What alternative do the authors offer to "being right" in a conflict?
2. What general principle or principles are violated by the seven "magic rules for ruining any discussion"? In other words, what general attitudes makes these moves destructive?
3. Which of the five steps for preparing to argue do you *least* often follow? What does that fact tell you about your way of "doing" conflict?
4. A fundamental, perhaps even a radically different, perspective or point of view is behind just about everything the Prathers say about "resolving issues

unmemorably." By "different," I mean different from the attitude we normally carry into a conflict. How would you describe this alternative point of view or perspective?

*T*his reading is an excerpt from a recent book that challenges one of Western culture's most basic beliefs about conflict. As you can tell by the title, the book's target is *blaming*, the widespread tendency people have to start dealing with a conflict by figuring out who or what is at fault so that they can clearly and solidly place blame. Jeffrey Kottler's attitude toward this common conviction is clear from his first sentence: "If you spent half as much time changing the ways you respond in conflict situations as you do trying to figure out who is at fault," he writes, "most of your troubles would soon vanish."

This will definitely not be easy for some people to hear. "If you don't figure out who's to blame," people often say, "how can you prevent something bad from happening again?" But as Kottler points out, this way of thinking overlooks how fault-finding and blaming actually affect communication in conflict. Most adversaries respond to blaming with more of the same, which means that the process makes the conflict worse rather than better. It is helpful to determine the causes of disastrous situations for the purposes of not repeating the same mistakes, "but only when the focus is on enlightenment rather than on assigning guilt." And there's a big difference between those two motives.

Echoing some of what I say in Chapter 2, Kottler argues that it is also often impossible to determine who is at fault, partly because "conflicted relationships tend to perpetuate themselves" until they have a life of their own. Whenever you're in this kind of relationship, the most fruitful first step is to take responsibility for your part of the whole without blaming either others or yourself.

With the help of some examples from his own life, Kottler distinguishes the "linear causality" that often operates in the natural world from the "circular causality" that governs the human world. The basic difference is that when cause-and-effect are understood to operate in a straight line (linear), cause can reliably be separated from effect and there is a predictable relationship between them. So there is linear causality between a temperature of 32°F or 0°C and water freezing. But the human world is much more complicated. One person doesn't disrespect another just "because she is insensitive." As Kottler explains, one person's perceptions and behaviors intermingle with the other person's perceptions and behaviors in a complex of expectations, attributions, and subtle nonverbal indicators that leave each person feeling that their opposite conclusions ("it's her fault"; "no, it's his fault") are entirely justified.

The best way to change this negative spiral is to take responsibility for your part of the conflict. Importantly, this does not mean blaming yourself. Taking responsibility "involves an internal process wherein you address a series of introspective inquiries," and Kottler describes how this process of internal questions and answers can work.

There are four basic questions to work through: (1) How are you disowning the problem? In what ways are you unaware of or actively denying your part in the whole? (2) In what ways are you making excuses for yourself? Just about all humans have a natural tendency to protect their own ego, and this can promote a level of defensiveness (as Jack Gibb talks about in a previous reading) that makes problems worse. Kottler urges us to reflect on our own version of this tendency. (3) What are your favorite scapegoats for diverting blame away from yourself? This is another common defense mechanism that Kottler encourages us to work away from. (4) What might you do internally to feel more in control over what happens externally? This question can help you understand the impact of the ways you might be talking to yourself about the conflict situation.

If Kottler were a communication professional rather than a counseling psychologist, he might emphasize more strongly the interpersonal aspects of working through these four questions. It can be helpful, for example, for parties to the same conflict to help each other respond to them. But whether the questions are considered individually or in conversations, they can help conflict parties significantly improve their communication with each other.

TAKING RESPONSIBILITY WITHOUT BLAMING

Jeffrey Kottler

. . . If you spent half as much time changing the ways you respond in conflict situations as you do trying to figure out who is at fault, most of your troubles would soon vanish. Most people are obsessed with identifying the culprit who is responsible for a dispute. On the one hand, if you can justify that it is *they* who were negligent or irresponsible, you may rub your hands together in glee and rest easy in the knowledge that at least you are not the one who created the mess, even if you do have to live with it. If, on the other hand, you frankly admit (or you are trapped into doing so) that *you*, not they, are responsible, then you can just as easily fall into the trap of feeling guilty and remorseful.

Since most of the time adversaries are not willing to accept blame, even when all evidence points toward them, it is largely a futile exercise trying to figure out who is at fault. Of course, it is helpful to determine the causes of disas-

Excerpt from *Beyond Blame: A New Way of Resolving Conflicts in Relationships* by Jeffrey Kottler, 1994. Reprinted by permission of Jossey–Bass, Inc. as publisher.

trous situations for the purposes of not repeating the same mistakes and learning from these failures, but only when the focus is on enlightenment rather than
on assigning guilt.

This distinction is especially important when you consider that interpersonal conflicts are almost always the consequence of collective efforts. Even if it
were possible to discern who is at fault, what difference would it make? You are
still both stuck with the problem.

WHO IS TO BLAME?

. . . Determining who is at fault is an impossible task. The process described
[here] requires that you identify who and what sets you off, understand the
causes and origins of your entrenched patterns, and work through your discomfort until you are willing to accept greater responsibility for your troubles.
You may not always be able to discover a single person or event that is causing
your difficulties.

Conflicted relationships tend to perpetuate themselves, playing off interactions, carrying forward with a momentum that appears to have a life of its own.
Any intention on the part of one person is predicated on the best prediction of
what another person might do. If you are expecting a person to act deviously,
you will prepare yourself for betrayal by cloaking your own behavior in deception. Conflicts are thus self-sustaining cycles of response and counterresponse,
as illustrated in the following case of a mother- and daughter-in-law.

From the very beginning, Fran and Tina regarded one another with suspicion. Fran believed her son was making a mistake by getting married too young,
and she channeled these feelings into resentment toward Tina (it is often easier
to show disappointment or anger to a stranger than to a loved one). Tina, in turn,
resented her mother-in-law for what she felt was excessive meddling. Each was
convinced the other had ulterior motives for sabotaging her relationship with
Brian, the son/husband. And, naturally, both were acting out a struggle that was
a reenactment of something they had experienced before: Fran did not want her
son to repeat the same mistakes she had made, and Tina had been so dominated
by her own mother throughout much of her life that she was determined not to
let this new mother control her life.

Tina held out an olive branch to her mother-in-law, inviting her to go to
lunch one day. Fran, expecting some hidden agenda, accepted reluctantly and
behaved with a certain amount of antagonism during the meal. Tina, perceiving
her mother-in-law as ungrateful, launched her own defensive campaign, an attack that Fran was expecting and so interpreted as aggression on her part. When
Brian heard the report that night from both combatants, each tried to convince
him that the other was at fault for the conflict.

The central theme of this stage in the process, taking responsibility without
blaming others or yourself, involves understanding the reciprocal nature of interpersonal difficulties. One of the most fascinating aspects of human behavior
is that we do not always obey the laws of the physical world, at least with regard

to what causes us to act. Whereas the laws of physics are based on a model of "linear causality," human behavior is best described as being based on "circular causality." What this means is that unlike the physical world, where it may be determined that one thing *causes* another, which in turn *causes* something else, human interactions are both causes *and* effects of what transpired previously.

This is as true for what is going on in your life now as it was for the circumstances of your past. At one time, I used to blame my mother for neglecting me, for instigating the continual arguments we had throughout my childhood and adolescence until I moved out at age seventeen. After all, she was an alcoholic. She was addicted to prescription tranquilizers, to food, to misery. When she died prematurely of cancer (and probably chronic depression), she provided me with the perfect scapegoat: it was *her* fault that I was continuously in conflict with other women in positions of authority.

Eventually, after studying the matter in depth over years of reflection, family research, journal writing, and therapy, I came to realize that my mother was only reacting to the forces of her own life—the ways she had been treated by her own parents, by my father, and even (it was difficult to admit) by my brothers and me. I realized that it was impossible to figure out who was at fault for the conflicts with my mother in the past, just as it is for those in the present.

It may appear as though a conflict results from a linear progression: I treat you disrespectfully because I am insensitive (or so you believe). Most situations are more complex: I felt slighted by you, even though you are unaware of this offense. I then approach you more tentatively in our next meeting, which you interpret as a lack of interest on my part. You begin to respond curtly, thereby reinforcing my feelings of rejection. I lash out next time, feeling totally justified but thereby appearing to be the one with the problem. You then innocently complain: "What is *his* problem?," never realizing your own role in the conflict. Most situations are even more complex than this since they involve more than two people.

You observe a family in action, for example. Thinking linearly, you see a child misbehaving, note that the parents argue between themselves before they decide what to do, and then, somewhat ineffectively, attempt to intervene to control their child. When you examine the situation in greater depth, you find that assigning blame is not as simple as you first thought. When the child misbehaves, his sister tattles to the mother, who promptly becomes angry. She then complains to the father, who punishes the child. The boy starts to pout and cry, sparking guilt in his sister, who got him in trouble. She then starts to act out herself, whining and complaining. The father and mother start arguing about whose fault this is. The boy then misbehaves again as a distraction, so his parents will stop fighting. The circular pattern continues round and round, each participant reacting to the other family members.

Who is at fault in this conflict? Is it the child who misbehaves? The sibling who manipulates the parents? The mother for being passive? The father for taking over? It is impossible to find the *single* source of this conflict, just as we cannot isolate who is causing whom to do what. All of their actions are interdependent, playing off of and reacting in response to each other's behavior. More often than not, circular causality is the most appropriate model for explaining what takes place during conflict situations.

THE INTROSPECTIVE PROCESS OF
ACCEPTING RESPONSIBILITY

Tanya and Samantha, two sisters who live in the same town, continuously bicker with one another over various imagined slights. Tanya invites their parents over for dinner one night but decides not to include her sister and her family at the gathering. Samantha becomes indignant when she learns of it and vows not to include Tanya and her family the next time there is a holiday get-together.

So who is at fault in this situation: Tanya for not including her sister at the first dinner? Samantha for being so petty that she reciprocated in kind, thereby escalating the conflict? How about their parents for constantly comparing the two sisters? Each time one sister checks in with her parents, she hears an up-to-date summary of all the successes the other sister has enjoyed during the previous week.

Of course, whatever conflict exists between them has its roots in interactions that began long ago, during childhood. The sisters grew up in competition with each other—vying to be the one who could get the best grades, the most popular boyfriend, the most successful husband, the most promising career, the largest home, the fanciest car, the brightest children. Clearly, neither one of them is solely responsible for their long-standing conflicts. Nor is it relevant, at this juncture, to blame their parents for pitting them against one another, or at least failing to neutralize their mutual antagonism.

The conclusion as to who is at fault for any situation is thus predicated on answering these questions: Is anyone responsible for what happened? What is the cause of the conflict? Who is to blame? When a person is held responsible for an event, does that mean that he or she is at fault? What am I doing inside my own head to deny responsibility for what has been happening in an effort to place blame elsewhere?

These are the questions Tanya considered when she came in to see me. She was sick and tired of enduring the constant strain in her relationship with Samantha. Was there anything she could do to stop the squabbles between them?

In order to break the blaming cycle in which each sister took turns finding fault with the other, collecting evidence to prove that the other one was to blame for the situation, it was necessary for Tanya to move away from such obsessive focus on what Samantha was up to and instead concentrate on what she could do to think more constructively about what was going on. This involved figuring out what button Samantha was pushing that elicited such resentment (the implication that she wasn't good enough), discovering where the origins of their struggles lay (a reenactment of their competition for their parents' approval), and harnessing her feelings of rejection and hurt as motivators to look inward rather than outward for the source of the difficulty.

Taking responsibility for the conflict does not mean blaming yourself instead of blaming the other person. Such a strategy can be just as counterproductive, sometimes even more so since it can involve a tendency toward self-pity and helplessness. At least when you are finding fault with others you are feeling feisty in the act of fighting back instead of withdrawing into a shell surrounded by the trophies of your failures.

Taking responsibility for the relationships in your life that are not going well without accepting blame for the troubles involves an internal process wherein you address a series of introspective inquiries. This procedure proved useful for Tanya in her efforts to regain more control over her perceptions of her sister and their relationship, even if she could not change their interactive patterns.

1. How Are You Disowning the Problem?

Notice the tendency to sidestep responsibility for what has happened before and what continues to take place in the conflicted relationship. For Tanya, this task proved to be quite easy with the assistance of her husband, who had listened far too long to her list of complaints.

"My husband pointed out to me how much time I spend thinking about my sister, bitching about what she is doing. He kids me that I may forget to make the kids' lunches, or to pick him up at the car dealership, but I have never forgotten a single episode of any injustice Samantha has inflicted on me. He is right. I do spend an inordinate amount of time denying that the problem between us is in any way my fault. Yet I can provide you with the longest list of reasons as to why I am so sure she is the one who is so unreasonable. I guess that only supports the argument that I am unwilling to take some responsibility for this mess."

2. In What Ways Are You Making Excuses for Yourself?

Part of the strategy for avoiding responsibility for the conflicts in your life is to construct a list of excuses, preferably as long as possible, that get you off the hook. If you are particularly bright, then you probably have developed especially good excuses that may not easily be discounted. Even if you are an amateur at this internal activity, it is likely that you have collected a list of favorites, such as:

I didn't do it.	I couldn't help it.
It was just dumb luck.	I didn't mean it.
I wasn't even there.	Don't look at me—she did it.
She asked for it.	Yes, but . . .
I didn't mean to do it.	Anyone would have done
It wasn't my fault.	the same thing.
I was just following orders.	She was asking for trouble.
I was just kidding.	I wasn't really trying.
It was just meant to be that way.	A bad temper runs in my family.

It wasn't me, it was the . . .   It was just an unfortunate
It wasn't me, and I don't know   situation.
who did it.   I didn't know the rules.
It wasn't a big deal.   Nobody told me.
I had no choice.

Recall a time recently when someone leveled blame at you for something that you did. What was your initial response? Before you had time to even think through your role and responsibility, to reflect on your degree of culpability, the first excuse was already out of your mouth. . . .

Such is the mechanism of excuse making as a self-protection cloak. You remain safe from criticism and keep assaults to a fragile self-image at bay, but in the process you never take the opportunity to identify the triggers that provoked your defensiveness. You are not able to understand what it is within you that feels threatened and vulnerable, nor are you able to talk things through, with yourself and others, to prevent further distortions in the future. . . .

If facing conflict without blame presents such wonderful opportunities for growth, why don't we do this more often? The answer is that it takes a tremendous amount of work. If you can get away with an excuse that deflects blame away from you, initially you keep your image clear. You stave off, at least temporarily, any of the effort associated with having to make changes. . . .

It is clearly a distortion of reality to deny your share of responsibility in *any* conflict. Even if you can convince someone you had no role in the disagreement (and that is doubtful), *you* know deep down inside that you are not totally blameless. Kidding yourself in one set of circumstances only leads to further self-deception in others. After a while, you will find it difficult to separate your fantasies about what is taking place from the actual objective events. In other words, you will believe your own lies and distortions, which further insulates you from receiving accurate information about the world and honest feedback about how you are perceived by others.

3. What Are Your Favorite Scapegoats for Diverting Blame Away from Yourself?

What are your favorite ways to divert attention and responsibility away from you and place it elsewhere? Is it poor genes? Bad luck? No support? A misunderstanding? Perhaps somebody else did it.

As with any self-respecting defense mechanism, blaming others for misdeeds allows you to maintain a positive self-image in light of attacks that are perceived as threatening. It buys you time until you can prepare a better excuse. It spreads around the focus of responsibility so that you do not bear the burden alone. Perhaps more important than rehabilitating your image in other people's eyes, blaming allows you to live with your own imperfections and still feel all right about yourself.

When a person is cornered into admitting that he or she did, in fact, do something, that it was intentional rather than accidental, and that he or she accepts responsibility for his or her actions, there is still a way to avoid blame: simply deny that there was anything wrong with what was done.

"Yes, you did tell me your concerns in confidence and ask me not to say anything to anyone else. Yes, I did promise I would honor your request. However, by keeping your feelings under wraps, by not confronting him with your concerns, by confiding in a few of us privately, you were only creating more divisiveness. I went to him and suggested that he approach you because I wanted the two of you to work things out. I felt an obligation not only to our relationship but also to the way we all get along."

Appealing to some greater good to explain one's actions is not the same as denying one's responsibility for creating a conflict. By offering a seemingly viable explanation, the individual accepts responsibility but denies any wrongdoing. The more comprehensible and rational the reasons, the more likely it is that he or she will not be held accountable.

Another means by which to disown responsibility is to *focus on the issue of intentionality:* you may have done it, but you did not mean to. This avoidance of blame goes something like this:

"There was no way I could have imagined that things would get this far out of control. I should not have been placed in this situation to begin with. I was just trying to be helpful."

A third possible response to an accusation is to imply that *you were coerced into acting this way.* You had no other choice; you were forced to do it.

"Hey, what would *you* have done? I could not risk doing anything else. I was in jeopardy, in such a vulnerable position that I was virtually forced to do it. I wish I could have acted otherwise, but there was just no other alternative."

Each of these denials of blame will only be employed when responsibility can be proven. Always the first choice is to *deny that you had anything to do with the situation in the first place.*

One of the best examples of using this type of excuse as a defense against blame comes from a favorite story of comedian Bill Cosby. It seems that one evening late at night, when Bill and his brother were supposed to be sleeping, they began wrestling around in bed. These tussles led to progressively more vigorous games, eventually culminating in "trampoline," in which they determined who could bounce the highest. When the bed came crashing down, the boys' father rushed into the room, ready to seek some revenge for his sleep being disrupted. "What is going on in here? Who broke this bed?"

Bill and his brother looked at one another. Even then showing signs that he was fast on his feet, Bill confidently proclaimed, "It was a robber! He came in through the window when we were sleeping. He woke us up jumping on the bed. Then he broke it! He escaped before we knew what happened."

"Son," his father calmly pointed out, "You don't have a window in this room. How could a robber come in through the window?"

Desperate to escape blame but never skipping a beat, Bill replied, "Well, Dad, he took it with him."

. . . It is counterproductive to blame others, but it can be just as destructive to blame yourself for unpleasant circumstances. Rather than dwelling on who is at fault, it is far better for you to accept responsibility for overcoming the problem and get on with the business of taking charge of this process and working things through. This effort is easier said than done, for the chief obstacles that get in the way of resolving conflicts are those unresolved issues that you have been ignoring.

4. What Might I Do Internally to Feel More in Control over What Happens Externally?

The consequence of accepting responsibility for a conflict is that you then have to do a tremendous amount of work on yourself in order to rectify matters. This has a lot less to do with things you do on the outside than with internal strategies you can adopt to feel more personal control and take responsibility for your internal feelings.

Attributing blame for conflict to someone or something outside of yourself represents a gross distortion of reality. Cognitive therapists (so called because they emphasize changing internal thinking patterns) have been writing for decades about the irrational beliefs people subscribe to that insist that feelings are reactions *caused* by what other people do:

"You *make* me so angry." (implying that the other person did something that created this feeling)

"You *made* me do it!" (insinuating that what the other person did necessarily caused this person's response)

"Why did you do that *to* me?" (signifying that the other person's actions were deliberately directed toward the speaker)

"If it were not for you . . . " (implying that if the other person did not exist, this person would not have any problems)

Actually, interpersonal struggles involve more than just one's chosen reaction to what has taken place. Certainly cognitive activity—that is, one's interpretation of others' actions—does influence how he or she feels about and responds to them. But in a complicated interaction between two people, individuals often trigger reactions in one another not only through their present behavior but through their unresolved issues as well.

When you attempt to assign blame for a problem, you are likely to follow one of three possible scenarios, none of which is strictly accurate.

1. *External blame:* "It is all your fault. If only you were different, then we would not have this problem between us."
2. *Scapegoat:* "We got manipulated into this conflict. If they had handled things differently, then you and I would not be having this problem."

Both of the above cognitive styles attribute blame to circumstances outside your control. You bear little responsibility for the situation, and so you have little power to change it. In the third case, you take total responsibility for the conflict.

3. *Internal blame:* "It *is* my fault. If I had reacted differently, then we would not be in this mess."

This is also a distortion of reality, since it is highly unlikely that anything is ever entirely one person's fault. Nevertheless, given a choice among the three blaming strategies, even with the remorse and guilt that accompany self-blame, this is still a more empowering way to think about your plight. At the very least, you are implying that you *choose* your reaction to what happened, meaning that you still can choose to think or act in a way that will produce a different reaction. Such personal responsibility is only possible, however, when you avoid the tendency to make excuses.

REVIEW QUESTIONS

1. What is the main practical problem with blaming that Kottler identifies?
2. Explain the difference between linear and circular causality. Give a concrete example of each.
3. What is a scapegoat, and how does scapegoating function in the process Kottler describes?
4. Blaming is important, some people say, because you have to know who was at fault to keep a bad thing from happening again. How does Kottler respond to this point?
5. "If facing conflict without blame presents such wonderful opportunities for growth," Kottler asks, "why don't we do this more often?" How does he respond to this question?
6. What is a defense mechanism?
7. What does Kottler suggest we substitute for "You make me so angry!" and "You made me do it!"

PROBES

1. Kottler emphasizes that taking responsibility for your part in a conflict does *not* mean placing blame on yourself. What's the difference? How can you take responsibility without blaming yourself?
2. Some people make Kottler's point by encouraging conflict participants to replace the understanding of "responsibility" that leads to blaming with an understanding of responsibility as "response-ability," the ability to respond. This is one rationale for the communication skill of "nexting" that I discuss in Chapter 2. Paraphrase Kottler's advice in this chapter by using the two constructs "response-ability" and "nexting."
3. When you read about Tanya, Samantha, and their parents, who did you believe was "at fault" in this situation?
4. What relationships do you notice between what Kottler calls "the blaming cycle" and the "communication spirals" that Bill Wilmot discusses in Chapter 9?

5. Which of Kottler's four questions most helps you move away from blaming?
6. Four ways to deny blame are to appeal to a greater good, claim you didn't mean to, say you were forced to, or deny any involvement. Which do you hear others using most in their conflicts with you? Which do you use most?

*I*nterpersonal conflicts over money, time, sex, and parenting issues are difficult enough to manage effectively. But often conflicts over abortion, religion in politics and education, legal rights for homosexuals, and environmental politics create even more intense and widespread polarization and division. These are examples of "moral conflicts," and the next reading is from a recent book by two communication researchers and teachers who have dedicated a large part of their lives to helping manage these kinds of disputes. Both Barnett Pearce and Stephen Littlejohn have taught and written about communication for several decades, and they have also worked as dialogue facilitators, mediators, and communication consultants for many different groups of people in "the real world." The following pages are taken from their book, *Moral Conflict: When Social Worlds Collide.*

The reading begins with a short report by Sally Miller Gearhart of a transformation she has undergone in her attitude toward conflict. This report is especially impressive to those of us who have been in Gearhart's classes or heard her speak. I can tell you from personal experience that she is a committed feminist social activist and educator who doesn't mince her words. If she can move from "normal" to what this reading calls "transcendent" discourse, just about anybody can.

After Gearhart's story, Pearce and Littlejohn describe normal discourse as the common kinds of communication that people experience in most conflicts—"attempts to persuade, frustrated diatribe, threats, and sometimes even violence." Transcendent discourse, on the other hand, suspends condemnations or blaming, aims to probe rather than persuade, and is designed to compare and critique rather than to win. Transcendent discourse can be used by a mediator, a judge, a critic, an audience, or the disputants themselves.

One important feature of transcendent discourse is that, when applied to intractable moral conflicts, it is not designed to resolve the issues but to humanize the ways in which they are engaged. Impatient people, activists, and some politicians may see this as impractical, because they believe it's necessary to reach a resolution so they can get on with business—determine a policy, draft a law, or define an agreement. But in the case of moral conflicts, it is actually those very expectations that are impractical and unrealistic. In moral conflicts people simply will not reach consensus, and "next-actions" still must be taken. This is where transcendent discourse is needed most.

Pearce and Littlejohn briefly review four specific, concrete, real-world examples where principles of transcendent discourse have been applied. One focused on the Greek-Turkish conflict in Cyprus in the 1960s; a second dealt with the border dispute between Somalia, Ethiopia and Kenya in the 1970s; a third grappled with the National Coal Policy in the United States in the late 1970s; and the fourth was the Syracuse Area Middle East Dialogue. Not all these projects has succeeded completely, but each has demonstrated the potential for transcendent discourse in the management of intractable social conflict.

Then Pearce and Littlejohn move to a discussion of the five general characteristics of transcendent discourse, or eloquence: It is (1) philosophical, (2) comparative, (3) dialogic, (4) critical, and (5) transformative. This way of communicating is philosophical in that it surfaces and deals with basic assumptions. It is comparative in that it tries to find ways to compare what look like mutually exclusive systems or options. This feature requires each person engaged in moral conflict to shift from experiencing the conflict from within his or her own moral order to viewing it more as an outsider.

Transcendent discourse is dialogic in that its purpose is to explore rather than convince or persuade. You might want to compare what Pearce and Littlejohn say in this section with William Isaacs's discussion of dialogue and David Bohm's treatment of communication in Chapter 2.

The fourth characteristic of transcendent eloquence, or discourse, is that it is critical, which means that it exposes the powers and limits of each side in the controversy. And the final feature is that it is transformative, which is to say that transcendent eloquence "reconstructs the context in which the conflict is to be understood." This way of communicating changes the frame that people are using to interpret what they hear. It alters the container in which the communicating is happening. This may be the most difficult of several difficult features of this way of communicating. When one side frames the dispute as "good versus evil" and the other side frames it as "freedom versus repression," what new frame can be created?

Pearce and Littlejohn offer some suggestions about this challenge and then conclude this reading with a sketch of some of the values and limits of transcendent discourse. They acknowledge that giving up "resolution" as a goal can be a significant limitation. But they also point out that humanizing the dispute can be profoundly important, and that there are at least three other important strengths of this form of communicating. They conclude with the admission that transcendent discourse is still uncommon in contemporary culture. But, they assert, "it does have value and needs to be nourished," especially because it is "the basis—perhaps the only honest basis—for hope."

NEW FORMS OF ELOQUENCE

W. Barnett Pearce and Stephen W. Littlejohn

Sally Miller Gearhart (1995), by her own description, is a retired activist. As she describes herself, "I've marched and rallied and picketed, raged and wept and threatened, crusaded and persuaded and brigaded" (p. 8). But something has changed in Gearhart's life. She now lives by a credo that she would have scorned in previous years. Instead of confronting, she is joining. We can think of no better way to introduce the subject of transcendent discourse than with her story.

> Five years ago when I'd see a logging truck loaded with redwoods or old oak, I'd shoot the driver a finger. He'd (could it ever be a she?) shoot one right back at me and then go home and put a bumper sticker on his truck that would read, "Hey, Environmentalist, try wiping your ass with a spotted owl!" Three years ago, I was a shade more gentle. I would stop dead in my tracks, glare at the driver of a logging truck and make sure he read my lips: "Fuck you, mister." Then he'd go home and add another bumper sticker to his truck: "Earth First! We'll log the other planets later."
>
> These days . . . I'm practicing acknowledging loggers as "fellow travellers on Planet Earth," as Trudy the bag lady would say, doing what they do just as I do what I do; I'm laying off any attempt to change or even judge them, and I'm trusting that acknowledgment of our kinship can make a positive difference in the texture of all our lives.
>
> When I meet an erstwhile "enemy," instead of moving immediately into horse posture or splitting the scene entirely (fight or flight), . . . I look for the joining point, the place where we are the same, where we can meet each other as beings who share the experience of living together on this planet. I introduce that into the conversation, and we talk about the thing that belongs to both of us. . . . When I can't find any common ground upon which to stand with some "enemy," like a logger, then I ask him to take me into his world for a day or two so I can hear him and his buddies talk about what it means to be out of work in a poor country with a family to feed.
>
> When all's said and done, I measure these encounters by my feelings. I like "joining" better than fighting or running away, better even than marching for or rallying to a cause. . . . I've learned a lot. I've learned that it is never individual men/people who are my "enemy" but complex systems of exploitation that have emerged from centuries of alienation and perpetuation of violence; it is these systems and that consciousness—not the people—that I can, with integrity, hope to change. I've learned that my pain, anger, and/or hatred accomplish nothing except to render me ineffectual and to increase the problem by adding to the pain, anger, and hatred that already burden the world. I've learned that whole

Excerpt from *Moral Conflict*, by W. Barnett Pearce and Stephen W. Littlejohn, 1997, pp. 151–167. Reprinted by permission of Sage Publications, Inc.

parts of my identified "enemy" are really my own self, walking around in different costume. And in the moments where we've found some joining space, I've learned that, though I still may not choose to spend time with him, I do feel kinship or love for that killer, that exploiter.

To tell the truth, I don't regret a single day of my past as an activist. I figure that the desire to stop injustices and heal the earth is an honest and an honorable one. It's a big part of who I have been as a being incarnated on this planet. That's why I've been here: to speak out and confront, to crusade and fight, to be involved in those struggles up to my eyeballs. I wouldn't know what I know, and probably wouldn't be making the changes I'm making, without those experiences of activism. But right now, I'm getting clear and unmistakable signals that it's time for another approach. If I can still hold strong to my standard of what is just and decent and appropriate behavior for human beings and yet to go about my life with a new awareness, with joy in the process instead of my former debilitating pain, and if I can do all this without creating and maintaining "enemies," then I have to try it. (pp. 8–11)

BEYOND NORMAL DISCOURSE

Normal discourse consists of attempts to persuade, frustrated diatribe, threats, and sometimes even violence. Is it possible to transcend these customary responses, to break the pattern, to engage those with whom we disagree on a new level, and to avoid the seemingly unavoidable spiral toward schism, degradation, and violence? We believe that these achievements may be possible if certain forms of transcendent discourse are employed.

Transcendent discourse goes beyond the normal communication of moral conflict. It can lead to the possibility of constructive dialogue, new contexts in which to understand differences, and new ways to compare and weigh alternative choices. Where normal discourse in moral conflict is condemnatory, transcendent discourse suspends execration. Where normal discourse tries to persuade, transcendent discourse aims to probe. Where normal discourse is designed to prevail, transcendent discourse seeks to compare and critique. Transcendent discourse can be employed by a mediator as a means of intervention, by a judge as a means of comparison, by a critic as a means of commentary, by an audience as a means of analysis, or by the disputants themselves as a means of transforming the conflict.

Intractable moral conflicts are not easily resolved and, in many cases, may not be resolvable. Indeed, many such conflicts should not be resolved, but they can be argued in more humane, enlightening, and respectful ways, at least "continuing the conversation" (Rorty, 1979, p. 394). Needed is a format or setting in which trust can be built between conflicting parties, a forum in which issues and options can be explored without attempts by one party to influence the other, and an atmosphere in which beliefs are put at risk of change, not by influence from the other party but by self-reflection.

Psychologist Herbert Kelman (1972) isolates three aspects of communication in conflict-transcending events that may change the dynamic of interaction:

The participants can learn new information about how the other side thinks; new ways of thinking about the issues and the conflict itself can be introduced; and participants can come to see their own communication patterns up close and to understand some of its problems. (pp. 192–194)

International relations scholar Terrell Northrup's (1989) analysis of intractable conflicts suggests that frozen conflicts can begin to thaw when two types of change come about. The first of these is a change in the dynamics of the relationship between the parties; the second, and most profound, is a change in the sense of identity by one or both sides in the conflict. Transcendent discourse is a form of communication that has the potential to accomplish either or both of these. In recent times, several attempts to achieve this level of communication have been made.

The Burton Experiment

As part of a program of studies on innovations in conflict resolution, Burton (1969) and his colleagues at the Centre for the Analysis of Conflict at University College, London, conducted a workshop in 1966 on the Greek-Turkish conflict in Cyprus. The weeklong session brought together two representatives from the Greek community, two from the Turkish community, and six social scientists.

The sessions were informal and relatively unstructured. The participants first presented their own views of the conflict, and the social scientists asked questions designed to clarify these positions. Next, the social scientists presented a number of models of conflict and asked the participants to discuss these and to apply them to their own dispute. Finally, toward the end of the week, the participants discussed possible ways to overcome the conflict. The social scientists provided insights into why a solution favored by one side was objectionable to the other. Throughout the workshop, the facilitator attempted to move the discussion away from accusation and blame toward analysis, self-reflection, and mutual understanding.

The session itself was at least partially successful in that the participants were able to talk to one another respectfully, make use of newly shared frames of reference, and gain information about one another's perspectives. At the least, certain citizens representing groups that had not been able to communicate with one another spent a week together exploring mutual concerns.

The Fermeda Workshop

The Fermeda Workshop was the brainchild of psychologist Leonard Doob (1970) and his colleagues at Yale University. It dealt with an intractable border dispute between Somalia, Ethiopia, and Kenya. After much difficulty securing government approval, Doob and his associates organized a workshop at the Hotel Fermeda in Switzerland. Participants included six Somalis, six Ethiopians, and six Kenyans, along with a small group of social scientists.

The workshop was two weeks in length and included sessions in which various theories of leadership and conflict were presented by the leaders. Unlike the Burton experiment, the Doob workshop did not begin with a discussion of the dispute itself. During the first few days, every attempt was made to avoid the topic. Instead, the leaders worked on creating an atmosphere in which the participants could get to know one another as individuals and to talk freely among themselves.

Then, in a second stage, the topic turned to the dispute. During this period, a role reversal exercise was used to help each participant develop empathy for the others. Finally, attention was directed at creating specific proposals for resolution of the conflict itself.

The workshop was successful in helping the participants to see the humanity of each of the parties in the dispute. Especially in the first phase, the participants did communicate freely. The experiment was less successful, however, in dealing with the conflict itself. Several of the participants refused to participate in the role reversal exercise, and, in the end, no consensus was reached on solutions.

The Doob experiment illustrates how difficult intractable conflict can be. Dealing on a higher level with the real issues that divide us and that involve us emotionally is hard to do, and many people simply refuse to cooperate in this type of exercise.

National Coal Policy Project

The National Coal Policy Project was an ambitious attempt at environmental conciliation, negotiation, and policy making in 1977 (Alexander, 1978). It followed a model known as policy dialogue, in which interested and conflicting parties attempt to resolve their differences on matters of general policy (Amy, 1987). The idea is that if a group can discuss ideas in the abstract out of the heat of a particular dispute, group members may be able to gain insights and generate acceptable ideas not possible in more immediately threatening circumstances.

The coal project was the brainchild of Gerald Decker, an industry executive with considerable credibility among both environmentalist and industrialist camps. He was interested in experimenting with policy dialogue and making use of a number of conflict resolution techniques. Decker met with leading environmentalists early in 1976 and, after considerable difficulty, persuaded most of them to participate in the talks. A number of industrial representatives were also induced to participate.

The talks were sponsored by Georgetown University's Center for Strategic and International Studies, which raised more than half a million dollars to support the project (Alexander, 1978). The participants were divided into five task groups. They went on a number of field trips to see the potential sites and impacts firsthand and respond to these as a group. In their talks, they were required to use "the rule of reason," which consists primarily of avoiding the deceptive tricks so commonly found in litigation: "Opponents should not . . . withhold data from each other or employ misleading tricks. They should not impugn motives or characters. They should avoid dogmatism, acknowledge uncertainties, and disclose personal interests and biases" (p. 101).

Although the bargaining was hard and the project certainly had its critics, the results seem to have exceeded all the participants' expectations. The two sides came to have a good deal of mutual respect, and a number of difficult issues were resolved. This project shows that deep conflicts can be transcended, at least on occasion, and such discourse can have a practical impact on the way things are done in the future.

Syracuse Area Middle East Dialogue

The Syracuse Area Middle East Dialogue (SAMED) has been a highly successful program bridging the Arab and Jewish communities in the greater Syracuse area on the Israeli-Palestinian problem (Schwartz, 1989). In fact, SAMED began something of a movement, which includes a variety of programs, including the American Coalition for Middle East Dialogue and the Seminar on Palestinian-Israel Reconciliation Efforts.

SAMED was a grassroots experiment in "Track II diplomacy," the involvement [of] ordinary citizens in informal and unofficial negotiations. The idea is that officials engaged in primary, or Track I, negotiations are unable to explore a full range of options because of political constraints. Citizens, who are somewhat removed from the immediate setting in which the dispute is occurring, however, do not have such constraints and may be somewhat freer to pursue a variety of alternatives (Davidson & Montville, 1982).

SAMED made use of the dialogue-group model, in which citizens sat together to discuss on a deep level the issues that separate them. The SAMED groups met regularly during an extended time, explored the issues, and attempted to reach consensus on certain ideas or courses of action.

SAMED began with only six persons in a pilot group—two Palestinians, two Jews, and two others—and they met frequently to plan the program and solicit members. An expanded dialogue group then met for more than a decade from once a month to once per quarter. The convener alternated between representatives from the two sides.

The group attempted to sort issues and tackle them systematically. Certain issues proved unmanageable at certain times, some were difficult but possible, and others fairly easy. Some issues had to be dropped and revisited later, and some remained intractable through a long period.

This project was highly successful. SAMED continued for a number of years, made contact and shared ideas with other dialogue groups, and even developed a consensus statement. Because of the duration of the project and the frequency of meetings, the members came to know one another well and appreciate the unique backgrounds and insights of each person. The members of the group did not always agree, but they continued to respect and talk to one another.

SAMED shows us that transcendent dialogue can be continual and long-term. People do not necessarily run away from it, and it can actually attract people and bring them back again and again. Once people see a new way of handling conflict, they may easily give up old patterns that seemed for so long to lead nowhere.

The projects discussed here represent ambitious and brave attempts to transcend difficult conflicts. They demonstrate that this is not an easy job but that with creativity and tenacity, it can be accomplished.

A DIFFERENT FORM OF ELOQUENCE

. . . *Eloquence* is the exemplary use of discourse within a rhetorical tradition. To be eloquent is to represent the highest form of expression within the frame of rules adopted by a moral community. Within a moral community, eloquent speech elicits attention, respect, and compliance. Between moral communities, however, it can create frustration, hatred, anger, and even violence.

Transcendent eloquence is an answer for people who are frustrated by the interminable character of moral disputes and long for something other than more of the same. As a form of speech that bridges or encompasses various moral communities, transcendent eloquence has five general characteristics; it is (1) philosophical, (2) comparative, (3) dialogic, (4) critical, and (5) transformative.

First, *transcendent eloquence is philosophical.* By this, we mean that it attempts to uncover the assumptions about knowledge, being, and values that lie behind the positions in conflict. As a philosophical discourse, transcendent eloquence is educational, aiming to help those involved to understand the basis of the conflicting belief systems on a deep level. It has the potential to create constructive reflection because it attempts to move the discussion from intractable struggle over issues to a more fundamental level at which the parties must pause and reflect.

The philosophical nature of transcendent discourse contrasts sharply with many traditional methods of dispute management, which are oriented toward interests, issues, and power and require disputants to itemize their objectives, make arguments for their interests, and use power. These methods are appropriate and effective in cases of conflict in which the disputants agree on the standards and means by which the conflict is to be conducted and settled, but they do not work well in cases in which the disputants' realities are incommensurate.

Many common methods of dispute resolution, including direct and representative democracy, litigation, and bargaining, fail to recognize just how deep many conflicts are. These methods certainly recognize the passion and commitment in moral disputes, but they often neglect the assumptive differences that lie behind this entrenchment. Political scientist Mona Harrington (1986) states that the failure to look at deep divisions "precludes real bargaining" and produces only superficial and temporary benefits. She concludes that "in the long run, by denying the seriousness of differences in society, the myth solidifies those differences and polarizes the groups bearing them" (p. 26). Ironically, then, if we ignore our axiomatic differences, we may end up more divided in our clash than might otherwise be the case.

The second characteristic is that *transcendent eloquence is comparative.* It attempts to create categories that can be used to compare otherwise incommensurate systems. It conceives a language with which people can talk with one another about their assumptions and see the relative powers and limits of each side. Stout (1988) refers to this type of language as a *creole*, a vocabulary in which two divergent groups can communicate and reason together.

We have already noted the inherent difficulty of comparing incommensurate systems. According to philosopher Richard Bernstein (1985), incommensurate and incompatible ways of thinking are not normally comparable because *from within either system,* there is no conceptual or logical frame sufficient to account for their differences. Therefore, such frames must be *created outside the conflicting positions.* This does not mean that the disputants themselves cannot do this, only that they have to get out of their own frame of reference to do so. Transcendence, thus, is a wholly creative act. It is a movement of the mind that enables one to surpass customary limits (Zwiebach, 1988.)

Comparability is an interpretive process of coming to understand each reality separately. It is a creative process of inventing a set of dimensions along which the two systems might be compared. As Bernstein (1985) expresses the process,

> The task of understanding an alien culture may require the imaginative elaboration of new genres, or the stretching of familiar genres, in order to compare what may be incommensurable. The art here is one of knowing what are the right questions to ask in approaching the strange practices of an alien culture. (p. 65)

Such comparison is always local and specific to the dispute in question because there can be no single, universal scheme that compares all systems.

Stout (1988) refers to this process of creating new categories as *bricolage,* which involves putting elements of a new moral language together. Like laying brickwork, it is the building of a new structure:

> My claim is simply that how the various fragments of moral language are related to each other and to the whole can be every bit as important as which parts are selected for retention or available for use in the first place. (p. 75)

Stout shows us that differences are created in discourse and that new discourse based on fragments of the old can and should be created to search for common ground.

Comparative ethnography is a discipline that creates models to compare cultures (Hymes, 1974; Philipsen, 1989). In comparative ethnography, incommensurate cultural systems are analyzed by creating a comparative model. In a sense, the parties in a moral conflict are different cultures, making the procedures of comparative ethnography apropos.

Transcendent eloquence, like comparative ethnography, aims to find or create a context within which the two sides can be compared on some dimension. Disputants themselves may then confront their differences on this new level. The aim is to transform the pattern of interaction between the conflicting parties so that it becomes more productive. The process involves a reconceptualization of the nature of the conflict and makes rational discourse between the parties possible. The transformed conflict forces spokespersons to deal directly with their own assumptions, which may give pause to see the rationality of the other side and even to open disputants to change.

In essence, this type of move is a shift from experiencing the conflict from within one's own moral order to viewing it from an outside, more objective position. Cooper (1981) refers to it as taking an "antidote" to one's own morality to understand how it compares with other, diverse forms (p. 31).

Spokespersons in the abortion debate normally speak different languages. The pro-choice advocates speak a language of individual rights and social welfare, whereas the pro-life advocates speak a language of scriptural authority and sanctity of biological life. This debate could be transformed into a dialogue about ethics and moral decision making, apart from the limited issue of abortion. Here a common language of moral decision making would need to be created. In this type of discussion, the parties would have the opportunity to understand the moral assumptions on which the claims of each side are based. Such an analysis would not center on whether a woman has the right to have an abortion; instead, it would focus on the criteria one uses to make a moral decision, any moral decision.

Another transcendent category that might be employed in the abortion debate is the definition of personhood apart from the specific question of whether a fetus is a person under the Constitution. As each side struggles to define personhood and to hear the definitions of the other side, both sides would be able to compare the conflicting positions on this issue (Gert, 1988; Goodman, 1988). The aim would be not to reach agreement but to understand better the basis for disagreement.

In sum, then, productive comparisons cannot be made in intractable conflicts until higher-level categories are created for this purpose, and when that is done, true dialogue on radical issues may occur. This experience can provide concepts that the participants never considered before, ideas that might be used as a common reference point in analyzing the statements and actions of each side.

The third characteristic is that *transcendent eloquence is dialogic.* It attempts to move the debate from statements designed to convince to statements designed to explore. It transforms a debate in which attributions are hurled back and forth into an interaction in which the relationship itself can be discussed. This approach changes from accusing and belittling and an attitude of exclusiveness to realizing that both sides are limited by the axioms of their respective realities and an attitude of inclusiveness.

The distinctive features of dialogue have been summarized by comparing it with monologue:

> In monologue, questions are asked to gain a speaking turn or to make a point; in dialogue, questions are asked to invite an answer. In monologue, one speaks in order to impress or impact on others; in dialogue, one speaks in order to take a turn to an interpersonal process that affects all participants. (Pearce, 1993, p. 61)

Thus, when we enter dialogue, we risk being changed.

Bernstein (1992) says this type of discourse "presupposes moral virtues—a certain 'good will'—at least in the willingness to really listen, to seek to understand what is genuinely other, different, alien, and the courage to risk one's more cherished prejudgments" (p. 51). . . .

In its ideal state, this type of dialogue creates the understanding that although we have deep moral differences, we are intelligent, well-meaning, and moral people. Showing that other people do not meet our criteria for intelligent moral probity and trustworthiness serves no good purpose. As such, transcendent eloquence should make participants aware and respectful of the moral tradition of opponents, even though they may continue to disagree.

We do not mean to suggest naively here that all participants in conflicts are well-meaning and moral people. Some are out to subvert others deliberately for personal gain, and such people can probably be found on both sides of most issues. If we start with the assumption that the other is mad, bad, or sick, however, we block ourselves from transcendent ways of dealing with the conflict and risk initiating a self-fulfilling prophecy in which the other becomes as despicable as we treat them. Starting assumptions are always risky; sometimes it is worth taking different risks for peace, as the Arab-Jewish dialogue well illustrates.

The dialogue-group model can be a practical means of transcending moral conflict. Legal scholar Richard Schwartz (1989) suggests that in dialogue groups, people with diametrically opposed views really can learn from one another, that such dialogue and intergroup learning can be expanded by creating a network of groups, and that official policy can even be affected by communicating ideas generated in such groups to policy makers. . . .

The fourth characteristic is that *transcendent eloquence is critical.* It exposes the powers and limits of each side in a controversy, and, more important, it exposes them to the advocates on both sides. It enables participants and viewers to weigh alternatives on the basis of these strengths and weaknesses. It deconstructs the assumed truth value of conflicting claims so that choices must be made, not on the basis of which side is correct according to some set of criteria or whose interests will be promoted or how decision makers happen to "feel" about the issue but on the basis of the powers and limits of the various positions when they are held up side by side. Transcendent eloquence, then, does not seek adjudication based on any foundational truth, nor does it employ the emotive method of choice deplored by MacIntyre (1981), in which one simply does what feels right.

Transcendent eloquence is critical, then, in a way that most traditional forms of discourse are not. Customary methods of managing disputes in our society are designed to clarify goals, articulate reasons, make choices, and compromise. They rarely compare the powers and limits of conflicting views directly, and they almost never allay assumed truths. . . .

The final characteristic of transcendent eloquence is that it is *transformative.* It reconstructs the context in which the conflict is to be understood. Any action or object—a wave of the hand, a facial expression, a manuscript, a piece of graffiti, a videotape—is always understood in relation to some context. Actions and contexts are closely related to one another. What we do and how we understand what is done depend on context, but the action in turn also serves to define the context in which it occurs. Each influences the other.

Within a moral conflict, then, what spokespersons say is interpreted within some context, which is in turn affected reflexively by their talk, gestures, writings, and actions. The Religious Right, for example, understands its dispute within a context of good against evil. In turn, statements made by advocates of the Religious Right, as well as those of their opponents, further bolster the context—a struggle of morality versus immorality. The other side, however, understands the struggle differently. For the liberals, the conflict is one between freedom of speech and religion and narrow-minded forces of repression. Their statements and actions and those of their conservative opponents are understood in this light and in turn reinforce their understanding of what is going on.

Most moral conflicts are stable. The patterns of understanding and acting are repeated over and over, and the participants rarely change their understandings of what is going on. Indeed, the context constitutes the accepted social worlds of each side. It is the moral imperative that galvanizes their actions. It is what they are. They become what they do. Their identities as warriors are determined by how they respond to the struggle. If people act toward others in hateful ways, they become filled with hate. Hate becomes the context.

It sometimes happens that people will speak and act in ways that transform the context so that their acts can be understood differently. To change the context means to change the identity of the community in which one acts.

For example, mediators can create new contexts within which the disputants can understand what is going on in new and more productive ways. In child custody disputes, for example, the mother and father may have different ways of understanding the situation, each in its own context. The wife may suggest that she should receive custody because of the sanctity of the mother-child relationship. The husband, on the other hand, may suggest that his wife has shown herself to be unfit and that he must therefore take custody. In this type of conflict, a mediator may attempt to create a new context that will change the issues, such as "the best interests of the child." This context does not focus exclusively on the mother-child relationship or the fitness of this particular mother but does focus on what is best for the child in these particular circumstances, which may be a more complex issue than the earlier framings would admit (Wynn, 1989). The notion of joint custody, now the option of choice in most states, grew from this type of contextual reconstruction. . . .

Transcendent discourse reconstructs contexts in large measure by changing the meaning of winning. In contemporary American life, winning as a cultural prescription has become a central virtue in the national culture. The self-help section of any bookstore contains shelf after shelf of books offering advice on how to win. We are deeply troubled if we do not have the most powerful military, the highest standard of living, the largest market share in computers and automobiles, and the most gold medals at the Olympic Games.

Many areas of life are expressed in the metaphor of winning. We do not simply want to reduce the use of drugs; we have a war on drugs. Political campaigns are not straightforward ways of presenting alternative candidates and platforms; they are contests in which the participants have game plans and that result in the declaration of a winner. The infatuation with winning causes us to focus on the "thrill of victory" and the "agony of defeat." In other words, winning is a pervasive context that defines our identities and drives our actions.

There are at least three positions we can take on winning. The first is to win at any price, the second is to count the costs and win if we can afford it, and the third is to rethink what winning means. The third option is contextual reconstruction.

The moral algebra of winning changes when we shift from being a partisan to looking at the conflict from outside. Whether Bill has more marbles than Betty does not really matter if the competition to take marbles is either irrelevant or itself the problem to be examined. In a transcendent mode, winning in the sense of prevailing over those who do not share our moral position may really equate to losing because in the process, we lose something more important. Winning in such situations can come to mean refusing to play the game of fight to the death.

Transcendent eloquence holds out the hope of transforming the context so that parties to the dispute can understand themselves, the opponent, the issues, and the relational patterns in different terms. This is what we mean by contextual reconstruction (Branham & Pearce, 1985). . . .

VALUES AND LIMITS OF
TRANSCENDENT DISCOURSE

Another way to understand the nature of transcendent eloquence is to consider what it is not. First, transcendent eloquence is not a method for resolving moral disputes, although, as the cases presented earlier in this chapter show, a number of resolution techniques may employ it in an attempt to deal more humanely, respectfully, and intelligently with moral conflict than is often the case. Transcendent discourse extends the hope of managing and coordinating moral conflicts without degradation, repression, or violence. When choices must be made between two morally incompatible positions—a frequent occurrence in contemporary society—transcendent discourse can provide a more rational basis for such decisions. Transcendent eloquence is also a way to promote constructive dialogue. It is a way to reduce harmful or destructive patterns of interaction. It can sometimes even lead to local, temporary solutions, where none have been found before.

Second, transcendent eloquence is not a neutral ground without values and commitments. It can create a new ground so that conflicts can be viewed in fresh ways, but that ground is never value-free. Transcendent eloquence is committed to reflection, to tempered judgment, and to humane talk.

Third, transcendent eloquence is not blindly relativistic. It lies somewhere between MacIntyre's (1981) *wistful alienation* and *utopian criticism* and Rorty's (1979) *smug approval* and *liberal apologetics*. It attempts to understand each position on an assumptive level before evaluating the powers and limits of the position. It makes judgments about positions by appropriateness in historical situations, and it promotes deep reflection by all participants so that they can make their own judgments.

Fourth, transcendent eloquence is not a panacea. It is a form that is appropriate in some situations and not in others. We are not suggesting that transcendent eloquence is the only appropriate response to moral conflict. Sometimes civility, tolerance, and rhetorical eloquence are appropriate. In the face of extreme oppression or violation of human rights, resistance, and revolution will sometimes be judged the only alternative. Moral conflicts do not usually necessitate such an extreme form, however, and transcendent eloquence becomes an appropriate and fruitful option on these many occasions.

We believe that when the salutary powers of transcendent eloquence are known and when it is made an option, this avenue often will be taken. We also suspect that those whose commitments lie with conflict management—people such as mediators, judges, counselors, and managers—will find this type of response inviting. It is especially appealing in situations in which the disputants are stuck in a rigid and harmful pattern of interaction or a pattern that prevents decisions from being made.

We believe transcendent eloquence is the best option in situations in which both conflicting parties subscribe to the Kantian ideal that human welfare must be an end in itself and never merely a means toward some other end. Most of the well-known moral conflicts in our own society fit these criteria.

Transcendent eloquence, then, is worthy of our consideration as a response to moral conflict. It can transform contempt into respect. It can minimize unreflective condemnation, and it can reduce violence. If we can see the rationality behind our opponent's position, we will no longer be able to characterize the opponent as insane, stupid, or misguided. When we realize the limits of our own philosophical assumptions, we will have more respect for the powers of our opponents' views. And, in the end, we will find the ability to disagree without silencing the other side through repression, injury and pain, or death.

This type of discourse is uncommon in our society. It is what Rorty (1979) calls "abnormal." But it does have value and needs to be nourished. It is, as Bernstein (1992) asserts, "the basis—perhaps the only honest basis—for hope" (p. 53).

REVIEW QUESTIONS

1. What is normal discourse? What are the main features of transcendent discourse?
2. Pearce and Littlejohn note that frozen conflicts can begin to thaw when there is a change in "the dynamics of the relationship between the parties" and "a change in the sense of identity by one or both sides." Explain what each of these means.
3. What is *Track II diplomacy?* Explain the significance of this term—and this phenomenon—in this context.
4. Explain how the jargon terms *creole* and *bricolage* clarify the comparative quality of transcendent discourse.
5. What point do Pearce and Littlejohn make about the win/lose perspective that pervades many moral conflicts?
6. What keeps transcendent eloquence from being "blindly relativistic"?

7. Explain the "Kantian ideal that human welfare must be an end in itself and never merely a means toward some other end."

PROBES

1. Paraphrase what you understand to be Sally Miller Gearhart's basic rationale (set of reasons) for making the change she reports she's made. How do you respond to her?
2. Why do you suppose several of the participants in the Fermeda workshop refused to participate in the role reversal exercise? What impact do you suppose this had on the outcome of this project?
3. Give an example of how the philosophical feature of transcendent discourse might be applied to a conflict between you and a member of your family.
4. Pearce and Littlejohn's discussion of the dialogic quality of transcendent discourse emphasizes a shift from resolution as a goal to exploration as a goal. In many situations, this would appear to be very unrealistic. But they argue that it is not unrealistic. How so? How do you respond to them on this point?
5. Test your understanding of what Pearce and Littlejohn call the "transformative" feature of transcendent discourse by identifying a general frame or basic perspective that could be substituted for both the "good versus evil" and "freedom versus restraint" frames held by many in the abortion controversy.

REFERENCES

Alexander, T. (1978, February 13). A promising try at environmental détente for coal. *Fortune, 97,* 94–102.

Amy, D. J. (1987). *The politics of environmental mediation.* New York: Columbia University Press.

Bernstein, R. J. (1985). *Beyond objectivism and relativism.* Philadelphia: University of Pennsylvania Press.

Bernstein, R. J. (1992). *The new constellation: The ethical-political horizon of modernity/postmodernity.* Cambridge, MA: MIT Press.

Branham, R. J., & Pearce, W. B. (1985). Between text and context: Toward a rhetoric of contextual reconstruction. *Quarterly Journal of Speech, 71,* 19–36.

Burton, J. W. (1969). *Conflict and communication: The use of controlled communication in international relations.* London: Macmillan.

Cooper, N. (1981). *The diversity of moral thinking.* Oxford: Clarendon.

Davidson, W. D., & Montville, J. V. (1982). Foreign policy according to Freud. *Foreign Policy, 45,* 145–157.

Doob, L. W. (Ed.). (1970). *Resolving conflict in Africa: The Fermeda workshop.* New Haven, CT: Yale University Press.

Gearhart, S. M. (1995, September). Notes from a recovering activist. *Sojurner: The Women's Forum, 21*(1) 8–11.

Gert, B. (1988). *Morality: A new justification of the moral rules.* New York: Oxford University Press.

Goodman, M. (1988). *What is a person?* Clifton, NJ: Humana.

Harrington, M. (1986). *The dream of deliverance in American politics.* New York: Knopf.

Hymes, D. (1974). *Foundations in sociolinguistics: An ethnographic approach.* Philadelphia: University of Pennsylvania Press.

Kelman, H. C. (1972). The problem-solving workshop in conflict resolution. In R. L. Merritt (Ed.), *Communication in international politics* (pp. 168–204). Urbana: University of Illinois Press.

MacIntyre, A. (1981). *After virtue: A study in moral theory.* Notre Dame, IN: University of Notre Dame Press.

Northrup, T. A. (1989). The dynamic of identity in personal and social conflict. In L. Kriesberg, T. A. Northrup, & S. J. Thorson (Eds.), *Intractable conflicts and their transformation* (pp. 55–82). Syracuse, NY: Syracuse University Press.

Pearce, W. B. (1993). Achieving dialogue with "the other" in the postmodern world. In P. Gaunt (Ed.), *Beyond agendas: New directions in communication research* (pp. 59–74). Westport, CT: Greenwood.

Philipsen, G. (1989). An ethnographic approach to communication studies. In B. Dervin, L. Grossberg, B. J. O'Keefe, & E. Wartella (Eds.), *Rethinking communication: Paradigm exemplars* (pp. 258–268). Newbury Park, CA: Sage.

Rorty, R. (1979). *Philosophy and the mirror of nature.* Princeton, NJ: Princeton University Press.

Schwartz, R. D. (1989). Arab-Jewish dialogue in the United States. In L. Kriesberg, T. A. Northrup, & S. J. Thorson (Eds.), *Intractable conflicts and their transformation* (pp. 180–209). Syracuse, NY: Syracuse University Press.

Stout, J. (1988). *Ethics after babel: The languages of morals and their discontents.* Boston: Beacon.

Wynn, R. L. (1989). Custody disputes and the victims. In L. Kriesberg, T. A. Northrup, & S. J. Thorson (Eds.), *Intractable conflicts and their transformation* (pp. 83–92). Syracuse, NY: Syracuse University Press.

Zwiebach, B. (1988). *The common life: Ambiguity, agreement, and the structure of morals.* Philadelphia: Temple University Press.

CHAPTER 14

Bridging Cultures

*F*or more than 25 years, educational psychologist David Johnson has been helping teachers and schools in North America, Central America, Europe, Africa, Asia, the Middle East, and the Pacific Rim take advantage of the benefits of collaborative and cooperative learning. One of the fruits of his labor is the 1997 edition of his book *Reaching Out: Interpersonal Effectiveness and Self-Actualization,* from which I've taken the next reading. This is a basic introduction to the attitudes and skills of connecting with people who are different from you.

Johnson begins with the point that, although globalization is a fact that is making diversity among acquaintances, classmates, co-workers, and neighbors increasingly inevitable, it is in some ways not "natural" for humans to want to get along with diverse others. For 200,000 years, as he puts it, humans lived in small hunting and gathering groups, interacting infrequently with others. But today we are regularly thrown together with cultural strangers. Both men and women in what have traditionally been single-sex jobs (firefighter, nurse, mail carrier, parking checker) are having to team with opposite-sex colleagues. Older and younger workers are forced to collaborate, and Blacks, Latinos, Asians, Caucasians, Arabs, Pacific Islanders, and members of other ethnic groups are thrown together with those with different, and sometimes competing, identities.

The chapter this reading was taken from explains six steps for building relationships with diverse peers, and this excerpt discusses four of the six: Accept yourself, lower barriers, recognize that diversity is a valuable resource, and work to clarify misunderstandings. The first step echoes some of what is in the readings about self-awareness in Chapter 4. Johnson encourages you to reflect on your own identity, which can be subdivided into your self-schema, gender identity, and ethnic identity, as a first step toward connecting effectively with people different from you.

Then he offers some suggestions about lowering three barriers: prejudice, the tendency to blame the victim, and cultural conflict. Prejudice—manifested in ethnocentrism, stereotyping, or discrimination—can be a major hurdle, but Johnson explains four specific ways to overcome it. Blaming the victim occurs when people "attribute the cause of discrimination or misfortune to the personal characteristics and actions of the victim." In this section, Johnson reviews some of the information about external and internal attributions that is discussed by Trenholm and Jensen in Chapter 5, and shows how careful attributions can enhance your experience. Culture clash is the third barrier Johnson explains.

The next section of the reading explains some specific ways in which diversity can be openly recognized and genuinely valued. Johnson suggests four steps that can help lead toward profitable collaboration among diverse people.

The final section of this reading highlights the importance of clarifying miscommunications. Johnson could have said a great deal more here than he does, but this section does remind us how language sensitivity and a developed awareness of stylistic differences among diverse communicators can help people deal effectively with those who are different from themselves. Johnson ends this section with seven specific suggestions, and the first is, "Use all the communication skills discussed in this book." Even though "this book" he was talking about was *Reaching Out*, you can interpret it as a reference to *Bridges Not Walls*. As Johnson recognizes, the skills developed in all 18 chapters of this book can be brought to bear on the project of improving relationships among diverse people.

You may have already thought through the ideas that Johnson discusses here. But if you haven't (or if you have, and would still appreciate a reminder), this is an excellent introduction to the frame of mind and some of the specific skills that are needed in order to bridge differences between you and people you might initially think of as "strangers."

BUILDING RELATIONSHIPS WITH DIVERSE OTHERS

David W. Johnson

INTRODUCTION

We live in one world. The problems that face each person, each community, each country cannot be solved without global cooperation and joint action. Economically, for example, there has been a globalization of business reflected in the increase in multinational companies, coproduction agreements, and offshore operations. As globalization becomes the norm, more and more companies must translate their local and national perspectives into a world view. Companies that are staffed by individuals skilled in building relationships with diverse peers have an advantage in the global market.

Interacting effectively with peers from different cultures, ethnic groups, social classes, and historical backgrounds does not come naturally. For 200,000 years humans lived in small hunting and gathering groups, interacting only infrequently with other nearby small groups. Today we are required to communicate effectively with people cross-culturally, through the generations, among races, between genders, and across those subtle but pervasive barriers of class. No wonder this feels uncomfortable—we have never been required to do it before!

Diversity among your acquaintances, classmates, co-workers, neighbors, and friends is increasingly inevitable. North America, Europe, and many other

parts of the world are becoming more and more diverse in terms of culture, ethnicity, religion, age, physical qualities, and gender. You will be expected to interact effectively with people with a wide variety of characteristics and from a
wide variety of backgrounds. In order to build relationships with diverse peers,
you must

1. Accept yourself.
2. Lower the barriers to building relationships with diverse peers.
3. Recognize that diversity exists and is a valuable resource. . . .
4. Clarify misunderstandings.

ACCEPTING YOURSELF

> *If I am not for myself, who will be for me? But if I am only*
> *for myself, what am I?*
> —The Talmud

Two basic human needs are to

1. Join with others in a cooperative effort to achieve something great.
2. Be a unique and separate individual who is valued and respected in one's
   own right.

In order to meet this second need, you must accept yourself as you are and
build a distinct image of yourself as a certain kind of person who has an identity differentiated and discernible from others. The greater your self-acceptance,
the more stable and integrated your personal identity. Building a coherent, stable, and integrated identity that summarizes who you are as a separate, autonomous, and unique individual is the first step in building constructive relationships with diverse peers.

The Person You Think You Are

What kind of person are you? How would you describe yourself to someone
who does not know you? Would your description be disjointed and contradictory, or would it be organized and consistent? Would it change from day to day,
or would it stay the same over a period of years? Do you like yourself, or do you
feel a basic sense of shame and contempt when you think of yourself? We all
need a strong and integrated sense of personal identity that serves as an anchor
in life.

Early philosophers advised us to "know thyself" and poets have told us, "To
thine own self be true." We have taken their advice. Hundreds of books have
been written dealing with how to get to know yourself and the *Oxford English
Dictionary* lists more than 100 words that focus on the self, from *self-abasement* to
self-wisdom. When you form a conception of who you are as a person you have
an identity.

Your **identity** is a consistent set of attitudes that defines who you are. It is a subjective self-image that is a type of cognitive structure called a self-schema. A **self-schema** is a generalization about the self, derived from past experience, that organizes and guides your understanding of the information you learn about yourself from interacting with others. You have multiple schemas, multiple identities, and multiple selves. They include your view of your physical characteristics (height, weight, sex, hair and eye color, general appearance), your social roles (student or teacher, child or parent, employee or employer), the activities you engage in (playing the piano, dancing, reading), your abilities (skills, achievements), your attitudes and interests (liking rock and roll, favoring equal rights for females), and your general personality traits (extrovert or introvert, impulsive or reflective, sensible or scatterbrained). Your **gender identity** is your fundamental sense of your maleness or femaleness. Your **ethnic identity** is your sense of belonging to one particular ethnic group. Your identity consists not only of various self-schemas that you currently possess but of selves that you would like to be or that you imagine you might be. These potential selves include ideals that you would like to attain and standards that you feel you should meet (the "ought" self). They can originate from your own thoughts or from the messages of others.

Each of your self-schemas is viewed as being positive or negative. You generally look at yourself in an evaluative way, approving or disapproving of your behavior and characteristics. Your self-schemas are arranged in a hierarchy. The more important an identity is, or the higher it stands in the hierarchy, the more likely it is to influence your choices and your behavior.

To cope with stress you need more than one self. The diversity and complexity of the identity reduces the stress you experience. Self-complexity provides a buffer against stressful events. If you have only one or two major self-schemas, any negative event is going to have an impact on most aspects of your identity. The woman who sees herself primarily as a wife, for example, is likely to be devastated if her husband says he wants an immediate divorce. In contrast, the individual who has a more complex representation of self may be more protected from negative events that primarily involve only one or two of several roles. The woman who sees herself not only as wife, but also as a mother, lawyer, friend, and tennis player will have other roles to fall back on when impending divorce threatens her role of spouse. People with more complex identities are less prone to depression and illness; they also experience less severe mood swings following success or failure in one particular area of performance. . . .

Some of the Benefits of Self-Acceptance

There is a common saying that goes, "I can't be right for someone else if I'm not right for me!" **Self-acceptance** is a high regard for yourself or, conversely, a lack of cynicism about yourself. There are a number of benefits to accepting yourself as you are, and a relationship exists among self-acceptance, self-disclosure, and being accepted by others. The more self-accepting you are, the greater your self-disclosure tends to be. The greater your self-disclosure, the more others accept you. And the more others accept you, the more you accept yourself. A high level of self-acceptance, furthermore, is reflected in psychological health. Psychologically healthy people see themselves as being liked, capable, worthy, and acceptable to other people. All of these perceptions are based on self-acceptance. Considerable evidence abounds that self-acceptance and acceptance of others are related. If you think well of yourself you tend to think well of others. You also tend to assume that others will like you, an expectation that often becomes a self-fulfilling prophecy.

DIFFICULTIES WITH DIVERSITY

Once you are accepting of yourself, you are in a position to be accepting of others. There are, however, a number of barriers to accepting diverse peers. They include prejudice, the tendency to blame the victim, and cultural conflict.

Prejudice

> *To know one's self is wisdom, but to know one's neighbor is genius.*
>
> —Minna Antrim (author)

Building relationships with diverse peers is not easy. The first barrier is prejudice. Prejudice, stereotyping, and discrimination begin with categorizing. In order to understand other people and yourself, categories must be used. **Categorizing** is a basic human cognitive process of conceptualizing objects and people as members of groups. We categorize people on the basis of *inherited traits* (culture, sex, ethnic membership, physical features) or *acquired traits* (education, occupation, lifestyle, customs). Categorizing and generalizing are often helpful in processing information and making decisions. At times, however, they malfunction and result in stereotyping and prejudice.

To be prejudiced means to prejudge. **Prejudice** can be defined as an unjustified negative attitude toward a person based solely on that individual's membership in a particular group. Prejudices are judgments made about others that establish a superiority/inferiority belief system. If one person dislikes another simply because that other person is a member of an ethnic group, sex, or religion, that is prejudice.

One common form of prejudice is ethnocentrism. **Ethnocentrism** is the tendency to regard our own ethnic group, culture, or nation as better or more correct than others. The word is derived from *ethnic*, meaning a group united by similar customs, characteristics, race, or other common factors, and *center*. When ethnocentrism is present, the standards and values of our culture are used as a yardstick to measure the worth of other ethnic groups. Ethnocentrism is often perpetuated by **cultural conditioning.** As children we are raised to fit into a particular culture. We are conditioned to respond to various situations as we see others in our culture react.

Prejudices are often associated with stereotypes. A **stereotype** is a set of beliefs about the characteristics of the people in a group that is applied to almost all members of that group. Typically, stereotypes are widely held beliefs within a group and focus on what other cultural and ethnic groups, or socioeconomic classes are "really like." Women have been stereotyped as more emotional than men. Men have been stereotyped as more competitive than women. Tall, dark, and handsome men have been stereotyped as mysterious. Stereotypes distort and exaggerate in ways that support an underlying prejudice or fundamental bias against members of other groups. Stereotypes are resistant to change because people believe information that confirms their stereotypes more readily than evidence that challenges them. Stereotypes almost always have a detrimental effect on those targeted, interfering with the victim's ability to be productive and live a high quality life.

Stereotypes reflect an **illusionary correlation** between two unrelated factors, such as being poor and lazy. Negative traits are easy to acquire and hard to lose. When you meet one poor person who is lazy you may tend to see all poor people as lazy. From then on, any poor person who is not hard at work the moment you notice him or her may be perceived to be lazy. Our prejudiced stereotype of poor people being lazy is protected in three ways. Our prejudice makes us notice the negative traits we ascribe to the groups we are prejudiced against. We tend to have a *false consensus bias* by believing that most other people share our stereotypes (i.e., see poor people as being lazy). We tend to see our own behavior and judgments as quite common and appropriate, and to view alternative responses as uncommon and often inappropriate. Finally, we often develop a rationale and explanation to justify our stereotypes and prejudices.

When prejudice is put into action, it is discrimination. **Discrimination** is an action taken to harm a group or any of its members. It is a negative, often aggressive action aimed at the target of prejudice. Discrimination is aimed at denying members of the targeted groups treatment and opportunities equal to those afforded to the dominant group. When discrimination is based on race or sex, it is referred to as racism or sexism.

Diversity among people can either be a valued resource generating energy, vitality, and creativity, or it can be a source of prejudice, stereotyping, and discrimination. To reduce your prejudices and use of stereotypes, these steps may be helpful:

1. Admit that you have prejudices (everyone does, you are no exception) and commit yourself to reducing them.
2. Identify the stereotypes that reflect your prejudices and modify them.
3. Identify the actions that reflect your prejudices and modify them.
4. Seek feedback from diverse friends and colleagues about how well you are communicating respect for and valuing of diversity.

Blaming the Victim

It is commonly believed that the world is a just place where people generally get what they deserve. If we win the lottery, it must be because we are nice people who deserve some good luck. If we are robbed, it must be because we are careless and want to be punished for past misdeeds. Any person who is mugged in a dark alley while carrying a great deal of cash may be seen as asking to be robbed. Most people tend to believe that they deserve what happens to them. Most people also believe that others also get what they deserve in the world. It is all too easy to forget that victims do not have the benefit of hindsight to guide their actions.

When someone is a victim of prejudice, stereotyping, and discrimination, all too often they are seen as doing *something* wrong. **Blaming the victim** occurs when we attribute the cause of discrimination or misfortune to the personal characteristics and actions of the victim. The situation is examined for potential causes that will enable us to maintain our belief in a just world. If the victim can be blamed for causing the discrimination, then we can believe that the future is predictable and controllable because we will get what we deserve.

Blaming the victim occurs as we try to attribute a cause to events. We constantly interpret the meaning of our behavior and events that occur in our lives. Many times we want to figure out *why* we acted in a particular way or why a certain outcome occurred. If we get angry when someone infers we are stupid, but we could care less when someone calls us clumsy, we want to know why we are so sensitive about our intelligence. When we are standing on a street corner after a rainstorm and a car splashes us with water, we want to know whether it was caused by our carelessness, the driver's meanness, or just bad luck. This process of explaining or inferring the causes of events has been termed **causal attribution.** An attribution is an inference drawn about the causes of a behavior or event. . . .

In trying to understand why a behavior or event occurred, we generally choose to attribute causes either to

1. Internal, personal factors (such as effort and ability)
2. External, situational factors (such as luck or the behavior/personality of other people)

For example, if you do well on a test, you can attribute it to your hard work and great intelligence (an internal attribution) or to the fact that the test was incredibly easy (an external attribution). When a friend drops out of school, you can attribute it to a lack of motivation (an internal attribution) or lack of money (an external attribution).

People make causal attributions to explain their successes and failures. These are *self-serving* attributions, designed to permit us to take credit for positive outcomes and to avoid blame for negative ones. We have a systematic tendency to claim our successes are due to our ability and efforts while our failures are due to bad luck, evil people, or a lack of effort. We also have a systematic tendency to claim responsibility for the success of group efforts ("It was all my idea in the first place and I did most of the work") and avoid responsibility for group failures ("If the other members had tried harder, this would not have happened.")....

Attributing the causes of others' failure and misfortune to their actions rather than to prejudice and discrimination can be a barrier to building constructive relationships with diverse peers. Bad things do happen to good people. Racism does exist. Innocent bystanders do get shot. It is usually a good idea to suspend any tendency to blame the victim when interacting with diverse peers.

Culture Clash

Another common barrier to building relationships with diverse peers is cultural clashes. A **culture clash** is a conflict over basic values that occurs among individuals from different cultures. The most common form is members of minority groups' questioning the values of the majority. Common reactions by majority group members when their values are being questioned are feeling:

1. *Threatened:* Their responses include avoidance, denial, and defensiveness.
2. *Confused:* Their responses include seeking more information in an attempt to redefine the problem.
3. *Enhanced:* Their responses include heightened anticipation, awareness, and positive actions that lead to solving the problem.

Many cultural clashes develop from threatening, to confusing, to enhancing. Once they are enhancing, they are no longer a barrier.

As prejudice, stereotyping, and discrimination are reduced, the tendency to blame the victim is avoided, and cultural clashes become enhancing, the stage is set for recognizing and valuing diversity.

RECOGNIZING AND VALUING DIVERSITY

In order to actualize the positive potential of diversity, you must recognize that diversity exists and then learn to value and respect fundamental differences among people. This is especially true in countries in which widely diverse groups of people live. The United States, for example, is a nation of many cultures, races, languages, and religions. In the last eight years alone, over 7.8 million people journeying from over 150 different countries and speaking dozens of different languages made the United States their new home. America's pluralism and diversity has many positive values, such as being a source of energy and creativity that increases the vitality of American society. Diversity among collaborators has been found to contribute to achievement and productivity, creative problem solving, growth in cognitive and moral reasoning, perspective-taking ability, and general sophistication in interacting and working with peers from a variety of cultural and ethnic backgrounds (Johnson & Johnson, 1989).

Within a relationship, a community, an organization, a society or a world, the goal is not to assimilate all groups so that everyone is alike. The goal is to work together to achieve mutual goals while recognizing cultural diversity and learning to value and respect fundamental differences while working together to achieve mutual goals. Creating a *unum* from *pluribus* is done in basically four steps. *First, you develop an appreciation for your own religious, ethnic, or cultural background.* Your identification with the culture and homeland of your ancestors must be recognized and valued. The assumption is that respect for your cultural heritage will translate into self-respect.

Second, you develop an appreciation and respect for the religious, ethnic, and cultural backgrounds of others. A critical aspect of developing an ethnic and cultural identity is whether ethnocentricity is inherent in your definition of yourself. An ingroup identity must be developed in a way that does not lead to rejection of outgroups. There are many examples where being a member of one group requires the rejection of other groups. There are also many examples where being a member of one group requires the valuing and respect for other groups. Outgroups need to be seen as collaborators and resources rather than competitors and threats. Express respect for diverse backgrounds and value them as a resource that increases the quality of your life and adds to the viability of your society. The degree to which your ingroup identity leads to respect for and valuing of outgroups depends on developing a superordinate identity that includes both your own and all other groups.

Third, you develop a strong superordinate identity that transcends the differences between your own and all other groups. Being an American, for example, is creedal rather than racial or ancestral. The United States is a nation that unites as one people the descendants of many cultures, races, religions, and ethnic groups through an identification with America and democracy. And America has grown increasingly diverse in social and cultural composition. Each cultural group is part of the whole and members of each new immigrant group, while modifying and enriching our national identity, learn they are first and foremost Americans. America is one of the few successful examples of a pluralistic society where different groups clashed but ultimately learned to live together through achieving a sense of common nationhood. In our diversity, there has always been a broad recognition that we are one people. Whatever our origins, we are all Americans.

Fourth, you adopt a pluralistic set of values concerning democracy, freedom, liberty, equality, justice, the rights of individuals, and the responsibilities of citizenship. It is these values that form the American creed. We respect basic human rights, listen to dissenters instead of jailing them, and have a multiparty political system, a free press, free speech, freedom of religion, and freedom of assembly. These values were shaped by millions of people from many different backgrounds. Americans are a multicultural people knitted together by a common set of political and moral values.

Diverse individuals from different cultural, ethnic, social class, and language backgrounds come together primarily in school, career, and community settings.

Sometimes the results are positive and individuals get to know each other, appreciate and value the vitality of diversity, learn how to use diversity for creative problem solving and enhanced productivity, and internalize a common superordinate identity that binds them together. If diversity is to be a source of creativity and energy, individuals must value and seek out diversity rather than fear and reject it. Doing so will eventually result in cross-cultural friendships. . . .

CLARIFYING MISCOMMUNICATIONS

Imagine that you and several friends went to hear a speaker. Although the content was good, and the delivery entertaining, two of your friends walked out in protest. When you asked them why, they called your attention to the facts that the speaker continually said "you guys" even though half the audience was women, used only sports and military examples, only quoted males, and joked about senility and old age. Your friends were insulted.

Communication is actually one of the most complex aspects of managing relationships with diverse peers. To communicate effectively with people from a different cultural, ethnic, social class, historical background than yours you must increase your

1. *Language sensitivity:* knowledge of words and expressions that are appropriate and inappropriate in communicating with diverse groups. The use of language can play a powerful role in reinforcing stereotypes and garbling communication. To avoid this, individuals need to heighten their sensitivity and avoid using terms and expressions that ignore or devalue others.
2. *Awareness of stylistic elements of communication:* knowledge of the key elements of communication style and how diverse cultures use these elements to communicate. Without awareness of nuances in language and differences in style, the potential for garbled communication is enormous when interacting with diverse peers.

Your ability to communicate with credibility to diverse peers is closely linked to your use of language. You must be sophisticated enough to anticipate how your messages will be interpreted by the listener. If you are unaware of nuances and innuendoes contained in your message, then you will be more likely to miscommunicate. The words you choose often tell other people more about your values, attitudes, and socialization than you intend to reveal. Receivers will react to the subtleties conveyed and interpret the implied messages behind our words. The first step in establishing relationships with diverse peers, therefore, is to understand how language reinforces stereotypes and to adjust our usage accordingly.

You can never predict with certainty how every person will react to what you say. You can, however, minimize the possibility of miscommunicating by following some basic guidelines:

1. Use all the communication skills discussed in this book.
2. Negotiate for meaning whenever you think the other persons you are talking with misinterpreted what you said.

3. Use words that are inclusive rather than exclusive such as women, men, participants.
4. Avoid adjectives that spotlight specific groups and imply the individual is an exception, such as black doctor, woman pilot, older teacher, blind lawyer.
5. Use quotes, references, metaphors, and analogies that reflect diversity and are from diverse sources, for example, from Asian and African sources as well as from European and American.
6. Avoid terms that define, demean, or devalue others, such as cripple, girl, boy, agitator.
7. Be aware of the genealogy of words viewed as inappropriate by others. It is the connotations the receiver places on the words that are important, not your connotations. These connotations change over time so continual clarification is needed. There are loaded words that seem neutral to you but highly judgmental to people of diverse backgrounds. The word lady, for example, was a complement even a few years ago, but today it fails to take into account women's independence and equal status in society and, therefore, is offensive to many women. Words such as girls or gals are just as offensive.

SUMMARY

In a global village highly diverse individuals interact daily, study and work together, and live in the same community. Diversity among your acquaintances, classmates, co-workers, neighbors, and friends is inevitable. You will be expected to interact effectively with people with a wide variety of characteristics and from a wide variety of backgrounds. In order to gain the sophistication and skills needed to do so you must accept yourself, lower the barriers to building relationships with diverse peers, recognize that diversity exists and is a valuable resource, . . . and clarify misunderstandings.

All people need to believe that they are unique and separate individuals who are valued and respected in their own right. In order to do so, you must accept yourself as you are and build a coherent, stable, and integrated identity. Your identity helps you cope with stress, it provides stability and consistency to your life, and it directs what information is attended to, how it is organized, and how it is remembered. Your identity is built through your current relationships and identifications with real, historical, and fictional people. Actually, you have many interrelated identities. You have a family identity, a gender identity, and a country identity. An important aspect of your identity is your identification with your cultural, ethnic, historical, and religious background.

The more accepting you are of yourself, the more able you are to be accepting of others. But there are barriers to building positive relationships with diverse peers. The most notable barriers are prejudice, blaming the victim, and culture clash. Minimizing these barriers makes it easier to recognize that diversity exists and fundamental differences among people are to be both respected and valued. To do so you must respect your own heritage, respect the heritages of others, develop a superordinate identity that transcends the differences, and a pluralistic set of values.

Accepting yourself, minimizing the barriers, and respecting and valuing diversity set the stage for actually gaining cross-cultural sophistication. Being able to relate effectively to people from a variety of cultures depends on seeking opportunities to interact cross-culturally, building trust, so that enough candor exists that you can learn what is and what is not disrespectful and hurtful to them. It is only through building friendships with diverse peers that the insights required to understand how to interact appropriately with people from a wide variety of backgrounds can be obtained. Two requirements for developing such friendships are highlighting cooperative efforts to achieve mutual goals and clarifying miscommunications that arise while working together.

REVIEW QUESTIONS

1. Explain what Johnson means—as specifically as you can—when he says that globalization has made diversity increasingly inevitable.
2. What is a self-schema? Give an example of one of your own self-schemas.
3. Explain the connection Johnson makes between prejudice and discrimination.
4. Explain how blaming the victim can contribute to stereotyping.
5. What does Johnson mean by "a strong superordinate identity that transcends the differences between your own and all other groups"?
6. What is a pluralistic set of values?
7. Give an example of how (a) language sensitivity and (b) awareness of stylistic elements of communication could enhance relationships with diverse others.

PROBES

1. People who belong to such organizations as a militia, skinhead, or Ku Klux Klan group often argue for the importance of ethnic purity and exclusivity. Members of men-only and women-only groups make similar arguments about gender exclusivity. Johnson's basic assumption in this reading is that these arguments for exclusivity are naïve, because diversity is a fact of the contemporary world. What specific examples can you cite to support Johnson's assumption? Where do you notice the concrete evidence of increasing diversity?
2. *Why* does Johnson say that the first step toward successfully interacting with diverse others is to learn to accept yourself?
3. Cognitive scientists pretty much agree that categorization is a basic human mental function. Our brains naturally and constantly categorize almost everything we perceive. If this is true, then we automatically categorize the people we perceive. How, then, can a person possibly avoid prejudice?

4. As Johnson defines *culture clash,* it is inevitable. Various cultures will naturally have conflicts over basic values. Tell how he suggests we respond to this inevitability.

5. Which of the previous readings in this book do you think could contribute most directly to your efforts to bridge differences with diverse others?

REFERENCE

Johnson, D. W. & Johnson, R. (1989). *Cooperation and competition: Theory and research.* Edina, MN: Interaction Book Company.

*L*etty Cottin Pogrebin published an exhaustive book on friendship based on two very thorough friendship surveys, many additional published research reports, and interviews with almost 150 people ranging in age from early adolescence to 82 years and representing most of the spectrum of cultures and subcultures in the United States. The following reading consists of excerpts from Chapter 11 of her 16-chapter book. As the title indicates, the chapter deals with friendship across a variety of cultural boundaries, including color, culture, sexual preference, disability, and age. As with other readings, I chose this one because it blends sound research and straightforward writing, credible theory, and solid practice.

This rigorous but accessible flavor of Pogrebin's work emerges in the section right after the introduction. She begins with the obvious but important point that if you're going to cross a boundary, you'll find yourself doing a lot of explaining—to yourself, to each other, and to your respective communities. Then she takes a couple of pages to elaborate on what that "explaining" will probably consist of.

The next major section develops another potentially profound theme: Intercultural relationships consistently have to deal with the reality that the two persons might be "the same," but that they're also "never quite the same." She illustrates the point with examples from black/redneck white, Jewish/Irish-Catholic, Puerto Rican/white, and Spanish/Jewish relationships. Pogrebin's discussion of "moving in one another's world" extends the notion of "the same but never quite the same" to include challenges introduced by second and third languages and fundamental cultural values. She also discusses several "hazards of crossing" that emerge when fundamental differences in cultural values meet.

Under the heading "The Problem with 'Them' Is 'Us,' " Pogrebin discusses gay/straight, disabled/nondisabled, and young/aged relationships. All three topics became current only in the past decade as the minority rights movement spread to include gays and lesbians, the disabled, and "senior citizens," and government regulations made these groups increasingly visible. As the author notes, these groups warrant separate discussions, in part because "to a large degree, our society still wants to keep them out of sight—the gays and lesbians for 'flaunting their alternative life-styles,' the disabled for not 'getting better,' and the old for reminding us of our eventual fate."

Pogrebin's outline of the kinds of explaining one has to do about his or her gay/straight relationships accurately captures the last 10 years or so of my experience communicating with some gay and lesbian people. The strong relationship Kris and I have with Bill and John Paul, our "married" neighbors, is one example of some of the problems and much of the potential Pogrebin discusses. I also appreciate her summary of the contrasts between gay and straight views on homophobia, AIDS, lesbian politics, and acceptance.

Until recently, disabled persons in the United States made up perhaps an even more invisible subculture. Thanks in part to major changes in building codes affecting all public construction, wheelchair-bound, deaf, and blind persons are becoming increasingly visible. Pogrebin explains some of the unique problems the nondisabled can have establishing and maintaining relationships with these persons. As one quadriplegic succinctly puts it, "We need friends who won't treat us as weirdo asexual second-class children or expect us to be 'Super-crips'—miracle cripples who work like crazy to make themselves whole again. . . . We want to be accepted the way we are." Some nondisabled persons are guilty of exactly these charges and can be shocked to hear them expressed so bluntly.

In the final section of this reading, Pogrebin discusses cross-age friendships. She cites some studies that indicate that three-year-olds already have developed "ageist" perceptions of the elderly—believing that old people are sick, tired, and ugly. Other studies reveal the stereotypes older people have of children and teenagers. She discusses some of the typical reasons for cross-age miscommunication and then suggests some reasons why age can be immaterial to developing friendships. As the average age of the U.S. populace continues to increase, Pogrebin's comments will become more and more applicable and important.

I appreciate the breadth of application in this reading. I believe that Pogrebin is writing about some cutting-edge aspects of interpersonal communication and that her ideas are going to become increasingly important.

THE SAME AND DIFFERENT:

Crossing Boundaries of Color, Culture, Sexual Preference, Disability, and Age

Letty Cottin Pogrebin

On August 21, 1985, as they had done several times before, twenty-one men from a work unit at a factory in Mount Vernon, New York, each chipped in a dollar, signed a handwritten contract agreeing to "share the money equaly [sic] & fairly to each other," and bought a ticket in the New York State Lottery. The next day, their ticket was picked as one of three winners of the largest jackpot in history: $41 million.

The story of the Mount Vernon 21 captivated millions not just because of the size of the pot of gold but because of the rainbow of people who won it. Black, white, yellow, and brown had scribbled their names on that contract—Mariano Martinez, Chi Wah Tse, Jaroslaw Siwy, and Peter Lee—all immigrants from countries ranging from Paraguay to Poland, from Trinidad to Thailand.

"We're like a big family here," said Peter Lee. "We thought by pooling our efforts we would increase our luck—and we were right."[1]

The men's good fortune is a metaphor for the possibility that friendships across ethnic and racial boundaries may be the winning ticket for everyone. This is not to say that crossing boundaries is a snap. It isn't. There are checkpoints along the way where psychic border guards put up a fuss and credentials must be reviewed. We look at a prospective friend and ask, "Do they want something from me?" Is this someone who sees personal advantage in having a friend of another race at his school, in her company, at this moment in history? Is it Brotherhood Week? Does this person understand that "crossing friendships" require more care and feeding than in-group friendship, that it takes extra work?

EXPLAINING

Most of the extra work can be summed up in one word: *explaining*. Whatever the boundary being crossed—race, ethnicity, or any other social category—both partners in a crossing friendship usually find they have to do a lot of explaining—to themselves, to each other, and to their respective communities.

Explaining to Yourself

One way or another, you ask yourself, "What is the meaning of my being friends with someone not like me?"

In his classic study, *The Nature of Prejudice,* Gordon Allport distinguishes between the in-group, which is the group to which you factually belong, and the reference group, which is the group to which you relate or aspire.[2] Allport gives the example of Blacks who so wish to partake of white skin privilege that they seek only white friends, disdain their own group, and become self-hating. One could as easily cite Jews who assume a WASP identity or "Anglicized Chicanos" who gain education and facility in English and then sever their ties of kinship and friendship with other Mexican-Americans.[3]

When you have a friend from another racial or ethnic group, you ask yourself whether you are sincerely fond of this person or might be using him or her as an entrée into a group that is your unconscious reference group. The explaining you do to yourself helps you understand your own motivations. It helps you ascertain whether the friend complements or denies your identity, and whether your crossing friendships are in reasonable balance with your in-group relationships.

Explaining to Each Other

Ongoing mutual clarification is one of the healthiest characteristics of crossing friendships. The Black friend explains why your saying "going ape" offends him, and the Jewish friend reminds you she can't eat your famous barbecued pork. Both of you try to be honest about your cultural sore points and to forgive the other person's initial ignorance or insensitivities. You give one another the benefit of the doubt. Step by step, you discover which aspects of the other person's "in-groupness" you can share and where you must accept exclusion with grace.

David Osborne, a white, describes his close and treasured friendship with an American Indian from Montana: "Steve was tall and athletic—the classic image of the noble full-blooded Indian chief. We were in the same dorm in my freshman year at Stanford at a time when there were only one or two other Native Americans in the whole university. He had no choice but to live in a white world. Our friendship began when our English professor gave an assignment to write about race. Steve and I got together to talk about it. We explored stuff people don't usually discuss openly. After that, we started spending a lot of time together. We played intramural sports. We were amazingly honest with each other, but we were also comfortable being silent.

"When I drove him home for spring vacation, we stopped off at a battlefield that had seen a major war between Chief Joseph's tribe and the U.S. Cavalry. Suddenly it hit me that, had we lived then, Steve and I would have been fighting on opposite sides, and we talked about the past. Another time, an owl flew onto our windowsill and Steve was very frightened. He told me the owl was a symbol of bad luck to Indians. I took it very seriously. We were so in touch, so in sync, that I felt the plausibility of his superstitions. I was open to his mysticism."

Mutual respect, acceptance, tolerance for the faux pas and the occasional closed door, open discussion and patient mutual education, all this gives crossing friendships—when they work at all—a special kind of depth.

Explaining to Your Community of Origin

Accountability to one's own group can present the most difficult challenge to the maintenance of crossing friendships. In 1950 the authors of *The Lonely Crowd* said that interracial contact runs risks not only from whites but from Blacks who may "interpret friendliness as Uncle Tomism."[4] The intervening years have not eliminated such group censure.

In her article "Friendship in Black and White," Bebe Moore Campbell wrote: "For whites, the phrase 'nigger lover' and for Blacks, the accusation of 'trying to be white' are the pressure the group applies to discourage social interaction."[5] Even without overt attacks, people's worry about group reaction inspires self-censorship. Henry, a Black man with a fair complexion, told me he dropped a white friendship that became a touchy subject during the Black Power years. "We'd just come out of a period when many light-skinned Negroes tried to pass for white and I wasn't about to be mistaken for one of them," he explains. "My racial identity mattered more to me than any white friend."

Black-white friendships are "conducted underground," says Campbell, quoting a Black social worker, who chooses to limit her intimacy with whites rather than fight the system. "I'd feel comfortable at my white friend's parties because everybody there would be a liberal, but I'd never invite her to mine because I have some friends who just don't like white people and I didn't want anybody to be embarrassed."

If a white friend of mine said she hated Blacks, I would not just keep my Black friends away from her, I would find it impossible to maintain the friendship. However, the converse is not comparable. Most Blacks have at some point been wounded by racism, while whites have not been victimized from the other direction. Understanding the experiences *behind* the reaction allows decent Black people to remain friends with anti-white Blacks. That these Blacks may have reason to hate certain whites does not excuse their hating all whites, but it does explain it. . . .

Historically, of course, the biggest enemies of boundary-crossing friendships have not been Blacks or ethnic minorities but majority whites. Because whites gain the most from social inequality, they have the most to lose from crossing friendships, which, by their existence, deny the relevance of ethnic and racial hierarchies. More important, the empowered whites can put muscle behind their disapproval by restricting access to clubs, schools, and businesses.

If you sense that your community of origin condemns one of your crossing friendships, the amount of explaining or justifying you do will depend on how conformist you are and whether you feel entitled to a happiness of your own making. . . .

THE SAME BUT NEVER QUITE THE SAME

"I go coon hunting with Tobe Spencer," said former police officer L. C. Albritton about his Black friend in Camden, Alabama. "We're good friends. We stay in town during the day for all the hullabaloo and at night we go home and load up the truck with three dogs and go way down into the swamps. We let the dogs go and sit on a log, take out our knives and a big chew of tobacco . . . and just let the rest of the world go by."

Looking at a picture of himself and Spencer taken in 1966, Albritton mused: "It's funny that a police officer like me is standing up there smiling and talking to a nigger because we were having marches and trouble at that time. . . . Old Tobe Spencer—ain't nothing wrong with that nigger. He's always neat and clean as a pin. He'll help you too. Call him at midnight and he'll come running just like that."[6]

Two friends with the same leisure-time pleasures, two men at ease together in the lonely night of the swamps. Yet race makes a difference. Not only does the white man use the derogatory "nigger," but he differentiates his friend Tobe from the rest of "them" who, presumably, are not neat and clean and helpful. The *same but never quite the same.*

Leonard Fein, the editor of *Moment,* a magazine of progressive Jewish opinion, gave me "the controlling vignette" of his cross-ethnic friendships: "An Irish-Catholic couple was among our dearest friends, but on that morning in 1967 when we first heard that Israel was being bombed, my wife said, 'Who can we huddle with tonight to get through this ordeal,' and we picked three Jewish couples. Our Irish friends were deeply offended. 'Don't you think we would have felt for you?' they asked. 'Yes,' we said, 'but it wasn't sympathy we wanted, it was people with whom, if necessary, we could have mourned the death of Israel—and that could only be other Jews.'

"The following week, when the war was over, my wife and I went to Israel. The people who came to live in our house and take care of our children were our Irish friends. They had understood they were our closest friends yet they could never be exactly like us.". . .

For Raoul, a phenomenally successful advertising man, crossing friendships have been just about the only game in town. He reminisced with me about growing up in a Puerto Rican family in a Manhattan neighborhood populated mostly by Irish, Italians, and Jews:

"In the fifties I hung out with all kinds of guys. I sang on street corners—do-wopping in the night—played kick the can, and belonged to six different basketball clubs, from the Police Athletic League to the YMCA. My high school had 6000 kids in it—street kids who hung out in gangs like The Beacons, The Fanwoods, The Guinea Dukes, The Irish Lords, and The Diablos from Spanish Harlem and Jewish kids who never hung out because they were home studying. The gang members were bullies and punks who protected their own two-block area. They wore leather jackets and some of them carried zip guns and knives. I managed to be acceptable to all of them just because I was good at sports. I was the best athlete in the school and president of the class. So I was protected by the gangs and admired by the Jewish kids and I had a lot of friends."

Raoul's athletic prowess won him a scholarship to a large midwestern university where he was the first Puerto Rican to be encountered by some people. "They wanted me to sing the whole sound track of *West Side Story.* They asked to see my switchblade. And I was as amazed by the midwesterners as they were by me. My first hayride was a real shock. Same with hearing people saying 'Good morning' to each other. Every one of my friends—my roommate, teammates, and fraternity brothers, Blacks from Chicago and Detroit and whites from the farms—they were all gentle and nice. And gigantic and strong. Boy, if one of them had moved into my neighborhood back home, he'd have owned the block.

"After graduation, a college friend went to work in a New York City ad agency that played in a Central Park league and needed a softball pitcher. He had me brought in for an interview. Even though I knew nothing about advertising, I was a helluva pitcher, and the owner of the agency took sports seriously. So he hired me. I always say I had the only athletic scholarship in the history of advertising. I pitched for the agency, I played basketball with the owner, and I learned the business. So I found my friends and my career through sports. Even though I may have been a Spic to most everyone, sports opened all the doors."

The same but never quite the same. . . .

"At the beginning, because of difficulties of adaptation, we immigrants protect ourselves by getting together with people from the same culture who speak the same language," says Luis Marcos, a psychiatrist, who came to the United States from Seville, Spain. "Next, when we feel more comfortable, we reach out to people who do the same work we do, mostly those who help us or those we help in some way. Then we have a basis for friendship. My mentor, the director of psychiatry at Bellevue, is a native-born American and a Jew. He helped me in my area of research and now he's one of my best friends. I also began to teach and to make friends with my medical students as they grew and advanced."

That Marcos and his friends have the health profession in common has not prevented misunderstandings. "When we first went out for meals together, my impulse was to pay for both of us," he says of another doctor, a Black woman who taught him not to leave his own behavior unexamined. "It wasn't that I thought she couldn't afford to pay; we were equally able to pick up the check. It was just that the cultural habit of paying for a woman was ingrained in my personality. But she misconstrued it. She felt I was trying to take care of her and put her down as a Black, a professional, and a woman. In order for our friendship to survive, she had to explain how she experiences things that I don't even think about."

MOVING IN ONE ANOTHER'S WORLD

Ethnotherapist Judith Klein revels in her crossing friendships. "My interest in people who are different from me may be explained by the fact that I'm a twin. Many people look to be mirrored in friendship; I've had mirroring through my sister, so I can use friendship for other things. One thing I use it for is to extend my own life. People who aren't exactly like me enhance my knowledge and experience. They let me be a vicarious voyager in their world."

As much as friends try to explain one another's world, certain differences remain particular barriers to intimacy.

Luis Marcos mentions the language barrier. "No matter how well I speak, I can never overcome my accent," he says. "And some people mistake the way I talk for lack of comprehension. They are afraid I won't understand an American joke, or if I choose to use aggressive words, they don't think I mean it, they blame my 'language problem.' "

While many Americans assume people with an accent are ignorant, many ethnics assume, just as incorrectly, that someone *without* an accent is smart. Some Americans have a habit of blaming the other person for doing or saying whatever is not understandable to Americans. Ethnics also have been known to blame their own culture—to use their "foreignness" as an excuse for behavior for which an American would have to take personal responsibility. "I can't help it if we Latins are hot-tempered" is a way of generalizing one's culpability.

Of course, the strongest barrier to friendship is outright resistance. After two years of off-and-on living in Tokyo, Angie Smith came to terms with the fact that "the Japanese do not socialize the way we do." She found, as many have, that in Japan friendship is considered an obligation more than a pleasure and is almost always associated with business.[7]

"Three times I invited two couples for dinner—the men were my husband's business associates—and three times the men came and the women didn't," Smith recalls. "They sent charming little notes with flowers, but they would not have been comfortable in our house for an evening of social conversation. Yet these same Japanese women would go out to lunch with me and tell me more intimate things than they tell each other. While we were in Japan, I just had to get used to sex-divided socializing and not having any couple friendships."

When people's differences are grounded in racism rather than alien styles of socializing, it can be especially painful to move in the other person's world.

"I felt myself a slave and the idea of speaking to white people weighed me down," wrote Frederick Douglass a century ago.[8] Today, most Blacks refuse to be weighed down by whites. They do not "need" white friends. Some doubt that true friendship is possible between the races until institutional racism is destroyed. Feminists of every shade have debated the question "Is Sisterhood Possible?" Despite the issues that affect *all* women, such as sexual violence, many Black women resist working together for social change or organizing with white women because they believe most whites don't care enough about welfare reform, housing, teen pregnancies, or school dropouts—issues that are of primary concern to Blacks.

Bell Hooks, a writer and a professor of Afro-American studies, wrote: "All too frequently in the women's movement it was assumed one could be free of sexist thinking by simply adopting the appropriate feminist rhetoric; it was further assumed that identifying oneself as oppressed freed one from being an oppressor. To a very great extent, such thinking prevented white feminists from understanding and overcoming their own sexist-racist attitudes toward black women. They could pay lip service to the idea of sisterhood and solidarity between women but at the same time dismiss black women."[9]

Phyllis Marynick Palmer, a historian, says white women are confounded by Black women's strong family role and work experience, which challenge the white stereotype of female incapacity. White women also criticize Black women for making solidarity with their brothers a priority rather than confronting Black men's sexism. In turn, Black women get angry at white women who ignore "their own history of racism and the benefits that white women have gained at the expense of black women."[10] With all this, how could sisterhood be possible? How can friendship be possible?

"I would argue for the abandonment of the concept of sisterhood as a global construct based on unexamined assumptions about our similarities," answers Dill, "and I would substitute a more pluralistic approach that recognizes and accepts the objective differences between women."

Again the word "pluralistic" is associated with friendship. An emphasis on double consciousness, not a denial of differences. The importance of feeling both the same and different, of acknowledging "the essence of me," of understanding that friends need not *transcend* race or ethnicity but can embrace differences and be enriched by them. The people who have managed to incorporate these precepts say that they are pretty reliable guidelines for good crossing friendships. But sometimes it's harder than it looks. Sometimes, the "vicarious voyage" into another world can be a bad trip.

The Hazards of Crossing

"Anglo wannabes" are a particular peeve of David Hayes Bautista. "These are Anglos who wanna be so at home with us that they try too hard to go native. For instance, Mexicans have a certain way that we yell along with the music of mariachi band. When someone brought along an Anglo friend and yelled 'Yahoo, Yahoo' all night, every Chicano in the place squirmed."

Maxine Baca Zinn gives the reverse perspective: of a Chicano in an Anglo environment. "Once, when I was to speak at the University of California, a Chicana friend who was there told me that the minute I walked into that white academic world my spine straightened up. I carried myself differently. I talked differently around them and I didn't even know it." Was Zinn just nervous about giving her speech or did she tighten up in anticipation of the tensions Chicanos feel in non-Hispanic settings? She's not certain.

When Charlie Chin, a bartender, started work in a new place, a white coworker quipped, "One thing you have to watch out for, Charlie, are all the Chinks around here." I winced when Chin said this, but he told me, " I just smiled at the guy. I'm used to those jokes. That's the way whites break the ice with Asians. That's the American idea of being friendly.". . .

For another pair of friends, having different sensitivities did not destroy the relationship but did create a temporary misunderstanding. Yvonne, a Black woman, was offended when her white friend, Fran, came to visit, took off her shoes, and put her feet up on the couch. "I felt it showed her disregard for me and I blamed it on race," says Yvonne. "Black people believe the way you behave in someone's home indicates the respect you have for that person. Also, furniture means a lot to us because we buy it with such hard-won wages." Weeks later, Yvonne saw one of Fran's white friends do the same thing while sitting on Fran's couch. Yvonne realized that the behavior had nothing to do with lack of respect for Blacks. "For all I know millions of whites all over America put their feet up when they relax—I'd just never seen that part of their world before."

What Bill Tatum discovered about a couple of his white friends was not so easy to explain away. When the couple asked Tatum to take some food to Helen, their Black housekeeper who was sick, he asked her name and address. They knew her only as "Helen" but were able to get her address from their 6-year-old who had spent a week at her apartment when they had been on vacation.

"I arrived to find a filthy, urine-smelling building, with addicts hanging out on the front stoop. Rags were stuffed in the broken windows in Helen's apartment. She was wearing a bag of asafetida around her neck, a concoction made by southern Blacks to ward off bad luck and colds. She was old, sick, and feverish. She said she'd never been sick before and her employers—my friends—had provided her with no health insurance. Obviously, they'd never imagined where or how this poor woman might live—or else they wouldn't have left their little girl with her. They treated their Black housekeeper with none of the respect and concern they showed me, their Black *friend* and a member of their economic class."

Until that experience, if anyone had ever accused the couple of racism, Tatum says he'd have gone to the mat defending them. Now he has to square what he's seen with his old love for them and he is finding it very, very difficult.

He makes another point about moving in the world of white friends. "Some whites make me feel completely comfortable because they say exactly what they think even if it contradicts whatever I've said. But other whites never disagree with me on anything. They act as if Blacks can't defend their positions, or they're afraid it would look like a put-down to challenge what I say even though they would challenge a white person's opinion in a minute."

While Tatum resents whites' misguided protectiveness, he also finds fault with "many Blacks who are climbing socially and are too damned careful of what *they* say. They won't advance an opinion until they have a sense of what the white friend is thinking." Not only is that not good conversation, he says, "that's not good friendship."

THE PROBLEM WITH "THEM" IS "US"

If you're a young, heterosexual, nondisabled person and you do not have one friend who is either gay, old, or disabled, there might be something wrong with *you*. If you're gay, old, or disabled and all your friends are just like you, it may not be because you prefer it that way.

Gay people, the elderly, and disabled people get the same pleasure from companionship and intimacy and have the same problems with friendship as does anyone else. They merit a separate discussion in this book for the same reason that class, race, and ethnicity required special discussion: because on top of the usual friendship concerns, they experience additional barriers.

In essence, the barriers exist because we don't *know* each other. Many people—some of whom are homophobic (have a fear of homosexuality)—reach adulthood without ever to their knowledge meeting a homosexual or a lesbian. Many have neither known someone who is blind or deaf or who uses a wheelchair nor spent time with an old person other than their grandparents. That there are such things as Gay Pride marches, disability rights organizations, and the Gray Panthers does not mean that these groups have achieved equal treatment under the law or full humanity in the eyes of the world. To a large degree, our society still wants to keep them out of sight—the gays for "flaunting their alternative life-styles," the disabled for not "getting better," and the old for reminding us of our eventual fate.

As a result of our hang-ups, these populations may be even more segregated than racial or ethnic minorities. When these groups are segregated, "we" don't have to think about "them." Out of sight, out of mind, out of friendship. People told me they had no gay, elderly, or disabled friends because "we live in two different worlds" or because "they" are so different—meaning threatening, unsettling, or strange. Closer analysis reveals, however, that we *keep* them different by making this world so hard for them to live in and by defining human norms so narrowly. It is our world—the homophobic, youth-worshipping, disability-fearing world—that is threatening, unsettling, and strange to them. In other words, their biggest problem is us.

To make friends, we have to cross our self-made boundaries and grant to other people the right to be both distinctive and equal.

Gay-Straight Friendship

Forming relationships across gay-straight boundaries can be as challenging as crossing racial and ethnic lines because it too requires the extra work of "explaining":

- Explaining to yourself why, if you're gay, you need this straight friend ("Am I unconsciously trying to keep my heterosexual credentials in order?"), or why, if you're straight, you need this gay friend ("Am I a latent homosexual?")
- Explaining to each other what your lives are like—telling the straight friend what's behind the words "heavy leather" or explaining to the gay friend just why he *cannot* bring his transvestite lover to a Bar Mitzvah
- Explaining to your respective communities why you have such a close relationship with one of "them"

Gay-straight friendship is a challenge not only because the heterosexual world stigmatizes gays but because homosexual society is a culture unto itself. Straights who relate comfortably with their gay friends say they get along so well because they respect the distinctive qualities of gay culture—almost as if it were an ethnic group. Interestingly enough, a Toronto sociologist has determined that gay men have the same institutions, "sense of peoplehood," and friendship networks as an ethnic community; all that gays lack is the emphasis on family.[11] All in places where lesbians congregate, such as San Francisco, there are women's bars, music, bookstores, publications, folklore, and dress styles—an elaborate self-contained culture.[12]

Since gay men and lesbians have to function in a straight world during most of their lives, it's not too much to ask a straight friend to occasionally accommodate to an environment defined by homosexuals. But even when both friends accommodate, gay-straight relations can be strained by disagreements over provocative issues.

Gay-Straight Debate

The Gay's View	The Straight's View
ON HOMOPHOBIA	
You're not relaxed with me. You think gayness rubs off or friendship might lead to sex. You act like every gay person wants to seduce you. You fear others will think you're gay. You are repulsed by gay sex though you try to hide it. You bear some responsibility for the discrimination against gays and if you're my friend, you'll fight it with me.	I am the product of a traditional upbringing. I cannot help being afraid or ignorant of homosexuality. My religion taught me that homosexuality is a sin. I'm trying to overcome these biases and still be honest with you about my feelings. I support gay rights, but I cannot be responsible for everyone else's homophobia.
ON AIDS	
Ever since the AIDS epidemic, you have not touched me or drunk from a glass in my house. I resent your paranoia. I shouldn't have to watch my gay friends die and at the same time feel that my straight friends are treating me like a leper. If I did get AIDS, I'm afraid you would blame the victim and abandon me. Can I trust a friend like that?	I *am* afraid I don't know how contagious the AIDS virus is or how it's transmitted. From what I read, no one does. All I know is that AIDS is fatal, homosexuals are the primary victims, and you are a homosexual. I'm caught between my affection for you and my terror of the disease. I don't know what's right and you're in no position to tell me.
ON LESBIAN POLITICS	
Lesbianism is not just sexual, it's political. Every woman should call herself a lesbian, become woman-identified, and reject everything masculinist. Women who love men and live in the nuclear family contribute to the entrenchment of patriarchal power and the oppression of women. Authentic female friendship can only exist in lesbian communities. If you don't accept "lesbian" as a positive identity, it will be used to condemn all women who are not dependent on men.	I support lesbian rights and even lesbian separatism if lesbians choose it. I believe lesbian mothers must be permitted to keep their children. I oppose all discrimination and defamation of lesbians. I believe that lesbian feminists and straight women can work together and be friends, *but* I resent lesbian coercion and political strong-arming. I also resent your more-radical-than thou-attitude toward heterosexuals. Like you, what I do with my body is my business.
ON ACCEPTANCE	
You want me to act straight whenever having a gay friend might embarrass you. I'm not going to tone down my speech or dress to please your friends or family. I do not enjoy being treated as a second-class couple when my lover and I go out with you and your spouse. If you can kiss and hold hands, we should be able to show affection in public. If straights ask each other how they met or how long they have been married, they should ask us how we met and how long we've been together.	You refuse to understand how difficult it is to explain gay life-styles to a child or an 80-year-old. You make me feel like a square in comparison with your flashy gay friends. You treat married people like Mr. and Mrs. Tepid, as if the only true passion is gay passion. Your friends make me feel unwanted on gay turf and at political events when I'm there to support gay rights. You put down all straights before you know them. It's hard to be your friend if I can't introduce you to other people without your feeling hostile or judging their every word. . . .

Disabled and Nondisabled Friendship

About 36 million Americans have a disabling limitation in their hearing, seeing, speaking, walking, moving, or thinking. Few nondisabled people are as sensitive to the experiences of this population as are those with close friends who are disabled.

"Last week," recalls Barbara Spring, "I went to have a drink at a midtown hotel with a friend who uses a wheelchair. Obviously it's not important to this hotel to have disabled patrons because we had to wait for the so-called accessible elevator for thirty minutes. Anyone who waits with the disabled is amazed at how long the disabled have to wait for everything."

"In graduate school, one of my friends was a young man with cerebral palsy," says Rena Gropper. "Because he articulated slowly and with great difficulty, everyone thought he was dumb and always interrupted him, but if you let him finish, you hear how bright and original his thinking was."

Terry Keegan, an interpreter for the deaf, has become friends with many deaf people and roomed for two years with a coworker who is deaf. "If they don't understand what we're saying it's not because they're stupid but because we aren't speaking front face or we can't sign." Keegan believes all hearing people should learn 100 basic words in Ameslan, American Sign Language. "Historically, this wonderful language has been suppressed. Deaf people were forced to use speech, lipreading, and hearing aids so they would not look handicapped and would 'fit in' with the rest of us. Their hands were slapped when they tried to sign. This deprived them of a superior communication method. Deafness is not a pathology, it's a difference. When we deny deaf people their deafness, we deny them their identity."

Many nondisabled people have become sensitized to idioms that sound like racial epithets to the disabled, such as "the blind leading the blind" or "that's a lame excuse." Some find "handicapped" demeaning because it derives from "cap in hand." A man who wears leg braces says the issue is accuracy. "*I'm* not handicapped, people's attitudes about me handicap me." Merle Froschl, a nondisabled member of the Women and Disability Awareness Project, points out that the opposite of "disabled" is "*not* disabled"; thus, "nondisabled" is the most neutral term. Disabled people are infuriated by being contrasted with "normal" people—it implies that the disabled are "abnormal" and everyone else is perfect. And the term "able-bodied" inspires the question, Able to do what: Run a marathon? See without glasses? Isn't it all relative?

"Differently abled" and "physically challenged" had a brief vogue, but, says Harilyn Rousso, those terms "made me feel I really had something to hide." Rousso, a psychotherapist who has cerebral palsy, emphasizes, "Friends who care the most sometimes think they're doing you a favor by using euphemisms or saying 'I never think of you as disabled.' The reason they don't want to acknowledge my disability is that they think it's so negative. Meanwhile, I'm trying to recognize it as a valid part of me. I'm more complex than my disability and I don't want my friends to be obsessed by it. But it's clearly there, like my eye color, and I want my friends to appreciate and accept me with it."

The point is not that there is a "right way" to talk to people who are disabled but that friendship carries with it the obligation to *know thy friends,* their sore points and their preferences. That includes knowing what words hurt their feelings as well as when and how to help them do what they cannot do for themselves.

"Each disabled person sends out messages about what they need," says Froschl. "One friend who is blind makes me feel comfortable about taking her arm crossing the street, another dislikes physical contact and wants to negotiate by cane. I've learned not to automatically do things for disabled people since they often experience help as patronizing."

"I need someone to pour cream in my coffee, but in this culture, it's not acceptable to ask for help," say Rousso, adding that women's ordinary problems with dependence are intensified by disability. "I have to feel very comfortable with my friends before I can explain my needs openly and trust that their reaction will not humiliate both of us. For some people it raises too many anxieties."

Anxieties that surround the unknown are dissipated by familiarity. Maybe that explains why so many disabled-nondisabled friendships are composed of classmates or coworkers who spend a lot of time together.

"There are those who can deal with disability and those who can't," says Phil Draper, a quadriplegic whose spinal cord was injured in a car accident. "If they can't—if they get quiet or talk nervously or avoid our eyes—the work of the relationship falls entirely on us. We need friends who won't treat us as weirdo asexual second-class children or expect us to be 'Supercrips'—miracle cripples who work like crazy to make themselves whole again. Ninety-nine percent of us aren't going to be whole no matter what we do. We want to be accepted the way we are."

To accept friends like Phil Draper, the nondisabled have to confront their unconscious fears of vulnerability and death. In one study, 80 percent of nondisabled people said they would be comfortable having someone in a wheelchair as their friend. But "being in a wheelchair" came immediately after "blind" and "deaf-mute" as the affliction they themselves would least want to have.[13] If we fear being what our friend is, that feeling is somewhere in the friendship.

Nondisabled people also have to disavow the cult of perfectability. Disabled people are not going to "get better" because they are not "sick"; they are generally healthy people who are not allowed to function fully in this society—as friends or as anything else.

"Friendship is based on people's ability to communicate," says Judy Heumann, the first postpolio person to get a teacher's license in New York City and now a leader of the disability rights movement. "But barriers such as inaccessible homes make it hard for disabled people to just drop in. Spontaneity is something disabled people enjoy infrequently and the nondisabled take for granted.

"While more public places have ramps and bathrooms that accommodate wheelchairs, many parties still occur in inaccessible spaces. If I have to be carried upstairs or if I can't have a drink because I know I won't be able to use the bathroom later, I'll probably decide not to go at all. One way I measure my friends is by whether they have put in the effort and money to make their houses wheelchair-accessible. It shows their sensitivity to me as a person.

"Good friends are conscious of the fact that a movie theater or concert hall has to be accessible before I can join them; they share my anger and frustration if it's not. They understand why I'm not crazy about big parties where all the non-disabled are standing up and I'm at ass-level. It makes me able to function more as an equal within the group if people sit down to talk to me. I can't pretend I'm part of things if I can't hear anyone. I don't want to *not* be invited to large parties—I just want people to be sensitive to my needs.

"I always need help cooking, cleaning, driving, going to the bathroom, getting dressed. I pay an attendant to do most of those things for me but sometimes I have to ask a friend for help, which presents a lot of opportunities for rejection. Often, the friends who come through best are other disabled people whose disabilities complement mine. I can help a blind woman with her reading, child care, and traveling around town; she can do the physical things I need. And we don't have to appreciate each other's help, we can just accept it." . . .

Cross-Age Friendship

I am now 46, my husband is 51. Among our good friends are two couples who are old enough to be our parents. One woman, a poet, can be counted on for the latest word on political protests and promising writers. She and I once spent a month together at a writer's colony. The other woman—as energetic and as well-read as anyone I know—is also involved in progressive causes. Although the men of both couples have each had a life-threatening illness, the one with a heart condition is a brilliant civil liberties lawyer and the one who had a stroke is a prize-winning novelist with stunning imaginative powers. The lawyer taught our son to play chess when he was 5. The novelist has encouraged our daughters to write stories ever since they could read. The men have been fine surrogate grandfathers.

When I described these couples to someone my own age, he said, "Ah, it's easy to be friends with *interesting* old people, but what about the dull ones?" The answer is, I am not friends with dull young or middle-aged people so why should I want to be friends with dull old people? And why does he immediately think in terms of old people *not* being interesting? Perhaps the crux of the problem with cross-generational friendship is this *double* double standard. First, to think we "ought" to be friends with the elderly—as a class—denies old people the dignity of individuality and devalues their friendship through condescension. But second, to assume that those who are young or in mid-life will necessarily be more interesting and attractive than those over 65 maintains a double standard of expectation that cheats younger people of friends like ours.

Ageism hurts all ages. And it begins early: Studies show that 3-year-olds already see old people as sick, tired, and ugly and don't want to associate with them.[14] Older people also have their biases about youthful behavior. Some 70-year-olds think children are undependable, unappreciative, ask too many questions, and must be told what to do. They believe teenagers are callow, impatient, and unseasoned.[15]

The authors of *Grandparents/Grandchildren* write, "We shouldn't blame adolescents for not being adults. To become adults, the young need to be around adults."[16] But age segregation keeps us apart. Without benefit of mutual acquaintance, stereotypes mount, brick by brick, until there is a wall high enough to conceal the real human beings on either side.

Another big problem is miscommunication. Conversations between young and old often founder because "sensory, physical, or cognitive differences" cause "distortion, message failure, and social discomfort."[17] That's a fancy way of saying they can't understand each other. And anyone who has ever talked with a young person whose span of concentration is the length of a TV commercial or with an old person whose mind wanders to the blizzard of '48 when asked how to dress for today's weather will understand how each generation's communication style can be a problem for the other.

But stereotypes and miscommunication do not entirely account for the gulf between young and old. Homophily—the attraction to the similar self—is the missing link. Those who are going through the same thing at the same time find it comforting to have friends who mirror their problems and meet their needs, and, usually, people of similar chronological age are going through parallel experiences with wage-earning, setting up house, child-rearing, and other life-cycle events.

Age-mates also tend to have in common the same angle of vision on history and culture. Two 65-year-olds watching a film about the Depression or World War II can exchange memories and emotional responses that are unavailable to a 30-year-old who did not live through those cataclysms. And while a person of 18 and one of 75 might both love Vivaldi, their simultaneous appreciation for Bruce Springsteen is unlikely.

Claude Fischer's studies reveal that more than half of all friend-partners are fewer than five years apart. But the span is reduced to two years if their relationship dates back to their youth when age gradations matter the most and the places where youngsters meet—school, camp, military service, and entry-level jobs—are more age-segregated. Contrary to popular wisdom, elderly people, like the rest of us, prefer friends of their own age. The more old people there are in a given community the more likely it is that each one will have a preponderance of same-age friends. And, believe it or not, a majority of old people say they think it's more important for them to have age-mates than family as their intimates.

Given this overwhelming preference for homophily at every age, why am I on the bandwagon for cross-generational friendship? Because when it's good, it's very, very good—both for friends of different ages who are undergoing similar experiences at the same time and for friends of different ages who are enjoying their differences.

- A 38-year-old woman meets 22-year-olds in her contracts class at law school.
- A couple in their early forties enrolled in a natural childbirth course make friends with parents-to-be who are twenty years younger.
- Three fathers commiserate about the high cost of college; two are in their forties, the third is a 60-year-old educating his second family.

Age-crossing friendships become less unusual as Americans follow more idiosyncratic schedules for marrying, having children, and making career decisions.

But there are other reasons for feeling that age is immaterial to friendship. Marie Wilson, a 45-year-old foundation executive who has five children of high school age or older, told me, "My friends are in their early thirties, and they have kids under 8. But these women are where I am in my head. We became close working together on organizing self-help for the poor. Most women my age are more involved in suburban life or planning their own career moves."

Sharing important interests can be as strong a basis for friendship as is experiencing the same life-cycle events. However, without either of those links, the age difference can sit between the young and the old like a stranger. I'm not asking that we deny that difference but that we free ourselves from what Victoria Secunda calls "the tyranny of age assumptions"[18] and that we entertain the possibility of enriching ourselves through our differences. . . .

As we cross all these lines and meet at many points along the life cycle, people of diverse ages, like people of every class and condition, are discovering that we who are in so many ways "the same and different" can also be friends.

REVIEW QUESTIONS

1. According to the author, when we engage in a cross-cultural relationship, what do we typically need to explain about it to ourselves? To each other? To our friends?
2. What is meant by Pogrebin's label, "the same but never quite the same"?
3. In the paragraph before the heading "The Hazards of Crossing," the author distinguishes *double consciousness* from a *denial of differences*. What do those two terms mean?
4. The essay includes a story about a white couple asking their black friend, Bill Tatum, to take some food to their black housekeeper who lived in Harlem and was sick. Tatum was shocked to discover the housekeeper living in a filthy slum. What was racist about the white couple's "generosity"?
5. How accurate is Pogrebin's summary of each side's views in the section titled "Gay-Straight Debate"?
6. What is the point of the author's discussion of the words we use to label disabled persons?
7. Paraphrase the following comment by Pogrebin: "If we fear being what our friend *is*, that feeling is somewhere in the friendship."

PROBES

1. Which of the three kinds of explaining that Pogrebin describes has been most difficult for you?

2. That author claims that "many Americans assume people with an accent are ignorant" and that "many ethnics assume, just as incorrectly, that someone *without* an accent is smart." How is this distorted value mirrored in the major television networks' choice of news anchors and reporters?
3. You may be surprised to read a discussion of gay/straight relationships here. What might justify putting a discussion of this topic in this book?
4. Do you commonly think about relationships with disabled persons as examples of "intercultural communication"? What happens when you do?
5. What problems have you encountered in your relationships with older persons? What is the most helpful thing Pogrebin says about these relationships?

NOTES

1. L. Rohter, "Immigrant Factory Workers Share Dream, Luck and a Lotto Jackpot," *New York Times*, August 23, 1985.
2. G. Allport, *The Nature of Prejudice*, Doubleday, Anchor Press, 1958.
3. J. Provinzano, "Settling Out and Settling In." Papers presented at annual meeting of the American Anthropological Association, November 1974.
4. D. Riesman, R. Denney, and N. Glazer, *The Lonely Crowd: A Study of the Changing American Character*, Yale University Press, 1950.
5. B. M. Campbell, "Friendship in Black and White," Ms., August 1983.
6. B. Adelman, *Down Home: Camden, Alabama*, Times Books, Quadrangle, 1972.
7. R. Atsumi, "Tsukiai—Obligatory Personal Relationships of Japanese White Collar Employees," *Human Organization*, vol. 38, no. 1 (1979).
8. F. Douglass, *Narrative of the Life of Frederick Douglass, an American Slave*, New American Library, Signet, 1968.
9. B. Hooks, *Ain't I a Woman: Black Women and Feminism*, South End Press, 1981.
10. P. M. Palmer, "White Women/Black Women: The Dualism of Female Identity and Experience in the United States," *Feminist Studies*, Spring 1983.
11. S. O. Murray, "The Institutional Elaboration of a Quasi-Ethnic Community," *International Review of Modern Sociology*, vol. 9, no. 2 (1979).
12. J. C. Albro and C. Tully, "A Study of Lesbian Lifestyles in the Homosexual Micro-Culture and the Heterosexual Macro-Culture," *Journal of Homosexuality*, vol. 4, no. 4 (1979).
13. L. M. Shears and C. J. Jensema, "Social Acceptability of Anomalous Persons," *Exceptional Children*, October 1969.
14. R. K. Jantz et al., *Children's Attitudes Toward the Elderly*, University of Maryland Press, 1976.
15. A. G. Cryns and A. Monk, "Attitudes of the Aged Toward the Young," *Journal of Gerontology*, vol. 1 (1972); see also, C. Seefeld et al., "Elderly Persons' Attitude Toward Children,": *Educational Gerontology*, vol. 8, no. 4 (1982).
16. K. L. Woodward and A. Kornhaber, *Grandparents, Grandchildren: The Vital Connection* (Doubleday, Anchor Press, 1981), quoted in "Youth Is Maturing Later," *New York Times*, May 10, 1985.

17. L. J. Hess and R. Hess, "Inclusion, Affection, Control: The Pragmatics of Intergenerational Communication." Paper presented at the Conference on Communication and Gerontology of the Speech Communication Association, July 1981.
18. V. Secunda, *By Youth Possessed: The Denial of Age in America*, Bobbs-Merrill, 1984.

*T*his reading presents an American-Soviet case study of some of the challenges of bridging cultural differences. University of Massachusetts communication teacher and researcher Donal Carbaugh reports about what happened when talk-show host Phil Donohue transplanted his television show to Moscow in 1987. Carbaugh focuses on the first 3 minutes and 40 seconds of a show in which Donohue tried to engage his Soviet audience in a discussion of sexual activity and contraception. The result was partly a reflection of Moscow society in 1987; things have changed considerably since then. But this article is still an excellent example of what can happen when significantly different cultural assumptions and patterns clash.

With the help of a transcript of the crucial part of the show, Carbaugh focuses on the definitions of "selves" that characterized each of the cultures in this clash. Donohue, says Carbaugh, presumed that members of his Soviet audience might be interested in doing something about the unwanted pregnancies and irresponsible premarital sex that Donohue believed were widespread in Russia. But the speech that Donohue produces out of his definition of the situation is, from the standpoint of his Soviet audience, at least inappropriate, and maybe even incoherent. After several uncomfortable exchanges, one audience member says in English, "it is necessary to change the subject," which Donohue eventually does.

As Carbaugh explains, Donohue introduced topics, specific words, and a sequence of questioning that were understandable in U.S. culture as "problem talk"—a discussion of an important social problem. But this clashed directly with the Soviet assumption that one does not discuss sexual matters in public, especially with outsiders. This was a moral prescription that Donahue violated. The result, and this is one crucial point of Carbaugh's analysis, was not just that the two cultures clashed, but that the people involved moved immediately to explanations for the clash that increased the distance between them. "You Americans can't understand us," was one claim. Another was that these Americans, who are used to so many serious social problems in their own culture, are trying to *create* problems in Soviet society. From Donohue's U.S. perspective, the existence of serious social problems was obvious, and *talk* was a way to help solve them. But from the Soviet audience members' point of view, it was the American penchant for talking about such problems that in fact created them.

Carbaugh also contrasts the two views of the person that emerged in the American-Soviet exchange. The American person has two main parts, the outer and the inner, and speaking is a useful way to make inner things known to others. The Soviet person also has two main parts, but they are the body and the soul, and the soul experiences events that should not and cannot be put into words. This view of the person led Donohue's Soviet listeners to hear the topic of "sex" that Donohue wanted to discuss as being more animal than human. For them, sexual relations were an important part of the undiscussable essence of a marriage. All this helped render Donohue's talk profoundly inappropriate.

You may very well never try to discuss sexuality and contraception with people from a culture very different from your own. But you can still learn from this article how culturally "normal" ways of speaking presume a view of persons, and that cultures can clash when these views of persons differ. Situations like these are ripe for the application of the communication attitudes and skills that are discussed throughout this book.

MEDIATING CULTURAL SELVES:

Soviet and American Cultures in a Televised "Spacebridge"

Donal Carbaugh

CONVERSATION AND CULTURAL SELVES

The general capacity to be bound by moral rules may well belong to the individual, but the particular set of rules which transforms him into a human being derives from requirements established in the ritual organization of social encounters. (Goffman, 1967, p. 45)

Conversation, from one view, is everywhere a culturally situated accomplishment, shaped as it is by local codes, local expressions of what persons and social relations are (and should be), what persons can (and should) do, and what, if anything, can (and should) be felt. But nowhere do participants invoke the same codes, the same currents of culture, on all conversational occasions. Nor anywhere do these necessarily situate all participants in the same way. This latter dynamic—of crosscurrents in talk—is especially pronounced on intercultural and multicultural occasions when various communication codes—various beliefs about persons, actions, and feelings—become deeply perplexing one to the other.[1]

. . . This [reading] explores one such conversational occasion, a televised "Spacebridge," in which two different cultural currents are flowing—one Soviet, the other American.[2] The general theoretical approach informing the study

Excerpt from "Mediating Cultural Selves" by Donal Carbaugh from *Constructing the Self in a Mediated World*, ed. Debra Grodin & Thomas Lindolf, pp. 84–105. Reprinted by permission of Sage Publications, Inc.

of this occasion is elaborated elsewhere.[3] The analytical problem is one of hearing cultural systems in televised conversation, with the general response being one of treating seriously participants' own terms, the dimensions and domains of meaning they invoke, their cultural forms of expression, indigenous conversational rules (or structuring norms), and the meanings about persons, actions, and feelings implicated in these. These concepts, together, provide a general lens with which to view (or hear) culturally communicated meaning systems, with each separately bringing into focus a more specific theoretical concern with regard to particular televised moments. Through the application of the general framework, distinctive cultural currents in this conversation are discovered, with each being a local theory for conducting and interpreting this particular communicative action. . . .

The segment examined in this [reading] appeared as part of a weeklong series titled "Donahue in Russia." The series was taped in Moscow and broadcast in the United States during the week of February 9, 1987. The particular segment of concern to us here consists of the first 3 minutes and 40 seconds of the second program in the series. Other than a brief "talk-over" by Phil Donahue (that lasted 16.8 seconds), the segment—following Donahue's normal production format—underwent no postproduction editing. . . . If the following analyses attain some degree of success, that is, if different cultural features are unveiled, readers should be better positioned to hear and see how cultural selves have shaped this conversation and better positioned to understand why, as one Soviet (bilingual in Russian and English) put it, "They think they're talking about the same thing, but they're not." What, in this televised conversation, has led this person to this conclusion? How could she hear in this encounter (as did others who are members of both communities) not just one but two very different systems operating? How does one hear in this, and other mediated conversations, culture(s) and self at work?

TRANSCRIPT*

1a) DONAHUE: Would you kindly stand for one second, please?
2a) You had sex, when you were 18 years old?

3a) SOVIET MALE A: (trans.): Yes, that's when I started.
 b) (..........)
 c) (..........)

4a) D: Did you use contraceptive when you practiced sex at age 18?
     [Audience laughter]

5a) SMA (trans.): Yes.
 b) Yes.
 c) Да.

*Editor's note: This transcript includes two English translations and the Russian words actually spoken by Donohue's guests.

6a) D: Did you take care of this matter yourself or did the girl insist that
7a)   you do it?

8a) SMA (trans.): Yeah, I knew about it before.
  b) Well (.) I knew it before that (.)
  c) Ну я до этого знал

9a) Before that I knew quite a bit.
  b) I knew a lot before that (.)
  c) Я до того знал уже многое
     [PAN TO AUDIENCE LAUGHTER, SMILES]

10a) I knew how, when, what, etc. I was well prepared.
  b) Well before I knew how, what, why (.) I was well prepared.
  c) Ну до этого знал и как, что, чего... Был хорошо подготовлен.

11a) D: Are most Soviet boys conscientious, like you, in protecting the
12a)   girl from pregnancy?

13a) SMA (trans.): Basically, yes. Why don't you ask the others?
  b) Yes (.) basically, yes (.) But actually ask the people themselves.
  c) Да, в основном да. А вообще-то спросите у ребят самих
     [PAN TO AUDIENCE SMILES]

14a) D: Yes?

15a) Sov. FEMALE A (trans.): You talk as though everybody here was
  b) # You talk as if everyone present here is
  c) Вы так говорите как будто бы вот каждый из пресутствующих

16a) already involved in that. I think when most of my girlfriends had
  b) doing it. I don't know about that, most of my girlfriends
  c) этим занимается. Я не знаю , большенство моих подруг

17a) gotten married at 18 or 20, they were virgins,
  b) got married when they were 18 and 20, and they all were virgins. # (.)
  c) вышли замуж в 18 и 20 они были девушками.

18a) and before marriage they did not engage in sex.
  b) #Before marriage did not even plan on having sex or sexual life.
  c) До брака и вообще не собирались заниматься сексом и сексуальной
     жизнью.

19a) They were waiting for that one special man, for that one special
  b) They were waiting for their one # (.) and only (.)
  c) Они ждали своего одного единственного

20a) person, and they found that one special person.
  b) #marriage with one person # (.) and they found it.

21a) And most of their husbands also, for most of them their wife
  b) And for the majority of their husbands (.)
  c) И для большенства их мужей

22a) also was the first woman with whom they had ever had sexual relations.
  b) as well (.) for them their wife was their first girl. (.)
  c) тоже для них их жена была первая девушка.

23a)
  b) Woman that they liked.
  c) Женщина которая понравилась.

24a) D: Is it true with most girls, most young women are virgins when
25a)   they get married in the Soviet Union?

26a) SFA (trans.): Well, a great number of girls are virgins until marriage.
  b) Well, (.) in general, (.) the larger part of girls are virgins before marriage.
     They just start leading that type of life after marriage.
  c) Ну, ну в общем большая часть девушек является девушками до
    замужества. Они начинают только жить такой жизнью только после
    замужества.

27a) I don't really know, maybe not everybody.
  b) Well, I don't know, maybe not (*all/quite*).
  c) Ну я не знаю может быть не (*все/совсем*)

28a) Sov. Female B (trans.): You know, I just want to say
  b) #I want to say
  c) Я хочу сказать,

29a) that I think it's quite the opposite. You can't really say that it's
  b) on the contrary# well in my opinion if not to say that it is
  c) что наоборот, ну по-моему если не

30a) very good if a girl when she gets married is still a virgin, because
  b) negative (.) you definitely cannot say that it is very good, if the girl when
     getting married is still a virgin (.)
  c) отрицательное , то нельзя сказать что это очень хорошо если девушка
    выходя замуж еще девушка.

31a) I think quite the opposite. She should be quite sure
  b) #Because I think that by that time, she basically should be sure
  c) Потому что я считаю, тогда она вобщем-то уже должна быть уверенна

32a) of what her husband is as a man, that he'll be a real partner
  b) of her husband as a man # (.)
  c) в своем муже как мужчине

33a) for her, otherwise it could be a real tragedy.
  b) because otherwise it could be a tragedy. # (..........) #
  c) а иначе же может быть трагедия а иначе может быть трагедия (.......)

34a) And sex for a married couple is extremely important.
  b) It is very important # (..........) #
  c) Это очень важно(...............)

35a) After all, sex is 80% of happiness for a married couple
  b) Practically (.) makes up, #well, 80% of happiness.
  c) Практически, ну 80 % счастья занимает.

36a) but, of course, that depends on each individual woman.
  b) Of course it depends on every individual woman #
  c) Естественно это зависит от каждой женщины

37a) But for me I think that's very important.
  b) (..........)
  c) (..........)

38a) Sov. Female C: I think it is necessary to change the subject
39a) of conversation, because these questions are very deep
40a) to be concerned by us.
   [AUDIENCE APPLAUSE]
41a) D (speaking over tape): This is day two of our visit to the Soviet
42a) Union. In this hour Soviet teens give a powerful exchange on
43a) everything from religion to war. But unlike American teenagers,
44a) areas they were reluctant to discuss included dating,
45a) school and sexuality.

46a) Sov. Male B (trans.) (in response to an inaudible question by Donahue):
   It's not a surprise that American students can't
  b) (..........)
  c) (..........)

47a) understand us, because they have many more problems
  b) Much more serious problems than (.) ours because (..........)
  c) На много серьезнее проблемы чем у нас потому что (............)

48a) than we have, the criminality, drugs, etc. Secondly,
  b) (..........) Secondly (.)
  c) (..........) во вторых

49a) all boys and girls here are in somewhat different surroundings.
  b) all the young people here (.) found themselves (.) well, in (..........)
  c) все ребята сидящие здесь попали ну в (............)

50a) This is new to them. They've never been on television
  b) (..........) situation. (..........)
  c) (..........) ситуации (..........)

51a) and this is the reason why they can't immediately talk to you
  b) (..........)
  c) (..........)

52a) as they do in America, where they are probably more easy going.
  b) We are not used to (*hanging out*) more uptight (..........) not
  c) Мы не привыкли (*шагаться*) скованней (..............) не вероятно,

53a) and when they may even have experience of being on television.

  b) that they (*have ever been on television*).

  c) что они (*когда-нибудь были на телевиденье*)

54a) SOV. MALE C (trans.): What can we do if everything is all right here?

  b) Well, what can we do if everything is all right? (.)

  c) Ну что мы можем сделать если все в порядке?

55a) Should we create problems?

  b) Should we think up a problem?

  c) Что, проблему придумать?

56a) SOV. MALE D (trans.): We don't want to invent problems. Why?

  b) We don't want to invent ourselves the problems. Why?

  c) Мы не хотим придумывать себе проблем. Зачем?

    [LAUGHTER AND APPLAUSE]

57a) SOV. MALE E: School is likewise, sometimes you are happy

58a) and sometimes you express just no particular emotions,

59a) and that's all.

60a) D: All right, I will listen to your advice and I will change the
61a) subject.

RITUAL AND CULTURAL DISCOURSES

Some conversational episodes foreground a particular interactional goal: the remedy of improprieties. More than anyone, Goffman (1967) has drawn our attention to the ritualized form of this type of corrective process:

> When the participants in an undertaking or encounter fail to prevent the occurrence of an event that is expressively incompatible with the judgments of social worth that are being maintained, and when the event is of the kind that is difficult to overlook, then the participants are likely to give it accredited status as an incident—to ratify it as a threat that deserves direct official attention—and to proceed to try to correct for its effects. At this point one or more participants find themselves in an established state of ritual disequilibrium or disgrace, and an attempt must be made to reestablish a satisfactory ritual state for them. (p. 19)

. . . Let us look briefly at the ritual Donahue invokes here, then at the Soviet one that engulfs him.[4] It is no surprise that Donahue, in his opening segment, initiates discussion with a version of the ritual form that is familiar to him and his American audience. In his first utterances on lines 1-2, 4, 6-7, 11-12, and 24-25, Donahue inquires about sex, contraceptive use, pregnancy, and virginity. Topics such as these, Donahue presumes, provide an exigence for public discourse, just as similar topics do in his homeland, erected on the communal assumption, in Bitzer's (1968) terms, that there is an "imperfection marked by urgency" (p. 10). In this case, presumably, the imperfection consists of unwanted pregnancies and perhaps irresponsible premarital sex.[5] The scene is a rhetorical one in that Donahue presumes it can be positively modified, with a partial remedy possibly created through the means of public discourse. Donahue presumes his interlocutors can be influenced by televised discourse and thus can subsequently become "mediators of change" (Bitzer, 1968, p. 11) better equipped (or informed?) to redress these presumed imperfections. Donahue, then, attempts to co-create with his audience a kind of ritualized and rhetorical action, to display what he considers to be "a fitting response to a situation which needs and invites it" (Bitzer, 1968, p. 2). The exigence (e.g., the unwanted pregnancies), the means of responding (e.g., public discourse, confessions, truth-sayings), and its meanings (e.g., the remedy of a societal impropriety through public participation) all cohere from this view. Together, they provide a common and productive way to address social problems through open, public discussion, that is, by engaging in an American communication ritual. Donahue's interrogative utterances, as such, are not just journalistic questions or directives, they are moves in a culturally expressive—albeit ritually performed—game.[6]

The ritualized speech that Donahue presumes and initiates, however, from the standpoint of the Soviet expressive order, is inappropriate, even incoherent. Immediately at lines 2-4, Donahue's interlocutor is taken aback (i.e., literally steps back from Donahue) while others laugh out loud, smile broadly, and whisper in each other's ears. The exigence Donahue invites his audience to address (e.g., the unwanted pregnancies) becomes immediately supplanted by another of their own (i.e., the foreign talk show host's unusual conduct). This imperfection grows with mounting urgency until finally, on lines 38-40, a woman speaks in English, the first Soviet to do so, and tells Donahue, to the delighted applause of her "contemporaries,"[7] that "it is necessary to change the subject," which Donahue eventually, on lines 60-61, agrees to do.

An American Voice

Note the question by Donahue on line 2: "You had sex when you were 18 years old?" He probes the issue by asking further about "contraceptive use" (line 4) and who took "care of this matter" (6), "protecting the girl from pregnancy" (11-12). What exotic American tree is planted here, but later uprooted from Soviet soil? What must be presumed for these comments indeed to be intelligible?

Donahue's speech characterizes a kind of human activity, presumably coitus, as "had sex" and "practiced sex"; he refers to it as an activity that is "practiced," then associates this "practice" with a technique, the "use" [of] a "contraceptive"; probes which individual was responsible for its "use"; and mentions a biological motive for contraception ("protection from pregnancy"). Human procreative activity is communicated here, then, as "sex," as an experience one "has" or "practices" in a particular way, which involves as part of the practice the possibility of contraceptive use, with this use being a primary responsibility of one of the involved individuals, because "protection" from deleterious biological consequences is desirable or necessary. The symbolic structuring of the topic invoked by Donahue thus draws attention—and directs subsequent discussion—to at least three prominent American cultural domains: physical facts (who did this activity, at what age, with what biological consequences), technical utilities (what techniques or technologies were used), and individual actions (did *you* do it—who is responsible). The tone used for the discussion could be characterized as a "serious rationality" that foregrounds not the passionate bonds among persons, or their moral status, but "sex" as a factual, technical, "practice" among individuals.[8]

Note further the sequence of symbols used, from "sex" (2, 4) to protection from "pregnancy" (11-12). The symbolic sequence takes "sex" in the direction of a problem of unwanted pregnancy and brings closer to the interactional surface other projectable problems that are culturally associated with this, problems such as premarital sex, irresponsible sexual practices, single-parent families, abortion, venereal diseases, AIDS, issues of morality, welfare systems, the population explosion, and so on. To an American ear, exposed to such a system, all of this could come to pass rather naturally. One can hear, without too much strain or reflection, even if angered by this line of questioning, the kind of thing Donahue is "getting at."

This line of questioning demonstrates a kind of "problem talk," or self-help dialogue, that functions—in part—to foreground various imperfections and thus to motivate subsequent utterances. The communicative form, a round-the-rally of problems-responses, involves a three-part spiraling sequence that introduces a topic, renders it problematic, precipitating responses that redress or further elaborate the problems.[9] . . .

Hearing Donahue as one engaged in this culturally expressive practice, then, leads us to hear that one might discuss this topic (i.e., coitus) in public, that it might be called "sex," that it might be symbolically constituted as a physical, technical, individual activity, that facts about it might be discussed rationally and seriously, that it is discussed and discussable as problematic. All of this is at least intelligible (if not entirely acceptable) to an American audience. . . .

These beliefs about the person are associated with the beliefs about talk and implicate a system of cultural premises:

> The person has two main parts:
>   the physical (body) and, within it,
>   the nonmaterial (thought and feeling).
>
> The nonmaterial cannot be seen.
>
> It is a part of an inner world.
>
> Things are not part of that world.
>
> Other people can't know what things happen in that part.
>
> Speaking makes these things known to others and is a preferred action.

These premises create a cultural notion of person that includes a body and its "mindful" part, the nonmaterial seat of personal being, which becomes the cultural site of discursive action and feeling.[10]

Turning back to our utterance, then, by Donahue on line 2, he is asking for a factual disclosure (confession?) about a Soviet male's "individual self" (not the public's collective morality), about his physical experiences on an issue deemed publicly important and problematic. In so asking, he creates a cultural discursive space into which he expects his interlocutor to move. His hope is to create, with his Soviet interlocutors, a ritualized—albeit American—public discussion. So designed, it is presumed that each person—"self"—can (and should) rationally discuss his or her own experience, thoughts, and feelings, display a serious rationality about "sex," thereby help to remedy the difficult exigence, the presumed "problems" with the Soviet person and "society." These meanings, or something like them, must be hearable for his speech to make sense. With them, we hear a culture at work, upon a televised, intercultural occasion.

A Soviet Reply

Immediately upon hearing Donahue's first question, the Soviet audience is aroused. Eyebrows are raised, laughter ensues, torsoes wave back and forth, and startled glances are exchanged. At one level, and following the corrective action taken by the Soviet woman on lines 38-40, we might explain much by positing the Soviet rule: In public discussions, especially with outsiders, it is not preferable (even though possible) to discuss sexual matters. It is this moral proscription, evidently, that Donahue has violated with his line of questioning (1-2, 6-7, 11-12), thus precipitating the above reactions. The rule also accounts for some of the expressed embarrassment and reserve by the two Soviet women who spoke. As Donahue notes in his talk-over (line 44), "They were reluctant to discuss." For an American ear, we hear through this phrasing an implication that "something fishy is going on," perhaps more evidence of a "closed society"—people unable, perhaps even constrained by the state, to speak their mind. But, as stated, we have a negative, a general moral proscription, a how not to speak. What, then, is affirmed? What communication, from the standpoint of the Soviet expressive order, should be forthcoming? And what does it instantiate that is cultural? What does it say about persons, social relations, talk, and feeling?

At this point, the justifications offered by the Soviet males on lines 46-59 help orient our interpretation. Note that the utterances take on an agonistic form, a contrasting of "your" ways with "ours." A comment made consistently and recurrently throughout the dialogues appears on lines 46-47: You Americans "can't understand us." Although several reasons are given elsewhere by the Soviets for this (e.g., a biased and uninformed American media, poorly educated about Soviet culture and history), the reasons that express the difference here are that you "have many more problems than we have, the criminality, drugs, etc." and Americans are accustomed to "being on television" and talking a certain way, but we (the Soviets) are not. What is amplified and applauded, to the delight of the audience, is this: "What can we do if everything is all right here? Should we create problems? We don't want to invent problems. Why?"

These Soviets have heard Donahue plodding down a problem-strewn path that to them is incoherent—thus laughable—in this public context. "Should we create problems" just so we have something to talk with you about? There are at least two premises supporting the Soviets' question. First, we do not have these problems of premarital sex, drugs, and criminality. They are not parts of our lives. Indeed, during some interviewing, this position was asserted as an actual truth. Such things are said not to be part of some Soviet lives: "We don't hear about these things in our press, and we don't live with these kinds of people [drug users, criminals]. Sure, it might exist somewhere, but it's not part of my life, in my community." Given this as an uncontested discursive fact, then indeed "problems" such as these—at least for the immediate interactional moment—are ruled out of social existence. . . .

Listening with these Soviet rules, the form, and dimensions, one begins to hear in this talk a Soviet sense and, with it, to discover the various interactional sources of Donahue's breach. Here he brings to a public, collective forum, where shared virtues guide discussion, a private matter that he explores through personal, individual, and scientific or factual terms. The exigence he creates, or the "precipitating event" as Goffman called it, includes a configuration of at least these features: An improper topic (sex rather than the common morality of public life) is brought to a setting and discussed in an improper way (scientifically rational, technical, and individual rather than moral, passionate, and corporate) through an improper form (foregrounding societal problems rather than shared virtues) . . . Private expression involves more intensely passionate sayings that are, as the woman in lines 30-40 put it, "very deep to be concerned by us." Private discourse among insiders runs deeper and involves greater volubility. Soviet beliefs about public talk, then, orient to shared moral bases of life and distinguish a kind of *reserve* in *public* with *outsiders* from a greater *expressiveness* in *private* among *insiders*.

Our interpretation here can be extended by recourse to a central Russian cultural symbol, *dusa* (roughly, "soul"), which the Soviet woman's phrase, "very deep," and the above dimensions culturally invoke. The beliefs about the person associated with this cultural symbol and elaborated with this expressive system create, like the American system, a *persona* of two parts, but the deeply felt, focal symbolic site of being differs:[11]

The person has two main parts:
    the body and the soul.

One cannot see but one can feel the soul.

Because of the soul, things can happen in and among persons that cannot happen in anything other than persons.

These things can be good or bad.

Because of this part, a person can feel things that nothing other than persons can feel.

This symbolically constructed notion of the Soviet person identifies a dynamic integrative world that is "above all, emotional" and morally colored, *and* that holds strong transcendental overtones (Wierzbicka, 1989, p. 52). *Dusa* not only symbolizes a model person as a distinct physical body with a rational and mindful self within, but further contrasts this organismic entity with a kind of cosmological connectedness, with a transcendent moral (good or bad), deeply feeling, and distinctly interhuman realm. The desired locus of discourse, when forthcoming in public or in private, is not so much a rational, scientifically technical, individual utility as it is a passionate, morally connected, shared feeling.[12] As Pasternak put it in *Doctor Zhivago,* "You in others, that's what your soul [dusa] is.[13] Preferred Soviet sayings usher forth, at least generally and characteristically, as soul-felt and relational expressions more than individually mindful and factual disclosures.

The Soviet form for public discussion, conversational rules, and premises of personhood thus place us in a better position to hear this intercultural segment, especially the topic of "sex." Note that, for Soviets, the concept "sex" entitles an activity that is more in the animalistic domain than it is in the distinctively human. As such, it violates the Russian sense of "soul," for the deeper soul of the person can and should involve only those things that can happen in persons. As one Soviet woman put it: "Sex is something animals do." To discuss this topic in a factual, rational, scientific way, with regard to contraceptive techniques and "practices," in public terms of "animalistic mechanics," rather than in a proper moral tone of deep feeling that weds it with a common morality and with uniquely human sensual passion, all of this is rather incoherent, thus laughable to Soviets. It is easier to see, then, how a Soviet female, upon viewing the segment, discussed how the first male speaker was *put in the position* of being a "fool and jerk," for he was swept into more rational/factual disclosures of individual, personally problematic, and animalistic experiences with "sex." The proper tone, form, and meanings, matters of the soul, virtuous positions, and unified themes were being wholly supplanted and elided. . . .

The above interpretations offer several initial substantive findings with regard to Soviet and American patterns of televised communication, with each distinctive in its ritualized form. We find, on the one hand, a soulful collective conversing on the basis of morality, orienting to the possible virtues of societal life. On the other hand, we find mindful individuals conversing on the basis of factual information, disclosing their real personal experiences in response to societal problems and issues. The former might sense the latter, at times, as soulless (lacking morality, commitment, and loyalty to the common good), just as the latter might sense the former as mindless (lacking factual information and analytic abilities). These statements are, of course, generalities, characterizations of two distinctive discursive styles, but they capture some of the conversational and cultural bases in this mediated conduct, and they identify some of the sources whereby each conceives of and evaluates the other. This general reading, built as it is around the cultural selves of each, is erected on the particular televised dynamics detailed above (see Carbaugh, 1993b, pp. 195–196).[14] . . .

Thus cultural selves view and verbalize the life of television, sometimes in distinctively ritualized forms, such that, within this single televised event, one seeks facts while another speaks morality. To know how this is so, we must hear in televised conversation not only generic forms and channels but with them cultural beliefs about selves and media.

REVIEW QUESTIONS

1. Paraphrase Carbaugh's first statement, that "conversation . . . is everywhere a culturally situated accomplishment."
2. What does Carbaugh mean when he says Donohue's talk follows "a ritual form"?
3. What is problem talk?
4. Paraphrase Carbaugh's claim that the Soviet audience responded to Donohue's questioning as they did because "an improper topic . . . is brought to a setting and discussed in an improper way . . . through an improper form."
5. Explain the significance of the Russian sense of *dusa*, or "soul," in this exchange.
6. Paraphrase Carbaugh's next to last line: "one seeks facts while another speaks morality."

PROBES

1. How is Carbaugh's view of conversation and culture (expressed in his first paragraph) similar to the view of culture I introduced in Chapter 2?
2. What is the significance, in this exchange between Donohue and his Soviet audience, of Donohue's discussion of sex as a physical, almost technical, activity? How does this approach fit or fail to fit into Soviet expectations?
3. Contrast the American and Soviet views of the person that each begins, "The person has two main parts. . ." How do these two views help explain this specific culture clash?
4. How might Donohue have discussed sexuality and contraception in ways that were viewed as *appropriate* by his Soviet audience?
5. Think of a clash between two cultural groups familiar to you—youth versus elders, whites versus blacks, wealthy versus homeless, pro-life versus pro-choice. How might Carbaugh's analysis of this American–Soviet event inform your understanding of the more familiar intercultural clash?

NOTES

1. For a treatment of televised discourse as culturally coded, see Donald Carbaugh (1988, 1990b).
2. Throughout the chapter, I use the term *Soviet* because that was the main term used by my informants and because the patterns I report were produced by speakers from various ethnic groups within the now dismantled "Soviet Union." The term is, of course, not without its difficulties. I switch to the term *Russian* when the analysis suggests a distinctly Russian feature. Following standard usage, *American* refers to patterns prominent and distinctive within the United States.
3. The ethnographic approach derives from Dell Hymes (1972), with recent formulations in Gerry Philipsen (1987, 1990) and Carbaugh (1990a, 1990b, 1991, 1995).

4. The interpretations of the Soviet communication system were produced in collaboration with Olga Beloded, Diane Chornenkaya, Lazlo Dienes, Joseph Lake, and Vicki Rubinshteyn, among others.

5. As Donahue might know, part of the unspoken consensus in urban Soviet common culture is that many women have multiple abortions, with numbers in the twenties and thirties not uncommon. See Hedrick Smith (1976, pp. 187-191).

6. See Tamar Katriel and Gerry Philipsen (1981) and Carbaugh (1988, pp. 153-176).

7. See Clifford Geertz (1973, pp. 365-366).

8. A similar introduction to the topic of "sex" was made by an American medical doctor on a college campus who was conducting a "workshop on sex education and birth control." He began with, "Tonight we're going to talk about sex. We're here to talk about social things, not moral issues. Whether it's right or wrong, good or bad, you'll have to decide for yourself. We're just going to talk about sex" (reported in "Condoms, Spermicides?" 1991, p. 3).

9. See Carbaugh (1988, pp. 127-166).

10. This is adapted from Anna Wierzbicka (1989). For a related discussion of the person, see Rom Harré (1984).

11. The following formulation is adapted from Wierzbicka (1989).

12. Realizing this helped me reflect upon what had been a very puzzling situation. A Russian student had called me at home one evening and asked, with no explanation, the date of my birth. Later, I realized the student was making decisions about advisory committees and wanted to know my astrological sign as a way of interpreting the nature of our connection within a transcendentally connective, feeling-full domain. The inference I draw from this exchange is not, of course, that all Russians are astrologers or actors on cosmic feeling. What the exchange displays, I think, is a communicative instance of a cultural orientation that itself coheres activities in terms more passionate, transcendentally connected, and feeling-full than does the American, centered as it is in terms of scientific rationality, expressive technicality, and individual utility.

13. The quotation is taken from the Russian version; see Wierzbicka (1989, p. 54).

14. The primary data for this report were gathered in 1987-1990, prior to the dismantling of the Soviet Union. What effects these recent political developments may have on the patterns described here are currently unknown. For some informants, the patterns described here are very durable, even in the face of pressures to change. As one informant put it, "We don't know how to do it any other way," with "it" referring to their habitual patterns of expressive life. For the robustness and pervasiveness of traditional Russian styles, see Jane Kramer (1990). Whether these cultural dynamics apply more generally cannot be firmly asserted on the basis of this report. I can, however, add that I have witnessed the Soviet-Russian pattern identified here in many contexts in the United States, in Europe, and in Russia. Various readers of this report assure me they have observed these patterns in various places including in Israel among Russian immigrants. Perhaps most gratifying have been reactions by Russians, various scholars of Russian culture and history, and Russian

scholars themselves, the latter soliciting this chapter for publication in a Russian journal. I mention this not to claim any final word in the matter—in fact, I see what is here as only a beginning—but to suggest that this report, whatever its flaws, has struck at least some cultural chord. How broadly the Soviet and American patterns apply and, if so, how intercultural encounters between them display these patterns, and to what extent these apply to various contexts and media of communication—all of this warrants further study.

REFERENCES

Bitzer, L. (1968). The rhetorical situation. *Philosophy and Rhetoric, 1,* 1-14.

Carbaugh, D. (1988). *Talking American: Cultural discourses on Donahue.* Norwood, NJ: Ablex.

Carbaugh, D. (Ed.). (1990a). *Cultural communication and intercultural contact.* Hillsdale, NJ: Lawrence Erlbaum.

Carbaugh, D. (1990b). Intercultural communication. In D. Carbaugh (Ed.), *Cultural communication and intercultural contact* (pp. 151-175). Hillsdale, NJ: Lawrence Erlbaum.

Carbaugh, D. (1991). Communication and cultural interpretation. *Quarterly Journal of Speech, 77,* 336-342.

Carbaugh, D. (1993b). "Soul" and "self": Soviet and American cultures in conversation. *Quarterly Journal of Speech, 79,* 182-200.

Carbaugh, D. (1995). An ethnographic theory of communication. In D. Cushman & B. Kovacic (Eds.), *Watershed theories of human communication.* Albany: State University of New York Press.

Condoms, spermicides? Dr. Abel doesn't blush. (1991, May 13). *Collegian,* p. 3.

Geertz, C. (1973). *The interpretation of cultures.* New York: Basic Books.

Goffman, E. (1967). *Interaction ritual: Essays on face-to-face behavior.* New York: Pantheon.

Hymes, D. (1972). Models of the interaction of language and social life. In J. Gumperz & D. Hymes (Eds.), *Directions in sociolinguistics: The ethnography of communication* (pp. 35-71). New York: Holt, Rinehart & Winston.

Katriel, T., & Philipsen, G. (1981). "What we need is communication": "Communication" as a cultural category in some American speech. *Communication Monographs, 48,* 301-317.

Kramer, J. (1990, March 12). Letter from Europe. *New Yorker, 74,* 76-90.

Philipsen, G. (1987). The prospect for cultural communication. In L. Kincaid (Ed.), *Communication theory: Eastern and Western perspectives* (pp. 245-254). New York: Academic Press.

Philipsen, G. (1990). An ethnographic approach to communication studies. In B. Dervin, L. Grossberg, B. O'Keefe, & E. Wartella (Eds.), *Rethinking communication: Vol. 2. Paradigm exemplars* (pp. 258-268). Newbury Park, CA: Sage.

Smith, H. (1976). *The Russians.* New York: Ballantine.

Wierzbicka, A. (1989). Soul and mind: Linguistic evidence for ethnopsychology and cultural history. *American Anthropologist, 91,* 41-58.

PART SIX

Approaches to Interpersonal Communication

This final section of *Bridges Not Walls* is made up of four approaches to interpersonal communication: one by a teacher, one by a psychologist, one by a counselor, and one by a philosopher. These readings are meant to illustrate four different ways in which the concepts and skills discussed in the first 14 chapters can be organized into a coherent whole. Each of these final readings develops one way to approach interpersonally communicating with others. None of the four includes every single concept and skill discussed in the book, but all reflect a commitment to the basic beliefs that are in the other readings; namely, that communication is a collaborative process, not something one person does "to" somebody else, that communication affects our personal identities; that communication is culturally situated; that communication is as complex as the humans who engage in it; and that there's a direct link between the quality of our communicating and the quality of our lives.

Each approach reflects the main agenda of its author. C. Roland Christensen is a teacher at the Harvard Business School who wants his students to learn by communicating interpersonally with him, and with each other. Ruthellen Josselson is a psychologist committed to helping people connect as profoundly as they are capable of connecting. Carl R. Rogers was a psychotherapist who wanted his clients, and readers of his books, to experience the quality of communication that he knew could help make them healthier. And Martin Buber was a philosopher who wanted to help people deeply understand the connection between the quality of their communication and the quality of their existence.

I encourage you to use these four readings to give some unity to your experience with the first 14 chapters. Interpersonal communication is complex enough that it can be easy to get lost in the details of verbal and nonverbal cues, self-awareness, person perception, listening, self-expression, conflict, and intercultural difficulties. So you might want to read these final chapters as a respite from work on the specifics, or as a way to reconnect with the forest after having concentrated on the trees. On the other hand, you might want to read these as overviews and previews, *before* looking at the other chapters. But in any case, I encourage you to notice how these four people have synthesized the other ideas into a whole that works for them. They can be a guide to your efforts to do the same thing.

CHAPTER 15

A Teacher's Approach

*A*s I mentioned, C. Roland Christensen is a teacher at the Harvard Business School and senior editor of a book called *Education for Judgment: The Artistry of Discussion Leadership*. The book is a collection of essays by teachers who have given up lecturing in favor of collaborative learning through focused discussion. I like his book and use it as a text partly because its title acknowledges that facilitating a good classroom discussion is an *art*, not a *science*, which is to say that it includes some *unmeasurable* aspects and some *mystery*. Christensen is a teacher who clearly recognizes this, and who applies to his teaching large chunks of the approach to interpersonal communication that's been laid out in the earlier chapters of *Bridges Not Walls*.

One of these chunks is the commitment to the idea that communication is a relational thing, something that happens mutually, *between people*. Christensen expresses his version of this idea as the "fundamental insight" that "teaching and learning are inseparable, [a] reciprocal giving and receiving." As he discovered firsthand, when you apply this insight to an 80-student classroom, the results can create cognitive overload. But they can also be gratifying as you find that students are deeply involved "both intellectually and with their guts." As a result of his first experiences, Christensen reports, he wanted to find out how this electrifying, yet overwhelming, process works.

When other teachers could only tell him, "Play it by ear," he went to those responsible for his survival, his students. He discovered that, directly or indirectly, they would let him know what worked and what didn't. He also figured out that the complex process could be understood in terms of three basic activities: questioning, listening, and responding to student responses. He explains some of the insights students taught him about these activities under six headings. First, students can play a significant role in constructing the day's agenda. Second, student logic can be different from—but nonetheless as useful as—the teacher's logic. Third, timing is crucial, and fourth, the types of questions affect how the discussion goes. Fifth, students can often communicate more effectively than the instructor because of their "rough and ready emotional profiles of one another," and finally, students build a class *culture* which affects all the class activities. These are all specific ways students contribute materially to the "teaching" process, and, Christensen believes, successful teaching begins when you recognize them.

In the major section of this essay, Christensen discusses five main "lessons" that he has learned about this approach to teaching. I could spend pages on each, but since he discusses them well, I'll just summarize them here. (1) *A teacher's openness and caring increase the student's learning opportunities.* Caring teachers don't just "coddle" students; they actually help them learn. (2) *Effective discussions require the classroom to become a learning space.* Intellectual hospitality and the safety that encourages risk-taking are two of its main features. (3) *Modest expectations are the most powerful of all.* Rather than trying to cover every possible topic or every possible reading, it works best to just help everybody learn a few ideas well. What a revolutionary idea! (4) *Instructors' patience promotes students' learning.* Inquiry and growth flourish under low pressure. The story in this section about the butterfly is super. (5) *Faith is the most essential ingredient in good teaching practice.* And to flesh out this idea, Christensen concludes with 10 items of "faith" that guide his teaching. I'll just mention a couple: "Involvement is critical to enduring learning." "Teaching is a moral act." "What my students become is as important as what they learn." "Fun has a critical place in teaching."

It's hard to read this essay without wishing that all your classes could be taught by Christensen, or somebody who approaches teaching and learning as he does. But I hope you can also see how this approach to classroom discussion is one exciting way to synthesize this book's approach to interpersonal communication.

EVERY STUDENT TEACHES AND EVERY TEACHER LEARNS:

The Reciprocal Gift of Discussion Teaching

C. Roland Christensen

It has been said that we live life forward but understand it backward. Looking back over years of discussion teaching, I see how intensely its process has intrigued, baffled, and intellectually nourished this practitioner—and the fascination shows no signs of abating. At its core lies a fundamental insight: teaching and learning are inseparable, parts of a single continuum—more Möbius strip than circle—of reciprocal giving and receiving. In discussion pedagogy students share the teaching task with the instructor and one another. All teach, and all learn. This view of the dynamic has implications for every aspect of discussion teaching, from fundamental assumptions to the finest points of classroom behavior. I make no claim to understand them all. But looking at teaching through the prism of reciprocity has allowed me to discern certain components of the process than can be named, described, studied, and communicated.

The reader should not be surprised to find "what I know," and, in particular, my descriptions of how I think while teaching, in the form of questions rather than statements. Four decades of discussion teaching leave their mark— in my case, an aversion to divorcing knowledge from challenge, dialogue, emotional engagement, and personal development. The quest for wisdom, as distinct from knowledge, will always remain open-ended.

This essay will present insights I have collected about the discussion teaching process with some details about the context that allowed me to see them. It will begin in the past, with my very first discussion class and fledgling efforts to learn how to learn about its mysteries. It will then continue with hypotheses about the nature of the process and the very powerful role students play in sharing its leadership with their instructors. And it will conclude in the present, with overarching "lessons learned" about values and the essential ingredient in all good teaching: faith.

EARLY YEARS: HOW I LEARNED TO LEARN ABOUT DISCUSSION TEACHING

Exploring the discussion process has been a wondrous adventure, a long journey within the confines of classroom walls. Like any productive educational enterprise, mine was aided by a fortunate synergy between instructor and institution. My colleagues on the faculty of the Harvard Business School honored teaching as a legitimate subject to be studied, as well as an action to be performed—an attitude that affected my perspective on everything that I saw, heard, and sensed as I taught, and my decisions on the best investment of my own intellectual resources.

My personal chain of discovery began with the first discussion class I ever taught: Tuesday, February 14, 1947. Yesterday. Remembered painfully, it was a bit like a session with a dental surgeon, sans novocaine. I was to teach an eighty-student section of the required second-year Business Policy course. The course mission was complex: to help students learn the functions, roles, and knowledge requirements of a general manager, with emphasis on the qualitative intricacies of strategic decision making. Underlying all this was the more basic goal of promoting the development of essential personal qualities: judgment, wisdom, and ethics.

Promptly at 8:30 A.M., having sweated through the weekend and Monday, I opened the door to Baker Library 101. It was a thin, cold room, with windows that rattled in the northeast wind and metal blinds stuck in various positions of closure. A slightly curved amphitheater format barely allowed space at the front for a platform, replete with brass rail and curtain that but partially hid the instructor's chair and desk. My suit coat over one arm—army exercise had changed my body frame and Harvard's salary did not allow for wardrobe refurbishment—and a folder of class notes in the other, I walked to the small platform, started up the three steps, tripped, and fell.

I blushed a bright red and knelt to gather my scattered papers. The room was quiet, except for an embarrassed half-laugh from the right, so brief it must have been squelched. I took a deep breath and, finally, stood up to look around at "them": scores of almost indistinguishable faces. A few smiled at me, thank heavens. My opening question—"Mr. Adams [you can imagine my reason for selecting him to start off], what is your diagnosis of the Consolidated Vultee situation?"—went well. But the remainder of the eighty minutes was a blur. My carefully prepared teaching plan, crafted to direct the group through an efficient analysis of the case that would reveal both the principles of Business Policy and my own indispensability to the discussion process, had minimal impact.

We were discussing a case about a company organizing for rapidly expanded military production during wartime, a topic still of high interest in 1947. The students wanted to pursue their own concerns and questions in ways that were meaningful to them. They agreed, disagreed, expressed confidence in (or incredulity at the naiveté of) their associates' suggestions. Infrequently, someone would admit confusion—a predicament appreciated and shared by the instructor. A few seemed bored, but most were deeply involved in the case, both intellectually and with their guts. There was no antagonism—all were polite—but the group permitted neither plan nor professor to get in its way.

When the class was over, I had heard hundreds and hundreds of words—verbal exchanges between and among the students, a multiplicity of conclusions, and an explosion of suggestions as to what the president of Consolidated Vultee should do. For me, it had been an academic Tower of Babel, a throw of conversational confetti. Most puzzling, however, was the reaction of the students. Seemingly, the class had made sense to them. Small groups stayed in the classroom after the discussion. Others left still carrying on their dialogue with an intensity that would have been difficult to contrive. Several commented, "Good class, professor." I thought, "Good class? Come on!"

The few steps back to my office felt like a stroll through a sandstorm. All I could remember of what had happened but minutes before were a few major themes and some dramatic statements. Students' comments fused; I couldn't recall who had said what or the responses those comments had triggered. A psychologist might have diagnosed my condition as cognitive overload: too much information to process too fast. How could I lead such a confusing process as this discussion had been? "It can't be done," I thought. "It simply can't be done!"

The only sensible course of action was to get help. Our faculty was the best, artists of the classroom, the teaching equivalents of Monet, Miró, and Jasper Johns. I asked senior colleagues to explain the discussion teaching process to me. Unfortunately, mastery of a creative activity does not guarantee the ability to explain it or help another master it. "Play it by ear, just play it by ear," was a typical response. For all their classroom genius, my colleagues treated teaching like the proverbial "black box": a container full of powerful mechanisms, but sealed.

During that first year of teaching, succeeding classes continued to listen much like the first one. The weeks marched by: dozens of class meetings, three times a week, with two eighty-person class groups. The discussions were spirited—decibels galore, dialogue, orations, even disquisitions. Crisp comments and pauses, murmurs, and mumbles. Themes did emerge in class, and the group often obtained reasonable consensus by the end of the session. Assumptions were tested and points proved. I had a good notion that cooperation powered the process, but even so, its dynamic eluded me. It was still a noisy mystery "out there." I felt like a stranger in the midst of the familiar. Nietzsche somewhere notes that all that is profound wears a mask. I wanted to look behind the mask that the learning process wore every day in the classroom.

Getting help became a puzzle, a pedagogical Rubik's cube. By now I had guessed that the students were responsible for my survival, thus far, in the classroom. Slowly this realization became a clue to learning about the mysterious process of discussion teaching. If colleagues couldn't "give" me the answer, perhaps I might find it with the students. After all, they were the reason it was working. I wondered if, somehow, those whom I supposedly led could help me learn how to lead. Perhaps I could work out a way to study what we all did in discussions and discover order in the apparent chaos. This would mean observing other teachers' classes and, as far as possible, my own.

I soon learned that mastery of course content wasn't the key. At the very beginning, I had, like most instructors, assumed that my job was to devise the clearest, most insightful analysis of the material possible, compose a list of questions to elicit that analysis in class, and then lead the students through my list in a courteous but authoritative manner. How starkly that assumption clashed with what I observed in class! When I tried to figure out what distinguished higher-from lower-quality discussion classes, I noticed that the better discussions were those in which the students asked particularly good questions—questions that often eclipsed those I had prepared. And the best discussions often modified or completely abandoned my neatly sequenced teaching plans. I was intrigued to realize that this aspect of good classes lay largely beyond my control, as did another common feature of productive discussions: students' listening to one another with attention and care. Good discussions frequently took paths that the group found reasonable but I had not foreseen. It seemed increasingly obvious that I neither could nor should try to control the discussion process. The students were my co-teachers.

Over time, such glimmers of insight brightened to beams of light that illuminated at least a portion of the contents of the black box of the discussion process. My early, overwhelmed conclusion, "It can't be done," evolved to, "It *can* be done, but not alone." But if the students were teaching, what was my job? To help them teach better. This meant that I needed not only to master the skills of leading the discussion process but also to devise ways to describe and explain the process to others.

Self-knowledge is the beginning of all knowledge. I had to find the teacher in myself before I could find the teacher in my students and gain understanding of how we all taught one another. Slowly, I learned to make my classroom observations more productive by focusing them. I started to try out tiny experiments. Instead of waiting for the class to assemble before making my appearance, for example, I tried arriving early to see what that might teach me about my students. The exercise proved valuable. Talking with students and watching them enter the room revealed much about their lives and interests—who played sports before class, who was under the weather or visibly fatigued that day, who had special interest in the day's topic (or, conversely, an apparent desire to hide). Coming to class early also allowed me to prepare a genial, cooperative atmosphere by welcoming students by name, and it gave me an opportunity to note students' subgroups.

Some other early experiments: I dropped my initial practice of calling opening speakers in alphabetical order and made choices based on some knowledge of students' backgrounds and interests. And I took a tip from a student who noted a preponderance of "whats" among my questions and tried more "whys." Simple, simple steps, rooted in practicality. But these were my first glimpses of the workings of the black box.

Finding time to reflect on the discussion as it unfolded in class was still like trying to meditate on a speeding fire engine. The after-class reprise was equally difficult. But I now had some ideas about why certain classes seemed more productive than others. Much of what we teachers do in the classroom seems intuitive. My task was to examine this apparently automatic behavior, show its workings, and identify areas in which judgment might play a part. "Process," whatever it might be, was clearly going to be the major focus of my attention.

Like most academics, I assumed that abstract principles of some sort would be my best guides. But my initial attempts, directed at understanding "process" in its purest sense, brought little practical reward. It seemed that the farther down the "abstraction ladder" I climbed, the closer I came to my real goal, an ever-deeper understanding of process. Near the bottom of the ladder, on the operational (how to) level, I began to make observations that truly dispelled confusion. When I came to class with a simple, practical teaching experiment in mind—something like evaluating the effect of calling on students seated in different parts of the room—I got results. Sometimes I focused on the art of questioning. What happens when I ask the same question of two students in succession? What is the effect of asking a delayed question—one to be answered after a moment of reflection—compared with asking the same question "cold"? Sometimes I concentrated on phrasing. What is the difference between using a student's name and simply gesturing? Or I concentrated on timing: How long can a silence last before restlessness sets in? I repeated these experiments from class to class, year to year, trying, like any researcher, to hold as many things constant as possible each time in order to evaluate the variable element.

Once I learned to focus on what a teacher says and does in the classroom, possibilities for experimentation and learning began to proliferate. The classroom proved to be a perfect laboratory for my nuts-and-bolts experiments with the discussion process. As an observer, of myself and other instructors in action, I truly began to learn. My experimental approach to the discussion process revealed that all participants, instructor included, spent most of their time either asking questions, listening to people's answers, or making some sort of response to those answers. I began to appreciate that these activities—questioning, listening, and response—were the most basic "stuff" of process. I also realized that every discussion produced rehearsals of data, analysis, questions, challenges, and syntheses, but not necessarily in a predictable sequence. This insight suggested that one of the instructor's most crucial tasks is linking—explicitly relating, and helping the students to relate, current points of argument to others that may have appeared earlier that day or in a previous discussion. This point, I realized, had important implications for teaching preparation as well as discussion management.

What I found inside the black box of the discussion process was an ever-changing flow of activities that resisted abstract analysis but yielded to disciplined observation and the application of very specific skills. To some extent, all of the essays in [*Education for Judgment*] examine aspects of these skills from the points of view of experienced practitioners, teachers at work. And what is our work? To create a favorable learning climate, to set a teaching/learning contract, to ask and respond to questions, listen to contributions, and promote the formation of groups in which students can teach themselves and one another. All these are practical approaches to a process that cannot be abstracted without substantial loss of identity, for the discussion process is a true slice of life. Guiding it takes skill, patience, and a basic faith that one may learn, with time and effort, to preside over disorder without disorientation.

SOME INSIGHTS ABOUT PROCESS AND STUDENTS' ROLE IN ITS LEADERSHIP

Seen in retrospect, my attempts to understand the workings of the discussion teaching process have much in common with the process itself. Both exhibit the disorderliness of discovery: even the most steadfast explorer cannot march straight through a jungle. Most attempts to capture the essence of the discussion process produce frustrations as well as insights. The very meaning of the phrase, for example, still teases our profession. The totality of a discussion includes the intellectual and emotional experiences of a whole roomful of people: material to occupy psychologists, neurologists, sociologists, anthropologists, and philosophers for years to come. My own quest for an enlightening definition produced little to help me choose which of ten vigorously waving hands to recognize. All processes are flows, either of activities or thoughts, but this basic definition gives one no handle on why some opening questions inspire lively debate while others trigger alienation or apathy, or why the comments of "student experts" sometimes help and sometimes hinder a discussion. Nor does it distinguish what happens in a discussion classroom from what happens on an assembly line.

I found the exercise of drawing distinctions more fruitful. Contrasting process with content provided practical help. Confusing mastery of material with mastery of the discussion process produces a common error: a controlling teaching style that creates bilateral frustration when students inevitably try to go their own ways. This lesson became clear to me as my students continued to offer polite, but stubborn resistance to my attempts to shepherd them through the meticulous analyses that had cost me so many hours of preparation. And when I examined my own initial inclination to choose opening speakers alphabetically from my class list, I found that it showed another typical novice's confusion: the failure to distinguish process from procedure. Procedures are logical and rigid sequences of actions, indispensable in making an arrest, performing an appendectomy, or accessing a computer file—but fatal to leading a meaningful group discussion. Discussions are liquid. They do not move in straight lines; they undulate.

Over the years, I have found the use of metaphor enriching to my understanding of the discussion process. What is a discussion, if not a voyage of exploration, with the leader as both captain and crew member? To appreciate the frequent reversals and indirections of the process, one may imagine a discussion class as a mountain climb, where even apparent reversals produce ascent. In the discussion process, "wrong" can be more helpful than "right"; an obtuse statement can spark a charged, enlightening debate that straightforward analysis could never provoke.

Discussion teaching is noisy. Messy, too. It greets an observer with a verbal cacophony—an unnerving scene for teachers unprepared for its energy. Good discussions unfold in unexpected ways that modify the programmed logic of a teaching plan. They pose new questions, uncover and gnaw away at sanctified assumptions, rejuvenate old topics with fresh insights, broaden perspectives, and create new paths of inquiry. But focused observation and systematic analysis can reveal meaning in the noise and logic in the disorder. The rough-and-tumble of classroom interchange contains opportunities that enhance the learning of both students and instructors. What unsettles a teacher may energize the students: less disorder, than new order. Discussion teaching demands a milieu of freedom, an openness that encourages students to share power over, and responsibility for, the leadership and conduct of a class.

In discussion teaching, tidiness can tyrannize. Messiness can work miracles. To succeed, the enterprise requires the active contribution, not merely cooperation, of the discussion group. Mutual collaboration—reciprocity of effort—is not only engaging and exciting for students, it is also imperative for the discussion leader. However impressive your experience or skills, you will have difficulty in questioning, listening, and responding while simultaneously observing, synthesizing, reflecting, and evaluating the discussion dialogue, and planning for the rest of the class. A teacher would need more than one pair of eyes and ears to carry out such a task—it really *can't* be done alone!

This realization suggests a further point: a great deal of essential information—factors that condition the instructional choices of the moment—emerges only in action as the process unfolds. Should an idea be explored in greater depth or overviewed in a hurry? Should the class move on to another topic? Would it be helpful to raise or lower the abstraction level of the argument? What does the group understand? What is missing? What topics need to be covered again? What questions are bothering or intriguing the group? What new avenues of exploration should we investigate now? It helps to remember that the teacher does not bear the sole responsibility for answering these questions. Students control a surprisingly large part of the turf of discussion leadership. They participate in critical "framework" decisions by influencing the agenda, sequence of topics, and allocation of time to various topics. They help determine the minute-by-minute direction of the discussion process and the quality of the dialogue. They contribute to the creation of a class culture, accept responsibility for their own

involvement, and teach their peers. They develop and practice the skills of leading and following. Without their co-leadership, there is no true discussion.

I have found it helpful to consider students' contribution to the leadership
of the discussion process under six broad categories. First, when responsibility
is collective, the students play a significant role in constructing the agenda of the
day. The instructor may find his or her preclass teaching plan influenced by the
addition of new topics of interest to student, suggestions for restating issues in
ways that provoke different questions, or requests that materials from previous
discussions be combined with the dialogue of the day. Sometimes the class will
simply reject the instructor's program. In these cases capitulation is advisable,
if not inevitable. Teaching is difficult enough when students want to learn, virtually impossible if they are uninterested. Given these circumstances, discussion
teachers do not, like lecturers, set the agenda; they manage its emergence, direction, and evolution.

Second, the students affect the sequence in which topics of the day are discussed. Teachers and students prepare differently. Instructors' plans exploit a
flow of inquiry that seems logical to them, consistent with course objectives, and
built on past experience with the material and students. But the instructor's
teaching logic may not match the students' learning logic. In discussion leadership, efficiency does not always equal effectiveness. Last year's—or last
hour's—discussion of a particular topic will never exactly predict the one that's
about to begin. Even very experienced instructors, who have been teaching
longer than their students have been studying (sometimes longer than their students have been alive), have an inferior command of one essential topic: their
students' agendas and learning styles. As a result, questions that an instructor
may wish to consider early may well be out of sync with the students' wishes
and needs.

Accordingly, a wise instructor prepares twice: both from his or her point of
view and, more important, from the students' point of view. How will participants be likely to approach the material? What paths of inquiry might they follow? When the instructor's approach differs from that of the students, the discussion may well tilt in the students' direction. The professor proposes, but the
class disposes.

The third aspect of the discussion that students influence is timing. When
their involvement in a question or topic is intense, it will be difficult for an instructor to redirect their energy. One can force a shift in topic, but students' interests, though denied, do not disappear. They reemerge, deftly inserted into
their responses to the instructor's new questions. The sensitive instructor will
"hear" the discontinuity and act accordingly.

Fourth, the types of questions students ask of one another and of the instructor play a critical role in directing the minute-by-minute flow of dialogue.
Their questions may be directionally neutral—"Where do we go next?"—or
may shift the discussion to another topic. The phrasing, tone, and delivery of
their questions and comments influence the mood and tempo of the class, encourage conflict, excitement, resolution, or reflection. The astute instructor will
listen carefully, and on several levels, to students' questions and also respect-

fully note the directive power in the students' choice of which individual or sub-group to address. This choice is another, crucial contribution students make to determining both the style and content of discussion.

Working and playing together over a period of time, students get to know their associates better than the instructor can—their itches and ouches, blind spots, areas of experience and wisdom, cares and concerns. And students possess current information about their peers to augment this background information. They are familiar with Rosa's or Juan's circumstances today, this minute. They know Herman's special interest in the topic and his mood. Was he worked over in an earlier class today? Is there a family crisis going on? This sort of student intelligence (in the military sense) lies mainly beyond an instructor's reach. But its power to maintain continuity or produce radical change in the direction of dialogue will show up in the classroom.

Such information can improve the quality of the group's communication. Effective communication—in which words encourage and advance understanding for others as well as the speaker—is difficult to achieve under the best of circumstances. Indeed, as the late Fritz Roethlisberger observed, the first law of communication is to expect miscommunication. Communication is even more complex in crowded classrooms, where dialogue is rapid-fire, personal commitment—even passion—accompanies many comments, and reflection time is limited. In such situations, students' intelligence does more to influence the flow of dialogue than the instructor's directions can.

Fifth, because students relate to one another as peers, they can often communicate more effectively than the instructor in class. Why? Not because they are more rigorous in thought, skilled in semantics and phonetics, or expert in their artistry of explanation. Rather, because they possess rough and ready emotional profiles of one another. In what fields does Ms. Peterson feel confident, have the knack of explaining, and the interest, patience, and ingenuity to state her message in a variety of ways? What are the barriers, the ignorance, bias, lack of interest, that limit Mr. Ripley's understanding and ability to listen?

Students also tend to share the language system of their generation, a common idiom of "go" and "no go" words and relevant metaphors ("needle in a haystack" might resonate less well than "contact lens in a swimming pool," for example). This, plus their knowledge of fellow students, brings them swiftly to the core of effective communication, speaking *to*, not *at*, one another.

Equally important, it is simpler and less threatening for participants to check and recheck each other's meaning than for the instructor to do so. They can accept "I don't understand what you said" more easily from a friend than a potential judge. Correction of the inevitable miscommunication is less complicated when it comes from a classmate than a teacher. When a fellow student says, "You didn't read me right. I meant this," or "Give me that again, Bill. Your assumptions are off base," the remark is less likely to be perceived as an accusation of ignorance or error, and more likely to be seen as a low-key request for help.

Finally, the sixth aspect of the discussion process that students influence heavily is class culture. Discussion groups derive tone and character from the way students work together in the daily routines of class. What is to be the balance between cooperation and competition? Where are the boundaries? What is acceptable and nonacceptable behavior? What are the responsibilities of a class member to himself or herself and the group? Obviously, all students should prepare, attend, and participate. It is difficult to experience a discussion in absentia. But what more? How will these particular participants work out the fundamental challenges of a member of a discussion group—when to stand out, when to blend in, when to lead, when to follow? How members of the group help one another through these complexities affects the context in which the discussions take place. The resolution of these problems contributes to the quality of the learning milieu.

The apparent disorder of a discussion class is, then, but a mask for a complicated teaching and learning process in which students play a vital, but far from obvious role in leadership. Only appreciation of, and attention to, process can help us teachers understand students' essential teaching contribution—a key understanding for effective educational discussions. Most important, the mask blinds us, as teachers, to a fundamental fact: we not only teach a course, but also simultaneously help the students learn how to teach one another. It is not enough to ask "good questions"; we must understand the art of questioning, listening, and responding constructively; model those skills in class for our students and, by so doing, demonstrate our respect for their importance.

LESSONS LEARNED

Years after that first disorienting class, I still regard the mysterious power of discussion teaching with awe. I have shed the youthful naiveté that led me to search for "the answer," but I still work away at pedagogical questions. Accommodation is the order of the years, but the decades have brought a measure of understanding. My belief in the essential magnificence of teaching grows ever stronger. What I have learned about the abiding conundrums of discussion pedagogy makes me even more certain that teaching is a great learning experience. And for the study of teaching, what better research laboratory than the classroom, where the teacher can experiment with the real "stuff" and test, modify, and retest all hypotheses? I have stressed the rewards of this pursuit, but I am also aware of its price. The gains in depth and specificity that come from "knowing more" increase the pressure for yet higher standards. As hands-on classroom knowledge builds, one can no longer turn to easy excuses—the students just didn't like the material; another course had a long report due this week; or (most common of all) I just had a bad day. None of these explanations works when one grasps the dynamics of classroom process. Higher standards are a constant reminder to do better.

In working up a "wish I had learned this earlier" list, I asked myself: Does my experience suggest one quintessential lesson? Perhaps the answer is yes. Teaching is a human activity. Intellect does not teach intellect; people teach people. No matter how factually accurate and time-tested our data, how clear cut and disciplined our analytical methods, or how practiced and skillful our pedagogical techniques, true learning emerges only when we honor the human factor. One measure of pedagogical maturity is the ability to augment technical expertise with attention to people.

Given this overarching proposition, I would like to offer some lessons learned from students, colleagues, and day-to-day classroom practice. Some of these lessons have been purchased at substantial personal cost. Many lessons had to be both learned and relearned. On reflection, I find none of them surprising. Why didn't I think of them earlier? No one reason. But is a lifetime in the classroom really long enough to figure out what effective teaching is all about?

1. A teacher's openness and caring increase the students' learning opportunities. When students perceive the instructor at the front of the room as distant and impersonal—a figurehead, not a friend—their learning opportunities suffer. "He lives in another world, guys; I don't know what turns his flame up. . . . I'm just line twelve on the class list." Enduring learning needs a human context, an emotional matrix, in which to grow. The teacher who provides that context and encourages it in the learning group must let students know him or her as more than an intellectual resource or mobile data base.

Our educational conventions put distance between teachers and students. Without sacrificing propriety or relinquishing our role as guides, we teachers need to open our worlds to students. Far too many people in public view become, as Dr. Grete Bibring put it, "individuals with faces that have never been lived in." Our students want and need to know what we stand for. The opposite side of this coin is our need to understand students as people. What are their ambitions, uncertainties, blind spots, and areas of excellence? When we open our wider worlds and appear "in the round," we also maximize our possibilities for learning about them. Openness brings mutual advantage because it permits mutual learning.

But openness is not enough. We must combine it with caring. Teachers must do more than feel concerned; we must actively look after and provide for the welfare of students. We must not only appreciate, but also become personally involved in, their progress. By so doing, we measurably enhance the potential for learning on both sides. One experienced associate noted that most students want to know how much you care before they care how much you know. His judgment, though paradoxical, makes sense to me. Caring converts impersonal offers of academic assistance into gifts, and every gift of learning enriches the giver as much as the recipient. Students sense the difference between perfunctory offers of help and true personal willingness to teach and learn with them. Openness increases a discussion leader's opportunities to help students. Caring makes the process work.

2. Effective discussions require the classroom to become a learning space. As a novice instructor I would have defined "learning space" physically, as the classroom. Baker 101 was an adequate room—satisfactory acoustics, lights in working order, enough chairs. I looked for nothing more. Over the years, however, my view of the classroom has grown metaphorical and far more demanding. A true learning space is psychological, not physical, and the teacher bears the primary responsibility for creating it.

I now view the discussion classroom as a joining ground where students, instructor, and ideas meet and commingle; a space where, as Henri Nouwen suggests, "students and teachers can enter into a fearless communication with each other and allow their respective life experiences to be their primary and most valuable source of growth and maturation."[1] The creation of such space requires a mutual trust in which teachers and learners (those shifting roles) can present themselves as colleagues in a common quest for truth. A genuine learning space is more than a container for this quest; it is a place where all feel free to question one another constructively and where an aggregation of competitive individuals, dedicated to personal goals, can become a learning group.

When we teachers create and support an atmosphere of intellectual hospitality, we help students believe that they have something of value to contribute. This belief, in turn, encourages them to risk trying out ideas—the risk that makes learning possible. Perhaps most important, it is only within a welcoming classroom space that we can obtain students' active involvement in discussions. Discussions that take place in true learning spaces engage students verbally and reflectively, intellectually and emotionally.

Above all, such spaces make risk-taking safe—as safe as it can be, that is. And safety—students' anticipation of aid and comfort in tough situations—is the greatest antidote to the discussion leader's ever-present, always unsettling challenge: silence. Joe isn't contributing very much anymore. What's going on? Is he reflecting on points made earlier, contemplating new questions to ask, wrestling with uncertainty, just feeling turned off—or is he scared? We teachers sometimes forget how difficult it is for students to develop the capacity for what Donald Schön calls cognitive risk-taking. A glance backward at our own student days may help us remember. Didn't we use silence to protect ourselves from questions—by peers, instructors, or ourselves (these last often the most painful)? In a safe space, members of a group with especially complex needs and concerns (that includes most of us, doesn't it?) can reveal their sensitivities and needs. When this happens, community is strengthened, and all benefit.

The creation and maintenance of a safe space is not very arduous, and its rewards are bountiful. David Riesman's metaphor of the teacher as host, or welcomer of guests, may serve as a useful guide. There is little cost but great value in learning something about students' backgrounds and current circumstances in time to welcome them personally to the upcoming dialogue. Similarly, the few moments we instructors devote to weaving "safety nets"—techniques for supporting students who run into trouble by taking on complex or unpopular points of argument—are well spent. Safety nets enable participants to walk the high wire of adventuresome thought and argument with daring bolstered by a sense of security.

When the instructor fosters the creation of a learning space in the classroom, everyone gains. The class becomes a community. A working partnership emerges between teacher and students, and risk-taking increases on both sides. We sometimes forget that instructors are as risk-averse as students. We hesitate to reveal our own uncertainties and areas of ignorance. We hold back from presenting positions in their early stages of development. We resist challenging popular points of view. But in a safe learning space, we can reveal what we know and need to know, and also what we are and would like to be.

3. Modest expectations are the most powerful of all. Teachers select their life's work for complex reasons, unique in every case. But one basic circumstance of our vocation unites us all: our work simultaneously allows us to serve the wider community and make significant contributions to the lives of the individual students entrusted to our care. Stories about master teachers give us pictures of what the great can do. Each of us has had some personal experience of the impact a teacher can make on a life by stimulating interest in a topic or field of study, providing a role model, or molding our basic values and beliefs. Teachers can accomplish so much of importance. But the contemplation of that accomplishment can overwhelm as well as inspire.

As my years in the classroom have multiplied, I have made the paradoxical discovery that modest expectations, particularly in the realm of content, trigger more effective learning than ambitious ones. Material learned in depth—with heart as well as head—stays with students, but broad-based lists of facts, techniques, and theories tend to fade. J. D. Salinger noted that the mark of immaturity is a desire to die nobly for a cause, but maturity brings the willingness to live humbly for one. Our colleague Abby Hansen suggests that discussion leaders' best songs are anthems of modest expectations. I have found that teaching practice improves when I fit my expectations about how much the group should cover in a given period to a quite modest standard. Thoroughness and depth compensate abundantly for the sacrifice of breadth. Retention of a few crucial things over time brings far more benefit than superficial mastery.

There are few tasks more difficult than evaluating the effect of our teaching. Trying to gauge success is like tossing coins into the Grand Canyon and waiting to hear the clink. How can we ever know just what we have contributed to a student's education? Teachers have much in common with performing artists, but our applause (or boos and hisses) may not come for years, if ever. Who knows what students retain a day, week, year, or decade after a seminar? It is chastening to be thanked by an alumnus for all you taught him only to realize, as the conversation continues, that he is praising a colleague, not you.

Gradually I have abandoned my interest in final outcomes—whatever they may be—and begun to derive satisfaction from the act of teaching itself. When I consider the innumerable gradations that intervene between success and failure, the complex natures of the parties involved, and the magnitude of the daily efforts that go unevaluated, I marvel at the imponderability of long-term effects. I have learned that wisdom and effectiveness lie in a constant struggle for improvement, rather than a quest for final results. Like virtue, teaching is its own reward. For me this means that if I practice and hone my skills, welcome observation and constructive criticism, and experiment and grow, my efforts may very well have an impact. Minor miracles do happen—often enough, in fact, to justify this hope.

4. Instructors' patience promotes students' learning. Patience, though a virtue of restraint, has the effect of energizing students. Inquiry, growth, and learning flourish under low pressure. Concepts and ideas are difficult to plant in our intellectual garden. They have erratic, individualized growing circles, and harvesting is always under the student's control—exam schedules to the contrary notwithstanding. Yet I found this simple lesson difficult to learn. Patience is not readily acquired.

Impatience comes more easily. Having worked through the process of understanding the applicability and limits of the ideas under study, we feel we know our subjects. The material is ours, and we forget the missteps we took on the way to this possession. But discussion teaching is not a straightforward dispensing of knowledge. Students have their own missteps to make; their journeys will not necessarily parallel ours. Discussion leaders who fail to appreciate the constructiveness of inefficiency make a serious error. Efficient teaching does not always equate with effective learning. On the contrary, students often discover valuable lessons at the ends of blind alleys—lessons that we teachers cannot anticipate before they unfold in the discussion. What seems like a digression may link the challenge of the moment to prior explorations. Apparent tangents examine questions of the students' creation, not because of any obvious link to the assignment of the day, but because they hold high, continuing intellectual interest for the students.

The syllabi we develop contribute to our impatience. There is always more to be taught than time to teach. A rigid, daily roster of material to cover pressures us to ignore crucial elements of context—school events, local and national circumstances, and personal matters. A colleague tells of a friend, a Civil War historian, who puts the point well: "In my class Grant has to arrive at Richmond before Thanksgiving, no matter what!"

The costs of such rigidity can be high, even cruel. As an unknown poet once said, "All the flowers of all the tomorrows are planted in the seeds of today." We need to nurture, tend, and let them mature at their own pace. Forcing can kill. Nikos Kazantzakis makes the point tellingly in *Zorba the Greek*:

> I remembered one morning when I discovered a cocoon in the bark of a tree, just as a butterfly was making a hole in its case and preparing to come out. I waited awhile, but it was too long appearing and I was impatient. I bent over it and breathed on it to warm it. I warmed it as quickly as I could and the miracle began to happen before my eyes, faster than life. The case opened, the butterfly started slowly crawling out and I shall never forget my horror when I saw how its wings were folded back and crumpled; the wretched butterfly tried with its whole trembling body to unfold them. Bending over it, I tried to help it breathe. In vain.
>
> It needed to be hatched out patiently and the unfolding of the wings should be a gradual process in the sun. Now it was too late. My breath had forced the butterfly to appear, all crumpled before its time. It struggled desperately and a few seconds later, died in the palm of my hand.
>
> That little body is, I do believe, the greatest weight I have on my conscience. For I realize today that it is a mortal sin to violate the great laws of nature. We

should not hurry, we should not be impatient, but we should confidently obey the eternal rhythm.[2]

This lesson has special meaning for teachers. We must bring to each class infinite patience, and moderate our critical judgments about students' progress. Walter Jackson Bate reminds us, in his biography of Samuel Johnson, how difficult it is to appreciate "the actual process and daily crawl of other people's experience."[3] But it is precisely this "daily crawl" that we must respect, protect, and honor. And we must, I submit, do it in a context of positive belief in students.

5. Faith is the most essential ingredient in good teaching practice. Thus far I have discussed in depth two essentials of discussion teaching: knowledge of pedagogical concepts and mastery of process skills. It is now time to consider the third essential: faith. Faith in the fundamental worth of our vocation, in the values that govern our relations with individual students and classes, and in the likelihood that at least some of the results we desire will be achieved. To me, faith is the indispensable dimension of teaching life. Why, then, is it so rarely mentioned? Perhaps because academicians may feel more comfortable with hard facts, logical analysis, and readily observable skills than with intangibles like belief. But without these intangibles—the "soul," if you will, that animates that mechanism inside the black box of discussion teaching—technique becomes mechanical, skills manipulative, and attitudes suspect.

Can faith be codified? I have found that certain insights have not only endured but assumed increasing significance for my teaching practice while other observations and theoretical constructs have faded or been replaced. I offer these articles of faith—so meaningful to me—not as prescriptions or dogma, but as a purely personal testament: *credo,* after all, means "I believe."

- I believe that the profession of teaching is crucial to the maintenance and advancement of civilization. Only our most talented—master crafts-people who perform to the highest possible standards—should undertake it. As Theodore Roethke put it in "Words for Young Writers," we need "more people that specialize in the impossible,"[4] and that is what teachers do. To me, teaching carries an awesome responsibility to encourage students to want to know, to show them how to know, and to insist that they ask and answer the question "For what purpose do *I* need to know?"
- I believe in the teachability of teaching. For the past two decades my pedagogical research, statements, and teaching objectives have centered on this fundamental conviction: good teachers are made, not born. We can observe, analyze, and communicate the artistry of discussion leadership to other practitioners. Effective teachers both practice and constantly search and research their own activities; their classrooms are both instructional arenas and laboratories.
- I believe that active involvement is critical to enduring learning. In discussion classes, students and teachers alike must give of themselves. Without involvement, the discussion of the day is but noise and its leadership a

charade. There's a world of difference between a lackadaisical game of "Simon Says" and the muscle-building that takes place when a committed coach leads an eager team through a workout. Involvement transforms passive, received knowledge into the active ability to apply that knowledge effectively.

- I believe that discussion leaders need to master both process skills as well as the substantive knowledge of their course. Without knowledge of process, instructors are limited in their effort to help students discover, assimilate, and retain course content. It is through command of process that the primacy of content is realized.

- I believe that teaching is a moral act. Ethical commitment must temper the balance we strike in selecting materials and working with them in class. Morality must shape our treatment of students—David Riesman calls teaching "power, with sympathy"—and the values we develop for the classroom community. As the late Professor Lon Fuller suggested, we must distinguish between a morality of duty—that which is formally and/or legally appropriate—and a morality of aspiration—a striving for excellence and idealism. The latter must govern.

- I believe that what my students become is as important as what they learn. The endpoint of teaching is as much human as intellectual growth. Where qualities of person are as central as qualities of mind—as is true in all professional education—we must engage the whole being of students so that they become open and receptive to multiple levels of understanding. And we must engage our whole selves as well. I teach not only what I know, but what I am.

- I believe that, in the words of Professor Charles Gragg, "teachers must also learn!"[5] We cannot truly teach unless we let ourselves experience the vicissitudes and exhilaration of exploration—the mastery and communication of ideas, coupled with the reception of new insights, and the never-ending desire to know more. Teaching and learning are inseparable; the process of education is a reciprocal gift.

- I believe that fun has a critical place in teaching. Great classes include multiple moods—verbal pyrotechnics, moments of stillness, measured, cadenced analyses, and flights of fancy—but always in a context of celebration. Fun permits breakouts from routine. It enlivens the humdrum and sustains generosity as all participants give and receive enjoyment along with wisdom. And fun can heal: it is difficult to dislike someone with whom you share a laugh. Humor can broaden the scope of the possible, but, as Samuel Johnson noted, "Nothing is more hopeless than a scheme of merriment."[6] In a context of good nature, fun will emerge unplanned from the inevitable incongruities of all extended conversations: the extrapolations that take comments to maximum exaggeration and the implosions that carry words and images to absurdity.

- I believe that the teacher's challenge in evaluating students is less to separate the gifted from the ordinary than to find the gifts of the ordinary. And I believe that we must communicate our evaluations in a manner that helps students understand their competence, or lack thereof, without destroying their confidence. Robert Frost said it well: "No figure [or letter] has ever caught the whole of it." At best, grades are imprecise measures even of academic achievement. They do not weigh the worth of a student as a person, now or in the future.

- I believe in the unlimited potential of every student. At first glance they range, like instructors, from mediocre to magnificent. But potential is invisible to the superficial gaze. It takes faith to discern it, but I have witnessed too many academic miracles to doubt its existence. I now view each student as "material for a work of art."

If I have faith, deep faith, in students' capacities for creativity and growth, how very much we can accomplish together. If, on the other hand, I fail to believe in that potential, my failure sows seeds of doubt. Students read our negative signals, however carefully cloaked, and retreat from creative risk to the "just possible." When this happens, everyone loses.

One student—call him Andy—was tottering between Low Pass and Unsatisfactory in my Business Policy course. Together we devised a remedial program. He would write five "dry run" exams before a "make-or-break" final that could determine whether he would graduate with his class. After each remedial exam, we would meet to discuss what he had written. Andy worked hard, but progress came slowly. At our last meeting, somewhat discouraged, I asked, "Andy, do you think you can handle the exam tomorrow?" He looked at me and said, oh so softly, "Professor Christensen, Professor Christensen, that's not it. The question is, do *you* think I can handle the exam? *Do you believe in me?*" His comment hit home—helped me. It reminded me of his strengths and the gains he had made. "Andy," I said, "would I spend this much time on a hopeless cause? Yes, I think you can pass this exam and take your degree. What's more, I know you will have a wonderful career. *I believe in you.*"

My words affected him visibly. He smiled, and I thought I could see his back straighten a bit as he left my office. He passed the final exam, graduated with his class, and went on to great success, in both business and civic affairs. Many people have benefited from Andy's capability and generosity—his family, our school, his community, and society in general.

We learn so much from our students. Andy and others like him taught me that if I round out my knowledge of Business Policy and skill at discussion management with faith in them, they can accomplish the improbable and enable me to do the same. For the reciprocity of teaching and learning—their inseparability—makes us share in our students' successes, just as we share in their failures. To give up on students is to give up on ourselves, and that I have never done.

REVIEW QUESTIONS

1. What is a Möbius strip? How does it help make Christensen's point in the first paragraph?
2. Christensen says he "soon learned that mastery of course content wasn't the key" to effective teaching. What was?

3. Describe the distinction Christensen makes between content and process and between process and procedures.
4. Paraphrase: "In discussion teaching, tidiness can tyrannize. Messiness can work miracles." "In discussion leadership, efficiency does not always equal effectiveness."
5. Explain the connection Christensen makes between a teacher's openness and his or her caring.
6. Give two clear examples of what Christensen means by "patience."
7. What does it mean to say that "teaching is a moral act?"

PROBES

1. It was relatively easy for Christensen to build this approach in a business-school class based on the case-study method. But other chapters of the book this essay appears in discuss applications of discussion teaching in political science, literature, and medical school (microscopic anatomy class). How might this approach be applied to each of the courses you are registered for this term?
2. On the one hand, Christensen emphasizes the application of specific, even mechanical skills—like asking questions of students in various parts of the room or using the students' name in the question versus not using his or her name. On the other hand, he clearly believes that excellent teaching involves more than just mechanics. How would you describe his view of this tension between mechanics, or rules, and intuition, or art?
3. What do you believe makes up the "class culture" Christensen talks about near the end of the essay? How does this culture affect what goes on in the classroom?
4. I think one of Christensen's most important insights is this: "Teaching is a human activity. Intellect does not teach intellect; people teach people." Paraphrase what you think this means and then respond. What would you expect the teacher who believes this to do, for example, with a syllabus, required readings, tests, office hours, and grading?
5. Give an example from your own experience of the importance of the class-room being a space where it is safe to take a cognitive risk.
6. Christensen says that he has gradually given up any interest in final outcomes—the degree to which his students achieve some particular goal in their education or in the "real world." What is his rationale for giving this up, and what has he substituted for it? How do you respond to this part of his essay?
7. How do you respond to all Christensen's talk about faith? Isn't this a pretty imprecise, abstract, and maybe even dangerous topic for something as concrete and practical as teaching? What justifies his discussion of it?

NOTES

1. Henri J. M. Nouwen, *Reaching Out* (Garden City, NY: Image Books, 1986), p. 85.
2. Nikos Kazantzakis, *Zorba the Greek,* tr. Carl Wildman (New York: Simon & Schuster, 1952), p. 120.
3. Walter Jackson Bate, *Samuel Johnson* (New York: Harcourt Brace Jovanovich, 1977), p. 233.
4. Theodore Roethke, *Straw for the Fire: From the Notebooks of Theodore Roethke, 1943–63,* selected and arranged by David Wagoner (Garden City, NY: Doubleday, 1972), p. 185.
5. Charles I. Gragg, "Teachers Also Must Learn," *Harvard Educational Review,* vol. 10 (1940), pp. 30–47.
6. Samuel Johnson, "The Idler," in vol. 2, no. 58, *The Works of Samuel Johnson,* ed. Robert Lynam (London: George Cowre, 1825).

CHAPTER 16

A Psychologist's Approach

R uthellen Josselson is a psychology professor at Towson State University in Maryland and a psychotherapist. This reading is from her book *The Space Between Us: Exploring the Dimensions of Human Relationships,* which she wrote for people who would like to better understand the experience of human relationships. Overall, she writes, her book "is for all who might like to join the dialogue about what we need from others."

This excerpt begins by sketching Josselson's basic model of human relationships, which consists of eight developmental dimensions, or stages, that, she argues, are the ways each human overcomes the space between people. I combined these early pages in her book with parts of her final chapter called "Notes on Love." Together these materials capture some of the central ideas that make up Josselson's approach to interpersonal communication.

As she reminds us here, the first contact humans experience is *holding,* being cradled in strong arms. Our need for this experience continues throughout our lives. A little later in our development we experience *attachment* to the most special person in our lives—usually our mother. When attached, it is as if we were overcoming the space by clinging, holding on. The third way of connecting emerges from the need to suck and is the first form of *passionate experience,* where others are the objects of our drives for gratification. Then we experience *eye to eye validation,* where we connect by being significant to someone else.

Next, Josselson says, we begin to notice that some others are bigger, stronger, and more able than we are, and we begin to *idealize and identify* with them. This form of connection is a way of expanding ourselves. As we grow through childhood, we discover the possibilities of engaging with others in companionship, which is a form of *mutuality,* the sixth stage of contact. This is followed, usually around adolescence, with a developed sense of belonging to one group rather than another, which Josselson calls *embeddedness* with others. The final stage in interpersonal development is to the position where we can *hold* another, and Josselson calls this *tending and care.* In these actions we cradle others, actually or symbolically, in our arms, thus completing the developmental circle.

As Josselson notes, these dimensions of contact overlap and sometimes unfold simultaneously, but they are still distinct. Healthy and complete development moves through all eight stages, and aspects of the need for each kind of contact continue as parts of our experience. Think, for example, of your own occasional longing just to be held by your mom, dad, or intimate partner, movements from idealization to mutuality on the job, and the continuing need to feel embedded in a group, which some people fill by joining organizations. One way to think about the concepts and skills discussed in the first 14 chapters of this book is as efforts to experience all eight of these dimensions of contact.

When Josselson turns to her discussion of "Notes on Love," she builds on these eight dimensions. For one thing, she emphasizes that no one love relationship can provide all eight dimensions of connection. We need the love of different people. She also notes that the higher orders of mutuality, passion, and tenderness are "probably available only to those who have had adequate experiences of attachment, holding, and (later) embeddedness."

In the section "Love and Culture," Josselson reminds us that cultural expectations can narrow our experience of love. Among some people, for example, the nuclear family, or its postdivorce remnant, is expected to perform functions formerly carried out by a whole community, and when it fails, the mother is usually blamed. We also compare ourselves with impossible cultural norms established by the media.

Near the end of the reading Josselson discusses the inevitability of conflict in love relationships, and the continuing tension between the separation that conflict can bring and the connection we desire. She notes that conflict can actually be a form of connection, and that the tension between distance and relation is part of the reality of human life.

There is gentle wisdom on these pages, and I hope some of it speaks to you.

OVERCOMING THE SPACE BETWEEN US

Ruthellen Josselson

There are eight primary ways in which we overcome the space between us. They involve, actually or metaphorically, a way of transcending space, of reaching through space (or being reached) and being in contact with each other. As each dimension emerges in the developmental history of the individual, each is concrete and basic. As development proceeds, each way of connecting becomes more symbolic, less physical and spatial, but no less crucial. Each dimension of relatedness has its own channel, its own origin and course. Understanding each dimension uniquely allows us to understand the confluence of the streams that create the character of relatedness in adult life.

Holding is the first interpersonal experience and represents security and a basic trust that what is essential will be provided. In holding, we experience ourselves as contained by another; powerful arms keep us from falling. Throughout life, we need to feel held in developmentally more mature idioms, but we continue to need to be contained, bounded, and grounded in order to grow.

A bit later in earliest development, babies learn to discriminate their mothers from the other people around, making possible *attachment* to this one very particular other person. The innate propensity to attach to others structures some of the most fundamental processes throughout life, including the painful

Excerpts from *The Space Between Us: Exploring the Dimensions of Human Relationships* by Ruthellen Josselson, 1996, pp. 6–8, 241–249. Reprinted by permission of Sage Publications, Inc.

vulnerability to loss that is part of our human core. When we are attached, it is as though we were clinging to someone, holding on with our limbs, keeping close. Throughout life, we continue to form attachments (if we are fortunate), and these are often at the center of our existence.

From the beginning of life, basic biological drives seek gratification. In infancy, the need to suck—the earliest form of libidinal life—forms a third configuration of interpersonal experience. Here, in the realm of *passionate experience,* others are objects of drive gratification. This pleasure-seeking orientation will organize experience in different ways and at different levels of intensity throughout the life course. Contacting others through our drives is the mode of passionate relating: overcoming separateness through sexual union or its symbolic expression. The pleasures of touch and the possibilities of uniting in boundaryless bliss are powerful means of transcending space.

In eye-to-eye relating, we overcome space through the communication of eye contact, finding ourselves in the other's eyes, having a place in the other. In *eye-to-eye validation,* we connect by existing in and for someone else. As early in development as we become able to know an other as an Other, we begin to use the other as a mirror to learn about ourselves. What the infant first sees in the mother's eyes forms a core of the infant's sense of self—the beginning of a process that continues in more refined and complex ways throughout life.

After existing for a time in this world of Others, we begin to notice that some are bigger, stronger, and more able to do things than we are ourselves. When we idealize and identify with others, we reach up for them, try to climb through the distance that separates us; we try to be where they are as a way of expanding ourselves. *Idealization and identification* are ways of linking to powerful others and striving to become like them (or to control them.)

As the person grows through childhood and the self matures and becomes more aware of others, the child eventually discovers the possibilities of engaging the self with others and becomes able to experience companionship, which is a form of *mutuality.* In mutuality, we stand side by side with someone, moving in harmony, creating a bond that is the product of both people—an emergent *we* in the space between.

When we are embedded with others, we "fit in" like a piece of a jigsaw puzzle; we are comfortable in our role, our "place." It is not usually until adolescence that the concern with having a place in society becomes paramount. Yet younger children also make important their sense of belonging to one group rather than another, differentiating themselves and at the same time experiencing communality. The experience is one of being part of, belonging—the dimension of *embeddedness* with others.

Finally, but all along, the developing person has been learning about taking care of others, offering the self to others' needs, bridging the space through *tending and care.* In tending, we hold others, cradling them (actually or symbolically) in our arms.

All of these modalities, then, are forms of reaching through the space that separates us, both physically and psychologically. Any given relationship may involve more than one of these dimensions, simultaneously or sequentially. The metaphor of spatial orientation is useful in cutting through confusing verbalizations to clarify how people are oriented toward each other and what they need to feel connected.

These dimensions of relatedness unfold simultaneously and often independently, although they may interpenetrate and incorporate each other. They are not, however, reducible one to another. Because human life is of a piece, the dimensions shade into one another; they do not stay separate and distinct (as well they should not). But each has its own coherent center; . . . each has its own metaphor and form of expression. Thinking in these terms allows us to move beyond thinking of all human connection as rooted in and metaphorically experienced as "good feeding."

How and toward whom love is expressed varies by culture. Yet there are certain fundamental human propensities for connection that find expression in some form universally. Social mores and traditions regulate the rituals and forms through which people are held or recognized or idealized, but the processes of these eight dimensions remain identifiable. . . .

NOTES ON LOVE

Love glitters because of its many facets; it captivates us because it is always unique, always singular in its expression. The question is not, What is love? but, What are loves? So much of human misunderstanding, however, derives from the mistaken assumption that *love* has a universally shared definition, as do words like *run* and *dog*, or even affect words such as *angry* and *happy*. But my experiences with love and needs for love are *not* the same as yours. Indeed, each person has a highly individual love "recipe" that idiosyncratically intermingles the eight dimensions of connection to others. The quality of love changes when it is composed of different dimensions.[1]

Although the cult of individualism often stresses that we should find the all-encompassing love in one individual, few individuals can satisfy all the love needs of another.[2] Yet people often feel like failures if their primary relationship does not satisfy all their relational needs. We need different dimensions of connection (in various combinations) from different people, and in turn we offer highly individual forms of responsiveness to others. . . .

Our common understanding of love implies either that the loved one is held in high esteem and intensely valued by the one who loves *or* that the love is a bond of attachment that can be taken for granted (along with the loved one)—a relationship neither esteemed nor necessarily intense. In addition, the common view of love presupposes a measure of exclusivity of the loved one, a sense of being special and different from those who are not loved.

When people talk about loving, however, they seem to experience little contradiction in the fact that they love their mother, their father, their grandmother, their aunt, their friend, their husband, their children, their mentor, and so on. All of these, however, are qualitatively different relationships that serve vastly different needs and exist on different dimensions of relational connection. . . .

There is no other word that is used for such a variety of emotional experiences. Love is the passion of one lover for another, the tenderness of parent for child, the attachment of old friends, the mutuality of shared experience, the gratitude for understanding and validation, the security of being adequately held, the admiration for someone who seems wonderful, and the joy of feeling at home. Perhaps what we mean when we say that we love is that we feel that the person we love is in some way essential for our existence.

In this fundamental existential sense, we can love and can be loved on any of the dimensions, exclusively or in combination. We love the one who holds us, because without that person we could not exist; and we love those we hold, because we mean so much to them. We love those to whom we are attached, because they are our emotional "home," where we will be taken in no matter what, and they are the people with whom our lives are intertwined. And we love those who mirror and recognize us, because without them we could not be. All these people we love with gratitude, for they give us ourselves. We also love those who are the objects of our passions, because they arouse and excite us and seem to embody all that would complete us. This person we wish to possess, exclusively and eternally. And we love those who embody our ideals, who stimulate us to reach beyond ourselves, who represent our becoming. We love those with whom we share ourselves, in play and in knowledge of one another. These are the people who walk with us through life, and they are irreplaceable. And we love those whom we tend and nurture, because they contain a part of us and testify to our value as human beings. We love, too, those with whom we are embedded; these people we love less personally but, especially in times of group distress, no less profoundly.

It may be that there are higher and lower forms of love, each building on the other. People who grew up deprived of adequate attachment experiences, for example, seek, above all, enduring attachment in later life. Such people—for example, child survivors of the Holocaust whose parents were taken from them and murdered—speak little as adults about a quest for passion or mutuality. For them, feeling bonded to special others in new attachments overshadows *all* other forms of relatedness (Moskowitz, 1983).

While healthy development requires some relational connection on all of the dimensions, the higher orders of mutuality, passion, and tenderness, for example, are probably available only to those who have had adequate experiences of attachment, holding, and (later) embeddedness. . . .

The labyrinths of our relationships with each other are created by our unique recipes for love. The arguments between spouses, between brothers and sisters, and between friends all begin with built-in—perhaps even unconscious—expectations of how one would treat and be treated if love bound the relationship. Thus "If you loved me, you would . . ." is a fundamental phrase of human misunderstanding.

Love and Culture

We have to be wary of love ideology that is based on cultural assumptions. Only recently, with the triumph of "therapeutic" ideals (Rieff, 1966), has "authentic feeling" become the ideological basis of love relationships. In contrast to previous eras, in which kinship or class or duty served to lead people to each other, our age anchors relationship in feeling.[3] The ideal is the heterosexual pair who are "in love," experiencing passion, tenderness, and attachment. Real relatedness among people—relatedness that sustains life, powers development, and shapes identity—is, however, far more complex.

Expectations about love are, to a large extent, dictated by culture.[4] That is dangerous only when people are confused as to what is a cultural ideal and what they can expect in reality. People are alarmed when they find themselves loving differently from others, for example. They are also confused by the idealization of love in a materialistic environment. When love is promoted as a commodity, it is hard to know when we have gotten our share. How much exactly are we entitled to? How do we know whether to stay with a relationship and try to improve it or simply move on? . . . Between our experience with another and our integration of that experience are multiple steps of meaning-making. . . .

The relational networks of our highly mobile, loosely organized society force people into increasingly smaller units of relational connection and at the same time idealize these units beyond their capacity to deliver. The current emphasis on marital "togetherness" often burdens the relationship beyond its endurance and so gives rise to an industry of self-help books and marriage counselors to try to keep it intact.

Similarly, the nuclear family is now asked to perform functions formerly carried out by a whole community, and when it fails in its task, it is usually the mother who is "blamed" (Luepnitz, 1988). As the extended family was fading out of existence in urban America in the 1950s, in response to rapidly increasing geographical mobility and the turn to the suburbs, the extremely popular television program "Father Knows Best" was romanticizing the nuclear family. No other television program has appeared so frequently in my patients' associations— associations related to their intense disappointment in their own families for not being like the TV family. They yearned for the calm understanding and compassion of that all-wise, ideal father, whom they were afraid all others had and they alone lacked.

We all secretly suspect that the reason that we do not get more from others is that we are undeserving, unacceptable. ("If only I could lose ten pounds, I would be loved as much as I want.") We compare our own experience of what others offer us with media images and come up short. We are ashamed to compare our experiences with others, because we may be exposed in our inadequacy. Thus many people live with the painful sense of having less loyal and interested friends than others do, less passionate spouses, less reliable attachment figures. To comfort and distract themselves, they seize on the current cultural and therapeutic message that what we really ought to do in life is learn to do it all ourselves. Love ourselves, take care of ourselves, draw wider boundaries. Be our own best friend! (I wonder how anything so absurd could have captured so many people.) Let's just not need each other, our culture urges.

Conflict and the Irrationalities of Love

The dimensional model of relatedness emphasizes the yearning for connection, but power, competition, and conflict are also present throughout. Within each of the dimensions of connection lurks the threat (and experience) of the opposite. We are most aware of being held when we begin to fall or feel smothered, for example. Nothing sharpens our sense of ourselves and our meaning for others as much as a heated argument or contest. Sometimes we most heighten our experience of a dimension of love when we veer into its absence or excess. . . .

Conflict is itself a form of connection, existing on each of the dimensions. Anger, envy, and contempt color all relationships. To speak of relational connection is not to imply seamless harmony or warm fuzziness or anything static and unchanging. Above all, relationships *move*. We discover the self though our conections with others, and our heightening of self-knowledge makes possible more complex and deeper ways of reaching others. As we grow, we refine and modify our connections. We never fully bridge the space between us, but we experience within our lives many ways of reaching across. . . .

To be unloved is unbearable because it means that we have no real meaning or importance to anyone. As humans, we are stuck with our inescapable need for the emotional responsiveness of another—a need kindled by the sparkle in our mother's eye, a need that serves no biological purpose and often causes us tremendous pain. But unless we know that we are somewhere part of the affective life of another, we cannot feel our own existence. This is why people who fear that they are unloved often work to be hated (hate being just another face of love in its intensity and its selectivity).

Conflict between us and those whom we take into our relational networks, conflict among the dimensions of our relational needs— these conflict generally must be lived with rather than "resolved." We can try to achieve a higher order of understanding and integration, or we can tear ourselves apart trying to insist on relational illusions or relational consistency. . . .

Marge, a thirty-five-year-old research subject, told of her own dreams of love. For years, while she was in her twenties, she was involved with a married man whom she idealized. He was in her profession, and she was always very stimulated talking to him about ideas. There was much mutuality between them, and wonderful sex. Yet she knew that his attachment to his wife was so strong that he would never leave her. What Marge was focused on was wanting just once to hear him tell her that he loved her. She felt that these would be the magic words that would let her know that she was a person of value. (He often told her that he loved being with her or loved making love to her, but he never said that he loved *her*.) Finally, after a five-year relationship, he said the magic words. And Marge said that she felt nothing. The declaration meant nothing. As in the wonderful "Do You Love Me?" song from *Fiddler on the Roof*, it did not change a thing. And she left him.

Consider also the insightful scene in the movie *Tootsie* where the Jessica Lange character confides to the female Dustin Hoffman character that her deepest fantasy is that someday a man will come up to her and say, with no ritual or small talk, "The simple truth is—I find you really interesting—and I'd really like to make love to you." Some days later, the Dustin Hoffman character, back as a man, obligingly does just that. And she throws her drink in his face. . . .

To understand relatedness, we must be able to encompass paradox and contradiction. Inner and outer, self and other, love and hate, fantasy and reality, rational and irrational, conscious and unconscious—all coexist within the relational frame.

Always there is the fear that love, in its many manifestations and dimensions, is not very scientific. And so we try to make love problems appear to be something else. People go to psychiatrists because they are lonely and feel unloved, and they are given medication: the "scientific" response.

A patient consults me for intractable stomach pain that physicians have been unable to treat medically. I am her fifth therapist. Others have told her that her problem is her oral dependency, her inhibited sexuality, possible sexual abuse (which she does not remember), repressed rage. She is talented, attractive, and sensitive but has no friends. What does she feel she needs? I ask her. "I need to have someone in my corner," she says. And that, I think, is the essence of it. So do we all.

REVIEW QUESTIONS

1. What is the main difference between the first two stages, holding and attachment?
2. What does Josselson mean when she says that when we connect in eye-to-eye validation, we "exist in and for someone else"?
3. Explain the difference between idealization and mutuality.
4. Why is it significant that the final stage of contact consists in giving to someone else the first stage of contact?
5. What point does Josselson make with her example of child survivors of the Holocaust?
6. What is the problem with the cultural idealization of love as the heterosexual pair who are experiencing passion, tenderness, and attachment?
7. What does it mean to say that "conflict is itself is a form of connection"?

PROBES

1. Notice how sexual passion is clearly a dimension of connectedness, but only one dimension out of eight. Especially in the midst of adolescence, when this dimension is heightened, it is difficult to keep sexuality in perspective. What are the benefits, and the dangers, of balancing your expectations for sexual contact in this way?
2. What was the first group you joined that gave you an early experience of embeddedness?
3. No one person, Josselson argues, can satisfy all of anyone's love needs. Does this mean that she doesn't believe in marriage? Explain.
4. Josselson suggests that some people live with the painful sense that they have less loyal and interested friends than others, or less passionate spouses. What misunderstanding can create this condition?

5. At the end of this reading, Josselson contrasts the "scientific" response to loneliness with another approach. What is it?

NOTES

1. Sternberg (1986) develops a theory that similarly schematizes love as multi-dimensional, resulting from different mixtures of ingredients. He describes eight forms of love by combining the following three components: intimacy (closeness, the emotional component), passion (arousal, the motivational component), and commitment (deciding to stay together, the cognitive component). His three factors seem best to correspond to what I call mutuality, passion, and attachment, respectively.
2. See Marris (1982) for further discussion of the ideological contexts of love relationships.
3. This idea is explored carefully and thoughtfully by Bellah and others (1985).
4. One central way in which a culture regulates how love is expressed is through its attitude toward homosexuality.

REFERENCES

Bellah, R. N., and others, (1985). *Habits of the heart.* New York: Harper Collins.

Leupnitz, D. A., (1988). *The family interpreted: Feminist theory in clinical practice.* New York: Basic Books.

Marris, P. (1982). Attachment and society. In C. M. Parkes & J. Stevenson-Hinde (eds.), *The place of attachment in human behavior.* New York: Basic Books.

Moskowitz, S., (1983). *Love despite hate.* New York: Schocken.

Rieff, P., (1966). *The triumph of the therapeutic.* New York: Harper Collins.

Sternberg, R. J. (1986). A triangular theory of love. *Psychological Review, 93:* 119–135.

CHAPTER 17

A Counselor's Approach

C arl Rogers was a psychotherapist and communication theorist who influenced many of the authors represented in this book. I highly recommend that you read at least one of his books—for example, *On Becoming a Person, Person to Person: The Process of Becoming Human,* or his most recent book, *A Way of Being.* In the 1950s Rogers was one of the half-dozen persons responsible for moving psychology away from an exclusive focus on Freudian psychodynamics and quantifiable variables to a concern with the whole person and communication relationships. By the time of his death in the late 1980s, he was known all over the world as a psychotherapist, group facilitator, and teacher.

This reading is made up of excerpts from a chapter in *A Way of Being.* Like many of his writings, this one was originally a talk he gave, in this case an invited speech at the California Institute of Technology. Rogers reports that as he prepared for the occasion, he became frustrated at his own efforts to describe what he believed about communication. So he decided to demonstrate rather than simply discuss, to endeavor, as he put it, "to *communicate,* rather than just to speak about the subject of communication."

In another place, Rogers wrote that over his lifetime he had discovered that "what is most personal is most general." This talk is evidence of this same insight. Rogers tries to stick close to his personal experiences with communication, and as he describes them, he finds himself talking about my experience—and probably yours, too. So this essay demonstrates how "what is most personal is most general."

One of the reasons I like much of what Rogers says is that he begins discussing communication by focusing not on talk but on listening. He describes what it means really to hear someone and to be heard, to be listened to by another. Over his 40 years as a psychotherapist, Rogers learned that complete hearing—listening, clarifying, and responding to all the levels at which the other is communicating—is one key to a therapeutic, growth-promoting relationship. The therapist, he argues, doesn't primarily need to be able to administer psychometric tests or interpret dreams. The most important thing is that he or she needs to make contact, to communicate interpersonally. As Rogers summarizes, "a creative, active, sensitive, accurate, emphatic, nonjudgmental listening is for me terribly important in a relationship."

The second of Rogers's three main points involves what he calls "congruence." This is his label for the state where "my experiencing of this moment is present in my awareness and when what is present in my awareness is present in my communication." As he explains in other writings, this does not mean that you impulsively blurt out every thought that enters your mind. Especially when you're experiencing mixed feelings, it's important to reflect on the dimensions of experience that deserve communicating. Rogers also believes that incongruence is often an outgrowth of fear.

The flip side of congruence, of course, is allowing and encouraging the other to be congruent too. As Rogers says, this is often the ultimate test for the leader, teacher, and parent. But when at least some measure of congruence characterizes both sides of a relationship, the communication is enriched by it.

Rogers's third learning is that what he's called "unconditional positive regard" or "nonpossessive warmth" is also vital to effective communication. People typically experience so much evaluation and criticism that when they feel accepted for who they are, they often blossom. As he notes, people can be appreciated just as we appreciate a sunset.

In other writings, Rogers has also clarified that he doesn't mean we should go around in a naïve fog, loving every terrorist, rapist, and sociopath who makes the front page. He worked extensively with "sick" persons, and he knew what it was like to apply the principle of unconditional positive regard to his communication with them. Often the key is to separate the person and the behavior so that you can accept the former while rejecting the latter. It is also important to remember that persons act in ways that make the most sense to them at the time they act. Observers may not be able to fathom the sense that some actions make, but if we want to communicate with these persons—without necessarily condoning what they do—positive regard helps.

When Rogers gave this talk, it was remarkable to hear a person being so open and straightforward in such a relatively "formal" situation. Rogers was often disarmingly direct in just that way. I hope his directness enables you to hear what he has to say. Carl Rogers had an approach to interpersonal communication that is very much worth getting to know.

Rogers is another "classic" writer who used "he" to mean "everyone." As with the essays by Gibb and Buber, I hope you can read beyond this language for the good ideas that are here.

EXPERIENCES IN COMMUNICATION

Carl R. Rogers

. . . What I would like to do is very simple indeed. I would like to share with you some of the things I have learned for myself in regard to communication. They are personal learnings growing out of my own experience. I am not attempting at all to say that you should learn or do these same things but I feel that if I can report my own experience honestly enough, perhaps you can check what I say against your own experience and decide as to its truth or falsity for you. . . . Another way of putting this is that some of my experiences in communicating with others have made me feel expanded, larger, enriched, and have accelerated my own growth. Very often in these experiences I feel that the other person has had similar reactions and that he too has been enriched, that his development and his functioning have moved forward. Then there have been other occasions in which the growth or development of each of us has been diminished or stopped or even reversed. . . .

The first simple feeling I want to share with you is my enjoyment when I can really *hear* someone. I think perhaps this has been a long-standing characteristic of mine. I can remember this in my early grammar school days. A child would ask the teacher a question and the teacher would give a perfectly good answer to a completely different question. A feeling of pain and distress would always strike me. My reaction was, "But you didn't hear him!" I felt a sort of childish despair at the lack of communication which was (and is) so common.

I believe I know why it is satisfying to me to hear someone. When I can really hear someone, it puts me in touch with him; it enriches my life. It is through hearing people that I have learned all that I know about individuals, about personality, about interpersonal relationships. . . .

When I say that I enjoy hearing someone, I mean, of course, hearing deeply. I mean that I hear the words, the thoughts, the feeling tones, the personal meaning, even the meaning that is below the conscious intent of the speaker. Sometimes too, in a message which superficially is not very important, I hear a deep human cry that lies buried and unknown far below the surface of the person.

So I have learned to ask myself, can I hear the sounds and sense the shape of this other person's inner world? Can I resonate to what he is saying so deeply that I sense the meanings he is afraid of yet would like to communicate, as well as those he knows?

I think, for example, of an interview I had with an adolescent boy. Like many an adolescent today he was saying at the outset of the interview that he had no goals. When I questioned him on this, he insisted even more strongly that he had no goals whatsoever, not even one. I said, "There isn't anything you want to do?" "Nothing. . . . Well, yeah, I want to keep on living." I remember distinctly my feeling at that moment. I resonated very deeply to this phrase. He might simply be telling me that, like everyone else, he wanted to live. On the other hand, he might be telling me—and this seemed to be a definite possibility—that at some point the question of whether or not to live had been a real issue with him. So I tried to resonate to him at all levels. I didn't know for certain what the message was. I simply wanted to be open to any of the meanings that this statement might have, including the possibility that he might at one time have considered suicide. My being willing and able to listen to him at all levels is perhaps one of the things that made it possible for him to tell me, before the end of the interview, that not long before he had been on the point of blowing his brains out. This little episode is an example of what I mean by wanting to really hear someone at all the levels at which he is endeavoring to communicate. . . .

I find, both in therapeutic interviews and in the intensive group experiences which have meant a great deal to me, that hearing has consequences. When I truly hear a person and the meanings that are important to him at that moment, hearing not simply his words, but him, and when I let him know that I have heard his own private personal meanings, many things happen. There is first of all a grateful look. He feels released. He wants to tell me more about his world. He surges forth in a new sense of freedom. He becomes more open to the process of change. . . .

Let me move on to a second learning that I would like to share with you. I like to *be heard.* A number of times in my life I have felt myself bursting with insoluble problems, or going round and round in tormented circles or, during one period, overcome by feelings of worthlessness and despair. I think I have been more fortunate than most in finding at these times individuals who have been able to hear me and thus to rescue me from the chaos of my feelings, individuals who have been able to hear my meanings a little more deeply than I have known them. These persons have heard me without judging me, diagnosing me, appraising me, evaluating me. They have just listened and clarified and responded to me at all the levels at which I was communicating. I can testify that when you are in psychological distress and someone really hears you without passing judgment on you, without trying to take responsibility for you, without trying to mold you, it feels damn good! At these times it has relaxed the tension in me. It has permitted me to bring out the frightening feelings, the guilts, the despair, the confusions that have been a part of my experience. When I have been listened to and when I have been heard, I am able to reperceive my world in a new way and to go on. It is astonishing how elements that seem insoluble become soluble when someone listens, how confusions that seem irremediable turn into relatively clear flowing streams when one is heard. I have deeply appreciated the times that I have experienced this sensitive, empathic, concentrated listening.

I dislike it myself when I can't hear another, when I do not understand him. If it is only a simple failure of comprehension or a failure to focus my attention on what he is saying or a difficulty in understanding his words, then I feel only a very mild dissatisfaction with myself. But what I really dislike in myself is not being able to hear the other person because I am so sure in advance of what he is about to say that I don't listen. It is only afterward that I realize that I have heard what I have already decided he is saying; I have failed really to listen. Or even worse are those times when I catch myself trying to twist his message to make it say what I want him to say, and then only hearing that. This can be a very subtle thing, and it is surprising how skillful I can be in doing it. Just by twisting his words a small amount, by distorting his meaning just a little, I can make it appear that he is not only saying the thing I want to hear, but that he is the person I want him to be. Only when I realize through his protest or through my own gradual recognition that I am subtly manipulating him, do I become disgusted with myself. I know too, from being on the receiving end of this, how frustrating it is to be received for what you are not, to be heard as saying something which you have not said. This creates anger and bafflement and disillusion.

This last statement indeed leads into the next learning that I want to share with you: I am terribly frustrated and shut into myself when I try to express something which is deeply me, which is a part of my own private, inner world, and the other person does not understand. When I take the gamble, the risk, of trying to share something that is very personal with another individual and it is not received and not understood, this is a very deflating and a very lonely experience. I have come to believe that such an experience makes some individuals psychotic. It causes them to give up hoping that anyone can understand them. Once they have lost that hope, then their own inner world, which becomes more and more bizarre, is the only place where they can live. They can no longer live in any shared human experience. I can sympathize with them because I know that when I try to share some feeling aspect of myself which is private, precious, and tentative, and when this communication is met by evaluation, by reassurance, by distortion of my meaning, my very strong reaction is, "Oh, what's the use!" At such a time, one knows what it is to be alone.

So, as you can readily see from what I have said thus far, a creative, active, sensitive, accurate, empathic, nonjudgmental listening is for me terribly important in a relationship. It is important for me to provide it; it has been extremely important, especially at certain times in my life, to receive it. I feel that I have grown within myself when I have provided it; I am very sure that I have grown and been released and enhanced when I have received this kind of listening.

Let me move on to another area of my learnings.

I find it very satisfying when I can be real, when I can be close to whatever it is that is going on within me. I like it when I can listen to myself. To really know what I am experiencing in the moment is by no means an easy thing, but I feel somewhat encouraged because I think that over the years I have been improving at it. I am convinced, however, that it is a lifelong task and that none of us ever is totally able to be comfortably close to all that is going on within our own experience.

In place of the term "realness" I have sometimes used the word "congruence." By this I mean when my experiencing of this moment is present in my awareness and when what is present in my awareness is present in my communication, then each of these three levels matches or is congruent. At such moments I am integrated or whole, I am completely in one piece. Most of the time, of course, I, like everyone else, exhibit some degree of incongruence. I have learned, however, that realness, or genuineness, or congruence—whatever term you wish to give it—is a fundamental basis for the best of communication.

What do I mean by being close to what is going on in me? Let me try to explain what I mean by describing what sometimes occurs in my work as a therapist. Sometimes a feeling "rises up in me" which seems to have no particular relationship to what is going on. Yet I have learned to accept and trust this feeling in my awareness and to try to communicate it to my client. For example, a client is talking to me and I suddenly feel an image of him as a pleading little boy, folding his hands in supplication, saying, "Please let me have this, please let me have this." I have learned that if I can be real in the relationship with him and express this feeling that has occurred in me, it is very likely to strike some deep note in him and to advance our relationship. . . .

I feel a sense of satisfaction when I can dare to communicate the realness in me to another. This is far from easy, partly because what I am experiencing keeps changing every moment. Usually there is a lag, sometimes of moments,

sometimes of days, weeks or months, between the experiencing and the communication: I experience something; I feel something, but only later do I dare to
communicate it, when it has become cool enough to risk sharing it with another.
But when I can communicate what is real in me at the moment that it occurs, I
feel genuine, spontaneous, and alive.

I am disappointed when I realize—and of course this realization always
comes afterward, after a lag of time—that I have been too frightened or too
threatened to let myself get close to what I am experiencing, and that consequently I have not been genuine or congruent. There immediately comes to
mind an instance that is somewhat painful to reveal. Some years ago I was invited to be a Fellow at the Center for Advanced Study in the Behavioral Sciences
at Stanford. The Fellows are a group of brilliant and well-informed scholars. I
suppose it is inevitable that there is a considerable amount of one-upmanship,
of showing off one's knowledge and achievements. It seems important for each
Fellow to impress the others, to be a little more assured, to be a little more
knowledgeable than he really is. I found myself doing this same thing—playing
a role of having greater certainty and greater competence than I really possess.
I can't tell you how disgusted with myself I felt as I realized what I was doing:
I was not being me, I was playing a part.

I regret it when I suppress my feelings too long and they burst forth in ways
that are distorted or attacking or hurtful. I have a friend whom I like very much
but who has one particular pattern of behavior that thoroughly annoys me. Because of the usual tendency to be nice, polite, and pleasant I kept this annoyance
to myself for too long and, when it finally burst its bounds, it came out not only
as annoyance but as an attack on him. This was hurtful, and it took us some time
to repair the relationship.

I am inwardly pleased when I have the strength to permit another person to
be his own realness and to be separate from me. I think that is often a very threatening possibility. In some ways I have found it an ultimate test of staff leadership and of parenthood. Can I freely permit this staff member or my son or my
daughter to become a separate person with ideas, purpose, and values which
may not be identical with my own? I think of one staff member this past year
who showed many flashes of brilliance but who clearly held values different
from mine and behaved in ways very different from the ways in which I would
behave. It was a real struggle, in which I feel I was only partially successful, to
let him be himself, to let him develop as a person entirely separate from me and
my ideas and my values. Yet to the extent that I was successful, I was pleased
with myself, because I think this permission to be a separate person is what
makes for the autonomous development of another individual.

I am angry with myself when I discover that I have been subtly controlling
and molding another person in my own image. This has been a very painful part
of my professional experience. I hate to have "disciples," students who have
molded themselves meticulously into the pattern that they feel I wish. Some of
the responsibility I place with them, but I cannot avoid the uncomfortable probability that in unknown ways I have subtly controlled such individuals and
made them into carbon copies of myself, instead of the separate professional
persons they have every right to become.

From what I have been saying, I trust it is clear that when I can permit real-ness in myself or sense it or permit it in another, I am very satisfied. When I cannot permit it in myself or fail to permit it in another, I am very distressed. When I am able to let myself be congruent and genuine, I often help the other person. When the other person is transparently real and congruent, he often helps me. In those rare moments when a deep realness in one meets a realness in the other, a memorable "I-thou relationship," as Martin Buber would call it, occurs. Such a deep and mutual personal encounter does not happen often, but I am convinced that unless it happens occasionally, we are not living as human beings.

I want to move on to another area of my learning in interpersonal relationships—one that has been slow and painful for me.

I feel warmed and fulfilled when I can let in the fact, or permit myself to feel, that someone cares for, accepts, admires, or prizes me. Because of elements in my past history, I suppose, it has been very difficult for me to do this. For a long time I tended almost automatically to brush aside any positive feelings aimed in my direction. My reaction was, "Who, me? You couldn't possibly care for me. You might like what I have done, or my achievements, but not me." This is one respect in which my own therapy helped me very much. I am not always able even now to let in such warm and loving feelings from others, but I find it very releasing when I can do so. I know that some people flatter me in order to gain something for themselves; some people praise me because they are afraid to be hostile. But I have come to recognize the fact that some people genuinely appreciate me, like me, love me, and I want to sense that fact and let it in. I think I have become less aloof as I have been able to take in and soak up those loving feelings.

I feel enriched when I can truly prize or care for or love another person and when I can let that feeling flow out to that person. Like many others, I used to fear being trapped by letting my feelings show. "If I care for him, he can control me." "If I love her, I am trying to control her." I think that I have moved a long way toward being less fearful in this respect. Like my clients, I too have slowly learned that tender, positive feelings are not dangerous either to give or to receive. . . .

I think of one governmental executive in a group in which I participated, a man with high responsibility and excellent technical training as an engineer. At the first meeting of the group he impressed me, and I think others, as being cold, aloof, somewhat bitter, resentful, and cynical. When he spoke of how he ran his office, it appeared that he administered it "by the book," without any warmth or human feeling. In one of the early sessions he was speaking of his wife, and a group member asked him, "Do you love your wife?" He paused for a long time and the questioner said, "O.K. That's answer enough." The executive said, "No. Wait a minute. The reason I didn't respond was that I was wondering, 'Have I ever loved anyone?' I don't really think I have ever *loved* anyone."

A few days later, he listened with great intensity as one member of the group revealed many personal feelings of isolation and loneliness and spoke of the extent to which he had been living behind a facade. The next morning the engineer said, "Last night I thought and thought about what he told us. I even wept quite a bit myself. I can't remember how long it has been since I have cried, and I really felt something. I think perhaps what I felt was love."

It is not surprising that before the week was over, he had thought through different ways of handling his growing son, on whom he had been placing very rigorous demands. He had also began to really appreciate the love his wife had extended to him—love that he now felt he could in some measure reciprocate.

Because of having less fear of giving or receiving positive feelings, I have become more able to appreciate individuals. I have come to believe that this ability is rather rare; so often, even with our children, we love them to control them rather than loving them because we appreciate them. One of the most satisfying feelings I know—and also one of the most growth-promoting experiences for the other person—comes from my appreciating this individual in the same way that I appreciate a sunset. People are just as wonderful as sunsets if I can let them *be.* In fact, perhaps the reason we can truly appreciate a sunset is that we cannot control it. When I look at a sunset as I did the other evening, I don't find myself saying, "Soften the orange a little on the right hand corner, and put a bit more purple along the base, and use a little more pink in the cloud color." I don't do that. I don't *try* to control a sunset. I watch it with awe as it unfolds. I like myself best when I can appreciate my staff member, my son, my daughter, my grandchildren, in this same way. I believe this is a somewhat Oriental attitude; for me it is a most satisfying one.

Another learning I would like to mention briefly is one of which I am not proud but which seems to be a fact. When I am not prized and appreciated, I not only *feel* very much diminished, but my behavior is actually affected by my feelings. When I am prized, I blossom and expand, I am an interesting individual. In a hostile or unappreciative group, I am just not much of anything. People wonder, with very good reason, how did he ever get a reputation? I wish I had the strength to be more similar in both kinds of groups, but actually the person I am in a warm and interested group is different from the person I am in a hostile or cold group.

Thus, prizing or loving and being prized or loved is experienced as very growth enhancing. A person who is loved appreciatively, not possessively, blooms and develops his own unique self. The person who loves nonpossessively is himself enriched. This, at least, has been my experience.

I could give you some of the research evidence which shows that these qualities I have mentioned—an ability to listen emphatically, a congruence or genuineness an acceptance or prizing of the other—when they are present in a relationship make for good communication and for constructive change in personality. But I feel that, somehow, research evidence is out of place in a talk such as I have been giving.

REVIEW QUESTIONS

1. What does Rogers mean by "hearing deeply"?
2. According to Rogers, what is the primary outcome of someone's being fully or deeply heard?
3. What does congruence mean? What does it *not* mean?

4. How does the fact that I am changing from moment to moment affect my being congruent?
5. At what points in his talk does Rogers suggest that the communication he is discussing is appropriate in nonintimate—that is, business or professional—settings?

PROBES

1. Which discussion of listening in Chapter 6 is closest to Rogers's description of hearing another and being heard?
2. How is Rogers's concept of congruence related to what McKay, Davis, and Fanning say about expressing in Chapter 7?
3. Do you think congruence helps create a defensive or a supportive communication climate (see Chapter 13)?
4. Did you ever feel uncomfortable as you read Rogers's words? What do those feelings tell you about one of the topics of Chapter 7, self-disclosure?
5. How do you think Anita Vangelisti, the author of "Messages That Hurt," in Chapter 8, would respond to what Rogers says here?

CHAPTER 18

A Philosopher's Approach

Martin Buber, a Jewish philosopher and teacher, was born and raised in Austria and Germany and died in 1965 in Israel. Throughout his life, Buber was both a "scholar," or "intellectual," and an intensely practical person interested in everyday life experiences. As an intellectual, he was hungry to learn and to write all he could about how humans relate with one another. As a practical person, he was determined to keep all his theorizing and scholarship firmly based on the concrete events he experienced every day. Because he was raised by his grandparents in Europe during the late nineteenth and early twentieth centuries (Buber's parents were divorced), lived through both world wars, was active in several political movements, and was a well-known, even famous, citizen of Israel, his life experiences are different in many ways from yours and mine. But for me, Buber's peculiar genius is that he can sense the part of his experience that is universal and can project that universal knowledge about human meetings through his European heritage and his "foreign" native language in such a way that he talks to me directly. In other words, even though he is in many ways very different from me, he says, "this is my experience; reflect on it a little and you might find that it's your experience too." Sometimes I stumble over Buber's language, the way he puts things. For example, like some other older authors in this book, Buber uses "man" when he means "human." But when I listen to him and do what he asks, I discover that he's right. It *is* my experience, only now I understand it better than I did before.

I don't know whether this one excerpt from Buber's writing will work this way for you. But the possibility is there if you will open yourself to hear him.[1] That's one thing about Buber's writings. Although he's a philosopher, he has been criticized because he doesn't state philosophical propositions and then try to verify and validate them with "proof." Instead, Buber insists that his reader try to meet him in a *conversation*, a dialogue. The main thing is for the reader to see whether his or her life experiences resonate with Buber's. This resonance is the only "proof" of the validity of Buber's ideas that the reader will receive. So far, millions of persons have experienced this resonance. Books by and about Buber, especially his *I and Thou*, have been translated into over 20 languages and are read around the world.

In almost all his writing, Buber begins by observing that each of us lives a twofold reality. One "fold" is made up of our interaction with objects—human and otherwise—in the world. In this model of living, we merely need to develop and maintain our ability to be "objective," to explain ourselves and the world with accurate theories and valid cause-and-effect formulations. But the other "fold" occurs when we become fully human *persons* in genuine relationships with others, when we meet another and "make the other present as a whole and as a unique being, as the person that he is."

The genuine relationship Buber talks about is the "highest form" of what I've been calling interpersonal communication. You've probably heard of Buber's term for it—an "*I-Thou* relationship."[2] According to Buber, the individual lives always in the world of *I-It*; the person can enter the world of *I-Thou*. Both worlds are necessary. You can't expect to communicate interpersonally with everyone in every situation. But you can only become a fully human person by sharing genuine interpersonal relationships with others. As Buber puts it, without *It* the person cannot live. But he who lives with *It* alone is not a person.

This article is taken from a talk Buber gave when he visited the United States in 1957. It's especially useful because it is a kind of summary of much of what he had written in the first 79 years of his life (he died when he was 87).

I've outlined the article to simplify it some and to show how clearly organized it actually is. As you can see from the outline, Buber's subject is interpersonal relationships, which he calls "man's personal dealings with one another," or "the interhuman." Like the rest of this book, Buber's article doesn't deal with some mystical spirit world in which we all become one. Rather, he's writing about communication between today's teachers and students, politicians and voters, dating partners, and between you and me. First, he explains some attitudes and actions that keep people from achieving "genuine dialogue." Then he describes the characteristics of this dialogue, or *I-Thou* relationship. In the outline I've paraphrased each point that he makes.

When you read the essay, you'll probably be able to see where several of the other writers in this book got some of their ideas. For example, compare Carl Rogers's explanation of "congruence" with what Buber says about "being and seeming."

Whether or not you note that kind of thing, however, read this article as thoughtfully as you can. It sums up everything in this book. And I know from the experience I have lived that it's worth understanding.

A reminder about his language: I pointed out in the Introduction that a few of the readings in *Bridges Not Walls* were written before we had learned about the destructive potential of the male bias in the English language. This is one of these readings. When I paraphrase Buber I remove this bias, and I have tried to soft-pedal it when I quote him. But it's still part of his writing, at least as it is now translated. Given what he believed about human beings—and given the strong intellectual influence his wife, Paula, had on him—I am sure that Buber would have been quick to correct the gender bias in his language if he had lived long enough to have the opportunity. I hope you can overlook this part of his writing and can hear his insights about *persons*.

OUTLINE OF MARTIN BUBER'S
"ELEMENTS OF THE INTERHUMAN"

I. Interhuman relationships are not the same as "social relationships."
   A. Social relationships can be very close, but no *existential* or person-to-person relation is necessarily involved.
   B. This is because the collective or social suppresses individual persons.
   C. But in the interhuman, person meets person. In other words, "the only thing that matters is that for each of the two [persons] the other happens as the particular other, that each becomes aware of the other and is thus related to him in such a way that he does not regard and use him as his object, but as his partner in a living event, even if it is no more than a boxing match."
   D. In short, "the sphere of the interhuman is one in which a person is confronted by the other. We [i.e., Buber] call its unfolding the dialogical."
II. There are three problems that get in the way of dialogue.
   A. The first problem is the duality of *being* and *seeming*. Dialogue won't happen if the people involved are only "seeming." They need to try to practice "being."
      1. "Seeming" in a relationship involves being concerned with your image, or front—with how you wish to appear.
      2. "Being" involves the spontaneous and unreserved presentation of what you really are in your personal dealings with the other.
      3. These two are generally found mixed together. The most we can do is to distinguish between persons in whose essential attitude one or the other (being or seeming) predominates.
      4. When seeming reigns, real interpersonal communication is impossible: "Whatever the meaning of the word 'truth' may be in other realms, in the interhuman realm it means that [people] communicate themselves to one another as what they are."
      5. The tendency toward seeming, however, is understandable.
         a. We *essentially* need personal confirmation, i.e., we can't live without being confirmed by other people.
         b. Seeming often appears to help us get the confirmation we need.
         c. Consequently, "to yield to seeming is [the human's] essential cowardice, to resist it is his [or her] essential courage."
      6. This view indicates that there is no such thing as "bad being," but rather people who are habitually content to "seem" and afraid to "be." "I have never known a young person who seemed to me irretrievably bad."
   B. The second problem involves the way we perceive others.
      1. Many fatalists thinkers, such as Jean-Paul Sartre, believe that we can ultimately know *only* ourselves, that "man has directly to do only with himself and his own affairs."

2. But the main prerequisite for dialogue is that you get in direct touch with the other, "that each person should regard his partner as the very one he is."
   a. This means becoming aware of the other person as an essentially unique being. "To be aware of a [person] . . . means in particular to perceive his wholeness as a person determined by the spirit: it means to perceive the dynamic centre which stamps his every utterance, action, and attitude with the recognizable sign of uniqueness."
   b. But this kind of awareness is impossible so long as I objectify the other.
3. Perceiving the other in this way is contrary to everything in our world that is scientifically analytic or reductive.
   a. This is not to say that the sciences are wrong, only that they are severely limited.
   b. What's dangerous is the extension of the scientific, analytic method to all of life, because it is very difficult for science to remain aware of the essential uniqueness of persons.
4. This kind of perception is called "personal making present." What enables us to do it is our capacity for "imagining the real" of the other.
   a. Imagining the real "is not a looking at the other but a bold swinging—demanding the most intensive stirring of one's being—into the life of the other."
   b. When I *imagine* what the other person is *really* thinking and feeling, I can make direct contact with him or her.

C. The third problem which impedes the growth of dialogue is the tendency toward imposition instead of unfolding.
   1. One way to affect a person is to impose yourself on him or her.
   2. Another way is to "find and further in the soul of the other the disposition toward" that which you have recognized in yourself as right.
      a. Unfolding is not simply "teaching," but rather *meeting*.
      b. It requires believing in the other person.
      c. It means working as a helper of the growth processes already going on in the other.
   3. The propagandist is the typical "imposer"; the teacher *can* be the correspondingly typical "unfolder."
   4. The ethic implied here is similar to Immanuel Kant's, i.e., persons should never be treated as means to an end, but only as ends in themselves.
      a. The only difference is that Buber stresses that persons exist not in isolation but in the interhuman, and
      b. for the interhuman to occur, there must be:
         (1) as little seeming as possible.
         (2) genuine perceiving ("personal making present") of the other, and
         (3) as little imposing as possible.

III. Summary of the characteristics of genuine dialogue:
A. Each person must turn toward and be open to the other, a "turning of the being."

   B. Each must make present the other by imagining the real.

   C. Each confirms the other's being; however, confirmation does not necessarily mean approval.

   D. Each must be authentically himself or herself.

      1. Each must say whatever she or he "has to say."

      2. Each cannot be ruled by thoughts of his or her own effect or effectiveness as a speaker.

   E. Where dialogue becomes genuine, "there is brought into being a memorable common fruitlessness which is to be found nowhere else."

   F. Speaking is not always essential; silence can be very important.

   G. Finally, all participants must be committed to dialogue; otherwise, it will fail.

Again, Buber's language sometimes can get in the way of understanding him. But if you listen carefully to him, I think you will be able to resonate with at least some of what he says.

ELEMENTS OF THE INTERHUMAN

Martin Buber

THE SOCIAL AND THE INTERHUMAN

It is usual to ascribe what takes place between men to the social realm, thereby blurring a basically important line of division between two essentially different areas of human life. I myself, when I began nearly fifty years ago to find my own bearings in the knowledge of society, making use of the then unknown concept of the interhuman, made the same error. From that time it became increasingly clear to me that we have to do here with a separate category of our existence, even a separate dimension, to use a mathematical term, and one with which we are so familiar that its peculiarity has hitherto almost escaped us. Yet insight into its peculiarity is extremely important not only for our thinking but also for our living.

We may speak of social phenomena wherever the life of a number of men, lived with one another, bound up together, brings in its train shared experiences and reactions. But to be thus bound up together means only that each individual existence is enclosed and contained in a group existence. It does not mean that between one member and another of the group there exists any kind of personal relation. They do feel that they belong together in a way that is, so to speak, fundamentally different from every possible belonging together with someone outside the group. And there do arise, especially in the life of smaller groups, contacts which frequently favour the birth of individual relations, but, on the other hand, frequently make it more difficult. In no case, however, does membership in a group necessarily involve an existential relation between one member and another. It is true that there have been groups in history which included highly sensitive and intimate relations between two of their members—as, for instance, in the homosexual relations among the Japanese samurai or among Doric warriors—and these were countenanced for the sake of the stricter cohesion of the group. But in general it must be said that the leading elements in groups, especially in the later course of human history, have rather been inclined to suppress the personal relation in favour of the purely collective element. Where this latter element reigns alone or is predominant, men feel themselves to be carried by the collectivity, which lifts them out of loneliness and fear of the world and lostness. When this happens—and for modern man it is an essential happening—the life between person and person seems to retreat more and more before the advance of the collective. The collective aims at holding in check the inclination to personal life. It is as though those who are bound together in groups should in the main be concerned only with the work of the group and should turn to the personal partners, who are tolerated by the group, only in secondary meetings.

The difference between the two realms became very palpable to me on one occasion when I had joined the procession through a large town of a movement to which I did not belong. I did it out of sympathy for the tragic development which I sensed was at hand in the destiny of a friend who was one of the leaders of the movement. While the procession was forming, I conversed with him and with another, a good-hearted "wild man," who also had the mark of death upon him. At that moment I still felt that the two men really were there, over against me, each of them a man near to me, near even in what was most remote from me; so different from me that my soul continually suffered from this difference, yet by virtue of this very difference confronting me with authentic being. Then the formations started off, and after a short time I was lifted out of all confrontation, drawn into the procession, falling in with its aimless step; and it was obviously the very same for the two with whom I had just exchanged human words. After a while we passed a café where I had been sitting the previous day with a musician whom I knew only slightly. The very moment we passed it the door opened, the musician stood on the threshold, saw me, apparently saw me alone, and waved to me. Straightway it seemed to me as though I were taken out of the procession and of the presence of my marching friends, and set there, confronting the musician. I forgot that I was walking along with the same step; I felt that I was standing over there by the man who had called out to me, and without a word, with a smile of understanding, was answering him. When consciousness of the facts returned to me, the procession, with my companions and myself at its head, had left the café behind.

The realm of the interhuman goes far beyond that of sympathy. Such simple happenings can be part of it as, for instance, when two strangers exchange glances in a crowded streetcar, at once to sink back again into the convenient state of wishing to know nothing about each other. But also every casual encounter between opponents belong to this realm, when it affects the opponent's attitude—that is, when something, however imperceptible, happens between the two, no matter whether it is marked at the time by any feeling or not. The only thing that matters is that for each of the two men the other happens as the particular other, that each becomes aware of the other and is thus related to him in such a way that he does not regard and use him as his object, but as his partner in a living event, even if it is no more than a boxing match. It is well known that some existentialists assert that the basic factor between men is that one is an object for the other. But so far as this is actually the case, the special reality of the interhuman, the fact of the contact, has been largely eliminated. It cannot indeed be entirely eliminated. As a crude example, take two men who are observing one another. The essential thing is not that the one makes the other his object, but the fact that he is not fully able to do so and the reason for his failure. We have in common with all existing things that we can be made objects of observation. But it is my privilege as man that by the hidden activity of my being I can establish an impassable barrier to objectification. Only in partnership can my being be perceived as an existing whole.

The sociologist may object to any separation of the social and the interhuman on the ground that society is actually built upon human relations, and the theory of these relations is therefore to be regarded as the very foundation of sociology. But here an ambiguity in the concept "relation" becomes evident. We speak, for instance, of a comradely relation between two men in their work, and do not merely mean what happens between them as comrades, but also a lasting disposition which is actualized in those happenings and which even includes purely psychological events such as the recollection of the absent comrade. But by the sphere of the interhuman I mean solely actual happenings between men, whether wholly mutual or tending to grow into mutual relations. For the participation of both partners is in principle indispensable. The sphere of the interhuman is one in which a person is confronted by the other. We call its unfolding the dialogical.

In accordance with this, it is basically erroneous to try to understand the interhuman phenomena as psychological. When two men converse together, the psychological is certainly an important part of the situation, as each listens and each prepares to speak. Yet this is only the hidden accompaniment to the conversation itself, the phonetic event fraught with meaning, whose meaning is to be found neither in one of the two partners nor in both together, but only in their dialogue itself, in this "between" which they live together.

BEING AND SEEMING

The essential problem of the sphere of the interhuman is the duality of being and seeming. Although it is a familiar fact that men are often troubled about the impression they make on others, this has been much more discussed in moral philosophy than in anthropology. Yet this is one of the most important subjects for anthropological study.

We may distinguish between two different types of human existence. The one proceeds from what one really is, the other from what one wishes to seem. In general, the two are found mixed together. There have probably been few men who were entirely independent of the impression they made on others, while there has scarcely existed one who was exclusively determined by the impression made by him. We must be content to distinguish between men in whose essential attitude the one or the other predominates.

This distinction is most powerfully at work, as its nature indicates, in the interhuman realm—that is, in men's personal dealings with one another.

Take as the simplest and yet quite clear example the situation in which two persons look at one another—the first belonging to the first type, the second to the second. The one who lives from his being looks at the other just as one looks at someone with whom he has personal dealings. His look is "spontaneous," "without reserve"; of course, he is not uninfluenced by the desire to make himself understood by the other, but he is uninfluenced by any thought of the idea of himself which he can or should awaken in the person whom he is looking at. His opposite is different. Since he is concerned with the image which his appearance, and especially his look or glance, produces in the other, he "makes" this look. With the help of the capacity, in greater or lesser degree peculiar to man, to make a definite element of his being appear in his look, he produces a look which is meant to have, and often enough does have, the effect of a spontaneous utterance—not only the utterance of a physical event supposed to be taking place at that very moment, but also, as it were, the reflection of a personal life of such-and-such a kind.

This must, however, be carefully distinguished from another area of seeming whose ontological legitimacy cannot be doubted. I mean the realm of "genuine seeming," where a lad, for instance, imitates his heroic model and while he is doing so is seized by the actuality of heroism, or a man plays the part of a destiny and conjures up authentic destiny. In this situation there is nothing false; the imitation is genuine imitation and the part played is genuine; the mask, too, is a mask and no deceit. But where the semblance originates from the lie and is permeated by it, the interhuman is threatened in its very existence. It is not that someone utters a lie, falsifies some account. The lie I mean does not take place in relation to particular facts, but in relation to existence itself, and it attacks interhuman existence as such. There are times when a man, to satisfy some stale conceit, forfeits the great chance of a true happening between I and Thou.

Let us now imagine two men, whose life is dominated by appearance, sitting and talking together. Call them Peter and Paul. Let us list the different configurations which are involved. First, there is Peter as he wishes to appear to Paul, and Paul as he wishes to appear to Peter. Then there is Peter as he really appears to Paul, that is, Paul's image of Peter, which in general does not in the least coincide with what Peter wishes Paul to see; and similarly there is the reverse situation. Further, there is Peter as he appears to himself, and Paul as he appears to himself. Lastly, there are the bodily Peter and the bodily Paul. Two living beings and six ghostly appearances, which mingle in many ways in the conversation between the two. Where is there room for any genuine interhuman life?

Whatever the meaning of the word "truth" may be in other realms, in the interhuman realm it means that men communicate themselves to one another as what they are. It does not depend on one saying to the other everything that occurs to him, but only on his letting no seeming creep in between himself and the other. It does not depend on one letting himself go before another, but on his granting to the man to whom he communicates himself a share in his being. This is a question of the authenticity of the interhuman, and where this is not to be found, neither is the human element itself authentic.

Therefore, as we begin to recognize the crisis of man as the crisis of what is between man and man, we must free the concept of uprightness from the thin moralistic tones which cling to it, and let it take its tone from the concept of bodily uprightness. If a presupposition of human life in primeval times is given in man's walking upright, the fulfillment of human life can only come through the soul's walking upright, through the great uprightness which is not tempted by any seeming because it has conquered all semblance.

But, one may ask, what if a man by his nature makes his life subservient to the images which he produces in others? Can he, in such a case, still become a man living from his being, can he escape from his nature?

The widespread tendency to live from the recurrent impression one makes instead of from the steadiness of one's being is not a "nature." It originates, in fact, on the other side of interhuman life itself, in men's dependence upon one another. It is no light thing to be confirmed in one's being by others, and seeming deceptively offers itself as a help in this. To yield to seeming is man's essential cowardice, to resist it is his essential courage. But this is not an inexorable state of affairs which is as it is and must so remain. One can struggle to come to oneself—that is, to come to confidence in being. One struggles, now more successfully, now less, but never in vain, even when one thinks he is defeated. One must at times pay dearly for life lived from the being; but it is never too dear. Yet is there not bad being, do weeds not grow everywhere? I have never known a young person who seemed to me irretrievably bad. Later indeed it becomes more and more difficult to penetrate the increasingly tough layer which has settled down on a man's being. Thus there arises the false perspective of the seemingly fixed "nature" which cannot be overcome. It is false; the foreground is deceitful; man as man can be redeemed.

Again we see Peter and Paul before us surrounded by the ghosts of the semblances. A ghost can be exorcized. Let us imagine that these two find it more and more repellent to be represented by ghosts. In each of them the will is stirred and strengthened to be confirmed in their being as what they really are and nothing else. We see the forces of real life at work as they drive out the ghosts, till the semblance vanishes and the depths of personal life call to one another.

PERSONAL MAKING PRESENT

By far the greater part of what is today called conversation among men would be more properly and precisely described as speechifying. In general, people do not really speak to one another, but each, although turned to the other, really speaks to a fictitious court of appeal whose life consists of nothing but listening to him. Chekhov has given poetic expression to this state of affairs in *The Cherry Orchard*, where the only use the members of a family make of their being together is to talk past one another. But it is Sartre who has raised to a principle of existence what in Chekhov still appears as the deficiency of a person who is shut up in himself. Sartre regards the walls between the partners in a conversation as simply impassable. For him it is inevitable human destiny that a man has directly to do only with himself and his own affairs. The inner existence of the other is his own concern, not mine; there is no direct relation with the other, nor can there be. This is perhaps the clearest expression of the wretched fatalism of modern man, which regards degeneration as the unchangeable nature of *Homo sapiens* and the misfortune of having run into a blind alley as his primal fate, and which brands every thought of a breakthrough as reactionary romanticism. He who really knows how far our generation has lost the way of true freedom, of free giving between I and Thou, must himself, by virtue of the demand implicit in every great knowledge of this kind, practice directness—even if he were the only man on earth who did it—and not depart from it until scoffers are struck with fear and hear in his voice the voice of their own suppressed longing.

The chief presupposition for the rise of genuine dialogue is that each should regard his partner as the very one he is. I become aware of him, aware that he is different, essentially different from myself, in the definite, unique way which is peculiar to him, and I accept whom I thus see, so that in full earnestness I can direct what I say to him as the person he is. Perhaps from time to time I must offer strict opposition to his view about the subject of our conversation. But I accept this person, the personal bearer of a conviction, in his definite being out of which his conviction has grown—even though I must try to show, bit by bit, the wrongness of this very conviction. I affirm the person I struggle with: I struggle with him as his partner, I confirm him as creature and as creation, I confirm him who is opposed to me as him who is over against me. It is true that it now depends on the other whether genuine dialogue, mutuality in speech arises between us. But if I thus give to the other who confronts me his legitimate standing as a man with whom I am ready to enter into dialogue, then I may trust him and suppose him to be also ready to deal with me as his partner.

But what does it mean to be "aware" of a man in the exact sense in which I use the word? To be aware of a thing or a being means, in quite general terms, to experience it as a whole and yet at the same time without reduction or abstraction, in all its concreteness. But a man, although he exists as a living being among living beings and even as a thing among things, is nevertheless something categorically different from all things and all beings. A man cannot really be grasped except on the basis of the gift of the spirit which belongs to man alone among all things, the spirit as sharing decisively in the personal life of the living man, that is, the spirit which determines the person. To be aware of a man, therefore, means in particular to perceive his wholeness as a person determined by the spirit; it means to perceive the dynamic centre which stamps his every utterance, action, and attitude with the recognizable sign of uniqueness. Such an awareness is impossible, however, if and so long as the other is the separated object of my contemplation or even observation, for this wholeness and its centre do not let themselves be known to contemplation or observation. It is only possible when I step into an elemental relation with the other, that is, when he becomes present to me. Hence I designate awareness in this special sense as "personal making present."

The perception of one's fellow man as a whole, as a unity, and as unique—even if his wholeness, unity, and uniqueness are only partly developed, as is usually the case—is opposed in our time by almost everything that is commonly understood as specifically modern. In our time there predominates an analytical, reductive, and deriving look between man and man. This look is analytical, or rather pseudo analytical, since it treats the whole being as put together and therefore able to be taken apart—not only the so-called unconscious which is accessible to relative objectification, but also the psychic stream itself, which can never, in fact, be grasped as an object. This look is a reductive one because it tries to contract the manifold person, who is nourished by the microcosmic richness of the possible, to some schematically surveyable and recurrent structures. And this look is a deriving one because it supposes it can grasp what a man has become, or even is becoming, in genetic formulae, and it thinks that even the dynamic central principle of the individual in this becoming can be represented by a general concept. An effort is being made today radically to destroy the mystery between man and man. The personal life, the ever-near mystery, once the source of the stillest enthusiasms, is levelled down.

What I have just said is not an attack on the analytical method of the human sciences, a method which is indispensable wherever it furthers knowledge of a phenomenon without impairing the essentially different knowledge of its uniqueness that transcends the valid circle of the method. The science of man that makes use of the analytical method must accordingly always keep in view the boundary of such a contemplation, which stretches like a horizon around it. This duty makes the transportation of the method into life dubious; for it is excessively difficult to see where the boundary is in life.

If we want to do today's work and prepare tomorrow's with clear sight, then we must develop in ourselves and in the next generation a gift which lives in man's inwardness as a Cinderella, one day to be a princess. Some call it intuition, but that is not a wholly unambiguous concept. I prefer the name "imagining the real," for in its essential being this gift is not a looking at the other, but a bold swinging—demanding the most intensive stirring of one's being—into the life of the other. This is the nature of all genuine imagining, only that here the realm of my action is not the all-possible, but the particular real person who confronts me, whom I can attempt to make present to myself just in this way, and not otherwise, in his wholeness, unity, and uniqueness, and with his dynamic centre which realizes all these things ever anew.

Let it be said again that all this can only take place in a living partnership, that is, when I stand in a common situation with the other and expose myself vitally to his share in the situation as really his share. It is true that my basic attitude can remain unanswered, and the dialogue can die in seed. But if mutuality stirs, then the interhuman blossoms into genuine dialogue.

IMPOSITION AND UNFOLDING

I have referred to two things which impede the growth of life between men: the invasion of seeming, and the inadequacy of perception. We are now faced with a third, plainer than the others, and in this critical hour more powerful and more dangerous than ever.

There are two basic ways of affecting men in their views and their attitude to life. In the first a man tries to impose himself, his opinion and his attitude, on the other in such a way that the latter feels the psychical result of the action to be his own insight, which has only been freed by the influence. In the second basic way of affecting others, as man wishes to find and to further in the soul of the other the disposition toward what he has recognized in himself as the right. Because it is the right, it must also be alive in the microcosm of the other, as one possibility. The other need only be opened out in this potentiality of his; moreover, this opening out takes place not essentially by teaching, but by meeting, by existential communication between someone that is in actual being and someone that is in a process of becoming. The first way has been most powerfully developed in the realm of propaganda, the second in that of education.

The propagandist I have in mind, who imposes himself, is not in the least concerned with the person whom he desires to influence, as a person; various individual qualities are of importance only in so far as he can exploit them to win the other and must get to know them for this purpose. In his indifference to everything personal the propagandist goes a substantial distance beyond the party for which he works. For the party, persons in their difference are of significance because each can be used according to his special qualities in a particular function. It is true that the personal is considered only in respect of the specific use to which it can be put, but within these limits it is recognized in practice. To propaganda as such, on the other hand, individual qualities are rather looked on as a burden, for propaganda is concerned simply with *more*—more members, more adherents, an increasing extent of support. Political methods, where they rule in an extreme form, as here, simply mean winning power over the other by depersonalizing him. This kind of propaganda enters upon different relations with force; it supplements it or replaces it, according to the need or the prospects, but it is in the last analysis nothing but sublimated violence, which has become imperceptible as such. It places men's souls under a pressure which allows the illusion of autonomy. Political methods at their height mean the effective abolition of the human factor.

The educator whom I have in mind lives in a world of individuals, a certain number of whom are always at any one time committed to his care. He sees each of these individuals as in a position to become a unique, single person, and thus the bearer of a special task of existence which can be fulfilled through him and through him alone. He sees every personal life as engaged in such a process of actualization, and he knows from his own experience that the forces making for actualization are all the time involved in a microcosmic struggle with counter-forces. He has come to see himself as a helper of the actualizing forces. He knows these forces; they have shaped and they still shape him. Now he puts this person shaped by them at their disposal for a new struggle and a new work. He cannot wish to impose himself, for he believes in the effect of the actualizing forces, that is, he believes that in every man what is right is established in a single and uniquely personal way. No other way may be imposed on a man, but another way, that of the educator, may and must unfold what is right, as in this case it struggles for achievement, and help it to develop.

The propagandist, who imposes himself, does not really believe in his own cause, for he does not trust it to attain its effect of its own power without his special methods, whose symbols are the loudspeaker and the television advertisement. The educator who unfolds what is there believes in the primal power which has scattered itself, and still scatters itself, in all human beings in order that it may grow up in each man in the special form of that man. He is confident that this growth needs at each moment only that help which is given in meeting and that he is called to supply that help.

I have illustrated the character of the two basic attitudes and their relation to one another by means of two extremely antithetical examples. But wherever men have dealings with one another, one or the other attitude is to be found to be in more or less degree.

These two principles of imposing oneself on someone and helping someone to unfold should not be confused with concepts such as arrogance and humility. A man can be arrogant without wishing to impose himself on others, and it is not enough to be humble in order to help another unfold. Arrogance and humility are dispositions of the soul, psychological fact with a moral accent, while imposition and helping to unfold are events between men, anthropological facts which point to an ontology, the ontology of the interhuman.

In the moral realm Kant expressed the essential principle that one's fellow man must never be thought of and treated merely as a means, but always at the same time as an independent end. The principle is expressed as an "ought" which is sustained by the idea of human dignity. My point of view, which is near to Kant's in its essential features, has another source and goal. It is concerned with the presuppositions of the interhuman. Man exists anthropologically not in his isolation, but in the completeness of the relation between man and man; what humanity is can be properly grasped only in vital reciprocity. For the proper existence of the interhuman it is necessary, as I have shown, that the semblance does not intervene to spoil the relation of personal being to personal being. It is further necessary, as I have also shown, that each one means and makes present the other in his personal being. That neither should wish to impose himself on the other is the third basic presupposition of the interhuman. These presuppositions do not include the demand that one should influence the other in his unfolding; that is, however, an element that is suited to lead to a higher stage of the interhuman.

That there resides in every man the possibility of attaining authentic human existence in the special way peculiar to him can be grasped in the Aristotelian image of entelechy, innate self-realization; but one must note that it is an entelechy of the work of creation. It would be mistaken to speak here of individuation alone. Individuation is only the indispensable personal stamp of all realization of human existence. The self as such is not ultimately the essential, but the meaning of human existence given in creation again and again fulfills itself as self. The help that men give each other in becoming a self leads the life between men to its height. The dynamic glory of the being of man is first bodily present in the relation between two men each of whom in meaning the other also means the highest to which this person is called, and serves the self-realization of this human life as one true to creation without wishing to impose on the other anything of his own realization.

GENUINE DIALOGUE

We must now summarize and clarify the marks of genuine dialogue.

In genuine dialogue the turning to the partner takes place in all truth, that is, it is a turning of the being. Every speaker "means" the partner of partners to whom he turns as this personal existence. To "mean" someone in this connection is at the same time to exercise that degree of making present which is possible to the speaker at that moment. The experiencing senses and the imagining of the real which completes the findings of the senses work together to make the other present as a whole and as a unique being, as the person that he is. But the speaker does not merely perceive the one who is present to him in this way; he receives him as his partner, and that means that he confirms this other being, so far as it is for him to confirm. The true turning of his person to the other includes this confirmation, this acceptance. Of course, such a confirmation does not mean approval; but no matter in what I am against the other, by accepting him as my partner in genuine dialogue I have affirmed him as a person.

Further, if genuine dialogue is to arise, everyone who takes part in it must bring himself into it. And that also means that he must be willing on each occasion to say what is really in his mind about the subject of the conversation. And that means further that on each occasion he makes the contribution of his spirit without reduction and without shifting his ground. Even men of great integrity are under the illusion that they are not bound to say everything "they have to say." But in the great faithfulness which is the climate of genuine dialogue, what I have to say at any one time already has in me the character of something that wishes to be uttered, and I must not keep it back, keep it in myself. It bears for me the unmistakable sign which indicates that it belongs to the common life of the word. Where the dialogical word genuinely exists, it must be given its right by keeping nothing back. To keep nothing back is the exact opposite of unreserved speech. Everything depends on the legitimacy of "what I have to say."

And of course I must also be intent to raise into an inner word and then into a spoken word what I have to say at this moment but do not yet possess as speech. To speak is both nature and work, something that grows and something that is made, and where it appears dialogically, in the climate of great faithfulness, it has to fulfill ever anew the unity of the two.

Associated with this is that overcoming of semblance to which I have referred. In the atmosphere of genuine dialogue, he who is ruled by the thought of his own effect as the speaker of what he has to speak has a destructive effect. If, instead of what has to be said, I try to bring attention to my *I*, I have irrevocably miscarried what I had to say; it enters the dialogue as a failure and the dialogue is a failure. Because genuine dialogue is an ontological sphere which is constituted by the authenticity of being, every invasion of semblance must damage it.

But where the dialogue is fulfilled in its being, between partners who have turned to one another in truth, who express themselves without reserve and are free of the desire for semblance, there is brought into being a memorable common fruitfulness which is to be found nowhere else. At such times, at each such time, the word arises in a substantial way between men who have been seized in their depths and opened out by the dynamic of an elemental togetherness. The interhuman opens out what otherwise remains unopened.

This phenomenon is indeed well known in dialogue between two persons; but I have also sometimes experienced it in a dialogue in which several have taken part.

About Easter of 1914 there met a group consisting of representatives of several European nations for a three-day discussion that was intended to be preliminary to further talks. We wanted to discuss together how the catastrophe, which we all believed was imminent, could be avoided. Without our having agreed beforehand on any sort of modalities for our talk, all the presuppositions of genuine dialogue were fulfilled. From the first hour immediacy reigned between all of us, some of whom had just got to know one another; everyone spoke with an unheard-of unreserve, and clearly not a single one of the participants was in bondage to semblance. In respect of its purpose the meeting must be described as a failure (though even now in my heart it is still not a certainty that it had to be a failure); the irony of the situation was that we arranged the final discussion for the middle of August, and in the course of events the group was soon broken up. Nevertheless, in the time that followed, not one of the participants doubted that he shared in a triumph of the interhuman.

One more point must be noted. Of course it is not necessary for all who are joined in a genuine dialogue actually to speak; those who keep silent can on occasion be especially important. But each must be determined not to withdraw when the course of the conversation makes it proper for him to say what he has to say. No one, of course, can know in advance what it is that he has to say; genuine dialogue cannot be arranged beforehand. It has indeed its basic order in itself from the beginning, but nothing can be determined, the course is of the spirit, and some discover what they have to say only when they catch the call of the spirit.

But it is also a matter of course that all the participants, without exception, must be of such nature that they are capable of satisfying the presuppositions of genuine dialogue and are ready to do so. The genuineness of the dialogue is called in question as soon as even a small number of those present are felt by themselves and by the others as not being expected to take any active part. Such a state of affairs can lead to very serious problems.

I had a friend whom I account one of the most considerable men of our age. He was a master of conversation, and he loved it: his genuineness as a speaker was evident. But once it happened that he was sitting with two friends and with the three wives, and a conversation arose in which by its nature the women were clearly not joining, although their presence in fact had a great influence. The conversation among the men soon developed into a duel between two of them (I was the third). The other "duelist," also a friend of mine, was of a noble nature; he too was a man of true conversation, but given more to objective fairness than to the play of the intellect, and a stranger to any controversy. The friend whom I have called a master of conversation did not speak with his usual composure and strength, but he scintillated, he fought, he triumphed. The dialogue was destroyed.

REVIEW QUESTIONS

1. What distinction does Buber make between the social and the interhuman?
2. What feature of interpersonal contact does Buber say can characterize even "a boxing match"?
3. What does Buber mean when he says that "it is basically erroneous to try to understand the interhuman phenomena as psychological"?
4. Does Buber say that a person can practice "being" consistently, all the time? Explain.
5. Paraphrase the last sentence in the first paragraph under the heading, "Personal Making Present." What is Buber challenging his reader to do here?
6. Identify three possible things that a person who is imposing could impose on his or her conversational partner. In other words, what is (are) imposed when a person is imposing? What is unfolded when a person is unfolding?
7. What does Buber mean when he says that "to keep nothing back is the exact opposite of unreserved speech"?

PROBES

1. What does it mean to you when Buber says that social contacts don't involve an existential relation, but that interhuman contacts do?
2. How is Buber's discussion of "being" and "seeming" similar to and different from Rogers's discussion of "congruence" (Chapter 17)?
3. For Buber, does "being" mean total honesty? Is "seeming" lying?
4. What circumstances make it difficult for you to "be"? How can you best help others to "be" instead of "seem"?

5. How do Buber's comments about the way we perceive others relate to the discussion of person perception in Chapter 5?
6. It sounds as if Buber is saying that science *cannot* be used to study human life. Is he saying that? Do you agree with him? Why or why not?
7. How is Buber's discussion of "imagining the real" related to what Stewart and Logan (Chapter 6) and Rogers (Chapter 17) say about empathy?
8. Which teacher that you've had has functioned most as an "imposer?" Which teacher has been most consistently an "unfolder?"
9. What does "personal making present" mean to you? What do you need to do in order to perceive someone that way?
10. Have you ever experienced a silent "dialogue" of the kind Buber mentions here? What happened?

NOTES

1. You might also be interested in other things written by or about Buber. For starters I recommend Aubrey Hodes, *Martin Buber: An Intimate Portrait* (New York: Viking, 1971); or Hilary Evans Bender, *Monarch Notes: The Philosophy of Martin Buber* (New York: Monarch, 1974). Maurice Friedman has written the definitive Buber biography, and I'd especially recommend the third volume, *Martin Buber's Life and Work: The Later Years, 1945–1965* (New York: Dutton, 1983). Buber's most important and influential book is *I and Thou*, trans. Walter Kaufmann (New York: Scribner, 1970).
2. Buber's translators always point out that this "thou" is not the religious term of formal address. It is a translation of the German *Du*, the familiar form of the pronoun "you." As Walter Kaufmann, one of Buber's translators, explains, "German lovers say *Du* to one another and so do friends. *Du* is spontaneous and unpretentious, remote from formality, pomp, and dignity."

Ideas are clean. They soar in the serene supernal. I can take them out and look at them, they fit in books, they lead me down that narrow way. And in the morning they are there. Ideas are straight—
But the world is round, and a
messy mortal is my friend.
Come walk with me in the mud. . . .

—Hugh Prather

Photo Credits

CO-1: © Tim McGuire
CO-2: © Ed Bock/The Stock Market
CO-3: © Tom & DeeAnn McCarthy: The Stock Market
CO-4: © Spencer Grant/Stock Boston
CO-5: © Paul Barton: The Stock Market
CO-6: © Arthur Tilley: FPG International
CO-7: © Bob Krist/The Stock Market
CO-8: © Zigy Kaluzny: Tony Stone Images
CO-9: © Ed Bock: The Stock Market
CO-10: © Jerry Howard/Stock Boston
CO-11: © Jim Cummins: FPG International
CO-12: © Frank Priegue: International Stock
CO-13: © Andrea Pizzi: The Stock Market
CO-14: © Joel Gordon
CO-15: Brooks Kraft
CO-16: Photo courtesy of Ruthellen Josselson
CO-17: John T. Wood
CO-18: © Corbis-Bettmann

Index